A Dictionary for the Modern Singer

DICTIONARIES FOR THE MODERN MUSICIAN

Series Editor: David Daniels

Contributions to **Dictionaries for the Modern Musician** offer both the novice and the advanced artist lists of key terms designed to fully cover the field of study and performance for major instruments and classes of instruments, as well as the workings of musicians in areas from conducting to composing. Focusing primarily on the knowledge required by the *contemporary* musical student and teacher, performer, and professional, each dictionary is a must-have for any musician's personal library!

A Dictionary for the Modern Singer by Matthew Hoch, 2014

A Dictionary for the Modern Singer

Matthew Hoch

ROWMAN & LITTLEFIELD
Lanham • Boulder • New York • London

Published by Rowman & Littlefield
A wholly owned subsidary of The Rowman & Littlefield Publishing Group, Inc.
4501 Forbes Boulevard, Suite 200, Lanham, Maryland 20706
www.rowman.com

Unit A, Whitacre Mews, 26-34 Stannary Street, London SE11 4AB

British Library Cataloguing in Publication Information Available

Library of Congress Cataloging-in-Publication Data

The hardback edition of this book was previously cataloged by the Library of Congress as follows:

Hoch, Matthew, 1975–, author.
A dictionary for the modern singer / Matthew Hoch.
    pages cm. — (Dictionaries for the modern musician)
Includes bibliographical references.
1. Vocal music—Dictionaries. 2. Singing—Dictionaries. I. Title.
ML102.V6H63 2014
782.003—dc23
                                                            2013043295

ISBN 978-0-8108-8655-1 (cloth : alk. paper)
ISBN 978-1-4422-7669-7 (pbk. : alk. paper)
ISBN 978-0-8108-8656-8 (ebook)

To my wife, Theresa,
and my three children,
Hannah, Sofie, and Zachary.

Contents

Foreword

Every academic and/or artistic discipline has at its root level a requisite body of knowledge. An understanding of that body of knowledge is necessary to effectively communicate within the discipline. Without a command of these basic tenets, individuals must often discuss intricacies in grossly general terms. In the case of music, and in this case, specifically singing, a large part of the initial training is taken up with the acquisition of that body of knowledge. All too often, information comes to individuals from less than credible sources. Then the process of information acquisition is compromised, and effective communication is inhibited rather than enhanced. To that end, the author has undertaken the present volume to facilitate the acquisition of accurate knowledge of the "jargon" of singing.

As a young voice student, my life would have been much less stressful had such a volume existed. There is no doubt that my ability to accurately communicate would have been enhanced. As a professor of singing at a university, I have for years cobbled together rudimentary vocabulary lists for my students. With the publication of this book, I will no longer question what I left out or forgot to include. Instead, I will hand them a copy of *A Dictionary for the Modern Singer*. From the terms *a tempo* to *zydeco*, accurate, clear, and concise definitions and explanations are offered for all aspects of the vocal art.

Author Matthew Hoch has compiled a tool that will be useful the first time it is opened. I believe it will become a standard reference tool for the training of singers. The more advanced singer will also find it valuable, offering a standard to measure individual perception and knowledge. Singing, with its widely varied schools of thought, pedagogy, genre, and aesthetic, is certainly a subjective art. As such, it can only benefit from a more unified and agreed upon vernacular. When we employ terms and concepts with a common meaning, the potential for understanding will certainly be enhanced. With enhanced understanding comes the potential for new knowledge. Growing the best of the art of singing is close to the heart of virtually every singer. Thanks to Dr. Hoch for taking a giant step in that direction with the publication of *A Dictionary for the Modern Singer*.

Donald Simonson, DM
Past president, National Association of Teachers of Singing
Professor and chair of voice, Iowa State University

Acknowledgments

There are numerous individuals from my past and present I would like to thank, all of whom have made this book possible. I am deeply indebted to my colleagues and supervisors at Scarecrow Press: Bennett Graff, senior acquisitions editor, as well as David Daniels, general editor for the Dictionaries for the Modern Musician series. Mr. Daniels was intimately involved with the shaping of the manuscript, reading virtually every entry and offering keen advice honed by decades in the trenches of the publishing industry. I am grateful for his wisdom throughout this entire process.

I am grateful for my position at Auburn University and the institution's consummate support of faculty research. Specifically, I would like to thank Dr. Sara Lynn Baird, chair of the Music Department, as well as Dr. Paula Brobrowski, associate dean of research for the College of Liberal Arts, for the summer research grant that made the completion of this manuscript possible.

Thank you to Dr. Donald Simonson, professor and chair of voice at Iowa State University, and past president of the National Association of Teachers of Singing (NATS), for enthusiastically agreeing to write the foreword to this book. Dr. Simonson was my master teacher at the 2006 NATS Intern Program and was an invaluable mentor to me during the formative stages of my career as an academic, scholar, and pedagogue. He remains one of the individuals to whom I turn for professional advice. He is both the correct and perfect person to write the foreword to *A Dictionary for the Modern Singer*.

While most of this book's content fell squarely into my zone of comfort, there were a few areas that were outside of my realm of competency. I am deeply grateful to Matthew Edwards of Shenandoah University for his numerous contributions to this book in the area of contemporary commercial music (CCM) styles, especially his expertise in rock/pop and audio technology. In this capacity, Mr. Edwards was involved in this project from the beginning, from the initial selection of terms to the proofing of final entries. The initial drafts of most of the audio technology terms were also written by him, as well as the contributing essay "What Every Singer Needs to Know about Audio Technology," which appears in the latter part of this dictionary. Without his expertise, this book would have been considerably less rich as a resource for CCM singers and pedagogues.

I am also indebted to the authors of the other four guest essays included in the book. Jeannette LoVetri and Dr. Heather Hunnicutt offer expert perspectives from their respective fields of research. The articles by John Nix and Dr. Dean Southern are reprinted with permission, originally appearing in the *Journal of Singing* and *Classical Singer* magazine. I am grateful to Dr. Richard Sjoerdsma and Sara Thomas—editors of these respective publications—for allowing for their inclusion in this book. Thanks also to Dr. Karen Wicklund for her appendix, "The Singer's Ten Steps to Wellness," which appears in her book *Singing Voice Rehabilitation: A Guide for the Voice Teacher and Speech-Language Pathologist*. This section is reprinted in appendix K courtesy of Cengage Learning. Dr. Suzanne Draayer is responsible for the collation and prototype definitions of the terms related to nineteenth-century Spanish song, and they are referenced here with her permission.

I am immensely grateful to Dr. Cheri Montgomery of Vanderbilt University for her preparation of the International Phonetic Alphabet (IPA) charts that appear in appendix A of this book. They are printed here with her permission.

I solicited help with several other definitions as well: A special thanks to Dr. Linda Lister for "yoga," Dr. David Meyer and Patricia Campbell for "squall," and Daniel Shigo for related entries on Lamperti, Klein, both Garcías, and the *coup de glotte*. The "aria" entry owes much to David Daniels and John Yaffé and was appropriated with their permission from their recent book, *Arias, Ensembles, and Choruses: An Expert Finder for Orchestras*, also published by Scarecrow.

Thank you to Dr. Scott McCoy for his proofing of several definitions and for granting permission to reprint anatomical images from his book *Your Voice: An Inside View*. Appendix J, "Listening to Singers," is also indebted to this publication. Thanks also to Dr. Ingo Titze of the National Center for Voice and Speech (NCVS) for his permission in reprinting the NCVS medicine chart that appears on their website (www.ncvs.org). Jeannette LoVetri also assisted me in refining the perilous "belt" definition.

For many of these definitions, I was more of an editor than a writer, as various pedagogical and industry terms have been defined numerous times over by many of the best and brightest scholars in our field. I owe much to the authors who have shaped my own pedagogical knowledge, including Richard Miller, James Stark, and Berton Coffin, in addition to those already mentioned here. Dozens—if not hundreds—of reference books were consulted during the writing of the manuscript, all of which are listed comprehensively in this book's bibliography.

During the final stages of the manuscript preparation, I engaged several colleagues as proofreaders. Two deserve special mention: Dr. Stephanie Tingler of the University of Georgia read through every definition, catching typos and offering many valuable insights. Likewise, Judith Nicosia of Rutgers University read through substantial portions of the manuscript and offered some in-depth advice on various entries. Other proofreaders included Lynn Thompson, Jennifer Piazza-Pick, Sarah Hall, Jessica Kasinski, Kate Maroney, Kyle Wheatley, Jennifer Lasarz, Kirsten Kunkle, Ashley Conway, Stephanie Adrian, and Joy Rotz. Many other colleagues helped to shape the initial selection of terms at the beginning of the project. I am grateful to Marc St Laurent, David Sabella-Mills, Marilee David, Debra Hughes, Ben Caston, Karen Calloway, Robert McTyre, and Janet Wooten for their suggestions.

My voice teachers, coaches, and theory and musicology teachers were also influential, as well as the many artists with whom I had the privilege of participating with in master classes and other professional development opportunities throughout the years. I am also grateful to my conductors, particularly Donald Nally, who was a pivotal influence during my first year of college and who later reentered my professional and personal life on numerous occasions; my summer at the Spoleto Festival in Italy in 2001 and our 2008 recording with his professional new music ensemble, the Crossing, were two of the most memorable. Helmuth Rilling was also a significant influence during my eight wonderful summers at the Oregon Bach Festival from 2005–2012. Dr. Dennis Shrock, under whom I sang in the Santa Fe Desert Chorale in 2003, and my accomplished choral colleagues and friends from the SFDC and OBF, have also contributed immeasurably to my choral knowledge.

To my many students throughout the years, who have probably taught me more about singing and teaching—and myself—than any teacher ever could have, I am deeply grateful that you have been a part of my life and career.

And to so many musicians and colleagues who have shaped my musical knowledge and life during the past two decades, my most sincere thanks. I would not be the musician, scholar, and person I am today without their mentoring and guidance.

Finally, I am deeply indebted to my wife, Theresa, for her patience and tolerance during my many months of intense and hermitic writing. This book was written in my "spare time," while juggling my university and church positions, as well as a rigorous performance and conference schedule. An unexpected summer move to a new city and jobs in 2012 also threw many curveballs into our busy life together. Finishing this book on time often meant shirking my responsibilities as a husband and father: locking myself in my office, ignoring my family, and relying on her to referee our three rambunctious children, do laundry, and cook meals. Not a day goes by when I take her for granted, and she—perhaps more than anyone else—is responsible for the timely completion of this ambitious project.

Introduction

I love glossaries. As an avid nonfiction reader, they are my favorite part of a book and the first part that I read. I love digesting little nuggets of information as I prepare to dive into a more expanded treatment of a particular topic. I am also—for better or worse—a "curious generalist." I enjoy all aspects and styles of vocal music and am always hungry to expand my breadth of knowledge. While this has been something of a hindrance when refining a more focused article topic or conference presentation, it has proven to be beneficial when teaching undergraduate students, which is perhaps my greatest passion.

When the opportunity presented itself to author *A Dictionary for the Modern Singer* for Scarecrow Press, I enthusiastically accepted the challenge before I realized the complexity of the project. The purpose of this book, like its instrumental companions in the series, is to provide a handy one-volume reference for the readership: singers, students of singing, teachers of singing, and vocal music enthusiasts. Initial parameters had to be set to define the audience and scope, as a topic this broad could have easily been an encyclopedia as opposed to the 256-page book my contract called for. (The end result wound up being significantly longer.)

Toward the beginning of the project, one preliminary reader expressed a concern about trying to accomplish so much in one volume. Indeed, wouldn't it be clearer to issue separate dictionaries for classical pedagogy, musical theatre terminology, voice science, and other subtopics? Perhaps, but that is not the conception of the Dictionaries for the Modern Musician series; this is a one-volume reference guide for the modern singer, with all of the complexities that involves.

Before the reader dives into the pages of this volume, the following are a few general comments about what this book is and what it is not. These have been some of the guiding principles behind this book and its series:

It is a modern, practical dictionary (*not* an historical one).
It is a generalist's dictionary (*not* a specialist's one).
There is an emphasis on breadth (rather than depth).
There is an emphasis on brevity (as opposed to length).

A Dictionary for the Modern Singer is a generalist's resource. It is not a pedagogy dictionary, a voice science dictionary, or a diction resource. Yet, it is, in a way, all of these things—and more—at the same time. And it fills a unique gap in the singer and voice teacher's library. While many specialist resources have been published, this is perhaps the first general lexicon of its kind. An emphasis was placed on breadth rather than depth, on brevity rather than comprehensiveness. When working on the initial draft of the dictionary, my series editor, David Daniels, said to me, "Imagine that you are putting together a resource for one of your students. What are the most essential things you want them to know about singing?" This advice has guided me throughout the course of eighteen months and numerous drafts of this dictionary as I routinely refined the work and made (sometimes difficult) decisions about various inclusions and exclusions.

As a result of this breadth, no single topic is covered exhaustively, or even adequately, for that matter. The reader who wishes to know more about any particular subject is strongly encouraged to pursue the resources outlined in this book's extensive bibliography. The bibliography—an essential feature of this dictionary—is organized by topic and with its own table of contents for easy reference.

While every work of scholarship is permeated with opinion, personal style, and a certain degree of subjectivity, I have made every effort to present the material as objectively as possible, usually consulting multiple resources when writing definitions. When a controversial subject or individual is covered, I have made every attempt to present both sides of the issue. While it is probably impossible for 100 percent of the readership to agree with every definition in this book, it is my hope that the majority of readers will find these definitions to be in the mainstream and—collectively—a helpful introduction to many aspects of singing.

My focus on the singer inexorably led to certain choices. Thus, while every undergraduate singer should certainly be familiar with sonata-allegro form, this is, by and large, an instrumental form and therefore not included here. Likewise, while *ritornellos* are a significant stylistic feature of baroque arias, they, too, are instrumental in nature. And while Wagner's *leitmotif* and Berlioz's *idée fixe* may be two terms equally worthy of knowing, the *leitmotif* appears in operas and is hence included, whereas the *idée fixe* figures most prominently in an orchestral work (*Symphonie fantastique*) and does not appear here.

Another significant decision that was made early in the process was to deliberately not include entries devoted to specific composers and their works. Since an effort was made to address a plethora of genres and styles, listing composers and their works would have instantly multiplied the length of the book in unmanageable ways. The student of singing is encouraged to consult the composer and work lists found in the appendixes of this book, as well as the bibliography. Similarly, poets and librettists—even ones as important as Heinrich Heine and Oscar Hammerstein II—are also excluded. Important singers, however, are included, particularly those who represent the most significant figures in their respective genres (Dietrich Fischer-Dieskau and German *Lieder*) or whose names are inextricably linked with particular idiomatic style (Amália Rodrigues and *Fado*).

The only real predecessor this book has is Cornelius Reid's *A Dictionary of Vocal Terminology*. The present book differs from Reid's 1984 work in several ways. First, as previously stated, it is a generalist's resource as opposed to a pedagogy dictionary. Also, when pedagogy is addressed, I have tried to represent a mainstream opinion and not base my definitions on any one "school" of pedagogy. In addition, I have favored much shorter, concise definitions that stand in contrast to many of Reid's longer essays. Finally, I made a conscious effort to consult Reid's work as little as possible while writing my own book, so as not to be unduly

influenced by it in one way or another. Thirty years after Reid's seminal work, it is my hope that *A Dictionary for the Modern Singer* will reflect many of the advances that have taken place within the realm of fact-based pedagogy.

For the slippery and extensive topic of the German Fach System, the twenty-nine *Fächer* of the thirteenth edition of Rudolf Kloiber's *Handbuch der Oper* (2011) was used as the objective standard. In addition, other unofficial and non-German *Fächer* occasionally appear as additional entries. Dates for musical works are also included whenever this seemed practical. Musicals are occasionally accompanied by two dates, reflecting both the West End and Broadway production years.

Due to Scarecrow's desire for a modern, practical resource, I also thought that it was essential to include as many contemporary commercial music (CCM) and world music styles as possible within the constraints of this book. Perhaps no instrument is capable of the diverse styles possible with the human voice, and I hope that singers of all genres will find opportunities to expand themselves and broaden their horizons by reading these pages.

In the end, although many judgment calls were made, a dictionary was written. The biggest project of my life was also quite fulfilling on many levels. It is my hope that the reader will find this book worthy of ownership and helpful in his or her personal journey in the ever-expanding world of singing.

Matthew Hoch
Auburn, Alabama
May 31, 2013

THE DICTIONARY

A

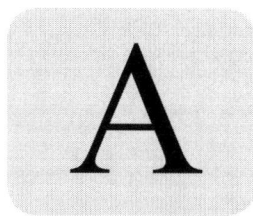

a cappella. Literally, "in the church **style**," but throughout time the phrase has come to mean to sing without instrumental **accompaniment**.

a tempo (It). Return to the previous **tempo**.

A=415. A **pitch standard** used when performing **early music**, indicating that A4 has a **frequency (pitch)** of 415 **Hz**. It is a tuning commonly used in early music **ensembles** that consider **historically informed performance practice (HIPP)** and use period instruments. A=415 refers to a downward retuning of the orchestra. Singers who perform **baroque** repertories will often be asked to sing at A=415, which is approximately one **half step** lower than **A=440**. Even singers who do not have **absolute pitch** are likely to have a strong sense of where particular notes are in their own vocal mechanism, so that for them, performing at A=415 is akin to transposing everything, and at first it may be disorienting. One can grow accustomed to it, however.

A=440. The modern **pitch standard** for music, indicating that A4 has a **frequency (pitch)** of 440 **Hz**. Modern instruments are tuned according to this A=440 standard. A=440 was not standardized until 1926, so performers of **early music** who pay attention to **historically informed performance practice (HIPP)** may adopt other pitch standards. **A=415** is a common tuning for early music **ensembles**.

AATS. Abbreviation for **American Academy of Teachers of Singing**.

ABA. A kind of **ternary form**. A **song** or **aria** with a contrasting section of music (B) inserted between two principal (A) sections. The B section usually offers a contrasting mood to the A section.

abdominal breathing. A breathing **technique** that only involves the muscles of the abdomen and not the rib expansion or **balanced breathing** associated with *appoggio*. See *National Schools of Singing*.

abduction. Movement of the **vocal folds** away from the midline of the **glottis**.

abductor spasmodic dysphonia (abductor SD). See **spasmodic dysphonia (SD)**.

Abgesang. The B section of a **bar form** (AAB) occurring after two *Stollen* (the A sections).

absolute pitch. The ability to recognize or produce a specific **pitch** without the need or use of an external pitch source (for example, a **pitch pipe**, **tuning fork**, or musical instrument). Absolute pitch is sometimes called perfect pitch, with which it is synonymous; however, the term *absolute pitch* is preferred in most **professional** circles. Although virtually all successful musicians have excellent **relative pitch**, only some develop and/or possess absolute pitch. While absolute pitch is occasionally useful, its practical value is subject to debate. Absolute pitch has more to do with hearing the unique color (chroma) of each individual pitch as opposed to hearing **frequency** (how high or low the pitch is). Pitch memory from previous musical experiences also seems to play a significant **role**, with some individuals possessing an uncanny ability to retain specific pitches in their long-term memory. The perception of pitch may change with age, a condition falling medically under the heading "paracusis" (a general term for various hearing defects). The subject's cochlea (an organ of hearing) shrinks as a result of the aging process, causing a note that had been perceived as A, for example, to excite a different area of the cochlea and **register** as B♭. Throughout time, with successive shrinkage, the same note A may be perceived as B♮ or even C. This can be very alarming to a musician, as, for instance, when a familiar piece is rendered unrecognizable by being in the "wrong" **key**—rather like seeing an acquaintance whose hair has been dyed. Who *is* this person who is both familiar and unfamiliar? Music psychologists tend to see the absolute pitch phenomenon as a graduated spectrum rather than as a black-and-white innate ability: Some individuals' sense of pitch is more "absolute" than others.

academic. 1. Used among singers to refer to a vocal specialist who is also a scholar, and sometimes a scholar first and foremost. While many academics are also performers, academics usually do not depend on performing for their livelihood, and their primary contribution to the vocal community is through their research on a particular aspect of singing or vocal literature. Early music specialists and professors of singing are usually considered academics.

2. A pejorative term sometimes used when a performance seems too studied, too rigid, or not expressive enough. A natural, instinctive performance is usually thought of as the antithesis of an "academic" performance.

Academy of Finnish Art Song. An organization based in Helsinki, Finland, devoted to the study, performance, and presentation of **Finnish art song**. The Academy of Finnish Art Song is supported by the Finnish Cultural Foundation and has published two important books: *Singing in Finnish* (2005) and *Singing in Swedish* (2009). These resources are available in English translation and include **IPA transcriptions** of 141 **songs** in Finnish and Finland-Swedish.

accelerando (**It**). Gradually faster.

accent. 1. In singing, a specific type of articulation that is harsher and more pronounced than usual.

2. In **diction**, can refer to the accented syllable of a word.

3. In diction, can refer to a regionalism that influences one's **pronunciation**. In this sense, it is similar to **dialect**, but less inclusive.

accent aigu (´). A French **diacritical marking** that—when placed over an *é*—indicates a closed [e] **vowel**. As French is essentially a language without word stress, this diacritical mark influences **pronunciation** only. The *accent aigu* looks identical to the Italian *accento acuto*, but these are best thought of as two distinct (albeit identical-looking) diacritical markings, each of which serves a unique and specific function within its respective language.

accent circonflexe (**Fr**). See **circumflex**.

accent d'insistence. An aspect of French **diction** that permits the singer to subtly add his or her own **accents** and inflections to certain syllables to convey a specific meaning. French is essentially a language without word stress, as opposed to German, Italian, and English, which have very emphatic stress patterns. Employing just a little of the *accent d'insistence* can greatly alter the meaning of a particular phrase. This property of the French language becomes increasingly important for advanced singers who wish to express themselves artistically. The *accent d'insistence* should not be confused with the **accent d'intensité**.

accent d'intensité. An aspect of French **pronunciation** that occurs in words of two or more syllables. In these words, the final syllable takes on a slight stress, and this stress is called the *accent d'intensité*. All other syllables remain equally unstressed. The *accent d'intensité* never applies to the final **mute e**. The *accent d'intensité* should not be confused with the **accent d'insistence**.

accent grave (`). French **diacritical mark** literally meaning "grave **accent**." The *accent grave* appears over the **vowels** *è*, *à*, and *où* in certain words in the French language. When it appears over the letter *e*, it affects the **pronunciation** of the vowel, rendering an open [ɛ]. In other instances (*à* and *où*), it has no effect on pronunciation.

accento acuto (´). The Italian term for the French **accent aigu**. Historically, the *accento acuto* was a bit esoteric and redundant; it was an Italian term that only pertained to French **diction** (since the *accento acuto* was not used in the Italian language—only the **accento grave** was used). Modern Italian, however, has seen some instances of the *accento acuto* replacing the *accento grave*. In these cases, the *accento acuto* can signal closed [e] **vowels**, thus bringing the marking more in line with the French usage. Examples include *perché* [per'ke], *sé* [se], and *né* [ne]. Modern Italian also tends to use the *accento acuto* over the final *i* or *u*. Examples include *partí* [par'ti] and *lassú* [las'su].

accento grave (`). The most common **diacritical mark** in Italian, most commonly found over final stressed **vowels** in **polysyllabic** words. It is also used in certain **monosyllabic** words that have different meanings but are otherwise spelled the same. (For example: "là" means "there," whereas "la" means "the" or "it.") Unlike the French **accent grave**, the Italian *accento grave* over an *è* or *ò* does not necessarily indicate that the vowel is open. On the contrary, there are many examples of closed stressed vowels that use an *accento grave*. Examples include *perchè* [per'ke], *sè* [se], and *nè* [ne]. In modern Italian, however, some of these final vowels have replaced the *accento grave* with the **accento acuto**. In these cases, some effort has been made to distinguish closed *e*'s [e] from open ones [ɛ], bringing the function of the *accento grave* more in line with the French usage. Examples of the modern *accento grave* include *caffè* [kafˈfɛ] and *ahimè* [aiˈmɛ].

acceptance angle. The angle—measured from the axis of a **microphone**—to which a microphone can pick up **acoustic** energy. Acceptance angles are usually indicated on a **pickup pattern diagram**. For more information, see the essay entitled "What Every Singer Needs to Know about Audio Technology."

accompanied recitative. See *recitativo accompagnato*.

accompaniment. Instrumental music that supports the singer. In the **classical** tradition, this is usually a piano (or occasionally a harpsichord, lute, or guitar), chamber **ensemble**, or orchestra. In **popular music** or **world music** traditions, accompanying instruments may vary widely from **style** to style.

accompanist. One who accompanies a singer or group of singers. Usually a pianist, but can refer to anyone who plays an **accompanimental** instrument.

ACDA. Abbreviation for the **American Choral Directors Association**.

ach-laut* [χ].** In **diction**, a voiceless velar **fricative** that is an idiomatic hallmark of the German language. *Ach-lauts* [χ] occur when *ch* follows the vowels *a*, *o*, and *u*, whereas ***ich-lauts [ç] occur when *ch* follows any other **vowel**—including *ä*, *ö*, and *ü*, or a consonant.

acid reflux. The common name for **gastroesophageal reflux disease (GERD)** or **laryngopharyngeal reflux disease (LPRD)**. Both conditions involve reflux of stomach contents as a result of normal physiological barriers to the reflux of gastric contents into the esophagus.

acoustic singing. Singing without the aid of electronic **amplification**. The opposite of **amplified singing**.

acoustics. The physics of sound. The discipline of acoustics involves sound **production**, propagation, and perception. Any instrument operates according to basic principles of acoustics, and the human voice is no exception. Subtle decisions that a singer makes regarding the use of his or her resonators (the **laryngopharynx**, **oral cavity**, and **nasopharynx**) fall under the laws of acoustics and greatly influence the resulting musical sound, projection, and **tone quality** produced. Although many accredited schools of music no longer offer acoustics courses as part of their required curricula for music majors, it is essential that all musicians—including singers—understand some of the fundamental concepts of acoustics.

acquired laryngeal webs. One of the two basic types of **laryngeal webs**. Acquired laryngeal webs are brought on by external trauma or illness. **Congenital laryngeal webs**—the other category—occur during embryonic development.

act. One large section of a stage **production**. In contemporary culture, **operas**, **operettas**, **musicals**, and **revues** are usually divided into two acts. Historically, however, the number of acts varies. French **baroque opera** established a **five-act** structure (based in part on **Renaissance** ideals, when plays were written in five acts, imitating classical Greek ideals). The five-act structure persisted through the *grand opéras* of Meyerbeer, Berlioz, and Halévy. **Italian operas** by Mozart, Donizetti, and Verdi ranged anywhere from two to four acts.

acting school. See **acting technique**.

acting technique. A specific **methodology** or philosophy regarding acting that includes movement and stage performance. Acting schools are often associated with and named after single individuals who are designated as a specific school's creator and founder. **Constantin Stanislavski, Lee Strasberg, Uta Hagen, Stella Adler, Michael Chekhov, Anne Bogart,** and **Sanford Meisner** are several important examples of individuals who have founded specific acting schools. Sometimes, a "school" is simply synonymous with a tradition: A performer of the school has not necessarily attended a specific program of instruction; rather, he or she simply subscribes to the movement's ideals and traditions. **Musical theatre** performers and—to a lesser extent—**opera** singers are part of the world of **theatre** and are likely to encounter **stage directors** who come from particular "schools" of acting. A basic understanding of the major schools is requisite for the **professional** theatrical singer. While it is still possible to find performers who remain devoted to a particular acting school, it is far more common in contemporary practice to encounter performers who draw upon **techniques** derived from a wide variety of sources. The contemporary actor tends to be more of a hybrid of various **styles** and schools.

action. A theatrical term/concept describing the movement or development of a **plot**.

acute laryngitis. A type of **laryngitis** brought on by a virus that often results in total, short-term voice loss. One generally recovers from acute laryngitis in a matter of weeks. Acute laryngitis is one of the three types of physically based laryngitis, along with **chronic laryngitis** and **fungal laryngitis**.

adagio (It). At ease or comfortable. Adagio is usually slower than **andante** but not as slow as **largo**.

Adam's apple. A common term referring to the protruding "bump" at the front of the **thyroid cartilage**. The Adam's apple is easy to see and feel, as this "bump" is located at the front and center of one's throat. Students of **classical** singing often look in the mirror at their Adam's apple to gauge whether it is raised or remains in a lowered position while singing. A lowered Adam's apple indicates a stable larynx, which is an essential ingredient in cultivating a *bel canto*, classical **tone quality**. A raised Adam's apple, on the other hand, indicates a "high larynx," which encourages a more speech-like, shallow **quality** that is undesirable in classical singing.

adduction. Movement of the **vocal folds** toward the midline of the **glottis**.

adductor spasmodic dysphonia (adductor SD). See **spasmodic dysphonia (SD)**.

Adler, Stella (1901–1992). American actress and acting teacher. Adler is most famous for developing an **acting technique** that is widely practiced and referenced by students and teachers of **theatre**. Adler was the only American actress who studied with **Constantin Stanislavski**. She initially collaborated with **Lee Strasberg** in the Group Theatre, but Adler left the collective after disagreements with Strasberg regarding the nuances of acting technique. Adler's approach to Stanislavski's teachings was more pragmatic and less extreme than those who subscribed to Strasberg's **Method**. Adler founded the Stella Adler Studio of Acting in New York City in 1949, which emphasized a balance between **emotional recall** and imagination. Her acting philosophy is summarized in her book, *The Technique of Acting* (1988). In theatrical training, Adler's method is one of the most frequently referenced acting techniques, along with those of **Michael Chekhov**, **Sanford Meisner**, **Uta Hagen**, **Viola Spolin**, Constantin Stanislavski, Lee Strasberg, and **Anne Bogart**.

Aeolian. A mode built on the sixth **scale degree** of the **major** scale. Aeolian mode is the same as **natural minor**.

affections. See **doctrine of affections**.

affricate. In **diction**, describes a **manner of articulation** in which **consonants** are produced via a **plosive** stop that is followed by a **fricative**. Common examples of fricative

consonants include [dz], [ts], [dʒ], and [tʃ]. Sometimes called "affricative." See also **lateral**, **nasal**.

afterglow. A party that follows a **concert** of **barbershop-style** music. In addition to food and revelry, there is almost always more singing. In this respect, an afterglow is an informal concert that takes place after a more formal concert (or show).

agent. A businessperson who "manages" a singer, assisting, arranging schedules, and helping to secure engagements (or **gigs**). In **theatre**, it is not uncommon to have more than one agent. Not to be confused with **casting director**, which is a completely different (albeit related) profession. Although one sometimes hears the term *casting agent*, there is technically no such thing.

aggiustamento. Italian term referring to **vowel** modification or **formant tuning**.

agility. The ability for a singer's voice to move easily, quickly, and accurately. See also *bel canto*, **coloratura**, *fioratura*, **flexibility**, **melisma**.

agitato (It). Agitated.

Agnus Dei. One of the five standard parts of the **Ordinary** in a Catholic **Mass**.

air. English synonym for **song** or melody. Often seen in association with songs or **arias** in the eighteenth-century British repertory.

air de cour. A **song** for voice and **accompaniment** that was popular in France during the early **baroque** era.

Aksu, Sezen (b. 1954). Turkish singer of **world music**, excelling in multiple **genres** and **styles**. Aksu is the most famous Turkish singer in the world, renowned for her **interpretations** in **classical**, **popular**, and folk idioms. She is also known for pursuing a political agenda with her music, using her fame to speak out on social and secular issues in Muslim Turkey, particularly discrimination against women and ethnic minorities. She has been a constant presence in the world music scene since 1980.

aleatoric music. A twentieth-century compositional innovation that eliminates traditional concepts of **form** and structure and instead allows for the element of chance. Performers are empowered to make individual decisions regarding time, form, structure, and order of content. Also known as chance music. Charles Ives (1874–1954), Henry Cowell (1897–1965), and John Cage (1912–1992) are usually named as significant aleatoric music pioneers.

Alexander Technique. A type of **bodywork** conceived by Frederick Matthias Alexander (1869–1955) intended to help individuals move intelligently and mindfully through life. Individuals who study the Alexander Technique increase their physical self-awareness and attempt to solve problems related to unnecessary tension and effort in the body. The goal of the **technique** is to restore freedom and **expression** to the body and mind. In his lifetime, Alexander wrote four treatises that define and clarify his technique: *Man's Supreme Inheritance* (1910, rev. 1918), *Constructive Conscious Control of the Individual* (1923), *The Use of the Self* (1932), and *The Universal Constant in Living* (1941). Many singers explore the Alexander Technique and view it as an essential tool in assisting with good **posture** and resolving issues involving undesired physical tension.

allargando **(It).** Broadening.

allegretto **(It).** Less fast than allegro. *Allegretto* often implies a lighter texture and character as well.

allegro **(It).** Quick or fast.

alleluia. See **alleluia-verse**.

alleluia-verse. One of the five standard parts of the **Proper** in a Catholic **Mass**.

Alt-Bachisches Archiv. A collection of music composed by members of the Bach family prior to Johann Sebastian Bach (1685–1750).

alternatim. In **medieval** music, the alternation of **Gregorian chant** with **polyphony**. Sections are usually governed by the **liturgical** text. The earliest **polyphonic genres**—for example, the conductus and *organum*—are examples of the kind of polyphonic compositions that were juxtaposed to (or, *in alternatim* with) Gregorian chant. Sacred compositions performed in the *alternatim* style persisted through the early decades of the **Renaissance** era and were particularly a feature of many *Magnificat* settings during these later years.

alternative (also called alt rock). A **style** of **rock** music that emerged in the 1980s and became popular during the 1990s. Although alternative is a wide umbrella that encompasses numerous different styles, many alternative musicians have been influenced by **punk**, which is an important precursor of the **genre**. In the 1990s, a hard-edged successor to alternative appeared called **grunge**.

alto. 1. In a four-part (**SATB**) **voicing**, the second highest part in **choral music**, usually performed by female **mezzo-sopranos** and male **countertenors**. Historically, it derives its name from **Latin**—*altus* ("high")—referring to its relationship with the **tenor** voice (which it is "higher" than).

2. Short for **contralto**, the lowest designation for a **classical** female **voice type**. Male altos are usually called countertenors, although they are usually designated as **altos** on choral **rosters**.

alveolar. An adjective used in **diction** that describes **consonants** that utilize the tip of the tongue and the ridge behind the upper teeth. Almost all examples of alveolar consonants occur in the English and American **pronunciations** of [d], [t], [z], [s], [l], [n], [ɾ], and [ɹ]. Most of these consonants are **dental** (i.e., employing the tongue tip against the upper teeth) in Italian, French, and German. Refers to a specific **point of articulation**. See also **alveolar**, **bilabial**, **labiodental**, **palatal**, **prepalatal**, **velar**.

alveolar ridge. The jaw ridge above the front teeth at the front of the roof of the mouth.

amateur. A nonprofessional musician. Unlike **professionals**, amateur musicians are not paid, but perform because they love to make music. (The etymology of the word *amateur* roughly means "one who loves.") Amateur does not necessarily imply anything pejorative about the level of performance; however, some amateur **ensembles** hold their own against professional ones. The **Grammy Award**-winning Atlanta Symphony Chorus and Mormon Tabernacle Choir are both examples of excellent amateur, all-volunteer ensembles.

ambit. Term sometimes used to refer to the **pitch (frequency)** variation of a singer's **vibrato**. Ambits can be described as wide (with much frequency variation) or narrow (with little frequency variation).

Ambrosian chant. The **medieval liturgical chant** of Milan. Similar in compositional **style** to **monophonic Gregorian chant**.

Ameling, Elly (b. 1933). Dutch **soprano**. Ameling was born in Rotterdam and began studying singing in her teens. After studying the French *mélodie* in Paris with **Pierre Bernac**, she won important singing competitions in Holland and Geneva. She made her **professional** debut in 1953, which marked the beginning of a forty-five-year career as a recitalist and **oratorio** singer. Ameling is held in particularly high regard for her **interpretation** of French *mélodies* and German *Lieder*, and she has recorded prolifically in both **genres**. She is also well-known for her performances of Bach **cantatas**. Ameling was knighted by the queen of the Netherlands in 1971.

American Academy of Teachers of Singing (AATS). Select, prestigious society of singing teachers. Founded in 1922, in New York City, the group has expanded in recent years to include accomplished **pedagogues** from throughout the United States. Membership is by invitation only. AATS regularly publishes articles related to the singing profession, many of which are jointly published in the *Journal of Singing* (the official journal of the **National Association of Teachers of Singing**). Limited to only forty members at any given time, election to the AATS remains a great honor and is a sort of "lifetime achievement" award among voice pedagogues.

American art song. Art song written by American composers, most of whom set American poems. After early European-styled experiments by such Boston composers as Amy Beach (1867–1944) and Edward MacDowell (1860–1908), Charles Ives (1874–1954) is considered to be the founder of a more distinctive and truly "American" art song. Many of Ives's compositional innovations were so radical that they were rejected by the conservative musical circles of the time, and he was forced to self-publish his *114 Songs* in 1922. Posterity would later judge this volume to be perhaps the most historically significant **song collection** ever published. Other important twentieth-century American art song composers include Charles Griffes (1884–1920), Virgil Thomson (1896–1989), Ernst Bacon (1898–1990), Aaron Copland (1900–1990), Theodore Chanler (1902–1951), Samuel Barber (1910–1981), Paul Bowles (1910–1999), Ned Rorem (b. 1923), Dominick Argento (b. 1927), and Richard Hundley (b. 1931). In recent years, younger composers, including Stephen Paulus (b. 1949), Libby Larsen (b. 1950), John Musto (b. 1954), and Lori Laitman (b. 1955), have made an indelible mark on the American art song **repertory**.

American Choral Directors Association (ACDA). Founded in 1959, the ACDA is a nonprofit music-education organization whose central purpose is to promote excellence in **choral music** through performance, composition, publication, research, and teaching. In addition, ACDA strives through arts advocacy to elevate choral music's position in American society. ACDA is particularly known for its national and regional conferences, as well as for its monthly publication, the *Choral Journal*.

American opera. A **genre** of **opera** written by American composers with **libretti** that are often set in a variety of American locales. The **folk opera** is an important **subgenre** of American opera that evokes specific regions of the United States through both the story and music. Some of the most famous American operas can also be called folk operas: George Gershwin's *Porgy and Bess* (1935) is set in the Deep South of Charleston, South Carolina;

Douglas Moore's *The Ballad of Baby Doe* (1956) in the American West (Colorado); Carlisle Floyd's *Susannah* (1955) in rural Appalachia; and Aaron Copland's *The Tender Land* (1954) on a farm in Minnesota. Samuel Barber (1910–1981) and especially Gian Carlo Menotti (1911–2007) contributed many operas to the **repertory**, albeit with a more European-derived **style**. At four and a half hours in length, Philip Glass's *Einstein on the Beach* (1976) is opera's most precocious venture into **minimalism**, another distinctly American artistic movement of the late twentieth century. The genre of American opera continues to grow, with new repertoire being written on a regular basis. The **Metropolitan Opera** has mounted **productions** of several new American operas in recent decades, namely John Corigliano's *The Ghosts of Versailles* (1991), John Harbison's *The Great Gatsby* (1999), and William Bolcom's *A View from the Bridge* (2002).

American operetta. A **form** of light **opera** that emerged in New York City in the early decades of the twentieth century. American **operetta** is a **repertory** distinct from **Viennese operetta** and **English comic opera**. While New York certainly enjoyed numerous imports from **Gilbert and Sullivan** and Franz Lehár (1870–1948), the principal composers of American operetta were Victor Herbert (1859–1924), Rudolf Friml (1879–1972), and Sigmund Romberg (1887–1951), all of whom lived and worked in New York. Ironically, none of these composers were born in the United States: Herbert was born in Ireland, Romberg in Hungary, and Friml in Czechoslovakia. Herbert's operettas appeared first, during the first decade of the twentieth century; his most famous works include *Babes in Toyland* (1903), *The Red Mill* (1906), and *Naughty Marietta* (1910). Friml's star rose after Herbert's, during the 1920s; his most famous works—*Rose Marie* (1924), *The Vagabond King* (1925), and *The Three Musketeers* (1928)—all date from this period. Romberg was the most European of the three, and his most popular works—*The Student Prince* (1924), *The Desert Song* (1926), and *The New Moon* (1928)—are very much in the **style** of Viennese operetta.

American r. A retroflex [ɹ] sound idiomatic to the English language, especially common in American **dialects**. While present and welcomed in **contemporary commercial music (CCM) styles**—for example, **popular music** and **musical theatre**—American "r" sounds are undesirable in most forms of **classical** singing, particularly **choral music**. While solo artists typically use them judiciously in American **opera** and **art song**, American r's are also generally avoided when singing British **repertoire**. In these instances, they are either replaced with a **flipped r** or **rolled r**, or omitted altogether. (See also **omitted r**.) The American student of singing must work diligently to avoid excessive use of the retroflex [ɹ].

American Speech and Hearing Association (ASHA). The American professional association for audiologists; **speech-language pathologists (CCC-SLPs)**; and speech, language, and hearing scientists. ASHA is something of a sister organization to the **National Association of Teachers of Singing (NATS)**, **New York Singing Teachers Association (NYSTA)**, **American Academy of Teachers of Singing (AATS)**, **National Center for Voice and Speech (NCVS)**, Voice and Speech Trainers Association (VASTA), and **Voice Foundation**. The organization's research and programs indirectly—and sometimes directly—impact teachers of singing. ASHA sponsors four peer-reviewed journals, including the *American Journal of Audiology* (AJA), *American Journal of Speech-Language Pathology* (AJSLP), *Journal of Speech, Language, and Hearing Research* (JSLHR), and *Language, Speech, and Hearing Services in Schools* (LSHSS). There are more than 150,000 members of ASHA.

amplification. Augmenting the volume and **quality** of singing through artificial, electronic means.

amplified singing. Singing that benefits from electronic **amplification**, as in **genres** that require a **microphone**. This includes virtually all **contemporary commercial music (CCM) styles**, including **pop**, **rock**, **jazz**, **country**, and **musical theatre**. The opposite of **acoustic singing**. **Processed singing** goes one step further, as it both amplifies and electronically alters the singer's natural voice.

amplitude. 1. The magnitude of **compressions** within a sound wave. Amplitude is measured in **decibels (dB)**. In practical terms, amplitude refers to how loud a sound is.

2. In singing, amplitude is an adjective used by voice teachers and choral **conductors** that refers—rather unscientifically—to the **pitch** variation of one's **vibrato**. In general, if a singer controls the amplitude of his or her vibrato, he or she is bringing more pitch centricity to the sound, which may be desirable in softer singing, **early music**, and **ensemble** singing. Conversely, a vibrato with wider amplitude is going to have more pitch fluctuation, thus making it harder for the individual voice to blend with other singers. In this sense, amplitude is a colloquial synonym for **ambit**, which is often used to refer to the pitch (**frequency**) fluctuation of a singer's vibrato.

anacrusis. A pickup; a rhythmically unstressed note or notes at the beginning of a musical passage.

anatomy. The branch of science concerned with the bodily structure of humans, animals, and other organisms. Anatomy also describes the bodily structure of an organism.

andante **(It).** Going, moving, or running. *Andante* is usually somewhat faster than *adagio*, but not as fast as *allegro*. Due to the ambiguity of the translation as it relates to **tempo**, the term *andante* can be problematic to interpret, especially when combined with other modifiers. For example, does *più andante* mean faster or slower? The Italian term means "going, moving, or running," but many musicians have come to believe that *andante* is a slow tempo. This bifurcation is a source of confusion among performers.

andantino. Italian **expressive marking** literally meaning "a little andante." Typically, *andantino* is interpreted as a bit faster than *andante*.

Anderson, Marian (1897–1993). African American **contralto**. Anderson was raised in Philadelphia and auditioned for further study at the Philadelphia Music Academy, where she was denied admittance on racial grounds. She went on to make her debut with the New York Philharmonic Orchestra in 1925, followed by a successful **recital** in Wigmore Hall in London in 1930. Due to the lack of stage opportunities, Anderson's career consisted mostly of **concert** work. After being denied a recital opportunity at Constitution Hall in Washington, DC, in 1939, Eleanor Roosevelt and other prominent Americans sponsored a concert for her at the Lincoln Memorial; the event drew an audience of more than 75,000 people. At the invitation of **Rudolf Bing**, Anderson made her **Metropolitan Opera** debut in 1955, in the **role** of Ulrica in Verdi's *Un ballo in maschera*, becoming the first black performer in the history of the **company**. She is considered to be an icon of the civil rights movement, paving the way for many African American singers in the United States. Anderson died in Portland, Oregon, in 1993, at the age of ninety-six.

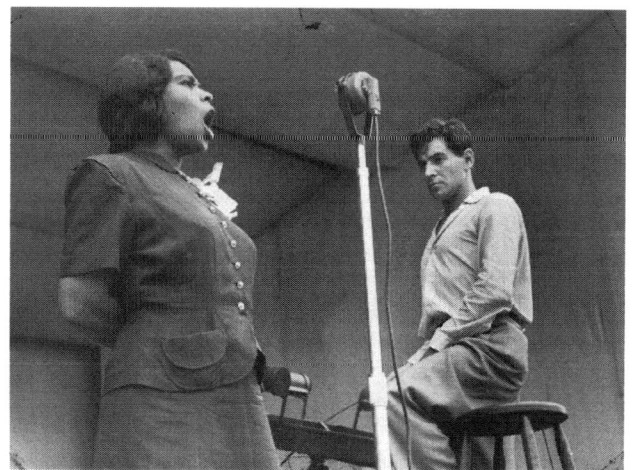

Figure 1. Leonard Bernstein rehearsing with singer Marian Anderson at Lewisohn Stadium, New York, June 1947. *Courtesy Library of Congress.*

Andrews, Julie (b. 1935). English singer and actress, and an iconic performer in the **musical theatre genre**. A former child actress, Andrews made her **West End Theatre** debut in 1948, and her **Broadway** debut in 1954, appearing in both instances as Polly Browne in Sandy Wilson's *The Boy Friend*. She went on to star in Lerner and Loewe's *My Fair Lady* (1956) and *Camelot* (1960), and became a television sensation in 1957, when she appeared in Rodgers and Hammerstein's *Cinderella*. She achieved Hollywood fame with *Mary Poppins* (1964) and *The Sound of Music* (1965), winning an Academy Award for the **role** of Mary Poppins. More than any other singer of her generation, Andrews perfectly exemplifies the "legit" leading-lady **soprano** of the classic Broadway era. She occasionally deviated from her **operetta**-like delivery when performing character **songs**, for example, those of Eliza Doolittle in *My Fair Lady*.

Anfang **(Ger).** Beginning.

Anglican chant. Harmonized **formulas** for singing psalms and canticles in **Anglican church music**. Anglican chant formulas usually consist of a series of **homophonic chords** that can be used interchangeably with various psalm texts. The psalms are then pointed (reconciled with the selected formula) by the **choirmaster** or organist. **Classical singers** who pursue a **church job** must often sing Anglican chant and may be asked to **sight read** in this **style** during their **audition**. Anglican chant should not be confused with **Gregorian chant** and its many **medieval** cousins.

Anglican church music. A specific **repertory** of choral and organ music performed and used **liturgically** in Anglican churches worldwide and in the Episcopal church in the United States. Anglican church music can be categorized into several principal **subgenres**, including **anthems** (both **full anthems** and **verse anthems**), services (most commonly morning services and **evening services**), **hymns**, responses, and psalmody. The psalms are usually set to **Anglican chant**. While Anglican church music is generally not used liturgically outside of Anglican and Episcopal worship services, many of the anthems have found their way into the mainstream choral **repertory**. Another interesting aspect of the **genre** is that it has never fallen out of fashion. The core repertoire and **style** of worship in most Anglican and Episcopal churches is virtually the same as it was in the nineteenth century. **Professional** choral singers who pursue **church jobs** quickly gain proficiency with this repertoire and liturgy.

animato **(It).** Animated.

antagonist. A muscle that directly opposes another muscle. Most muscles in the body are paired with an antagonistic muscle. See **muscle antagonism**.

anthem. 1. A piece of **choral music**, usually in the Anglican tradition, used in **liturgical** worship. See also **full anthem**, **verse anthem**.

2. A **musical theatre ballad** that idiomatically expresses the attitudes or desires of a particular character. Usually occurs late in the show. See also **eleven o'clock number**.

anticipation. 1. In **contemporary commercial music (CCM) styles**, occurs when a singer purposefully comes in before the notated **pitch**. An anticipation is a stylized rhythmic choice and the opposite of **backphrasing**.

2. An **ornament** that consists of a metrically weak **dissonant** note that is immediately reharmonized as a **consonance**.

antiphon. A **liturgical chant** that precedes and follows a psalm or canticle in liturgical worship. The **Marian antiphons** and *O* **antiphons** are two specific types.

antiphonal. An adjective that describes a piece of music where two or more **ensembles** perform in alternation with one another.

aphonia. The inability to phonate; the loss of one's voice.

aphonic. One who suffers from **aphonia**.

apocopation. In Italian **diction**, the elimination of the final **vowel** of a word. This happens frequently in literary Italian, and the composer must deal with this phenomenon when he sets the text. Likewise, singers need to recognize apocopated words as truncations of the original word. Examples include *ancora = ancor* and *amore = amor*. Apocopation does not alter the **syllabic** stress of the word; the same syllable is still stressed regardless of whether it is then followed by a final vowel. Apocopation also occurs in Spanish.

Appelman, D. Ralph (1908–1993). American **voice pedagogue** best known as the author of *The Science of Vocal Pedagogy* (1967). This treatise, along with William Vennard's ***Singing: The Mechanism and the Technic*** (1967), helped to inaugurate the modern era of **fact-based voice pedagogy**.

appoggiatura. A specific **ornament** that occurs when a **dissonant pitch** falls on a strong metric **beat**. *Appoggiaturas* can resolve by step either upward or downward. The Italian meaning of the term is "leaning," and the *appoggiatura* must be "leaned upon"—that is, the *appoggiatura* must be sung with more emphasis than the note to which it resolves. Singers of **early music** must be skilled and knowledgeable in their implementation and execution of *appoggiaturas* and other ornaments, because the

interpretation of *appoggiaturas* can vary considerably from one historical period to another.

appoggio. An Italian term used in vocal **technique** to describe a specific type of **breath management**. *Appoggio* remains the most widely practiced breath management technique used by **classical singers** and taught by **voice pedagogues** of all **genres** and **styles**. **Fact-based voice pedagogy** and modern voice science seem to affirm *appoggio* as the most efficient technique for breath management during singing. The word *appoggio* comes from the Italian word *appoggiare*, which means "to lean on." In *The Structure of Singing* (1986), **Richard Miller** offers a simple, one-line definition of *appoggio*: "the establishment of dynamic balance between the inspiratory, phonatory, and resonatory systems in singing." While few would argue with this explanation, the specific physiology that informs *appoggio* necessitates a longer and more complex definition, and *appoggio*—while widely practiced—remains a technique that often eludes or confuses the novice student of singing. While voice pedagogues may strive to establish good breath management with their students, they also tend to approach the teaching of *appoggio* in different ways and with a variety of different exercises.

The vast majority of contemporary voice teachers, however, agree that good *appoggio* involves a coordination of **thoracic breathing** and **abdominal breathing**. In this sense, *appoggio* replaces other methods of breathing, the most common three being **clavicular breathing** (which is almost never used in classical singing), thoracic breathing, and abdominal breathing (the latter two being hallmarks of other national schools of singing). Thoracic–abdominal breathing—essentially a synonym for *appoggio*—is also descriptively known as **balanced breathing**, and its hallmark is the efficient use of distinct and different muscles during both **inhalation** and **exhalation**. In *appoggio*, the primary muscles of inhalation are the **diaphragm** and the **external intercostal muscles**. The primary muscles of exhalation are six in number. They include the **internal intercostal muscles** and five muscle pairs: the **internal oblique abdominis muscles**, **external oblique abdominis muscles**, **transverse abdominis muscles**, **rectus abdominis muscles**, and **quadratus lumborum muscles**. Each of the muscles of exhalation work in coordination and balance with one another. During inhalation, the muscles of exhalation are relaxed, while the muscles of inhalation are engaged, and, conversely, during exhalation, the muscles of inhalation are relaxed, while the muscles of exhalation are engaged. In good *appoggio*, expansion occurs around the base of the **thorax** and lower abdomen, and this expansion is then efficiently maintained during **phonation**.

As efficient breath management offers a good foundation for any style of singing, *appoggio* is a technique that extends beyond classical singing and can be practiced with equal success by singers of all genres and styles, including **contemporary commercial music (CCM)** styles.

apprenticeship. Term often used interchangeably with **young artist program (YAP)** in the field of **opera**. Apprentices generally **cover** principal artists who sing leading **roles** and perform *comprimario* **roles**. Wolf Trap, Santa Fe, Houston Grand, Sarasota, Central City, Des Moines Metro, Ash Lawn, and Chautauqua are examples of well-known apprenticeships for aspiring opera singers. **Art song** apprenticeships—for example, those found at such summer festivals as **Tanglewood** and **Ravinia**—are usually called fellowships.

approximate. To bring the **vocal folds** together.

aria. An **opera**, **oratorio**, or **cantata** excerpt for one solo singer. In **number operas**, arias are always stand-alone movements, but in **through-composed operatic** works, arias are simply solo sections that occur within the larger symphonic framework. **Classical singers** often excerpt arias for use in **concert** and **audition** settings. *Aria* is a term that has evolved during the last five centuries or so. When opera was invented around the beginning of the seventeenth century, the term came to be used for lyrical, more reflective, vocal solos, as opposed to the intervening material (intended mostly to further the action). At first, these arias tended to be accompanied by **continuo** only, but gradually larger instrumental **ensembles** appeared as *ritornelli*, or were even interspersed among vocal phrases and—ultimately—appeared as **accompaniment** to the voice.

By the eighteenth century, the *da capo* aria had become the dominant **form** of aria, with increasingly long sections often separated from one another by ritornellos (short instrumental passages interspersed throughout a piece). The B-section was generally in a contrasting **key** or mood, and the *da capo* (the return of the A section) invited **ornamentation** on the part of the singer. **Cadenzas** could be inserted at the ends of both sections. The ubiquity of the *da capo* form made it possible to evoke surprise when expectations were not realized; for example, the B section of Handel's "Why Do the Nations So Furiously Rage Together?" (*Messiah*, 1742) is followed not by a *da capo*, but by a **chorus**—"Let us break their bonds asunder"—back in the **tonic key**. The **ground bass aria** was another standard aria form during the **baroque** era, most famously employed in two arias from Purcell's *Dido and Aeneas* (1889): "Ah! Belinda, I Am Pressed with Torment" and "When I Am Laid in Earth," otherwise known as Dido's Lament.

In the baroque era, composers sometimes designated movements for two singers as arias (often with one of the singers singing a **chorale** tune, as in a Bach **cantata**), but this is more of a period definition of the term, and movements like these are more practically thought of as **duets** by modern singers. In both the baroque and the **classical** eras, arias are frequently preceded by **recitatives** (both *recitativo secco* and *recitativo accompagnato*). Subsequently, a general loosening of the form led to *dal segno* arias (in which the return of the A section is shortened), to rondo arias, to arias climaxing with a *stretta* (a fast and bravura showpiece), and even insertions of **dramatic** recitative between sections of the aria. Contributing even more to this loosening was the incorporation of *pertichini*: lines for other characters, or for the chorus, intruding into the solo **number**. In concert performance, the *pertichini* can sometimes be omitted, or cut, without doing too much violence to the music.

In the nineteenth century, a sort of "double aria" became a prominent means of solo display: a slow and expressive aria, known as the *cantabile* or *cavatina*, followed by a fast and brilliant aria, the *cabaletta*. The whole was often preceded by a *scena* in an accompanied—by a keyboard or an orchestra—recitative **style**, and perhaps another *scena* might intervene between the *cavatina* and the *cabaletta*. Sometimes, with the addition of the *pertichini*, the complex becomes extended to the point that the connection between *cavatina* and *cabaletta* is dissipated and almost lost. An example of this is "De miei bollenti spiriti" and "O mio rimorso," from Verdi's *La traviata*. The result of the double aria as a compositional form is that a given aria may come to be known by multiple titles: the first words of the *cavatina*, and/ or of the *cabaletta*, or even an introductory recitative or *scena*—not to mention such descriptive names as Lucia's "Mad Scene" from Donizetti's *Lucia di Lammermoor* (1835), Yaroslavna's "Lament" from Borodin's *Prince Igor* (1874), or the "Bell Song" from Délibes's *Lakmé* (1883).

aria for two. An **operatic aria** that is sung directly to another character onstage. Rodolfo's "Che gelida manina" and Mimì's "Sì, mi chiamano Mimì"—both from Puccini's *La bohème* (1896)—are two famous examples.

aria package. A **repertoire** of **arias**—usually five—taken to **auditions** by young artists and by singers auditioning for graduate school and **young artist programs (YAPs)**. Aria packages usually feature an aria in each of the principal four languages—Italian, French, German, and English—and one additional aria, either a fifth language or, more often, a contrasting aria in one of the original four languages. The singer usually chooses his or her first aria, after which the judges decide which one will be performed next. Although a singer will usually only sing two arias, all five must be prepared and ready.

arie antiche **(It).** Ancient **arias**. The vast *oeuvre* of baroque and early **classical** Italian arias. Most *arie antiche* were originally written for **Italian operas**, but the **accompaniments** have been reconceived and romanticized for piano. The *arie antiche* was largely revived for an important collection edited and published by Allessandro Parisotti (1853–1913), entitled *Arie antiche: ad una voce per canto e pianoforte* (1890). In New York, the publisher G. Schirmer collected twenty-four of Parisotti's **songs** and republished them as *24 Italian Songs and Arias* (1894), which became the most frequently owned vocal anthology in American studios. Composers represented in the anthology include Giulio Caccini (c. 1551–1618), Alessandro Scarlatti (1660–1725), and Giovanni Battista Pergolesi (1710–1736). These **romantic** arrangements are frequently appropriated into singers' **repertoires** and are considered by many to be a part of the **Italian art song genre**.

arietta. An Italian term referring to a "small" **aria** or **song** that is shorter and less elaborate than an aria. *Ariettas* are often sung by supporting (*comprimario*) characters in **Italian operas** of the **classical** and **baroque** periods.

arioso. An Italian term used by composers to refer to a passage that is usually more lyrical than a **recitative**, but shorter in duration and less lyrical than an **aria**. In the **baroque** era, brief *ariosos* often occurred in the middle of recitative movements, with melodic material emerging from a recitative-like texture and then—after a short time—returning there again. Johann Sebastian Bach (1685–1750) often used an *arioso* at the end of a recitative to establish a more expressive mood, whether of sadness, hopefulness, or confidence.

Armenian chant. **Liturgical chant** developed by the Armenian Apostolic Church beginning in the year 552. Armenian chant is **monophonic** and similar in compositional **style** to **Gregorian chant**.

Armstrong, Louis (1901–1971). **Jazz** singer and trumpet player, and one of the most famous of all jazz musicians. Nicknamed "Satchmo," he began his long career in the 1920s, when he played New Orleans-**style** jazz with his band, the Hot Fives and Sevens. He further established himself during the **swing** era and beyond, becoming something of an anachronism (albeit a very popular one) by the 1950s and 1960s, maintaining his dated, idiosyncratic style until his death in 1971. His title track from the **musical** *Hello Dolly!* (1964)—a throwback to the jazz style of the 1930s—became a No. 1 Billboard hit during an era saturated by Beatles records. To this day, there has not been another **Broadway** tune that has achieved anything close to this kind of popularity.

Armstrong is unequivocally one of the most influential singers in history. He is credited as the first singer to depart from the European **operetta**-derived style of sustained, **open-throated** singing, instead favoring short, *staccato* utterances reminiscent of instrumental **riffs** in **uptunes**. Armstrong also developed a completely novel approach to **vocal production**, disregarding traditional notions of vocal beauty and cultivating a gravely, earthy **tone quality**; all conventions of traditional vocalism were turned on their ear for the sake of style. These attributes alone would have secured Armstrong's place in the pantheon of vocal history, but he also achieved another first, becoming the first jazz performer of eminence to **improvise** vocally as an instrumentalist would (and as he did on his trumpet). His 1926 recording of the **song** "Heebie Jeebies" is often cited as the first recorded example of **scat** singing.

ars antiqua. Early French **polyphony** during the **medieval** period. *Ars antiqua* refers to the **polyphonic** music written before the *ars nova*.

ars nova. A **style** of **polyphony** that emerged in fourteenth-century France. *Ars nova* music was innovative metrically, allowing for double and triple division of note values, thus permitting greater rhythmic complexity.

ars subtilior. A **style** of **polyphony** that emerged in southern France and northern Italy during the late fourteenth and early fifteenth centuries. *Ars subtilior* music was extremely complex in rhythm and notation.

art music. Another name for Western **classical** music from the **medieval** through the **modern** period.

art rock. A **subgenre** of **rock** music characterized by its use of larger forms and more complex **harmonies** and rhythms. Synonymous with progressive rock (or prog rock).

art song. A composition for voice and piano intended for private or **concert** performance. Art songs are usually short in length and are settings of poems. More than any other **genre**, the art song is the place where a composer attempts to synthesize the poet's words with music through vivid text painting in both the vocal line and the piano **accompaniment**.

Art song had its formal beginnings in the late eighteenth century, around the same time as the invention and proliferation of the piano. The art song **repertoire** consists of many **subgenres**, most of which are categorized by the language of the poetry. As the language of the **song** often (but not always) categorizes it according to a particular nation or culture, this delineation is helpful for discussion and study. For example, the German

Lied will have different compositional and stylistic features than the French *mélodie*. **Russian art song** and **Italian art song** are two other distinct subgenres. **English art song** and **American art song** share the same language (English), but they are usually studied as two separate subgenres due to their distinct **styles** and stylistic **interpretations**. The same is true of **Spanish art song** and **Latin American art song**, which set different poets and feature distinct **pronunciations** of the same (Spanish) language. Cosmopolitan composers like Franz Liszt (1811–1886) dabbled in several subgenres at once, writing German *Lieder*, French *mélodies*, and Italian art songs. **Nordic art song** (sometimes called **Scandinavian art song**) is perhaps the most confusing subgenre to categorize, as many of its composers were multilingual, setting German, Swedish, Norwegian, Danish, and Finnish poetry with equal fluency and comfort.

Multiple art songs intended to be performed together and in a prescribed order are known as **song cycles**. Song cycles often (but not always) maintain a cohesive narrative and are settings of poems from the same poet. **Song collections** are usually larger volumes of songs that are published together, but from which songs can be excerpted in performance without regard to the others within the **opus**. And a third type, the **song set**, indicates a short grouping of songs that is usually published under a single opus **number** and not necessarily intended to be performed as a cohesive group. The composer's intentions are occasionally unclear, and it is difficult to distinguish a song collection (or set) from a song cycle. Likewise, performers often permit themselves to cohesively perform entire song collections in published order in both concert performances and on recordings. See also **folk music**, *Kunstlied*, **pop**.

articulators. In discussions pertaining to **voice pedagogy**, **vocal production**, and vocal **technique**, usually refers to the lips, teeth, tongue, mandible/jaw, and **glottis**. Other articulators include the **alveolar ridge**, **hard palate**, **soft palate**, **uvula**, and pharyngeal wall. Articulators can be divided into two categories: Speech organs that move (for example, the tongue) are active articulators, whereas ones that do not (fpr instance, the hard palate) are passive articulators.

aryepiglottic fold. Muscular structure found at the top of the **larynx**. The aryepiglottic fold's function is to help pull the **epiglottis** down to cover the **vocal folds** and **glottis**—and by extension the **trachea** (windpipe)—during swallowing. This area of the **vocal tract** is also the probable source of the **singer's formant**, making the aryepiglottic fold relevant to the phenomenon of **singer's resonance** or **ring**. The aryepiglottic fold is sometimes called the laryngeal collar or epilarynx. See the anatomical drawings located in appendix B.

arytenoid cartilages. One of the three principal cartilages of the **larynx**. Unlike the **cricoid cartilage** and **thyroid cartilage**, there are two arytenoid cartilages, both of which are attached to the top of the posterior surface of the cricoid cartilage. They are shaped like two pointed horns and attached to the cricoid cartilage via two synovial joints. These synovial joints allow the arytenoids to pivot and slide together and apart. As the arytenoids are the posterior attachment point for the **vocal folds**, it is this movement within the larynx that allows the vocal folds to **approximate** (i.e., come together for **phonation**). The arytenoids are also the connecting point for the muscles that open and close the **glottis**. See the anatomical drawings located in appendix B.

ASHA. Abbreviation for the **American Speech and Hearing Association**.

aspirate. A **consonant** sounded with an audible release of breath. In English, French, Italian, and German, [k] is the most common aspirate consonant. In English, this would include the consonants [p] and [t] as well.

aspirated *h*. See *h aspiré*.

assai **(It).** Very.

assez **(Fr).** Enough.

audio spectrum. The audio spectrum of a sound source visually displays the **amplitude** of **frequencies** up to 20,000 **Hz**. The audio spectrum is made up of a combination of **harmonics** and **formants**. When working with audio technology, a **flat** response produces no alterations in the frequency spectrum of the signal. A **cut** reduces the amplitude of frequencies within a specified **range**. A **boost** increases the amplitude of frequencies within a specified range. Also known as frequency spectrum.

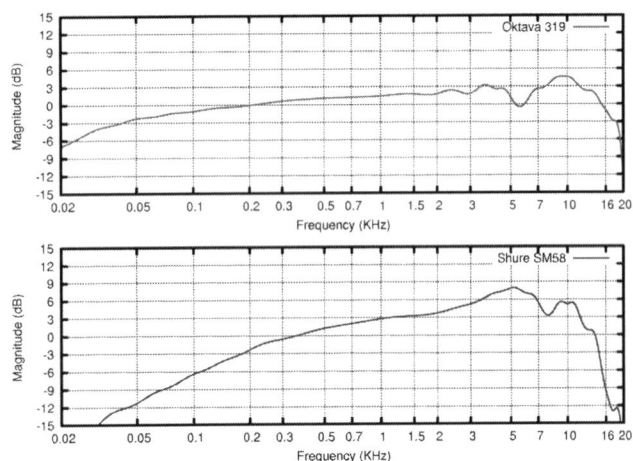

Figure 2. Audio spectrum graph of two different microphones. *Courtesy Creative Commons.*

audition. A sample performance given by a singer when being considered for an **operatic** or **musical theatre role**, a **church job**, or admission into a college or university degree program. A competition is a specific type of audition where singers compete for one or several prizes (usually monetary awards and titles).

augmented sixth chord. A **chord** in **tonal music** that immediately precedes a **dominant** chord. The chord derives its name from the augmented sixth **interval** found between its **bass** note—almost always the ♭6 scale degree—and the ♯4 scale degree above it. The third note in an augmented sixth chord is always the **tonic**, but the fourth **pitch** can vary, creating three "flavors" of augmented sixth chords: the **Italian augmented sixth (It+6)**, which has a doubled tonic; the French augmented sixth (**Fr+6**), which adds the second scale degree; and the German augmented sixth (**Ger+6**), which adds a ♭3 scale degree. Of the three varieties, the Ger+6 chord is perhaps the most interesting because it can be **enharmonically** respelled as a dominant seventh chord, thus allowing the composer to modulate to a distantly related **key**. Composers of German *Lieder* make frequent use of augmented sixth chords to expressively highlight certain words of the poetic text.

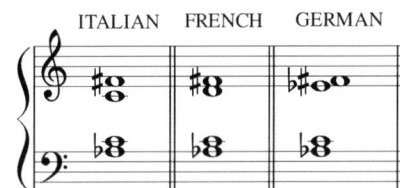

Figure 3. Italian, French, and German augmented sixth chords. *Courtesy Creative Commons.*

ausdrucksvoll **(Ger).** Expressive. See also *mit Ausdruck* ("with **expression**").

Auto-Tune. A digital sound processing (DSP) technology developed by Dr. Harold Hildebrand in 1997, to correct **pitch** errors in digitally recorded music. The technology works by using mathematical algorithms and autocorrelation to analyze and alter the pitch of an audio signal based on user settings. Auto-Tune is now available for both prerecorded and live sound enhancement and enables a wide **range** of applications, from subtle pitch correction to extreme pitch alteration. As this technology has rapidly become a standard part of the commercial music industry, a performer of **contemporary commercial music (CCM)** styles is likely to encounter Auto-Tune.

auxiliary tone. See **neighboring tone**.

avant-garde **(Fr).** "Advance guard" or "vanguard." Refers to people or works of art that are either experimental or innovative.

avec **(Fr).** With.

axial alignment. The ideal body alignment for singing. See also **Alexander Technique**, **Body Mapping**, **noble posture**.

axis. An imaginary line that extends from the center of a **microphone's diaphragm** to the center of the sound source. In **pickup pattern diagrams**, the axis is usually notated by a zero (or 0°). An **acoustic** signal directed along this line toward the center of the diaphragm is described as being "on-axis." A sound source positioned at any angle other than directly into the center of the microphone diaphragm is described as being "off-axis." For more information, see the essay entitled "What Every Singer Needs to Know about Audio Technology."

B

bachata. Spanish-language popular **song genre** that has its roots in the Dominican Republic. The texts are usually about love and romance. The *bachata* is a twentieth-century genre that derives its name from the Caribbean **dance** of the same name.

bachelor of music (BM). The standard undergraduate degree in vocal performance. Most **classical singers** desiring a career in classical singing go on to earn their **master of music (MM)** in voice performance after their BM is completed. It should be noted, however, that many singers go on to MM programs and **professional** careers without an undergraduate degree in performance. Coming to singing a bit later in life is idiomatic to vocalists. Pianists and violinists, for example, who are serious about having professional careers almost never do this; their serious study of performance must begin much earlier in life, usually during childhood.

back vowel. Describes a **vowel** in which the arch of the tongue is back with the tip down during **enunciation.** [u], [ʊ], [o], [õ], [ɔ], [ɑ], and [ɑ̃] are common examples of back vowels. See also **central vowel, closed vowel, front vowel, mixed vowel, nasal vowels, open vowel.**

backbeating. To emphasize **beats** 2 and 4 in **rock styles.** Often used interchangeably with **backphrasing,** which deals with delivery of the text and is slightly more involved.

backphrasing. The practice of singing behind the **beat.** An essential element of **RnB** and **hip-hop**-influenced vocal music in contemporary **pop** and **musical theatre styles.**

balada árabe. A type of nineteenth-century Spanish **song** literally meaning "Arabian **ballad**" that features exotic **harmonies** and highly decorated melodies and **accompaniments.** The **form** derives its name from the

era of the Moorish occupation of Spain (approximately between the years 711 and 1492). The subject of *balada árabe* texts was almost always a love story.

balanced breathing. Another name for *appoggio.*

balanced onset. An onset that is neither too harsh nor underenergized. This type of onset is the perfect balance between a **breathy onset** and a **glottal attack,** neither of which is desirable in **classical** singing.

Baldwin, Dalton (b. 1931). American **collaborative pianist** and coach. Baldwin is best known for his three-decade collaboration with the French baritone **Gérard Souzay,** with whom he made many legendary recordings of French *mélodies* for the EMI label, including the complete **songs** of Gabriel Fauré (1845–1924), Claude Debussy (1862–1918), Maurice Ravel (1875–1937), and Francis Poulenc (1899–1963). In this series, Baldwin also accompanied other **art song** luminaries, including **Elly Ameling, Teresa Berganza,** Nicolai Gedda (b. 1925), José van Dam (b. 1940), Jessye Norman (b. 1945), and Frederica von Stade (b. 1945). Baldwin has also had a long affiliation with Westminster Choir College and frequently gives master classes in the United States and France.

ballad. 1. A specific kind of *Lied* that sets a German Romantic poem. These ballads take their name from the poetic **genre** of the same name and usually consist of many strophes—sometimes dozens—threaded together by a single narrative. Similar to the **melodrama,** the singer becomes a **bard** or storyteller. Important composers of the German ballad include Johann Friedrich Reichardt (1752–1814), Carl Friedrich Zelter (1758–1832), Johann Rudolf Zumsteeg (1760–1802), Franz Schubert (1797–1828), Robert Schumann (1810–1856), and, perhaps most important of all, Carl Loewe (1796–1869).

2. A slow **jazz song**, often about love gained or lost.

3. One of the three types of French fixed forms (*formes fixes*). In this case, always carries the French spelling (*ballade*).

4. A **medieval** English narrative song. These songs were passed orally from generation to generation, and virtually no music from this genre survives.

ballad opera. An eighteenth-century **genre** of English **musical theatre** that incorporated well-known popular **songs** that were usually by a variety of disparate composers. The tunes were given new texts and a fresh **libretto**, and the *pastiche* was performed in a full-length, coherent form. The genre was short-lived and soon fell out of fashion. John Gay's *The Beggar's Opera* (1732) remains the quintessential example of the ballad opera.

ballade. One of the three *formes fixes*, along with the *rondeau* and *virelai*. The *ballade* has a repetitive **verse** pattern of aab, with the b section acting as a **refrain**.

ballet. During the **Renaissance** era, a **homophonic** secular **song** in a quick **tempo**. Balletts are notable for their nonsense **refrains**, the most common of which is "fa-la-la." The first ballets appeared in Italy, but the **genre** soon spread to England and France as well. Thus, examples of the ballet can be found in Italian, English, and French. The genre bears considerable similarity to the **madrigal**.

bandwidth. In audio technology, the distance between the lowest and highest **frequencies** within a defined set of frequencies. Bandwidth is measured in **hertz (Hz)** and is most often encountered when working with **equalization** settings. The setting on an **equalizer** used to change the bandwidth is called the "Q."

bar form. AAB **song form**, consisting of two *Stollen* and an *Abgesang*. Bar form was originated by German *Minnesingers* and *Meistersingers* during the **medieval** period of music history, and the **form** was famously resurrected in certain pieces of German **art music**, most notably in Schubert's **song** "Die Forelle," D550 (1817) and Wagner's **music drama** *Die Meistersinger von Nürnberg* (1868), where it was used as the very exemplar of hidebound conservatism.

barbershop. A four-part, **unaccompanied** vocal **style** of American **popular music**. **Barbershop harmony** is traditionally performed by four male singers, with one person singing each part. The four parts are called the lead (who sings the melody), the **bass**, the **baritone**, and the **tenor** (a kind of descant to the melody that is sung above the lead part in **falsetto**). Barbershop singing reached its height in popularity during the early decades of the twentieth century, primarily drawing its **repertoire**

from the **Tin Pan Alley** and **Great American Songbook** repertory. Unapologetically anachronistic, barbershop harmony recalls a specific era in American popular music, surviving today largely through the sponsorship of the Barbershop Harmony Society, also known as SPEBSQSA (the Society for the Preservation and Encouragement of Barbershop Quartet Singing in America). While usually performed by a **quartet**, the same repertory may be performed by a barbershop chorus, with multiple singers on a part. Barbershop choruses can be very small (with as few as sixteen voices) to very large (numbering in the hundreds).

barbershop harmony. The specific type of four-part **harmony** developed by the Amercian **barbershop quartet**, consisting predominantly of various types of seventh **chords**. The tendency for each part "to sing its own note" and the avoidance of triadic **harmonies** is the most significant hallmark of the **barbershop style** and gives the **genre** its own idiosyncratic flavor. According to the Barbershop Harmony Society, a four-part *a cappella* **song** cannot truly be a called a piece of **barbershop** music unless it is comprised of at least 35 to 60 percent **dominant** seventh chords.

barbershop quartet. A distinctly American **genre** of four-part *a cappella* singing, traditionally for male voices. The **golden age** of **barbershop** singing was roughly synonymous with the time period associated with **Tin Pan Alley** and the American **sheet music** industry, from the 1890s through the early 1930s. The decline in popularity of barbershop singing led to the founding of the Society for the Preservation and Encouragement of Barbershop Quartet Singing in America (SPEBSQSA) in 1938.

The four parts in a barbershop quartet are the **lead**, **tenor**, **baritone** (usually called **bari**), and **bass**. The lead almost always sings the melody, while the other three voices harmonize with the tune. The tenor voice is always sung in **falsetto**, giving prominence to the lead voice, which is the second highest in the four-part structure. The fact that the melody is not the highest voice is one of the features that gives **barbershop** singing its own distinctive sound. The core barbershop **repertoire** predominantly features melodies and **lyrics** found in popular tunes from the first decades of the twentieth century. While early experiments in the barbershop **style** were probably **improvisational**, a notated repertory soon emerged that ensured **harmonic** consistency from performance to performance. Barbershop quartet singing involves understanding some jargon terms associated with the genre, for example, **woodshedding**, **tags**, and **polecat songs**.

The barbershop quartet inspired two notable spinoff **ensembles**: the female barbershop quartet (represented by the organizations **Sweet Adelines International** and

Harmony, Incorporated) and the barbershop **chorus**. Both incarnations perform the same repertoire as the barbershop quartet: the women singing up an **octave** and the chorus with multiple singers on each of the four parts. Female **barbershoppers** still utilize the same voice part labels as their male counterparts: lead, tenor, bari, and bass.

barbershopper. A devoted singer of **barbershop** music. Often a member of the Barbershop Harmony Society or one of the two female barbershop societies: **Sweet Adelines International** or **Harmony, Incorporated**.

bard. A **medieval** singer, poet, and storyteller.

bari. Short for **baritone**, the second-lowest part in a **barbershop quartet** and four-part **barbershop harmony**. The bari voice is the least prominent of the four voices and fills the **harmonically** crucial **role** of providing the fourth **pitch** in a close **harmony style** laden with seventh **chords**.

baritenor. A **musical theatre voice type** that describes a male singer with a wide **range** and colors reminiscent of both **baritone** and **tenor** voices. Baritenors often maintain a baritone **tessitura**, but they also need to possess (and sustain) multiple high notes. Unlike **operatic** tenors, however, the higher range of a baritenor is often **belted** and does not necessarily reflect the warmth and beauty expected of **classical** high baritones. (The baritenor does not usually employ **cover**.) Most modern **musicals** written in a contemporary **style** make regular use of the baritenor. Quintessential baritenor **roles** on **Broadway** include Enjolras in *Les Misérables* (1985/87) and Tom Collins in *Rent* (1996).

baritone. 1. One of the seven principal **classical** voice categories and the generic term for a medium-pitched male **voice type**. The **Kloiber Fach System** identifies four types of baritones: the *lyrischer Bariton*, *Kavalierbariton*, *Heldenbariton*, and *Charakterbariton*. The **Verdi baritone** and **patter baritone** represent other varieties. (While the *Heldenbariton* is a rough equivalent to the Verdi baritone, the latter category is technically not part of the **German Fach System**.) During the first two centuries of **opera** history, baritones were not labeled as such and were simply known as "**basses**." All bass **roles**, regardless of **range** and **tessitura**, were lumped together into one category. Beginning in the nineteenth century, however, the baritone emerged as a separate (again, generic) *Fach* in and of itself. After Mozart, however, composers made a distinction between baritones and basses, writing specific roles and **repertoire** for each voice type.

2. In **choral music**, the label often given to higher basses that sing the Bass I part in eight-part *divisi*.

baroque. One of the six major epochs of music history. The baroque period is the third era, roughly spanning the years 1600–1750. It is preceded by the **Renaissance** era (1400–1600) and followed by the **classical** era (1750–1825). The dawn of the baroque period coincides with the rise of instrumental music and the birth of **opera**, thus making the era especially important and relevant to vocalists. In addition to opera, other vocal **genres** extant during the baroque period include **oratorio**, **passions**, **anthems**, **chorales**, **masques**, **cantatas** (both **sacred** and **secular**), incidental music plays, and the **vocal concerto**.

baroque dance. The **baroque** era of music, rhythm, and **meter** is often indebted to standard **dance** forms, such as the bourée, chaconne, passacaglia, gavotte, gigue, and sarabande, each of which had its own idiomatic **quality**. For baroque dances in triple meter, **hemiola** is an essential rhythmic grouping that must be observed by the astute singer.

baroque opera. The **baroque** era began with the birth of **opera**. The earliest operas were the result of experiments undertaken in Florence by the **Florentine Camerata**, who aspired to create fully sung, instrumentally accompanied drama. Set in the monodic **style**—essentially a single voice with instrumental **accompaniment**—the subjects of these earliest operatic experiments were almost always mythological in nature. Claudio Monteverdi (1567–1643), who was from Cremona and not a member of the Florentine Camerata, is given credit for composing the first **operatic** masterpiece with *Orfeo* (1607). In 1643, Monteverdi again moved the **genre** forward with *L'incoronazione di Poppea*, the first opera that set a historical rather than a mythological subject. By this time, hundreds of operas were being composed throughout Italy, and major cities began building **opera houses** to serve as venues for the popular new art form. In France, Jean-Baptiste Lully (1632–1687) and Jean-Philippe Rameau (1683–1764) created their own distinct version of **French opera**. These works emphasized lavish **spectacle** and introduced new conventions, for instance, a ballet in Act IV of the **five-act** structure.

In addition to Paris, Rome, Milan, Venice, and Naples, London was the other great center of baroque opera. Henry Purcell (1659–1695) experimented with setting the English vernacular with his opera *Dido and Aeneas* (1689). This work, based on excerpts from Virgil's *The Aeneid* (c. 29–19 BCE), is noteworthy for its masterful use of **ground bass aria** form, the second important idiomatic baroque **aria form** (along with the *da capo* aria). But it was George Frideric Handel (1685–1759) who emerged as England's towering operatic figure. Handel's operas—all written in Italian—were largely rooted in the Italian *opera seria* tradition and were showcases for **virtuosic** singing, especially in the final A section of *da capo* arias.

Bartoli, Cecilia (b. 1966). Italian **mezzo-soprano**. Bartoli was born in Rome and made her **operatic** debut at an early age, singing the **role** of the Shepherd Boy in Puccini's *Tosca* in 1974, at the age of eight. After formal studies at the Academy of Saint Cecilia in Rome, she made an international name for herself with the role of Rosina in Rossini's *Il barbiere di Siviglia*, which she performed in Cologne, Zurich, and at the Schwetzingen Festival. She quickly earned a reputation as one of the world's leading Rossini singers, with a flawless articulate **coloratura**. A high mezzo-soprano, Bartoli also embraces several **soprano** roles, including several by Mozart: Susanna in *Le nozze di Figaro*, Zerlina and Donna Elvira in *Don Giovanni*, and Despina in *Così fan tutte*. Her operatic **repertoire** also includes works by George Frideric Handel (1685–1759), Christoph Willibald Gluck (1714–1787), and Joseph Haydn (1732–1809). Her worldwide fame was, in part, secured by her prolific recording career, and she is perhaps the most recorded mezzo-soprano in recent decades.

baryton-Martin. The French label for a type of high **baritone** who exemplifies certain aesthetic qualities, including a **reedy**, higher upper **register** that is light in **quality**. The *baryton-Martin* is a distinctly French "Fach" that has no equivalency in the **German Fach System**. The *baryton-Martin* was named after the French singer Jean-Blaise Martin (1768–1837), who exemplified this **voice type**. The only **opera role** in the mainstream **repertory** that qualifies as a true *bartyon-Martin* role is the title role in Debussy's *Pelléas et Mélisande* (1902). Although the label is seldom applied to singers in the twentieth century, it is best exemplified by **Pierre Bernac**, whose singing was characteristic of the *baryton-Martin*. The label is virtually never used with non-French singers.

bass. 1. The lowest of the seven principal voice categories, lower than (and distinct from) **baritone**. The **Kloiber Fach System** identifies four types of basses: the *Spielbaß (Baßbuffo)*, *schwerer Spielbaß (schwerer Baßbuffo)*, *Charakterbaß (Baßbariton)*, and *seriöser Baß*. The *basso cantabile*, *basse chantante*, and *basso profondo* are other frequently referenced varieties.

2. The lowest choral part in four-voice divisi. Can also refer to the Bass II part if "baritone" is used to label the Bass I part.

bass-baritone. Roughly equivalent to the *Charakterbaß Fach* in the **Kloiber Fach System**, the bass-baritone label is more frequently used in a more general sense to refer to either young **bass** voices who possess a more pliant, **lyric quality**, or bass voices that can sing in the higher **tessitura**, thus embodying some of the qualities of the **baritone** voice as well. Bass-baritones usually sing more lyrically and with a less heavy quality than

basses. Many bass-baritones have a **range** that extends as low as the bass and virtually as high as the **baritone**, making them unique in the male vocal world of two **octave** ranges or less. Joseph Haydn (1732–1809) wrote almost exclusively for the bass-baritone in his **oratorios** and masses, making such works a challenge for many contemporary baritones and basses.

basse chantante. The French equivalent of the Italian *basso cantabile*.

basso buffo. A **stock character** in Italian **comic opera** of the eighteenth and early nineteenth centuries. *Basso buffos* are comic **basses**, and their singing **style** is blustery, as opposed to lyrical, in character. Examples include Dr. Bartolo in Rossini's *Il barbiere di Siviglia* (1816), Dr. Dulcamarapo in Donizetti's *L'elisir d'amore* (1832), and the title **role** in Donizetti's *Don Pasquale* (1843).

basso cantabile. A **voice type**, and a term used to describe a singing, lyrical **bass** or **bass-baritone** voice. *Basso cantabiles* are usually lighter, more flexible voices that do not have the weight or power of **dramatic baritones** or basses, for example, the *Charakterbariton*, *Heldenbariton*, or *seriöser Baß*. The *basso cantabile* is ideally suited for the florid **baroque** music of George Frideric Handel (1685–1759) or Alessandro Scarlatti (1660–1725). Not one of the official twenty-nine categories in the **Kloiber Fach System**. The French term for this voice type is *basse chantante*.

basso continuo. Term used interchangeably with *continuo*.

basso profondo. Italian term literally meaning "profound **bass**" or "deep bass," used to describe a bass who can sing in an exceptionally low **range**. Although this term is frequently used, it is not an official category in the **Kloiber Fach System**.

basso seguente (It). "Following **bass**." A **baroque** predecessor of the *basso continuo*.

Battle, Kathleen (b. 1948). African American **soprano**. Battle is a light **lyric coloratura** soprano known for her **agility** and incomparable technical facility. She was born in Portsmouth, Ohio, as the youngest of seven children. She attended the Cincinnati College-Conservatory of Music and began her career as a public-school music teacher. Battle made her professional debut at the *Festival dei Due Mondi* in Spoleto, Italy, as the soprano soloist in Brahms's *Ein deutsches Requiem*, Op. 45. This performance led to an illustrious career as a soloist, first in **oratorio** and later in **opera**. During the 1980s, she performed in most of the world's great **opera houses**, excelling in the **roles** of George Frideric Handel (1685–1759),

Wolfgang Amadeus Mozart (1756–1791), and Gaetano Donizetti (1797–1848). She was a favorite soprano of the **Metropolitan Opera** for more than a decade, but in 1994, after a prolonged period of strain with the management, she was fired for "unprofessional behavior." After this high-profile dismissal, Battle returned to **concert** and **recital** singing. She has performed for two popes, John Paul II (1920–2005) and Benedict XVI (b. 1927).

Bauchaussenstütz. A German **breath management technique** roughly meaning "belly breathing." *Bauchaussenstütz* is an alternative to *appoggio* that involves intentional pressure in the abdominal wall as opposed to rib expansion and **thoracic breathing** and **abdominal breathing**. **Richard Miller** discusses—and discourages—the *Bauchaussenstütz* technique in his 1977 treatise, *National Schools of Singing*. The *Bauchaussenstütz* technique is generally not practiced by North American singers and singing teachers.

Bay Psalm Book. The first **psalter** published in North America, in 1640. Its full title is *The Whole Booke of Psalms Faithfully Translated into English Metre*. The first edition uses forty-eight tunes, in combination with six metrical patterns, during which the 150 psalms are **chanted** in **liturgical** worship.

Bayreuth Festspielhaus. An **opera house** north of Bayreuth, Germany, designed by Richard Wagner (1813–1883) and dedicated solely to the performance of his **music dramas**. The Bayreuth Festspielhaus—translated as the "Bayreuth Festival Theatre"—was built from 1872 to 1876, and was principally funded by Wagner's patron, Ludwig II of Bavaria (1845–1886). The first performance to take place in the Bayreuth Festspielhaus was the world **premiere**, four-evening performance of *Der Ring des Nibelungen* (1876). The opera house is noteworthy for its completely hidden orchestra pit, which is below the stage and covered by a hood, making it completely invisible to the audience. This and other structural features were conceived by Wagner to increase the illusion of **dramatic realism**. Each year, the Bayreuth Festspielhaus hosts a festival—called the Bayreuth Festspiel—dedicated to the music dramas of Wagner. The Bayreuth Festspielhaus is a lifetime pilgrimage for many Wagner enthusiasts worldwide.

Beard, John (1717–1791). English **tenor** known for his long association with George Frideric Handel (1685–1759). Beard sang more parts under Handel's direction than any other singer, including **roles** in ten **operas** and all of Handel's English **oratorios** except *The Choice of Hercules* (1751), which had no leading tenor. Unlike many tenors of his day, Beard had a full, heroic tenor voice that was heard to particular advantage in the title roles of *Samson* (1743), *Judas Maccabeus* (1747), and *Jephtha* (1752). Hailed as the greatest tenor of his day, Beard did much to establish the tenor voice during an age when **castrati** and **sopranos** reigned supreme.

Figure 5. Painting: A scene from "Love in a Village," by Isaac Bickerstaffe. Act 1, Scene 2, with Edward Shuter as Justice Woodcock, John Beard as Hawthorn, and John Dunstall as Hodge, Oil on Canvas, 1767. *Courtesy Creative Commons.*

beat. 1. In music, a single **pulse** within a measure.
2. In **theatre**, the timing of a particular action.
3. In **acoustics**, the phenomenon that results when two **unison pitches** are not exactly **in-tune**.

beat boxing. Percussive sounds made through **phonation**. Beat boxing occurs in many types of **contemporary commercial music (CCM) styles**. Sometimes called vocal percussion.

beats per minute (BPM). Used interchangeably with **MM** (the abbreviation for "Maelzel's Metronome").

Figure 4. Photochrom print of the Bayreuth Festspielhaus, c. 1895. *Courtesy Library of Congress.*

beaucoup (Fr). "A lot" or "many."

Begleitung (Ger). **Accompaniment**.

Beijing opera. See **Peking opera**.

bel canto. 1. An Italian phrase meaning "beautiful singing," referring to a flexible, **coloratura style** of singing. In this sense, *bel canto* was used to describe the florid **operas** of George Frideric Handel (1685–1759), the **arias** from which showcased the **virtuosity** of the singer. The same phrase was used to describe florid singing in later eras of **Italian opera** as well.

　2. A label for the specific brand of Italian opera that emerged at the beginning of the nineteenth century in Italy, featuring florid-style singing and **legato** Italian melodies. Gioacchino Rossini (1792–1868), Gaetano Donizetti (1797–1848), and Vincenzo Bellini (1801–1835) represent the apotheosis of the **genre**. Many of Giuseppe Verdi's (1813–1901) operas retain elements of the *bel canto* school of Italian opera.

　3. A school of **voice pedagogy** roughly equivalent to the **International Italian School**. While the specific tenets that define *bel canto* **pedagogy** can be somewhat ambiguous—and vary widely from teacher to teacher, all of whom may claim to subscribe to *bel canto* ideals—a practical definition assumes a reverence to the **treatises** and method books of the great Italian **pedagogues**, with an emphasis on the central **canon** of Italian **operatic repertoire**. Some pedagogues have defined the *bel canto* school of pedagogy more narrowly, for instance, Lucie Manén, in her 1987 treatise, *Bel Canto*. See also the contemporary definition of *bel canto* written by James Stark (b. 1938), which is discussed in appendix D.

Bel Canto/Can Belto. A series of **musical theatre workshops** designed by **voice pedagogue** Mary Saunders Barton (b. 1945) of Penn State University. The workshops focus on the vocal **technique** behind musical theatre singing, encouraging healthy approaches to the **belt** voice and other elements of the musical theatre **style**.

bel canto **opera.** A specific kind of **Italian opera** from the first half of the nineteenth century that emphasizes beautiful melodies, florid singing, and simple **accompanimental** patterns in the orchestra. The **dramatic** works of Gioacchino Rossini (1792–1868), Gaetano Donizetti (1797–1848), and Vincenzo Bellini (1801–1835) are often categorized as *bel canto* operas.

belt. A frequently encountered term that can refer to a **style**, **register**, and **technique** used by singers who perform in nonclassical styles. Because the word *belt* can mean so many things, it is often a confusing term to discuss and difficult to define precisely. Indeed, belt can serve as a noun (indicating the register or technique), an adjective (describing the **tone quality** or sound), or a verb (describing what the singer is doing). Perhaps no other word in singing is as multifarious.

　Most singing teachers would agree that belt is most frequently associated with the female **chest** voice (or the **TA-dominant** or **mode 1** register). As **classical** female singers largely avoid this register (with the possible exception of **dramatic**, "Verdi" mezzos)—instead favoring head voice (or the **CT-dominant** or **mode 2** register)—the belt sound emerged as a distinctly different, refreshing commercial sound in the late 1920s, when **Ethel Merman** did much to popularize the new technique. Heralded as having a "voice like a trumpet," Merman could project to the back row of the **theatre** without the assistance of a **microphone**. Belting became an enduring aspect of the **musical theatre** style, and it became equally ubiquitous among female singers in most forms of contemporary **popular music** as well.

　While women are most frequently cited in discussions involving belting, men can also belt. Since men (with the exception of **countertenors**) already sing in their chest voices, their belt may sound less distinctive than the female belt. Male belting usually involves brighter, spread **vowels** in the higher register, with the complete absence of **cover** or **operatic head voice**.

　Belting has been a major source of controversy among **voice pedagogues** for more than half a century. This controversy usually centers around two points of contention: 1) disagreement regarding the definition of what constitutes a belt voice, and 2) whether it is possible to belt in a healthy way. Regarding the first point, if one is to accept that the belt describes chest-dominant register, then one can answer the second point by saying "it depends." If the female belts in a lower **range**, then the singer has little to fear in terms of her vocal health, but the higher one belts, the more precarious the issue becomes. The most common solution to this conundrum is the use of **mix**—essentially the introduction of CT-dominant activity with brighter vowel choices—in the higher belt range. Mix can be either heady or chesty in **quality**, giving rise to the terms head mix, chest mix, or other variants. The belt voice remains one of the most fascinating topics currently explored and discussed by modern singers and **pedagogues**.

belt-mix. A term frequently used by **contemporary commercial music (CCM)** and **musical theatre pedagogues** to refer to a female, **TA-dominant** "pop" sound, but often with a **range** extension on top. While a true **belt** might be delivered in 100 percent **chest** voice—and at a lower range and **tessitura**—a female who uses a belt-mix is often capable of singing in a higher range, employing CT activity, in combination with brighter **vowel** choices.

belter. A singer who **belts**.

belty. Used to describe a particular voice or **song** that has **belt**-like qualities. See also **brassy**.

Benedictus. Part of the *Sanctus* (sometimes called *Sanctus-Benedictus*), which is one of the five parts of the **Ordinary** in a Catholic **Mass**.

Beneventan chant. A **repertory** of **Latin liturgical chant** that was written in Southern Italy from the tenth through thirteenth centuries. Stylistically, there is little compositional difference between Beneventan and **Gregorian chant**.

Berberian, Cathy (1925–1983). American **soprano** and composer renowned for her supreme musicianship and **interpretation** of **new music**. Berberian studied at Columbia University and New York University, receiving an eclectic education that included training in music, writing, dancing, and pantomime. She also worked with an Armenian **dance** group and studied voice in Milan. She married the *avant-garde* composer Luciano Berio (1925–2003) in 1950. In her early thirties, she burst onto the international new music scene when she was discovered by John Cage (1912–1992), whose *Aria with Fontana Mix* she **premiered** in 1958. Berberian made her **Tanglewood** debut in 1960, with the premiere of Berio's *Circles*. The list of composers who wrote pieces specifically for Berberian's voice includes Igor Stravinsky (1882–1971), Roman Haubenstock-Ramati (1919–1994), Hans Werner Henze (1926–2012), and Sylvano Bussotti (b. 1931). In addition to new music, Berberian also actively performed **baroque opera**, specializing in the works of Claudio Monteverdi (1567–1643).

berceuse (Fr). Lullaby. Also called *Schlummerlied*, **slumber song**, *Wiegenlied*.

Berganza, Teresa (b. 1935). Spanish **mezzo-soprano**. Berganza was born in Madrid, where she studied voice and piano at the Madrid Conservatory while still in her teens. She made her **concert** and **operatic** debuts soon after graduation and quickly established a **professional** opera career. Known for her technical **virtuosity**—particularly with florid singing—she was respected for her flawless **interpretations** of **coloratura roles**, especially Dorabella in Mozart's *Così fan tutte*, Rosina in Rossini's *Il barbiere di Siviglia*, and the title role in Rossini's *La cenerentola*. Berganza made her **Metropolitan Opera** debut in 1967, as Cherubino in Mozart's *Le nozze di Figaro*. Her **recital repertoire** includes German *Lieder*, French *mélodies*, **Russian art song**, and—most significant—**Spanish art songs**, which she has recorded prolifically. Her recorded legacy is preserved on *The*

Spanish Soul, a three-disc set that was released in 2008, which captures Berganza at the height of her interpretive and technical prowess.

bergerette. A fifteenth-century French **polyphonic secular song**. The *bergerette* was essentially a one-**verse** *virelai*, which is one of the *formes fixes*.

Bernac, Pierre (1899–1979). French **baritone** and teacher of singing. Bernac was born in Paris and did not begin singing **lessons** until the age of eighteen, when his first voice teacher was the composer André Caplet (1878–1925). While he was still in his twenties, he met the composer Francis Poulenc (1899–1963), with whom he would begin a long collaborative relationship and partnership. Poulenc wrote more than ninety **songs** for Bernac's voice, and Bernac **premiered** six of Poulenc's most important **song cycles**: *Chansons gaillardes* (1926), *Cinq poèmes de Paul Éluard* (1935), *Tel jour, telle nuit* (1937), *Banalités* (1940), *Calligrammes* (1948), and *La fraîcheur et le feu* (1950). Bernac's only **opera role** was Pelléas in Debussy's *Pelléas et Mélisande*, which he performed twice in 1933. Bernac's voice can be classified as a *baryton-Martin*, a distinctly French label that describes a light, **reedy**, high baritone. Today, Bernac is primarily remembered for his two influential books: *The Interpretation of French Song* (1970) and *Francis Poulenc: A Man and His Songs* (1977). Both are owned and regularly referenced by most singers and teachers of singing.

Bernoulli effect. See **Bernoulli's principle**.

Bernoulli's principle (Bernoulli effect). Law of physics coined by Daniel Bernoulli that states that air (fluid) in motion has less pressure or density than when immobile, thus producing suction. If flow is constantly maintained, air will speed up at a constricted rate, with a decrease in pressure occurring at that point. Bernoulli's principle is often cited by **voice pedagogues** and voice scientists as playing a **role** in **vocal fold adduction**.

bewegt, bewegter (Ger). Agitated, more agitated.

bhajan. A Hindu religious **song** that pays homage to various Hindu deities.

Bhosle, Asha (b. 1933). Indian singer, best known as a **playback singer** in the Bollywood film industry. Bhosle's career began in 1963, and has spanned six decades. Known for her wide vocal **range** and stylistic versatility, she has recorded more than 12,000 **songs**, most of which have appeared on the soundtracks of more than 1,000 Bollywood films, making Bhosle perhaps the most recognizable voice in India.

bidirectional pattern. In audio technology, a descriptive phrase used to describe how a **microphone** will respond to **acoustic** energy directed at it. A bidirectional pattern is a **pickup pattern** that consists of two large circular pickup zones emanating from the front and back of the microphone's **diaphragm**. Figure 6 offers a visualization of a bidirectional pickup pattern. The bidirectional pattern is not particularly useful for singers; a practical application would be an interview situation where two speakers are sitting across from one another. For more information, see the essay entitled "What Every Singer Needs to Know about Audio Technology."

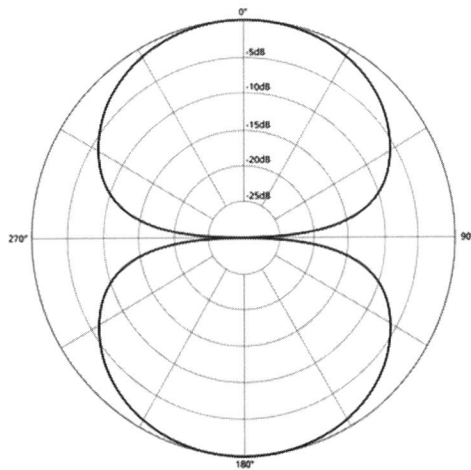

Figure 6. Bidirectional microphone pattern. *Courtesy Creative Commons.*

big band. A large **jazz ensemble** popular in American music from 1935–1945. Big bands consisted of five saxophones, three or four trumpets, three or four trombones, and a rhythm section (piano, bass, and drums). Singers were often featured as soloists in big band **concerts**. Also called a swing band.

big band era. The era of American **popular music** history that was dominated by **big band** literature, from 1935–1945. Also called the swing band era.

bilabial. In **diction**, a **point of articulation** that describes **consonants** that are produced with both lips. Examples of bilabial consonants include [b], [p], [m], [w], and [ʍ]. See also **alveolar, dental, labiodental, palatal, prepalatal, velar.**

bilateral. Describes vocal pathologies that occur on both **vocal folds**. The opposite of **unilateral** (which means to occur on only one vocal fold).

Bing, Rudolf (1902–1997). Austrian-born **opera impresario** best known for his **role** as general manager of the **Metropolitan Opera** from 1950–1972. Under his leadership, the Metropolitan Opera enjoyed a period of great flourishing, and Bing fostered the careers of many European and American opera singers. He is the author of two books, *5000 Nights at the Opera* (1972) and *A Knight at the Opera* (1981).

Björk (b. 1965). Icelandic singer and songwriter, known for her unique voice and interesting compositions. Now known to the world as simply Björk, she was born Björk Guðmundsdóttir in Reykjavík and learned piano at an early age. She was heavily influenced by **punk** music in high school and sang in several bands, one of which (the Sugarcubes) eventually achieved international recognition. Moving on to a highly successful solo career, Björk went on to release seven internationally acclaimed albums from 1993–2011. Fusing together multiple **genres**, including **rock, jazz**, techno, **dance, classical**, and **folk music**, Björk's recordings are usually highly digitized and deliberately overprocessed, giving them a distinctly idiomatic sound. Her voice—somewhat disembodied but beautiful—seems to come from another world. Also acclaimed as an actress, she starred in the Lars von Trier (b. 1956) film *Dancer in the Dark* (2000), winning numerous awards for her performance, including Best Actress at the Cannes Film Festival.

bleat. Literally, the wavering cry made by a goat or sheep. Used pejoratively to describe an ugly, distasteful sound made by a singer (usually a **tenor**). Also used less frequently as a synonym for **tremolo** (a fast **vibrato**).

blend. When multiple singers strive to sing in perfect **ensemble** with one another, they are trying to achieve blend. Blend is a combination of many separate singing elements, and singers must match **pitches**, rhythm, and **vowels**, as well as achieve a good balance with one another. In choral singing, **straight tone** is often employed to achieve blend, as well as tuning **formants** in such a way that minimizes the individual **singer's resonance** or **ring**. It is, of course, possible to blend and still sing in **harmony**, which adds an additional layer of complexity to blending. Singers must tune sonorities vertically to achieve the desired overtones present in blended singing.

block (verb). To stage a character in an **opera, operetta**, or **musical**.

blocking. The **choreographed** stage movements of a character in a stage **production**.

blue note. In **jazz** and **blues**, a note that is sung (or played) at a slightly lower **pitch** than the "correct" diatonic note of the major **scale**. Blue notes are inserted deliberately and for an expressive purpose. They are frequently used for the third and seventh **scale degrees** of the prevailing **key**, and sometimes also for the fifth.

bluegrass. A fast-paced, high-octane **subgenre** of **country** music inspired by the **folk music** of the Appalachian region of the United States. While bluegrass is frequently thought of as an instrumental **genre**—with its characteristic fiddles, banjos, and mandolins—it has also produced vocal artists that are inextricably linked with the genre. Examples of bluegrass singers include the Stanley Brothers (Carter and Ralph), the famous duo of Lester Flatt (1914–1979) and Earl Scruggs (1924–2012), Ricky Skaggs (b. 1954), and Alison Krauss (b. 1971). Bluegrass vocal **harmony** may contain anywhere from two to four parts and features **chords** in close position with a **dissonant** harmony in the top voice. In this respect, bluegrass vocal music is similar in **style** to **barbershop** music.

blues. An African American **genre** that emerged in the early twentieth century, and an important forerunner of **jazz** and **rock 'n' roll**. There are three basic types of blues: **country blues**, **classic blues**, and **urban blues**. Country blues, which came first, emerged in the Mississippi Delta and East Texas at the turn of the twentieth century. This **subgenre** usually featured a male singer with a steel-stringed **acoustic** guitar. **Robert Johnson** and Charley Patton (1891–1934) are famous exponents of the country blues **style**. In classic blues, which flourished during the 1920s, a blues singer was accompanied by a either a pianist or jazz band in a more formal venue. Ma Rainey (1886–1939) and Bessie Smith (1894–1937) are two of the most well-known names in the classic blues genre. Urban blues (which eventually developed into **rhythm and blues**) added electric **amplification** to the sound, as well as more **virtuosic** instrumental playing. This style was performed in larger cities, especially Chicago, during the late 1940s. Howlin' Wolf (1910–1976) and B. B. King (b. 1925) are examples of urban blues musicians. Blues subgenres make extensive use of the **twelve-bar blues**, which forms the basis of the style.

BM. Abbreviation for the **bachelor of music** degree. The BM has become the standard undergraduate vocal performance degree, largely replacing the BFA, BA, and (occasionally) the BS. Most National Association of Schools of Music-accredited colleges and universities now offer the BM degree.

Body Mapping. A type of **bodywork** developed by William Conable (b. 1940), a professor of cello at Ohio State University from 1972–2008. Body Mapping is essentially the study of how human anatomy applies to musical performance. Body Mapping does not change what one does, but rather how one does it. In this sense, it is similar to the **Alexander Technique** (which Conable also studied intensively). Conable's wife Barbara (b. 1940) founded Andover Educators in 1998, an organization devoted to teaching the principles of Body Mapping. Many singers, instrumentalists, and conductors practice the study.

bodywork. A type of therapeutic or physical development **technique** that involves working with the human body. As the body is the singer's instrument, these techniques can be a beneficial part of a singer's training, especially with such issues as **posture**, breathing, and physical endurance onstage. Various types of bodywork systems and techniques include the **Alexander Technique**, **Body Mapping**, **Feldenkrais**, and **yoga**, among many others.

Bogart, Anne (b. 1951). American **theatre** and **opera director**, and the author of four frequently referenced theatrical books: *The Director Prepares: Seven Essays on Art and Theatre* (2001), *The Viewpoints Book: A Practical Guide to Viewpoints and Composition* (2005), *And Then, You Act: Making Art in an Unpredictable World* (2007), and *Conversations with Anne* (2012). Bogart is also the creator of Viewpoints, an acting **technique** that is based on **ensemble** building and group **improvisation**.

bolero. A Spanish **dance** in **triple meter**, recognized for its characteristic triplets, usually occurring on the second half of the first **beat**. The most famous instrumental example is Ravel's orchestral work (eponymously entitled *Bolero*), but the rhythm can also be heard in vocal **genres**, usually when the composer is trying to evoke the exotic. The *bolero* is famously heard in certain **songs** in the **musical theatre genre**, for example, "The Impossible Dream," from Mitch Leigh's *Man of La Mancha* (1965), and "A Trip to the Library," from Bock and Harnick's *She Loves Me* (1963).

Figure 7. *Bolero* rhythmic pattern. *Courtesy Creative Commons.*

book. 1. The **libretto** of a **musical**. 2. A **musical theatre** singer's **audition** folder, consisting of many **cuts** in various **styles**.

boost. When working with audio technology, a boost increases the **amplitude** of **frequencies** within a specified **range**. See also **audio spectrum**.

bossa nova. Brazilian **genre** of **popular music**. Literally translating as the "new thing," *bossa nova* emerged in the mid-1950s and built on the tradition established by *samba*. *Bossa nova* fused together elements of *samba* with the **harmonic** and melodic complexity of **jazz**, particularly the "cool jazz" movement that had emerged in the United States. **João Gilberto** is perhaps the world's most famous exponent of *bossa nova*.

boy soprano. A young male singer with an unchanged voice. In the Anglican tradition, boy **sopranos** (or **trebles**) sing the soprano parts, and **countertenors** sing the **alto** parts.

BPM. Abbreviation for **beats per minute**. Used interchangeably with **MM** (the abbreviation for "Maelzel's Metronome").

brassy. A subjective adjective that describes a vocal sound that is "bright"; "**resonant**"; and favors more forward, front **vowels**. More specifically, it is usually used to describe a **TA-dominant** or "**belty**" voice. Brassy is a desirable **quality** in the **classic Broadway repertoire**, but it can be used pejoratively when assessing **classical singers** (particularly **mezzo-sopranos**). Also used as a synonym for belty.

break. 1. A slang but commonly used term for the place in the singing voice where two **registers** meet. Roughly synonymous with *passaggio*.

2. When used as a verb, a dated, slang term for the phenomenon that occurs when an adolescent male's voice changes. "When my voice broke" more accurately means "when my voice changed." The male **vocal folds** become thicker and longer during puberty, and unchanged voices become adult ones.

breath cycle. The endless sequential cycle of **inhaling** and **exhaling**.

breath management. Refers to breathing **technique**, and control of the **exhalation** in particular. See also *appoggio*.

breath mark. A comma-like marking instructing the singer to pause briefly. Also called a *Luftpause*.

"breathe the vowel." A pedagogical concept that instructs the student singer to set up the correct **acoustic** space before he or she **phonates**. While this is technically not a **fact-based** thing to say (**vowels** cannot be "breathed"), it is a concept that is easily understood and frequently practiced by many singers and voice teachers.

breathing school (national). See *National Schools of Singing*.

breathing technique. See *appoggio*.

breathy. A subjective adjective that describes a vocal sound that is not fully **adducted**. In a breathy sound, a certain percentage of the airflow is not used efficiently and "escapes" through the **glottis**, preventing the listener from hearing a clear **tone quality**. When one's tone quality is "breathy," one can literally hear unused air along with the singer's **phonation**.

breathy onset. Refers to an unclean **onset** that is imbalanced, with the **vocal folds** not **approximating** fully. The opposite of a harsh or glottal onset. Singers, especially **classical singers**, always strive to achieve a **balanced onset**.

breeches role. See **pants role**.

breit (Ger). Broad.

Brel, Jacques (1929–1978). Belgian singer and songwriter. Brel was born and raised in Brussels, and began a somewhat ordinary life working in his father's cardboard factory. He didn't begin writing **songs** and performing them in the Brussels **cabaret** circuit until after he married and had his first child. Brel gained a wide following in Belgium and France and secured worldwide fame in the latter part of his career. He was particularly highly regarded for his literate and thoughtful **lyrics**. In 1968, an **Off-Broadway revue** entitled *Jacques Brel Is Alive and Well and Living in Paris* opened, featuring English translations of some of Brel's most well-known songs.

Broadway. 1. A **theatre** district in New York City. Most Broadway theatres are located between West 40th Street and West 54th Street, and from west of Sixth Avenue to east of Eighth Avenue. This area includes Times Square. Broadway is also the name of an actual street, and some—but not most—of the theatres are actually on Broadway.

2. A synonym for both American **musical theatre** (broadly) or New York musical theatre (specifically). Since the vast majority of new **musicals** have some sort of genesis or impact in the New York theatre community, the distinction is barely worth noting. To most people, Broadway equals musical theatre, which equals the New York City musical theatre scene. **Off-Broadway** theatre is also a part of New York, and while this **repertoire** is smaller and more intimate in scale, it is still considered by many to be the same repertoire. Only industry **professionals** would quibble about the distinction.

Brown, Oren Lathrop (1909–2004). American **voice pedagogue** and the author of *Discover Your Voice: How to Develop Healthy Voice Habits* (1996), his most famous **treatise**. During the peak of his career, he was a faculty member at the Juilliard School from 1972–1991. One of Brown's principal interests was vocal pathologies and **voice therapy**, and he was one of the first eminent

American voice teachers (along with **William Vennard** and **Ralph Appelman**) to incorporate voice science into his teaching. Brown was also extremely active in the **New York Singing Teachers Association (NYSTA)** and one of the founders of NYSTA's Professional Development Program, which was named after him upon his death in 2004.

buccal speech. An alternative way of speaking that does not utilize the lungs or **larynx**. In buccal speech, air is stored in the **oral cavity** (usually the cheek), which acts as an alternate lung. The air is then sent into the mouth, where speech is created without the engagement of the **vocal folds**. Buccal speech is also widely known as "Donald Duck talk," as the famous Disney character is the quintessential example of bucchal speech in the mass media. Some **new music** performers use buccal speech as an **extended technique**.

buffo. A label for a comic character in **Italian opera**. See also *basso buffo*, *schwerer Spielbaß* (*schwerer Baßbuffo*), *Spielbaß* (*Baßbuffo*).

Buika, Concha (b. 1972). Spanish singer born in Equatorial Guinea. Buika was raised on the Spanish-speaking island of Majorca, where she was one of the only people of African descent in her neighborhood. There, she absorbed a wide variety of Spanish influences. Her unique music is an amalgam of many **genres**, including **flamenco**, *copla*, *bachata*, **soul**, *rumba*, and **jazz**. At the height of her career, she is one of the most well-known figures in today's international **world music** scene.

bunraku. A kind of traditional Japanese puppet **theatre** that involves **chanting**. The vocal **style** is similar to *Noh* and *kabuki*.

burden. A synonym for **refrain** that was sometimes used during the **medieval** and **Renaissance** eras.

Burgundian school. Refers to a specific group of early **Renaissance** composers, their music, and the musical **style** in which they wrote. The most important composers of the Burgundian school included Guillaume Du Fay (c. 1397–1474), Gilles Binchois (c. 1400–1460), and Anton Busnois (c. 1430–1492). Most of the composers were in some way affiliated with the court of the Dukes of Burgundy, a duchy in eastern France and the low countries during the fifteenth century.

burlesque. A comic, theatrical English **genre** that satirized a well-known serious story. Frequent subjects included mythology and well-respected plays and **operas**. The burlesque fell out of fashion after the nineteenth century.

burletta. The Italian translation of **burlesque**, this term was used in England in the late eighteenth and early nineteenth centuries to refer to Italian **comic operas**. The English also satirized such works using the same *burletta* label.

Byzantine chant. The **medieval liturgical chant** of Eastern Orthodox Christian churches. Similar in compositional **style** to **monophonic Gregorian chant**.

C

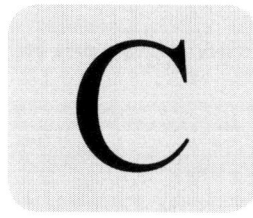

cabaret. A **genre** in the **musical theatre style** that is usually performed in small "cabarets" or nightclubs by singing entertainers. Cabaret casts are often small, and there is usually no narrative or other **production** elements (costumes, sets, scenery, etc.) generally associated with musical theatre productions. **Cabaret songs** are best thought of as musical theatre **songs** that stand alone and are not from **musicals**. See also **Nancy LaMott, trunk songs**.

cabaret singer. A singer who works in a **cabaret** nightclub singing **cabaret songs**. **Nancy LaMott** is an example of a cabaret singer, as well as the character Sally Bowles in the Kander and Ebb **musical** *Cabaret* (1966).

cabaret song. A **song** in the **musical theatre style** sung by a **cabaret singer**. They are often written by musical theatre composers and **lyricists** but are usually intended for **cabaret** performance and are not written for a specific **musical**.

cabaletta. In **Italian opera**, the concluding portion (coda) of an **aria** or **duet**, always in a fast **tempo** intended to give a rousing, audience-pleasing conclusion. *Cabalettas* were most routinely employed in the **operas** of Gioacchino Rossini (1792–1868), but they can also be found in subsequent works written by Gaetano Donizetti (1797–1848), Vincenzo Bellini (1801–1835), and the early works of Giuseppe Verdi (1813–1901). Quintessential examples of the *cabaletta* are the final sections of the famous arias "Largo al factotum" and "Una voce poco fa" from Rossini's *Il barbiere di Siviglia* (1816).

caccia. Fourteenth-century Italian **genre** literally meaning "hunt." The *caccia* is also a **form** featuring two voices in **canon** over an untexted **tenor** voice.

cadence. A concluding **harmonic** or melodic **formula** in a **phrase** or section of music. Cadence points are relevant to singers mostly for expressive reasons; the singer should be aware of them so that he or she can be cognizant of subtle **tempo** and dynamic shifts that reflect the structure of the music. For **Renaissance** and **baroque** soloists, cadences are also traditional places where **ornamentation** is expected. Cadence points are even more important to choral singers, as the experienced chorister will need to watch the **conductor** carefully and control his or her **vibrato** accordingly. At cadences, choral conductors will often request **straight-tone** singing.

cadenza. A highly embellished—often **improvised**—passage that occurs at a final **cadence** in a piece of music. Vocal cadenzas usually appear at the end of **arias** in the Italian *bel canto* tradition. While cadenzas are sometimes performed as originally notated by the composer, singers sometimes substitute traditional cadenzas with alternate cadenzas passed down to younger generations by great singers. Many **classical singers** own entire collections of cadenzas, for example, the famous volumes *Variazioni-cadenze tradizioni per canto* (1977), edited by Luigi Ricci (1893–1981), and *Coloratura Cadenzas* (1943), edited by Estelle Liebling (1880–1970).

call. Another name for a **traditional belt technique**, as opposed to a **cry**, which is a label for a **contemporary belt**.

call-and-response. An alternation of musical material between two performers or two groups of performers. The most common **form** of call-and-response occurs when a soloist/leader sings a phrase that is immediately echoed by the rest of the group (or **chorus**). Many forms of African indigenous music make use of call-and-response, and the African American **work songs** and **field hollers** of the nineteenth century retain this convention. These **genres** were important precursors of the **blues** and **jazz** that form the foundation of modern American **popular music**.

Callas, Maria (1923–1977). Iconic Greek **operatic soprano** of American birth. Callas is inarguably one of the most famous—and unique—singers of all time. After an early childhood in the United States, Callas returned to Greece in 1937, where she sang the title **role** in Puccini's *Tosca* in 1942, at the age of nineteen. Her international career began in her twenties when she sang a series of **dramatic operatic roles** in Italian **theatres**; these included the title roles in Wagner's *Tristan und Isolde*, Verdi's *Aida*, and Puccini's *Turandot*. Ironically, Callas eventually moved into the florid ***bel canto* repertoire**, the literature through which she achieved her greatest acclaim. The title role in Bellini's *Norma* is widely considered to be her greatest *parte*, with "Casta diva"—Norma's Act I **cavatina**—heralded as Callas's signature **aria**. With this role, she made her debut at **Covent Garden** in 1952, and at the **Metropolitan Opera** in 1956. Although Callas's career was not one of great longevity—she encountered a troublesome series of vocal problems in the 1960s—her eminence as one of **opera's** most artistic singers (and best singing actresses) is universally acknowledged. While her technically insecure voice is not one of the most beautiful on record, her performances rank among the most intelligent and expressive ever recorded.

cambiata. 1. A "changing voice." Usually refers to a specific vocal line in an **octavo** of developmental **choral music**, written for an adolescent boy with a limited **range**. The *cambiata* line often appears between the **alto** and **baritone** line in a four-part SACB texture.

2. A five-note **ornament** that occurs when the second note is **dissonant** but the third is **consonant**.

Cambridge Music Handbooks. A series of short handbooks published by Cambridge University Press. Each is a monograph devoted to a particular musical work, with extensive analysis and commentary. To date, there are ten Cambridge Music Handbooks on major choral works, all of which are highly prized by choral **directors** and **professional** choristers; these books are devoted to Monteverdi's *Vespers* (1610), Handel's *Messiah* (1742), Bach's *B Minor Mass* (1749), Haydn's *Creation* (1798), Beethoven's *Missa Solemnis*, Op. 123 (1824), Brahms's *Ein deutsches Requiem*, Op. 45 (1868), Verdi's *Requiem* (1874), Janáček's *Glagolitic Mass* (1927), Tippett's *Child of Our Time* (1944), and Britten's *War Requiem* (1962). There are also three additional books devoted to vocal works: Schubert's *Die schöne Müllerin* (1823), Mahler's *Das Lied von der Erde* (1911), and Schoenberg's *Pierrot lunaire*, Op. 21 (1912). All should be owned and studied by the modern singer. **Operas** are covered in another Cambridge University Press series, the **Cambridge Opera Handbooks**.

Cambridge Opera Handbooks. A series of short handbooks published by Cambridge University Press. Each is a monograph devoted to a particular **opera**, with extensive analysis and commentary. Still in production, there are currently more than forty titles in print. Composers represented include Claudio Monteverdi (1567–1643), Christoph Willibald Gluck (1714–1787), Wolfgang Amadeus Mozart (1756–1791), Ludwig van Beethoven (1770–1827), Hector Berlioz (1803–1869), Richard Wagner (1813–1883), Giuseppe Verdi (1813–1901), Georges Bizet (1838–1875), Leoš Janáček (1854–1928), Giacomo Puccini (1858–1924), Claude Debussy (1862–1918), Richard Strauss (1864–1949), Igor Stravinsky (1882–1971), Alban Berg (1885–1935), Kurt Weill (1900–1950), and Benjamin Britten (1913–1976).

***canción*.** Spanish word literally meaning "**song**." Usually refers to a rustic, folk-like song that is further described by an accompanying adjective: *canción andaluza*, *canción habanera*, and so forth.

***canción andaluza*.** A nineteenth-century Spanish **song** type that is defined primarily by its texts, which depict various aspects of Spanish culture, including bullfights, **flamenco** clubs, and various cities in Spain. The *canción andaluza* is usually rich in **ornaments**, especially **trills** and other short, repetitive melodic devices.

***canción española*.** One of the most idiomatically Spanish of the nineteenth-century Spanish **song** types, the *canción española* often incorporates rhythms from traditional Spanish dances, including the ***bolero*, *polo*,** or ***seguidilla*.** These songs take a variety of different **forms,** but they are often multisectional, with each section denoting a different mood or **color.** The *canción española* is often quite theatrical in nature.

***canción habanera*.** A **song** written in the **style** of a ***habanera*,** usually adopting the distinctive rhythmic **motive** of the *habanera* dance, which was brought from Cuba to Spain in the mid-to-late nineteenth century. The *habanera* was distinctive in its rhythmic style and intensely popular in late nineteenth-century Spain.

canción lírica*.** Literally translating as "lyrical **song**," the *canción lírica* is the most European of the nineteenth-century Spanish song types, adopting many of the characteristics of its cousins, the German ***Lied and French ***mélodie*.** These features included chromaticism, **dissonance**, independence of the piano **accompaniment**, and vivid **expression** of the poetic text.

canon. 1. A composition that features the same melody performed by several voices that enter at different and regular time **intervals** to create a simple **polyphonic** composition. In the **folk music** tradition, canons are often called rounds. The famous **Broadway song** "Fugue for Tinhorns" from Loesser's *Guys and Dolls* (1950) is an example of a canon. (It is not a **fugue** at all.)

    2. A general law, rule, or principle by which something is judged. In music (and literature), a canon is an accepted body of works that have stood the test of time. **Opera** companies, for instance, generally program works that are from the standard **operatic** canon.

    3. The **choirmaster** and **director** of music in a Catholic or Anglican cathedral.

canso (Provençal). See *canzo*.

cantabile (It). 1. Songlike.

    2. In the *bel canto* **opera style** established by Gioacchino Rossini (1792–1868), the slow and lyrical opening section of an **aria** or **duet**. The *cantabile* is usually followed by the *tempo di mezzo* and *cabaletta*.

cantaor (Sp). Singer.

cantata. 1. In the seventeenth and eighteenth centuries, a multimovement piece for voice and **continuo** consisting of **recitatives** and **arias**. These cantatas were usually settings of secular texts in Italian and French. The early solo cantatas of George Frideric Handel (1685–1759) are of this type.

    2. A **genre** of Lutheran church music in the eighteenth century. These cantatas were frequently based on **chorale** tunes, which provide some of the melodic and contrapuntal material for the work. The full **homophonic** chorale is then presented as the last movement of the cantata. Soloists offer recitatives and arias between choral movements. These cantatas were usually sacred and fully orchestrated. The roughly 200 sacred cantatas of Johann Sebastian Bach (1685–1750) are quintessential examples of this genre.

    3. In later eras, a sacred work for soloists, **choirs**, and orchestra (or organ). These cantatas are still in several movements but are usually shorter than a full-length **oratorio**. There are numerous examples in the contemporary church music **repertory**, including the *Christmas Cantata* (1957) of Daniel Pinkham (1923–2006)

cante jondo (Sp). "Deep **song**." A singing **style** found in **flamenco** music.

canticle. **Liturgical**, psalm-like text that is usually sung in a service of worship. Canticles are Biblical but are not from the 150 Psalms of David. Some of the most famous canticles include the Song of Mary (*Magnificat*), the Song of Simeon (*Nunc dimittis*), the Song of Moses (*Cantemus Domino*), the Song of Zechariah (*Benedictus Dominus Deus*), and the Three Songs of Isaiah (*Ecce, Deus*; *Quærite Dominum*; *Surge, illuminare*).

Canticle of Mary. See *Magnificat*.

Canticle of Simeon. See *Nunc dimittis*.

cantiga. A medieval **monophonic secular song** in Spanish or Portuguese.

cantilena (Lat) Song. A **medieval** or **Renaissance polyphonic song** that is not based on a **cantus firmus**.

cantillation. In the Jewish tradition, describes the singing of the **cantor**.

cantonial style. In the Lutheran **chorale** tradition, the setting of the chorale tune in the highest voice, with the lower voices singing in **harmony**.

cantor. The person who leads worship—both vocally and musically—in the Judeo-Christian tradition. The cantor will often sing an initial **chant** or **liturgical** melody that is then imitated in response by the congregation. Cantors also sing portions of scripture as soloists. **Yossele Rosenblatt** is regarded as the most famous cantor in modern history. Although cantors are most famously associated with Judaic liturgical practice, there are cantors in the Christian tradition as well.

cantorial. An adjective that describes the singing **style** of the **cantor**.

cantoris. In an Anglican church with a divided chancel, the cantoris is the left side of the **choir** (the same side as the **cantor**). The cantoris side faces the **decani**, which is the right side of the choir.

cantus firmus. An existing melody—usually a **chant**—upon which a **polyphonic** work is based.

canzo (It). An Italian **monoponic secular song** of the **medieval** era. Each **stanza** had six or seven lines. The melody of the first two lines is repeated once, with new material occurring in the last two or three lines, creating a kind of **bar form**. Sometimes spelled *canso* in the Provençal tradition.

canzona (*canzon*) (It). An Italian instrumental work of the late **Renaissance** that literally translates as "**song**." The **genre** derives its name from the vocal music it imitates; *canzonas* are essentially instrumental arrangements of French **chansons** and Italian **madrigals**.

canzone Napoletana (It). See **Neapolitan song**.

canzonetta (*canzonet*) (It). A sixteenth-century Italian and English secular **song genre**. *Canzonettas* are similar to the **madrigal** genre, but they were usually **homophonic** in texture.

cardioid pattern. In audio technology, a descriptive phrase used to describe how a **microphone** will respond to **acoustic** energy directed at it. A cardioid pattern is a **pickup pattern** that is in the shape of an upside-down heart. Figure 8 offers a visualization of a cardioid pickup pattern. These polar patterns are subject to **proximity effect**, and this setup can be useful to vocalists who wish to exclude acoustic energy coming toward the backside of the microphone. For more information, see the essay entitled "What Every Singer Needs to Know about Audio Technology."

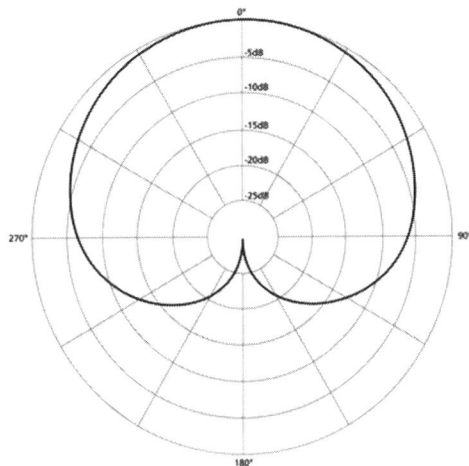

Figure 8. Cardioid microphone pattern. *Courtesy Creative Commons.*

careful. A mnemonic device for students of French **diction**. The four **consonants** in the word careful—*c*, *r*, *f*, and *l*—are often—but not always—ones that are pronounced when they occur at the end of French words. Examples include "parc" [paɾk], "chef" [ʃɛf], "ciel" [sjɛl], and "mer" [mɛɾ]. Exceptions include "blanc" [blɑ̃], "baiser" [beze], "clef" [kle], and "gentil" [ʒɑ̃ti].

carol. English **Renaissance song** in several **stanzas** with a **refrain** (or **burden**). The texts of carols are usually religious in nature and often seasonal; Christmas is a common theme.

Cartilages of Santorini. See **corniculate cartilages**.

Caruso, Enrico (1873–1921). Italian **tenor**, and one of the most famous singers of all time. Caruso spent the early part of his career in Italy, with successful performances in Naples, Palermo, Milan, and Rome. He made his **Covent Garden** debut in 1902, as the Duke of Mantua in Verdi's *Rigoletto*. He performed the same **role** at the **Metropolitan Opera** one year later, in 1903, beginning a

long association with the **company**. With the **Met**, Caruso performed 850 performances of thirty-eight roles, most of them Italian roles in the **verismo** vein. He was renowned as an interpreter of Puccini, performing Rodolfo in *La bohème*, Cavaradossi in *Tosca*, and creating the role of Dick Johnson in *La fanciulla del West* in 1910. He also performed Canio in Leoncavallo's *Pagliacci*, and many roles by Giuseppe Verdi (1813–1901), including Alfredo in *La traviata*, Riccardo in *Un ballo in maschera*, and Radames in *Aida*. His career was cut short when he died of a lung ailment in 1921. Perhaps more than any other single factor, Caruso's celebrity status and meteoric rise to fame was secured by the invention of the gramophone recording, which coincidentally occurred at the same time that his career began to flourish. He was one of the first **opera** singers whose *oeuvre* is prolifically preserved on a series of famous recordings that date back to 1902. Caruso's complete recordings are still widely available on CD.

Figure 9. Enrico Caruso in *Aida.* Photograph by Herman Mishkin. *Courtesy Historic Broadway Photographs.*

Castel, Nico (b. 1931). Portuguese-born multilinguist and character **tenor** of the **operatic** stage. Although Castel has had an impressive career as a tenor in *comprimario* **roles**, he is primarily known to the international singing community as one of the world's foremost authorities on singer's **diction**. His numerous multiline **librettos**—consisting of the text, a word-for-word translation, an **IPA transcription**, and sometimes a more understandable rephrasing of the text (clarifying idiomatic phrases, etc.)—are published by Leyerle Publications. Empathetic to the needs of the **classical singer**, he frequently makes diction adjustments (for instance, **vowel** modification, including **vocalic harmonization**) to assist the performer with technically difficult passages. Colloquially, **opera** singers refer to their "Nico," a slang term for one of his librettos, which they reference exhaustively while preparing their **role**.

Castilian. The traditional **pronunciation** of continental, European Spanish, as opposed to **Standard American Spanish (SAS)**, the pronunciation variants found in Mexico, Central America, and South America. Today, when one refers to Castilian Spanish, they are usually using this term as a synonym for Standard European Spanish **(SES)**. In addition to being the standard Spanish pronunciation for **classical singers**, Castilian Spanish is also the language standard for both television and radio speakers.

casting director. In **musical theatre**, the person hired by the producing **theatre** or **company** to cast the show, usually by contacting **agents** and **auditioning** potential "fits" for each **role**. Casting directors are distinct from agents, and "casting agent" (which is frequently heard) is an erroneous hybrid term that is factually incorrect, since agents and casting directors are almost always two separate professions.

castrato (pl. castrati). A male singer who is castrated before puberty. Castration at an early age caused a truncation of **laryngeal** growth while the **chest** and lungs continued to mature toward an adult size. The result was an adult male singer with the range of a **soprano** (soprano castrato) or **mezzo-soprano** (**alto** castrato) who was capable of great **agility** and singing unusually long phrases. Castration was practiced in Italy from the sixteenth through the nineteenth centuries. As this practice is no longer in use today, **countertenors** usually inhabit the **operatic** roles once written for castrati, although the countertenor's **tone quality** is likely warmer in comparison to that of the castrati. Famous castrati include **Senesino**, **Farinelli**, and **Alesandro Moreschi**—also known as the "last castrato," whose shrill, androgynous voice is preserved on record, giving the modern listener an aural glimpse into the era of the castrato.

catalog show. A **genre** of **musical theatre** that is a type of **revue**, presenting an evening of previously written **songs**, often by a single composer or composer–**lyricist** team. Catalog shows are sometimes—but not always—connected by narrative script. *Ain't Misbehavin'* (1978), *Buddy* (1990), and *Mamma Mia!* (2001) are examples of catalog shows, respectively presenting retrospectives on the music of Fats Waller (1904–1943), Buddy Holly (1936–1959), and ABBA. The catalog show is also called a compilation show. Catalog shows that present songs originally recorded by **popular music** artists are sometimes called **jukebox musicals**.

catch. An English **canon** that sets a secular, bawdy text. Catches are usually written for three male voices.

catch breath. A short, quick breath taken in between phrases, often when there is not enough time to fully exhale and take a deeper, more nourishing breath. Extended **melismatic** passages in the works of Johann Sebastian Bach (1685–1750), for instance, may require multiple catch breaths.

cavatina. A type of **aria** in **Italian opera** during the late eighteenth and early nineteenth centuries. *Cavatinas* were labeled as such by the composer and were sometimes difficult to distinguish from arias proper. *Cavatinas* were sometimes shorter in length than arias, and they were often used as **entrance arias** to introduce characters to the audience. *Cavatinas* can also be part of a longer aria structure, offering a slow introduction that then moves into a *scena* and then a faster *cabaletta*. An example of this type of *cavatina* is "Ah, fors'è lui" from Verdi's *La traviata* (1853). Wolfgang Amadeus Mozart (1756–1791) seemed to consistently use the term *cavatina* to denote a simple, **strophic** aria as opposed to a *da capo* or **through-composed** one. "Porgi amor, qualche ristoro" from *Le nozze di Figaro* (1786) is a quintessential example of a Mozart cavatina.

CCC. Abbreviation for **Certificate of Clinical Competency**.

CCC-SLP. A **speech-language pathologist (SLP)** who has also earned his or her **Certificate of Clinical Competency**.

CCM. Abbreviation for **contemporary commercial music**.

CDP. Abbreviation for **cricothyroid dominant production**. **CT-dominant** is another frequently used adjective.

Cecilia. See **Saint Cecilia**.

Cecilian movement. A desire by composers of church music in Germany and Austria during the nineteenth century to return to the **Renaissance style** of **polyphonic** composition. The choral **motets** of Anton Bruckner (1824–1896) are often associated with the Cecilian movement.

cédez (Fr). Give way, relax (in **tempo**).

central vowel. A **vowel** in which the tongue maintains a central position during **enunciation**. [ə], [ɜ], and [ʌ] are examples of frequently sung central vowels. See also **back vowel, closed vowel, front vowel, mixed vowel, nasal vowels, open vowel**.

Certificate of Clinical Competency (CCC). Certificate awarded to a **speech-language pathologist (SLP)** after he or she has completed his or her clinical fellowship year.

Chaliapin, Feodor (1873–1938). Russian **bass**. Chaliapin was born in a small village and was largely self-taught, performing with many small provincial companies before acquiring formal training at the age of nineteen. He soon moved on to important performances in St. Petersburg and Moscow, where he sang many of the bass **roles** of the core **Russian opera** literature, including the title role in Musorgsky's *Boris Godunov*. Chaliapin began performing internationally in 1901, with an appearance at **La Scala** as the title role in Boito's *Mefistofele*. He reprised the same role at his **Metropolitan Opera** debut in 1907. He created the title role in Massenet's *Don Quichotte* in London, in 1910. Chaliapin made more than 200 recordings and appeared in two films, including *The Adventures of Don Quixote* (1933), by G. W. Pabst (1885–1967). It was for this film that Maurice Ravel (1875–1937) and Jacques Ibert (1890–1962) wrote their famous "Don Quichotte" **songs**, which were to be sung by Chaliapin; only Ibert's song was ultimately used in the film. Chaliapin is widely regarded as the best operatic bass of his day and one of the great singing actors in **operatic** history.

chamber music. A piece of music written for a small **ensemble**. In vocal music, chamber music usually refers to a **song** or **song cycle** with instrumental **accompaniment** other than orchestra, usually with one instrument on a part. The **repertoire** of vocal chamber music is vast. Three examples of famous vocal chamber works are *Der Hirt auf dem Felsen*, D965 (1828), by Franz Schubert (1797–1828), for **soprano**, clarinet, and piano; the *Chansons madécasses* (1926), by Maurice Ravel (1875–1937), for voice, flute, cello, and piano; and *Dover Beach*, Op. 3 (1931), by Samuel Barber (1910–1981), for **baritone** and string quartet.

chance music. See **aleatoric music**.

changing voice. See *cambiata*.

chanson. A French word meaning "**song**." Today, *chanson* usually refers to a French popular song. In contrast, French **art songs** are called *mélodies*. In the **medieval** and **Renaissance** eras, *chanson* referred to various types of **polyphonic** secular songs.

chanson de geste (Fr). **Song** of deeds. A type of **medieval** French **monophonic secular song** illuminating the deeds of national heroes.

chansonnier (Fr). Songbook. A manuscript collection of secular **songs** with French words. Usually used to refer to songs from the **medieval** and **Renaissance** eras.

chant. 1. A verb usually referring to when a soloist (usually a **cantor**) sings scripture and other sacred texts in **liturgical** worship.

2. A body of **medieval monophonic** vocal **repertoire** written for use in liturgical worship. **Gregorian chant** is the most well-known version of this kind of chant, but there are others as well, including **Byzantine**, **Ambrosian**, **Mozarbic**, **Gallican**, **Armenian**, and **Old Roman** varieties. Although chant usually refers to the **plainsong-style** chant of the Western Christian church, Muslims also chant their scripture (the Qur'an), developing a distinctly non-Western style that is still universally practiced today throughout the Muslim world. See also **Qur'anic chant**.

chant notation. See **four-line staff**.

chanter **(Fr).** To sing.

chanteur manqué **(Fr).** "Lacking singer." A pejorative term for a singer who lacks vocal talent or **technique**.

character actor/actress. A standard **type** in **musical theatre**. Character actors are generally "sidekick" roles of secondary importance to the **leading man** or **leading woman**. The stereotypical character **role** is comic in nature, utilizes a **character voice**, and sometimes dances. Quintessential character roles include Will Parker and Ado Annie in Rodgers and Hammerstein's *Oklahoma!* (1943). A character actor or actress occasionally finds his or her way into a leading role. Annie Oakley, for example—the lead role in *Annie Get Your Gun* (1946), by Irving Berlin (1888–1989)—combines aspects of the character actress and the leading lady. Character actresses are almost always expected to **belt** and never utilize a **legit** voice, as leading ladies and **ingénues** might.

character voice. In **musical theatre**, a **nonlegit** voice used by a **character actor or actress**. For women, a character voice almost always necessitates utilizing either a **belt** or **mix**.

characterization. In **opera** or **musical theatre**, describes the musical–orchestral highlighting of a particular aspect of a character's personality. The composer achieves characterization primarily through text painting.

Charakterbariton. German *Fach* that literally translates as "character **baritone**." In the **Kloiber Fach System**, the *Charakterbariton* is positioned one spot lower on the chart than the *Heldenbariton* and one spot higher than the *Spielbaß (Baßbuffo)*. Examples of *Charakterbariton* **roles** include Schaunard in Puccini's *La bohème* (1896), Scarpia in Puccini's *Tosca* (1900), Beckmesser in Wagner's *Die Meistersinger von Nürnberg* (1868), and Alberich in Wagner's *Das Rheingold* (1862) and *Siegfried* (1876). See the *Fach* chart in appendix C.

Charakterbaß (Baßbariton). German *Fach* that literally translates as "character **bass**" or "**bass-baritone**." In the **Kloiber Fach System**, the *Charakterbaß (Baßbariton)* is positioned one spot lower on the chart than the *schwerer Spielbaß (schwerer Baßbuffo)* and one spot higher than the *seriöser Baß*. Examples of *Charakterbaß (Baßbariton)* roles include Monterone in Verdi's *Rigoletto* (1851), Timur in Puccini's *Turandot* (1926), and Alberich in Wagner's *Der Ring des Nibelungen* (1876). See the *Fach* chart in appendix C.

Charaktersopran. German *Fach* that literally translates as "character **soprano**." In the **Kloiber Fach System**, the *Charaktersopran* is positioned one spot lower on the chart than a *dramatischer Sopran* and one spot higher than the *koloratur-Mezzosopran*. The smallest of the categories in the Kloiber Fach System, there are only three *Charaktersopran* roles: La Folie in Rameau's *Platée* (1745), Volpino in Haydn's *Lo speziale* (1768), and Melisande in Debussy's *Pelléas et Mélisande* (1902). See the *Fach* chart in appendix C.

Charaktertenor. German *Fach* that literally translates as "character **tenor**." In the **Kloiber Fach System**, the *Charaktertenor* is positioned one spot lower on the chart than the *Heldentenor* and one spot higher than the *lyrischer Bariton*. Examples of *Charaktertenor* roles include Dr. Cajus in Verdi's *Falstaff* (1893), Mime in Wagner's *Das Rheingold* (1862) and *Siegfried* (1876), Herodes in Strauss's *Salome* (1905), and Mao Tse-tung in Adams's *Nixon in China* (1987). See the *Fach* chart in appendix C.

Charles, Ray (1930–2004). American **rhythm and blues** singer who is credited as one of the pioneers of the **soul genre**. Charles was born in Albany, Georgia, and grew up in Greenville, Florida. He went blind at the age of six due to untreated glaucoma. He left a school for the deaf and blind when he was fifteen years old to tour northern and central Florida with a **jazz** combo. He then moved to Seattle, were he recorded his first rhythm and blues hits. This launched a major performance and recording career that reached its zenith in the 1960s. Although Charles continued to perform for the next three decades, his legacy rests on many of his earliest recordings. Charles's mature **style** fused together elements of **gospel** with traditional **blues**, which formed a new style that would come to be labeled as soul. The moans and grunts—which were directly appropriated from Black Holiness and Apostolic churches—had an overtly secular and sexual connotation in his music. Unlike many of his rhythm and blues contemporaries, Charles made major inroads into the white community, which embraced his music. His life was immortalized in the 2004 biopic film *Ray*, which introduced his music to a new generation of listeners.

chart. What **jazz** and **rock** musicians call the **score**.

chazzan. A Jewish **cantor**. See also *hazzan*.

Chekhov, Michael (1891–1955). Russian American actor, **director**, author, and **theatre** practitioner. Chekhov is most famous for founding an **acting technique** that is widely practiced and referenced by students and teachers of theatre. The central tenets of the Chekhov technique include an emphasis on a "psycho-physical approach," which includes transformation, following impulse, using one's imagination, and exploring inner and outer gesture. In theatrical training, Chekhov's method is one of the most frequently referenced acting techniques, along with those of **Stella Adler**, **Sanford Meisner**, **Uta Hagen**, **Viola Spolin**, **Anne Bogart**, **Constantin Stanislavski**, and **Lee Strasberg**.

Chenier, Clifton (1925–1987). Black Creole American accordionist and singer whose name is inextricably linked with the *zydeco* **genre**. Chenier grew up in a musical family, often playing in makeshift **ensembles** with his father, uncle, and brother. He made his first recording in 1954, of traditional **blues** material, and later moved into recording more traditional French music at the encouragement of his **producer**. This led to his most well-known album, *Louisiana Blues and Zydeco* (1965), which secured Chenier's eminence in the zydeco genre. He is credited with both popularizing and revitalizing the genre. In 1984, Chenier won both a **Grammy Award** and a National Heritage Fellowship from the National Endowment for the Arts. He is widely regarded as the "King of Zydeco."

chest. The common name for a **TA-dominant (mode 1) register** in singing. Also sometimes referred to as *voce di petto*, **ring register**, **modal** register, **heavy mechanism**, or **belt**. As chest is the natural register of human speech, it is often the preferred register in theatrical **genres** of singing and **popular music**.

chiaroscuro. Italian term derived from art history meaning "bright-dark" or "light and shadows." In the Italian *bel canto* tradition of singing, *chiaroscuro* refers to the balance between bright and dark vocal **timbres**. In this sense, *chiaroscuro* is an ideal toward which the **classical singer** should strive: the perfect balance of **resonance** and a beautiful, rich **tone quality**.

choir. An **ensemble** of singers. In the narrow sense, choir has a sacred connotation, labeling a church-affiliated ensemble that performs within the context of **liturgical** worship. In contemporary usage, however, choir tends to be used interchangeably with such synonyms as **chorus** and **chorale**, and many secular schools, colleges, and universities have vocal ensembles that are labeled as choirs.

choirmaster. The choir **director** in an Anglican, Episcopal, or Lutheran church.

chops. A slang term, used by performers of **jazz**, **popular music**, and **musical theatre** that refers to **technique**. A singer with "good chops" is technically skilled at what he or she does.

choral artist. See **chorister**.

choral division. The faculty, **ensembles**, and courses involved with **choral music** at a conservatory, college, or university. Sometimes, the choral division is not its own entity and is simply part of the **vocal division**. An institutional choral division is not to be confused with choral *divisi*, which are part splits—such as Soprano 1 and Soprano 2—that can occur within a **choral score**.

choral music. A **genre** of **repertoire** that includes any piece of music that is written for an **ensemble** of singers. The genre of choral music is vast, including one-on-a-part *a cappella* Renaissance **motets**, as well as symphonic choral **masterworks** that employ hundreds of singers and instrumentalists. The history of choral music is inextricably entwined with the **sacred music** of the Christian church, dating back to the **monophonic chants** of the **medieval** period, which were sung by unison ensembles of monks. Most of the music that survives from the medieval and Renaissance eras qualifies as choral music, as instrumental music had yet been notated, and there were comparatively few secular solo genres. Important medieval and Renaissance genres of choral music include **plainsong**, *organum*, the conductus, the **Mass**, motet, **liturgical drama**, and **polyphonic secular song**, including the *ballade*, *virelai*, *rondeau*, **madrigal**, *chanson*, *frottola*, *lauda*, *villancico*, and *canzona*. The most important composers of medieval and Renaissance choral music included Guillaume de Machaut (c. 1300–1377), Guillaume Du Fay (c. 1397–1474), Josquin des Prez (c. 1450–1521), and Giovanni Pierluigi da Palestrina (c. 1525–1594).

The **baroque** era introduced instrumental **accompaniment** to choral genres, and the **oratorio**—perfected by George Frideric Handel (1685–1759)—was perhaps the most significant choral development of the new era. Also in England, church musicians like Henry Purcell (1659–1695) composed **full anthems**, **verse anthems**, and **evening services**, usually with organ accompaniment. In Germany, the Lutheran **cantata** and the **Passion** genres emerged, which reached their fruition with the works of Johann Sebastian Bach (1685–1750). The **classical** era showed a particular allegiance to the Mass genre, with important settings by Wolfgang Amadeus Mozart (1756–1791) and Franz Schubert (1797–1828), while Joseph Haydn (1732–1809) composed the era's two most

important oratorios with *Die Schöpfung* (*The Creation*, 1798) and *Die Jahreszeiten* (*The Seasons*, 1801).

The first important choral works of the **romantic** era were two late works of Ludwig van Beethoven (1770–1827): the *Missa solemnis in D major*, Op. 123 (1824) and the *Symphony No. 9 in D minor*, Op. 125 (1824). The latter was one of the first major symphonic works to incorporate the use of a **chorus**, a tradition later continued by Gustav Mahler (1860–1911). Both the oratorio, as well as the Mass and **Requiem** genres, continued to flourish throughout the nineteenth century. Some of the most important choral works of the romantic era were the oratorios *Paulus*, Op. 36 (*St. Paul*, 1836) and *Elias*, Op. 70 (*Elijah*, 1846), by Felix Mendelssohn (1809–1847); *Ein deutsches Requiem*, Op. 45 (1868), by Johannes Brahms (1833–1897); and **Latin** Requiems by Hector Berlioz (1803–1869), Giuseppe Verdi (1813–1901), and Gabriel Fauré (1845–1924). Mendelssohn, Brahms, and Anton Bruckner (1824–1896) also contributed a number of short choral works that form a major part of the romantic choral repertory. Robert Schumann (1810–1856) occupies a unique place in discussions of nineteenth-century choral music; while he was prolific, he composed comparatively little sacred music, focusing instead on **partsongs** and secular oratorios, for example, *Das Paradies und die Peri*, Op. 50 (1843).

In the twentieth century, choral music continued to proliferate, although with less loyalty to the traditional Mass and motet genres. England—the most important contributor to twentieth-century choral repertory—remained devoted to the oratorio. Noteworthy works included *The Dream of Gerontius*, Op. 38 (1900), by Edward Elgar (1857–1934); *Belshazzar's Feast* (1931), by William Walton (1902–1983); *A Child of Our Time* (1944), by Michael Tippett (1905–1998); and the *War Requiem* (1962), by Benjamin Britten (1913–1976). In Germany, *Carmina Burana* (1937), by Carl Orff (1895–1982), became perhaps the most frequently performed twentieth-century choral work, accessible to many amateur choral societies. The most famous modern French work is the *Requiem*, Op. 9 (1947), by Maurice Duruflé (1902–1986), but there were many other contributions to the repertory by such important French composers as Claude Debussy (1862–1918) and Francis Poulenc (1899–1963), as well as Swiss composers Frank Martin (1890–1974) and Arthur Honegger (1892–1955). Italy's most important choral composers were Luigi Dallapiccola (1904–1975) and Luigi Nono (1924–1990). Numerous composers from the United States contributed to the repertoire, most of them—like Samuel Barber (1910–1981) and the Italian-born Gian Carlo Menotti (1911–2007)—focusing on shorter choral works. And a number of other countries produced important composers of choral music as well. Leoš Janáček (1854–1928) came from the Czech Republic, Einojuhani Rautavaara (b. 1928) from Finland, Arvo Pärt (b. 1935) and Veljo Tormis (b. 1930) from Estonia, Sven-David Sandström (b. 1942) from Sweden, and—perhaps most important—Karol Szymanowski (1882–1937), Krzysztof Penderecki (b. 1933), and Henryk Górecki (1933–2010) from Poland. The Russian choral repertoire is also vast, with important twentieth-century works by Sergei Rachmaninoff (1873–1943) and Igor Stravinsky (1882–1971).

Choral Public Domain Library (CPDL). An online **sheet music** archive for **choral music** in the **public domain**. Choral musicians, **conductors**, and musicologists regularly download music from CPDL free of charge. The website also archives detailed information about composers and **repertoire**, making CPDL an essential research tool for choral repertoire enthusiasts.

choral score. A **score** that publishes only the choral parts, as opposed to a **vocal score** (or **piano-vocal score**), which publishes the choral parts with the **piano reduction**. Choral scores are almost universally loathed by **choristers**, many of whom shell out their own money to purchase the more expensive and helpful vocal score.

chorale. 1. A German **hymn** in the Lutheran church. Lutheran **cantatas** are based on chorale tunes.
2. Another name for a **chorus**.

chord. A group of three or more **pitches** sounded simultaneously. In **tonal music**, chords are usually **functional** in nature, meaning that they fit into a **harmonic progression**. In **posttonal** music, chords may be **nonfunctional**, dissonant **tone clusters**.

chord progression. See **harmonic progression**.

choreographer. The person who conceives, teaches, and supervises the dance **numbers** in a **musical**, **operetta**, or **opera**.

choreography. The planned **dance** steps of a **musical theatre** or **opera production**.

chorister. A singer who sings in a choral **ensemble**, either an **amateur** or **professional** one. Also called a choral artist.

chorus. An **ensemble** of singers. In the narrow sense, chorus has a secular connotation, but in contemporary usage, this seems erroneous, as many choruses perform **sacred music**, for instance, many of the great **Latin Mass** settings of the Western **canon**. (It is probably true, however, that ensembles that regularly sing in **liturgical** worship are called church choirs, not church choruses.)

chorus master. One who prepares the **chorus** for a **conductor**. It is common practice to enlist a separate chorus

master in the **genres** of **opera** and **symphonic choral music**.

chromatic fixed do. A type of *solfège* in which C is always *do* and a unique **solmization** syllable is assigned to each chromatic note of the **scale**.

chronic laryngitis. A type of **laryngitis** that is not brought on by sudden illness, but rather through environmental or health conditions. Common causes of chronic laryngitis include smoking, overuse of alcohol, poor hydration, or **acid reflux**. Chronic laryngitis is generally treatable through lifestyle change and over-the-counter medications (in the case of reflux). Chronic laryngitis is one of the three basic types of laryngitis, along with **acute laryngitis** and **fungal laryngitis**.

church job. A paid singing position—usually as a **chorister** or **cantor**—at a church or synagogue.

church Latin (ecclesiastical Latin). The **standard Roman pronunciation** of **Latin**, authorized by Pope Pius X (1835–1914) in 1903. These rules advocate a standard **pronunciation** of Latin for all choral works written after the year 1903, regardless of the composer's nationality or the work's country of origin. Church Latin is essentially an Italian way of pronouncing Latin, although scholars would argue that there are subtle differences between the church Latin and true Italianate Latin. Some choral **directors**, for example, the late **Robert Shaw**, have advocated that the rules of church Latin should be applied retroactively to pretwentieth-century works as well, thus prioritizing a systematic pronunciation standard and pedagogical simplicity over **historically informed performance practice (HIPP)**. As the **conductor** ultimately determines the pronunciation method used for a particular performance, the **oratorio** singer and choral artist must be equally comfortable performing in several Latin variants.

church modes. The eight basic **modes** (or diatonic **scales**) that originated in the **chant repertory** of the **medieval** era. The eight church modes include the following: **Dorian**, **Phrygian**, **Lydian**, **Mixolydian**, **Hypodorian**, **Hypophrygian**, **Hypolydian**, and **Hypomixolydian**. A thorough understanding of the church modes is crucial to the performer of **early music**, as virtually all sacred vocal music—much of which was based on **Gregorian chant**—was written in one of the eight church modes.

church music. See **sacred music**.

circle song. A kind of group vocal **improvisation** developed and popularized by vocal artist **Bobby McFerrin**. In a circle song, a group leader **improvises** melodies,

motives, and **riffs**, which he or she then passes along to the rest of the circle. Those individuals are then free to **ornament** and embellish the composition. Circle songs bear some similarity to the compositional process of certain forms of Eastern (including Indian) **classical** music, although circle songs are always a group effort rather than the work of a soloist.

circumflex (^). A French **diacritical marking** that can appear over each of the five cardinal **vowels**—â, ê, î, ô, û—and also the vowel combinations aî, aû, oî, and oû. The circumflex only affects pronunciation in three situations: â = dark [ɑ], ê = open [ɛ], and ô = closed [o]. French vowels with a circumflex are also lengthened when they precede a pronounced consonant. In French, the circumflex is known as the *accent circonflexe*. The circumflex is also occasionally encountered in old Italian, where it indicates a letter that has been omitted (*côre* = *cuore*, e.g.). An Italian circumflex has no effect on pronunciation.

classic blues. One of the three basic **subgenres** of **blues**, along with **country blues** and **urban blues**. Classic blues flourished during the 1920s and featured a blues singer accompanied by a either a pianist or **jazz** band. Ma Rainey (1886–1939) and Bessie Smith (1894–1937) are two of the most well-known names in the classic blues **genre**.

classic Broadway. A general category that refers to the **Broadway** era that began with *Oklahoma!* (1943) and ended with *Hair* (1968). *Oklahoma!* is considered by many Broadway historians to be the first true **musical**; before *Oklahoma!*, the Broadway industry was fragmented into the disparate **genres** of **musical comedies**, **revues**, and **operettas**. And *Hair* is given credit as being the first **rock** musical; beginning with *Hair*, rock would continue to infiltrate the very fabric of Broadway. Classic Broadway is also used as an adjective: the musicals and **songs** written between 1943–1967 are considered to be the "classic Broadway **canon**," and singers from this era are said to have the "classic Broadway sound." Some of the most important composers and **lyricists** of the classic Broadway era include Cole Porter (1891–1964), Irving Berlin (1888–1989), Frank Loesser (1910–1969), Richard Rodgers (1902–1979) and Oscar Hammerstein II (1895–1960), Richard Adler (1921–2012) and Jerry Ross (1926–1955), Alan Jay Lerner (1918–1986) and Frederick Loewe (1901–1988), and Jerry Bock (1928–2010) and Sheldon Harnick (b. 1924). Singers who exemplify the classic Broadway sound include **Julie Andrews**, Mary Martin (1913–1990), Alfred Drake (1914–1992), John Raitt (1917–2005), Howard Keel (1919–2004), and Gordon MacRae (1921–1986).

classical. 1. An era of Western music spanning from roughly 1750–1825. The roots of the classic period begin earlier, however, around 1730. The classical era is immediately preceded by the **baroque** era and is followed by the **romantic** era. Stylistically, the classical era sought to revive the Greek ideals of symmetry, balance, proportion, and **form** in art. **Expression** was universal and **objective** instead of personal and subjective. The epicenter of the classical era was Vienna, and the primary vocal **genres** written during this period included **operas**, **Masses**, and **concert arias**. The principal composers of classical-era music include Joseph Haydn (1732–1809) and Wolfgang Amadeus Mozart (1756–1791), and the early works of Ludwig van Beethoven (1770–1827) and Franz Schubert (1797–1828) also fall squarely into the Viennese classical style.
2. A general, "catchall" term for Western **art music**. In this sense, classical music extends to music that was written during periods other than the classical period proper (1750–1825).

classical singer. A vocal performer of Western **art music**. Most individuals who call themselves classical singers focus on the **repertory** written between 1600 to the present day. (Performers of **medieval** and **Renaissance** works are usually considered to be **early music** performers or choral artists.) Although the classical vocal repertory is vast, there is a certain degree of stylistic uniformity that can be aurally observed in a majority of the repertoire. While there are subtle stylistic shifts and nuances that must be observed as one moves between repertoires, much of the music can be approached utilizing the same basic vocal **technique**. In some instances in twentieth- and twenty-first-century **opera**, **extended techniques** are required of the performer.

classical sound. The largely agreed upon *bel canto* aesthetic of singing cultivated by the **International Italian School**. The classical sound is remarkably consistent across **voice types** and principal solo **genres** of the **classical** style, including **opera**, **oratorio**, **art song**, and chamber music, although some forms of **new music** and **early music** fall outside the mainstream.

clausula. In **Notre Dame polyphony**, a short section of *organum*—either in two, three, or four voices—that closes with a **cadence**. A clausula is a **polyphonic** elaboration of a section of **monophonic chant**.

clavicular breathing. A method of breathing that is high in nature, involving the shoulders (clavicular refers to the clavicles). Clavicular breathing is generally undesirable in singing due to one's inability to control the **exhalation**. See also *appoggio*.

closed quotient (CQ). In voice science, refers to the percentage of time that the **glottis** is closed during each cycle of **vocal fold oscillation**.

closed vowel. Describes a **vowel** that requires a rounding or spreading of the lips and less space between the articulators. Closed vowels are the opposite of **open vowels**. Common examples include [i], [e],[u], [o], [y], and [ø]. See also **back vowel**, **central vowel**, **front vowel**, **mixed vowel**, **nasal vowel**.

cluster. A group of **dissonant pitches** comprising a **chord** that cannot be analyzed by means of traditional music theory. Clustertone sonorities are a hallmark of certain kinds of contemporary **choral music**. Also called a **tone cluster**.

coach (vocal coach). See **collaborative pianist**.

Cody, Radmilla (b. 1974). Native American singer of the Navajo tribe. Cody was raised in the Navajo Nation and began singing traditional Navajo music at an early age. When she was twenty-three, she participated in and won the Miss Navajo contest, which brought her national attention. After her tenure as Miss Navajo, she embarked on a recording career. From 2000–2011, she recorded five nationally released albums. Her **songs** offer a combination of traditional Navajo music and contemporary **popular music**. Cody is perhaps the most well-known Native American performer in the entertainment industry.

Coffin, Berton (1910–1987). American **voice pedagogue** most famous for his scholarly publications and his influence on a generation of voice pedagogues. Coffin's most important scholarship was published in *The Sounds of Singing: Vocal Techniques with Vowel-Pitch Charts* (1976, rev. 1987) and *Overtones of Bel Canto: Phonetic Basis of Artistic Singing with 100 Chromatic Vowel-Chart Exercises* (1980). These two books are two of the most important treatises of the **fact-based** school of **voice pedagogy**, advocating systematic **vowel** modification in various parts of the vocal **range** to achieve **resonance** via scientific and **acoustic** principles. Coffin also edited *Historical Vocal Pedagogy Classics* (published posthumously in 1989), a one-stop shop of historically important pedagogical writings that all teachers of singing must eventually read. Coffin taught at the University of Colorado Boulder for more than thirty years and was president of the **National Association of Teachers of Singing (NATS)** from 1968–1970. Along with **Richard Miller**, **Cornelius Reid**, and **Oren Lathrop Brown**, Coffin ranks as one of the most influential American **classical** voice pedagogues of the twentieth century.

colla parte **(It).** With the parts. An instruction to instrumentalists that invites them to play with the choral parts. For example, in the eighteenth century, it was common for three trombones to play the **alto**, **tenor**, and **bass** choral parts *colla parte*, with a zink or cornetto sometimes doubling the **soprano** part as well.

collaborative pianist (collaborative artist). A more respectful name for a singer's **accompanist**, recognizing his or her **role** as an equal—rather than as a subordinate—collaborator in the artistic process. A collaborative pianist who works on musical issues with less experienced singers is often called a coach (or vocal coach).

color. A word used to describe the **quality** of one's voice. Usually darker, richer voices are said to have more "color." A singer's color—along with **range** and **tessitura**—is often a significant factor in determining one's **voice type** or *Fach*. Roughly equivalent to **timbre**.

coloratura. Fast, **melismatic** singing. Coloratura passages in vocal music are either written out by the composer or improvised by the singer during **ornamentation**. Examples of coloratura singing can be found in all eras, but coloratura singing was especially popular in the **operatic repertory** from George Frideric Handel (1685–1759) through the *bel canto* operas of Gioacchino Rossini (1792–1868), Gaetano Donizetti (1797–1848), and Vincenzo Bellini (1801–1835). The Queen of the Night, an iconic character in Mozart's *Die Zauberflöte* (1791), sings two of the most famous coloratura **arias** in the repertory. Coloratura is roughly synonymous with *fioratura*, although the latter term sometimes implies improvised ornamentation. It is also used as an adjective in three of the 29 *Fachs* of the **Kloiber Fach System**: the *lyrischer Koloratursopran*, *dramatischer Koloratursopran* and the *koloratur-Mezzosopran*.

comédie-ballet. A seventeenth-century French theatrical **genre** featuring lavish **spectacle**, singing, and dancing.

comic opera. Not to be confused with the nineteenth-century French **genre** *opéra comique*. Although an accurate literal translation, this is a separate genre in its own right. See also **English comic opera**.

commedia dell'arte. A **genre** of **improvised** Italian **theatre** that flourished for approximately 200 years, from the early sixteenth through the eighteenth centuries. *Commedia dell'arte* featured various **stock characters**, including Pantalone, Scaramuccia, Columbina, Pedrolino (Pierrot), Arlecchino (Harlequin), and Pulcinella (Punch). *Commedia dell'arte* was an important forerunner of **opera**.

commission. A piece of **new music** that is requested from a composer for a specific organization, individual, or event. Commissions are contracted well in advance of the event for a sum of money.

communion. Another name for the Eucharist—the sharing of bread and wine in remembrance of the crucifixion of Christ—in a Christian worship service. The communion is also one of the five standard parts of the **Proper** in a Catholic **Mass**.

community theatre. An all-volunteer **theatre company**, often in a small city or town.

company. A group of theatrical performers. Sometimes called a **troupe**.

compensatory tension. Unnecessary tension that interferes with singing. Compensatory tension usually emerges when a singer is attempting to resolve a specific technical challenge but is ultimately unsuccessful due to a technical miscalculation, which thus results in unwanted tension.

compilation show. See **catalog show**.

Complete Vocal Technique (CVT). A vocal **technique** developed by Danish pedagogue Catherine Sadolin (b. 1958). The primary philosophy behind CVT is that singing is not as difficult as many people think it is, and that the most important aspect of the technique is **expression**, which allows singers to convey their individual artistic choices through the music they choose to sing. The method also uses four basic technical "**modes**" of singing: **neutral**, **curbing**, **overdrive**, and **edge**. The first educational video produced on the CVT was called *Rough, Ready, and Able*. It was released in 1991. Subsequent releases of Sadolin's works in other languages include English and Swedish (1996), German (2009), French (2010), and Spanish (2012).

compound duple. A two-**beat meter** in which each beat is divided into a three-part **subdivision**. See also **compound meter**.

compound meter. When each **beat** of a measure is divided into three **subdivisions**. There are three kinds of compound meter: **compound duple**, which has two beats per measure; **compound triple**, which has three beats per measure; and **compound quadruple**, which has four beats per measure.

compound quadruple. A four-**beat meter** in which each beat is divided into a three-part **subdivision**. See also **compound meter**.

compound triple. A three-**beat meter** in which each beat is divided into a three-part **subdivision**. See also **compound meter**.

compression. 1. In **acoustics**, an increase in density or a pressurization of air molecules. Compression is the opposite of **rarefaction**. Both compression and rarefaction travel in waves.

2. A vocal processing effect used to smooth out dynamic changes in **amplified singers**. A compression of the **amplitude** of the music by electronic means.

3. Within the **Speech Level Singing (SLS)** method, compression is used to describe the pressure with which the **vocal folds** vibrate. High compression indicates strong vocal fold **adduction**, whereas a low compression indicates weak vocal fold adduction.

compression wave. See **compression**.

comprimario **role.** A smaller, supporting **role** in an **opera**.

con moto **(It).** With motion.

concept album. In **musical theatre**, an album of **songs** from a forthcoming **musical** that is released a year or two prior to the actual show to generate buzz and excitement. Andrew Lloyd Webber (b. 1948) and Tim Rice (b. 1944) successfully used concept albums to promote their musicals *Jesus Christ Superstar* (1971–1972) and *Evita* (1978–1979).

concept musical. In **musical theatre**, a show that is conceived around a central idea or concept rather than a traditional narrative **plot**. Concept musicals often tell their stories in a nonlinear way, presenting brief tableaus that are not necessarily delivered in chronological order. Some of the most famous concept musicals in history include Rodgers and Hammerstein's *Allegro* (1947), Stephen Sondheim's *Company* (1970), and Hamlisch and Kleban's *A Chorus Line* (1975).

concert. A musical performance in a **recital** hall or other nontheatrical venue.

concert aria. An **aria** that is written for voice and orchestra as opposed to for an **opera** or **oratorio**. Concert arias are occasionally arias that were originally intended to be part of an opera **score** but were ultimately cut or otherwise not included in the theatrical work. Wolfgang Amadeus Mozart (1756–1791) wrote many concert arias for voice and orchestra.

concert music. For singers, **repertoire** composed for solo voice and orchestra. Concert music is distinct from **opera**, **art song**, and **chamber music**. Barber's *Knoxville:*

Summer of 1915 (composed in 1947) is an example of a piece of concert music, as are Mozart's numerous **concert arias**. The German term is ***Konzertmusik***.

concert opera. An **opera** that is performed without staging (or with partial staging), and usually in **concert** attire, as opposed to in costumes. It is also the custom to perform concert versions of operas **on-book** as opposed to memorized. Concert operas are a much simpler and less expensive way to experience works from the **operatic repertory**.

concerted madrigal. Refers to a late, instrumentally accompanied **madrigal** from the early **baroque** era.

condenser microphone. A **microphone** designed with two parallel, electrically charged, thin metal plates. The anterior plate is free moving, while the posterior plate is fixed. A layer of insulation lies between the two plates. When the anterior plate is sent into motion by **acoustic** vibrations, the charge between the two plates is altered, resulting in a fluctuation of the electrical current. Those fluctuations are transmitted to the amplifier through the microphone cable for processing by the sound system. For more information, see the essay entitled "What Every Singer Needs to Know about Audio Technology."

conditional ballad. A type of **song** developed by **lyricist** Oscar Hammerstein II (1895–1960) as a way of inserting a love **duet** into the first **act** of an **operetta** or **musical**, thus giving the characters an opportunity to sing together before they actually fall in love. In these **ballads**—actually duets—the characters daydream about what it would be like to actually be in love. Quintessential examples include "Make Believe" from *Show Boat* (1927), "People Will Say We're in Love" from *Oklahoma!* (1943), and "If I Loved You" from *Carousel* (1945).

conductor. The person who physically directs an **ensemble**—either an orchestra, **choir**, **opera**, or **musical theatre production**. Conductors can either use a baton—which is generally preferred when conducting instrumental ensembles—or their hands and arms to coordinate the entrance of various parts and maintain good rhythmic ensemble. In addition to conducting final performances, the conductor is also responsible for **rehearsal** and preparation of an ensemble. In **musical theatre** and opera, the conductor is usually (although not always) the same person as the **musical director**. In musical theatre, there will occasionally be a pit orchestra conductor who is a separate individual than the musical director, who works with the singers.

congenital laryngeal webs. One of the two basic types of **laryngeal webs**. Congenital laryngeal webs occur during embryonic development. The other type are **acquired laryngeal webs**, which are brought on by external trauma or illness.

consonance. An **interval** or **harmony** that is considered to be stable and therefore does not require **resolution**. The opposite of **dissonance**.

consonant. 1. One of two principal categories of **phonetic sounds** (along with **vowels**). Consonants are pronounced with the **articulators**—for example, the tongue, lips, and **glottis**—and are classified by three large categories: **point of articulation**, **manner of articulation**, and whether the consonant is **voiced** or **unvoiced**.
2. An adjective pertaining to **consonance**.

consonant cluster. Three or more **consonant** sounds adjacent to one another. Occurs frequently in German in such words as "Angstschweiß" and "Pflichte."

consonant pair. Two **consonants** that are only different from one another in the sense that one is **voiced** and the other is **unvoiced**. Common consonant pairs include [b] and [p], [d] and [t], [g] and [k], [v] and [f], [z] and [s], [ʒ] and [ʃ], and [θ] and [ð].

consort song. A English **Renaissance song** written for voice and consort of viols.

constant voice injury. A type of **vocal injury** that will not change throughout time, and a permanent injury with which one must cope. Constant voice injuries are rare. One example includes the virilization of the **vocal folds** of the female **larynx** due to the administration of androgens. One of the three basic types of voice injuries, along with **progressive voice injuries** and **episodic voice injuries**.

constrictor muscles. One of three pairs of muscles that form the pharyngeal wall.

contact ulcers. A voice disorder that occurs when ulcerative sores appear at or near the **vocal process** (the point of connection at the **arytenoid** for the **vocal ligaments**). Contact ulcers occur either **unilaterally** or **bilaterally** and are usually caused by trauma or illness. They can usually be resolved through lifestyle changes and **voice therapy**.

contemporary belt. In **contemporary commercial music (CCM)**, a higher **belt style** needed to perform contemporary **popular music** and modern **musical theatre repertoire**. Also called **belt-mix** or **superbelt**.

contemporary Christian music. Sometimes used as a synonym with **praise music**, contemporary Christian music is an even broader label, including **pop** artists who sing Christian **lyrics** but do not necessarily work for a church or use their music in a **liturgical** context. Thus, the phrase contemporary Christian music usually refers to the industry and the **genre**, whereas praise music refers to music that is actually used in a worship service. The two flavors of the genre largely draw from the same **repertoire** of **songs** and conventions.

contemporary commercial music (CCM). A term coined by Jeannette LoVetri (b. 1949) to describe any nonclassical vocal **genre**. Thus, the term "CCM style" indicates any nonclassical singing style. Such styles vary widely, and CCM includes the genres of **musical theatre**, **rock**, **pop**, **country**, **jazz**, **blues**, **R&B**, **gospel**, **world music**, and virtually every **subgenre** or variation of these principal categories. During the past two decades, the CCM abbreviation has been appropriated widely among singing teachers, and many different schools of CCM **pedagogy** have emerged throughout the United States and abroad. Various **voice pedagogues** have made names for themselves by billing themselves as the disseminator of a specific kind of philosophical approach toward the **technique** of CCM singing. A few of these techniques—too numerous to list comprehensively—include **Somatic Voicework (SVW)**, **Speech Level Singing (SLS)**, and **Estill Voice Training (EVT)**.

continuo. A feature of **ensemble** music in the seventeenth and eighteenth centuries, consisting of a **bass** line played on a melodic instrument, together with a **chord**-playing instrument (usually either a harpsichord or organ); the actual music of the latter was **improvised** by the skilled player, although it is often written out in modern editions. While some **cantata** movements and **vocal concertos** were written for voice and continuo (without additional instruments), this kind of **accompaniment** is most frequently heard in the **recitatives** of **operas**, **oratorios**, and cantatas. Continuo accompaniment remained in vogue for dry recitative (or *recitativo secco*) through the operas of Wolfgang Amadeus Mozart (1756–1791) and Gioacchino Rossini (1792–1868). It was finally rendered obsolete with the death of the **number opera** in the early nineteenth century, when operatic **scores** became more seamless and **symphonic** in nature.

contrafactum. A vocal work in the **medieval** and **Renaissance** eras in which a new sacred text replaces an original secular one.

contralto. One of the seven principal **classical** voice categories and the lowest of the three female **voice types**. The **German Fach System** identifies four subcategories of **contraltos**: the *Spielalt*, *lyrischer Alt*, *dramatischer Alt*, and *tiefer Alt*. Although the *Fach* system makes a clear distinction between **mezzo-sopranos** and contraltos, the **opera** profession does not, and many mezzo-sopranos also sing much of the contralto **repertoire** outlined by the **Kloiber Fach System**. The three mezzo-soprano categories in the *Fach* system include the *koloratur-Mezzosopran*, *lyrischer Mezzosopran*, and *dramatischer Mezzosopran*. Outside of Germany, few female singers label themselves as contraltos.

contratenor (Lat). Against the **tenor**. In **medieval** counterpoint, a contrapuntal line written "against" the tenor part. Not to be confused with the German *Fach* of the same name. See also *Contratenor (Countertenor)*.

contratenor (countertenor). A category in the **German Fach System**. The *contratenor (countertenor)* is the highest male category in the twenty-nine **Kloiber Fach System** designations, stationed one spot below the *tiefer Alt* on the chart and one spot above the *haute-contre*. *Contratenors (countertenors)* are essentially male falsettists. *Contratenor (countertenor)* **roles** include Nerone in Monteverdi's *L'incoronazione di Poppea* (1643); Oberon in Britten's *A Midsummer Night's Dream* (1960); and many roles by Handel, including the title roles in *Ariodante* (1735), *Giulio Cesare* (1724), *Orlando* (1733), *Rinaldo* (1611), and *Tamerlano* (1724). Most of the **baroque** roles in the *contratenor (countertenor)* category were originally written for **castrati**. See the *Fach* chart in appendix C.

coon song. A dated, racist term for a specific type of **song** written in African American **dialect** or with black musical characteristics. Popular during the latter half of the nineteenth century and the beginning of the twentieth century. See **minstrel show**, **minstrel song**, **parlor song**, **plantation song**.

coordinated register. See **mixed register**.

copertura. The **technique** of singing with a *voce chiusa* **timbre** as opposed to a *voce aperta* timbre.

coping cards. A **technique** borrowed from psychotherapy used in the management of **musical performance anxiety (MPA)**. The singer writes down positive statements about his or her capabilities on cards while in a normal mental state to refer to during times when experiencing MPA.

copla. A Spanish **song genre** that has been in use since the fourteenth century. The term *copla* derives from the poetic form of the same name, which consists of four-line poetic **stanzas** with an ABCB rhyme scheme. The genre found renewed popularity among popular musicians in the twentieth century. Sometimes called *copla andaluza*, which means "Andalusian *copla*."

copla andaluza. See *copla*.

cori spezzati (It). Broken (divided) **choirs**. Refers to two or more choirs that are separated spatially during performance. St. Mark's Basilica in Venice was famous for its *cori spezzati* during the late **Renaissance** era, and much music was composed for its two choirs, who performed **antiphonally**.

corniculate cartilages (cartilages of Santorini). Two small conical points located at the top of each of the two **arytenoid cartilages**. Historically called the cartilages of Santorini, they were named after the Italian physician Giovanni Domenico Santorini (1681–1737).

count singing. A choral **rehearsal technique** popularized by **Robert Shaw**. When count singing, choral singers replace the text with the number of the **beat** that they're singing. Some **consonants** are pronounced, however, and placed on rests in the music. Count singing is a repetitive exercise that is meant to intellectually engage singers—particularly **amateur** singers—and make them cognitively aware of the importance of rhythm in good **ensemble** singing. Count singing is still practiced by an entire generation of Shaw's students, many of whom are choral **directors** throughout the United States.

countermelody. A second tune written by a composer designed to be sung (or played) simultaneously with the original melody. Countermelodies occur frequently in **operatic** and **musical theatre genres**.

countertenor. One of the seven basic **voice types**, countertenors are essentially male singers who choose to sing in their **falsetto** (or **CT/mode 2**) **register**. While all countertenors are naturally **tenors**, **baritones**, or **basses** (as their voices have changed after puberty), the successful countertenor does not cross train between two different *Fächer*; most countertenors are exclusively countertenors. Due to the location of their natural second *passaggio*, tenors tend to become **mezzo-soprano** countertenors, whereas baritones and basses tend to become **soprano** countertenors. The countertenor phenomenon is a relatively recent one that began proliferating in the latter half of the twentieth century, largely through the pioneering efforts of such **early music** singers as Alfred Deller (1912–1979) and Russell Oberlin (b. 1928). In addition to singing **art songs** and mezzo-soprano **roles** in **baroque oratorios**, countertenors often specialize in the baroque **operatic** roles once inhabited by **castratos**. While there are some similarities, it must be remembered that castrato singers had a distinct **timbre** due to different physical and **laryngeal** configurations. Thus, castratos and countertenors should be thought of as two separate voice types. See also *contratenor (countertenor)*.

country (country and western). A **style** of American **popular music** that dates from the early decades of the twentieth century, when record companies began to capitalize on the dissemination of white "hillbilly" music of the American South. From its earliest days, the vocal style of country music featured a distinctive rustic **twang**, a **quality** that has endured throughout the **genre's** long history. Idiomatic **accompanimental** instruments include the banjo and violin. In the 1930s, dissemination of the style throughout the United States occurred largely through radio airplay. Nashville's **Grand Ole Opry** also played a significant **role** in popularizing the genre. As the decades wore on, country's sound became less **acoustic** and more amplified and spawned several **subgenres**, including honky tonk, western **swing**, and **country rock**. **Bluegrass** is another subgenre that is deliberately anachronistic, clinging to its Appalachian roots. Now almost 100 years old, country music remains one of the most enduring genres of popular music in the United States.

country and western. See **country**.

country blues. One of the three basic **subgenres** of **blues**, along with **classic blues** and **urban blues**. Country blues emerged in the Mississippi Delta and East Texas at the turn of the twentieth century. This subgenre usually featured a male singer with a steel-stringed **acoustic** guitar. **Robert Johnson** and Charley Patton (1891–1934) are famous exponents of the country blues **style**.

country pop. A **fusion genre** that combines elements of **country** with aspects of **pop**. Most contemporary country music is probably more accurately labeled as country pop or **country rock**.

country rock. A **fusion genre** that combines elements of **country** with aspects of **rock**. Most contemporary country music is probably more accurately labeled as country rock or **country pop**.

coup de glotte (Fr). A French **voice pedagogy** term literally meaning "stroke of the **glottis**." The *coup de glotte* concept is attributed to **Manuel García** (1805–1906), who described the ideal **onset** for singing. When the theory of the *coup de glotte* was first published in *A Complete Treatise on the Art of Singing* (1841, rev. 1872), critics of García mistakenly thought that he was advocating a harsh **glottal attack**, a point that García subsequently clarified in his 1872 revision to the *Traité* and in *Hints on Singing* (1894); rather, he was encouraging a **balanced onset**, along with ideal **breath management** and **placement**.

court (Fr). Short.

Covent Garden. A district in London on the eastern edge of the West End, known to **opera** lovers as the home of the Royal Opera House, one of the world's most famous **operatic venues**. The Royal Opera House is simply called "Covent Garden" by most opera enthusiasts. The original **opera house** was built in 1732. The current building is the third structure due to fires that destroyed the first two in 1808 and 1857, respectively. Covent Garden seats 2,256 people and consists of four tiers of boxes and balconies. In addition to being England's premiere opera house, Covent Garden is also the home of the Royal Ballet.

cover. 1. The term for an **understudy** in **opera**. Covers have an opportunity to perform the **role** should the actual singer who is cast become ill or otherwise incapacitated. Apprentices and young artists often cover lead roles while simultaneously performing *comprimario* or **chorus** roles.

2. In **classical** vocal **technique**, a term that usually refers to the **vowel** modification that occurs when men sing at the top of their vocal **range**. Refers to the **turning** that must occur above the *secondo passaggio* to give the impression of a seamless, even **tone quality**. If a singer does not cover, the tone quality will likely become too bright and spread and be incongruent with the classical aesthetic. The concept of cover is controversial only because voice teachers are not consistent in their use of the word, with different **pedagogues** intending different things when they mention the word *cover*. While cover (referring to vowel modification) is a normal aspect of advanced male vocal technique, covering can also refer to an artificial darkening of the voice that a singer might pretentiously use if attempting to sound older than he actually is. Such "dishonest" singing is likely to result in compensatory, extraneous tension and is, of course, undesirable.

3. In **popular music**, a new recording or performance of a song originally released by another artist (with whom that song is usually associated). A cover recording can occasionally become more popular than the original.

4. The outermost layer of the **vocal fold** that consists of the **stratified squamous epithelium** and superficial layer of the **lamina propria** (**Reinke's space**).

CPDL. Abbreviation for **Choral Public Domain Library**.

CQ. Abbreviation for **closed quotient**.

crack, cracking. See **pitch break**.

creative artist. Term used in juxtaposition to an **interpretive artist**. In music, a creative artist composes a piece of music, which the interpretive artist—the performer or **conductor**—then performs.

Credo. One of the five standard parts of the **Ordinary** in a Catholic **Mass**.

crescendo (It). To get louder or grow in volume.

cricoarytenoid muscles. Muscles that connect the **cricoid cartilage** to the **arytenoid cartilage**. There are two types of cricoarytenoid muscles, each of which serves a different physiological function: the paired **lateral cricoarytenoid (LCA)** muscles serve as the primary adductors of the **vocal folds**, and the paired **posterior cricoarytenoid (PCA)** muscles act as the primary abductors of the vocal folds. See the anatomical drawings in appendix B.

cricoid cartilage. One of the three principal cartilages of the **larynx**, located below the **thyroid cartilage**. The cricoid cartilage is shaped like a signet ring. See the anatomical drawings in appendix B.

cricothyroid dominant production. See **CT-dominant**.

cricothyroid muscles. Paired muscles that connect the **cricoid cartilage** to the **thyroid cartilage**. When engaged, the cricothyroid muscles elongate the **vocal folds**, making them the **larynx's** primary **pitch**-control muscles. There are two types of cricothyroid muslces: *pars recta* (vertical) and *pars oblique* (more horizontal). See the anatomical drawings in appendix B.

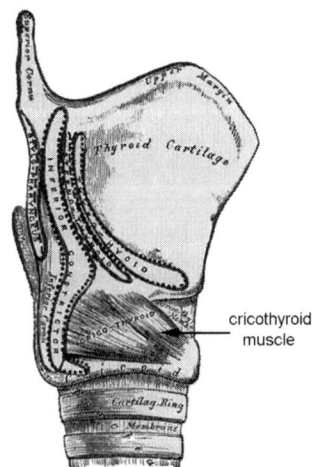

Figure 10. Cricothyroid cartilage and muscle. *Courtesy Gray's Anatomy,* with labeling by Scott McCoy; reprinted with permission from *Your Voice: An Inside View* (2004).

croon. To sing in a soft, low voice, often in a sentimental style. Crooning is often a stylistic feature of popular **ballads**. Crooners generally use **microphones**.

cry. In **contemporary commercial music (CCM)**, a higher **belt style** needed to perform contemporary **popular**

music and modern **musical theatre repertoire**. Also called **pop wail**, **belt-mix**, or **superbelt**.

CT. Abbreviation for **cricothyroid**.

CT-dominant. An adjective that describes a type of singing that is in **mode 2** or **operatic head voice**. All female **classical** singers sing in a CT-dominant **style**, as do **countertenors**.

curbing. One of the four vocal **modes** described in the **Complete Vocal Technique (CVT)** method. Curbing is described as a "half metallic" mode that resembles the sound of a wail, moan, or whine. Curbing is used in **popular music** when a sound with some metal is desired in lower **pitches** at a medium volume. It is also found in **classical** vocal music when men are singing at medium volume throughout their **range** and when women are singing at a louder volume in the middle part of their voice (and sometimes at lower pitches as well). See also **edge**, **neutral**, **overdrive**.

cut. 1. A small portion of a **song**, usually only thirty to forty-five seconds in length. **Musical theatre auditions** usually consist of several cuts as opposed to entire performances of songs. Contrasting cuts allow auditioners to assess a singing actor's versatility as opposed to just one aspect of his or her **technique**.

2. To deliberately shorten a piece of music, usually by removing a section from the middle or eliminating a repeat.

3. In audio technology, a cut reduces the **amplitude** of **frequencies** within a specified **range**. See also **audio spectrum**.

CVT. Abbreviation for **Complete Vocal Technique**.

cyst. See **vocal fold cysts**.

D

da capo aria. A **baroque aria** in **ABA form**, found with great prevalence in early eighteenth-century **operas** and **oratorios**. _Da capo_ arias generally feature a very short text—two to four lines per section of music—with an instrumental treatment of the vocal line. The voice sings **melismatic** passages on the repeated text. The B section offers a sharp contrast (in **style**, **key**, mode, or tempo), after which _da capo_ is indicated. The performer then repeats the A section, adding significant **ornamentation**. The _da capo_ aria is an island of stasis in an opera or oratorio, rarely involving any action or advancing the **plot**. It is a vehicle whereby composer and performer can show their ability to express strong emotion, as well as technical ability.

dance. While technically its own discipline and unrelated to the art of singing, dance plays a significant **role** in the **interpretation** of music from some eras. **Baroque** music, for instance, is often based on basic dance rhythms, for example, the _bourée_, gavotte, gigue, minuet, sarabande, allemande, chaconne, passacaglia, and courante. Understanding the subtle differences between these dances is essential knowledge to the performer of **early music**. Likewise, one cannot understand **Viennese operetta** without knowledge of the **waltz**, which performers cast in roles will likely have to physically dance as well. **Musical theatre** performers are expected to be triple threats, with the ability to dance, as well as act and sing.

Daniel sitteth. A mnemonic device for students of English **diction**, reminding them to insert a [j] glide after the six **consonants** or consonant groups in this phrase—_d_, _n_, _l_, _s_, _t_, and _th_—whenever they are followed by an [u] sound that is spelled either _u_ or _ew_. Examples include "news" [njuz], "lute" [ljut], and "suit" [sjut]. This rule is especially helpful for American students, who tend to omit the [j] glide in their **dialectical pronunciation** of these words. Exceptions include l in combination with other consonants, for instance, "flute" [flut] and "influence" [ˈInfluɛns].

dB. Abbreviation for **decibel**.

DCA. Abbreviation for **director of choral activities**.

de la Isla, Camarón (1950–1992). Spanish singer considered by many to be the greatest of all **flamenco** singers. De la Isla was born in San Fernando, Cadiz, Spain, to a basket-weaving mother and blacksmith father. Although his real name was José Monje Cruz, his uncle nicknamed him Camerón (which means "shrimp") because he was blonde and fair-skinned. After winning a singing contest at the age of sixteen, he moved to Madrid, where he began his career as a flamenco singer. He soon met the guitarist Paco de Lucía (b. 1947), with whom he had a longtime collaboration and recorded fourteen albums. De la Isla was the most famous flamenco singer of the second half of the twentieth century, and he contributed numerous innovations to the **genre**, for example, the addition of an electric bass. He is also credited as the inventor of _nuevo flamenco_, a contemporary incarnation of the traditional genre.

de Los Angeles, Victoria. See **Los Angeles, Victoria de**.

decani. In an Anglican church with a divided chancel, the decani is the right side of the **choir**. The decani side faces the **cantoris**, which is the left side of the choir.

decibel (dB). In voice science, the most common measurement for **amplitude**. Subjectively, a measurement for how loud something is. Normal conversations, for example, are usually at a level of about 60 dB, whereas a jet engine clocks in at 135 dB. Sounds that measure at greater than 120 dB can be harmful to the human ears. Sounds greater than 170 dB can be lethal.

Deckung (Ger). See **cover**.

declamation. Refers to the stressed and lengthened syllables of a particular language, as well as the natural rise and fall of speech. Composers of vocal music pay particular attention to declamation when setting their text. For example, a short, unaccented syllable will almost never be set on a sustained high note. Good text-setting will make languages sound and feel "natural." Declamation does not concern itself with the meanings of individual words, however, and it should not be confused with text painting, which is when a composer illustrates the meaning of particular words via specific compositional devices.

declamatory. Delivered in a speech-like style with an emphasis on word meaning.

decrescendo (It). To become softer or decrease in volume.

de-essing. A recording-studio **technique** that uses electronic processors to reduce such **sibilant consonants** as [s], [z], and [ʃ]. De-essers can also be used in live performances.

deep lamina propria. The innermost layer of the **lamina propria**.

dental. 1. In the study of **diction**, a **point of articulation** that describes **consonants** that involve the tip of the tongue and the back of the upper row of teeth. Common examples of dental consonants include [z], [s], [l], [θ], and [ð]. See also **alveolar, bilabial, labiodental, palatal, prepalatal, velar**.
2. A mnemonic device for the student of Italian, French, and Spanish diction that reminds the singer to dentalize (place the tongue on the back of the teeth) the four consonants in the word dental: *d, n, t,* and *l*. In English and German diction, these four consonants tend to be pronounced with the tongue touching the **alveolar ridge**.

derivative. A pejorative term that refers to a singer's expressive **style** and **tone quality**. If a singer is either consciously imitating or overly influenced by a more famous performer, then he or she is said to have a derivative style. No singer ever became iconic by imitating someone else's style; therefore, it is quintessentially important for the singer to develop his or her own unique artistry.

descant. 1. In Anglican hymnody, a nonmelodic higher **treble** line that usually occurs only during the last **verse** of the **hymn**. Can broadly refer to any high, nonmelodic **harmony** in **choral music**, usually executed by the **sopranos**.
2. An obsolete term for the soprano part in choral music.

Deutsche Grammophon Gesellschaft (DGG). A major record label based in Germany. DGG is legendary for the **quality** of its sound recordings and remains one of the preeminent labels in **classical** music. In addition to chronicling many of the world's great **opera** singers in their signature **roles** throughout the past fifty years, DGG was also **Dietrich Fischer-Dieskau's** label of choice for many of his most famous recordings, including his comprehensive Schubert recordings with the late **Gerald Moore**.

DGG. Abbreviation for **Deutsche Grammophon Gesellschaft**.

dhrupad. Ancient, sacred Indian vocal **genre** of the Hindustani tradition. Almost exclusively performed by male singers and accompanied by such instruments as the tanpura (a four-stringed drone instrument) and the pakhawaj (a barrel-shaped, two-headed drum).

diacritical marking. An additional symbol added to letters in some languages, often indicating stress or **pronunciation**. Italian, French, and German—three core languages for **classical singers**—all use diacritical markings extensively. The most common examples include the *accento grave* (ˋ), *accento acuto* (ˊ), *accent grave* (ˋ), *accent aigu* (ˊ), **circumflex** (ˆ), and *diérèse* (dieresis) or *umlaut* (¨).

dialect. A particular **form** of language that is unique to a certain geographical region or ethnic group. While one's **accent** is a part of one's dialect, dialect can also include unique vocabulary words, **pronunciations**, and grammar structures. In singer's **diction**, usually only the accent and pronunciation related to the dialect is germane.

dialect song. A type of **musical theatre song** that is sung in a specific **dialect**. Examples are manifold, ranging from the Irish-flavored songs in Ahrens and Flaherty's *A Man of No Importance* (2002) to the long and rich history of African American **musicals**.

diaphragm. 1. A large, dome-shaped muscle that separates the contents of the human **thorax** and the abdomen, and one of the two primary muscles of **inspiration** (along with the **external intercostal muscles**). The diaphragm is the second-largest muscle of the human body, exceeded only by the *gluteus maximus* (buttocks) muscles. It is also one of only two unpaired muscles in the body, the other being the *orbicularis oris* (the sphincter-like muscle around the mouth).
The diaphragm is at its greatest point of contraction when the singer has most fully inhaled. During **expiration**, the diaphragm returns to a relaxed position. Through good *appoggio* **technique**, the singer can learn how to use **antagonistic** muscles to control the relaxation

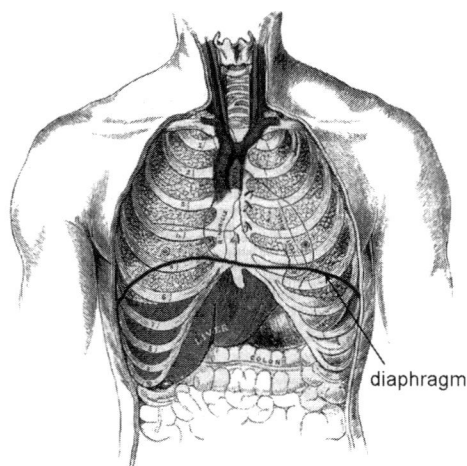

Figure 11. Location of diaphragm in thorax/torso. *Courtesy Gray's Anatomy,* with labeling by Scott McCoy; reprinted with permission from *Your Voice: An Inside View* (2004).

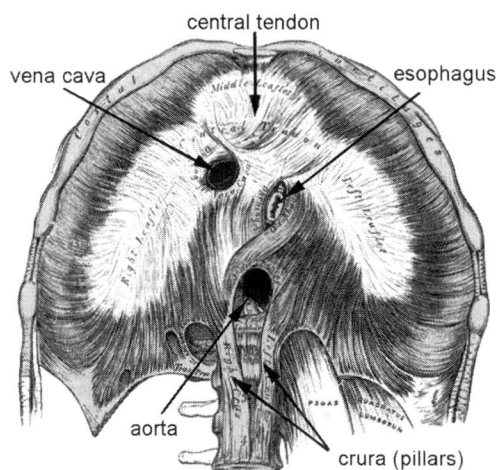

Figure 12. Inferior view of diaphragm. *Courtesy Gray's Anatomy,* with labeling by Scott McCoy; reprinted with permission from *Your Voice: An Inside View* (2004).

of the diaphragm, preventing its immediate collapse. Thus, the singer's concept of **support** (control of the **exhalation**) has much to do with diaphragmatic control. While the diaphragm is technically a voluntary muscle, it is difficult for a singer to exert direct, conscious control of it. Rather, the singer learns to control its movement through deliberately contracting other muscles (for example, the external intercostal muscles).

There are many misconceptions about the diaphragm among singers, voice teachers, and choral **directors**. Many use the term casually without a **fact-based** understanding of its **role** and function. The phrase "sing from your diaphragm" is frequently used, even though the diaphragm only contracts during inspiration (and singing—in the Western sense—while inhaling is impossible). Likewise, the phrase "breathe from your diaphragm" is a rather pointless remark, since *all* breathing (regardless of whether one is a singer) involves the diaphragm, whether one breathes well or poorly, with *appoggio* or not. While the diaphragm's central role during breathing certainly merits some discussion as it pertains to singing, many fact-based teachers of singing consider the diaphragm to be an overrated muscle and view excessive mention of it during teaching to be superfluous. Likewise, many singers and choral directors use the term casually and erroneously.

2. In a **microphone**, the name for a thin mylar dome that is attached to a magnetic coil. **Acoustic** vibrations set the diaphragm into motion, which alters the magnetic field and produces an electric signal that is transmitted to the amplifier.

diaphragmatic-costal breathing. Engaging the **diaphragm** and **external intercostal muscles** to create space for **inhalation**. An accepted element of **balanced breathing** (***appoggio***).

diaspora. A Greek word that means "scattering" or "dispersing." Diaspora specifically deals with the scattering of people and cultures away from their original homeland. Diaspora is a particularly relevant topic in the discussion of many types of **world music**, as new **genres** are often the result of the melting pot that occurs when various cultures merge their traditions. **Blues** and **jazz**, for instance, are largely the result of African diaspora in the United States.

diction. The discipline and study of text **pronunciation**. The **classical singer** largely approaches the study of diction as the mastery of the correct pronunciation of foreign languages, the "big four" being Italian, German, French, and English. For choral and **oratorio** singers, **Latin** is also an essential language (both **church Latin** and **Germanic Latin**). In addition, experienced classical singers often venture into Spanish, Russian, Czech, and Nordic languages. Virtually all textbooks that approach singer's diction do so utilizing the **International Phonetic Alphabet (IPA)**, which has become the universal tool in diction **pedagogy** (particularly in North America). Furthermore, published IPA transcriptions are now available for virtually all of the standard **art song** and **operatic** literature, making foreign-language **repertoire** more accessible than ever to both the student and advanced singer.

For nonclassical singers, diction is also a topic worthy of study and consideration. **Musical theatre** performers, for instance, almost always sing in the vernacular, but they will utilize different kinds of diction in different situations; for instance, the **style** of music they are singing and whether they are **amplified**. Within each language, there are also numerous **accents**, regionalisms, and **dialects** to master. **Opera** singers must also weigh these factors. For example, the **comic operas** of **Gilbert and Sullivan** require a different kind of English than Gershwin's *Porgy and Bess* (1935) or Floyd's *Susannah* (1955).

Many terms in this book are diction-related. See also *accent aigu* (´), *accent d'insistence*, *accent d'intensité*, *accent grave* (`), *accento acuto* (´), *accento grave* (`), *ach-laut* [χ], affricate, alveolar, American *r*, apocopation, back vowel, bilabial, <u>ca</u>reful, Castilian, central vowel, circumflex (^), closed vowel, consonant, Da<u>nie</u>l <u>sit</u>teth, dental, diacritical marking, *dièrèse* (dieresis) (¨), diphthong, falling diphthong, flipped *r* [ɾ], fricative, front vowel, glide, glottal, guttural *r*, har<u>mo</u>ni<u>ou</u>sly, *ich-laut* [ç], labiodental, lateral, manner of articulation, mixed vowel, nasal, nasal vowels, open vowel, palatal, peak of the tongue arch, plosive, point of articulation, polysyllabic, prepalatal, quality (1), Received Pronunciation (RP), rising diphthong, rolled *r*, shadow vowel, Standard American Spanish (SAS), syllabification, triphthong, *umlaut* (¨), unvoiced, velar, vocalic harmonization, voiced, vowel, vowel chart.

diegetic. An adjective used to describe music that occurs in an onstage **production** that is a realistic part of the action on the stage. Examples of diegetic **songs** would include a mother singing a **lullaby** to her baby or a drinking song.

dièrèse **(dieresis) (¨).** A French diacritical mark that indicates the separation of two **vowels** that are adjacent to one another. Examples include *haïr* [aˈiɾ] and *foëne* [fɔˈɛn(ə)]. Although a dieresis looks identical to a German *umlaut* (¨), they are best thought of as two distinct **diacritical marks** that function differently in each respective language.

dieresis. See *dièrèse*.

diminished scale. See **octatonic scale**.

diphthong. A combination of two **vowels** in the same syllable of a word. In English and German, the two vowels are of comparable length (although one often sustains the first vowel for a longer duration in **classical** singing). In Italian, one of the two vowels is significantly longer depending upon whether the singer is dealing with a **rising diphthong** or a **falling diphthong**. While there are many examples in English and Italian, German only has three diphthongs: [ae], [ao], and [ɔø].

diplophonia. A voice disorder characterized by a "double voice." Diplophonia is either the result of **phonation** from two different **sources**—for example, the true **vocal folds** and the **false vocal folds**—or it can occur if there is a pathology (for instance, a cyst or **lesion**) in one of the two vocal folds.

direct laryngosopy. See **laryngoscope (laryngosopy)**.

directional pattern. See **pickup pattern**.

director. Someone in a position of authority over an aspect of a **musical production**. Can refer to a **stage director**, **musiccal director**, choral **conductor**, **opera** conductor, or **producer**.

director of choral activities (DCA). The principal choral **conductor** at a university, college, or conservatory. The DCA almost always conducts the elite, **auditioned ensemble**, teaches conducting courses, and serves as the chief administrator for the **choral division**, overseeing budgets and planning choral events, joint major works (with other ensembles), and tours and other trips. DCAs also frequently serve as guest clinicians for **honor choirs**, usually for the purpose of recruiting.

disaster song. A Depression-era American folk or commercial **song** that had a theme of death, destruction, or disaster. Great tragedies were a favorite theme, for example, the sinking of the Titanic in 1912, or the crashing of the Hindenburg in 1937. Also called a **murder ballad**.

disorder. See **voice disorder**.

dissonance. An **interval** or **harmony** that is considered to be unstable and therefore requires **resolution** to a **consonance**.

dissonant. An adjective pertaining to **dissonance**.

diva. An Italian term denoting a female **opera** singer, usually the leading lady (or *prima donna*) in an opera **production**; however, the term is more frequently used in the pejorative sense to refer to a singer—usually an opera singer—who exemplifies the negative stereotypes associated with singers. These stereotypes include such qualities as being difficult to work with or caring more about being the center of attention than the overall artistic product.

divisi **(It).** The separation of a singer within a single choral section (**soprano, alto, tenor,** or **bass**) into higher and lower subsections. In most choirs, eight-part *divisi* is standard, with each member of a section being assigned a number—either 1 or 2 (1 is higher, 2 is lower)—so that **choristers** are clear about which note to sing when their section divides. *Divisi* is often abbreviated as "div."

DMA. Abbreviation for the **doctor of musical arts** degree.

doctor of musical arts (DMA). The terminal degree in vocal performance, usually only pursued by singers desiring a career in academia. Most accredited colleges and universities require their music faculties to hold doctoral degrees for appointment at the rank of assistant, associate, or full professor and for tenure eligibility. DMAs are not common among full-time **professional classical singers**, who usually embark on performance careers after earning their **master of music (MM)**. At Indiana University, Northwestern University, and Florida State University, the DMA is simply the "doctor of music" (DM).

doctrine of affections. A belief upheld during the **baroque** era that the principal **objective** of music is to arouse passions (or "affections") in the listener. By extension, this notion also maintained that each section of a piece of music should have only one unifying affection. As a result, much of the baroque **repertoire** has a terraced structure, with new affections (**tempo**, **key**, **dynamic**, or **style**) only occurring after a piece—or section of a piece—has concluded.

dodecaphonic music. See **twelve-tone music (dodecaphonic music)**.

dominant. In **tonal music**, the fifth **scale degree** and the **chord** built on that note (V).

Domingo, Placido (b. 1941). Spanish **tenor** of international acclaim. Born in Spain, Domingo's family emigrated to Mexico in 1950, where Domingo studied piano, **conducting**, and singing. At the age of sixteen, he began singing **baritone roles** in *zarzuelas* before debuting as Alfredo in Verdi's *La traviata* in Monterrey in 1961. After several years of performing with the Israeli National Opera, Domingo made his New York City Opera debut as Pinkerton in Puccini's *Madama Butterfly* in 1965. He made his **Metropolitan Opera** debut in 1968, as Maurizio in Cilea's *Adriana Lecouvreur*, and his **La Scala** debut in 1969, as the title role in Verdi's *Ernani*. His international fame secured, Domingo became an untiring performer, performing more than 140 different **operatic** roles throughout the next four decades. Known for his consummate musicianship, keen intelligence, warm stage presence, and passionate singing, he became particularly renowned for his portrayal of the title role in Verdi's *Otello*, a role that he recorded three times. Also a conductor, Domingo made his conducting debut at the New York City Opera in 1973, and at the Metropolitan Opera in 1984. He became artistic **director** of the Washington National Opera in 1996, and of the Los Angeles Opera in 2000. Now in its fifth decade, Domingo's career rivals the longevity of virtually any **opera** singer in history.

Dorian. One of the eight **church modes**.

double bill. Two one-**act** events, often **operas**, presented on the same evening.

double motet. A thirteenth-century **motet** for three voices, with different texts in the *duplum* and *triplum*.

downbeat. The strong, first **beat** of a **meter**. In **hypermeter**, **downbeats** are felt less frequently, but almost always still regularly (every several measures).

dramatic. An adjective used to describe a heavier voice with a richer **operatic color**. Dramatic singers are sometimes singers who begin their careers in one *Fach* and later attempt higher **repertoire**. For instance, some **mezzo-sopranos** become dramatic **sopranos**, and some **baritones** become *Heldentenors*.

dramatic bass. A seldom-used term for *seriöser Baß*, as opposed to comical **basses** or *basso buffos*. See also *Spielbaß (Baßbuffo)*, *schwerer Spielbaß (schwerer Baßbuffo)*.

dramatic baritone. See *Heldenbariton*.

dramatic contralto. See *dramatischer Alt*.

dramatic mezzo-soprano. See *dramatischer Mezzosopran*.

dramatic soprano. See *dramatischer Sopran*.

dramatic tenor. See *Heldentenor*.

dramatischer Alt. German *Fach* that literally translates as "**dramatic contralto**." The *dramatischer Alt* is the second-lowest female category in the **Kloiber Fach System**, surpassed only by the *tiefer Alt* designation. The *lyrischer Alt* is considered to be one *Fach* higher on the chart than the *dramatischer Alt*. Examples of *dramatischer Alt* **roles** include Lucia in Mascagni's *Cavalleria rusticana* (1890), the Witch in Humperdinck's *Hänsel und Gretel* (1893), and the Mother in Menotti's *The Consul* (1950). See the *Fach* chart in appendix C.

dramatischer Koloratursopran. German *Fach* that literally translates as "**dramatic coloratura soprano**." In the **Kloiber Fach System**, the *dramatischer Koloratursopran* is heavier than the *lyrischer Koloratursopran* and positioned one spot higher on the chart than the *lyrischer Sopran*. Examples of *dramatischer Koloratursopran* **roles** include Poppea in Monteverdi's *L'incoronazione di Poppea* (1643); Cleopatra in Handel's *Giulio Cesare* (1724); Manon in Puccini's *Manon Lescaut* (1893); and several roles by Wolfgang Amadeus Mozart (1756–1791), including Donna Anna in *Don Giovanni* (1787), Fiordiligi in *Così fan tutte* (1790), and the Königin der Nacht in *Die Zauberflöte* (1791). See the *Fach* chart in appendix C.

dramatischer Mezzosopran. German *Fach* that literally translates as "**dramatic mezzo-soprano.**" In the **Kloiber Fach system,** the *dramatischer Mezzosopran* is heavier than the *lyrischer Mezzosopran*, but it is positioned one *Fach* higher on the chart than the *Spielalt*. Examples of *dramatischer Mezzosopran* **roles** include Fricka in Wagner's *Der Ring des Nibelungen* (1876), Dalila in Saint-Saëns's *Samson et Dalila* (1877), Laura in Ponchielli's *La Gioconda* (1876), Octavian in Strauss's *Der Rosenkavalier* (1911), and Judith in Bartók's *Bluebeard's Castle* (1918). See the *Fach* chart in appendix C.

dramatischer Sopran. German *Fach* that literally translates as "**dramatic soprano.**" In the **Kloiber Fach System,** the *dramatischer Sopran* is heavier than the *jugendlich-dramatischer Sopran*, but it is positioned one *Fach* higher on the chart than the *Charaktersopran*. Examples of *dramatischer Sopran* **roles** include Leonore in Beethoven's *Fidelio* (1805, rev. 1814); Lady Billows in Britten's *Albert Herring* (1947); the title roles in Puccini's *Tosca* (1900), *Suor Angelica* (1918), and *Turandot* (1926); the title roles in Strauss's *Salome* (1905), *Elektra* (1909), and *Ariadne auf Naxos* (1916); and several roles by Richard Wagner (1813–1883), including Isolde in *Tristan und Isolde* (1865) and Brünnhilde in *Die Walküre* (1870), *Siegfried* (1876), and *Götterdämmerung* (1876). See the *Fach* chart in appendix C.

dramma giocoso. A hybrid **Italian operatic genre** of the eighteenth century, combining characteristics of the **opera seria** and **opera buffa**. Mozart's *Don Giovanni* (1787) is the quintessential example of the *dramma giocoso*.

drone. A constant **pitch** or pitches over which a piece of music is performed or constructed. Drones can either be sung or played on an instrument, for instance, a tambura or bagpipes. Drones are common in some **forms** of **world music,** and scholars believe that they were an integral part of **early music.** In the latter case, drones were most likely sung along with **monophonic chants, tropes,** and **sequences,** for example, in the music of Hildegard von Bingen (1098–1179). Drones also exist in certain **medieval polyphonic** compositions, namely Perotin's four-voice *organa*, and they have been utilized by such twentieth-century choral composers as Arvo Pärt (b. 1935) and John Tavener (b. 1944). These types of drones, however, are perhaps more accurately described as **pedal points.**

dry recitative. See *recitativo secco*.

duet. A type of **ensemble** for two singers or instrumentalists. There are countless examples of duets from the **opera** and **musical theatre repertory,** and many *Lied* and *mélodie* composers also included duets in their **song oeuvres.**

dummy lyric. A temporary **lyric** inserted by a **lyricist** until a real one is written, usually during a **workshop** of a new **musical theatre** work.

duple meter. A **meter** with two **beats**. There are two basic types of duple meter: **simple duple** and **compound duple.**

duplum. In **medieval polyphony,** the second voice from the bottom. The *duplum* is immediately above the **tenor.**

Duprez, Gilbert-Louis (1806–1896). Nineteenth-century French **tenor** and singing teacher who is primarily remembered in the annals of **opera** history as the first tenor—on April 19, 1837—to sing a **high C** in full **operatic head voice.** (During the *bel canto* age, virtually all tenors sang their high notes in **falsetto.**) The famed example occurred during Arnold's Act IV **aria** of *Guillaume Tell*, by Gioacchino Rossini (1792–1868). Rossini actually hated the new sound, describing it as the "squawk of a capon whose throat is being cut," but the public was enraptured, and DuPrez forever changed what was expected out of the **operatic** tenor.

Figure 13. Caricature of Gilbert-Louis Duprez. *Courtesy Panthéon Charivarique.*

Dur (Ger). Major, as in E-Dur (E major).

duration. How long a note is sustained in singing. In voice science, duration is a means of **objectively** measuring singing. Similar measurements include **frequency (pitch)** and **amplitude** (volume).

dynamic markings. Markings by the composer to indicate how loud or soft a musical passage should be.

dynamic microphone. A **microphone** designed with a thin mylar dome (the **diaphragm**), which is attached to a magnetic coil. **Acoustic** vibrations set the diaphragm into motion, which alters the magnetic field and produces an electric signal that is transmitted to the amplifier. For more information, see the essay entitled "What Every Singer Needs to Know about Audio Technology."

dynamics. How loud or soft a musical passage should be. Indicated by **dynamic markings**.

dysphonia. A pathological term that describes any abnormality in the singing (or speaking) voice. Describes the voice not **phonating** properly. Often characterized by hoarseness. See also **dysphonia puberum**.

dysphonia puberum. Medical term for the common voice changes that occur in adolescent boys during puberty.

dysphonic. One who suffers from **dysphonia**.

E

early music. A broad term generally referring to the musical **repertories** of the preclassical age: the **medieval**, **Renaissance**, and **baroque** periods. Early music performers tend to be specialists, as many of the **techniques** required represent a significant departure from mainstream vocal repertoires and **styles**. The natural inclinations of a singer's individual instrument also play a significant **role**. Voices that are valued in the early music community will not necessarily be valued by the mainstream **operatic** community, and vice-versa. For example, a vocalist who excels when singing Puccini might not be heard to best advantage in the music of Josquin des Prez (c. 1450–1521) or Hildegard von Bingen (1098–1179). Many early music specialists are often **academics** as well, researching new repertories, reading from original notation, and having a thorough understanding of **ornamentation**. Understanding period language and **diction** and having knowledge of social and historical contexts is paramount.

early music performance practice. See **historically informed performance practice (HIPP)**.

ecclesiastical Latin. See **church Latin (ecclesiastical Latin)**.

échappée. See **escape tone**.

ectasias. See **vascular ectasias**.

edge. One of the four vocal **modes** described in **Complete Vocal Technique (CVT)**. Edge is described as a "full metallic mode" that is "light, aggressive, sharp, and screaming." The **quality** can be found in heavy **rock** and **gospel** in a high vocal-**range pitches** at loud volumes. Edge is roughly equivalent to what many **voice pedagogues** would call **belting**. In **classical singing**, edge is only found in the male voice at high pitches and loud volumes. See also **curbing, neutral, overdrive**.

Edwardian comic opera. A label for **English comic opera (operetta)** that flourished after the breakup of **Gilbert and Sullivan**. Principal composers and **librettists** include Ivan Caryll (1861–1921), Lionel Monckton (1861–1924), and Sidney Jones (1861–1946). The Edwardian comic opera **repertory** has fallen almost completely out of fashion. It is kept alive primarily through such preservation societies as the Ohio Light Opera Company. See also **West End Theatre**.

EGG. Abbreviation for **electroglottograph**.

eight revolutionary operas. A specific type of **musical theatre** commissioned by Mao Zedong (1893–1976) after the founding of the People's Republic of China in 1949. These "**operas**"—actually five **Peking operas**, two **ballet** dramas, and one symphonic piece—were part of his planned "Cultural Revolution," which took place between 1966–1976. The eight revolutionary operas were watered down, simplistic works intended to be easily accessible to the masses. They were also highly censored, with an antirevolutionary polemic permeating the narratives. After the end of the Cultural Revolution in 1976, and the arrest of Zedong's wife, Jiang Qing (1914–1991), who was largely responsible for artistic endeavors during the Cultural Revolution, more traditional Chinese dramatic works began to be composed once again. While the eight revolutionary operas are of great historical importance, they are almost never revived today.

ein wenig **(Ger).** A little.

einfach **(Ger).** Simple.

electret condenser microphone. A type of **condenser microphone** that relies on a permanently charged element within the **diaphragm** to transduce **acoustic** energy, thus eliminating the need for **phantom power**. Electret condenser microphones are commonly found in smaller recording devices, for example, iPhones, laptop computers, or head-mounted performance **microphones**. For more information, see the essay entitled "What Every Singer Needs to Know about Audio Technology."

electroglottograph (EGG). A tool used to obtain **objective** measurements of certain aspects of the singing voice, used extensively by voice scientists and **vocologists**. The EGG is a noninvasive device that uses electrical signals to measure relative contact between the **vocal folds**, assessing both the **frequency** of the **glottal** cycle, as well as the **closed quotient**. The EGG is one of the two principal signals used in **VoceVista** (the other being the **microphone** itself).

eleven o'clock number. A powerful musical **number**—usually a **ballad**—that is sung by a principal character in the final fifteen minutes of a **Broadway musical**. Eleven o'clock numbers are usually in the penultimate position, immediately preceding a final **ensemble** number. "Memory" from Andrew Lloyd Webber's *Cats* (1981–1982) and "What I Did for Love" from Marvin Hamlisch's *A Chorus Line* (1976) are quintessential examples of the eleven o'clock number. See also **showstopper**.

elision. A salient aspect of French **diction**, where two words are joined together, usually to preserve **legato** or avoid the presence of a **glottal** stop. In French, elisions always occur when the preceding word ends in a **mute** *e* and the next word begins with a **vowel** or *h*. In this situation, mute *e* is dropped, and the **consonant** before the mute *e* then connects directly with the vowel sound that begins the next word. For example, "elle est" becomes [ɛlɛ]. Elision is not to be confused with liaison, which is the sounding of a normally silent final consonant before a word beginning with a vowel or *h* ("deux heures" = [døzœr]).

Elision can also occur in Italian diction. Here, when a word begins with a vowel or *h*, the vowel ending the previous word is often dropped altogether or shortened ("che allumi" becomes "ch'allumi"). Finally, *i* and *u* can morph into **glides**: [j] and [w] ("degli antichi" is pronounced [deʎʎjan'tiki]). Also in Italian, if the same vowel that ends a word also begins the next one, it is usually treated as a single, interrupted vowel sound ("ci incontrammo" becomes "c'incontrammo").

emerging artist. A young **classical** musician who is in his or her final stages of training, poised to enter a **professional** career. Essentially synonymous with **young artist**.

emotional memory. See **emotional recall**.

emotional recall (emotional memory). An acting term/concept usually associated with **Constantin Stanislavski**

and part of an actor's training in the **Method**. In its pure, ideal form, emotional recall requires that a performer personally experience an emotion or situation before he or she acts it. The actor must then remember those sensations and recall them, thus bringing **realism** and depth to the performance. Actors who practice emotional recall less narrowly may use their imagination or study someone else's situation to enhance realism. **Musical theatre** performers must be familiar with the concept of emotional recall regardless of whether they personally consider themselves to be **Method actors**.

Empfindung **(Ger).** Feeling.

en pressant **(Fr).** Hurrying.

en retenant **(Fr).** Slowing.

encore **(Fr).** Again. Also used to label an additional **song** or **aria** at the end of a **recital** or **concert**, usually prompted by demand via a **standing ovation**.

endoscope (endoscopy). An instrument that a physician uses to see inside the body. Endoscopes are inserted directly into the organ. Endoscopy literally means "looking inside."

engaged. Singing that is **supported**, or utilizes good *appoggio* technique.

English art song. Piano-accompanied **genre** that emerged in England as a successor of **Victorian art song**. Principal composers include Ralph Vaughan Williams (1872–1958), Roger Quilter (1877–1953), John Ireland (1879–1962), George Butterworth (1885–1916), Ivor Gurney (1890–1937), and Benjamin Britten (1913–1976).

English comic opera. A specific **genre** of light **opera** referring to the English spin on the genre most ubiquitously exemplified by the thirteen surviving **comic operas** of William Schwenck Gilbert (1836–1911) and Arthur Sullivan (1842–1900). These works are often referred to collectively as **G&S** works. They usually featured a two-**act** structure with dialogue. The **librettos** usually satirize some aspect of Victorian British society, and excessive confusion and mayhem is almost always resolved neatly (although not always logically) in the final moments of the evening. Essential to the **Gilbert and Sullivan formula** was their own set of **stock characters**: the attractive **ingénue** (the **soprano**); the pining **tenor** (her love interest); the bad **bass**; the uglier and older **mezzo-soprano**; and—most idiomatically to Gilbert and Sullivan—the **patter baritone**, who is usually the central comic figure of the work. Gilbert and Sullivan's comic operas are unapologetically dated but still enjoy frequent revivals.

In contemporary **productions**, there is a tradition of updating certain comic references to relatively obscure Victorian places, institutions, and conditions, so that they now refer to local situations that are immediate to the particular audience. For example, "Knightsbridge" becomes "Brooklyn" for a New York audience, and Josephine's reference to "Gillows" becomes "Filene's Basement" when performed in Boston. Along the same lines, performers often write new final **verses**, with local or contemporary references, to some of the comic patter songs, for example, "I Am the Very Model of a Modern Major General." Gilbert and Sullivan comic operas are the only works that are still performed from the English comic opera **repertory**. One generation later, a body of work sometimes referred to as **Edwardian comic operas** succeeded Gilbert and Sullivan's Victorian works, but these comic operas have never secured a permanent place in the light opera repertory.

English madrigal. A type of **Renaissance madrigal** that was written in England and set in English texts. The English madrigal was a successor to the **Italian madrigal**.

English opera. English-language **opera** that flourished in England. Henry Purcell (1659–1695) composed the first masterpiece of English opera with Dido and Aeneas (1689), a retelling of the myth by Virgil (70–19 BC). Toward the end of the **baroque** era, London became one of Europe's most important centers for opera. Although George Frideric Handel (1685–1759) is often thought of as an English composer, his operas are in Italian. Thus, for this reason, he is usually not considered to be a composer of English opera; however, the **concert** works *Acis and Galatea* (1718) and *Semele* (1743) do sometimes receive **operatic** stagings. After the baroque era, English opera experienced a long dormancy that did not awaken until the twentieth century with the operatic works of Ralph Vaughan Williams (1872–1958) and Benjamin Britten (1913–1976), who is often regarded as the most important English composer since Purcell. Harrison Birtwistle (b. 1934), Peter Maxwell Davies (b. 1934), Oliver Knussen (b. 1952), and Thomas Adès (b. 1971) have also made important contributions to the **genre**.

English operetta. A **genre** of British light **opera** championed by such composers as Arthur Sullivan (1842–1900), Lionel Monckton (1861–1924), and Ivor Novello (1893–1951). Technically, Sullivan labeled his works **comic operas** rather than **operettas**. See also **English comic opera**.

enharmonic. Adjective that describes two notes that are notated differently but sound alike. Examples include D♯ and E♭ or B♯ and C♮. **Chords** can also be enharmonic; for example, a **Ger+6** chord in C minor (A♭-C-E♭-F♯) can be respelled as a dominant seventh chord in D♭ major (A♭-C-E♭-G♭).

ensemble. 1. A specific group of singers or instrumentalists. Different musical works, **genres**, and **style** periods require different types of ensembles. Composers and **conductors** also make specific decisions on what ensembles are required for a specific work. For example, does a choral **motet** call for sixteen or 120 voices? If the composer does not specify, then the conductor must make a decision according to type of work, historical context, and other factors.

2. How well two or more musicians perform together with particular regard to rhythmic synchronicity. For example, if a choral group has "good ensemble," that is a way of saying that they are singing with excellent rhythmic precision.

3. An **operatic** or **musical-theatre** excerpt for two or more soloists.

ensemble finale. In eighteenth-century **operatic** convention, the practice of bringing every (living) principal character onstage for a final, concluding musical **number**. In addition to ensemble finales that occur at the ends of **operas**, they can also occur at the halfway point, either at the end of Act I (in a two-**act** opera) or Act II (in a four-act opera). Mozart's opera *Le nozze di Figaro* (1786) includes two of the most famous examples of the ensemble finale, occurring at the ends of Acts II and IV, respectively.

ENT. Commonly used abbreviation for "ear, nose, and throat" doctor. See also **otolaryngologist**.

entr'acte. An orchestral piece played before the second **act** of a two-act **musical** or **operetta**. Literally meaning "between acts" in French, the entr'acte serves as a type of **overture** for the second act.

entrance aria. An **opera aria** that introduces a character to the audience. Figaro's "Largo al factotum" from Rossini's *Il barbiere di Siviglia* (1816) is perhaps the most famous entrance aria in the **operatic repertory**.

enunciation. The act of speaking or singing **phonetic sounds**. Synonym of articulation.

epiglottis. A leaf-shaped cartilage found at the top of the **larynx**. The epiglottis is attached to the **cricoid cartilage**, where it serves as a valve to direct swallowed food into the esophagus and away from the **trachea** (windpipe). The epiglottis is one of the three single cartilages of the larynx, along with the cricoid cartilage and **thyroid cartilage**. See the anatomical drawings in appendix B.

episodic voice injury. A type of **vocal injury** that alternates between periods of distress and symptom-free periods. **Spasmodic dysphonia** is an example of an episodic voice injury. One of the three basic types of voice injuries, along with **progressive voice injuries** and **constant voice injuries**.

epithelial dysplasia: carcinoma. Cancerous growths in the **larynx**. The scientific name for **laryngeal** cancer.

epithelial hyperplasia: hyperkeratosis. Benign, noncancerous lesions in the **larynx**.

epithelial hyperplasia: leukoplakia. Precancerous growths in the **larynx**.

equal temperament. The artificial division of an **octave** into twelve equal parts, enabling one to use any of the twelve **pitches** as the first **scale degree** in either a **major key** or **minor key**. Equal temperament can only occur if each pitch is tuned according to a slight compromise. The piano, for example, is an equal-tempered instrument. Equal temperament is the opposite of **just intonation**, which means that slight modifications can be made to achieve perfect **intonation** à la the ratios first established by Pythagoras (570–495 BCE). **Choirs** and orchestras tend to adjust intonation on a situational basis, so that one encounters a mix of equal temperament and just intonation, as each musician adapts the pitch of individual notes to the surrounding ambiance. **Early music** groups, on the other hand, may rigorously adopt particular historic temperaments, for example, "1/4-comma meantone," "1/6-comma meantone," "Werckmeister," and the like. The singer must rely on his or her ears and experience to successfully and flexibly adapt to both of these commonly used intonation systems.

equalization. The process of adjusting the **amplitude** of specific **frequencies** within a sound signal.

equalizer. A common component of stereo and recording systems that allows the user to make specific adjustments to **frequencies** within the sound spectrum. The most common types of equalizers found in **professional** sound equipment are **shelf equalizers**, **parametric equalizers**, and **graphic equalizers**.

ernst (Ger). Serious, grave, or solemn. Famously used by Johannes Brahms (1833–1897) as the title of his final four-**song** collection *Vier ernste Gesänge*, Op. 121 (1896). In this sense, the songs are "serious" in the sense that they are settings of sacred texts (see also *Geistliche*). Most *Lieder* are settings of secular poems.

erst (Ger). First. Usually precedes a noun (e.g., "erstes tempo"). "Erst" is the adverb; "erste" is the adjective. Other **forms**, for instance, "erstes," are merely inflected adjectives.

escape tone. An **ornament** that consists of a metrically weak **dissonant** note that is approached by step and left by leap in the opposite direction. Also called an *échappée*.

esquinazo. A **serenade** sung in Chile during the nighttime or at dawn, usually in honor of a religious figure.

Estill Voice Training (EVT). A voice training program developed in 1988, by the **singing voice specialist** and **voice pedagogue** Jo Estill (1921–2010). The Estill method attempts to "deconstruct" various elements of **vocal production**, instructing the singer on how to control these functions on an individual basis. Estill Voice Training International, LLC, administrates a series of courses and certification programs that are offered at various locations throughout Europe, Australia, and the United States.

Ethiopic chant. The **liturgical chant** of the Ethiopian Orthodox Church. Manuscripts date from the late sixteenth century.

ethnic and border music. A **genre** of music distinct from **world music** only in the sense that these folk and popular **styles** take place within and near the borders of the United States (as opposed to elsewhere in the world). *Zydeco*, mariachi, and *ranchera* are three examples of ethnic and border music that utilize singers.

etwas (Ger). Somewhat. Usually precedes an adjective. (i.e., "etwas geschwind" = "somewhat fast").

EUOUAE. The **vowels** of *seculorum amen*. Often replaces the text at the end of **Gregorian chants**.

evangelist. The narrator of an **oratorio** or **Passion**, a **role** almost always assigned to a **tenor**.

evening service. A specific **genre** of **Anglican church music** that is written for evening prayer (a short evening prayer service with no Eucharist). Evening services are in two parts that are performed separately, separated by the reading of scripture. These two movements are settings of the canticles *Magnificat* and *Nunc dimittis*. Evening service refers to just these two movements of music, whereas evensong refers to the entire prayer service (which usually contains an additional **anthem**, **Anglican chant**, and organ preludes and postludes). An evensong is an evening prayer service offered as part of the **liturgy**

in Anglican churches. The term *evensong* is often used (incorrectly) as a substitute term for evening service, the sung canticles of an evensong.

evensong. See **evening service**.

EVT. Abbreviation for **Estill Voice Training**.

exercise. See **vocalise**.

exhalation. The part of the **breath cycle** in which air exits the lungs. The opposite of **inhalation**.

exoticism. A fascination with non-European cultures that emerged in the arts during the nineteenth century. The more "exotic" (i.e., unlike Western Europe), the more interesting. **Opera** was particularly influenced by the exoticism craze, and many operas written during this period were set in exotic locales. The most famous examples include Bizet's *Carmen* (1875), Puccini's *Madama Butterfly* (1904), Delibes's *Lakmé* (1883), Verdi's *Aida* (1871), and Puccini's *La fanciulla del West* (1910). The composer occasionally made efforts to incorporate indigenous musical references into the **score**. For example, Bizet incorporated Spanish **dances**—for instance, the *seguidilla* and *habanera*—and folk-like modalities in *Carmen*. But more often, exoticism was accomplished through the location, story, sets, and costumes alone. For example, there is nothing particularly Egyptian about the music in Verdi's *Aida*, nor anything particularly American about the music in Puccini's *La fanciulla del West*. Exoticism also involves certain stereotypes that enhance ambiance but don't necessarily accurately depict exotic locations, namely the prevalent use of augmented seconds in *Aida* and the banjo imitations in *La fanciulla del West*. **Orientalism** was a specific type of exoticism that reflected a European fascination with the Far East. This late nineteenth-century obsession was specifically parodied in **Gilbert and Sullivan's English comic opera** *The Mikado* (1885).

expiration. See **exhalation**.

expiration (primary muscles of). In the Italian *appoggio* breathing technique, there are six primary muscles of expiration. These include the **internal intercostal muscles**, **rectus abdominis muscles, external oblique abdominis muscles, internal oblique abdominis muscles, transverse abdominis muscles,** and **quadratus lumborum muscles**. See the anatomical drawings in appendix B.

explode. To pronounce a final or internal **consonant** with a **shadow vowel**, thus increasing its audibility to the audience. Exploded consonants are desired in **classical singing genres**, which are **acoustic** in nature and do not depend on electronic **amplification**. See also **acoustic singing, amplified singing**.

expression. The act of conveying mood, **color**, and sentiment through singing. All aspects of singing are relevant to expression, including **diction, musicality,** and stage presence.

expressionism. A German artistic movement originating in Vienna in the early twentieth century. Expressionism had its beginnings in visual art (particularly painting) and literature, but the movement soon influenced composers as well. Expressionist composers believed that music should reflect the inner consciousness of its creator, and that the composer should "express" his or her personal feelings about the subject. As a result, expressionistic music tends to be highly emotional and provocative, often shocking its listeners through exaggerated and distorted content. Death, blood, and violence, for example, are not uncommon subjects. Arnold Schoenberg's *Pierrot lunaire*, Op. 21 (1912) and Alban Berg's **opera** *Wozzeck* (1922) are two of the most frequently studied and performed expressionistic works in the vocal **repertoire**.

expressive marking. Markings in a musical **score** that provide specific interpretive instructions for the performers. Expressive markings can be either **objective** (e.g., "**legato**" or "soft") or subjective (e.g., "expressively," or "with feeling"). Many expressive markings are in Italian, French, and German. Singers who speak English as their first language must develop a comprehensive knowledge of expressive markings in foreign languages to be able to correctly interpret scores (or at least own a good music dictionary). **Tempo markings** (often in Italian) are a specific kind of expressive marking that are frequently encountered in **classical genres** and **styles**, often accompanied by **metronome markings**.

extended technique. A nontraditional sound required by the singer for certain types of contemporary **repertoires**. Musicians of all instruments who perform *avant-garde* contemporary **art music** must familiarize themselves with extended techniques, and vocalists are no exception. A brief list of specific extended vocal **techniques** includes **buccal speech, glottal fry, growling, inhaled singing, multiphonics,** screaming, *Sprechstimme*, overtone singing, **ululation**, vocal **tremolo, vocal trills,** and **yodeling**. Prominent composers whose works require extended vocal techniques include Arnold Schoenberg (1874–1951), John Cage (1912–1992), György Ligeti (1923–2006), Luciano Berio (1925–2003), Hans Werner Henze (1926–2012), Karlheinz Stockhausen (1928–2007), George Crumb (b. 1929), and Peter Maxwell Davies (b. 1934). Notable singers who specialize in extended vocal techniques include Cathy Berbarian

(1925–1983), Bethany Beardslee (b. 1925), Jan De-Gaetani (1933–1989), Phyllis Bryn-Julson (b. 1945), and Joan Heller (b. 1944). Meredith Monk (b. 1942) deserves special mention as a creative artist who both composes and then performs works that explore the limits of the capabilities of the human voice.

extended tertian. **Harmonies** that consist of multiple **pitches**—five or more—that are stacked in **intervals** of thirds. Similar to **quartal** (stacked in fourths) or **quintal** (stacked in fifths) sonorities. Extended tertian sonorities have long been a feature of **jazz** and are also a hallmark of certain kinds of contemporary **choral music**.

external intercostal muscles. Along with the **diaphragm**, one of the two primary muscles of **inspiration**. The external intercostal muscles are the outermost layer of muscles on the inside of the **thorax**.

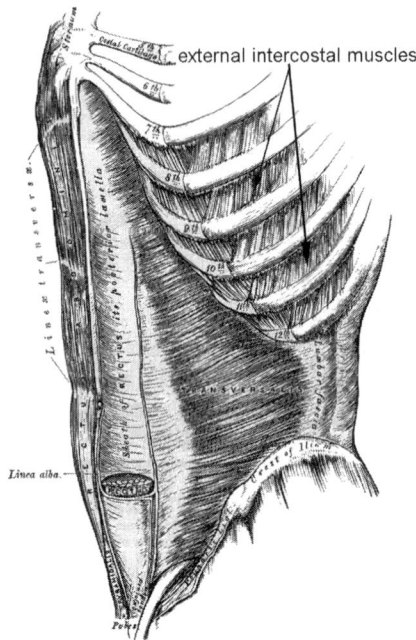

Figure 14. External intercostal muscles. *Courtesy Gray's Anatomy*, with labeling by Scott McCoy; reprinted with permission from *Your Voice: An Inside View* (2004).

external oblique abdominis muscles. In the Italian *appoggio* breathing technique, one of the six primary muscles of **expiration**. The other five include the **internal intercostal muscles**, **transverse abdominis muscles**, **internal oblique abdominis muscles**, **rectus abdominis muscles**, and **quadratus lumborum muscles**.

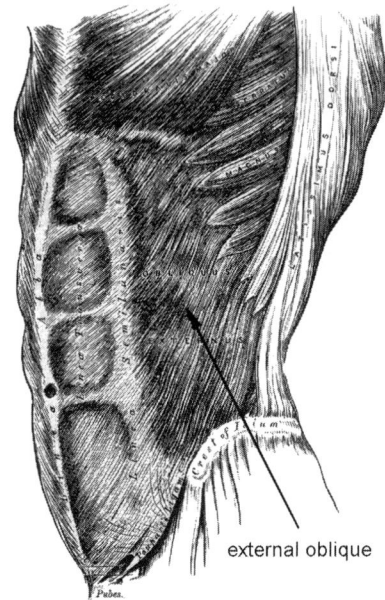

Figure 15. External oblique abdominis muscles. *Courtesy Gray's Anatomy*, with labeling by Scott McCoy; reprinted with permission from *Your Voice: An Inside View* (2004).

extravaganza. A nineteenth-century **genre** of **musical theatre** with an emphasis on **spectacle**: lavish sets, costumes, and technical achievement. *The Black Crook* (1866) is a quintessential example of an extravaganza. The **production** values of the extravaganza have their roots in French *grand opéra*. Although the label as a genre went out of fashion by the early twentieth century, the lavish **operettas** mounted during the first three decades of the twentieth century retained some of the idiomatic features of the extravaganza. Sometimes called a spectacle, with which it is synonymous.

extrinsic laryngeal muscles. A complex series of muscles that connect the **larynx** to other surrounding structures, including the **sternum** and **hyoid bone**. There are two subdivisions of extrinsic laryngeal muscles: the infrahyoid group (which directly connect to the larynx) and the suprahyoid group (which do not directly connect to the larynx but still affect **laryngeal** movement). The four muscles of the infrahyoid group include the stenohyoid muscles, sternothryoid muscle, thyrohyoid muscle, and omohyoid muscles. The six muscles of the suprahyoid group include the stylohyoid muscle; anterior and posterior diagastric muscles; and geniohyoid, hyloglossus, and mylohyoid mucles. See the anatomical drawings in appendix B.

F

F₀. The abbreviation for **fundamental frequency**.

Fach (pl. Fächer). In **classical singing** (specifically **operatic** singing), one's specific **voice type**. By extension, one's *Fach* also dictates which operatic **roles** one would sing. Narrowly, the *Fach* system refers to the **Kloiber Fach System** or **German Fach System**, which is traditionally used in the **opera houses** of Germany and Austria. These companies make regular use of **house singers**—singers who remain in residency for an extended period of time, performing multiple roles in the **repertory**. European opera houses, even smaller ones, tend to be repertoire houses that program seasons in repertory—that is, multiple productions running at the same time. The *Fach* system is generally not used in other parts of the world, and **professional** singers from all nationalities generally sing roles from multiple *Fächer* once their careers are established.

Designed by Rudolf Kloiber (1899–1973), the *Fach* system consists of twenty-nine categories, most of which are subcategories of the six basic voice types: **soprano, mezzo-soprano, contralto, tenor, baritone,** and **bass**. See appendix C for a chart that further clarifies the Kloiber Fach System. A list of these categories is as follows (as categorized by Kloiber, in rough order from highest to lowest): *Soubrette, lyrischer Koloratursopran, dramatischer Koloratursopran, lyrischer Sopran, jugendlich-dramatischer Sopran, dramatischer Sopran, Charaktersopran, koloratur-Mezzosopran, lyrischer Mezzosopran, dramatischer Mezzosopran, Spielalt, lyrischer Alt, dramatischer Alt, tiefer Alt, contratenor (countertenor), haute-contre, Spieltenor (Tenorbuffo), lyrischer Tenor, jugendlicher Heldentenor, Heldentenor, Charaktertenor, lyrischer Bariton, Kavalierbariton, Heldenbariton, Charakterbariton, Spielbaß (Baßbuffo), schwerer Spielbaß (schwerer Baßbuffo), Charakterbaß (Baßbariton),* and *seriöser Baß*. To understand these labels, it is important to know the roles associated with each, as literal translations can be misleading. For example, even though *Charakterbariton* literally means "character baritone," a more accurate English translation might be "**dramatic** baritone," as the *Charakterbariton Fach* includes such roles as Scarpia in Puccini's *Tosca* (1900) and Alberich in Wagner's *Das Rheingold* (1862) and *Siegfried* (1876), as opposed to comic roles like Major-General Stanley in **Gilbert and Sullivan's** *The Pirates of Penzance* (1879). (Comic roles are often in the *Spielbaß* category, although the *Fach* system does not account for **English comic opera** roles.) And *lyrischer Sopran* literally translates as lyric soprano, but a North American soprano who labels herself as such is likely to sing such roles as Mimì in Puccini's *La bohème* (1896) and the title role in Puccini's *Tosca* (1900), two roles that are technically not in the *lyrischer Sopran Fach*. Many singers can comfortably sing roles from several *Fächer*, and they do, but house singers are generally contracted for a specific *Fach*, and they are not obligated to sing roles that fall outside of it. Thus, the *Fach* system can do much to protect the singer, who might otherwise be asked to sing inappropriate repertoire.

It is also common practice for many singers and **voice pedagogues** to use descriptive labels for singers that are not official categories in the *Fach* system. The ***baryton-Martin***, for example, is a distinctly French category that has nothing to do with the *Fach* system and little to do with **opera**. And popular **genres**, for example, **musical theatre**, have no codified system in place, the result being that one encounters a wide variety of descriptive labels (for instance, **baritenor** and **belter**). The numerous translations into English, French, and Italian further complicate the art and practice of voice classification. See appendix C for a chart that further clarifies the German Fach System.

Fach system. Synonymous with **German Fach System** and **Kloiber Fach System**. See also *Fach*.

fact-based. An adjective that describes a pedagogical concept that is **objective** and based on science as opposed to one that is subjective, empirical, or based on the traditions of a former generation. **Fact-based voice pedagogy** is a modern school of voice pedagogy that incorporates science and objective facts about the voice, in addition to conventional wisdom and subjective sensation. **William Vennard** and **Richard Miller** are two seminal, pioneering figures in the modern era of fact-based **pedagogy**. Fact-based **pedagogues** reject traditional maxims that defy physical reality. "Sing from your **diaphragm**!" is one such saying: Since the diaphragm is a muscle of **inhalation**, this statement is false, as no one sings as they inhale; rather, singing occurs on the **exhalation**. "Sing through your third eye!" is another, as no one, of course, actually has a third eye.

Fact-based pedagogy does not reject every *bel canto* tradition, however. Rather, it expands and clarifies certain phenomena in singing. Not mutually exclusive to one another, some old-school concepts can also be fact-based, as modern science has proven that many of the instincts of *bel canto* pedagogues (for example, Francesco Lamperti [1811–1892] and the younger **Manuel García**) are compatible with the findings and measurements of modern **vocology**.

fact-based voice pedagogy. See **fact-based**.

fado. A Portuguese **song genre**. The songs are usually **strophic** in **form**, with **lyrics** laden with longing and regret. *Fado* is usually accompanied by a twelve-stringed guitar—called a *guitarra portuguesa*—a *violao* (a smaller guitar), or an accordion. *Fado* has its roots in the African and Moorish culture that has historically dominated the Iberian Peninsula. **Amália Rodrigues** is the quintessential exponent of the genre.

Fairuz (b. 1935). Lebanese singer, and one of the most famous musicians in the Arab world. To the Lebanese, Fairuz's **songs** evoke a distinct nationalism, with many of her songs expressing nostalgia for village life in Lebanon. Fairuz has never left her native Lebanon (even during civil war), and many in her country revere her as a patriot. She was also active as an actress in the Lebanese **theatre** scene. After the death of **Umm Kulthum**, Fairuz quickly rose in stature to become the Middle East's greatest living diva. Later in her career, she began using Western instruments and **harmonies**, creating unique **fusion** sounds in her later recordings.

falling diphthong. Two **vowel** sounds in the same syllable with a lengthening of the first vowel. Falling diphthongs are especially important in Italian **diction**. Examples include such frequent monosyllabic words as "mia" [mi:a], "tua" [tu:a], and "io" [i:o] (as well as many others).

false vocal fold contraction (FVF contraction). A **technique** used by some **heavy metal** singers and **scream artists** that (they believe) safely allows them to produce **grit** and other gravelly vocal qualities; however, as the **false vocal folds** are located above the actual **vocal folds**, it is next to impossible to see what the real vocal folds are actually doing during FVF contraction, which leads some **voice pedagogues** to speculate that the sound resulting from FVF contracting is actually coming from **glottal fry** occurring at the level of the real vocal folds. FVF contraction is a relatively new topic in **voice pedagogy** that is in need of further study and discernment.

false vocal fold retraction (FVF retraction). This concept comes from the **Estill Voice Training (EVT)** method, which suggests that the singer can move the ventricular folds apart to open the throat. Singers are guided into this position through the imagery of a silent laugh.

false vocal folds. A pair of ventricular folds that are positioned directly above the **vocal folds** in the **larynx**. The false vocal folds get their name because of their position, and because they resemble—in some ways—the true vocal folds. The false vocal folds can neither be adducted nor tensed. Thus, they have absolutely nothing to do with normal **phonation**. Some people can, however, bring the false vocal folds into contact with one another through the abnormal constriction of the entire larynx. When this happens, a raspy, undesirable sound can be produced. Also called the vestibular folds.

falsetto. Another name for **head** voice. Although falsetto technically describes any **CT-dominant/mode 2 production**—either male or female—falsetto is almost exclusively used among voice **professionals** to describe the male head voice, which generally is not used by men in **classical singing**. The big exception to this practice is the **countertenor**, who develops his falsetto (or head voice) similar to the way that female classical singers do. Some **voice pedagogues** and voice scientists make a distinction between head voice and falsetto, citing more **thyroarytenoid** activity—or "mix"—in the head voice; in this definition of falsetto, the thyroarytenoid muscle is completely unengaged.

fantasia. The second **act** of a **minstrel show**. Also called an **olio**.

Farinelli (1705–1782). A celebrated Italian **castrato** who remains one of the most famous singers in the history of **opera**. Farinelli was born Carlo Maria Michelangelo Nicola Broschi in the small village of Andria (now Apulia) in southeast Italy. His father, a local composer and the *maestro di cappella* of the city's cathedral, recognized his musical talent at an early age. When Broschi's father suddenly died in 1717, it seems likely that the family's perilous financial situation may have inspired the decision for Carlo to be castrated and pursue a musical career as a singer. (Successful opera singers were some of the most lucrative professions of the day.) After Broschi's castration, his singing career progressed rapidly, and he quickly became famous throughout Italy. By the time of his Viennese debut in 1724, Broschi had already adopted the stage name of Farinelli. During the course of the next two decades, he would perform throughout Europe, with extended engagements in London and Madrid. Along with **Senesino** (another castrato), Farinelli was the most famous opera singer of his day, although he never formed a relationship with any one composer the way Senesino developed a mutual loyalty with George Frideric Handel (1685–1759). Nevertheless, Farinelli **premiered** many **roles** in lesser-known works by a variety of composers, the most important of whom was Johann Adolph Hasse (1699–1783). Farinelli retired in 1759 and lived the last twenty-three years of his life in retirement in Bologna. His life was dramatized in the 1994 film *Farinelli*, which makes considerable departures from the historical accuracy of actual events.

Figure 16. Portrait of Farinelli, c. 1720.

feedback. In audio technology, feedback refers to the phenomenon that happens when a **microphone** picks up **acoustic** vibrations from the speaker system, amplifies them, sends them back through the system, and repeats the process again. When this happens, the resulting sound is a surge in **amplitude** of the signal within the **frequency range** that the microphone is amplifying. For more information, see the essay entitled "What Every Singer Needs to Know about Audio Technology."

Feldenkrais. A type of **bodywork** practiced by singers that promotes body awareness. The Feldenkrais method was conceived and designed by Moshé Feldenkrais (1904–1984), who sought to reduce pain and limitations in movement through a series of exercises rooted in self-awareness and ease of facility. Many of Feldenkrais's prolific writings were published during his lifetime and are available in posthumous editions.

feurig (Ger). Fiery.

field holler. A specific kind of African American **work song**. Usually in **call-and-response form**, it begins with a musical leader "calling out" in a high, loud voice, sometimes breaking into **falsetto**, with the responding **chorus** echoing the musical material stated by the leader. Field hollers are an essential forerunner of **blues**, **jazz**, **gospel**, and **spiritual genres**.

final. The most important note of a **church mode**. After text is **chanted** on the **reciting tone**, it **cadences** at the final.

fine (It). End.

fine amour (Fr). Refined love. *Fine amour* is a concept cultivated by the *troubadours* and *trouvères* that refers to admiring an ideal, unattainable woman from afar.

Finnish art song. A vast **repertory** of **art song** in the Finnish language that has gained increasing international exposure in recent decades. The most well-known Finnish art song composers include Toivo Kuula (1883–1918), Leevi Madetoja (1887–1947), Erkii Melartin (1875–1937), Oskar Merikanto (1868–1924), and—most important—Yrjö Kilpinen (1892–1959). Jean Sibelius (1865–1957) also contributed some important settings of Finnish poems. The **Academy of Finnish Art Song** has produced several English-language publications aimed at increasing the awareness and encouraging the performance of this vast body of repertoire. See also **Finnish diction, Nordic art song**.

Finnish diction. The study of singing in Finnish. **Songs** in Finnish represent a rich treasure trove of songs for the recitalist, and the language is quite accessible and easier to learn than the three Scandinavian languages: Swedish, Norwegian, and Danish. While these other three languages share some common characteristics, Finnish is unique among the Nordic languages and is part of the Finnic language family, having more in common with Estonian than the Scandinavian languages. **Finnish art song** is quite accessible, and there is no reason for the undergraduate singer not to explore it.

fioratura. **Virtuosic** passages in vocal music comprised of quickly moving notes that demand great technical **flexibility** from the singer. *Fioratura* is roughly synonymous with **coloratura**, although the former term often implies some degree of improvised **ornamentation**.

first inversion. See **inversion**.

first *passaggio*. See ***primo passaggio***.

first practice. See ***prima prattica***.

first run. In **theatre**, describes the performances that take place between a show's opening night and the closing down of a **production**.

Fischer-Dieskau, Dietrich (1925–2012). German **baritone** and the world's most recognizable figure in the **genre** of German *Lieder*. Fischer-Dieskau's name is inextricably linked with the genre. In addition to **recital** singing, he also maintained an active performance career in **opera**, **oratorio**, and **chamber music**. Considered by some to be the best musician of all singers, many important twentieth-century composers, including Samuel Barber (1910–1981), Benjamin Britten (1913–1976), Hans Werner Henze (1926–2012), and Aribert Reimann (b. 1936), specifically wrote works for Fischer-Dieskau's voice. Fischer-Dieskau performed comfortably in many languages, including Russian, Hungarian, and Hebrew. As a recording artist, his recording career spanned six decades and almost perfectly encapsulated the advent and longevity of the LP record. His hundreds of recordings have earned him the reputation as the most recorded artist in history; indeed, if one plays all of his recordings back-to-back, no one has recorded more material than Dietrich Fischer-Dieskau. He collaborated with many of the world's great pianists and had a long and productive collaborative relationship with the great English pianist **Gerald Moore**, with whom he recorded every Schubert song suitable to the male voice.

Fitzgerald, Ella (1917–1996). One of history's most acclaimed **jazz** singers, renowned for her vocal **virtuosity**, rich **tone quality**, consummate **musicianship**, and unrivalled ability to **scat**. Fitzgerald was born in Virginia and raised in Yonkers, New York, where she heard jazz music from an early age. In the 1930s, she began performing in Harlem nightclubs and was discovered by Chick Webb (1905–1939) in 1934, when she won a singing contest at the Apollo Theater. In 1938, she achieved widespread fame for her famous rendition of "A Tisket, a Tasket," a **song** that she had written herself. From 1956–1964, she recorded a series of "songbooks" for Verve records, recording many popular selections from the **Great American Songbook**, including George Gershwin (1898–1937) and Ira Gershwin (1896–1983), Irving Berlin (1888–1989), Jerome Kern (1885–1945), Johnny Mercer (1909–1976), Duke

Ellington (1899–1974), Harold Arlen (1905–1986), Cole Porter (1891–1964), and Richard Rodgers (1902–1979) and Lorenz Hart (1895–1943). Duke Ellington famously referred to Fitzgerald as the "First Lady of Jazz."

Figure 17. Portrait of Ella Fitzgerald, Dizzy Gillespie, Ray Brown, Milt Jackson, and Timme Rosenkrantz at Downbeat, New York, New York, c. 1947. *Courtesy Library of Congress.*

five-act opera. An **opera** comprised of five **acts**, a structure originally advocated by the **classical** dramatists of Greece and Rome, and later practiced by the **Renaissance** dramatists—as well as authors of the earliest operas—who imitated the ideals of their classical predecessors. As a result, most early operas adopted this structure as well. In France, Jean-Baptiste Lully (1632–1687) championed the structure, introducing other conventions (most famously a **formulaic ballet** in Act IV). Jean-Philippe Rameau (1683–1764) continued this tradition one generation later, and the five-act structure persisted through the ***grand opéras*** of Giacomo Meyerbeer (1791–1864), Fromental Halévy (1799–1862), and Hector Berlioz (1803–1869). Outside of France, composers and **librettists** abandoned the five-act tradition much sooner, and Handel and Mozart regularly utilized two-, three-, and four-act structures. By the mid-nineteenth century, composers no longer felt bound to the five-act tradition, but, historically, it remains one of the most influential and widely practiced **forms** in opera.

five great sequences. The most important **Latin sequences** used in **liturgical** worship. The five great sequences are the ***Stabat Mater***, *Dies Irae*, *Lauda Sion*, *Veni Sancte Spiritus*, and *Victimae Paschali Laudes*.

fixed *do*. A type of ***solfège*** in which C is always *do*, regardless of the **key**. Primarily used in Europe.

flageolet register. The highest vocal **range** in the female voice, usually only occurring at the **pitch** of C6 or higher. While technically an extreme end of the **cricothyroid register** (and not a truly unique register in and of itself), the flageolet register resembles cricothyroid register in function, although more acute and extreme. In flageolet register, only the edges of the **vocal folds** are **approximated**, and there is high **subglottic** pressure and considerable longitudinal tension in the **vocal ligaments**. Only a small portion of the **opera** and **art song repertory** requires frequent use of the flageolet register, although it should be accessed and practiced with regularity by all **classical sopranos**. See also **flute register**, **whistle register**.

flamenco. A **repertory** of both music and **dance** that evolved in Andalusia, in southern Spain. Although its specific origins are unclear, flamenco may have developed as a result of Arab-speaking peoples and their influence in the region. Flamenco's ties to gypsy culture also seem strong. In addition to singing, dancing, snapping, and foot-stamping are also essential features of flamenco. A specific type of singing associated with flamenco is the *cante jondo*, which literally means "deep **song**." Guitars are featured prominently in flamenco, and songs are often composed in the **Phrygian mode**. The *seguidilla* and the *soleá* are specific song types. **Camarón de la Isla** is widely regarded as one of the greatest flamenco singers of all time and is the most well-known exponent of the **genre**.

flat. When working with audio technology, a response produces no alterations in the **frequency** spectrum of the signal. See also **audio spectrum**.

Fleming, Renée (b. 1959). American **soprano** and one of the most famous living **opera** singers. Fleming actively performs a wide **repertoire** ranging from George Frideric Handel (1685–1759) to Richard Strauss (1864–1949) to American **jazz standards**. Fleming was born in Indiana, Pennsylvania, and raised in Rochester, New York. After her undergraduate years at SUNY Potsdam, she pursued graduate study at the Eastman School of Music, followed by a residency with the Juilliard Opera Center. She won the Richard Tucker Award in 1990, after which she went on to an illustrious career in opera. Her signature **operatic roles** include Countess Almaviva in Mozart's *Le nozze di Figaro*, Violetta in Verdi's *La traviata*, Desdemona in Verdi's *Otello*, and the title role in Massenet's *Manon*. She has also recorded **art songs** in several languages, as well as **musical theatre** and jazz standards.

flexibility. An aspect of vocal **technique** that pertains to **agility** and how well the voice moves. Many **treatises**—for example, *The Structure of Singing* (1986),

by **Richard Miller**, and other historical technique books from the International Italian School—devote specific exercises to improving flexibility, and most **voice pedagogues** address flexibility during the **warm-up** portion of the voice **lesson**.

flipped r [ɾ]. A single flip of the *r*, used frequently in **classical singing** in all four of the major languages—Italian, French, German, and English—in certain circumstances. Utilizes the [ɾ] symbol in the **International Phonetic Alphabet (IPA)**. See also **American r**, **rolled r**.

flooding. A **technique** borrowed from the mental health profession and used for the management of **musical performance anxiety (MPA)**. During flooding, a performer is flooded with bad experiences—for instance, distractions, poor preparation, and so forth—during a mock performance, for example, a **studio class**.

flop. A term usually used in the **musical theatre** industry to describe an unsuccessful show that closes before it recoups its **production** expenses, thus losing instead of making money.

Florentine Camerata. An academy of scholars, poets, musicians, and scientists who met at the home of count Giovanni de' Bardi (1534–1612) in Florence during the final decades of the sixteenth century. Their discussions about Greek artistic ideals—and music and drama specifically—led to the earliest experiments in **opera** during the final years of the century. Known members of the Florentine Camerata included the composers Emilio de' Cavalieri (c. 1550–1602), Jacopo Peri (1561–1633), and Giulio Caccini (c. 1551–1618); the poet Ottavio Rinuccini (1562–1621); and Vincenzo Galilei (c. 1520–1591), father of the astronomer Galileo Galilei (1564–1642).

flute register. A commonly used term that refers to **flageolet register**.

fly space. The area above a stage where curtains, lights, and scenery are hung.

focus. A concept used regularly by **voice pedagogues** that describes a sound that is more concentrated, **resonant**, and fully adducted. Focus can usually be achieved through a combination of **vowel** modification, *aggiustamento*, **resonance** adjustment, **formant tuning**, and *appoggio* under the tutelage of an experienced teacher. While focus is certainly a desirable attribute of a cultivated **classical technique**, it is also possible for a voice to be too focused (as a result of **compensatory tension** or excessive tension). One can always have too much of a good thing, and this maxim is especially true in vocal technique.

folk music. 1. The indigenous music of a nation or people, usually passed down through oral tradition (as opposed to being written down). Many **genres** of **world music** are also folk-like in nature, being indigenous or ritualistic. Thus, folk music is most often used to describe Western music of the oral tradition, although Western music is certainly not the only kind of folk music. Many composers incorporate the folk music of their countries into their musical **scores** to express their own specific nationalism. This is especially prevalent in the genres of **art song** and **opera**.

2. A genre of **popular music**, also known as **folk rock**, that is a **fusion** of the folk music and **rock** genres. Examples of folk singers include Bob Dylan (b. 1941), Joan Baez (b. 1941), Joni Mitchell (b. 1943), and Cat Stevens (b. 1948).

folk opera. An **operatic** work set in a particular geographical region and incorporating indigenous music from that region. *Porgy and Bess* (1935), by George Gershwin (1898–1937)—set in Charleston, South Carolina—is regarded as the quintessential folk opera, with an all African American cast singing a score infused with **jazz**, **spirituals**, and gospel music. Other examples of folk opera include *Down in the Valley* (1945), by Kurt Weill (1900–1950); *The Tender Land* (1954), by Aaron Copland (1900–1990); *Susannah* (1955), by Carlisle Floyd (b. 1926); and *The Ballad of Baby Doe* (1956), by Douglas Moore (1893–1969).

folk rock. A **fusion genre** of **rock** that incorporates elements of **folk music**.

forced resonance. A type of musical **resonance** that operates under the principle of mass and compliance. Stringed instruments operate under this principle: the vibration of the strings transfers through the bridge to the body of the instrument. Forced resonance is also known as conductive resonance.

foreign languages. See **diction**.

form. The structure of a piece of music. Like instrumental music, vocal forms have their own sets of patterns, with different stock forms being in vogue during different eras of music history. In the **art song genre**, for example, there are four principal **song forms**: **strophic**, modified strophic, **scenic**, and **through-composed**. And while the **32-bar song form** was common in **popular music** during the first half of the twentieth century, contemporary popular music often prefers a **verse-chorus song form**. While form is most easily distilled in such shorter forms as **songs** and **arias**, larger vocal works, for example, **operas** and **oratorios**, can also be analyzed in terms of overall formal structure. In these larger works, many smaller forms may coexist within the overall structure.

For instance, a **baroque** opera might contain both *da capo* **arias** and **ground bass arias**, which were two of the most common aria forms of the baroque era.

formant. Specific **resonances** created by the **vocal tract** and a fundamental concept in the study of **acoustics** as it relates to singing. Formants occur naturally in the **oral cavity** and **pharynx** and interact with the **harmonic series** of the **fundamental frequency** being sung. As a result, some **harmonics** are strengthened, while others are attenuated. The vocal tract has many formants, but the first five are most essential to the singer. The first two formants determine the **vowel**, and formants 3 through 5 are often referred to as the **singer's formant**. The singer's formant is an important element of resonance in **classical singing** that is used to enhance projection. Formants are a difficult concept to understand, with chapters of **voice pedagogy** and voice science books devoted to the study of them.

formant tracking. See **formant tuning**.

formant tuning (formant tracking). **Vowel** modification (or substitution) to enhance **resonance** through coordinating vowels with the **pitch** being sung. Formant tuning is used by **classical singers** to produce an even musical **scale**, and by **contemporary commercial music (CCM)** singers to permit high-pitched **belting**.

formes fixes **(Fr).** Literally meaning "fixed **forms**," a group of secular **polyphonic song forms** that flourished in France during the late **medieval** and early **Renaissance** eras. The three principal *formes fixes* were the *ballade*, *rondeau*, and *virelai*, each of which had its own idiomatic musical and lyrical structure. A related form, the *bergerette*, flourished later than the other three *formes fixes*.

formula. The **harmonic progression**—usually in four parts—to which **Anglican chant** is sung. Various texts (usually psalms) can be "pointed" (syllabically set) to virtually any formula, creating thousands of possible combinations.

forte, fortissimo **(It).** Loud, very loud.

four-line staff. A **medieval** staff used in the notation of **Gregorian chant**. **Early music** performers and church musicians who specialize in **plainsong** must be fluent in reading **neumes** on four-line staves. See also *Liber Usualis*.

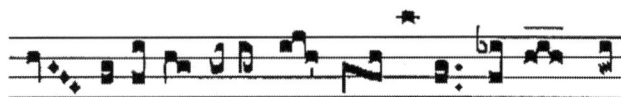

Figure 18. Four-line staff used in chant notation. *Courtesy Creative Commons.*

fourth wall. An acting term/concept referring to the imaginary "wall" at the front of the stage in a traditional proscenium stage. Singers in **operas** and **musicals** implicitly acknowledge the presence of this "fourth wall" largely by interacting with one another and not directly acknowledging the audience's presence. Thus, the audience is permitted to "peer into" a private scenario by "seeing through" this fourth wall. Occasionally, performers deliberately break through the fourth wall and speak or interact directly with the audience. This occurs most frequently in **musical comedies** and light opera.

Fr+6. Abbreviation for **French augmented sixth**.

Franklin, Aretha (b. 1942). American singer and songwriter. Franklin was born in Memphis, Tennessee, and raised in Detroit, Michigan, where she was exposed to **gospel** music at an early age. She signed with Columbia Records at the age of eighteen and began recording **rhythm and blues songs**. In 1968, she moved to the Atlantic Records label, with whom she quickly soared to national fame. During this time, Franklin became closely associated with the **soul genre**, and she is still considered by many to be the "Queen of Soul." She has won eighteen Grammy Awards and is one of the best-selling female artists of all time.

free resonance. The type of **resonance** that occurs as the result of vibrations of air molecules and reflections of soundwaves within a void. Singers utilize free resonance (as opposed to **forced resonance**, which depends on a mechanical connection from a vibrator to a resonator). To function as a free resonator, a structure must be hollow, have volume, and have an opening through which soundwaves can exit. All wind instruments, including organs, also operate according to free resonance principles.

free singing. A broad, imprecise, and subjective concept that is almost universally encouraged by singing teachers and practiced by the vast majority of solo **classical singers**. Implies that the voice is free of any extraneous tension and that the production is healthy. Free singing can also refer to vibrant, **resonant** singing with presence of a strong **singer's formant** and wider **vibrato amplitude**.

Thus, while free singing almost always bears a positive connotation among **opera** singers and **classical** soloists, it is a more controversial concept among choral artists. While some aspects of free singing are good in all circumstances (minimal tension, healthy production, etc.), other aspects (for example, the presence of **singer's resonance** and vibrato) can negatively impact **blend** and **intonation**. **Professional** choral singers must develop the **technique** to rein in certain aspects of free singing to conform to the style mandated by the **conductor**.

French art song. See *mélodie*.

French augmented sixth (Fr+6). See **augmented sixth chord**.

French opera. French-language **opera**, the basic **repertoire** of which stretches from the mid-**baroque** era with **five-act operas** of Jean-Baptiste Lully (1632–1687) through *Pelléas et Mélisande* (1902), an impressionistic work by Claude Debussy (1862–1918). During the baroque era, the *grand opera* style flourished. After Lully's success at the court of King Louis IV, Jean-Philippie Rameau (1683–1764) became his principal successor, writing operas in a similar style, although more **harmonically** daring. Giacomo Meyerbeer (1791–1864), Fromental Halévy (1799–1862), and Hector Berlioz (1803–1869) continued the *grand opera* tradition, which fell out of fashion due to the rise of two nineteenth-century **subgenres** of French opera: *opéra comique* and *opéra lyrique* (lyric opera). The *opéra comique* was usually not comical in nature; rather, it was shorter in length, written for a smaller house, and contained dialogue (some of which was later orchestrated into **recitatives**). *Carmen* (1875), by Georges Bizet (1838–1875), is a quintessential example of the *opéra comique*. The *opéra lyrique* included the seamless melodic works of Jules Massenet (1842–1912) and Charles Gounod (1818–1893). These lyric operas were shorter in length and more accessible than *grand operas*. During the nineteenth century, the *opéra bouffe*—a light-hearted, comical, and often risqué theatrical work—also emerged. Jacques Offenbach (1819–1880) was the most famous composer of *opéra bouffes*, and his *Orphée aux enfers* (1858) is considered to be the apotheosis of the **genre**.

French r. See **guttural r**.

frequency (Hz). The **objective** measurement of vibrations per second, measured in **hertz (Hz)**. For example, the **pitch** A4 is measured at 440 Hz. In singing, **frequency** can be measured by the number of times the **vocal folds** close per second on any given pitch. The vocal folds of a singer singing an A4 will vibrate 440 times per second. While frequency is closely related to pitch, it is not quite a synonym due to the fact that frequency is an objective measurement and pitch is a subjective perception, incorporating other issues, including **vibrato** and **timbre**. Frequency is closely associated with **period** and **wavelength**.

frequency response. A quantitative measurement of a **microphone's** ability to reproduce an **acoustic** signal. Frequency response graphs often display **frequencies** from 20 to 20,000 Hz and display **amplitude** variations of –20 to +20 dB.

frequency spectrum. See **audio spectrum**.

fricative. In the study of **diction**, describes a **manner of articulation** in which **consonants** are produced by directing the air flow past a set of **articulators**. Common examples of fricative consonants include [v], [f], [z], [s], and [ʃ]. See also **affricate**, **lateral**, **nasal**, **plosive**.

frisch **(Ger).** Fresh, youthful, or spritely.

fröhlich **(Ger).** Happy, lively, or joyful.

front vowel. Describes a **vowel** in which the arch of the tongue is forward with the tip down during **enunciation**. [i], [I], [e], [ɛ], [a], [æ] are common examples of front vowels. See also **back vowel**, **central vowel**, **closed vowel**, **mixed vowel**, **nasal vowels**, **open vowel**.

frottola. An Italian **polyphonic** secular **song** that proliferated during the **Renaissance** era. While the texts often dealt with rustic themes, the *frottola* should be regarded as **art music**, with originally composed melodies as opposed to appropriated folk tunes. Most *frottolas* made use of a repeated rhythmic **formula** suggestive of a rustic **dance**.

fry. Could refer to vocal fry, **glottal fry**, **pulse**, or *Schnarrbass*.

fugue. A **polyphonic** composition with various voices entering imitatively with the same subject. Unlike a **canon**, different voices enter at different **pitch** levels, usually at the **interval** of a fifth.

full anthem. An Anglican **anthem** sung in **liturgical** worship with no soloists during the **Renaissance** and baroque eras. A full anthem differs from a **verse anthem**, which has soloists that alternate their solo passages with the full **chorus**.

full lyric. See **lyric**.

full score. An orchestral **score** that notates every instrumental part with its own line. Full scores are used by **conductors** and occasionally by singers and instrumentalists who perform **chamber music**.

functional. In music theory, describes a **chord** that can be analyzed in a way that makes sense with tonal **harmony**. Functional chords follow predictable rules and observe correct **voice leading**.

fundamental (fundamental frequency). In **acoustics**, the lowest **frequency** in a **harmonic series**, and thus the first **harmonic**. Abbreviated as F_0. **Pitch** is always identified by the fundamental frequency. For example, **A=440 Hz**.

fungal laryngitis. A type of **laryngitis** that results from a fungal or yeast infection. Asthmatics who take steroid inhalers also place themselves at risk for suffering from fungal laryngitis. Fungal laryngitis is one of the three basic types of laryngitis, along with **acute laryngitis** and **chronic laryngitis**.

fusion. Any **genre** that is a melding of two or more forerunners. For example, **rockabilly** is a fusion of **country** music and **rock 'n' roll**.

FVF contraction. See **false vocal fold contraction**.

FVF retraction. See **false vocal fold retraction**.

G

G&S. Abbreviation for **Gilbert and Sullivan**.

Gallican chant. The **Latin chant** of the churches of Gaul (**medieval** France). Similar in compositional style to **monophonic Gregorian chant**.

García, Manuel (1775–1832). Manuel García was a **tenor**, composer, and father of a historic school of singing. García studied with Giovanni Anzani (d. 1815), who was, in turn, a student of Nicola Porpora (1686–1768). Porpora is considered to be one of the greatest voice teachers of the Italian school of singing. García's three children—**Manuel García** (1805–1906), **Maria Malibran**, and **Pauline Viardot**—were proponents of their father's teaching. García's *Exercises and Method for Singing with Accompaniment for the Piano Forte* (1824) was expanded by his son, who furthered his father's method by giving it a physiological basis.

García, Manuel (1805–1906). Manuel García was the son of the famous **tenor** who was also named **Manuel García** (1775–1832). The younger García codified his father's teaching in *A Complete Treatise on the Art of Singing* (1841, rev. 1872), which assigned physiological causes to **tone**, differentiating between the action of the **glottis** and the **pharynx**. García is considered the father of voice science, being the first person to use the **laryngoscope** to investigate the inner workings of the **larynx** in *Observations of the Human Voice* (1855). His teaching on vocal **onset**, the *coup de glotte* ("stroke of the glottis"), was the source of controversy, which he later clarified in *Hints on Singing* (1894). García is credited with restoring the voice of **Jenny Lind**, the "Swedish Nightingale."

Gardel, Carlos (1890–1935). Argentine singer celebrated throughout Latin America as the eminent vocal interpreter of the **tango**. The vocal version of the tango is sometimes called the *tango canción*. The illegitimate son of a French woman, he spent his youth as a street performer, perfecting his skills as an actor and dancer. The **lyrics** of tango **songs**—the vocal extension of the tango **dance**—were almost always political in nature. He is dubbed by many as the "Father of the Tango."

gastroesophageal reflux disease (GERD). One of the two major types of reflux disease (along with **laryngopharyngeal reflux disease [LPRD]**) caused by gastric acid migrating into the esophagus. If acid proceeds to spill into the **larynx** and **vocal folds**, it then becomes LPRD. GERD can be controlled by over-the-counter medicines, as well as dietary choices and the avoidance of eating within a certain time frame (usually two to three hours) before going to sleep.

***Geistliche* (Ger).** Of the spirit. *Geistliche* is a German adjective meaning sacred. The term was famously used by Hugo Wolf (1860–1903) to describe the first ten **songs**—the *Geistliche Lieder*—of his *Spanisches Liederbuch* (1889) **song collection**. The remaining thirty-four songs (the secular ones) were designated as *Weltliche Lieder* (secular songs; *Weltliche* means "of the world").

***género chico*.** A Spanish **genre** of **musical theatre** with spoken dialogue and **songs**.

genre. In music, a frequently used term that attempts to categorize music according to type, **forms**, and **style**. There are often many **subgenres** within a **genre**. This occurs in **opera**. For instance, opera is a genre in and of itself, but there are many types (subgenres) of opera, for example, Italian *opera seria*, French *grand opéra*, German **music dramas**, and American **folk operas**. Each of these subgenres can also be discussed and studied as individual genres in their own right.

Ger+6. Abbreviation for **German augmented sixth**.

GERD. Abbreviation for **gastroesophageal reflux disease**.

German art song. See *Lied*.

German augmented sixth. See **augmented sixth chord**.

German Fach System. Another name for the **Kloiber Fach System**. Sometimes, the "German Fach System" can be used to label an expansion of Kloiber's system (for instance, if an additional, non-Kloiber subcategory is added or discussed). See also *Fach*.

German opera. The younger cousin of **Italian opera** and **French opera**, German opera did not develop into a significant **genre** until the late eighteenth and early nineteenth centuries, when *Singspiels* and **German Romantic opera** began to emerge. Richard Wagner (1813–1883) then reinvented the art form with his **music dramas**, bold and innovative experiments that elevated the entire **operatic** genre to new levels of sophistication. In the twentieth century, Richard Strauss (1864–1949), Hans Pfitzner (1869–1949), Alban Berg (1885–1935), Karlheinz Stockhausen (1928–2007), and Aribert Riemann (b. 1936) added significant works to the **repertory**.

German Romantic opera. The name given to the lyrical **operas** by German composers in the German language that were composed during the **romantic** era, before the advent of the **music dramas** of Richard Wagner (1813–1883), which incorporated a network of *leitmotifs* and were written in a more progressive **style**. The three quintessential examples of German Romantic opera include Wagner's *Die fliegende Holländer* (1843), *Tannhäuser* (1845), and *Lohengrin* (1850). Precursors to these three works include *Der Freischütz* (1821), by Carl Maria von Weber, which can also be described as a *Singspiel*, and—in some respects—Beethoven's *Fidelio* (1905, rev. 1914), although this is a unique work that tends to defy broader classification. Other composers—seldom performed today—include Heinrich Marschner (1795–1861), Albert Lortzing (1801–1851), and Friedrich von Flotow (1812–1883). Many of these early German Romantic operas contained strong elements of folklore and magic, giving them the sometimes-used **subgenre** label *Zauberoper*, literally meaning "magic opera."

German Romanticism. A German poetic movement that arose immediately after the French Revolution in the German cities of Berlin and Jena. The movement soon spread to Heidelberg, Dresden, Vienna, and Munich. Important German Romantic poets included Novalis (1772–1801), Friedrich Schlegel (1772–1829), Ludwig Tieck (1773–1853), Clemens Brentano (1778–1842), and Joseph von Eichendorff (1778–1857). These poets developed in the shadow of Johann Wolfgang von Goethe (1749–1832), whose poems—while rooted in the **classical** tradition—featured many elements of German Romanticism. German Romantic poems were profoundly metaphorical; for example, wandering represents individuality, the forest evokes mystery, and night alludes to death itself. A basic understanding of German Romanticism is essential for performers of *Lieder*, just as a basic understanding of **symbolism** is indispensible to performers of French *mélodies*.

Germanic Latin. A way of pronouncing **Latin** that departs from the standard Roman pronunciation—usually referred to as **church Latin**—that was authorized by Pope Pius X (1835–1914) in 1903. Germanic Latin attempts to replicate the **pronunciation** that would have been practiced by performers of Latin **repertoire** in Germany, Austria, and other Eastern European countries prior to the twentieth century. While Germanic Latin is only one variant of pretwentieth-century Latin (Anglican Latin and French Latin are two others), it is by far the most frequently practiced alternative pronunciation due to the sheer amount of repertoire to emerge from Austria and Germany during the **baroque**, **classical**, and **romantic** eras. Indeed, all of the **Mass** settings of Johann Sebastian Bach (1685–1750), Wolfgang Amadeus Mozart (1756–1791), Joseph Haydn (1732–1809), Franz Schubert (1797–1828), Ludwig van Beethoven (1770–1827), and Anton Bruckner (1824–1896) are more accurately pronounced using Germanic Latin, making comfort with the pronunciation an essential skill for the experienced **oratorio** singer or choral artist.

Gesamtkunstwerk. German term literally meaning "complete artwork." Richard Wagner coined the term *Gesamtkunstwerk* to describe his later **operas**—which he called **music dramas**—to emphasize the equal importance of all elements of the **operatic production**. To Wagner, the ideal music drama should not only be about the music; it should also emphasize the best poetry, art direction, sets, costumes, stage **technique**, architecture, and literary achievement (through the **libretto**). Wagner's quest to achieve the idea *Gesamtkunstwerk* inspired him to build a custom-designed **opera house** at Bayreuth to stage his final music dramas. The **Bayreuth Festspielhaus** was the first to feature a sunken orchestra pit, and the backstage area offered many state-of-the-art technical innovations.

geschwind (Ger). Quick or fast.

ghazal. An Indian secular **song** that describes women in an amorous way. Sung in Urdu or Persian, ghazals are usually based on North Indian ragas.

gig. Colloquial term for "performance" used in the **musical theatre**, **jazz**, and **popular music** communities. "Gigs" are often regular opportunities for which musicians are paid. **Classical singers** have adopted the term for these types of routine performances, for instance, **church jobs** (i.e., "church gig.").

Gilbert and Sullivan (G&S). An English composer–librettist team and the collective label given to the thirteen surviving **English comic operas** of William Schwenck Gilbert (1836–1911) and Arthur Sullivan (1842–1900). These works are often collectively referred to as **G&S** works. The thirteen **comic operas** include *Trial by Jury* (1875), *The Sorcerer* (1877), *HMS Pinafore* (1878), *The Pirates of Penzance* (1879), *Patience* (1881), *Iolanthe* (1882), *Princess Ida* (1884), *The Mikado* (1885), *Ruddigore* (1887), *The Yeomen of the Guard* (1888), *The Gondoliers* (1888), *Utopia Limited* (1893), and *The Grand Duke* (1896). The G&S comic operas are also sometimes called the **Savoy Operas**, named after the Savoy Theatre, where most of them were **premiered**.

Figure 19. Caricature of Gilbert and Sullivan. *Courtesy Naxos Music.*

Gilberto, João (b. 1931). Brazilian popular singer, composer, and guitarist. His name is inextricably linked with the Brazilian *bossa nova* style, which consists of syncopated patterns over a **samba beat**. Gilberto exploded into fame in 1959, when he released *Chega de Saudade*, a recording of arrangements by Antônio Carlos Jobim (1927–1994). This recording revealed a new singing style and solidified Gilberto's reputation as the icon of *bossa nova* vocal aesthetics. In 1962, Gilberto took part in the Bossa Nova Carnegie Hall Concert, after which he moved to New York. His most famous recording—a collaboration with Stan Getz entitled *Getz/Gilberto*—was released in 1963. It won six **Grammy Awards** and sold almost 1 million copies. Gilberto's wife, Astrud Gilberto

(b. 1940), sang the album's most famous **song**, "The Girl from Ipanema," making her an overnight sensation and an iconic singer in her own right.

glide. In the study of **diction**, a glide is a short **vowel** sound that immediately yields to a longer vowel sound within the same syllable. The most frequently encountered glides are [j] and [w], which are short versions of [i] and [u], respectively. In French diction, the singer also encounters [ɥ], which is a short version of the **mixed vowel** [y].

glissando (pl: *glissandi*) (It). A slide from one **pitch** to another. Similar to *portamento*.

Gloria. One of the five standard parts of the **Ordinary** in a Catholic **Mass**.

glottal. A **point of articulation** in **diction** that involves airflow and the opening between the **vocal folds**.

glottal attack. A vocal iteration in which **phonation** begins with a harsher, often audible articulation initiated by the sudden release of air built up behind fully **approximated vocal folds**. While glottal attacks are often discouraged in **classical voice pedagogy** (**voice pedagogues** usually encourage their students to strive for a **balanced onset**), their presence as a salient feature of German, English, and Nordic **diction** makes them impossible to avoid altogether. Singers and voice teachers generally try to find a moderate and delicate balance between correct **declamation** of the language while simultaneously preserving **legato**. Although glottal attacks share some similarities with **plosive consonants**, they are a unique **manner of articulation** and an entity unto themselves. Only **vowels** can begin with glottal attacks.

glottal chink. See **mutational chink**.

glottal fry. **Phonation** at the lowest **pitches** of the voice, either male or female. Produces an imprecise phonation reminiscent of "clicking." Minimal airflow is needed to produce glottal fry. Sometimes used as a therapeutic **technique**. Also called **pulse**.

glottal stop. To stop **phonation** suddenly by abruptly closing the **glottis**.

glottis. The space between the unapproximated **vocal folds**.

golden age. A term used in both **opera** and **musical theatre** that looks back on a former era of singing with admiration and respect. Historians and teachers of singing who use the term often do so under the pretense that the former era represented something greater than the present one. When one uses the term *golden age*, they are not referencing a clearly defined historical era with beginning and end dates. Rather, the term is a wistful and nostalgic **expression** of approbation applied subjectively by the user.

golden era of song. See **Great American Songbook**.

Goliard songs. The secular **Latin songs** of the **Goliards** during the **medieval** era.

Goliards. A group of clergy during the twelfth and thirteenth centuries who wrote secular, satirical **Latin** poetry for sung performance. These songs were called **Goliard songs** and were often about drinking.

gorgheggi. Florid **vocalises** in the Italian tradition.

gorgia. An improvised **ornamentation** associated with Italian vocal music of the early seventeenth century. See also **coloratura**, *fioratura*.

gospel. An African American style of sacred **choral music** and a closely related **genre** (and successor) to **blues** and the **spiritual**. Originally written for and still used in worship services, it has also developed into a solo genre, with **Mahalia Jackson** as its most famous exponent. Gospel music features simple melodies that are embellished through **improvisation**. Shouts, groans, and howls also augment this idiomatic musical **style**. Gospel singing can most authentically be performed *a cappella* or accompanied by the piano, Hammond organ, guitar, or a rhythm section (bass and drums).

gradual. One of the five standard parts of the **Proper** in a Catholic **Mass**.

Grammy Awards. Originally called the Gramophone Awards, the Grammys are annual awards given by the National Academy of Recording Arts and Sciences to recognize outstanding recordings in the music industry. The number of awards has fluctuated throughout time, and the 2012 restructuring of the awards delineated seventy-eight distinct award categories. Although the televised Grammy Award prime time special only tends to feature commercial music artists, there are several categories devoted to **classical** music, including Best Opera Recording, Best Choral Performance, and Best Classical Vocal Solo.

grand (Fr). Large.

grand motet. Large, multimovement **motets** composed in France during the **baroque** era.

Grand Ole Opry. A weekly **country** music stage **concert** that is broadcast from Nashville, Tennessee. The first Grand Ole Opry broadcast occurred on November 28, 1925, and it remains one of the longest-running broadcasts in the history of music of any **genre**. The Grand Ole Opry House can be thought of as the Carnegie Hall of country music, with the greatest performers in the genre making appearances there. In addition to country music, the Grand Ole Opry has also welcomed performers of **bluegrass**, **gospel**, and **folk music**.

grand opéra. 1. **Genre** of **French opera** that prevailed from the mid-seventeenth century—with the **operas** of Jean-Baptiste Lully (1632–1687) and Jean-Phillipe Rameau (1683–1764)—and persisted through the early nineteenth century. *Grand opéras* had five **acts**. While the *grand opéra* was in vogue, Paris was the center of the **operatic** universe, and many **Italian opera** composers also tried their hand at writing them. The era of *grand opéra* ended in the early eighteenth century with the works of Giacomo Meyerbeer (1791–1864), Fromental Halévy (1799–1862), and Hector Berlioz (1803–1869).

2. An imprecise, catchall term that commonly denotes any work from the mainstream, **classic–romantic** opera **repertory**. In this sense, "grand opera" (without the *accent aigu*) is distinct from more intimate **baroque** repertories and **forms** of light opera. This use of the term should not be confused with *grand opéra* in the more narrow sense, the specific brand of grandiose French opera that existed from the mid-seventeenth to the early nineteenth centuries (Lully to Berlioz).

Grant, Amy (b. 1960). American popular singer and **contemporary Christian music** artist. The best-selling Christian artist of all time, having sold more than 30 million records, she is also known as the "Queen of Christian Pop." After getting her start in contemporary Christian music, Grant crossed over into mainstream **popular music**, recording "The Next Time I Fall," a No. 1 hit, with Peter Cetera (b. 1944). Her secular solo album *Heart in Motion* (1991) produced the No. 1 single "Baby Baby."

granulomas. Benign growths of inflammatory tissue occurring at the **vocal processes**. Granulomas are usually preceded by **contact ulcers**. Also called vocal process granulomas.

graphic equalizer. In audio technology, an instrument that separates the **frequencies** of the **audio spectrum** into a specific number of frequency **bandwidths** (called bands). For example, a ten-band graphic equalizer would typically have sliders for frequencies of approximately 31 **Hz**, 62 Hz, 125 Hz, 250 Hz, 500 Hz, 1 kHz, 2 kHz, 4 kHz, 8 kHz, and 16 kHz. Each slider can be moved up and down from the centerline (0 **dB**) to **boost** or **cut** the frequencies within a predefined bandwidth (called "Q"). For more information, see the essay entitled "What Every Singer Needs to Know about Audio Technology."

Graphical Auto-Tune. A version of **Auto-Tune** that utilizes a graphical interface, allowing engineers to make precise adjustments to individual **pitches** and portions of pitches. Graphical Auto-Tune is better suited for fixing small errors in a recording.

grave (**It**). Slow and serious.

grave accent (`). English term for the *accent grave* **diacritical marking** that is encountered in French. Called the *accento grave* in Italian.

Grawemeyer Award. An annual award given by the University of Louisville. The Grawemeyer Awards honor specific achievements in five categories: education, the improvement of world order, religion, psychology, and music composition. The composition award is the oldest of the Grawemeyer Awards and was first presented in 1985. Vocal works that have won the Grawemeyer Award for Music Composition have included four **operas** and two **art song** cycles. A comprehensive list of these works appears in appendix F.

Great American Songbook. The Great American Songbook is a conceptual term referring to the vast catalog of **popular music** that came out of **Tin Pan Alley** between World War I and World War II. It is not a literal book, as the **repertoire** of the Great American Songbook is far too vast to be conflated into a single volume. The repertoire primarily draws from popular **songs** from the 1920s, 1930s, and 1940s by such composers as Irving Berlin (1888–1989), Jerome Kern (1885–1945), and Cole Porter (1891–1964), as well as such composer–**lyricist** teams as Richard Rodgers (1902–1979) and Lorenz Hart (1895–1943) and George Gershwin (1898–1937) and Ira Gershwin (1896–1983). While most of these songs were originally written for **Broadway musical comedies** and **revues**, they were quickly appropriated as jazz standards and sold as **sheet music** for home performance. They are still heard as such today, and while musicians still recognize many tunes from the Great American Songbook, few remember their original context within a particular show. The popularity of sheet music and the Great American Songbook quickly declined after the invention and widespread proliferation of the phonograph and LP records in the late 1940s.

great sequence. See **five great sequences**.

Great White Way. Nickname for the Broadway Theatre District, which is located between 42nd Street and 53rd Street, encompassing Times Square. Historically—in the late nineteenth century—the New York Theatre District was a bit larger, stretching all the way to 23rd Street. This lower section of the Theatre District—from 23rd Street to 34th Street—was famously illuminated with many electrical advertising signs, a novelty that became popular during the 1890s. City folks began referring to this section of town as the "Great White Way" in reference to the brightness of the lights.

Gregorian chant. The **repertory** of **liturgical** plainchant that arose in the Roman Catholic Church during the **medieval** era, and much of which is still in use today. Most of the sacred Western choral repertory during the medieval and **Renaissance** eras was based on Gregorian chant, and this repertory influenced choral composition in later eras as well. Gregorian chant is one of many types of plainchant, but it is the **chant** repertory that is most frequently heard and most relevant to the study of Western **art music**.

Figure 20. Gregorian chant excerpt from the *Liber Usualis. Courtesy Creative Commons.*

Gregorian chant notation. A type of **neumatic** notation found in the *Liber Usualis*.

griot. See *jali*.

grit. The gravelly sound produced by **rock** singers. Although grit can sound like a vocally damaged voice to **classical singers**, some **contemporary commercial music (CCM) pedagogues** argue that the sound can be produced in a healthy way, particularly with the aid of a **microphone** and a certain degree of vocal processing.

ground bass aria. One of two specific **aria forms** of the **baroque** era (along with the *da capo* aria). Ground bass arias are similar to instrumental chaconnes and passacaglias in that they are constructed over a simple **bass** line that is repeated exactly and indefinitely throughout the course of the entire aria. The composer's task is to ingeniously and creatively construct chord progressions and phrases in spite of the constraint provided by the bass line. Henry Purcell (1659–1695) was renowned as a composer of ground bass arias, and his **opera** *Dido and Aeneas* (1688) contains two of the most famous examples: "Ah! Belinda, I Am Pressed with Torment" and "When I Am Laid in Earth," otherwise known as Dido's Lament.

growling. A low, **guttural vocalization**. Growling is applied in some types of **heavy metal** music and utilized by **new music** performers as an **extended technique**.

grunge. A **subgenre** of **alternative rock** that emerged in the 1980s. Grunge is particularly associated with the Seattle area in the Northwestern United States. Distorted electric guitars and apathetic **lyrics** are typical characteristics of the **style**. The vocal style of grunge is similar to **hard rock**. The popularity of grunge peaked in the early 1990s with such groups as Nirvana and Pearl Jam.

Gunn, Nathan (b. 1970). American **baritone**, famous for his early development, rich voice, acting skills, and exceptionally good looks. By his mid-thirties, Gunn had appeared in most of the world's major **opera houses** in more than a dozen principal **roles**. Known for his physique (as one of opera's "buff baritones"), he is perhaps the only **classical singer** to have been labeled by *People* magazine as one of the "sexiest men alive." Devoted to teaching, Gunn and his wife, pianist Julie Jordan Gunn, were appointed to the music faculty of the University of Illinois in 2007.

guttural. A speech sound that is created in the back of the **oral cavity**. Guttural literally means "of the throat."

guttural r. Also known as the French *r* due to its idiomatic use in the French spoken language. The guttural *r* is essentially an **unvoiced uvular fricative** [x], and it is often heard in French **forms** of **popular music**—for example, the *chanson*—as well as in French **musical theatre**. Traditionally, it has almost never been used in French **classical singing**, although there has been a recent movement to begin incorporating it, especially in European musical circles.

Gypsy music. See **Romani music**.

H

h aspiré. In the French language, words that begin with *h* fall into two categories: aspirated *h* (*h aspiré*) and unaspirated *h* (*h inaspiré*). While the [h] is not pronounced in either case, the singer must conscientiously know which type of *h* he or she is dealing with, as the *h aspiré* forbids liaison. The singer must conscientiously look up each word that begins with *h* in a dictionary, where each aspirated *h* will be marked, often with a ' or † symbol. Unaspirated *h* will have no such marking. Examples of the *h aspiré* include "haricot" ("les haricots" = [lɛ aɾiko]) and "haies" ("des haies" = [dɛ ɛ]).

h inaspiré. Opposite of the *h aspiré*. Unaspirated *h* allows for the possibility of liaison. Examples of *h inaspiré* include "hommes" ("les hommes" = [lɛzɔm]) and "hiver" ("en hiver" = [ãnivɛɾ]). See *h aspiré* for a detailed explanation regarding the distinction between *h aspiré* and *h inaspiré*.

habanera. A nineteenth-century Cuban **dance** and **song**, known for its slow **tempo**, **duple meter**, and distinctive rhythm: a dotted-eighth note, followed by a sixteenth note, followed by two eighth notes (then repeated). The name is derived from the city of Havana ("Habana"). The term is often (incorrectly) misspelled with a tilde over the *n* (*habañera*). Even though the *habanera* originated in Cuba, it achieved widespread popularity in Europe, especially in Spain. Georges Bizet (1838–1875) famously wrote one of Carmen's **arias**—"L'amour est un oiseau rebelle," from *Carmen* (1875)—in the style of a *habanera*. Its influence is also felt in many **Spanish art songs**, as well as instrumental works from the late nineteenth and early twentieth centuries.

habilitation. The process of physically learning and keeping new skills. The opposite of **rehabilitation**, which means to regain skills that have been lost.

Hagen, Uta (1919–2004). German-born American actress and acting teacher. Hagen is most famous for developing an **acting technique** that is widely practiced and referenced by students and teachers of **theatre**. She is mostly known to students of acting through her two highly influential textbooks: *Respect for Acting* (1973) and *A Challenge for the Actor* (1993). Her **technique** emphasizes **realistic** acting, which advocates the "transference" or "substitution" of one's own psyche into that of the character being portrayed. Although Hagen was one of the only major twentieth-century acting teachers who was not associated with the ideas of **Constantin Stanislavski** or the **Method**, her philosophy does congeal with some of the ideas put forth by **Lee Strasberg**, **Stella Adler**, and **Sanford Meisner**. Hagen was herself an accomplished actress and a three-time winner of the **Tony Award**. In theatrical training, Hagen's method is one of the most frequently referenced acting techniques, along with those of Stanislavski, Strasberg, Adler, Meisner, **Michael Chekhov**, **Viola Spolin**, and **Anne Bogart**.

half step. The smallest standard **interval** in Western music and the fundamental building block of Western melody and **harmony**. Each **octave** contains twelve half steps, and two half steps equal one **whole step**. All tonal and modal **modes** are constructed from unique patterns of whole and half steps.

Hampson, Thomas (b. 1955). American **lyric baritone** and one of the world's most preeminent and famous **classical singers**. Hampson was born in Elkhart, Indiana, and raised in Spokane, Washington. After earning a BFA in voice performance from Fort Wright College, he continued his studies at the Music Academy of the West with Marital Singher (1904–1990), and at the Merola Opera Program in San Francisco, where he met **Elisabeth Schwarzkopf**. Hampson won the **Metropolitan Opera**

National Council (MONC) auditions in 1981, a win that helped to launch a long and distinguished career. Now in his fourth decade of nonstop engagements, he has appeared in all of the world's major **opera houses** and produced more than 170 commercial recordings. In addition to his ever-expanding **repertory** of **opera roles**, Hampson is a distinguished **concert** singer, particularly devoted to **American art song** and German *Lieder*. He is world renowned for his unparalleled **interpretations** of the **orchestral songs** of Gustav Mahler (1860–1911).

hard mix. In **contemporary commercial music (CCM)**, a higher **belt style** needed to perform contemporary **popular music** and modern **musical theatre repertoire**. Similar to **belt-mix** or **superbelt**, but usually with more **twang** or **noise (fry)** in the sound.

hard palate. The hard, bony portion of the front of the **palate** (the roof of the mouth).

hard rock. A **subgenre** of **rock** that is louder, edgier, and uses amplified instruments and distortion. Hard rock is an important precursor of **heavy metal**, but it is more melodic than its successor.

harmonic. Upper **harmonics** in the **harmonic series**. Harmonics are synonymous with overtones, although they are numbered differently: the lowest **tone** in the series is termed the first harmonic, but the next is the first overtone (although the second harmonic).

harmonic minor. A **minor scale** with a raised seventh **scale degree**.

harmonic progression. A series of **chords** in **tonal music** that follow the proper rules of **harmony** and **voice leading**.

harmonic series. The "overtone series" that is an essential property of musical sound. In singing, every sound is comprised of simultaneously occurring interrelated **frequencies** at different **amplitudes**. The **pitch** uttered by the singer is also the lowest pitch in the series, and this is also known as the **fundamental frequency**. **Harmonics** then exist above the fundamental frequency in whole-number multiples (x1, x2, x3, x4, etc.).

The aggregate of the fundamental frequency and its **overtones** is called the harmonic series. The harmonic series plays an essential **role** in singing and the **resonance** of the singing voice. Variations in the strength of specific harmonics in the harmonic series are the reason why no two voices sound alike, even if they are singing the same pitches; in other words, the harmonic series has everything to do with the **color** of an individual voice. In **acoustic** terms, each singer has his or her own unique

spectral envelope. While harmonics are present in all **styles** of music, some styles of **world music** make explicit use of audible harmonics. **Tuvan throat singing** is a quintessential example.

Figure 21. The harmonic series. *Courtesy Creative Commons.*

harmoniously. A mnemonic device for students of Italian **diction**. The five **consonants** in the word harmoniously—*r*, *m*, *n*, *s*, and *l*—assist with **syllabification** of Italian words. Syllabification always occurs after these five letters when they occur as initial letters in consonant groups. Examples include "sem-bian-te" and "ris-pon-de."

harmony. Two or more musical **tones** sounding simultaneously. Aspects of harmony include simultaneous **intervals**, **chords**, and **tone clusters**.

Harmony, Incorporated. One of two female **barbershop** societies, along with **Sweet Adelines International**. Harmony, Incorporated split away from Sweet Adelines International in 1957, after a dispute regarding whether to admit African American members. As a result, Harmony, Incorporated became the world's first racially integrated barbershop society. Both Sweet Adelines International and the Society for the Preservation and Encouragement of Barbershop Quartet Singing in America followed suit several years later.

harpsichord. A stringed keyboard instrument in use from the sixteenth through the eighteenth centuries, before the invention of the piano. Singers who program **secular music** from the **baroque** and early **classical** eras should seek the use of a harpsichord to better realize the intentions of the composer. **Sacred music** from these eras often sounds best with a **portative organ**.

haute-contre. 1. Historically, a specific type of French **classical voice type**. *Haute-contres* were not **countertenors** or **castratos**, but they made extensive use of **falsetto** when singing higher notes or passages. *Haute-contres* can generally be classified as **tenors** with higher **ranges**; however, *haute-contres* still sang tenor **roles**, as opposed to the **soprano** and **mezzo-soprano repertory** inhabited by the **baroque** castrati and the contemporary countertenor.

2. One of the twenty-nine designations in the **Kloiber Fach System**, and the smallest *Fach* category. All designated *haute-contre* roles are from only three composers:

Jean-Baptiste Lully (1632–1687), Jean-Philippe Rameau (1683–1764), and Christoph Willibald Gluck (1714–1787). Specific *haute-contre* roles include the title role in Lully's *Atys* (1676), Castor in Rameau's *Castor et Pullux* (1737), and Orfeo in Gluck's *Orfeo ed Euridice* (1762). See the *Fach* chart in appendix C.

hazzan. A Jewish **cantor**. See also *chazzan*.

head. The common name for a **CT-dominant (mode 2) register** in singing. Sometimes referred to as *voce di testa*, **loft** register, or **light mechanism**. Although head is not the natural register of human speech, it is the preferred register for female voices in **classical genres** of singing.

heavy mechanism. Subjective term used by **voice pedagogues** that can either refer to "loudness" or "heaviness" in the voice, often caused by an increase in **thyroarytenoid** activity. Voice pedagogues may caution their singers against undue strain by discouraging them from using "too heavy of a mechanism" in a particular passage of a **song** or **aria**.

heavy metal. A **subgenre** of **rock** characterized by high **amplification**, **virtuosic** instrumental **riffs**, and a distorted vocal **tone quality**. The **genre** flourished in the late 1960s and early 1970s in the United States. Jimi Hendrix (1942–1970) was an important early exponent of the **style**. Heavy metal enjoyed a resurgence of popularity in the 1980s. In 2007, American **voice pedagogue** Melissa Cross (b. 1956) released two DVDs entitled *The Zen of Screaming* and *The Zen of Screaming 2*, which construct a pedagogical framework for singers who wish to attempt the heavy metal style.

heiter (Ger). Serene, merry, or cheerful.

Heldenbariton. Literally, German for "heroic **baritone**." *Heldenbaritons* are male voices that sing in the baritone **range** with exceptional power and volume, with a **color** reminiscent of **basses**. In the **Kloiber Fach System**, this type of baritone is heavier than the *Kavalierbariton*, but it is stationed one spot higher on the chart than the *Charakterbariton*. Examples of *Helenbariton* **roles** include the title roles in Debussy's *Pelléas et Mélisande* (1898) and Bartók's *Duke Bluebeard's Castle* (1918), and Dr. Schön in Berg's *Lulu* (1835), as well as many roles in Wagner's **music dramas**, including Hans Sachs in *Die Meistersinger von Nürnberg* (1868), Wotan in *Die Walküre* (1870) and *Siegfried* (1876), and Amfortas and Klingsor in *Parsifal* (1878). See the *Fach* chart in appendix C.

Heldentenor. Literally, German for "heroic **tenor**." *Heldentenors* are male voices that sing in the tenor **range** with exceptional power and volume, with a **color** reminiscent of **baritones**. In the **Kloiber Fach System**, this type of tenor is heavier than the *jugendlicher Heldentenor*, but it is stationed one spot higher on the chart than the *Charaktertenor*. Examples of *Heldentenor* **roles** are Aeneas in Berlioz's *Les Troyens* (1858), Otello in Verdi's *Otello* (1887), and Peter Grimes in Britten's *Peter Grimes* (1945), as well as many of Wagner's greatest roles, including Tristan in *Tristan und Isolde* (1865), Stolzing in *Die Meistersinger von Nürnberg* (1868), and Siegfried in *Siegfried* (1876) and *Götterdämmerung* (1876). Many *Heldentenors* begin their careers as baritones before transitioning into the *Heldentenor* **repertory**. Singers who followed this path include Lauritz Melchior (1890–1973) and **Placido Domingo**. See the *Fach* chart in appendix C.

hemiola. A rhythmic phenomenon that frequently occurs in quick **triple meters**. Hemiola is the "layering" of a larger, augmented feeling of three over two smaller groupings of three (usually full measures), so that the normal 3+3 feeling is reorganized as 2+2+2. While hemiola is most commonly found at **cadence** points in **baroque** music, there are examples of this phenomenon in all eras and **styles**, including folk and popular **genres**. The **chorus** of Leonard Bernstein's "America" (from *West Side Story*, 1957) is a famous example of hemiola in contemporary **popular music**.

Figure 22. An example of the hemiola rhythmic pattern. *Courtesy Creative Commons.*

hemorrhage. See **vocal fold hemorrhage**.

Hertz (Hz). The scientific measurement for **frequency**, calculated in cycles per second. In music, Hertz (**Hz**) **objectively** measures **pitch** (e.g., **A=440** Hz).

heureux (Fr). Happy.

high C. Refers to C5, the pinnacle of achievement for the **operatic tenor**. The **aria** "Ah mes amis quel jour de fête! . . . Pour mon âme," from Donizetti's *La fille du régiment* (1840), is famous for its nine high Cs.

high lonesome. A melodic **style** of **bluegrass**.

highlife. A **genre** of **world music** that originated in Ghana, in West Africa, during the twentieth century. The primary features of highlife include group vocals over guitars and wind instruments (usually saxophones and trumpets) accompanied by a synthesized rhythm section. E. T. Mensah (1919–1996) is widely regarded as the "King of Highlife" and is the principal exponent of the genre.

Hints on Singing. An 1894 treatise by **Manuel García** (1805–1906). *Hints on Singing* is a distillation of García's earlier groundbreaking *A Complete Treatise on the Art of Singing* (1841, rev. 1872), which clarifies earlier teachings on vocal **onset** (*coup de glotte*) and was the first book to illustrate modifications of the **pharynx** that affect vocal **timbre**. The work was edited by one of García's students, **Herman Klein**.

hip-hop. Form of **popular music** that is closely related to and descended from the **rap genre**. Hip-hop is associated with the African American community and closely linked with other urban cultural trends, included breakdancing, graffiti art, MCing, and DJing. While generally accepted as a genre of vocal music, the actual role of singing is minimized in hip-hop music, usually being relegated to samples: a prerecorded, often processed melodic section used as a sort of **refrain**.

HIPP. Abbreviation for **historically informed performance practice**.

historia (pl. *historiae*). A **Latin** term that literally means either "history" or "a narrative of past events." *Historiae* were German musical settings of nativity, **Passion**, or resurrection stories during the **medieval**, **Renaissance**, and **baroque** eras.

historical pedagogy. Voice pedagogy that predates the scientific or **fact-based** era of singing that emerged during the second half of the twentieth century. Historical pedagogy was primarily passed down from singing teacher to student and through historically significant **treatises**. The most important historical pedagogues include **Pier Francesco Tosi**, **Manuel García** (1805–1906), **Mathilde Marchesi**, **Julius Stockhausen**, **Giovanni Battista Lamperti**, **William Shakespeare**, and **Lilli Lehmann**. Most of their writings were anthologized by **Berton Coffin** his 1989 book *Historical Vocal Pedagogy Classics*.

historically informed performance practice (HIPP). A relatively recent school of performance practice that seeks to replicate, as closely as possible, the original intentions of the composer. Singers who prioritize HIPP often sing at **A=415**, with period instruments, with a **straight tone** (or less **vibrato**), and with **ornamentation** appropriate to the **style** and time period. **Diction** is also an area that is highly scrutinized by HIPP performers; one might sing with older forms of **pronunciation** (i.e., Old French) or in **Germanic Latin** or French Latin (or another variants).

historicus. The **evangelist** or narrator in an **oratorio** or **Passion**.

hocket. In **medieval polyphonic** vocal music, the practice of splitting a single melody between two vocal lines in rapid alteration. The melodic line emerges when both parts are sung simultaneously. Hocket can also refer to any piece of music or passage that is composed via hocket **technique**.

Figure 23. An example of the Hocket Compositional Technique. *Courtesy Creative Commons.*

Holiday, Billie (1915–1959). African American **jazz** singer. Holiday was born Eleanora Fagan in Baltimore, Maryland. Abandoned by her father at a young age, she followed her mother to New York City, where she began singing in night clubs during her teenage years. In 1933, she was discovered by talent scout and **producer** John Hammond (1910–1987), who arranged for Holiday to record with clarinetist and bandleader Benny Goodman (1909–1986). During the course of the next decade, she secured her fame by going on to sing and record with some of the most famous jazz musicians of her day. Although Holiday is almost universally regarded as one of the most famous jazz singers of all time, she is unique in two principal respects: First, she is one of the only great jazz singers who did not **improvise** (see **scat**). Second, almost everyone agrees that she did not possess a great vocal instrument. In some respects, this makes her fame and universal acclaim even more profound, as she secured her reputation on almost purely expressive and artistic terms as opposed to technical or **virtuosic** prowess. Holiday struggled with substance abuse and abusive relationships throughout her life. When her health suffered, she lost most of her earnings as her voice deteriorated. After a **concert** in Boston in 1959, cardiac arrest sent her into a coma, from which she never awoke; she died of liver and kidney failure a short time later.

homophony. One of the three principal textures of music, the term describes multiple voices that move together in more or less the same rhythm. It is different from **monophony** in that each voice has its own distinct **pitch**, thus creating **harmony**. See also **polyphony**.

honor choir (sometimes honors choir). An elite, usually **auditioned ensemble** of student singers. While high school honor choirs are probably the most commonly found type of honor choir, middle school and children's honor ensembles have become increasingly common. Honor choirs have become immensely popular throughout the United States, and they remain one of the signature programs sponsored by such national and state music education and choral associations as the **National Association for Music Education (NAfME)** and **American Choral Directors Association (ACDA)**. From a music education perspective, there are numerous positives about the honor choir experience. Most obviously, honor choirs give students the experience of singing in an elite ensemble with an accomplished music educator. **Voice pedagogues**, however, often express concern about the abusive nature of the honor choir **rehearsal** schedules, which often place adolescent voices in rehearsals for up to ten hours per day for several days in a row. Another common criticism is that the **repertoire** of honor choirs often lacks musical substance, with students learning short **octavos** as opposed to being exposed to major works by major composers. It is fair to say, however, that honor choirs are not going away any time soon, and they are an essential part of any singer's precollege musical education.

Horne, Marilyn (b. 1934). American **mezzo-soprano**. Horne was born in Bradford, Pennsylvania, and moved to Long Beach, California, when she was eleven years old. In 1952, she enrolled as a voice major at the University of Southern California, where she studied with **William Vennard** and participated in master classes with Lotte Lehmann (1888–1976). Known for her warm **tone quality**, keen **coloratura**, and consummate musicianship, Horne soon established a **professional** career in a wide variety of **repertoire** ranging from the title role in Handel's *Rinaldo* to Marie in Berg's *Wozzeck*. Her extensive **opera** career has been prolifically preserved on record. In recent decades, Horne has been increasingly dedicated to the mentoring and support of young **classical singers**. Since 1997, she has directed the voice program at the Music Academy of the West in Santa Barbara, California, and she collaborates with Carnegie Hall on "The Song Continues," a festival program for emerging **art song** performers in Weill and Zankel **recital** halls in New York City.

hot. An ambiguous word sometimes used as a superlative adjective when describing **contemporary commercial music (CCM) voice types**. Profoundly subjective, a "hot" voice may also be an "exciting" one. They can be found in the **musical theatre** listings, for instance, those found in such weekly publications as *Backstage*.

house singer. A house singer is a staff singer in a European **opera house**, for example, those found in Germany. Young American **opera** singers—as well as young artists

from other countries—often seek out jobs as house singers during the early stages of their careers. Singers can both **audition** for these opportunities in major metropolitan centers (like New York City) or seek placement as a house singer with the assistance of their agents. If desired, one can remain a house singer for his or her entire career. House singers usually adhere rather rigidly to the **German Fach System**, only singing **roles** within their particular *Fach*, and performing multiple roles **in repertory** (simultaneously on alternating nights).

HPV. Abbreviation for **human papilloma virus**.

human papilloma virus (HPV). A virus of more than 100 varieties, four or five of which directly affect the human **larynx**, resulting in papillomas (similar to warts) on the larynx, throat, and **vocal folds**. Hoarseness and voice changes are common symptoms of HPV.

hymn. While this term can narrowly only refer to the text of a particular hymn setting, it is commonly used to refer to both the text and music within a Christian worship service. A hymn is comprised of three principal elements: the text, the **hymn tune**, and the harmonization. Several of these elements can be combined interchangeably with one another. (For example, there can be many settings of the same texts and several harmonizations of the same hymn tunes, even within a single hymnal.)

hymn tune. The melody of a **hymn**. Hymn tunes form a body of **repertoire** independent from hymn harmonizations and hymn texts. These three entities—tunes, harmonizations, and texts—can be mixed and matched to form the vast **genre** of hymnody. The same hymn tune is often repeated within a single hymnal, albeit paired with different harmonizations or texts. Hymn tunes, which are known by their names as opposed to their composers, are usually listed in all capital letters. ELLACOME, CWM RHONDDA, and HYFRYDOL are examples of common hymn tunes.

hyoid bone. A horseshoe-shaped bone that lies between the chin and the **thyroid cartilage**. The hyoid bone is connected to the **larynx** via the **thyrohyoid membrane**.

hypercardioid pattern. In audio technology, a descriptive phrase used to describe how a **microphone** will respond to **acoustic** energy directed at it. A hypercardioid pattern is a **pickup pattern** with a **cardioid pattern** shape on the anterior of the **diaphragm** and a medium-sized circular pattern shape emanating from the posterior of the diaphragm. This pattern is similar to the cardioid, with a slightly narrower **acceptance angle**. Figure 24 offers a visualization of a hypercardioid pickup pattern. Unlike a standard cardioid microphone, a hypercardioid microphone responds to noise from the posterior of the diaphragm, as well as the anterior. This allows the microphone to pick up some of the room's natural **reverb**, but it can also amplify unwanted room noise and contribute to **feedback**. For more information, see the essay entitled "What Every Singer Needs to Know about Audio Technology."

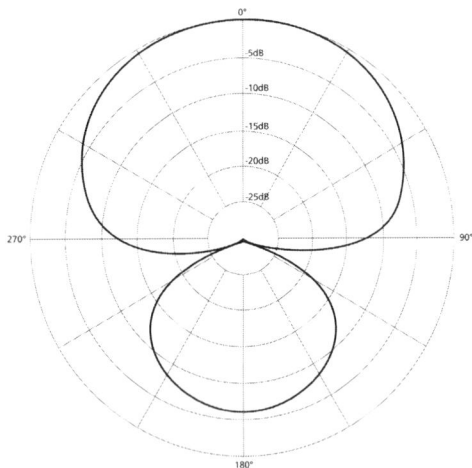

Figure 24. The hypercardioid microphone pattern.
Courtesy Creative Commons.

hyperfunction. "Excess functioning." In **voice pedagogy**, this term specifically refers to a hyperfunctioning of the **vocal folds** due to excess tension or forcing within the **laryngeal** region, ventricular (false) vocal fold **phonation**, anteroposterior laryngeal "squeezing," and harsh **glottal onsets**. Hyperfunction is usually the result of poor or underdeveloped vocal **technique**, but it can also be caused by specific **voice disorders** or pathologies. The opposite of **hypofunction**.

Hyperion Records. A London-based, independent **classical** music record label particularly noteworthy for its encyclopedic catalog of **art songs**, particularly German *Lieder* and French *mélodies*. The record **company** is most notable for its relationship with **collaborative pianist Graham Johnson**, who has pursued a series of daunting projects for Hyperion, including the complete **songs** of Franz Schubert (1797–1828) on thirty-seven CDs. These recordings are packaged with perhaps the most extensively researched and exhaustive liner notes ever written, and many singers and pianists confess to buying the CDs simply to read the program notes. Johnson has also recorded the complete songs of Robert Schumann

(1810–1856), and he recently began a series on the complete songs of Johannes Brahms (1833–1897). Johnson's recordings of French *mélodies* for the Hyperion label are also impressive, and he has finished projects on the complete recordings of Charles Gounod (1818–1893), Camille Saint-Saëns (1835–1921), Georges Bizet (1838–1875), Emmanuel Chabrier (1841–1894), Gabriel Fauré (1845–1924), Ernest Chausson (1855–1899), Déotat de Séverac (1872–1921), Reynaldo Hahn (1874–1947), and Louis Durey (1888–1979). Other notable pianists who have undertaken projects for Hyperion include Roger Vignoles (b. 1945), who is currently recording the complete songs of Richard Strauss (1864–1949) and Julius Drake (b. 1959), who is doing the same with the complete songs of Franz Liszt (1811–1886).

hypermeter. When the music "feels" as if the **meter** is larger than notated, the performer (either consciously or unconsciously) imposes a broader metrical structure. This phenomenon may be thought of as bar groupings that form their own meter on the hyper level. This often occurs in quick **triple meters**. For example, if each group of four measures constitutes one vocal **phrase**, then the performer is probably singing in a **compound quadruple** hypermeter (as opposed to four measures of a very fast **simple triple** meter). Thus, a **downbeat** is only felt once every four measures as opposed to every measure. Poulenc's "Marc Chagall" from *Le travail du peintre* (1956) is an example of a **song** that is best learned and felt in hypermeter.

Hypodorian. One of the eight **church modes**.

hypofunction. "Underfunctioning." In **voice pedagogy**, this term specifically refers to a hypofunctioning of the **vocal folds**, that is, an underfunctioning vocal mechanism. Vocal hypofunction is marked by low intensity, lack of vibration, and insufficient **glottal** closure. Hypofunction is usually the result of poor or underdeveloped vocal **technique**, but it can also be caused by specific **voice disorders** or pathologies. The opposite of **hyperfunction**.

Hypolydian. One of the eight **church modes**.

Hypomixolydian. One of the eight **church modes**.

Hypophrygian. One of the eight **church modes**.

Hz. Abbreviation for **Hertz**.

I

IA. Abbreviation for **interarytenoid**.

ich-laut **[ç].** In **diction**, a voiceless **palatal fricative** that is an idiomatic hallmark of the German language. *Ich-lauts* [ç] occur when *ch* follows any **vowel** aside from *a*, *o*, and *u*—including *ä*, *ö*, and *ü*—or any **consonant**, whereas *ach-lauts* [χ] simply occur when *ch* follows *a*, *o*, and *u*.

ICVT. Abbreviation for **International Congress of Voice Teachers**.

idiopathic. Describes a disease or disorder that arises from an unknown cause. Some **voice disorders** are classified as idiopathic.

imagery. An imaginative, nonfact-based way of describing **vocal processes**. Many voice teachers—in both historical and contemporary contexts—have used imagery when teaching their students.

imbongi. A performer of *izibongo*.

imitation Mass. See **parody Mass**.

immer **(Ger).** "Always."

implode. To understate an internal or final **consonant** (as one might in speech), omitting **shadow vowels** and thus making the consonant less audible to the audience. It is common for consonants to be imploded in amplified **genres** and such **contemporary commercial music (CCM) styles** as **popular music**, **musical theatre**, and **jazz**. **Exploded** consonants (the opposite of imploded) are more necessary in **acoustic singing**.

imposto **(It).** "Impose." An imprecise Italian term sometimes referenced in *bel canto* **treatises**. Some **voice pedagogues** use the term *imposto* to describe **placement** or refer to a **sympathetic resonance** or feeling in the bridge of the nose.

impresario. The **producer**/financer of a musical event, for instance, an **opera** or opera **company.** Historically important impresarios include Louis Désiré-Véron (1798–1867), director of the Paris Opera, and—to an extent—Richard Wagner (1813–1883), who directed his **opera house** at **Bayreuth**. (Wagner was an unusual impresario in that he was also the composer, **librettist**, and **production** designer.) Most impresarios confine themselves to management and finance. Contemporary impresarios are known simply as producers. In the **genre** of **musical theatre**, **Hal Prince** and **Cameron Mackintosh** are two of the most famous examples.

impressionism. A French artistic movement used to describe a particular musical **style** that flourished during the last decade of the nineteenth century and the first decade of the twentieth century. Claude Debussy (1862–1918) is credited as its founder and—for all practical purposes—is the only significant exponent of the style. Musical impressionism is named after the visual art movement of the same name, which featured the play of light and color in nature. (Claude Monet's painting entitled *Impression, soleil levant* inspired a critic to coin the term in 1874.) Debussy's mature vocal music was written firmly in the impressionistic style. His songs from this period do not feature traditional melodies and instead rely almost exclusively on setting the vocal lines according to the natural **declamation** of the French language. His piano **accompaniments** depict poetic atmospheres through the use of such impressionist compositional **techniques** as planing (parallel fifths and **octaves**), **modes** outside of major and minor, and **whole-tone scales**. Traditional **voice leading** and **harmonic progressions** are virtually ignored. Debussy's **opera** *Pelléas et Mélisande* (1902) utilizes these same techniques, making it the only significant impressionist opera in the international **repertory**. This work is a five-**act** setting of the **symbolist** play by Maurice Maeterlinck (1862–1949), and it originally starred the great Scottish American **soprano** Mary Garden (1874–1967). Impressionism can be contrasted with **expressionism**, a distinctly German artistic movement that focused on humans and subjective (often extreme) emotional content.

improvisation. A piece of music, section of music, or **ornamentation** that is made up spontaneously by the performer and is not part of the written **score**. Improvisation is a salient feature of **jazz** and other **forms** of **popular music**, and many forms of Western **art music** have improvisational elements, for example, **baroque** ornamental flourishes and the **cadenzas** of *bel canto* **operas**.

IMSLP. Abbreviation for **International Music Score Library Project**.

in repertory. Refers to the practice of mounting multiple **operas** or **musicals** in the same house at the same time, shifting between **productions** depending upon the night of the week. The **Metropolitan Opera**, for example, often offers five or six different productions within any given week. Regional houses, however, which may only mount three or four distinct productions per year, do not offer their shows in **repertory**. Rather, one production closes before another opens.

incidental music. Additional music written for a play. Many of the songs of Henry Purcell (1659–1695) were originally conceived as incidental music.

incipit **(Lat).** Beginning. Indicates the short **chant** fragments sung by a soloist immediately before the *Gloria* and *Credo* movements of a **Mass** setting.

incomplete mutation. See **mutational chink**.

indie. Slang for "independent." In **musical theatre** and **popular music**, a term used to describe small, independent record companies. The term can also be applied to a recording that these companies produce.

indirect laryngosopy. See **laryngoscope (laryngosopy)**.

ingénue. A specific **type** in **musical theatre**. Ingénues are almost always young characters in their late teens or early twenties who are involved in romantic relationships or are the object of another leading character's attraction. Ingénues are of secondary importance to the **leading man** and/or **leading woman**. Ingénue characters can be

the principal characters within their own subplot. (Note: In the original French, "ingénue" would be a young woman, as a young man would be spelled "ingénu." But in contemporary English usage, the same spelling is used to label either gender.)

inhalation. The part of the **breath cycle** in which air enters the lungs. The opposite of **exhalation**.

inhaled singing. An **extended technique** that involves singing while inhaling as opposed to exhaling. The result is a sound rooted in **glottal fry**. While some **pitch** variation is possible, the **technique** is limited in scope compared to traditional singing.

injury. See **vocal injury**.

innig **(Ger).** Heartfelt, sincere, or fervent.

inspiration. See **inhalation**.

inspiration (primary muscles of). In the Italian *appoggio* breathing **technique**, there are two primary muscles of inspiration. These include the **external intercostal muscles** and the **diaphragm**. See the anatomical drawings in appendix B.

instrument. Among vocalists and singing teachers, refers to the singer's voice, usually when discussing unique qualities of the voice. For example, if a singer has a "good instrument," it often means that they possess good natural **tone quality**. Or the singer may talk about the capabilities of his or her instrument, assessing its natural qualities or *Fach*.

integrated. Adjective that describes a **musical theatre** work where **songs** grow naturally out of the dramatic action. *Oklahoma!* (1943) was praised as an integrated **musical**, whereas many of the show's predecessors—**musical comedies** of the 1920s and 1930s—were not.

interarytenoid (IA). A muscle of the **larynx** that connects the two **arytenoid cartilages**. The interarytenoid muscle helps to seal the posterior of the **glottis** during **phonation**. The interarytenoid muscles are divided into two parts: transverse (unpaired) and oblique (paired).

intercostal muscles. See **external intercostal muscles**, **internal intercostal muscles**.

intermediate lamina propria. The middle layer of the **lamina propria**.

interlude. An instrumental section of music played between two other things. See also **postlude, prelude**.

intermède. A work performed in between the **acts** of a **French opera** or play, sometimes theatrical and **operatic** in **quality**. Similar in some ways to the Italian *intermezzo*, the French *intermède* developed independently and occurred slightly earlier in opera history. Sometimes refers to an independent, short, lighthearted work, for example, Rousseau's *Le devin du village* (1752).

intermezzo. A short, Italian **comic opera** that was originally written to be performed "in the middle" of a longer, serious **opera** (hence its name). Pergolesi's *La serva padrona* (1733) is a famous example of an *intermezzo*, first performed between the **acts** of Pergolesi's **opera seria**, *Il prigionier superbo* (1733). Many of these *intermezzos* eventually came to be divorced from the original operas that framed them, becoming independent theatrical works in their own right.

internal intercostal muscles. In the Italian *appoggio* breathing **technique**, one of the six primary muscles of expiration. The other five include the **rectus abdominis muscles, external oblique abdominis muscles, internal oblique abdominis muscles, transverse abdominis muscles,** and **quadratus lumborum muscles.**

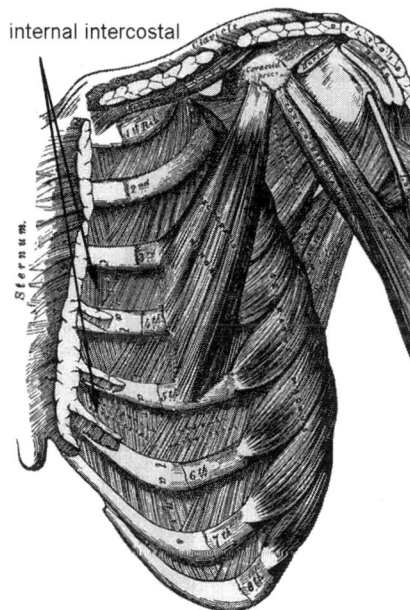

Figure 25. Internal intercostal muscles. *Courtesy Gray's Anatomy,* with labeling by Scott McCoy; reprinted with permission from *Your Voice: An Inside View* (2004).

internal oblique abdominis muscles. In the Italian *appoggio* breathing **technique**, one of the six primary muscles of expiration. The other five include the **rectus abdominis muscles, external oblique abdominis muscles, internal intercostal muscles, transverse abdominis muscles,** and **quadratus lumborum muscles.**

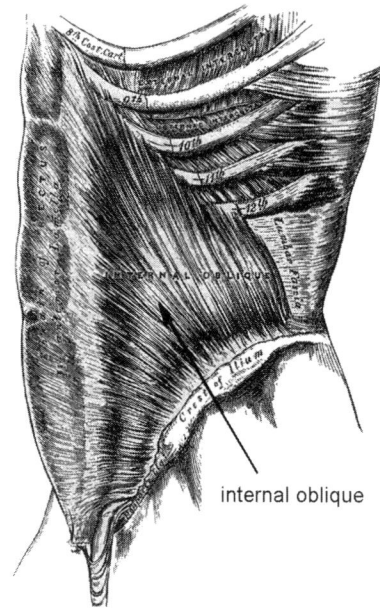

Figure 26. Internal oblique abdominis muscles. *Courtesy Gray's Anatomy,* with labeling by Scott McCoy; reprinted with permission from *Your Voice: An Inside View* (2004).

International Congress of Voice Teachers (ICVT). International conference for **voice pedagogues** usually held only once every four years. The first eight ICVT events were held in Strasbourg, France (1987); Philadelphia, Pennsylvania, United States (1991); Auckland, New Zealand (1994); London, England (1997); Helsinki, Finland (2001); Vancouver, British Columbia, Canada (2005); Paris, France (2009); and Brisbane, Queensland, Australia (2013). The next conference will be held in Stockholm, Sweden (2017).

International Italian School. An inclusive, unofficial international school of **classical voice pedagogy**. Indicative of a mainstream, often **fact-based**, school of **pedagogy** in which **pedagogues** strive for their students to sing with good **posture,** *appoggio,* and an open/free sound. Canonical **opera arias** and **art songs** from the **baroque** through the **romantic** eras comprise the staple **repertoire** of the International Italian School. The Italian adjective primarily refers to the approach to vocal **technique**, and this "Italian" technique is applied to repertoire in languages other than Italian (most typically German, French, and English). For example, although he is an American pedagogue, **Richard Miller's** widely practiced **systematic** approach to voice pedagogy falls squarely into the International Italian School. Miller is also a stalwart advocate of the *appoggio* breathing technique associated with the Italian school and practiced by most North American singers and singing teachers.

International Music Score Library Project (IMSLP). An online **sheet music** archive for music in the **public**

domain. Musicians and musicologists regularly download music from IMSLP free of charge. The website also archives detailed information about composers and **repertoire**, making IMSLP an essential research tool for performers and musicologists.

International Phonetic Alphabet (IPA). An internationally used alphabetic system of phonetic notation primarily based on the **Latin** alphabet. The IPA is the most commonly used phonetic notation system in the world, and it is almost universally used by all linguists, choral **directors**, performers, and teachers of singing. The "international" nature of the IPA system allows it to be universally applied and adapted for all languages and **dialects**. See the charts in appendix A for more details about the IPA.

International Phonetic Association. Established in 1886, in Paris, the International Phonetic Association is the oldest and most well-known organization for phoneticians in the world. Perhaps most relevant to singers and voice teachers, the International Phonetic Association establishes, promotes, and maintains the **International Phonetic Alphabet (IPA)**, the most recent version of which was published in 2005. The International Phonetic Association issues two principal publications, the *Handbook of the International Phonetic Association* (1999) and the *Journal of the International Phonetic Association* (1886–present).

interpolation. An additional **song**—sometimes by a completely different composer—that is added to an **operetta** or **musical**, usually at the request of one of the leading performers. Interpolations were used to showcase particular singers and did nothing whatsoever to advance the **plot**. The practice of interpolating largely fell out of fashion after the early decades of the twentieth century, with the notable exception of Johann Strauss's *Die Fledermaus* (1874), which famously interpolates surprise **numbers** into Act II (sometimes with outside guests who are not even billed in the show).

interpretation. A performer's unique rendition of a musical work. Schubert's *Winterreise*, D911 (1828), for example, has been recorded hundreds of times, but each performer has offered his or her own interpretation by subtly varying **tempi**, dynamics, and other stylistic nuances.

interpretative artist. A musician who "interprets" the creative work of someone else, for instance, the composer. Singers and **conductors** are examples of interpretive artists. In music, the opposite of a **creative artist**.

interval. The distance in **pitch** between two notes.

intervocalic. Refers to a **consonant** that falls between two **vowel** sounds.

intrinsic laryngeal muscles. The muscles that interconnect the cartilages of the **larynx**. The intrinsic laryngeal muscles include the paired thyroarytenoid muscles, the paired **cricothyroid muscles** (categorized as *pars recta* and *pars oblique*), the **lateral cricoarytenoids (LCA)**, the **posterior cricoarytenoids (PCA)**, and the **interarytenoids** (categorized as transverse and oblique). See the anatomical drawings in appendix B.

intonation. How **in-tune** or "well-centered" a singer's **pitches** are. Good intonation is desirable in all **styles**. Beginning students sometimes confuse the definition of intonation with **tone quality**, which instead refers to the beauty or **quality** of sound produced.

introit. One of the five standard parts of the **Proper** in a Catholic **Mass**.

in tune. Descriptive adjective used by musicians to refer to how "centered" **pitches** are. When one sings with good **intonation**, he or she is singing "in-tune." If intonation is not good, then he or she is **"out of tune."**

inversion. A tertian **chord** with either the third, fifth, or—in the case of seventh chords—the seventh on the bottom. A chord with the third on the bottom is in first inversion, a chord with the fifth on the bottom is in second inversion, and a chord with the seventh on the bottom is in third inversion. Chords that are not inverted are in **root position**.

Ionian. A **mode** built on the first **scale degree** of the **major scale**. Thus, Ionian mode is the same as major.

IPA. Abbreviation for the **International Phonetic Alphabet**. Also the abbreviation for the **International Phonetic Association**, but the abbreviation is usually used to refer to the former, not the latter.

IPA transcription. The phonetics of a **song** or **aria** transcribed into the **International Phonetic Alphabet (IPA)** for the singer. Many **classical singers** hand copy IPA transcriptions into their **scores**.

Isla, Camerón de la. See **de la Isla, Camerón**.

isometric. A music theory term encountered in the **medieval repertoire** of music history (see **isorhythm**). Can also refer to a system of body exercises in which one muscle is pitted against another.

isorhythm. A modern term for a compositional **technique** used during the **medieval** era. Isorhythm combines two specific elements: a talea (a repeated rhythmic pattern) and a color (a repeated melody). As the repetitions of the talea and color do not necessary coincide with one another, new and interesting rhythmic juxtapositions emerge. Isorhythm was most memorably used in the **isorhythmic motet**. **Isometric** is a frequently encountered synonym for isorhythmic.

isorhythmic motet. A **medieval** vocal composition that makes use of **isorhythm**.

It+6. Abbreviation for **Italian augmented sixth**.

Italian art song. Piano-accompanied **song genre** that developed in Italy beginning in the nineteenth century. Although the Italian art song appeared as a genre during the same century as the German *Lied* and French *mélodie*, it flourished independently and was not influenced by its cousin genres. In general, the Italian art song emulates the same ideals as *bel canto* **opera**, preferring beautiful, florid melodies and simple **accompaniments**. Text-to-music relationships are not as specific, and piano accompaniments do "paint" the texts in the same way as *Lieder* or *mélodies*. In this respect, these early Italian art songs resemble **Neapolitan songs** in their populist style and folk-like simplicity. Perhaps not unexpectedly, four of the principal composers of these songs also excelled in composing **operas**: Gioacchino Rossini (1792–1868), Gaetano Donizetti (1797–1848), Vincenzo Bellini (1801–1835), and Giuseppe Verdi (1813–1901). The most important Italian art song composers of a younger generation include Paolo Tosti (1846–1916), Ottorino Resphighi (1879–1936), and Stefano Donaudy (1879–1925).

Due in large part to an important collection edited and published by Allessandro Parisotti (1853–1913) entitled *Arie antiche: ad una voce per canto e pianoforte* (1890), many Italian songs and **arias** from the **baroque** and early **classical** eras emerged at the turn of the century and became immensely popular amongst singers. Most of these songs were originally written for **Italian operas**, but the accompaniments were reconceived and romanticized for piano. In New York, the publisher G. Schirmer collected twenty-four of Parisotti's songs and republished them as *24 Italian Songs and Arias* (1894), which became the most frequently owned vocal anthology in American studios. Composers represented in the anthology include Giulio Caccini (c. 1551–1618), Alessandro Scarlatti (1660–1725), and Giovanni Battista Pergolesi (1710–1736). These **romantic** arrangements are frequently appropriated into singers' **repertoires** and are considered by many to be a part of the Italian art song genre.

Italian augmented sixth. See **augmented sixth chord**.

Italian madrigal. A type of **Renaissance madrigal** that was written in Italy and set in Italian texts. The Italian madrigal was succeeded by the **English madrigal**.

Italian opera. Opera composed in the Italian language. Italian opera traces its origins back to the last decade of the sixteenth century and the earliest **monodic** experiments of the **Florentine Camerata**. These operas—by Emilio de' Cavalieri (c. 1550–1602), Giulio Caccini (c. 1551–1618), Jacopo Peri (1561–1633), and others—were dramatic settings of mythological subjects. Claudio Monteverdi (1567–1643) composed the first **operatic masterwork** in this vein with his *Orfeo* (1607). Several decades later, Monteverdi again moved the **genre** forward with *L'incoronazione di Poppea* (1743), the first opera based on a historical (rather than mythological) subject. By the mid-seventeenth century, opera was flourishing in most of the major cities in Italy, which were building **opera houses** to accommodate the new genre. Italian operatic genres—especially the conventions of the *opera seria*—spread internationally, and Italian was considered by many composers to be the proper language for opera, a notion that would persist through the end of the eighteenth century. London became an important center for Italian opera during the late **baroque** period with the works of George Frideric Handel (1685–1759) and Christoph Willibald Gluck (1714–1787), and Wolfgang Amadeus Mozart (1756–1791) continued the Italian opera tradition in Vienna, although Mozart's works were distinctly Viennese in style.

The early nineteenth century was dominated by the *bel canto* Italian operas of Gioacchino Rossini (1792–1868), Gaetano Donizetti (1797–1848), and Vincenzo Bellini (1801–1835), and this tradition was built upon by Giuseppe Verdi (1813–1901), the towering figure of Italian opera during the nineteenth century. Toward the end of the century, *verismo* was introduced in the works of Ruggero Leoncavallo (1857–1919), Pietro Mascagni (1863–1945), and Giacomo Puccini (1858–1924). In addition to the aforementioned composers, Francesco Cavalli (1602–1676), Alessandro Scarlatti (1660–1725), Giovanni Battista Pergolesi (1710–1736), Domenico Cimarosa (1749–1801), Amilcare Ponchielli (1834–1886), Alfredo Catalani (1854–1893), and Umberto Giordano (1867–1948) have also made important contributions to the **canon** of Italian opera.

Italianate Latin. See **church Latin**.

izibongo. Zulu praise poems. *Izibongo*—which means "praises" or "surname" in Zulu—are not religious in nature. Rather, they are sung in deference to one's superiors (in stature, rank, or wealth). *Izibongo* are often performed by an *imbongi*, a professional praise-singer.

J

jácara. In seventeenth-century Spain, a sung *romance* depicting the life of a scoundrel-like character, usually performed between the **acts** of plays. The *jácara* is an antecedent of the *tonadilla*. Some sources also indicate that sacred *jácaras* were also composed around this time, and these works are preserved in selected **polyphonic** manuscripts.

Jackson, Mahalia (1911–1972). American **gospel** singer who is perhaps the most famous gospel singer in history. Born in New Orleans, Jackson later moved to Chicago, where she met Thomas A. Dorsey, commonly referred to as the "Father of Gospel Music." Dorsey mentored her, and Jackson began her touring and recording career shortly thereafter. During the course of her long career, she recorded more than thirty full-length albums and numerous singles, twelve of which earned "gold" status (selling more than 1 million copies). In addition to being a singer, Jackson was also known as a prominent civil rights activist and was a featured performer at the 1963 March on Washington, the site of Dr. Martin Luther King's legendary "I Have a Dream" speech. Jackson is the winner of six **Grammy Awards** and has been featured on a U.S. postal stamp.

Figure 27. Mahalia Jackson at the Prayer Pilgrimage for Freedom in Washington, DC, May 17, 1957. *Courtesy Library of Congress.*

Jackson, Michael (1958–2009). American singer and songwriter widely known as the "King of Pop." Jackson was born in Gary, Indiana, as the eighth of ten children. With four of his brothers—Jackie (b. 1951), Tito (b. 1953), Jermaine (b. 1954), and Marlon (b. 1957)—Michael was a member of the Jackson 5, a successful **soul** and **R&B** group that recorded with Motown beginning in 1968. Jackson began a series of efforts as a solo artist throughout the 1970s, an endeavor that found full fruition with the release of *Off the Wall* (1979), a highly successful album that ultimately sold more than 20 million copies. His next solo album, *Thriller* (1983), became the best-selling album of all time, selling more than 65 million copies and solidifying Jackson as one of the greatest stars in the history of the entertainment industry. Although his career persisted throughout the next two decades, he never regained his soaring popularity of the 1980s. The final years of his career were plagued by a series of scandals and lawsuits, and he suffered cardiac arrest in the summer of 2009.

jali **(pl.** *jalolu***).** A wandering singer of the Manding caste in West Africa, roughly equivalent to the medieval *troubadour*. In French, the *jali* is called a *griot*.

jam. In **jazz**, **rock**, and other **contemporary commercial music (CCM) styles**, a verb meaning to **improvise** in an informal setting.

Jara, Víctor (1934–1973). Chilean singer, particularly famous for his revolutionary **songs**. During the early 1970s, Jarra became world famous for his socially conscious songs, most of which depicted class struggle under the notorious presidency of Salvador Allende (1908–1973). Jarra was later captured, tortured, and killed by the Chilean military, making him an iconic martyr throughout Latin America.

jazz. Distinctly American musical idiom that combines elements of African rhythm and European **harmony**. Jazz was almost exclusively created by African Americans at the beginning of the twentieth century, and it has its roots in **spirituals**, **work songs**, and **field hollers** of former African American slaves. **Blues** is the most significant forerunner of jazz. It forms the basis of most of the **genre's** earliest experiments. Like European **classical** music, jazz went through many movements throughout the course of its comparatively short history. Some of these principal movements include ragtime, classic "New Orleans" jazz, hot jazz, **swing**, bebop, cool, hard bop, *bossa nova*, modal, and free jazz. Contemporary jazz since 1970 has consisted of many different types of **fusion** genres. In addition to the blues, **improvisation** is another essential element of jazz, and virtually all jazz performers improvise regularly regardless of the specific jazz **style** they are performing. Jazz singers have existed since the blues era, and they have been an important part of jazz history since its beginning. Iconic jazz singers from the classic jazz, swing, and bebop eras include **Louis Armstrong**, **Ella Fitzgerald**, Tony Bennett (b. 1926), **Billie Holiday**, **Frank Sinatra**, and Mel Tormé (1925–1999). More contemporary jazz singers include Diana Krall (b. 1964) and Harry Connick Jr. (b. 1967). Unlike instrumentalists, not all jazz singers improvise, but those that do adopt an instrumental-like, **syllabic** language known as **scat**.

jazz rock. A type of **fusion genre** that mixes together elements of **jazz** and **rock**.

jazz standard. See **standard**.

jitter. Voice science term for a short-term fluctuation in **frequency** (**pitch**).

Johnson, Graham (b. 1950). Rhodesian-born, British-based pianist and **collaborative pianist**. Johnson is particularly well-known as a champion of the **art song repertoire**, especially the German *Lied* and French *mélodie*. He studied at the Royal Academy of Music and later privately with **Gerald Moore** and Geoffrey Parsons (1929–1995). In 1976, he founded a project known as the Songmakers Almanac, which is devoted to exploring neglected and underperformed works in the art song **genre**. Johnson has had a long-standing relationship with London's Wigmore Hall, where he has planned numerous festivals and performed hundreds of **concerts**. Although Johnson's principal career has been as a collaborative pianist, he is perhaps even more revered by the singing community for his formidable work as a scholar.

As the chief architect behind an extensive series of recordings for the London-based **Hyperion Records**, he pursued a series of daunting projects, including recording the complete **songs** of Franz Schubert (1797–1828) on thirty-seven CDs. These recordings are packaged with perhaps the most extensively researched and exhaustive

liner notes ever written, and many singers and pianists confess to buying the CDs simply to read the program notes. He has also recorded the complete songs of Robert Schumann (1810–1856) and recently began a series on the complete songs of Johannes Brahms (1833–1897). His recordings of French mélodies for the Hyperion label are also impressive, and Johnson has finished projects on the complete recordings of Charles Gounod (1818–1893), Camille Saint-Saëns (1835–1921), Georges Bizet (1838–1875), Emmanuel Chabrier (1841–1894), Gabriel Fauré (1845–1924), Ernest Chausson (1855–1899), Déotat de Séverac (1872–1921), Reynaldo Hahn (1874–1947), and Louis Durey (1888–1979).

Johnson, Robert (1911–1938). American **blues** singer, songwriter, and guitarist, and one of the most influential blues musicians of all time. Johnson's reputation lay in relative obscurity until 1961, when some of his recordings were reissued on the Columbia label. His fame reached unprecedented heights in 1990, when Sony/Columbia reissued his complete recordings. His poorly documented life and mysterious death at the age of twenty-seven have only increased his iconic and legendary status among blues, **jazz**, and **rock** musicians. A Faustian myth is perpetuated that he sold his soul to the devil in exchange for his musical gifts.

Jolson, Al (1886–1950). Russian American singer and actor. Jolson was born into a Jewish family in the small village of Srednik in present-day Lithuania. When he was five, his family moved to New York City. Raised in New York, Jolson was steeped in music from an early age, both at the synagogue and through the Jewish vaudeville community, with whom he began performing while still in his teens. He became especially well-known for performing

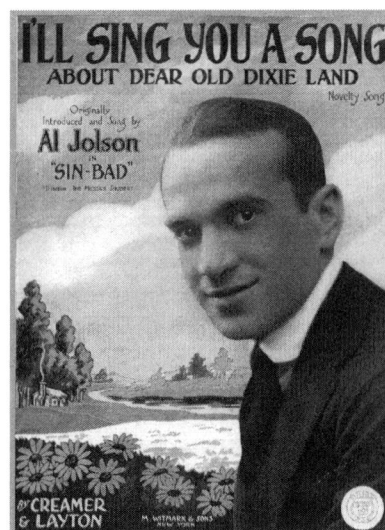

Figure 28. Cover of the sheet music for "I'll Sing You a Song," popularized by Al Jolson.

in blackface and singing **jazz** and **blues**. History remembers Jolson as the star of the 1927 film *The Jazz Singer*, where he sang on-screen in the first nationally distributed talking picture. At the peak of his career, he was the highest-paid professional singer in the United States and was dubbed by many as the "World's Greatest Entertainer."

Jones, Warren (b. 1951). American **collaborative pianist**. Jones earned his **bachelor of music (BM)** from the New England Conservatory and his **master of music (MM)** from the San Francisco Conservatory. During the course of his lauded career, he has accompanied the greatest singers of his day, including **Marilyn Horne**, Håkan Hagegård (b. 1945), Samuel Ramey (b. 1942), **Kathleen Battle**, Bo Skovus (b. 1962), and Kiri Te Kanawa (b. 1944). Known for his sensitive playing and the pianistic **colors** he brings to music, Jones is also an avid **chamber music** performer and a champion of **new music**. For ten years, he was an assistant **conductor** at the **Metropolitan Opera**.

jongleur. A wandering French street musician during the **medieval** era.

jota. A fast, **triple-meter genre** of **song** and **dance** originating from Northern Spain. A quintessential form of Spanish **folk music**, the *jota* has profoundly influenced the Spanish **art song** genre. Many of these songs can authentically be called *jotas*. See also *habanera, seguidilla*.

jubilus. The **melisma** sung on the final syllable of the word *alleluia* in **Gregorian chant**; the term may also refer more generically to **melismatic vocalization**. Also called a *neuma*.

jukebox musical. Also called a **catalog show** or anthology **musical**, the jukebox musical is a contemporary **revue** that features the greatest hits of a single artist or musical group. Essentially a string of well-known **songs**, a loose (and usually thin) **plot** strings the tunes together into a sort of cohesive narrative. The **genre** appropriately derives its name from the fact that the original artist's legacy exists through recorded singles (as one would hear on a jukebox) as opposed to written-down compositions.

Well-known examples of the jukebox musical include *Mamma Mia!* (1999/2001, ABBA), *All Shook Up* (2004, Elvis Presley), *Movin' Out* (2002, Billy Joel), and *Lennon* (2005, John Lennon). *Rock of Ages* (2009) represents an interesting twist on the genre, congealing some of the most famous **rock** songs of the 1980s from a variety of solo artists and **heavy metal** groups.

jugendlich-dramatischer Sopran. In the **Kloiber Fach System**, a type of **soprano** that is powerful and young. A *jugendlich-dramatischer Sopran* (literally translating to "young **dramatic** soprano") is somewhat heavier than the *lyrischer Sopran*, but not quite as heavy as the *dramatischer Sopran*. It is roughly equivalent to what many English-speaking singers and voice teachers would call a **lyric-*spinto*** soprano. Examples of *jugendlich-dramatischer Sopran* **roles** are Elsa in Wagner's *Lohengrin* (1850), Mimì in Puccini's *La bohème* (1896), Jenůfa in Janácek's *Jenůfa* (1904), and Marie in Berg's *Wozzeck* (1922). See the *Fach* chart in appendix C.

jugendlicher Heldentenor. In the **Kloiber Fach System**, a type of **tenor** that is powerful and young. A *jugendlicher Heldentenor* (literally translating to "young heroic tenor") is somewhat heavier than the *lyrischer Tenor*, but not quite as heavy as the *Heldentenor*. It is roughly equivalent to what many English-speaking singers and voice teachers would call a **lyric** *Heldentenor* or young *Heldentenor*. Examples of *jugendlicher Heldentenor* **roles** are Raoul in Meyerbeer's *Les Hugenots* (1836), Samson in Saint-Saëns's *Samson et Dalila* (1877), Rudolfo in Puccini's *La bohème* (1896), and Palestrina in Pfitzner's *Palestrina* (1917). See the *Fach* chart in appendix C.

just intonation. Also called "true" or "pure" **intonation**, just intonation refers to a nontempered tuning system that aligns itself with the natural **harmonics** found in nature. Ratios as outlined by Pythagoras (570–495 BCE)—"acoustically pure" ones—are retained. Thus, to a musician, just intonation is, in a sense, the opposite of **equal temperament**. **Unaccompanied choirs** and string sections of orchestras tune their fifths according to just intonation, thus achieving a greater harmonic spectrum and richer overtones.

K

kabuki. A highly influential and world-renowned **genre** of Japanese **musical theatre**, standing alongside *Noh* and *bunraku*. Out of these three, *kabuki* is the most well-known outside of Japan, and many Western scholars and performers have been fascinated with the genre. *Kabuki* was developed during the late seventeenth and early eighteenth centuries in Edo (now Tokyo). There is considerably more movement and visual **spectacle** in *kabuki* than in other **forms** of Japanese musical theatre. The singing **style** in kabuki theatre is distinctly non-Western in nature, with a bright **timbre** and absence of warmth and **vibrato**. Closely following the **declamation** of the language, there is a similarity between the kabuki vocal style and *Sprechstimme.*

Kahn, Nusrat Fateh Ali (1948–1997). Pakistani singer specializing in performance of the *qawwali* **genre**. Kahn was born in Lyallpur, Pakistan, and gave his first public performance at the age of sixteen. His reputation quickly spread beyond Pakistan when he began recording for the British label Oriental Star Agencies. He made **professional** appearances in more than forty different countries. Kahn gained worldwide exposure when his music was featured predominantly in Martin Scorsese's controversial film *The Last Temptation of Christ* (1988).

Kamakawiwo'ole, Israel (1959–1997). Hawaiian singer. Kamakawiwo'ole was born in Honolulu and began performing while still in his teens, quickly gaining a Hawaiian reputation that eventually spread throughout the continental United States. In addition to his singing, Kamakawiwo'ole is famous for his ukulele playing and the incorporation of **reggae** and **jazz** into his compositions. His most famous **song** is his "Somewhere over the Rainbow/What a Wonderful World" **medley**, which was released in 1993. He died at the age of thirty-eight due to health complications brought on by severe obesity.

Kantorei. The singers and instrumentalists in a German cathedral, chapel, or court.

Kapellmeister **(Ger).** Chapel master. The principal musician in a German cathedral, chapel, or court.

Katz, Martin (b. 1945). American pianist and vocal coach. During the past forty years, Katz collaborated with some of the world's greatest singers, including **Marilyn Horne**, Frederica von Stade (b. 1945), **Kathleen Battle**, David Daniels (b. 1966), Karita Mattila (b. 1960), and José Carreras (b. 1946). In 2003, he founded SongFest in Los Angeles, a festival devoted to the championing of **art song** and the encouragement of young singers. Katz has taught at the University of Michigan for more than twenty years, and, in 2009, he released his first book, *The Complete Collaborator.*

Kavalierbariton. A category in the **Kloiber Fach System** that characterizes a **lyric baritone** (or *lyrischer Bariton*) with a **dramatic edge**. The *Kavalierbariton* is considered to be heavier than the *lyrischer Bariton*, but lighter than the *Heldenbariton*. Examples of the *Kavalierbariton* include Count Almaviva in Mozart's *Le nozze di Figaro* (1786), the title **role** in Mozart's *Don Giovanni* (1787), Escamillo in Bizet's *Carmen*, Ford in Verdi's *Falstaff* (1893), and the title role in Adams's *Nixon in China* (1987). See the *Fach* chart in appendix C.

Keita, Salif (b. 1949). Malian singer. Keita was born in the village of Djoliba. At an early age, he was cast out of his family due to his albinism. He began performing at an early age and eventually moved to Paris to pursue a musical career. Keita's music represents a **fusion** of West African **styles** with Western **popular music**. His stature as the greatest singer in Mali's history is especially noteworthy due to the fact that Mali's rigid caste system forbade him from becoming a **professional** singer. Now a seasoned artist of international acclaim, Keita has been dubbed the "Golden Voice of Africa."

key. One of the most basic of all music theory concepts, keys specifically describe the 24 **major** and **minor modes** within **tonal music**. **Key signatures** in **scores**—containing anywhere from zero to seven sharps or flats—indicate the key to the performers. While traditionally it has been heresy in **opera** to change the key of an **aria** (thus making the aria "easier" with respect to certain high notes, etc.), it us quite commonplace to adapt the keys of **songs** in **Broadway musicals** to better suit the voices of specific performers. Likewise, **art songs** are often published and performed in a variety of keys, regardless of the key that was originally sanctioned by the composer.

key signature. Sharps or flats printed at the beginning of a line of music that indicate the **key** of a composition.

Khaled (b. 1960). Algerian singer known as the "King of *Raï*." Born in Oran, Khaled began performing and recording while still in his teens. His **reedy** vocal **style** is both expressive and **dramatic**. Khaled is no stranger to controversy and is an outspoken critic of the beliefs and practices of fundamentalist Muslims. He is the most internationally famous singer from the Arab-speaking world. Khaled is the master of the *raï* **genre**, the name of which means "opinion" in Arabic.

khoomei. See **Tuvan throat singing**.

khyal. Popular **song form** in north Indian (Hindustani) **classical** tradition. *Khyals* are similar to *thumri* in **style** and form, but they have significantly less **improvisation**. Sometimes spelled "*khayal*" or "*kheyal*."

kinesthetic. A learning **style** that refers to learning by physical engagement. Although it incorporates other learning styles as well—for example, auditory, visual, reading, and writing—singing is an activity that involves a certain amount of kinesthetic learning.

kirtan. A Bengali folk song in **call-and-response form**. Sung as a part of Bhakti devotional traditions in India.

Klein, Herman (1856–1934). English music critic, author, and **voice pedagogue**. Klein studied singing with **Manuel García** (1805–1906); taught at the Guildhall School of Music, London; and was the first chairman of the **National Association of Teachers of Singing (NATS)** (the organization that later became the **New York Singing Teachers Association [NYSTA]**) in New York. The book *Herman Klein and the Gramophone* (1990) contains Klein's criticism of singing and early recording

technology, as well as the essay "The *Bel Canto*: With Particular Reference to the Singing of Mozart" (1923), which articulates many of García's principles.

klezmer. A type of **world music** closely associated with the Jews of Eastern Europe. Although the klezmer **style** dates back to the fifteenth century, it was not given its current label until the early part of the twentieth century. Klezmer's distinctive sound derives from its own unique set of **modes**, combined with characteristic, folk-like **dance** rhythms. Historically an instrumental **genre**—the violin and clarinet are frequently heard—Klezmer vocalists are becoming more and more common, often weaving traditional Yiddish songs into the instrumental fabric.

Kloiber Fach System. The **German Fach System** that is named after its inventor, Rudolf Kloiber (1899–1973). See also *Fach*.

kokett **(Ger).** Coquettish or flirtatious.

koloratur-Mezzosopran. A category in the **Kloiber Fach System** that literally translates as "**coloratura mezzosoprano**." The *koloratur-Mezzosopran* is the highest mezzo-soprano *Fach*, positioned one spot lower on the chart than the *Charaktersopran* and one spot higher than the *lyrischer Mezzosopran*. A smaller *Fach* category, examples of *koloratur-Mezzosopran* **roles** include the title role in Handel's *Rinaldo* (1711) and several roles by Gioacchino Rossini (1792–1868), including Isabella in *L'italiana in Algeri* (1813), Rosina in *Il barbiere di Siviglia* (1816), Angelina in *La centerentola* (1817), and the title role in *Tancredi* (1813). See the *Fach* chart in appendix C.

Konzertmusik **(Ger).** See **concert music**.

Koopman, Ton (b. 1944). Dutch choral **conductor**. Koopman was born in Zwolle, Overijssel, the Netherlands, and later studied organ and harpsichord at the Sweelinck Conservatory and musicology at the University of Amsterdam. He quickly earned a reputation as a prodigious talent and won many awards as a student musician. From 1978–1988, he was professor of harpsichord at the Sweelinck Conservatory and, in 1988, was appointed professor of harpsichord at the conservatory in The Hague. In 1979, Koopman founded the Amsterdam Baroque Orchestra, and, in 1992, he founded the Amsterdam Baroque Choir. Shortly after his establishment of this choral **ensemble**, he embarked on an ambitious project to record the complete **cantatas** of Johann Sebastian Bach (1685–1750), a venture that was completed in 2005. That same year, he began a second daunting pursuit, aspiring to record the complete choral works of Dietrich Buxtehude (1637–1707). Koopman is the darling of the **early music** community, championing **historically informed performance practice (HIPP)** in his live performances and recordings. Koopman's all-**professional** ensembles are small, streamlined forces that play entirely on period instruments at **baroque pitch** level (**A=415**). His cerebral singers ably execute deft **ornamentation**, **straight-tone** singing, and informed period **diction**. Also an accomplished organist, Koopman has recorded extensively as an organ soloist. Completed projects include the complete organ works of Bach and Buxtehude.

Koranic chant. See **Qur'anic chant**.

kräftig **(Ger).** Strong or energetic.

kriti. South Indian Carnatic Hindu praise music. *Kritis* are sung in Teluga, Tamil, or Sanskrit and usually accompanied by a mridangam (a wooden, double-headed drum) or tambura (a long-necked string instrument).

Kulthum, Umm (1904–1975). Egyptian singer and arguably the most famous Middle Eastern singer of all time. Kulthum was born in a rural village in the Nile Delta, in Egypt, and began singing at an early age, being taught by her father to **chant** the Qur'an (see **Qur'anic chant**). She was vaulted into fame during the 1930s due to the support of Arabic radio stations and by earning the respect of famous Arabic instrumentalists, who were enthusiastic to collaborate with her. At the peak of her career, she achieved almost goddess-like stature in the Arabic world, with millions tuning into her weekly Thursday-night live broadcasts. Like many other famous popular singers of the twentieth century, Kulthum was also known as an actress, appearing in several films. In addition to her distinctive vocal **style**, which was characterized by **virtuosic riffs** and other **improvisations**, Kulthum also was famous for her expressive use of a handkerchief and tendency to collapse at the end of a performance—fully spent—before being carried off the stage.

While the Western spelling of her name varies widely, "Umm Kulthum" has become standardized in scholarship through the seminal work of Virginia Danielson (b. 1949), author of *The Voice of Egypt: Umm Kulthum, Arabic Song, and Egyptian Society in the Twentieth Century* (1997). In this book, Danielson highlights Kulthum's eminence and influence: "Imagine a singer with the virtuosity of Joan Sutherland or Ella Fitzgerald, the public persona of Eleanor Roosevelt and the audience of Elvis Presley, and you have Umm Kulthum, the most accomplished singer of her century in the Arab World."

Kunstlied **(Ger).** Art song.

Kyrie. One of the five standard parts of the **Ordinary** in a Catholic **Mass**.

L

La Scala. Italian **opera house** in Milan, Italy, and one of the most famous opera houses in the world. Audiences at La Scala are (in)famous for their enthusiasm and candor: no cheers—or boos—in the world are more wild and raucous. Although officially named the Teatro alla Scala, the opera house is known throughout the world as simply "La Scala."

Figure 29. Teatro alla Scala (La Scala), Milan, Italy. *Courtesy Creative Commons.*

labiodental. In the study of **diction**, a **point of articulation** for **consonants** that involves the lower lip and upper row of teeth. Common examples of labiodental consonants include [v], [f], and [pf]. See also **alveolar**, **bilabial**, **dental**, **palatal**, **prepalatal**, **velar**.

laboratory. A workspace for the **vocologist** or **voice pedagogue** that utilizes some sort of scientific technology or equipment for data collection related to singing. Many laboratories make use of scientific measurements, for instance, those calculated by **VoceVista** and other **professional** voice software or scientific equipment. Sometimes abbreviated as "lab."

lai. A **monophonic secular song** of the **medieval** era. One of the *formes fixes*. The musical **form** was AA, BB, CC, and so forth—one melody for every two lines of poetry— similar to the **sequence**. The melody is repeated for the second line of each pair. The poetry was often about the Virgin Mary. *Lais* were sung by the *trouvères* and *Minnesingers*. Also spelled *lay*. See also *ballade*, *rondeaux*, *virelai*.

Laine, Cleo (b. 1927). English **jazz** singer and actress known for her exceptional **range** and **virtuosic scat** singing. A prolific recording artist, Laine's discography ranks among the most extensive of all jazz vocalists. She is widely regarded as one of the best jazz vocalists of all time, standing alongside such names as **Ella Fitzgerald**, **Billie Holiday**, Carmen McRae (1920–1994), and Sarah Vaughan (1924–1990). Laine has appeared on **Broadway** and won a **Grammy Award** in 1983. She was also honored with the Order of the British Empire (OBE) in 1979 and knighted (DBE) in 1997.

lamentations. Choral settings of **verses** from the *Lamentations of Jeremiah*. Each verse begins with letters of the Hebrew alphabet, which are presented in alphabetical order: Alpeh, Beth, Gimel, Daleth, etc. Usually performed during Holy Week in **liturgical** services.

lamina propria. A layer of the **vocal fold** body located in between the **stratified squamous epithelium** and the thyroarytenoid muscle. The lamina propria is divided into three layers: the **superficial lamina propria**, **intermediate lamina propria**, and **deep lamina propria**.

LaMott, Nancy (1951–1995). American **cabaret singer** based in New York City. Through a longtime friendship with composer and pianist David Friedman (b. 1950), LaMott recorded six albums that achieved cult status within the **cabaret** industry. These albums include *Beautiful Baby* (1991), *Come Rain or Come Shine* (1992), *My Foolish Heart* (1993), *Just in Time for Christmas*

(1994), *Listen to My Heart* (1995), and *What's Good about Goodbye?* (1996). Friedman later collected many of his **songs** (most of which were recorded by LaMott) in an **Off-Broadway catalog show** entitled *Listen to My Heart: The Songs of David Friedman* (2003). LaMott died of uterine cancer when she was only forty-four years old. Since her untimely death, her stature has grown significantly amongst New York City cabaret artists.

Lamperti, Giovanni Battista (1839–1910). Italian singing teacher and son of **voice pedagogue** Francesco Lamperti (1811–1892). Along with the younger **Manuel García** (1805–1906), Lamperti is one of the only historically important voice pedagogues who still exerts tremendous influence on contemporary voice teachers. Lamperti only published one book, *The Technics of Bel Canto* (1905), but his work is widely known through *Vocal Wisdom: Maxims of Giovanni Battista Lamperti* (1931), a collection of pedagogical maxims and advice compiled from the notebooks of one of his students, William Earl Brown (1863–1945). Although Lamperti is frequently associated with the younger García, each had a distinct philosophical approach to the art of singing. García's **pedagogy** tended to be scientific and progressive and research-based in nature, whereas the Lamperti School represented one of the last blasts of old-school empiricism.

langsam, langsamer **(Ger).** Slow, slower.

languages. See **diction**.

largamente **(It).** Broadly.

larghetto **(It).** A little slow. Usually slightly faster than *largo*, but slower than *adagio*.

largo **(It).** Very slow. The slowest of the commonly used Italian **tempo** markings, slower than *larghetto* or *adagio*.

laryngeal. Adjective that means "pertaining to the **larynx**."

laryngeal tube. Section of the **vocal tract** that contains the **larynx**.

laryngeal vestibule. The portion of the cavity of the **larynx** that is above the **vocal folds**. The **false vocal folds** are located in the laryngeal vestibule.

laryngeal web. A **voice disorder** that results in a web-like spread across the **glottis** between the **vocal folds**. Laryngeal webs can be of two types: **congenital laryngeal webs** (developed embryonically) or **acquired laryngeal webs** (brought about through trauma or infection). Webs can usually be resolved through surgery, **voice therapy**, and **vocal rest**.

laryngitis. A type of **voice disorder** that involves the swelling and irritation of the **larynx**, often resulting in voice impairment or loss. The causes of laryngitis are wide-ranging, and the disorder can be categorized into four basic types: **acute laryngitis**, **chronic laryngitis**, **traumatic laryngitis**, and **fungal laryngitis**.

laryngologist. An **otolaryngologist (ENT)** who receives further training, specializing in disorders of the voice, airway, and swallowing. Laryngologists are qualified to perform **phonosurgery**, a surgical procedure aimed at improving the voice.

laryngopharyngeal reflux disease (LPRD). One of the two major types of reflux disease (along with **gastroesophageal reflux disease [GERD]**), LPRD (or sometimes labeled as simply LPR) is **acid reflux** that involves the **larynx**. LPRD is caused by gastric acid migrating into the esophagus and spilling out onto the **vocal folds**. LPRD can be controlled by over-the-counter medicines, as well as dietary choices and the avoidance of eating within a certain time frame (usually two to three hours) before sleeping.

laryngopharynx. Another name for the **pharynx**.

laryngoscope (laryngoscopy). An instrument used by an **otolaryngologist (ENT)** or **speech-language pathologist (SLP)** that allows the clinician to view the **vocal folds** of the client. The laryngoscope can either be used through direct laryngoscopy (inserted into the mouth of the client) or indirect laryngoscopy (via a fiber-optic scope through the nose, for example). The laryngoscope was first used in 1854, when **Manuel García** (1805–1906) became the first man to use a laryngoscope to view the functioning **glottis** and **larynx** of a human. In the twenty-first century, most ENTs and SLPs use **video laryngoscopes**.

larynx (pl. larynges). The part of the human body that houses the **vocal folds**. For this reason, the larynx is colloquially referred to as the voice box. The larynx is comprised of three principal cartilages: the **cricoid**, the **thyroid**, and the two **arytenoids**. These cartilages protect the two vocal folds, which serve as the vibration **source** in singing. The larynx is often mispronounced as "larnyx," and the young singer should make an early effort to ensure a correct **pronunciation** of this vital area of vocal anatomy.

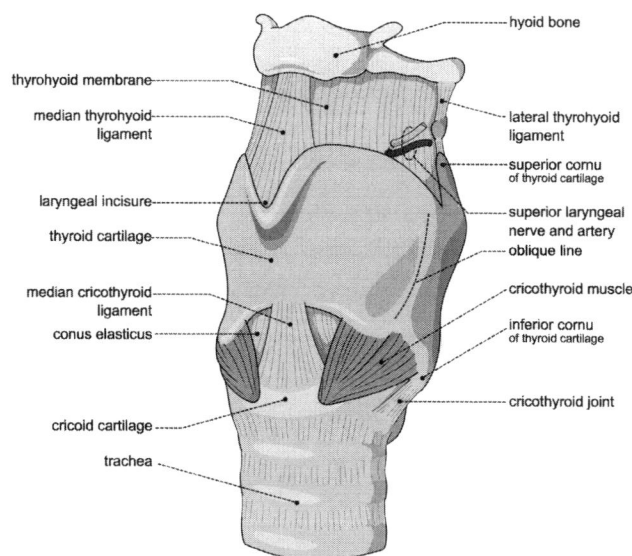

Figure 30. Anatomical drawing of the human larynx. *Courtesy Creative Commons.*

lateral. In the study of **diction**, describes a **manner of articulation** in which **consonants** are produced by directing **vocalized tone** over the sides of the tongue. Common examples of lateral consonants include [l] and [ʎ]. See also **affricate, fricative, nasal, plosive.**

lateral cricoarytenoids (LCA). One of the two types of paired **cricoarytenoid muscles**. The lateral cricoarytenoids function as **vocal fold** adductors.

Latin. A fundamental language in singing. As Latin was the language of the early Christian church (and thus the language of **Gregorian chant**), more **choral music** sets Latin texts than perhaps any other language. The aspiring singer will need proficiency in pronouncing Latin in all of its variants. See also **church Latin, Germanic Latin.**

Latin American art song. While Spanish-language **art song** performance has traditionally focused on the literature from the country of Spain, recent inroads have been made to explore the **repertoires** of Latin America. This repertoire is generally settings of Portuguese and Spanish texts. **Standard American Spanish (SAS) pronunciation** is applied to the **songs** in Spanish, with subtle variations existing between different countries and cultures. The most important composers of Latin American art song include Albert Ginastera (1916–1983), Carlos Guastavino (1912–2000), Francisco Ernani Braga (1868–1945), and Heitor Villa-Lobos (1887–1959). Many other composers also contribute to this vast repertoire.

lauda. A nonliturgical Italian religious **song**. *Laudas* originated during the **medieval** era, and examples can still be found dating from the mid-nineteenth century.

laudate psalms. The last three psalms of the **psalter**: 148 (*Laudate Dominum de caelis*), 149 (*Cantate Domino*), and 150 (*Laudate Dominum in sanctis ejus*).

lay. Alternate spelling for *lai.*

LCA. Abbreviation for **lateral cricoarytenoids**.

leading man/woman. A specific **type** in **musical theatre**. A leading man or woman is usually a principal character—usually neither old nor young—who is depicted as being a strong protagonist. In the **classic Broadway** tradition, leading men and women generally sing in a more **legit style** than the actors in supporting character **roles**.

leading motive. See *leitmotif.*

leading tone. In **tonal music**, the seventh **scale degree**. In both **major keys** and **minor keys**, leading tones are always one **half step** below the **tonic**.

lebendig **(Ger).** Brisk, lively. Synonym of *lebhaft.*

lebhaft **(Ger).** Brisk, lively. Synonym of *lebendig.*

Lee Silverman Voice Treatment (LSVT). A systematic treatment for **voice disorders** that develop in clients who suffer from Parkinson's disease. LSVT can also be used with individuals who suffer from stroke, multiple sclerosis, cerebral palsy, and Down syndrome.

legato. An essential aspect of **classical** vocal **technique**, legato describes the constant quest for the singer to strive for a seamless, well-supported, and **resonant** vocal line. The singer and voice teacher pursue this ideal primarily through breath control, optimal **acoustic** space, and tension release. While **consonants** necessarily interrupt the vocal line, the singer strives to make them as unobtrusive as possible, often compromising **diction** (especially in higher passages) in an effort to preserve the integrity of the legato. One of the reasons that Italian is often thought of as the perfect language for **opera**—and singing in general is due to the natural legato inherent in the Italian language: Italian **vowels** are optimal for singer's resonance, there are no **glottal attacks**, and Italian consonants do not interrupt the flow of language as they do in nonlegato languages (like English and German). When a singer does encounter a nonlegato language, he or she must make every effort to sing legato in spite of the challenges presented by the text. A seamless legato will also help to enhance **singer's resonance** and unlock the full projection potential of the voice.

While solo **classical singers** almost always strive for legato at all times, legato is often undesirable in choral singing, which depends more on a seamless blend and crisper, shorter delineation in faster articulated passages. Resonance in choral **ensembles** is achieved through blend, **intonation**, and perfect tuning of the overtones. A legato voice—in the classical, *bel canto* sense—would be likely to stick out in a choral ensemble.

légère, légèrement **(Fr).** Lightly or nimbly.

leggiero **(It).** Light or agile. Sometimes used as an adjective to describe voices that are particularly flexible and capable of clean **coloratura**. A *leggiero* **tenor**, for instance, might sing the **role** of Almaviva in Rossini's *Il barbiere di Siviglia* (1816).

legit. In **musical theatre**, to sing "legit" means to sing in a **classical style**. This word can also be used as an adjective. In many works of classic **Broadway**, **leading men** and **leading women** and **ingénues** were often the "legit" singers, whereas supporting **roles** (for example, **character actors and actresses**) were the "nonlegit" singers.

Lehmann, Lilli (1848–1929). German **soprano** and **voice pedagogue**. Lehmann was born into a musical family in Würzburg. Both of her parents were **opera** singers, and she was exposed to the **operatic repertoire** from an early age. Lehmann made her **professional** debut in Berlin in 1870, and she was soon performing Wagnerian **roles** in Bayreuth, London, and New York. She was particularly well-known for her portrayals of Isolde in *Tristan und Isolde* (1865) and Brünnhilde in *Der Ring des Nibelungen* (1876), but she was also famous for singing the title role in Bellini's *Norma* (1831). Lehmann founded the International Summer Academy at the Mozarteum in Salzburg in 1916. Today, she is perhaps best remembered for her pedagogical **treatise**, which is boldly entitled *How to Sing* (1902).

Leich. German name for *lai*.

leicht **(Ger).** Light or nimble.

Leidenschaftlich **(Ger).** Passionately.

leiser **(Ger).** More gently.

leitmotif. A musical device brought to its most extensive and characteristic use by Richard Wagner (1813–1883) and used in his **music dramas**. *Leitmotifs* are short musical **motives** that represent a specific character, object, emotion, action, or place. Many *leitmotifs* can be combined contrapuntally and simultaneously within a musical **score**, thus making the score itself a programmatic depiction of the dramatic action occurring on the stage.

lent **(Fr).** Slow.

lento **(It).** Slow.

lesions and masses (of the vocal fold). A broad category of **voice disorders** that includes **vascular ectasias**, **vocal fold hemorrhages**, polyps, **nodules**, **vocal fold cysts**, **contact ulcers**, and **granulomas**. See individual entries for more information about each of these disorders.

Lessac-Madsen Resonant Voice Therapy (LMRVT). A kind of **voice therapy** conceived, developed, and implemented by Katerine Verdolini (b. 1952). LMRVT is a holistic, evidence-based approach that presents a systematic way to therapeutically resolve certain kinds of **hyperfunctional** and **hypofunctional voice disorders**. LMRVT is especially popular in the **theatre** community among teachers of acting.

lesson. A one-on-one private session with a voice teacher, usually focusing on one or more aspects of vocal **technique**. A public voice lesson with outside observers is usually referred to as a **master class**.

Levine, James (b. 1943). American **conductor** and pianist best known for his long tenure as **musical director** and principal conductor of the **Metropolitan Opera** in New York City. Levine was born in Cincinnati, Ohio, to a musical family. He excelled at the piano, performing a concerto with the Cincinnati Symphony Orchestra at the age of ten. During the 1960s, he became the assistant conductor of the Cleveland Orchestra under George Szell (1897–1970) before venturing into the **operatic repertory**. He made his debut at the Metropolitan Opera in 1971, and became its principal conductor in 1973. Under his leadership, the Metropolitan Opera orchestra grew in stature and is now regarded as one of the finest orchestras in the world. In addition to **opera**, Levine also has extensive experience conducting the orchestral repertoire, with many guest appearances worldwide. He served as the musical director of the Boston Symphony Orchestra from 2004–2011.

Liber Usualis. A 1,900-page book of **Gregorian chants** intended for use in **liturgical** worship. The *Liber Usualis* is a comprehensive collection and the most widely used anthology of **chant** in common use. The book was compiled by the monks of the Abbey of Solesmes in France in 1896, and it has been revised in numerous editions. The *Liber Usualis* utilizes **neumatic** notation on a **four-line staff**. All chants are organized by season and liturgical service.

librettist. The person who writes the **libretto** of an **opera** or **operetta**.

libretto (pl. libretti). The written words of an **opera**. Called a **book** in **musical theatre**.

lick. In **rock** and **pop** music, a short vocal **improvisation**. The term *lick* is sometimes used interchangeably with **riff**, although riffs tend to be longer than licks.

Lied* (pl. *Lieder*).** Name given to a German **art song**. The **genre** as a whole is known as ***Lieder, which is the plural of *Lied* (meaning "**songs**"). *Lied* can also refer to any German-language song regardless of the nationality of the composer. Of all the art song languages, the *Lied* genre is probably the vastest. There are literally thousands of *Lieder*, many of which were written by some of the greatest composers of all time. The *Lied* genre is closely linked with the advent of **German Romanticism** and the flowering of German Romantic poetry. This proliferation of **romantic** literature occurred at the same time as the rise in popularity of the newly invented piano, which made the early nineteenth century ripe for *Lieder* composition. Composers were attracted to the small-scale nature of the genre and expressive possibilities offered by the combination of human voice and the piano.

Important pioneers of the German *Lied* genre include Johann Friedrich Reichardt (1752–1814), Johann Rudolf Zumsteeg (1760–1802), and Carl Friedrich Zelter (1758–1832). These early experiments were basically **strophic** in **style**, with a simple **accompaniment** (intended for **amateur** performance) and little real text-to-music relationships. The *Lieder* of Franz Schubert (1797–1828) marked a major step forward in compositional style, with the use of varied **forms** (strophic, modified strophic, **scenic**, and **through-composed**) and a true synthesis of poetry and music. In Schubert's *Lieder*, the piano accompaniment played a significant **role** in text painting, and many of the piano parts were **virtuosic** in difficulty. Schubert wrote more than 600 songs and is considered by many to be the "Father of the German Lied." Ludwig van Beethoven (1770–1827) and Carl Loewe (1796–1869) also composed some important *Lieder*, and Robert Schumann (1810–1856), Johannes Brahms (1833–1897), Hugo Wolf (1860–1903), and Richard Strauss (1864–1949) made significant contributions to the genre throughout the remainder of the nineteenth century. The orchestrated *Lieder* of Gustav Mahler (1860–1911) also comprise an important corner of the **repertory**. Twentieth-century *Lieder* were written by Hans Pfitzner (1869–1949), Arnold Schoenberg (1874–1951), Alban Berg (1885–1935), and others.

Liederabend* (pl. *Liederabende*).** An evening of **art song** in an intimate venue, usually the living room or parlor of a private home. While the name *Liederabend* implies that only German art songs are performed, contemporary *Liederabende*—if they occur—may program art songs in multiple languages. Franz Schubert (1797–1828) was famous for hosting *Liederabende* to introduce his newly written **songs**. These evenings were also known as ***Schubertiads, and the **barito**ne Johann Michael Vogl (1768–1840) was the most famous performer who attended these events.

***Liederbuch* (pl. *Liederbücher*).** A German word literally meaning "songbook." *Lied* composers applied this label to specific **song collections** that they composed. The two most famous *Liederbücher* in the **repertory** are the *Spanisches Liederbuch* (1889) and the *Italienisches Liederbuch* (1996), both by Hugo Wolf (1860–1903). Interestingly, although their titles translate as "Spanish Songbook" and "Italian Songbook," respectively, they are settings of German translations of Spanish and Italian poetry. A *Liederbuch* is different than a **song cycle** in that it is a collection of individual **songs** as opposed to a group of songs with a single unifying feature, for instance, a narrative or poetic theme. In theory, one can sing excerpts from a *Liederbuch* more easily than a song cycle. In practice, however, the line between a song collection and a song cycle can become somewhat blurred and controversial.

***Liederkreis*.** A German term meaning **song cycle**. Robert Schumann (1810–1856) is generally credited with coining the term, as he specifically gave two of his song cycles the title "*Liederkreis*": Op. 24 (1840) and Op. 39 (1840), respectively; however, while Schumann made progressive leaps in the development of the **genre**, the *Liederkreis* has important predecessors, with Beethoven's *An die ferne Geliebte*, Op. 98 (1816) and Schubert's two narrative song cycles, *Die schöne Müllerin*, D795 (1823) and *Winterreise*, D911 (1828). Johannes Brahms (1833–1897) and Richard Strauss (1864–1949) also made significant contributions to the genre.

light lyric. See **lyric**.

light mechanism. Subjective term used by **voice pedagogues** that can either refer to an **underengaged (undersupported)** sound or a **tone quality** that is predominantly produced via **cricothryroid** activity.

Lind, Jenny (1820–1887). Swedish **opera** singer often referred to as the "Swedish Nightingale." Lind was one of the most popular singers of the nineteenth century, with a successful career in Europe. In 1850, she toured the United States, which secured her worldwide fame and legacy. She was one of the most famous pupils of the younger **Manuel García** (1805–1906).

lining out. A form of *a cappella* hymnody or psalmody in which a leader (often called a **cantor**, clerk, or **precentor**) introduces the **hymn tune** to the congregation. The congregation then sings the subsequent **verse**. Lining out is somewhat similar to **call-and-response**, except that in lining out, the soloist is only utilized at the beginning of the performance. In other words, there is only one call; the rest of the piece is all response.

lip trill. A "buzzing" of the lips. Lip trills are a **semioccluded vocal tract** exercise that are commonly used during vocal **warm-ups** and in **technique lessons**.

lirico spinto (**It**). See *spinto*.

listesso (**It**). The same.

liturgical. Adjective pertaining to **liturgy**.

liturgical drama. A sacred play set to music and performed as part of the **liturgy**. The liturgical drama is an important **medieval** precursor to **opera**. *Ordo Virtutum* (1152), by Hildegard von Bingen (1098–1179), is the most famous example of a liturgical drama and one of the only complete works of its kind to survive to the present day.

liturgy. The formally organized service rites of the Christian church. Liturgy affects the church on macro levels—structuring seasons and a three-year rotation of scripture—as well micro levels, for example, prescribing the respective order of each individual service. Musical compositions written for the church set specific **liturgical** texts, each of which are used at a specific point and for a specific purpose in the liturgy.

LMRVT. Abbreviation for **Lessac-Madsen Resonant Voice Therapy**.

Locrian. A **mode** built on the seventh **scale degree** of the **major scale**. Due to the tritone (d5) that exists between the first and fifth scale degrees, Locrian mode has no **dominant** scale degree and thus is almost never used.

loft. 1. A subjective singing **timbre** that is the opposite of **twang**. Loft is often described as lacking brightness, **edge**, or **nasality**. It is often achieved by enlarging the **pharynx** and engaging (lifting) the **soft palate**.

2. Another name for the **operatic head voice**, **CT**, or **mode 2** register.

long (**Fr**). Long.

l'Oranaise, Reinette (1918–1998). French singer of Arab-Andalus music. L'Oranaise was born in Tiaret, in central Algeria, and stricken blind by smallpox at the age of two. She studied at a school for the blind in Algiers, where she was encouraged to pursue music. In 1938, she moved to Paris, where she lived off and on until her death. L'Oranaise particularly excelled at the *raï* genre, which she helped introduce to a wider European audience. At

the time of her death, she was regarded by many as the "First Lady of North African Music."

Los Angeles, Victoria de (1923–2005). Spanish **soprano**. Los Angeles was born in Barcelona and studied the piano, guitar, and singing at a young age. She made her **operatic** debut in Barcelona in 1941, at the age of eighteen, in the **role** of Mimì in Puccini's *La bohème* and soon became one of the most well-known **classical singers** in Spain. She made her **Covent Garden** debut in 1950 (again as Mimì), and her **Metropolitan Opera** debut in 1951, in the role of Marguerite in Gounod's *Faust*. Although her operatic career was long and successful, she is perhaps most highly regarded for her **recital** singing, particularly her **interpretation** of *Lieder*, *mélodies*, and—especially—**Spanish art songs**. Her devotion to Spanish **song** from the **medieval** era to the present day has been comprehensively preserved in a legendary four-disc collection by EMI records entitled *Songs of Spain* (1999). Los Angeles maintained a longtime collaborative relationship with the English pianist **Gerald Moore**.

low larynx. A prevailing concept widely practiced by singers and voice teachers that suggests that the lower the **larynx**, the better the **tone quality**. While the low larynx concept predates the **fact-based** era of voice teaching, there is considerable truth behind the concept, as more pharyngeal space—which also comes from an **open throat** and engaged **soft palate**, in addition to the low larynx—generally cultivates a tone quality desirable in **classical singing**, provided that **compensatory tension** does not result in an effort to place the larynx in an unnaturally low position. The low larynx concept is generally not as desirable in **contemporary commercial music (CCM)** styles, which strive for a more speech-like **quality** and do not require the same kind of pharyngeal space as **classical genres**.

LPRD. Abbreviation for **laryngopharyngeal reflux disease**.

LSVT. Abbreviation for **Lee Silverman Voice Treatment**.

Luftpause (**pl.** *Luftpausen*) (**Ger**). Air pause. The German term for short "lift" or breath mark.

lullaby. A cradle **song**, often imitative of a folk song. Lullabies are used to sing a person (usually a baby) to sleep. Metrically, lullabies are often in triple time and usually feature a regular, repeated rhythm in the **accompaniment**. See also *berceuse*, *Schlummerlied*, **slumber song**, *Wiegenlied*.

lute song. A **Renaissance** or **baroque** vocal solo originally written for voice with lute **accompaniment**. The lute song is most idiomatically an English **genre**, and the most famous and prolific composers of lute songs are John Dowland (1563–1626) and Thomas Campion (1567–1620). In modern performances of this **repertoire**, a **classical** guitar often accompanies the singer instead of an actual Renaissance lute.

Lutheran Mass. A **genre** of sacred **choral music** that sets only the first two movements of the **Mass Ordinary**—the *Kyrie* and *Gloria*. The other three movements—the *Credo*, *Sanctus*, and *Agnus Dei*—are not part of the Lutheran Mass. Bach composed four Lutheran Masses in 1738: BWV 233 in F major, BWV 234 in A major, BWV 235 in G minor, and BWV 236 in G major.

lutte vocale. Italian *bel canto* term that refers to *appoggio*, specifically the **muscle antagonism** between the primary muscles of **inspiration** and **expiration**. Literally meaning "vocal struggle," the term was coined by the physiologist Louis Mandl (1812–1881) and popularized through the writings **Giovanni Battista Lamperti**.

Lydian. One of the eight **church modes**.

lyric. 1. The words of a popular or **musical theatre song**, written by a **lyricist**. Often used in the plural when referring to multiple songs, for example, "Lyrics by Lorenz Hart."

2. To have a melodic **quality**. Often used as an adjective to describe singers who sing in a lighter, more melodic way than their more **dramatic** colleagues (as in a lyric tenor or lyric baritone). With female **classical singers**, however—for instance, lyric sopranos and lyric mezzo-sopranos—a lyric sound is often thought of as a richer one, although not as heavy as a *spinto* or dramatic singer. The term *light lyric* is sometimes used, especially with female singers. In this sense, the term *full lyric* is the opposite of light lyric.

lyric baritone. See *lyrischer Bariton*.

lyric coloratura soprano. See *lyrischer Koloratursopran*.

lyric mezzo-soprano. See *lyrischer Mezzosopran*.

lyric opera. Form of nineteenth-century **French opera** that lies somewhere in between *opéra comique* and *grand opéra*. Lyric operas are generally **through-composed** and not **number operas**, and they usually contain no spoken **dialogue**. *Faust* (1859) and *Roméo et Juliette* (1867), by Charles Gounod (1818–1893), are two examples. See also *opéra lyrique*.

lyric soprano. See *lyrischer Sopran*.

lyric tenor. See *lyrischer Tenor*.

lyricist. The person who writes the **lyrics** of a popular or **musical theatre song**. In **opera**, the lyricist is known as the **librettist**.

lyrischer Alt. German *Fach* that literally translates as "**lyric contralto**." The *lyrischer Alt Fach* is the third-lowest female category in the **Kloiber Fach System**, surpassed only by the *dramatischer Alt* and *tiefer Alt* designations. The *Spielalt* is considered to be one *Fach* higher on the chart than the *lyrischer Alt*. Examples of *lyrischer Alt* **roles** include Mrs. Quickly in Verdi's *Falstaff* (1893), Ciesca in Puccini's *Gianni Schicchi* (1918), and Floßhilde in Wagner's *Der Ring des Nibelungen* (1876). See the *Fach* chart in appendix C.

lyrischer Bariton. German *Fach* that literally translates as "**lyric baritone**." In the **Kloiber Fach System**, the *lyrischer Bariton* is the highest baritone *Fach*, one notch lower on the chart than the *Charaktertenor*, but lighter than the *Kavalierbariton*. Examples of *lyrischer Bariton* **roles** include Billy Budd in Britten's *Billy Budd* (1951), Belcore in Donizetti's *L'elisir d'amore* (1832), Malatesta in Donizetti's *Don Pasquale* (1842), Guglielmo in Mozart's *Così fan tutte* (1790), Papageno in Mozart's *Die Zauberflöte* (1791), and Harlekin in Strauss's *Ariadne auf Naxos* (1916). See the *Fach* chart in appendix C.

lyrischer Koloratursopran (Koloratursoubrette). German *Fach* that literally translates as "**lyric coloratura soprano**." In the **Kloiber Fach System**, the *lyrischer Koloratursopran (Koloratursoubrette)* is one spot lower on the chart than the *Soubrette*, but lighter than the *dramatischer Koloratursopran*. Examples of *lyrischer Koloratursopran (Koloratursoubrette)* **roles** include Blonde in Mozart's *Die Entführung aus dem Serail* (1782), Musetta in Puccini's *La bohème* (1896), and Sophie in Strauss's *Der Rosenkavalier* (1911). See the *Fach* chart in appendix C.

lyrischer Mezzosopran. German *Fach* that literally translates as "**lyric mezzo-soprano**." In the **Kloiber Fach System**, the *lyrischer Mezzosopran* is heavier than the *koloratur-Mezzosopran*, but lighter than the *dramatischer Mezzosopran*. Examples of *lyrischer Mezzosopran* **roles** include Mercédès in Bizet's *Carmen* (1875); Charlotte in Massenet's *Werther* (1892); Hänsel in Humperdinck's *Hänsel und Gretel* (1893); Suzuki in Puccini's *Madama Butterfly* (1904); and several roles by Mozart, including Cherubino in *Le nozze di Figaro* (1786) and Dorabella in *Così fan tutte* (1790). See the *Fach* chart in appendix C.

lyrischer Sopran. German *Fach* that literally translates as "**lyric soprano.**" In the **Kloiber Fach System**, the *lyrischer Sopran* is positioned one spot lower on the chart than the ***dramatischer Koloratursopran*** and one spot higher than the ***jugendlich-dramatischer Sopran***. Examples of *lyrischer Sopran* **roles** include Michaëla in Bizet's *Carmen* (1875); Sophie in Massenet's *Werther* (1892); and many roles by Mozart, including Susanna in *Le nozze di Figaro* (1786), Zerlina in *Don Giovanni* (1787), and Pamina in *Die Zauberflöte* (1791). See the *Fach* chart in appendix C.

lyrischer Tenor. German *Fach* that literally translates as "**lyric tenor.**" In the **Kloiber Fach System**, the *lyrischer Tenor* is positioned one spot lower on the chart than the ***Spieltenor (Tenorbuffo)***, but it is lighter than the ***jugendlicher Heldentenor***. Examples of *lyrischer Tenor* **roles** include Ernesto in Donizetti's *Don Pasquale* (1842); Alfredo in Verdi's *La traviata* (1853); Pinkerton in Puccini's *Madama Butterfly* (1904); and many roles by Mozart, including Ottavio in *Don Giovanni* (1787), Ferrando in *Così fan tutte* (1790), and Tamino in *Die Zauberflöte* (1791). See the *Fach* chart in appendix C.

M

Maal, Baaba (b. 1953). Senegalese singer and guitarist. Born in Podor, on the Senegal River, Maal is the son of a fisherman. A lifelong musician, he did not achieve worldwide acclaim until much later in his life. Maal is the most famous Senegalese singer after **Youssou N'Dour**.

Mackintosh, Cameron (b. 1946). British theatrical **producer** known for his numerous commercially successful **megamusicals**. His notable productions include *Cats* (1981–1982), *Les Misérables* (1985–1987), *The Phantom of the Opera* (1986–1988), *Miss Saigon* (1989–1991), and *Mary Poppins* (2004–2006). He was knighted in 1996 and is one of the wealthy figures in the entertainment industry.

mad scene. A **scene**—usually in **opera**—in which a leading character portrays insanity, often through a dramatic **aria** or *scena*. Famous mad scenes include those of Ophelia in Thomas's *Hamlet* (1868), Wozzeck's in Berg's *Wozzeck* (1925), Peter Grimes's in Britten's *Peter Grimes* (1945), and—most famous of all—Lucia's in Donizetti's *Lucia di Lammermoor* (1835).

Madonna (b. 1958). American singer, songwriter, and actress, and one of the most iconic of all American **pop** artists. Madonna was born in Bay City, Michigan, in 1958, and she moved to New York City in 1977 to pursue a career in modern **dance**. Her vocal **style** is wide-ranging in **color**, shifting from a bubble-gum pop style to seductive warmth, even between tracks on the same album. Madonna is particularly known for reinventing her image on an almost yearly basis, as well as her penchant for generating controversy. She is known as the "Queen of Pop" and remains one of the most important figures in the American recording industry.

madrigal. A **Renaissance genre** of vocal music that consists of secular texts set in a **polyphonic style**. The two schools of madrigal composition included the **Italian madrigal** (which came first) and **English madrigal** (which appropriated many of the conventions of the Italian school). Although the French also dabbled in the madrigal genre, these polyphonic secular **songs** are technically called *chansons*.

madrigal comedy. A specific kind of **madrigal cycle** where the narrative is lighthearted in nature. An important precursor of **opera**.

madrigal cycle. A series of **madrigals** meant to be performed in sequence so as to tell a distinct narrative. Claudio Monteverdi (1567–1678) wrote the most famous madrigal cycles, which he grouped into various "books" of madrigals. When lighthearted in nature, often called a **madrigal comedy**. Madrigal cycles were an important precursor of **opera**.

madrigalism. A term used to describe various text painting devices prevalent in the **Renaissance madrigal**. The first **operas** written in the early **baroque** era owed much to madrigalism, appropriating many of the conventions of the madrigal **genre**.

maestoso **(It).** Majestic.

maestro **(It).** Master. Refers to an accomplished musician, usually the **conductor** of an orchestra or **opera production**.

maestro della musica **(It).** Master of music. The principal musician in an Italian court.

maestro di capella **(It).** Master of the chapel. The principal musician in an Italian chapel or cathedral.

magic opera. See *Zauberoper*.

Magnificat. A canticle from Luke 1:46–55, also called the Canticle of Mary or Song of Mary. The *Magnificat* is performed at Roman Catholic services during Vespers and in Anglican services during evensong. Many composers have also written choral-orchestral settings of the *Magnificat*, including Antonio Vivaldi (1678–1741), Johann Sebastian Bach (1685–1750), and Franz Schubert (1797–1828).

maître de chapelle (Fr). Master of the chapel. The principal musician in a French chapel or cathedral.

maître de musique (Fr). Master of music. The principal musician in a French court.

major mode (key). One of the two principal **modes** of **tonal music**, the twelve **major keys** follow a specific **formula** of whole and half steps: WWHWWWH.

makam. See *maqam*.

male rock falsetto. A **CT-dominant** (**falsetto**-based) sound with some **thyroarytenoid** engagement of the **vocal folds**. Used in **rock** and **pop** music that is exceptionally high in nature. Also called a **reinforced falsetto**.

male soprano. A high **countertenor** who sings in the **soprano range**. Some (but not most) singers and voice teachers make a distinction between this **voice type** and the countertenor, whereas others designate some countertenors as soprano countertenors and **mezzo-soprano** countertenors. Depending upon the location of the male second *passaggio*, **baritones** tend to become soprano countertenors, whereas **tenors** tend to become mezzo-soprano countertenors.

Malibran, Maria (1808–1836). Spanish **mezzo-soprano** who was the daughter of **Manuel García** (1775–1832) and the sister of **Pauline Viardot** and **Manuel García** (1805–1906). After early study with her father, she went on to one of the most distinguished careers in Europe. Malibran excelled in the *bel canto* **roles** of Gioacchino Rossini (1792–1868) and Vincenzo Bellini (1801–1835), and she created the title roles in Halévy's *Clari* (1828) and Donizetti's *Maria Stuarda* (1835). Malibran was held in especially high regard for her great **flexibility** and **musicianship**. She died prematurely at the age of twenty-eight when she fell from her horse during the Manchester Festival in England.

Mancini, Giovanni Battista (1714–1800). Italian **castrato** and voice teacher. Mancini was born in Ascoli Piceno and studied singing in Naples and Bologna. Although he wrote several **treatises** on singing, he is best known for *Practical Reflections on the Figurative Art of Singing* (1776), which appeared in the United States in an English translation in 1912.

manner of articulation. A **diction** term that refers to how a singer directs air past his or her **articulators** when pronouncing a **consonant**. Teachers and students must address various manners of articulation when perfecting the **pronunciation** of languages. Examples of specific manners of articulation include **plosive**, **fricative**, **affricates**, **nasal**, and **lateral** consonants. See also **point of articulation**.

maqam (*makam*). A set of Arabic **modes** prevalent in many forms of Middle Eastern music, including Turkish music.

marcato. Marked, stressed, or emphasized. See **nonlegato**.

Märchenoper (pl. *Märchenopern*). Roughly translated as "fairy-tale **opera**," the *Märchenoper* was a specific type of early **German Romantic opera** that featured fairy tale and magical thematic content. The **genre** was short-lived, and most *Märchenopern* that composers labeled as such wound up being dismal failures. Two successful works that seem to fit the criteria of the genre are *Oberon* (1826), by Carl Maria von Weber (1786–1826), and *Hans Heiling* (1833), by Heinrich Marschner (1795–1861). The *Märchenoper* is almost indistinguishable from the *Zauberoper* genre.

Marchesi, Mathilde (1821–1913). German **mezzo-soprano** and **voice pedagogue**. After an early career as a **concert** singer—and a single **opera role** (Rosina in Rossini's *Il barbiere di Siviglia*)—Marchesi devoted herself to teaching beginning in 1854. She is best known today for her numerous sets of vocal exercises, most of which were published under the French title *L'art du chant*. She is also the author of *Ecole Marchesi: method de chant théorique et pratique* (1886), which is widely available in its 1903 English translation.

Marian antiphons. An **antiphon** in praise of the Virgin Mary sung at the end of compline. The four Marian antiphons are *Alma Redemptoris Mater* ("Nourishing Mother of the Redeemer"), *Ave Regina caelorum* ("Hail, Queen of Heaven"), *Regina caeli laetare* ("Rejoice, Queen of Heaven"), and *Salve Regina* ("Hail, Queen").

marking. The practice of not singing in full voice, usually when combatting illness or "saving" a tired voice for a performance. The practice of marking is controversial, and **conductors** react to marking with various levels of patience. A prevailing opinion asserts that if the singer is healthy, has a solid **technique**, and is singing appropriate **repertoire**, then marking is not necessary.

Martin baritone (*baryton*). See *baryton-Martin*.

mask. See **masque** ("mask" is an alternate spelling for both definitions).

masque. 1. An English entertainment **genre** popular during the **baroque** era. The masque literally featured masks, costumes, scenery, dancing, poetry, and music. The subject matter was usually mythological or allegorical in nature. The most famous examples of the masque were written by Henry Purcell (1659–1695), whose *King Arthur* (1691) and *The Fairy Queen* (1692) represent the best works of the genre. In the twentieth century, Ralph Vaughan Williams (1872–1958) revived the genre with *Job: A Masque for Dancing* (1931).

2. French word for "mask," which is related to the concept of **placement** in vocal **technique**. The masque—or masque resonance (as the concept is often taught)—is a purely subjective concept, as it deals with perceived sensations related to the zygomatic and nasal regions of the face. As sensation may differ from singer to singer, many teachers prefer to forgo this concept altogether, instead focusing on **vowel** modification and **formant tuning** to achieve optimal **resonance**. (These voice teachers also feel that "placement" is essentially the same thing as vowel modification and formant tuning.)

masque resonance. See masque (2).

Mass. 1. A musical setting of the **Ordinary** portions of the Roman Catholic **liturgical** service. The Mass is one of the most ubiquitous **subgenres** in **choral music**, with landmark Mass settings existing from the **medieval** period to the present day. Medieval settings of the Mass include multiple **Gregorian chant** settings, in addition to the first **polyphonic** setting by Guillaume de Machaut (c. 1300–1377). The polyphonic Mass exploded during the **Renaissance** era, with a prolific number of Masses composed by Johannes Ockeghem (1410–1497), Jacob Obrecht (1457–1505), Josquin des Prez (c. 1450–1521), Tomás Luis de Victoria (1548–1611), Giovanni Pierluigi de Palestrina (1525–1594), and others. The *B Minor Mass* of Johann Sebastian Bach (1685 1750) is the most significant setting of the **baroque** era, and multiple settings by Wolfgang Amadeus Mozart (1756–1791), Joseph Haydn (1732–1809), Ludwig van Beethoven (1770–1827), and Franz Schubert (1797–1828) represent the Viennese Mass, a specific take on the **genre** prominent during the **classical** era. Beethoven's *Missa solemnis* ushered in the **romantic** era, with other significant settings written during the nineteenth century by Anton Bruckner (1824–1896) and others. By the twentieth century, the popularity of the Mass as a musical genre had declined significantly; the most important twentieth-century settings included those by Igor Stravinsky (1882–1971) and

Frank Martin (1890–1974). It should be noted that the majority of the post-Renaissance settings were conceived as **concert** works; they were intended for concert rather than liturgical use. The **Requiem** Mass is a related genre that closely parallels the history of the Mass.

2. Lowercase, a kind of **voice disorder**. See also **lesions and masses**.

***mässig* (Ger).** Moderately.

master class. A public **lesson** or coaching given to a singer by a more experienced **professional** singer, **voice pedagogue**, or vocal coach. If the clinician is a professional singer or voice pedagogue, he or she will tend to focus on the singer, addressing issues related to vocal **technique**, **diction**, **expression**, and stage presence. Vocal coaches, who are usually pianists, will focus on the aforementioned aspects, in addition to the collaboration; he or she will typically work with both the singer and the pianist, addressing issues of **ensemble**, balance, and collaborative sensitivity.

master of music (MM). The standard graduate degree for vocal performance. The MM is usually the terminal degree for **professional classical** performers. In contrast to **musical theatre** performers, most **classical singers** go to graduate school to earn their MM degree before embarking on a career in performance. Many singers with a MM degree also teach at colleges and universities, usually at the rank of adjunct or instructor.

masterwork. A subjective, ill-defined term that is reserved for the greatest works of a particular composer or **genre**. While specific criteria for what constitutes a masterwork are not enumerated, the term is most frequently used among vocalists when discussing long choral-orchestral works by major composers. For instance, most choral enthusiasts would regard Brahms's *Ein deutsches Requiem*, Op. 45 (1868) as a masterwork, whereas his short *a cappella* motet, *Warum ist das Licht gegeben dem Mühlseligen*, Op. 74, No. 1 (1879)—while still an excellent piece—is not.

***mbalax*.** A syncopated **form** of **dance** music from Senegal. Popularized throughout the world by **Youssou N'Dour**, who is considered to be the principal exponent of the **style**.

McClosky, David Blair (1902–1988). Boston-based **opera** singer and voice teacher. Born in Oswego, New York, McClosky graduated from the New England Conservatory and appeared more than twenty times as a soloist with the Boston Symphony Orchestra in the 1930s and 1940s. As a voice teacher, he served on the voice faculties of Boston University and the Boston Conservatory.

In the later years of his career, McClosky became highly regarded as a vocal health specialist, collaborating with **otolaryngologists (ENTs)** at several medical centers throughout the city and earning a reputation as a voice teacher who worked with injured singers. (In the twenty-first century, one might regard McClosky as a **singing voice specialist (SVS)**, but this term did not exist at the time.) McClosky was the private vocal coach of U.S. president John F. Kennedy (1917–1963) during his 1960 presidential campaign. McClosky's book *Your Voice at Its Best* (1959) was reissued in its fifth edition in 2011, and it includes material from another book of his entitled *Voice in Song and Speech* (1984). In 1979, McClosky also founded the **McClosky Institute of Voice (MIV)**, a nonprofit organization devoted to the enhancement of the healthy voice and the treatment of **voice disorders** without surgery.

McClosky Institute of Voice (MIV). A nonprofit organization founded in 1979, by David Blair McClosky, devoted to the enhancement of the healthy voice and the treatment of **voice disorders** without surgery. Since 1982, MIV has offered annual seminars and workshops related to voice and vocal health in Boston and other parts of the United States. Since McClosky's death in 1988, MIV has been perpetuated by his students and other disciples, many of whom are recognized as "Certified McClosky Vocal Technicians" (CMVTs), graduates of a certification program that was instituted in 1996.

McDonald, Audra (b. 1970). An American singing actress best known for her work in the **musical theatre genre**. McDonald was born in Berlin, Germany, and raised in Fresno, California, eventually moving to New York to study **classical singing** at the Juilliard School. After graduating from Juilliard, she found early success on **Broadway**, winning three **Tony Awards** by the age of twenty-eight for her **role**s in *Carousel* (1994 revival), *Master Class* (1996), and *Ragtime* (1998). She went on to win two additional Tony Awards in *A Raisin in the Sun* (2004 revival) and *Porgy and Bess* (2012 revival). McDonald is widely regarded as one of the finest singers in the Broadway industry.

McFerrin, Bobby (b. 1950). American vocalist and **conductor**, and one of the most unique and idiosyncratic artists in the history of singing. McFerrin cannot be categorized as a performer of any one particular **genre**, as he fuses together elements of **classical** music, **jazz**, **popular music**, and **world music** in his performances. McFerrin is a composer, as well as an **interpretive artist**, often making his own arrangements of well-known **repertoire**. Although he may be best known for the 1988 hit song "Don't Worry, Be Happy," this **song** is an anomaly in McFerrin's *oeuvre* and is not representative of his typical style. He is also a skilled improviser, and **improvisations** are a central element of his live performances. As of 2013, McFerrin has won ten **Grammy Awards**.

mechanistic. Performed without spontaneity, spirit, or individuality. Lacking **singer's instinct**. See also **academic**.

median. In **tonal music**, the third **scale degree** and the **chord** built on that note (III).

medication. Perhaps more than any instrumentalist, good physical health is of quintessential importance to the singer; however, many medications have direct and adverse effects on the singer's voice and vocal health. Serious singers should actively share their medical conditions with their singing teachers and consult reference books related to vocal health to ensure that it is safe to sing while under the influence of certain medications. See appendix L for a list of medications and their effects on singers.

medieval. The first of the six major eras in music. Although the medieval period—or Middle Ages—lasted for approximately 1,000 years (from 400 to 1400), the study of Western music begins when music began to be written down for the first time, which occurred during the eighth century. The period ends with the emergence of the **Renaissance** in the first decades of the fifteenth century. As little instrumental music was written down during the medieval era, virtually all medieval music is relevant to vocalists. Medieval **genres** include **plainsong**, *organum*, the conductus, **Mass**, **motet**, **liturgical drama**, and **monophonic secular song** (sung by *troubadours*, *trouvères*, *Minnesingers*, and *Meistersingers*). Suberas that occurred during the medieval period include the *ars antiqua*, *ars nova*, and *ars subtilior*.

medley. A collection of disparate tunes that are combined by an arranger or composer into a seamless piece of music. **Overtures** of **musicals** and **operettas** are frequently medleys of tunes from the show.

megamusical. A financially lucrative, blockbuster **musical** with wide audience appeal and lots of technical **spectacle**. The British **producer Cameron Mackintosh** is largely responsible for the advent of the megamusical. Notable examples of the **genre** include *Les Misérables* (1985–1987), *The Phantom of the Opera* (1986–1988), and *Miss Saigon* (1989–1991).

Meisner, Sanford (1905–1997). American actor and acting teacher. Meisner is most famous for developing an **acting technique** that is widely practiced and referenced by students and teachers of **theatre**. Rooted in the **Method acting** of **Constantin Stanislavski**, Meisner developed his **technique** after years of early training under **Lee Strasberg** and **Stella Adler**. Meisner soon distanced himself from his mentors, however, and his philosophy developed in a parallel way alongside of their respective techniques. The Meisner technique advocates a systematic series of progressive, interdependent training exercises that focus on **improvisation**, emotional access, and personal response to an existing textual work. In theatrical training, Meisner's method is one of the most frequently referenced acting techniques, along with those of Stanislavski, Strasberg, Adler, **Michael Chekhov**, **Uta Hagen**, **Anne Bogart**, and **Viola Spolin**.

Meistersinger. Literally translated as "master singer," *Meistersingers* were poet-composers from Germany who wrote and performed **monophonic secular songs** from the fourteenth through seventeenth centuries. *Meistersingers* were often members of guilds, and this culture was explored in the **music drama** *Die Meistersinger von Nürnberg* (1868), by Richard Wagner (1813–1883). The *Meistersingers* built on the traditions established by the *Minnesingers*, who preceded them.

mele. A unique type of Hawaiian singing that is a part of the hula **dance**. The *mele* is also prevalent throughout Polynesia.

melisma. A portion of a vocal line where numerous notes are set to one syllable. In **Gregorian chant** singing, one of the three possible ways to set a text; **syllabic** and **neumatic** are the other two. Melismas are usually relatively short, often comprised of only one or two vocal **phrases**. An entire piece set to one syllable, for example, is usually called a **vocalise** rather than a melisma.

melismatic. A type of text setting where one syllable is set to many notes. See also **coloratura**, *fioratura*, **neumatic**, **syllabic**.

melodía. Nineteenth-century Spanish **song** type. While the musical **forms** of the *melodía* are diverse in nature, the texts usually describe such earthy themes as love, yearning, human jealousy, advice to young lovers, and even death.

melodic minor. A **minor scale** that raises both the sixth and seventh **scale degrees** in ascending passages and returns to **natural minor** on descending ones.

mélodie. A vast body of **art song repertoire** in the French language. The French equivalent of the German *Lied* genre, the *mélodie* was directly inspired by the early nineteenth-century compositions of Franz Schubert (1797–1828) and Robert Schumann (1810–1856), as well as by the French *romance*, a kind of **strophic**,

piano-accompanied parlor **song** that dates from the late eighteenth century. Hector Berlioz (1803–1869), Charles Gounod (1818–1893), Georges Bizet (1838–1875), and Jules Massenet (1842–1912) contributed the earliest works to the *mélodie* genre. Just as German *Lieder* achieved maturity through keener text-to-music relationships and a more expressive and innovative use of the piano **accompaniment**, the French *mélodie* likewise reached maturity in the 1880s, most notably through the songs of Gabriel Fauré (1845–1924), Henri Duparc (1848–1933), and Claude Debussy (1862–1918). Other notable composers of the mature *mélodie* include Ernest Chausson (1855–1899), Emmanuel Chabrier (1841–1894), and Maurice Ravel (1875–1937). Francis Poulenc (1899–1963) and Jacques Leguerney (1906–1997) represent a twentieth-century climax of the French *mélodie*, contributing some of the greatest works in the entire art song genre.

melodrama. A **form** of **musical theatre** that combines spoken dialogue with underscoring. Several of the great *Lied* and *mélodie* composers also tried their hand at melodramas, and the performer of **art songs** might encounter some of these pieces grouped together with their published **songs**. Some famous examples include *Schön Hedwig*, Op. 106 (1848) and *Zwei Balladen*, Op. 122 (1852), by Robert Schumann (1810–1856); *Enoch Arden*, Op. 38 (1897), by Richard Strauss (1864–1949); and *L'histoire de Babar* (1940), by Francis Poulenc (1899–1963).

même (**Fr**). Same.

MENC. Abbreviation for **Music Educators National Conference**. In 2011, MENC changed its name to the **National Association for Music Education (NAfME)**.

meno mosso (**It**). Less motion.

merchandizing. The selling of goods and commercial items associated with a particular show, usually a work of **musical theatre**. The 1907 American **production** of Franz Lehár's *The Merry Widow* is credited with the birth of merchandizing through souvenirs—"Merry Widow" cigars, chocolates, scarves, and so forth—a practice that has been a staple commercial practice of the **Broadway** industry ever since.

Merman, Ethel (1908–1984). American singing actress and one of the most influential singers of all time. Merman was one of only a handful of singers who fundamentally changed notions about the capabilities of the human voice. She was one of the first female singers who performed almost exclusively in a **belt style**, carrying a robust, **TA-dominant quality** up to B4 and C5. She was said to have a "voice like a trumpet," with the ability to carry to the last row of the **theatre** without the aid of a **microphone**. Merman enjoyed close relationships with some of the greatest **Broadway** composers of the twentieth century, including George Gershwin (1898–1937), Cole Porter (1891–1964), Irving Berlin (1888–1989), and Jule Styne (1905–1994). Her signature **roles** (all of which she **premiered**) included Kate Fothergill in *Girl Crazy* (1930), Reno Sweeney in *Anything Goes* (1934), Annie Oakley in *Annie Get Your Gun* (1946), Sally Adams in *Call Me Madam* (1950), and Gypsy Rose Lee in *Gypsy* (1959). Through these roles and others, she gave world-premiere performances of many of the most well-known **songs** of the **Great American Songbook**, including "I Got Rhythm," "You're the Top," "Anything Goes," "I Get a Kick Out of You," "There's No Business Like Show Business," and "Everything's Coming Up Roses."

Merrill, Robert (1917–2004). American **operatic baritone** of the twentieth century. A native New Yorker, Merrill was born in Brooklyn to Jewish parents of Polish descent. After an early career as a semiprofessional baseball player, he decided to pursue singing **lessons**. After the death of **Leonard Warren** in 1960, Merrill became the principal baritone of the **Metropolitan Opera**. His signature **roles** included Enrico in Donizetti's *Lucia di Lammermoor*; Escamillo in Bizet's *Carmen*; Valentin in Gounod's *Faust*; and many Verdi baritone roles, including the title role in *Rigoletto*, Count di Luna in *Il trovatore*, Germont in *La traviata*, Rodrigo in *Don Carlo*, Amonasro in *Aida*, and Iago in *Othello*.

messa di voce. Italian term literally meaning "placing the voice." *Messa di voce* exercises are performed with a gradual **crescendo** followed by a **descresendo**. Not to be confused with *mezza voce.*

messe basse **(Fr).** Low **Mass.** A shorter French Mass without a *Credo.* The French equivalent of the Italian *missa brevis.*

messe basse solennelle **(Fr).** Low solemn **Mass.** Another name for a *messe basse.*

The Met. Colloquial term for the **Metropolitan Opera House.** This nickname is a bit confusing, as the Metropolitan Museum of Art in New York City is also known by many as "The Met."

meter (metre). The grouping of rhythmic impulses in poetry and music. There are seven common meters: **simple duple** meter, **simple triple** meter, **simple quadruple** meter, **compound duple** meter, **compound triple** meter, **compound quadruple** meter, and complex meter. Unless one is dealing with freely unstructured music, for example, some **forms** of **aleatoric music** or contemporary **art music**, the vast majority of Western and **world music** falls into one of these seven meters.

Method, the. A frequently used term among actors that refers to **Method acting**.

Method acting. A school of acting that subscribes to the **Method** of **Constantin Stanislavski. Lee Strasberg** is usually credited as the founder of the Method, which uses Stanislavski's systematic progression of **techniques** encouraging actors to get in touch with their personal emotions that they can then apply to their performances. To Stanislavski (and Strasberg), one must access real, personal emotions if one is to be believable onstage. Actors who subscribe to the Method strive to literally become their characters, drawing from life experience and inhabiting their character on the stage and off.

method actor. An actor (or singer) who learns and executes his or her **roles** exclusively according to the teachings of **Constantin Stanislavski** and his disciple, **Lee Strasberg**. While many actors—the majority—value and respect Stanislavski's teachings, most actors today possess theatrical training from a wide variety of sources. Generally speaking, only Stanislavski purists who practice the **Method** exclusively refer to themselves as Method actors.

method book. See technique book.

methodologist. A **voice pedagogue** who designs a specific vocal curriculum or **sequence** of **vocalizations** for a singer in training. Methodologists usually systemize their approach by writing method books or **technique books**. **Nicola Vaccai, Mathilde Marchesi,** and **Heinrich Panofka** are three of the most famous methodologists in the history of **voice pedagogy**. Their method books are still in frequent use today.

metronome. A device used to indicate the **tempo** of a composition. Metronomes audibly (and sometimes visually—through a blinking light) sound regular **beats**, and the musician can adjust the **frequency** of the beats to set the desired speed. Analog metronomes have existed since the early nineteenth century, but, in recent years, virtually all musicians use electronic metronomes. Some of the latter permit the user to tap a button at a certain tempo, yielding a digital readout of the number of **beats per minute (BPM)**. Metronomes are indispensible practice tools for all musicians, including singers and **conductors**.

metronome marking. The measurement for the **tempo** of music in number of **beats per minute (BPM)**. Metronome markings are often indicated with the abbreviation

MM, which actually stands for "Maelzel's Metronome," in homage to Johann Nepomuk Maelzel (1772–1838), the inventor of the **metronome**. (Conveniently, MM also serves as an abbreviation for "metronome marking.") If the metronome marking is sixty, this means that each **beat** lasts exactly one second (to create a *larghetto* tempo). Most pieces of music written from the **romantic** era onward contain metronome markings, which are usually provided by the composer. If the piece does not contain a metronome marking, the tempo can then be determined by the performer, who considers such issues as tradition—how the fast the **song** or **aria** is usually performed—and the speed at which his or her individual voice is heard to best advantage. Singers should always provide specific metronome markings to their **accompanist** to assist them in their preparation for a **rehearsal** or performance.

Metropolitan Opera House. The principal **opera house** in New York City and the United States, and one of the largest and most prestigious venues for **professional opera** in the world. **The Met**—as it is colloquially known—opened in 1966, and it is located at Lincoln Center in New York City. As an organization, the Metropolitan Opera dates back much further. For the first part of its history—from 1883–1966—the **company** performed in the "Old Met," an opera house on **Broadway** and 39th Street. The current Metropolitan Opera House contains 3,800 seats and 195 standing-room places. The backstage area and fly space are capable of great technical feats, and the facility smoothly rotates up to four different opera **productions** each week of its season. The Met usually performs twenty-seven different opera productions each season.

Figure 31. Program cover, Metropolitan Opera House, 1935. *Courtesy Creative Commons.*

Metropolitan Opera National Council (MONC) auditions. An annual singing competition hosted and sponsored by the **Metropolitan Opera** in New York City. Established in 1954, its purpose is to discover and develop young singers with the potential for significant careers in **opera**. MONC auditions begin at the district level in all fifty states. District winners then progress to one of fourteen regional competitions, and the winners of the regional competitions advance to the semifinal round at the Metropolitan Opera House. Approximately ten finalists are selected from the semifinal round to sing in the final round, which occurs onstage at **The Met**, accompanied by the Metropolitan Opera orchestra. Five singers are then awarded the grand prize of $15,000 each. Winning the MONC auditions is one of the most prestigious honors that a young opera singer can achieve. In 2008, a feature-length documentary was released entitled *The Audition*, which chronicles the journey of a group of aspiring opera singers from the district level to the national finals.

mezza voce. Italian term literally meaning "half voice." Refers to a softer dynamic level. Not to be confused with *messa di voce.*

mezzo forte **(It).** Somewhat loud.

mezzo piano **(It).** Somewhat soft.

mezzo-soprano. The second highest of the seven principal **classical** voice categories. The **German Fach System** identifies three subcategories of **mezzo-sopranos**: the *koloratur-Mezzosopran*, *lyrischer Mezzosopran*, and *dramatischer Mezzosopran*. Although the *Fach* system makes a clear distinction between mezzo-sopranos and **contraltos**, the **opera** profession does not, and many mezzo-sopranos also sing much of the contralto **repertoire** outlined by the **Kloiber Fach System**. The four contralto categories in the *Fach* system include the *Spielalt*, *lyrischer Alt*, *dramatischer Alt*, and *tiefer Alt*. Outside of Germany, few female singers label themselves as contraltos.

microphone. A piece of electronic equipment that converts **acoustic** sounds into electrical signals. There are three basic types of microphones: **dynamic microphones**, **condenser microphones**, and **ribbon microphones**. Emile Berliner (1851–1929) invented the microphone in 1876, and they became a fixture in the **pop** music industry throughout the course of the twentieth century. The advent of the microphone has perhaps influenced popular singing **styles** more than any other single factor.

microphone sensitivity. In **amplified singing**, measurement of the input-to-output ratio; the input is measured in **decibels**, and the output is measured in voltage. In the United States, most **microphones** use a measurement system that results in a negative number, for example, −54dBV/Pa (1.85mV). The higher the number, the more sensitive the microphone; therefore, a microphone with a sensitivity of −60dBV/Pa is considered to be less sensitive than a microphone with a −54dBV/Pa rating. A microphone with higher sensitivity is often preferable for a softer sound source (i.e., the singer), whereas a microphone with a lower sensitivity is often preferable for a louder sound source.

Middle Ages. Another term for the **medieval** era.

Mighty Handful. A group of five nineteenth-century Russian composers who dedicated themselves to nationalistic principles. The members of the Mighty Handful were Aleksandr Borodin (1833–1887), César Cui (1835–1918), Mily Balakirev (1837–1910), Modest Musorgsky (1839–1881), and Nikolay Rimsky-Korsakov (1844–1908). They were also known as the **Russian Five**.

migration. See **vowel migration**.

Miller, Richard (1926–2009). Arguably the most prolific and important modern **classical voice pedagogue**, and inarguably one of the most influential among North American singing teachers. More modern singing teachers affirm Richard Miller's ideas than any other single **pedagogue**. His landmark 1986 **treatise**, *The Structure of Singing*, introduced a systematic approach to **voice pedagogy** that is widely in practice among singing teachers. Miller's long career as a singing teacher was spent almost entirely at the undergraduate institution of Oberlin College in Oberlin, Ohio. There, he founded the Otto B. Schoepfle Vocal Arts Center, one of the first **vocology laboratories** in the United States dedicated to studying the singing voice. In addition to *The Structure of Singing*, Miller's other books include *National Schools of Singing* (1977), *Training Tenor Voices* (1993), *On the Art of Singing* (1996), *Singing Schumann* (1999), *Training Soprano Voices* (2000), *Solutions for Singers* (2004), and *Securing Baritone, Bass-Baritone, and Bass Voices* (2008).

minimalism. An artistic movement that emerged in the United States during the twentieth century. Minimalism was originally a concept in the visual arts that favored simplicity as a means of **expression**, for instance, blank canvases and sculptures of blue cubes. Minimalism in music involves repetition of short melodic or **harmonic** fragments. Composers inspired by minimalist concepts included La Monte Young (b. 1935), Terry Riley (b. 1935), Steve Reich (b. 1936), and—most important to singers—Philip Glass (b. 1937). The towering example

of minimalism in **opera** is Glass's four-and-a-half hour *Einstein on the Beach* (1976), the original **production** of which was directed by Robert Wilson (b. 1941). During the course of four **acts** and five "knee plays," *Einstein on the Beach* is a **nonplot show** in which Glass and Wilson utilize a plethora of minimalist effects, including vocal texts that consist of nothing but numerals and a beam of light that slowly elevates from a horizontal to a vertical position throughout the span of twelve minutes.

Minnelieder. **Monophonic secular song repertory** sung by the ***Minnesingers*** in **medieval** Germany. The literal translation of *Minnelieder* is "love **songs**."

Minnesinger. Literally translating as "singers of love," the *Minnesingers* were the poet-composers of **medieval** Germany. Their **monophonic secular repertoire** is known as ***Minnelieder***, which literally translates as "love **songs**." The *Minnesingers* were precursors to the ***Meistersingers***, who built upon the traditions they established.

minor. One of the two principal **modes** of **tonal music**, along with **major**. The minor **mode** comes in three principal forms: **natural minor**, **harmonic minor**, and **melodic minor**. Natural minor—identical to the **Aeolian** mode—has no altered **scale degrees**, harmonic minor raises the seventh scale degree, and melodic minor raises both the sixth and seventh scale degrees in ascending passages and returns to natural minor on descending ones. Minor modes are directly related to their relative major cousins, and one can think of minor modes as ones that tonicize the sixth scale degree of the major scale. Singers of all **styles** must know their major and minor **scale** spellings inside and out.

minstrel. A thirteenth-century traveling musician. Some minstrels were employed by royal courts or cities.

minstrel show. A nineteenth-century musical-theatrical **genre** featuring performers (both black and white) in blackface, often satirizing the lives and situations of African Americans. Minstrel shows were divided into three **acts** and featured a variety of entertainments, including jokes, singing, dancing, and other special and obscure talents. The first act resembled a variety show and usually ended with a "walk-around" (a choral **number** performed in a semicircle) or a "cakewalk" (a plantation dance imitative of a white aristocratic ball). The second act was called an **olio** or **fantasia** and usually contained some sort of instrumental music or dancing. The third act was usually in the style of a **burlesque**. Original **songs** composed from the minstrel shows were called **minstrel songs**, and these songs achieved widespread popularity in the nineteenth century. Some of the most famous minstrel **troupes** included the Virginia Minstrels, Christy's Minstrels, and Bryant's Minstrels. Stephen Foster (1826–1864) was perhaps the nineteenth century's best-known composer of minstrel songs.

minstrel song. A **song** written for American **minstrel shows** in the nineteenth century. Performed in blackface, minstrel songs were usually upbeat and mimicked African American **dialect** and mannerisms. Stephen Foster (1826–1864) is the best-known composer of minstrel songs. "Oh, Susannah" (1848) is perhaps Foster's most famous minstrel song. Dan Emmett (1815–1904)—a composer who has largely been forgotten—also composed several enduring minstrel songs, including "Old Dan Tucker" (1843) and "Dixie" (1859).

minstrelsy. Another name for the **minstrel show genre**.

minyo. A type of Japanese folk **song**.

missa brevis **(It).** Brief **Mass**. An Italian term that describes a shorter Mass without a *Credo*. In France, the *missa brevis* is called a *messe basse*.

Missa pro defunctis. Another name for the **Requiem Mass**.

mit Ausdruck **(Ger).** With **expression**.

MIV. Abbreviation for the **McClosky Institute of Voice**.

mix. A **contemporary commercial music (CCM)** term used to describe a **register** that is somewhere in between **head (CT)** and **chest (TA)** voice. Some schools of CCM **pedagogy**—for instance, **Somatic Voicework (SVW)**—describe two different kinds of mix: head mix and chest mix. While mixing certainly occurs in **classical** music (see **mixed register**), the term is used with more frequency among CCM singers and teachers, particularly in the **musical theatre genre**, where mix often becomes necessary when singing high in the female **belt range**. The term *mix* is also used in combination with other words to subjectively describe various **timbres** and **styles**; examples include such hybrid terms as *belt-mix*, *pop-mix*, *rock-mix*, and others. The terminology, while used with frequency in musical theatre listings, is not at all standardized.

mixed formation. A type of choral formation in which the four sections (or choral parts) are not seated together. Instead, **sopranos**, **altos**, **tenors**, and **basses** are scattered throughout the **choir**, sometimes seated in **quartets**. While mixed formations tend to encourage freer singing and warmer **tone qualities**, side-effect problems may emerge, including excessive **vibrato**, **out-of-tune** singing, and the inability to blend within sections (due to sections not being seated together). Volume also tends to increase in mixed formation. The larger the choir, the more challenging it becomes to sing in mixed formation.

Some **conductors** experiment with using mixed formations in some **repertoires**, but not others. For instance, mixed formation may work well in accompanied **romantic choral music** (for example, Brahms and Schumann), but less well in *a cappella* **Renaissance** choral music (for instance, Palestrina and Victoria). While mixed formations are commonly employed (usually as a teaching tool) at the university and collegiate levels, they are almost never used by **professional** choral **ensembles** due to the challenges involved in achieving a unified **blend** and good **intonation**. Most professional choral ensembles seat sections together and strive to sound like **one voice** within their sections.

mixed register. Refers to a balance of **TA/mode 1** and **CT/mode 2** registration in singing. While the vocal folds are ultimately more engaged in one mode (**register**) than the other, modification of the acoustic space in the *zona di passaggio* can give the singer the feeling—and listener the perception—of a third ("mixed") register. The mixed register concept is controversial among voice pedagogues, many of whom do not acknowledge it as a true register. The term is most frequently encountered when discussing the middle range of the singer and in reference to the transition that occurs between chest (TA/mode 1) and head (CT/mode 2) voice. In this sense, mixed register refers to the gradual and subtle shifting between registers to eliminate abruptness and give the illusion of a smooth and seamless tone quality throughout the range of the singer. Also called coordinated register.

mixed vowel. A **vowel** that is formed as a combination of two other vowels through the manipulation of the tongue and lips. For instance, in the [y] mixed vowel, the tongue forms [i] while the lips form [u]. [Y], [y], [ø], and [œ] are the most common mixed vowels and are frequently used in German and French. In certain Scandinavian languages, other mixed vowels are also used, including [ɵ], [o], [ʉ], and [ɤ]; Russian utilizes [i]. See also **back vowel**, **central vowel**, **closed vowel**, **front vowel**, **nasal vowels**, **open vowel**.

Mixolydian. One of the eight **church modes**.

MM. 1. Abbreviation for "Maelzel's Metronome." See also **metronome marking**.
2. Abbreviation for the **master of music** degree.

modal. 1. Another name for **chest**, **TA**, or **mode 1 register**.
2. Describes music written in a **mode** other than a **major key** or **minor key**.

mode. 1. A specific type of **scale** or melody, defined by its sequence of **whole steps** and **half steps** within a single **octave**. Historically, the most common Western modes were the eight **church modes: Dorian, Hypodorian, Phrygian, Hypophrygian, Lydian, Hypolydian, Mixolydian,** and **Hypomixolydian.** In more recent centuries, however, there have been seven standard modes: **Ionian (major),** Dorian, Phrygian, Lydian, Mixolydian, **Aeolian (minor),** and **Locrian** (almost never used). Ionian and Aeolian—the major and minor modes—are the two modes of **tonal music,** which comprises most of the Western **canon.**

2. Can refer to one of the six rhythmic (as opposed to melodic) modes. Used during the **medieval** era.

3. Designation for one of the two principal vocal **registers: Mode 1** refers to **thyroarytenoid** (TA) register, or **chest** voice; **mode 2** refers to **cricothyroid** (CT) register, or **head** voice.

mode 1. Designation for **thyroarytenoid** (TA) or **chest register.**

mode 2. Designation for **cricothyroid** (CT) or **head register.**

moderato **(It).** Moderate. Faster than *andante*, but slower than *allegro*.

modern. The sixth and final of the principal eras of Western **art music,** the modern era encapsulates all music written since the end of the **romantic** era (around 1900). Discussions of the modern era are sometimes further delineated according to centuries: either twentieth or twenty-first century. The modern era is pluralistic in nature, with many examples of **posttonal** music intermingling with **neo-romantic** tonal compositions. Other movements, for example, **minimalism,** also make their impact. Perhaps most important, the modern era gives way to a plethora of **popular music genres,** relegating newly composed art music (to an extent) to **academic** and other **new music** communities. Many **classical** arts organizations primarily base their **repertoire** on the **tonal music canon** from the **baroque,** classical, and romantic eras. This is certainly true of **opera companies** and **art song** and **oratorio** societies.

modulation. A change from one **key** to another within the same piece of **tonal music.**

moins **(Fr).** Less.

moll **(Ger).** Minor, as in B-moll (B minor).

monadic. Adjective pertaining to **monody.**

MONC. Abbreviation for **Metropolitan Opera National Council.**

monitor. The electronic speaker placed in front of an **amplified singer,** allowing him or her to hear the other parts being amplified or recorded.

Monk, Meredith (b. 1942). Multifaceted American vocalist and composer. Monk's works are eclectic in nature and scope and often interdisciplinary in nature, combining music, **theatre, dance,** and even film in innovative and creative ways. Monk is probably best known for her singing and vocal compositions, most of which she has performed and recorded herself with the collaboration of other vocal artists. She is a pioneer of **extended techniques** for the voice, and her prolific output of **new music** for the voice is one of the most unusual and intriguing *oeuvres* in contemporary music. Her three operas—*Education of the Girlchild* (1973), *Quarry* (1976), and *Atlas* (1992)—stretch our understanding of the **genre** and its possibilities. While Monk does not altogether depart from traditional musical notation, the score only offers a starting point for the **interpretation** of her works. Her compositions and vocals can be heard on more than a dozen CDs, most of them recorded for the ECM label.

monody. A particular **style** of accompanied vocal solo that developed in Italy at the beginning of the **baroque** era (c. 1600). In monody, a **recitative**-like solo vocal line is accompanied by a *basso continuo*. Monody is closely associated with the beginnings of **opera.**

monophonic. An adjective pertaining to **monophony.**

monophonic secular song. Describes secular songs written for one voice during the **medieval** and early **Renaissance** eras. Monophonic secular songs were performed by the *troubadours, trouvères, Minnesingers,* and *Meistersingers*.

monophony. A musical texture consisting of a single **unaccompanied** melodic line.

monophthong. A **vowel** sound that remains constant throughout an entire syllable.

monosyllabic. Diction term referring to a word with one syllable.

Moore, Gerald (1899–1987). English **collaborative pianist** and one of the most famous *Lieder* **accompanists** of all time. Moore is especially well-known for his close collaborative relationships with **Dietrich Fischer-Dieskau, Elisabeth Schwarzkopf,** and **Victoria de Los Angeles,** three of the most famous artists in the history of the **art song genre.** Between 1966–1972, he recorded more than

400 Schubert *Lieder* with Fischer-Dieskau, including every Schubert *Lied* suitable to the male voice. Testament Records reissued his humorous spoken LP, entitled *The Unashamed Accompanist*, in 1999.

Moreschi, Alessandro (1858–1922). Italian singer of the late nineteenth century known throughout the world as the "Last Castrato." Moreschi seems to be the only **castrato** who made sound recordings. Born and raised in the town of Monte Compatri, he sang as a boy in the chapel of the Madonna del Castagno. Although the time of his castration is not known, Moreschi was singing in Rome as a castrato by 1870, and, in 1873, he was appointed as first **soprano** in the choir of the Papal Basilica of St. John Lateran. Moreschi earned his reputation in part for his exceptional high notes, which were heard to great advantage in some of the Papal **repertoire**, including the *Miserere*, by Gregorio Allegri (1582–1652). The extant recordings of Moreschi's androgynous, shrill, and eerie-sounding voice were made in Rome in 1902 and 1904, and they are widely available to twenty-first-century listeners. Because of his age and the early state of recording technology, these recordings may not be a faithful reproduction of the castrato voice.

moritat. A type of **ballad** sung at German street fairs that describes notorious deeds of legendary criminals. "Mack the Knife," from Weill's *The Threepenny Opera* (1928), is a famous example of a moritat from the **musical theatre genre**.

motet. A **polyphonic** piece of **choral music**. The term *motet* has meant different things at different times in music history. The earliest motets simply consisted of a descant added to a **clausula**. Thirteenth-century motets could be either sacred or secular, in **Latin** or French, often multitextual (with several texts occurring simultaneously in different voices), and almost always based on a **cantus firmus** derived from **Gregorian chant**. In the fourteenth century, many motets were **isorhythmic**. From the fifteenth century onward, any polyphonic setting of a sacred Latin text that was not part of a **Mass** was considered to be a motet. Beginning in the sixteenth century, the term *motet* could apply to polyphonic sacred compositions in any language.

motive. A short melody or rhythm that recurs later in a musical work.

movable do. A type of *solfège* in which *do* is assigned to the **tonic** of whatever **key** is predominant.

Mozarbic chant. The **medieval liturgical chant** of Spain. Similar in compositional **style** to **monophonic Gregorian chant**.

MPA. Abbreviation for **music performance anxiety**.

MTD. Abbreviation for **muscle tension dysphonia**.

MTNA. Abbreviation for the **Music Teachers National Association**.

mucosal edema. See **Reinke's edema**.

mucosal wave. A vibratory pattern that occurs on the **cover** of the superior surface of the **vocal folds** during **phonation**. A normal mucosal wave is a salient feature of a healthy singing voice.

mugam. **Classical** Azeri vocal music from the country of Azerbaijan in the former Soviet Republic. Set to Sufi-influenced poetry that praises Allah, it is a kind of throat singing with similarities to Tuvan *khoomei* and Swiss **yodeling styles**.

multiphonics. More than one **pitch** produced at the same time. While usually an instrumental **technique**, vocalists can also produce multiphonics, typically in one of two ways: through either throat singing or whistling while **phonating**. Performers of **new music** use multiphonics as an **extended technique**.

murder ballad. A Depression-era American folk or commercial **song** that has a theme of death, destruction, or disaster. Great tragedies were a favorite theme, for example, the sinking of the Titanic in 1912, or the crashing of the Hindenburg in 1937. Also called a **disaster song**.

muscle antagonism. The phenomenon that occurs in the human body when one muscle contracts and its paired muscle releases. Most muscles in the body are paired; the only two unpaired muscles in the body are the **diaphragm** and the *orbicularis oris* (the sphincter-like muscle around the mouth).

muscle tension dysphonia (MTD). A vocal pathology that occurs when there is excessive tension in the extrinsic and intrinsic muscles of the **larynx**. Symptoms of MTD include hoarseness, **laryngitis**, **vocal fatigue**, and discomfort when speaking or singing. If a singer is diagnosed with MTD, he or she should be treated by a medical **professional** who specializes in **voice disorders**, for instance, an **otolaryngologist (ENT)** or **speech-language pathologist (SLP)**.

music drama. The name that Richard Wagner (1813–1883) gave to his mature works, signifying that they went beyond the artistic intentions of traditional **opera**. With his music dramas, Wagner placed an equal value on every aspect of the **production**: the literary **quality** and origin of the **libretto**, the poetry, the scenery, the costumes, and even the architecture of the building. Wagner built the **Bayreuth Festspielhaus** to his specifications as a venue for mounting his music dramas. Wagner's music dramas include *Tristan und Isolde* (1865), *Die Meistersinger von Nürnberg* (1868), *Parsifal* (1878), and his four-part *Der Ring des Nibelungen* (1876).

Music Educators National Conference (MENC). Former name of the **National Association for Music Education (NAfME).**

music performance anxiety (MPA). A state of apprehension, uncertainty, and fear resulting from the anticipation of a realistic or fantasized threat in the context of a **musical** performance. Many singers experience MPA at some level, particularly during formative years of study.

Music Teachers National Association (MTNA). An American organization of independent and collegiate music teachers based in Cincinnati, Ohio. Founded in 1876, MTNA membership grew to more than 22,000 members in 2012. Primarily an organization for piano teachers, MTNA offers some services to voice teachers, especially with their annual national young artist competition in voice. MTNA also offers a national certification program. A singing teacher who completes the program is recognized as a Nationally Certified Teacher of Music (NCTM).

musica reservata **(It).** Reserved music. A term used during the **Renaissance** era to describe music that did not make use of explicit or obvious **word painting**.

musical. 1. A stage work with relatively equal emphasis on three distinct art **forms**: acting, singing, and dancing. As a **genre**, the modern **musical** did not formally emerge until 1943, when Rodgers and Hammerstein's *Oklahoma!* was widely recorded as the first musical. Before this date, three genres—**musical comedies**, **revues**, and European-**style operettas**—were the normal fare on **Broadway**, but the new style of *Oklahoma!* was highly influential, and critics and the public began referring to the new works that emerged simply as "musicals." The musical is the most important genre under the umbrella of the **musical theatre** style. Musicals are usually in two **acts** with a narrative **plot**. Other musical theatre genres include revues, **jukebox musicals**, **catalog shows**, **cabarets**, and contemporary **song cycles**. The **songs** from these cousin genres are almost identical in style to those found in the musical, but there is usually no coherent plot that binds an evening together.

2. A singer who is expressive on an aural level (as opposed to a physical level, i.e., stage presence, gestures) is said to be very "musical." See also **musicality**.

musical comedy. One of the three types of **Broadway** offerings (along with the **revue** and European-**style operetta**) during the first several decades of the twentieth century. Of the three types, musical comedy is the **genre** that is most closely related to **vaudeville**, with an emphasis on **dance** and comedy. Musical comedies usually had a loose **plot** in which a young man gets his girl after a series of humorous escapades. George M. Cohan (1878–1942) is perhaps the greatest and most prolific composer of musical comedies—and he also wrote the **lyrics** for them, acted in them, danced in them, produced them, and directed them.

musical director. The person who supervises the musical preparation and execution of an **opera**, **operetta**, or **musical**. In opera, the musical director usually serves as the **conductor** as well.

musical play. Early twentieth-century term given to a **musical theatre** work that had a **plot** of uncommon substance. *Show Boat* (1927) was dubbed by critics and fellow artists as a musical play due to its literary **quality**, controversial themes, and character depth. While "serious" **musicals** became more common in the second half of the twentieth century, *Show Boat* was a revolution with a firm eye on the future.

musical theatre. A theatrical **style** that combines music, acting, and **dance**, often in a lavish **spectacle**. Throughout its long history, musical theatre has always been closely linked with **popular music**, and musical theatre **songs** have often mirrored current trends in popular styles. Contemporary musical theatre **genres** include the **musical**—which is by far the most significant genre—but also **revues**, **jukebox musicals**, **catalog shows**, **cabarets**, and contemporary **song cycles**. Throughout most of its history, musical theatre as an art **form** evolved along two separate paths in two distinct cities: the **West End Theatre** of London and New York's **Broadway**. While each tradition draws upon a unique set of roots and precursors, significant cross-pollination began occurring by the end of the twentieth century, and in recent decades, both Broadway and the West End have shared similar **repertories**.

musicality. An aspect of performance that deals with how aurally expressive a musician is.

Musicians Earplugs. A trademarked brand of earplugs designed and developed by Etymotic. Musicians Earplugs were developed in response to hearing loss experienced by many **professional** and **amateur** musicians, who routinely expose themselves to unsafe **decibel** levels during **rehearsals** and performances. Musicians Earplugs can be purchased from licensed hearing professionals.

musicianship. Aspect of performance that deals with how accurate one is with their **interpretation** of the **score**. A singer who sings with good musicianship will be well-prepared and sing all **pitches**, rhythms, dynamics, and **expressive markings** with great integrity.

musique mesurée **(Fr)**. Measured music. Late sixteenth-century French **style** of text setting, especially in **polyphonic** *chansons*. In *musique mesurée*, long note values correspond to accented syllables of text. Also called *vers mesurée*.

mutational chink. A medical phenomenon that often occurs in the **larynges** of adolescent girls, where the **arytenoid cartilages** grow faster than the **interarytenoid** muscles. The result is the inability to attain full closure of the **vocal folds** during **phonation**, resulting in a chronic gap and an airy **tone quality**. During these years, the voice teacher must be sensitive to the mutational chink and not try to resolve the issue through excess tension. As long as no vocal pathologies emerge, the singer will outgrow the mutational chink as the interarytenoid muscles mature. Also known as glottal chink, incomplete mutation, and puberphonia.

mute *e*. The final *e* of a French word, unpronounced in speech. Mute *e*s are often set to music by the composer, but sometimes they are not, which makes the mute *e* one of the more complex issues one deals with in the study of French **diction**. In addition, mute *e*s are subject to **elision** when they are followed by words that begin with an initial **vowel** or *h*.

myoelastic-aerodynamic theory (of voice production). A theory of **vocal fold oscillation** developed in the 1950s and 1960s that explains **phonation** through **Bernoulli's principle**. The myoelastic-aerodynamic theory suggests that Bernoulli forces (negative pressure) assist in sucking the **vocal folds** together. After this occurs, air pressure builds beneath the closed **glottis**, eventually resulting in an opening of the glottis from bottom to top. As air flows through the glottis, velocity increases as pressure decreases. The vocal folds then act elastically, springing back shut (also from bottom to top) as air leaves the glottis. The process then repeats itself. This theory of voice **production** is still accepted by scientists, although it has been improved upon through the more recent **one-mass model** and **three-mass model**. A fourth theory is the **neurochronaxic theory of voice production**, which has long been rejected as a dated and incorrect theory.

N

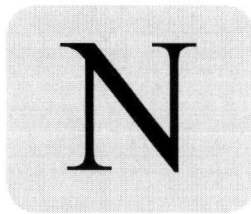

nach (Ger). After.

NAfME. Abbreviation for the **National Association for Music Education**, formerly known as the **Music Educators National Conference (MENC)**.

nasal. In the study of **diction**, describes a **manner of articulation** in which **consonants** are produced by directing **vocalized tone** through the **nasal cavity**. Common examples of nasal consonants include [m], [n], [ŋ], and [ɲ]. See also **affricate, fricative, lateral, plosive**.

nasal cavity (nasopharynx). One of the three primary resonators in the **vocal tract**, along with the **pharynx** and **oral cavity**.

nasal vowels. Four specific French **vowels**—[ɑ̃], [ɛ̃], [õ], and [œ̃]—that are deliberately colored by **nasal resonance** via a deliberate "lowering" (engagement) of the **soft palate**, thus forming new and distinct vowels. See also **back vowel, central vowel, closed vowel, front vowel, mixed vowel, open vowel**.

nasality. A **quality** in singing that occurs when one does not "lift" (or engage) the **soft palate**, thus opening up the nasal chamber to become part of the **singer's resonance**. In the Western **classical singing** tradition, nasality is considered an unbecoming quality. Thus, classical singers strive to almost never sing with a nasal sound, with the exception of when it is necessary in nasal **consonants**—[n], [m], [ɲ], and [ŋ]—and **nasal vowels**—[ɑ̃], [ɛ̃], [õ], and [œ̃].

In **musical theatre** and other popular **styles**, nasality is not necessarily considered to be a negative quality, as performers often desire a **tone quality** that is more representative of natural speech, which naturally retains a certain degree of nasality.

NASM. Abbreviation for **National Association of Schools of Music**.

nasopharynx. Another name for the **nasal cavity**.

National Association for Music Education (NAfME). The national organization for public-school music educators, including **musical directors**. NAfME marked its centennial in 2007, as the only association that addresses all aspects of music education. Through membership of more than 75,000 active, retired, and preservice music teachers, and with 60,000 honor students and supporters, NAfME serves millions of students nationwide through activities at all teaching levels, from preschool to graduate school. Until 2011, NAfME was known as the **Music Educators National Conference (MENC)**.

National Association of Schools of Music (NASM). A national accreditation agency for university, college, and conservatory schools of music and music departments, founded in 1924. Most programs that offer degrees in voice seek accreditation through this agency, with member schools listed online.

National Association of Teachers of Singing (NATS). The world's largest association of singing teachers, founded in 1944, and based in Jacksonville, Florida. NATS membership grew to more than 7,000 in the second decade of the twenty-first century. The association's members primarily come from the United States and Canada, with twenty-five other countries also represented. NATS hosts biennial national conventions, and chapters and regions host annual student **auditions**. The NATS Intern Program, a prestigious mentoring program for young teachers of singing, is also offered each summer. *The Journal of Singing*—the official publication of NATS—is published five times annually.

National Center for Voice and Speech (NCVS). A research and teaching institution based in Salt Lake City dedicated to studying the human voice and speech. The center is led by Ingo Titze (b. 1945), one of the world's most highly regarded **vocologists**. In addition to hosting year-round symposia on various topics, NCVS also offers an annual Summer Vocal Institute (SVI). Singing teachers and voice specialists who complete the four-course curriculum are awarded the Certificate in Vocology, the first credential of its kind in the United States. The NCVS also has a center at the University of Iowa in Iowa City.

National Opera Association (NOA). A national organization founded in 1955 that seeks to promote a greater appreciation of **opera** and **musical theatre** and encourages opera education programs in the United States. NOA hosts annual competitions in singing and for collegiate **opera** scenes and publishes an **academic** journal entitled *The Opera Journal.* NOA membership includes **professionals** from the United States, Canada, Europe, Asia, and Australia.

national school of breathing. See *National Schools of Singing*.

National Schools of Singing. An important **treatise** by **Richard Miller** that was first published in 1977, under the title *English, French, German, and Italian Techniques of Singing: A Study in National Tonal Preferences and How They Relate to Functional Efficiency in Singing.* To prepare for this study, Miller observed more than 700 voice **lessons** in 165 different studios in major schools and conservatories in England, France, Germany, and Italy, comparing nationalistic tendencies as they appeared in the respective countries. Among his most important observations is the conclusion that the Italian school—and particularly the *appoggio* breathing **technique**—is the most pedagogically efficient and should be practiced and advocated by all singers and singing teachers. Miller is also critical of the German "belly breathing" technique called *Bauchaussenstütz.* The book was revised and reissued twenty years later, in 1997, with the new title *National Schools of Singing: English French, German, and Italian Techniques of Singing Revisited.* The volume remains one of the most important books on singing published in the second half of the twentieth century.

nationalism. In music, the deliberate **expression** of one's nationality or regional heritage in a musical composition, usually through the use of folk melodies and **dance**. In vocal music, the texts of nationalistic music can also relate to the history of a particular country or people. In the nineteenth century, nationalism became a salient force in **art music**, when composers from outside the "big four" European countries—Germany, France, Italy, and England—began to impact the international **canon**. The **Russian Five** were distinctly nationalistic composers, as were Bedřich Smetana (1824–1884), Antonín Dvořák (1841–1904), and Leoš Janáček (1854–1928) in Czechoslovakia (now the Czech Republic); Béla Bartók (1881–1945) and Zoltán Kodály (1882–1967) in Hungary; Edvard Grieg (1843–1907) in Norway; Jean Sibelius (1865–1957) in Finland; and Charles Ives (1874–1954) in the United States.

NATS. Acronym for the **National Association of Teachers of Singing**.

natural minor. A **minor scale** with no altered **scale degrees**.

NCVS. Acronym for the **National Center for Voice and Speech**.

N'Dour, Youssou (b. 1959). Senegalese vocal artist. N'Dour is the world's most recognizable ambassador of the *mbalax* **style**, a syncopated **dance** music that originated in Senegal. Perhaps the most famous singer in Africa, N'Dour gained fame in the West through his vocals in the 1986 hit song "In Your Eyes," by Peter Gabriel (b. 1950). In 2012, N'Dour became Senegal's minister of tourism and culture.

Neapolitan chord. The ♭II **chord** of a **major key** or **minor key**, usually presented in first **inversion** as a substitute for a **subdominant** (IV) chord. Neapolitan chords appear in minor keys more often than major keys and are frequently used by *Lied* composers to expressively highlight certain words of the poetic text.

Figure 32. Neapolitan chord in C Minor. *Courtesy Creative Commons.*

Neapolitan song. A popular **song** from southern Italy dating from the early nineteenth century. The texts—which are usually sung by men—are either **serenades** or the complaints of a pining lover. The name "Neapolitan" derives from the region of origin, which was formerly the Kingdom of Naples. The southern **dialect** in which the songs are performed is sometimes called the Neapolitan language or Southern Italian. "O sole mio" is perhaps the most famous example of a Neapolitan song.

neighboring tone. 1. An **ornament** that consists of a **dissonant** note that is either one step higher or lower than a **consonant tone**. Also called an auxiliary tone.

2. In music theory, any note approached by stepwise motion.

neo-romantic. Describes twentieth- and twenty-first-century music that is written in a tonal, **romantic** style.

neumatic. 1. A type of text setting that is a middle ground between **syllabic** and **melismatic** settings, thus setting several notes per syllable of text. The neumatic adjective is almost exclusively used when describing **medieval monophonic** music, particularly **Gregorian chant**.

2. Describes a type of notation one encounters in the Gregorian chant **repertory**, which utilizes **neumes** as opposed to modern notation. Also called **Gregorian chant notation**.

neume. Any of the note shapes used in the notation of **Gregorian chant**. Neumes take many shapes and **forms**—each with a specific name and function—and are used in conjunction with the **four-line staff**. Performers of **chant** and **early music** must be familiar with neumes.

neurochronaxic theory (of voice production). A theory of **vocal fold oscillation** developed by French voice scientist Raoul Husson (1901–1967) that contends that nerve impulses from the brain are the sole cause of **vocal fold** vibration. This outdated theory has long been discredited scientifically in favor of the **myoelastic-aerodymic theory**, as well as the **one-mass model** and **three-mass model of voice production**.

neurogenic. Describes a disease or disorder that originates in the nerves or nervous tissue. The most common types of neurogenic **voice disorders** are **vocal fold paralysis**, **vocal fold paresis**, and **spasmodic dysphonia (SD)**.

neutral. One of the four vocal **modes** described in **Complete Vocal Technique (CVT)**. The neutral sound **quality** is described as being similar to the soft, soothing quality often heard when one sings a **lullaby**. Unlike the three other CVT modes—**curbing**, **edge**, and **overdrive**—there is no "metal" quality present in neutral mode.

new music. A label that describes contemporary **art music**. New music artists often **premiere** works of living composers, many of whom are **commissioned** to write new pieces. Vocalists who pursue new music **genres** may be asked to use **extended techniques**.

new wave. The **subgenre** of **rock** music played by numerous English and American bands beginning in the late 1970s. New wave music deliberately rejected **hard rock** and **heavy metal** in favor of a simpler, more intimate **style**. Elvis Costello (b. 1954) and Patti Smith (b. 1946) are two of the most recognizable singers associated with new wave.

New York Singing Teachers Association (NYSTA). International organization of singing teachers based in New York City. Founded in 1906, NYSTA is the oldest singing teachers association in the United States. Original members included such luminaries as **Enrico Caruso**, Emma Eames (1865–1952), Geraldine Farrar (1882–1967), Mary Garden (1874–1967), Ernestine Schumann-Heink (1861–1936), and Marcella Sembrich (1858–1935). NYSTA is especially dedicated to educational outreach, and its Professional Development Program (PDP) regularly delivers on-site and on-demand **pedagogy** courses through a series of core courses, including Vocal Anatomy and Physiology, Voice Acoustics and Resonance, Vocal Health for Voice Professionals, Singers Developmental Repertoire, and Comparative Voice Pedagogy. Singing teachers who complete the five-course core curriculum receive a certificate of completion. NYSTA's tagline is "Educating Voice Professionals Worldwide." *VOICEPrints*—the official journal of NYSTA—is published fives time annually.

nicht **(Ger).** Not. Almost always precedes an adjective (e.g., *nicht schnell*).

nicht schnell **(Ger).** Not fast.

nicht zu schnell **(Ger).** Not too fast.

Nixon, Marni (b. 1930). American **soprano**. Nixon is perhaps the most well-known **playback singer** in the United States, voicing the singing of several leading ladies in Hollywood films. Her most famous singing **roles** have included Deborah Kerr's Anna in *The King and I* (1956), Natalie Wood's Maria in *West Side Story* (1961), and Audrey Hepburn's Eliza Doolittle in *My Fair Lady* (1964). She is also accomplished as a **classical singer**, performing many **opera** and **oratorio** roles with major **companies** and symphony orchestras. A resident of New York City, Nixon is an active teacher and a longtime member of the **New York Singing Teachers Association (NYSTA)**.

Nō **(Jap).** See *Noh*.

NOA. Abbreviation for **National Opera Association**.

noble posture. The ideal **posture** for singing, which includes standing erect with a high **sternum**, allowing for good **axial alignment** with the opportunity for rib expansion. Noble posture is practiced by virtually all singers and teachers of singing.

noch **(Ger).** Still or yet.

nodes. See **nodules**.

nodules. A vocal pathology in which benign, callous-like **lesions** form on the **vocal folds**, often as a result of prolonged vocal abuse, including poor vocal **technique**, yelling, harsh **glottal attacks**, overuse of the voice, and poor vocal hygiene. Nodules interfere with **glottal** closure in the **larynx**, inhibiting vocal fold vibration and prohibiting full **adduction** of the vocal folds. The result is usually a weakened, breathy sound with a limited vocal **range**. Vocal nodules almost always occur **bilaterally** (in adjacent pairs) and in women. At first, nodules are soft in nature, but they harden after repeated abuse. Vocal nodules can often be healed with prolonged **voice therapy**, provided the singer also works to eliminate abusive practices and improve vocal hygiene. Vocal nodules are also commonly referred to as **nodes**.

Nogaku. See *Noh*.

Noh. Highly stylized **form** of Japanese drama that incorporates acting, singing, dancing, miming, and instrumental music. *Noh* singing is similar in **style** to that heard in *kabuki* **theatre**. Also spelled *Nō* or *Nogaku*.

noise. A **contemporary commercial music (CCM)** term referring to **fry** in the **tone quality** of the singer.

non troppo **(It).** Not too much.

nonfunctional. In music theory, describes a **chord** that cannot be analyzed in a way that makes sense with **tonal harmony**, i.e., it does not "function" in a tonal way. The **Tristan chord** from Wagner's *Tristan und Isolde* (1865) is the quintessential nonfunctional chord, with many other examples proliferating throughout the **posttonal** era of music.

nonlegato. An adjective that describes a passage of music that is not **legato** and is rather either *staccato* or **marcato** in **quality**. Nonlegato is a command or instruction most frequently uttered by choral **conductors**, who want a passage of **polyphonic** music to sound crisp, detached, and clean with an absence of singer's legato.

nonlegit. In **musical theatre**, to not sing in a **classical (legit)** style.

nonplot show. An **opera** or **musical** without a narrative story. Famous examples include Stephen Sondheim's *Company* (1970) and Philip Glass's *Einstein on the Beach* (1976). See also **concept musical**.

nonvibrato. An adjective that describes a singing **style** that is completely absent of **vibrato**; a **straight-tone** quality. Nonvibrato is a command or instruction most frequently uttered by choral **conductors**, who may desire to hear a piece, a section of a piece, or a **cadence** in a nonvibrato style. Nonvibrato is also a salient feature in solo styles of **early music**.

Nordic art song. A vast **repertoire** of **recital** music not often heard in the West due to the number of languages represented in the repertoire. A singer of Nordic art song must be comfortable singing in Danish, Norwegian, Swedish, and Finnish. While there is some repertoire from Iceland and the Faroe Islands, this literature is minimal compared to the **songs** that exist in the four principal languages. Nordic art song is frequently called **Scandinavian art song**, but Scandinavia proper only includes the countries of Denmark, Sweden, and Norway. Since **Finnish art song** is of such high **quality**—and since the ease of **Finnish diction** makes it a reasonable conquest for young singers—it is practical to include Finnish repertoire in discussions of Nordic art song. The most important composers of Nordic art song include Edvard Grieg (1843–1907), Jean Sibelius (1865–1957), Yrjö Kilpinen (1892–1959), Wilhelm Stenhammar (1871–1927), Hugo Alfvén (1872–1947), Ture Rangström (1884–1931), and Carl Nielsen (1865–1931).

Norton Critical Scores. A series of critical **scores** published by W. W. Norton & Company in New York. In addition to a scholarly *Urtext* edition of the score, each volume also consists of numerous essays on a particular musical work. Although the series is somewhat finite—it was discontinued in the 1980s for unclear reasons—each score is worth having in one's library. There are five Norton Critical Scores devoted to vocal works: Palestrina's *Pope Marcellus Mass* (1562), Purcell's *Dido and Aeneas* (1689), Bach's *Cantata No. 4* (1707) and *Cantata No. 140* (1731), and Schumann's *Dichterliebe* (1840).

notes inégales **(Fr).** Unequal notes.

Notre Dame polyphony. Early experiments in **medieval polyphony** that originated at the Cathedral of Notre Dame in Paris in the late twelfth and early thirteenth centuries. The Notre Dame school is credited with the invention of *organum*, and its principal composers include Léonin (fl. c. 1150–c. 1201) and Pérotin (fl. c. 1200).

number. An **aria**, **ensemble**, or **song** in an **opera**, **oratorio**, or **musical**.

number opera. An **opera** comprised of many separate pieces (or **numbers**), for instance, **arias**, **ensembles**, and **chorus**. **Recitative** is sung between numbers. Virtually all operas written during the **baroque** and **classical** periods were number operas. During the **romantic** era, number operas fell out of fashion in favor of **through-composed** operas.

Nunc dimittis. A canticle from Luke 2:29–32, also called the Canticle of Simeon or Song of Simeon. The *Nunc dimittis* is performed at Roman Catholic services during Compline and in Anglican services during evensong.

nut. A **Broadway** jargon term that refers to the weekly cost of running a **musical**.

NYSTA. Abbreviation for the **New York Singing Teachers Association**.

O

O **antiphons.** The seven **antiphons** sung at Vespers on the seven days preceding Christmas Eve. The *O* antiphons are *O Sapientia* ("O Wisdom"), *O Adonai* ("O Sacred Lord"), *O Radix Jesse* ("O Flower of Jesse's Stem"), *O Clavis David* ("O Key of David"), *O Oriens* ("O Radiant Dawn"), *O Rex Gentium* ("O King of All Nations"), and *O Emmanuel* ("O Emmanuel").

Obie Awards. Annual **Off-Broadway theatre** awards given by the *Village Voice* newspaper in New York City. The Obie Awards complement the **Tony Awards**, which are reserved for **Broadway** theatre.

objective. 1. In voice science, a type of data that can be measured scientifically, for example, **frequency, amplitude, spectral envelope,** or **duration.** Objective data contrasts with subjective perceptions. In voice teaching, describes **fact-based** teaching that incorporates principles of physiology and voice science.

2. An acting term that refers to what the character wants or is trying to get. An interpretive concept explored by singers of **musical theatre** and **opera.**

Observations on the Florid Song. A 1743 **treatise** by **Pier Francesco Tosi.** One of the earliest **voice pedagogy** treatises, *Observations on the Florid Song* also provides insight into the types of **ornaments** practiced by singers of the first half of the eighteenth century.

obstacle. An acting term that refers to what is preventing the character from achieving his or her goal. An interpretive concept explored by singers of **musical theatre** and **opera.**

octatonic scale. A **scale** with eight distinct **pitches.** Octatonic scales most often describe scales that alternate between **whole steps** and **half steps.** In **jazz** theory, these specific scales are called diminished scales. There are only three possible varieties of diminished scales.

Figure 33. Three incarnations of the octatonic scale. *Courtesy Creative Commons.*

octave. An **interval** of two **pitches** of the same name in which the higher pitch has twice the **frequency** of the lower pitch.

octavo (8ᵛᵒ). The name for a short, published choral composition. Historically, the term derives its name from the folding of a large sheet of paper into eight sections, resulting in sixteen printed pages (front and back), Hence, the term also came to mean a particular size: about eight to ten inches tall.

ode. A choral setting of a secular poem, usually **scored** for soloists, **chorus,** and orchestra. Odes were popular in England during the **baroque** era and were usually composed to honor members of royalty or saints.

oeuvre **(Fr).** Works. Refers to the complete body of works, usually the compositions of a particular composer or performing artist.

off-book. When a singing **role** is memorized. Certain genres—**opera** and solo **art song recitals**—are usually performed off-book.

Off-Broadway. A designation for New York City **professional theatre** (including plays and **musicals**) in venues with a seating capacity between 100 and 499. Off-Broadway **productions** tend to be small and more intimate than **Broadway** productions, with smaller cast sizes and orchestras. Some of **musical theatre's** greatest hits were originally Off-Broadway productions, including *The Fantasticks* (1960), which holds the record as the longest-running musical of all time, playing for forty-two years and 17,162 performances.

offertory. One of the five standard parts of the **Proper** in a Catholic **Mass**.

Off-Off-Broadway. A designation for New York City **professional theatre** in venues that are smaller than **Off-Broadway productions**, usually fewer than 100 seats.

offset. The end of a sung **pitch** or **phrase** when **phonation** ceases, and the opposite of **onset**. See also **release**.

Old Roman chant. A type of **medieval liturgical chant** preserved in a set of five Roman manuscripts. Essentially identical in **style** and an extension of the **Gregorian chant repertory**.

olio. The second **act** of a **minstrel show**. Also called a **fantasia**.

omitted *r***.** In English **diction**, the practice of omitting *r* altogether in certain situations. For instance, if *r* is immediately followed by a **consonant**: Lord [lɔd], earthly [ɜθli], and so forth. Omitting the *r* in these situations is standard practice when singing **English art song** and in most choral situations.

omnidirectional pattern. In audio technology, a descriptive **phrase** for how a **microphone** will respond to **acoustic** energy directed at it. An omnidirectional pattern is a **pickup pattern** with a circular shape entirely surrounding the microphone's **diaphragm**. Omnidirectional microphones pick up sound equally from all directions. Figure 34 offers a visualization of a shotgun pickup pattern. These microphones are often used for live recordings of acoustic performers, for example, orchestras, **choirs**, and **classical** vocalists. Omnidirectional microphones are not subject to the **proximity effect**, which improves their ability to accurately capture sound sources from a distance. For more information, see the essay entitled "What Every Singer Needs to Know about Audio Technology."

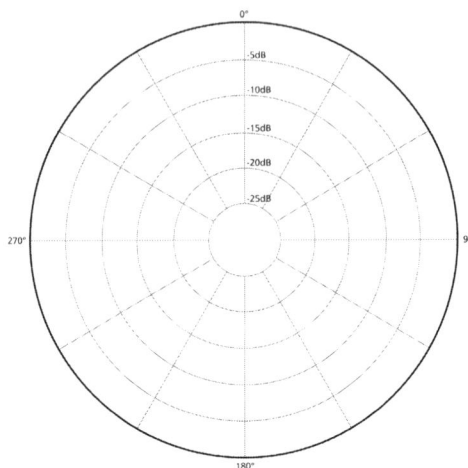

Figure 34. An omnidirectional microphone pattern. *Courtesy Creative Commons.*

on-book. When a singer uses the **score** as opposed to memorizing a **role**. Certain **genres**—**oratorio, chamber music**, and **choral music**—are usually performed on-book.

Ondar, Kongar-ool (1962–2013). A master of **Tuvan throat singing** and the world's most visible and famous *khoomei* singer. Ondar's first name literally translates to "loud boy," and during the latter part of his life, he was given a stipend and housing by the Tuvan government out of deference for his incomparable musical skills. Also involved in politics, Ondar was a member of the Great Khural of Tuva, the governing body of the country, a small republic in Central Asia. His singing can be heard on the soundtrack to the movie *Genghis Blues* (1999).

one-act opera. An **opera** in one **act**. One-act operas are often short in length and presented with other one-act (or short) operas as **double bill** or **triple bill**. Some of the most famous one-act operas are Mascagni's *Cavalleria rustiana* (1890), Strauss's *Salome* (1905), Menotti's *The Old Maid and the Thief* (1939), and Gilbert and Sullivan's *Trial by Jury* (1875). Giacomo Puccini (1858–1924) also composed a famous triptych of one-act operas: *Il tabarro, Suor Angelica*, and *Gianni Schicchi*. These operas were first performed at the **Metropolitan Opera** in 1918, as a triple bill known as *Il trittico*.

one-mass model (of voice production). A theory of **vocal fold oscillation** that builds upon the **myoelastic-aerodynamic theory**, making that theory more plausible by suggesting that sustainability of oscillation is made possible through inertia in the **vocal tract**. Unlike the myoelastic-aerodynamic model, the one-mass model includes the vocal tract and demonstrates that the air pressure above and below the **glottis** is asymmetrical. The one-mass model does not account for everything observed in vocal fold vibration, however, and the **three-mass model**

represents another evolution in our understanding of vocal fold oscillation.

one voice. A jargon term used by choral **conductors** and choral artists that means achieving a perfect **blend** within a section of a choral **ensemble**. The **sopranos**, for example, will listen carefully to one another, exactly matching **pitch**, **vowel**, and volume to sound like "one voice" within their section. **Straight-tone** singing and deliberately limiting the **singer's resonance** are common **techniques** used when a section strives to sound like one voice. Many choral conductors, for example, the late **Robert Shaw**, have advocated this "loss of identity" within one's section for the sake of the ensemble; ideally, a choral singer should not hear himself or herself, but become a seamless part of the choral fabric.

onset. The beginning of a singing **tone**. Onset describes not only the act, but also the **quality**, as there is a spectrum of different types of onsets. A **balanced onset** is the default position of good **classical singing technique**, being neither too "hard" (indicative of a harsh **glottal attack**) nor too "soft" (airy, with the **vocal folds** not fully **approximating**). The opposite of onset is **release**, which signifies the end of a singing tone. Release is sometimes referred to as **offset**.

open throat. A nonscientific term traditionally used by **voice pedagogues** to describe a sensation of freedom. In **objective** parameters, most singing teachers might agree that an open throat involves some combination of a lowered **larynx**, a high (or engaged) **soft palate**, and a tongue/jaw and pharyngeal area that is free of excess tension, especially in the constrictor muscles. An "open throat" is a concept that not only motivates singing efficiency, but also encourages a warm, round **tone quality** synonymous with the **classical** aesthetic. While a **contemporary commercial music (CCM)** singer might desire technical efficiency and freedom from excess tension in his or her singing, "open throat" might not be an ideal way to describe a **style** that is more closely related to natural speech. On the contrary, a singer who sings with an open throat is probably going for a sound that is the antithesis of speech.

open vowel. Describes a **vowel** that requires more space between the **articulators** than **closed vowels**. Common examples include [ɪ], [ɛ], [ɔ], [ʊ], [ʏ], and [œ]. See also **back vowel**, **central vowel**, **front vowel**, **mixed vowel**, **nasal vowels**.

opening night. See **premiere**.

opera. A prevailing and incomparably important **genre** in **classical singing**, opera can be simply defined as a "drama that is entirely sung." A thorough definition is far more complex, however, as the genre of opera has assumed radically different **forms** during the course of its 400-plus-year history. Most people would think of Beethoven's *Fidelio* (1805, rev. 1814), for instance, as an opera, even though it contains dialogue. On the other hand, most people would also regard *Les Misérables* (1985–1987) and *Phantom of the Opera* (1986–1988) as **musicals**, even though they are entirely sung. Perhaps a more accurate contemporary definition would also incorporate the intentions of the composer (whether he or she conceives of the work as an opera) and the singing **style** required to realize the intentions of the composer (i.e., some sort of **classical technique**).

The birth of opera occurred during the last decade of the sixteenth century as a result of musical experiments developed by members of the **Florentine Camerata**, a group of scholars, poets, and composers who met at the court of Giovanni de' Bardi (1534–1612). These operas, written in a **monodic** style, retold Greek myths that were the subject of dramas performed during the **Renaissance** era. Claudio Monteverdi (1567–1643) composed opera's first universally acclaimed **masterwork** with *Orfeo* (1607). Monteverdi proceeded to push boundaries with the new genre in *L'incoronazione di Poppea* (1643), the first opera based on a historical rather than mythological subject. Opera continued to grow in popularity throughout the **baroque** era. In addition to the major cities of Italy—Venice, Florence, Milan, and Naples—Paris and London also became important centers for opera. **French operas**, in their own distinctive style, were written by Jean-Baptiste Lully (an Italian *émigré*, 1632–1687) and Jean-Philippe Rameau (1683–1764). Henry Purcell (1659–1695) experimented with **English opera** in London with *Dido and Aeneas* (1689), but it was George Frideric Handel (1685–1759) who emerged as the late baroque's most successful and distinguished composer of opera with his **Italian operas** for London audiences.

The most important opera composer of the Viennese classical era was undoubtedly Wolfgang Amadeus Mozart (1756–1791), whose mature operas are still among the most frequently performed works in the world's **opera houses**. In Italy, *bel canto* **operas** emerged as the aesthetic convention of the day, with Gioacchino Rossini (1792–1868), Gaetano Donizetti (1797–1848), and Vincenzo Bellini (1801–1835) emerging as the three greatest exponents of the style. As the nineteenth century progressed, more distinct traditions flowered in Italy, France, and Germany. Giuseppe Verdi (1813–1901) built upon the *bel canto* traditions of his predecessors, becoming the **romantic** era's most important composer of Italian opera. After early experiments in Germany by Carl Maria von Weber (1786–1826), Richard Wagner (1813–1883) became the towering figure in **German opera**, reinventing the form—and perhaps music itself—with his mature

music dramas. In France, the most important opera composers were Hector Berlioz (1803–1869), Georges Bizet (1838–1875), Charles Gounod (1818–1893), and Jules Massenet (1842–1912). **Nationalism** in opera also emerged toward the end of the nineteenth century, with a proliferation of Russian, Czech, and even Polish operas, all of which explored their vernacular language and idiomatic histories and musical traditions.

The genre of opera continued to become more diverse by the beginning of the twentieth century. Giacomo Puccini (1858–1924) continued the Italian tradition with his *verismo* operas, and Richard Strauss (1864–1949) and Alban Berg (1885–1935) wrote the most important German operas of the first half of the century. Claude Debussy (1862–1918) created opera's only experiment in **impressionism** with *Pelléas et Mélisande* (1902). **American opera** also flourished, offering its own brand of nationalism. And the ***avant-garde*** operas of Karlheinz Stockhausen (1928–2007) and the **minimalistic** experiments of Philip Glass (b. 1937) stretched the very definition of the genre. Ultimately, however, these modernist works have made very little impact on the international **repertory**, which still favors the repertoire from Handel through Puccini. Romantic opera predominantly forms the core of the performance repertory.

Many additional terms in this book are opera-related. See also **aria**, **arietta**, **arioso**, **cabaletta**, **cantabile**, *cavatina*, *comédie-ballet*, *da capo* aria, *dramma giocoso*, **ensemble**, **ensemble finale**, **folk opera**, *grand opéra*, **ground bass aria**, *leitmotif*, **monody**, **number opera**, *opéra bouffe*, *opera buffa*, *opéra comique*, **opera house**, *opéra lyrique*, *opera semiseria*, *opera seria*, *recitatif mesuré*, *recitatif simple*, **recitative**, *recitativo accompagnato*, *recitativo secco*, *scena*, *stretta*, *tragédie en musique*.

Opéra Bastille. A 2,700-seat **opera house** in Paris, built from 1984–1989 to replace the **Palais Garnier** as the principal home for the Paris Opéra. In addition to being a larger house, the Opéra Bastille is a significant upgrade from the Palais Garnier, with elaborate facilities for set and **production** changes.

opéra bouffe. A **form** of French light **opera** that emerged in the mid-nineteenth century. An *opéra bouffe* was usually a satirical, comical work, often quite bawdy in nature. The **genre** derived its name from the Bouffes Parisiens, where many of the first *opéra bouffe* **productions** were **premiered**. The *opéra bouffe* was invented by the French composer Louis Auguste Florimond Ronger (1825–1892)—better known to history as Hervé—but the genre achieved popularity with the works of Jacques Offenbach (1819–1880). Offenbach's *Orphée aux enfers* (1858), which satirizes the Greek myth of **Orpheus**, is considered to be the quintessential *opéra bouffe*. It is no accident that Offenbach chose this myth—the same one

chosen by Claudio Monteverdi (1567–1643) and Christoph Willibald Gluck (1714–1787)—for his subject; the possibilities for satire could not have been richer.

opera buffa. A specific type of Italian **comic opera** that emerged during the eighteenth century. The *opera buffa* was often formulaic and contained **stock characters**, for example, the ***basso buffo***. The *opera buffa* may be contrasted with ***opera seria***, the serious (and also formulaic) **Italian operas** of the day.

opéra comique. A specific type of nineteenth-century **French opera** with dialogue. Although *opéra comique* literally translates as "**comic opera**," the **plot** of an *opéra comique* could be either comical or serious. These works were often performed at the Opéra-Comique, a Parisian opera **company** that still exists. *Carmen* (1875), by Georges Bizet (1838–1875)—an *opéra comique* that is far from comical—is the most well-known example of the **genre** that is still in the **repertory** today.

Figure 35. Actors of the *opéra comique*.

opera house. A **theatre** built specifically for **operatic productions**. **Operas** were originally performed in private venues, but their rapid rise in popularity at the beginning of the seventeenth century led to the construction of custom-made opera houses. The **Teatro San Cassiano** in Venice was built in 1637. It is generally recognized as the world's first opera house. A comprehensive list of the world's opera houses is not possible here, but a brief listing of some of the most famous examples would include the **Metropolitan Opera House** in New York, the Teatro alla Scala (more commonly known as **La Scala**) in Milan, the **Palais Garnier** in Paris, the Royal Opera House at **Covent Garden** in London, the **Teatro Colón** in Buenos Aires, and the **Bayreuth Festspielhaus** in Bayreuth, Germany.

opéra lyrique. **Operatic genre** that emerged in Paris in the latter half of the nineteenth century. See also **lyric opera**.

opera semiseria. A short-lived Italian **operatic genre** of the late eighteenth and early nineteenth centuries that blended together elements of **comic opera** and serious **opera**. Specifically, the *opera semiseria* usually contained the **virtuosic arias** of the *opera seria* and the **ensemble finales** of the *opera buffa*. *Opera semiseria* was similar in nature to the *dramma giocoso*, although composers usually specifically labeled their works as one or the other. *La sonnambula* (1831), by Vincenzo Bellini (1801–1835), is an example of an *opera semiseria*.

opera seria. Literally meaning "serious **opera**," the *opera seria* was a **genre** of **Italian opera** that emerged and remained prevalent throughout the eighteenth century. The *opera seria* adhered to a strict formal structure in three **acts**, with formulaic **stock characters** and frequent *da capo* arias. Pietro Metastasio (1698–1782) and Apostolo Zeno (1669–1750) were the two most famous **librettists** of *opera seria*, and these two men did much to clarify the formulaic structure and conventions of the genre. It should be noted that although the *opera seria* was an Italian genre, these works were composed throughout Europe—by Italians, Austrians, Germans, and even the English.

operatic. Adjective that means "in the **operatic style**." Can also describe a singing style that is "full throated" and reminiscent of **romantic** Italian singing **technique**. This latter use of the adjective—while prevalent in use—is a bit ironic, as a performance of an **aria** by George Frideric Handel (1685–1759) or Philip Glass (b. 1937) is likely to not be "operatic" in style, even though those excerpts are from **operas**.

operatic head voice. A kind of **vowel** modification—or **cover**—that male **classical singers** use in their higher **range**. Operatic head voice is **TA-dominant** and part of the coordinated or **mixed register**. The label is misleading, as operatic head voice is not a new **register**, nor is it head voice in any way (i.e., **falsetto**, a **CT-dominant** sound, or **mode 2** register). It is simply the selection of warmer, darker vowels to conform to the **classical** aesthetic of an even register and good **tone quality**.

OperaWorks. A holistic summer training program founded, developed, and directed by Ann Baltz (b. 1954). OperaWorks presents intensive summer and winter sessions in California and also engages in residencies at universities and conservatories. The program is multifaceted, with tracks for emerging and advanced artists, as well as voice teachers and **stage directors**.

operetta. In the narrow definition, operetta refers to the **waltz**-based **Viennese operetta** of the late nineteenth century; however, it is commonly used in a wide, "catch-all" sense referring to any **form** of light **opera** in any language. See also **American operetta**, **English comic opera**, *opéra bouffe*.

opus (Lat). "Work." A number assigned to a composer's work, often by a publisher. An opus number sometimes comprises several works, for instance, a **song set** that contains multiple **songs**. Opus numbers often indicate the chronological order in which a composer's works were published. Not all composers' works are catalogued according to opus numbers. In some cases, a scholar might posthumously organize a composer's *oeuvre*. The most common examples relevant to singers include Bach (BWV), Mozart (K), and Schubert (D). Opus is abbreviated as Op. (singular) or Opp. (plural). Sometimes works without opus numbers are catalogued with the abbreviation "WoO."

oración. See *plegaria*.

oral cavity (oropharynx). The part of the **vocal tract** that includes the mouth, tongue, and teeth.

Oranaise, Reinette l'. See **l'Oranaise, Reinette**.

oratorio. A **genre** of music for **chorus**, orchestra, and soloists. Oratorios generally have a biblical or religious narrative but are written for the **concert** hall as opposed to a **liturgical** worship service. Unlike **opera**, oratorios are generally not staged and do not feature sets and costumes. The oratorio proper is always set in the vernacular, although a loose and practical definition of the genre also includes some **Latin** works as well.

The earliest oratorio experiments were Italian **baroque** works, but the first oratorios that are still in the **repertory** were composed in Lutheran Germany by Heinrich Schütz (1585–1672) and Johann Sebastian Bach (1685–1750). Bach's *St John Passion*, BWV 245 (1724) and *St. Matthew Passion*, BWV 244 (1727) represent two of the greatest works in the genre. Perhaps the most important composer of oratorio in any era was George Frideric Handel (1685–1759), who devoted himself almost exclusively to the genre during the latter part of his long career in London. Franz Joseph Haydn (1732–1809) composed the **classical** era's most important oratorios with *Die Schöpfung* (*The Creation*, 1798) and *Die Jahreszeiten* (*The Seasons*, 1801), and Felix Mendelssohn became the **romantic** era's most important oratorio composer with *Paulus*, Op. 36 (*St. Paul*, 1836) and *Elias*, Op. 70 (*Elijah*, 1846). In the twentieth century, it was England that remained most devoted to the genre, with four essential oratorios: *The Dream of Gerontius*,

Op. 38 (1900), by Edward Elgar (1857–1934); *Belshazzar's Feast* (1931), by William Walton (1902–1983); *A Child of Our Time* (1944), by Michael Tippett (1905–1998); and the *War Requiem* (1962), by Benjamin Britten (1913–1976).

Although they do not fit the narrow definition of the oratorio due to the lack of a narrative biblical story and specific characters, the **Latin Mass** and **Requiem** genres are often thought of as a substantial part of the oratorio repertory, meeting most of the other oratorio definition criteria. Likewise, **cantatas**—for all intents and purposes—are little more than short oratorios. The active oratorio singer certainly thinks of all such works as a part of his or her oratorio repertoire.

orchestral song. A **song** with orchestral **accompaniment** (as opposed to piano accompaniment). Gustav Mahler (1860–1911), Richard Strauss (1864–1949), and Maurice Ravel (1875–1937) are the most famous composers of orchestral songs.

orchestral song cycle. A **song cycle** with orchestral **accompaniment** (as opposed to piano accompaniment). The most famous examples in the **repertoire** include Strauss's *Vier letzte Lieder* (1948) and Mahler's *Lieder eines fahrenden Gesellen* (1886), *Rückert-Lieder* (1904), and *Kindertotenlieder* (1904).

orchestrated song. See **orchestral song**.

orchestrated song cycle. See **orchestral song cycle**.

orchestration. Describes the instruments and forces that are used to accompany the singer of an **opera**, **oratorio**, or another piece of vocal music. Orchestrations usually represent the original **accompaniment**, but they occasionally come later as an elaboration of an original piano accompaniment. Orchestrations bear tremendous influence on what kind of voice (or *Fach*) a singer needs to possess to project over an instrumental accompaniment, as lighter voices may have difficulty projecting over heavy orchestrations. Some orchestrated songs and **arias** must be performed with orchestra and are not effective in **piano reduction**; Ravel's *Shéhérazade* (1904) is one such example.

Ordinary. The five separate texts of the **Mass** that do not change according to the **liturgical** calendar: *Kyrie*, *Gloria*, *Credo*, *Sanctus*, and *Agnus Dei*. A sixth part, the *Benedictus*, is actually part of the *Sanctus*, but it is often set as a different movement of the Mass in musical settings. Other parts of the five sections may be broken off into separate movements; Bach's *B Minor Mass*, BWV 232 (1749), for example, has twenty-seven separate movements. In addition to many **medieval** and **Renaissance** Mass settings, composers from the **baroque** era onward frequently set the Ordinary as five-movement choral-orchestral works. Some of the most well-known Mass settings in this vein include the *B Minor Mass*, BWV 232 (1749) of Johann Sebastian Bach (1685–1750), the six late Masses of Joseph Haydn (1732–1809), the *C Minor Mass*, K427 (1783) of Wolfgang Amadeus Mozart (1756–1791), the *Missa solemnis*, Op. 123 (1824) of Ludwig van Beethoven (1770–1827), and the six Masses of Franz Schubert (1797–1828).

organum **(pl. *organa*).** One of several **styles** of early **polyphony** most closely associated with the Notre Dame school that flourished around the twelfth century in France. An *organum* is a **polyphonic** composition in which additional voices, performed within **medieval** rhythmic **modes**, are composed over a portion of existing **chant**. The two *organum quadruplum* of Perotin (fl. 1200)—*Viderunt omnes* and *Sederunt principes*—represent the earliest known four-voice polyphonic compositions in Western music.

organum duplum. An *organum* written for two voices.

organum quadruplum. An *organum* written for four voices.

organum triplum. An *organum* written for three voices.

Orientalism. A kind of nineteenth-century exoticism that specifically addresses fascination with Eastern cultures.

ornamentation. The improvised or planned embellishment of a vocal or instrumental line, usually but not always through the addition of notes and rhythmic figures. While the definition of ornamentation is simple, the art and practice of ornamentation is nuanced and complex, with different rules and customs applying to different eras and **styles**. The singer of **early music** spends much of his or her time studying ornamentation.

oropharynx. Another name for the **oral cavity**.

Orpheus. A figure from Greek mythology who is especially relevant to musicians. Orpheus was considered to be the greatest mortal musician, and he played the lyre so well that he even had the power to control nature itself. When his bride Eurydice died, Orpheus even used his musical gifts to charm the king and queen of the Underworld, who returned Eurydice to Orpheus under the condition that he would not look at her until he returned to the land of the living. Impatient, Orpheus glanced back too quickly, thus losing Eurydice forever.

As the myth of Orpheus is a tribute to the power of music, the subject has always been an appealing one to composers of **opera**. Jacopo Peri (1561–1633) and Giulio

Caccini (1551–1618)—both members of the **Florentine Camerata**—composed early dramatic settings of the Orpheus myth in 1600 and 1602, respectively. And Claudio Monteverdi (1567–1643) chose the same subject for *Orfeo* (1607), widely considered to be the first **operatic masterwork**. In 1762, Christoph Willibald Gluck (1714–1787) chose the subject for his **reform opera**, *Orefo ed Euridice*, which deliberately sought to reinvent the operatic conventions of the time. Since the Orpheus theme was so ubiquitous, the subject was also ripe for parody, as Jacques Offenbach (1819–1880) exemplifies in his *opéra bouffe*, *Orphée aux enfers* (1858). Orpheus has been the subject of at least sixty known operas since the creation of the **genre**, as well as more than 100 **song** settings.

Figure 36. Athanasius Kircher: Orpheus tuning his lyre, with the subdued Cerberus at his feet, from *Musurgia universalis*, Book 3, frontispiece, 1650.

oscillation. 1. In **vocology**, a repeated back-and-forth movement. A vibration. See also **vocal fold oscillation**.
2. In electronic music, a signal that is used to create special audio effects, including **vibrato**, **tremolo**, and phasing. Not a synonym for vibrato, although it is occasionally—and erroneously—used that way.

oscillazione. Italian translation of **oscillation**.

ossia **(It).** Or. In a **score**, used to indicate an alternate passage that the performer is welcome to perform instead.

ostinato. A repetitive pattern, usually in the **accompaniment** of a piece of music.

otolaryngologist (ENT). A medical doctor who specializes in the study and treatment of the ears, nose, and throat (hence the common abbreviation ENT). An otolaryngologist is a medical doctor who can prescribe medicine to the injured or impaired singer. An ENT is also a part of the three-member **voice team**, the other two members being the **voice pedagogue** and **speech-language pathologist (SLP)**. An otolaryngologist who goes on to further specialization training in voice, airway, and swallowing disorders is simply called a **laryngologist**.

out of tune. An adjective used to describe singers with bad **intonation** (i.e., the **pitches** are not centered). In **choral music**, out-of-tune singing occurs when individual sections do not sound like **one voice** or sing with poor **blend**, failing to accurately match **vowels** within their section and in the **ensemble**.

overdrive. In **contemporary commercial music (CCM)**, a higher **belt style** needed to perform contemporary **popular music** and modern **musical theatre repertoire**. Similar to **belt-mix** or **superbelt**, but usually with a harder **edge** and increased **subglottal** pressure for a more **rock**-infused sound. Overdrive is also one of the two "full-metallic" **modes** described in **Complete Vocal Technique (CVT)**. In **classical** music, overdrive is mostly found in loud male singing, whereas females only use overdrive in the lowest part of the voice.

overtone series. See **harmonic series**.

overture. An orchestral piece played at the beginning of an **opera** or **musical**. Especially in musicals and **operettas**, overtures may offer a **medley** of tunes that will be heard throughout the course of the subsequent evening, a tradition that began with the overture to *Orphée aux enfers* (1858), by Jacques Offenbach (1819–1880). The term may also be used for a short orchestral work that is not attached to a **theatre** piece.

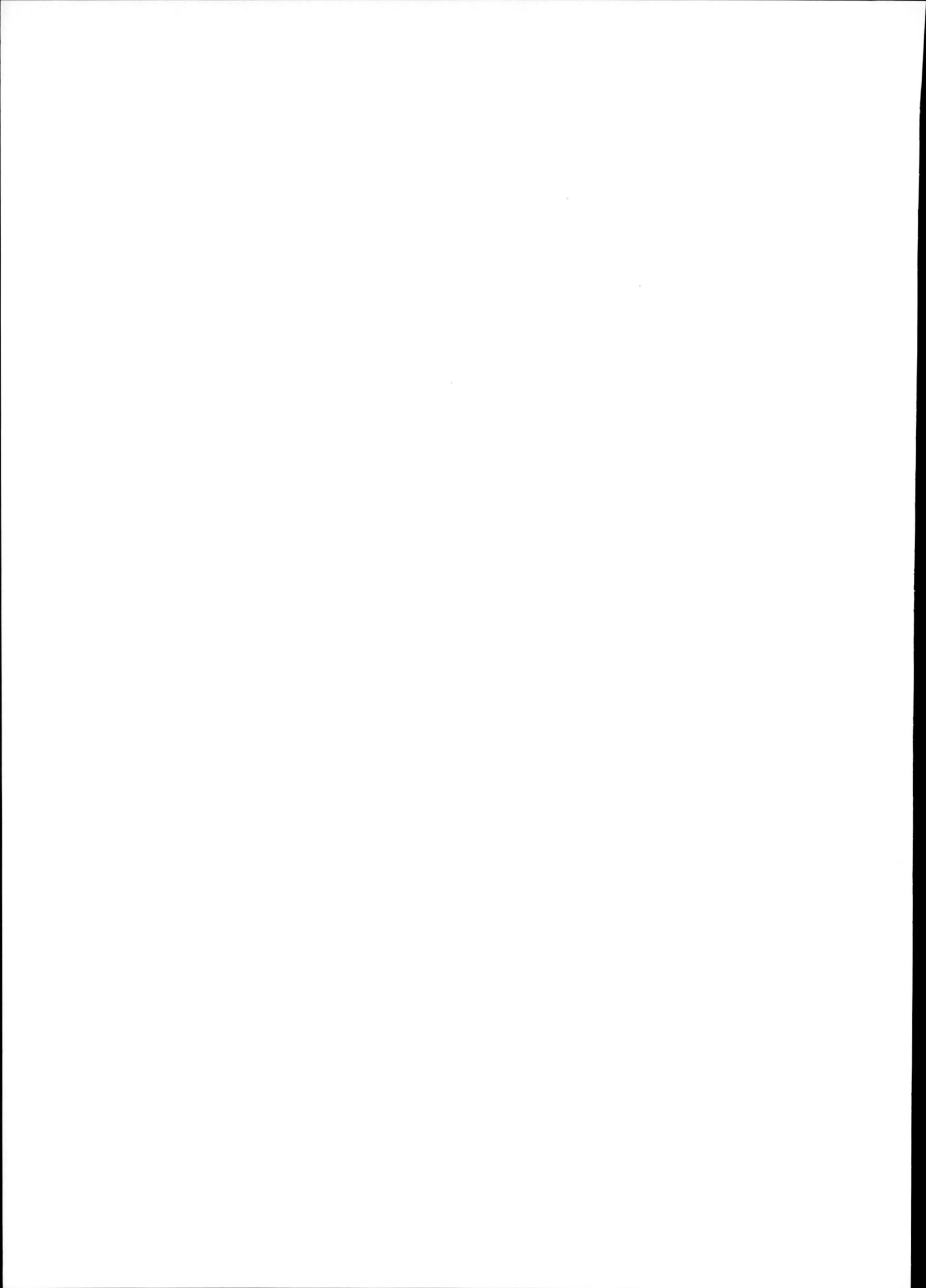

P

paean. An exuberant **song** of praise or thanksgiving.

Palais Garnier. An **opera house** in Paris built from 1861–1875. Erected specifically for the Paris Opéra, the Palais Garnier is often called simply the Opéra Garnier, Opéra de Paris, or simply the Opéra. From 1984–1989, the new and larger **Opéra Bastille** was built to house the Paris Opéra, and the Palais Garnier is now primarily used for **ballet productions**.

palatal. In the study of **diction**, refers to a specific **point of articulation** of a **consonant** involving the middle of the tongue and the **hard palate**. The **glide** [j] is the only common palatal consonant. See also **alveolar**, **bilabial**, **dental**, **labiodental**, **prepalatal**, **velar**.

palate. The roof of the mouth, formed by the palatine bone. Divided into the **hard palate** (front) and **soft palate** (back). Distinct from **palette**.

palette. The expressive **colors** a singer has at his or her disposal. Distinct from **palate**.

pan. An exceptionally negative review.

Panofka, Heinrich (1807–1887). German violinist, composer, and singing teacher best known today for his two widely available sets of **vocalises** (published as Op. 85 and Op. 86). Other **technique books** include *The Practical Singing Tutor* (London, 1852) and *L'art de chanter*, Op. 81 (Paris, 1854). Panofka also composed prolifically for the violin and wrote dozens of **songs**, few of which are still performed today.

pansori. A **genre** of traditional Korean music that features one singer (*sorikkun*) and one drummer (*gosu*). The text relates an epic story (*mandang*). A full performance of a pansori might take hours to complete.

pants role. In **opera**, a male **role** written to be performed by a female singer. The higher voice of a woman is typically meant to convey youth. Well-known pants roles include Cherubino in Mozart's *Le nozze di Figaro* (1786), Oscar in Verdi's *Un ballo in maschera* (1859), and Octavian in Strauss's *Der Rosenkavalier* (1911). Pants roles are also called *travesti*, breeches roles, or trouser roles. It should be noted that **baroque castrato** roles are not pants roles. Even if a **mezzo-soprano** performs a castrato role in a contemporary **production**—an increasingly rare occurrence due to the advent of the **countertenor**—these roles are male roles written to be performed by men. Countertenors almost never sing female roles. While technically they are not pants roles, there are a few female opera roles that are often sung by men. The most notable examples include the Sorceress in Purcell's *Dido and Aeneas* (1689) and the Witch in Humperdinck's *Hänsel und Gretel* (1893).

papering the house. In **musical theatre**, the giving away of free tickets so that a performance is well-attended. The practice of papering the house often occurs at the beginning of the **run** of a struggling show, in hopes that word of mouth will increase public enthusiasm, allowing the show to pick up steam and not have to close.

papilloma. See **human papilloma virus (HPV)**.

parametric equalizer. In audio technology, a type of **equalizer** that allows the user to control three primary parameters: **amplitude**, center **frequency**, and **bandwidth**. Parametric equalizers produce a bell-shaped curve with three settings used to adjust the frequency spectrum of an audio signal: the center frequency, width of frequencies to be adjusted, and amplitude of the adjustment (either **boost** or **cut**). The width of the frequencies to be adjusted is called the "Q." When adjusting the Q, a higher number will indicate a narrower band of frequencies, while a lower Q will indicate a wider band of frequencies. For more information, see the essay entitled "What Every Singer Needs to Know about Audio Technology."

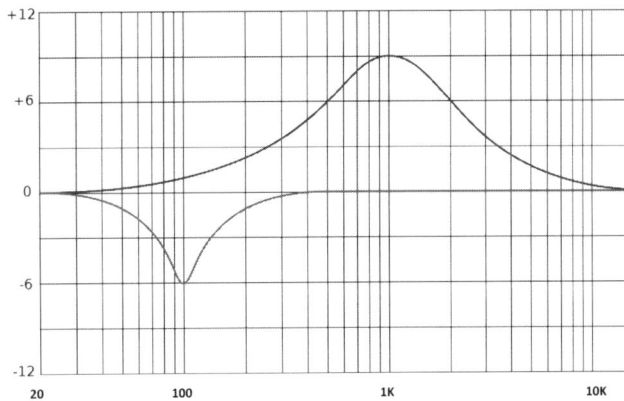

Figure 37. A parametric equalizer graph. *Courtesy Creative Commons.*

paraphrase Mass. A **polyphonic Renaissance** Mass in which each movement is based on the same **monophonic** melody—often a **chant**—that is paraphrased in most or all of the voices. A paraphrase Mass is distinct from **parody Mass**.

paresis. See **vocal fold paresis**.

parlando **(It).** Speaking. Used to instruct singers to deliver a vocal line in a speech-like way.

parlor song. A type of nineteenth-century American **song** for voice and piano. Parlor songs were sentimental in nature and intended for private performance. Published in the **form** of **sheet music** (often with elaborate cover art), the parlor song is an ancestor of the **Tin Pan Alley** song. Stephen Foster (1826–1864) was the most famous composer of parlor songs. Notable examples of the **genre** include "Sweetly She Sleeps, My Alice Fair" (1851) and "Jeanie with the Light Brown Hair" (1856).

parody Mass. A type of **polyphonic Renaissance Mass** in which each movement is based on the same polyphonic model—often a **madrigal**, *chanson*, or **motet**—and all voices of the model are used in the Mass. Also called an imitation Mass, but distinct from **paraphrase Mass**. The term *parody* refers to the replacement of the original text with the Mass text; it is not pejorative.

pars **(Fr).** Part. A self-contained section of a **Renaissance motet**.

partbook. Score containing only one line of **choral music**. **Polyphonic choral music** of the fifteenth and sixteenth centuries was usually printed in partbooks. The publication of partbooks largely fell out of practice after the **Renaissance** era. Choral musicians—unlike orchestral and wind musicians—are not used to this practice, and virtually all contemporary editions of Renaissance choral music are published in standard **choral score** (or **octavo**) format.

partsong. 1. In the **baroque** era, a **song** for more than one voice.

2. In the nineteenth century Viennese **style**, a *Lied* for more than one voice (usually four voices).

pas **(Fr).** Not.

passaggio. Literally meaning "passage" in Italian, the *passaggio* is a pivotal point in the vocal **register** where the singer must begin **vowel** modification to give the impression of a seamless **tone quality** throughout his or her vocal **range**. It is generally agreed that both men and women have two *passaggio* points, labeled the *primo passaggio* (first *passaggio*) and *secondo passaggio* (second *passaggio*). In women, the *primo passaggio* usually occurs between C4 and A4, and the *secondo passaggio* between E5 and A5. In men, the *primo passaggio* usually occurs between F3 and C4, and the *secondo passaggio* between C4 and A4 (the same location as the female *primo passaggio*). The location of specific *passaggio* points within these parameters varies from singer to singer, and the specific **pitch** level at which these transitions occur is one of several determining factors (along with **color** and **tessitura** comfort level) in establishing one's **voice type** (or *Fach*).

Passaggio points are also related to the finer nuances of **registration**. For instance, the location between the two *passaggio* points (in both female and male voices) is often considered to be the **mixed register**, regardless of the principal registration, which is determined at the **laryngeal** level. In female **classical singers**, the pitches located above the *secondo passaggio* are usually produced in a pure head voice (CT voice). Male classical singers usually employ vowel modification above their *secondo passaggio* to achieve the desired warmth and tone quality; they sometimes call this new "register" **operatic head voice** (even though it is not truly a new register). Although modern voice science has clarified the *passaggio* phenomenon—particularly among **fact-based voice pedagogues**—*passaggio* is still a point of controversy and discussion among voice teachers.

passing tone. An **ornament** that consists of a **dissonant** (nonharmonic) note connecting two **consonant** notes by stepwise motion.

Passion. A type of **oratorio** that recounts the arrest, trial, and Crucifixion of Jesus Christ. Passion settings have been used **liturgically** in the Christian church since its beginnings; some **plainsong** settings date back to the **medieval** era. While there are a number of **Renaissance** examples that predate them, the earliest Passions that remain a part of the **repertory** are the Lutheran Passions of Heinrich Schütz (1585–1672); Schütz composed settings of the *St. John*, *St. Luke*, and *St. Matthew* Passions in 1665 and 1666. The two surviving Passions of Johann Sebastian Bach—the *St. John Passion*, BWV 245 (1724) and the *St. Matthew Passion*, BWV 244 (1727)—represent the apotheosis of the **genre**. After the **baroque** era, the Passion fell out of favor as a genre of choice for many of the greatest composers; however, several Anglican Passions emerged in England in the late nineteenth century, notably *The Crucifixion* (1887), by John Stainer (1840–1901), and *Olivet to Calvary* (1904), by John Henry Maunder (1858–1920). Krzysztof Penderecki (b. 1933) **premiered** his setting of the *St. Luke Passion* in 1965. Daniel Pinkham (1923–2006) also premiered his setting of the *St. Mark Passion* in the same year.

pasticcio (It). Italian word meaning "meat pie" or "mess." In music, a *pasticcio* is an **operatic** work with a **score** comprised—either entirely or partly—of previously written **songs**, often by multiple composers. The *pasticcio* was common in eighteenth-century **Italian opera**, with such composers as Christoph Willibald Gluck (1714–1787) and George Frideric Handel (1685–1759) often borrowing from previous works when creating new ones. In **musical theatre**, *The Black Crook* (1866) is also an example of a *pasticcio*, as is *The Enchanted Island*, which was **premiered** in 2011, by the **Metropolitan Opera**.

pastiche (Fr). French word meaning "imitation." In music, *pastiche* is often used to describe a **medley**. Not the same as *pasticcio*.

pastoral opera. A short-lived **genre** of **baroque opera** closely related to the **masque**. The quintessential pastoral opera is in English and features shepherd-like characters against a bucolic backdrop. Mythological characters are also a common feature in pastoral **libretti**. Pastoral operas were a product of their time, and virtually none are still performed in the twenty-first century. The notable exception is Handel's *Acis and Galatea* (1718), which was labeled as a masque by the composer but is often presented fully staged in modern **productions**. *Dido and Aeneas* (1689), by Henry Purcell (1659–1695), also contains strong elements of pastoral opera.

pathology. See **voice disorder**.

patter baritone. The **stock character** in **Gilbert and Sullivan comic operas** who is the central comedic figure. The patter baritone always sings at least one **patter song**—a multiversed, nimble-tongued comic **number**—during the course of the evening. Virtually every Gilbert and Sullivan comic opera features a patter baritone; examples include Sir Joseph Porter in *HMS Pinafore* (1878), Major-General Stanley in *The Pirates of Penzance* (1879), the Lord High Chancellor in *Iolanthe* (1882), Ko-Ko in *The Mikado* (1885), and Jack Point in *The Yeoman of the Guard* (1888).

patter song. A comic **song**, usually in **strophic form**, that features a copious amount of rapidly delivered text. **Gilbert and Sullivan** were famous for their patter songs, which appear in almost all of their **comic operas**. Famous examples include "When I, Good Friends, Was Called to the Bar," from *Trial by Jury* (1875); "I Am the Very Model of a Modern Major General," from *The Pirates of Penzance* (1879); and "When You're Lying Awake with a Dismal Headache," from *Iolanthe* (1882). Patter songs are usually performed by the **patter baritone** (or comic baritone), a **stock character** that appears in all Gilbert and Sullivan comic operas.

Pavarotti, Luciano (1935–2007). Italian **tenor** and one of the most iconic and universally acclaimed singers of the second half of the twentieth century. Pavarotti gained international success as an **opera** singer while still in his late twenties, performing multiple **roles** at **Covent Garden** and **La Scala** before making his **Metropolitan Opera** debut in 1968, as Rodolfo in Puccini's *La bohème*. Pavarotti became an overnight sensation in 1972, when he sang the role of Tonio in Donizetti's *La fille du régiment*, also at **The Met**. With his nine effortless high Cs in "Ah! mes amis" (his signature **aria**), he enthralled the audience and earned seventeen curtain calls, a record that still stands at The Met. Pavarotti's fame as an opera singer surpassed virtually every other singer of his generation. The only possible rival to his celebrity was **Placido Domingo**, and during a pop-culture phenomenon of the 1990s, two of the famous "Three Tenors" were Pavarotti and Domingo; however, these two singers excelled in very different roles, and Pavarotti never ventured into the *spinto* and *Heldentenor* **repertoire** of Domingo. When Pavarotti performed the heaviest role of his career—the title in Verdi's *Otello*—he sang it in his own effective way. His *Otello* is perhaps the lightest and most lyrical preserved on record. Pavarotti sang his final opera performance in 2004—Cavaradossi in Puccini's *Tosca* at the Met—and retired in 2005. He died two years later, in 2007.

PCA. Abbreviation for **posterior cricoarytenoids**.

peak of the tongue arch. In **diction**, classifies whether a **vowel** is a **front vowel**, **central vowel**, or **back vowel**. Peak of the tongue arch is one of the two distinct properties of vowels, along with **quality** (**open vowels** and **closed vowels**). Vowels can be classified as "open and front," "closed and back," and so forth. See also **vowel chart**.

pear-shaped tone. A concept that originated in the historical *bel canto* school of Italian singing, this nonscientific term instructs the **classical singer** to imagine that his or her **acoustic** space (the **oral cavity** and **pharynx**) is shaped like a pear, with the larger end of the pear toward the back of the acoustic space and the "stem" of the conceptual pear sticking out of the front of the mouth. Similar to "yawning," the idea of a pear-shaped space supposedly encourages a **low larynx**, **open throat**, and raised (engaged) **soft palate**, all conditions that help cultivate a good **classical tone quality**. Some voice teachers also use the imagery of a "light bulb," which is similar in concept.

The pear shape has also been conjured in discussions of breathing **technique**. In these discussions, two models are usually evoked: the "pear-shape-down" paradigm and the "pear-shape-up" paradigm. In the former, the ribcage is free to move while pressure is exerted downward toward the pelvis and outward toward the abdomen. In the pear-shape-up paradigm, the ribcage is kept high and stable, and the diaphragm and abdomen are primarily used to pump the air. The second approach is widely favored among **voice pedagogues** and is more conducive to the Italian **breathing technique** known as *appoggio*.

pedagogue. One who teaches. See also **voice pedagogue**.

pedagogy. A method of teaching.

pedal point. A sustained note in a composition, often—but not always—in the lowest **register**. The other voices move while the pedal point is sustained.

Peking opera. Sometimes called Beijing opera, Peking opera is a dramatic art form that emerged and flourished during the later part of the Qing Dynasty (1644–1912) in Imperial China. Peking opera combined singing, instrumental music, **dance**, pantomime, and acrobatics, and was formulaic in nature, making use of four primary **stock characters**—respectively named *Sheng, Dan, Jing,* and *Chou*—and many supporting players. The **plots** were usually of traditional Chinese subjects. The singing in Peking opera was distinctly non-Western in **style**, bearing much similarity to the Eastern **classical singing** heard in *kabuki* theatre and *Noh* dramas. During the Cultural Revolution, Peking opera was replaced by the propagandist **eight revolutionary operas**, but the tradition was successfully revived after the arrest of the Gang of Four in 1976. The 1993 film *Farewell My Concubine* offers a glimpse into the world of Peking opera, and the film derives its name from a Peking opera of the same name.

perfect pitch. See **absolute pitch**.

performance practice. The idea that the **canon** of Western **classical** music contains a wide variety of **styles** and practices within the classical idiom, and that correct performance style varies according to specific eras, composers, regions, and traditions. While this idea may seem obvious—certainly **world music** and **popular music** routinely make these distinctions—the concept of **historically informed performance practice (HIPP)** is a relatively recent development among classical musicians. Emerging in the 1970s and encouraged by the **early music** communities, performance practice often uses different **pitch standards** from the prevailing **A=440** (**A=415** is frequently used), makes regular use of **period instruments**, and considers **diction** issues relevant to the time and place of the original performance of the work.

period. 1. In voice science, refers to one complete cycle of a wave or **oscillation**.

2. An era of music or an adjective that evokes a specific era in music (i.e., a **period instrument**).

3. In music theory, a group of measures that embrace a natural division of the melody. Periods are complete musical utterances that conclude with a **cadence**.

period instrument. An instrument used in **historically informed performance practice (HIPP)** that attempts to replicate sonorities heard at the original performance of a work.

petit (**Fr**). Small.

petit motet. French **baroque genre** of **choral music**. A *petit motet* is a small **sacred concerto** for one, two, or three voices and **continuo**.

peu à peu (**Fr**). Little by little.

phantastisch (**Ger**). Fantastic or fantastical.

phantom power. In audio technology, a way of transmitting electrical power through a **XLR microphone** cable to power the magnetic plates in a **condenser microphone**. Phantom power has no affect on **dynamic microphones**, but it can permanently damage **ribbon microphones**. For more information, see the essay entitled "What Every Singer Needs to Know about Audio Technology."

pharynx. The "throat area" portion of the **vocal tract** that connects the **larynx** to the **oral cavity**. See the anatomical drawings in appendix B.

phonation. The sound produced while singing (or speaking). When the **vocal folds approximate** and **vibrate**, phonation occurs.

phonation break. A brief interruption in **phonation** while singing or talking.

phoneme. The smallest phonetic unit in a language.

phonetic sounds. The sounds of spoken language, broken into two broad principal categories: **vowels** and **consonants**. The term *phonetic* can also be applied as an adjective to languages that tend to follow specific **pronunciation** rules (with few exceptions) and "look the way they sound." Thus, Italian, German, and Finnish are "phonetic" languages, whereas French and English are not.

phonosurgery. A surgical procedure performed by a **laryngologist** that is intended to improve the voice.

phrase. In vocal music, usually refers to a line sung in a single breath. Thus, "phrasing" refers to the action and plan of singing multiple phrases within an **aria** or **song**. Phrasing is a crucial element of singing that becomes entirely situational and defies specific rules. Multiple performances of standard literature sung by great singers may reveal different phrasing strategies.

Phrasing decisions are largely dependent upon three **objective** criteria: 1) how the composer sets the text musically, 2) the punctuation already inherent in the poetic text or **libretto**, and 3) the musical sense of the passage. As sensitive composers usually base their melodic content on the natural **declamation** of the line—how the line would be spoken—new phrases are often delineated by such phenomena as commas and periods. Multiple commas within a single melodic line, however, do not justify multiple phrases, which makes the art of phrasing more subjective.

A vocal phrase differs entirely from the definition of a phrase within the field of music theory. Music theorists generally agree that phrases are defined **harmonically**, with **cadences** marking the ends of phrases. Singers should be familiar with both meanings of the word and use the term distinctively when they converse or write about music.

Phrygian. One of the eight **church modes**.

physiology. The branch of biology that deals with the normal functions of living organisms and their parts. Physiology also describes the way in which a living organism or bodily part functions.

piano, pianissimo **(It).** Soft, very soft.

piano reduction. The recasting of an orchestral **score** into a two-line grand staff that can be read by pianists. **Vocal scores** used by singers feature piano reductions.

piano rehearsal. A **rehearsal** that takes place with a **rehearsal pianist** before the arrival of an orchestra. In **professional** choral situations, early piano rehearsals are under the direction of the **chorus master**, whereas later piano rehearsals are under the direction of the **conductor**.

piano-vocal score. A more precise term for what is usually termed a **vocal score**. Voice parts (of an **opera**, **oratorio**, or **song**) are included, along with a **piano reduction** of the orchestra **score**.

pickup. An anacrusis; rhythmically unstressed notes at the beginning of a musical passage.

pickup pattern. A term used to describe how a **microphone** responds to **acoustic** signals within 360 degrees of the center of the microphone's **diaphragm**. The pickup pattern is also known as a polar pattern or directional pattern.

pickup pattern diagram. A circular graph that displays information concerning the **frequency** response of a **microphone** at angles from 0 to 180 degrees from the center of the **diaphragm**. Pickup patterns are usually displayed with figures that resemble a heart shape or variations of an oval or circle. For more information, see the essay entitled "What Every Singer Needs to Know about Audio Technology."

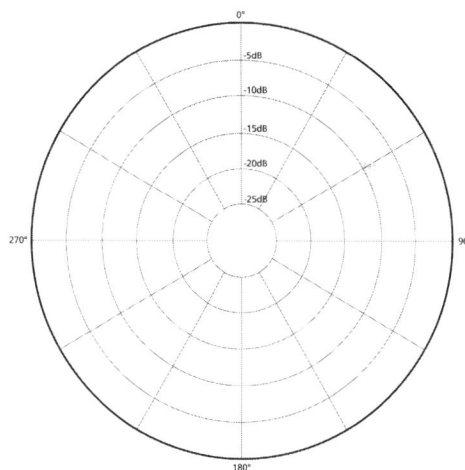

Figure 38. A polar microphone pattern. *Courtesy Creative Commons.*

pitch. The perceived **quality** of a sound according to its fundamental **frequency (Hz)**. How "high" or "low" a **pitch** is perceived to be is primarily dependent on its number of **oscillations** per second, measured in **Hertz (Hz)**. Pitches are perceived as being higher with increased frequency and lower with decreased frequency. Pitch should not be confused with **timbre**, which is a synonym for tone color. Today, pitch is universally standardized, with A4 equaling 440 Hz per second (**A=440**). See **pitch standard**.

pitch break. A sudden, unintentional shift into the **mode 2/ CT** register while singing (in a **TA-dominant style**) or speaking. Colloquially called cracking.

pitch pipe. A small device—usually circular in shape— that provides the chromatic **pitches** within a given **octave**. When one blows on the desired pitch, the pitch is sounded. Pitch pipes are often used during **rehearsals** of *a cappella* singing groups, particularly **amateur** groups and groups that specialize in **popular music** (for example, **barbershop quartets** and **choruses**). **Professional** and **semiprofessional** choruses that specialize in *a cappella* **classical choral music** usually prefer to get their pitches from **tuning forks** or chorus members with **absolute pitch**.

pitch standard. Refers to the system of tuning according to number of **frequencies (Hz)** per second, usually according to the era of music history in which a **genre** was originally written. **A=440** is the standard tuning for modern music of any genre. Various genres of **early music** (including **baroque** music) adopt alternate pitch standards, the most common of which is **A=415**. **Medieval** and **Renaissance** genres can be heard at a variety of pitch standards determined by the performers, as this represents an era before pitch standardization. (**Gregorian chant**, for example, can begin on any **pitch** level even though it is notated with specific pitches on a **four-line staff**.)

pitchy. An informal, pejorative term for a singer who either has insecure **technique** or is not singing his or her best. A pitchy singer may have an unstable **tone quality** and may, at times, sing **out-of-tune**.

più mosso (It). More motion.

placement. A prevalent, but subjective, concept in voice teaching that involves "placing" the voice to achieve optimal **resonance**. Some teachers who advocate correct placement do so through describing sensation, which is profoundly subjective, as the perception of sensation differs from singer to singer. Other teachers, however, view placement as synonymous with vocal modification, which makes the **technique** considerably more **objective** and **fact-based**.

plainsong. A **style** of **monophonic chant** from the **medieval** era. **Gregorian chant** is a type of plainsong.

Plançon, Pol (1851–1914). French **operatic bass** and one of the most acclaimed singers of his generation. Plançon made his debut at the Paris Opéra in 1883, as Méphistophélès in Gounod's *Faust*. During the next decade, he sang important **roles** in the world **premieres**

of Massenet's *Le Cid* (1885) and *La Navarraise* (1894), as well as Saint-Saëns's *Ascanio* (1890). Because of his reputation for seamless **legato**, unrivalled **flexibility**, and well-articulated **trills**, the French regarded Plançon as a *basse chantante*, the equivalent of the Italian *basso cantabile*.

plantation song. A later type of **minstrel song** that is nostalgic and sentimental for some aspects of the antebellum South. Stephen Foster's "Old Folks at Home" (1851) and "My Old Kentucky Home" (1853) are examples of plantation songs.

playback singer. A singer whose performance is prerecorded for use in movies. Playback singers usually record **songs** for soundtracks, and the actors and actresses cast in the film's **roles** lip-sync the songs. **Marni Nixon** is perhaps the most famous playback singer in the American film industry, whereas **Asha Bhosle** is known for her eminence as a playback singer in Bollywood (the Indian film industry).

plegaria. Nineteenth-century Spanish **song** type that is essentially a plea for help from the Virgin Mary. Also called an *oración*.

plosive. In the study of **diction**, describes a **manner of articulation** in which **consonants** are produced via a momentary closure of the air flow passage. Common examples of plosive consonants include [b], [p], [d], [t], [g], and [k].

plot. The narrative story of an **opera**, **operetta**, or **musical**.

plus (Fr). More.

point of articulation. A **diction** term that refers to the specific part of the lips, teeth, and tongue a singer uses when pronouncing a **consonant**. Teachers and students must address various points of articulation when perfecting the **pronunciation** of languages. Specific points of articulation include **bilabial**, **labiodental**, **dental**, **alveolar**, **prepalatal**, **palatal**, and **velar**. See also **manner of articulation**.

polar pattern. See **pickup pattern**.

polarity. The pattern emanating from the center of a **microphone's diaphragm** that indicates its ability to pick up **acoustic** energy.

polecat song. A standard **song** from the **barbershop repertoire**.

polyp. See **varix**.

polyphonic. Adjective pertaining to **polyphony**.

polyphonic choral music. While this label can apply to polyphonic choral music of any era, it is generally used among **conductors** and **choristers** to describe the **Renaissance polyphony** of such composers as Josquin des Prez (c. 1450–1521), Giovanni Pierluigi da Palestrina (C. 1525–1594), Tomás Luis de Victoria (1548–1611), and others.

polyphonic secular song. Describes secular songs for more than one voice part written during the **medieval** and **Renaissance** eras. Specific **subgenres** include the *virelai*, *ballade*, *rondeau*, *chanson*, *frottola*, *lauda*, *villancico*, *canzona*, and secular **motet**.

polyphony. One of the three principal textures of music, polyphony describes two or more voices moving simultaneously, each with its own **pitch** and rhythmic identity.

polysyllabic. Diction term referring to a word with more than one syllable.

pop. On one level, "pop" is simply an abbreviation for **popular music**, but in practical use, the term refers to a specific kind of lighter, melodic-driven popular music from the 1980s to the present day. This connotation of pop music is a **subgenre** that is distinct from other **forms** of popular music, for example, **rock**, **jazz**, **grunge**, **R&B**, and **hip-hop**.

pop filter. A round, mesh-like disc that is placed in front of a **microphone** in a recording studio to help eliminate aspirated sounds ("pops") and wind noise. Also called a windscreen.

pop-mix. A description of a **contemporary commercial music (CCM)** singing **style** sometimes found in **musical theatre audition** listings (for instance, those found in *Backstage*). The subjective term may imply a **TA-dominant**, "lighter" **mix** associated with contemporary **pop** music (as opposed to **classic Broadway** or harder, edgier styles).

pop opera. A label sometimes given to a **rock opera** in a lighter, more contemporary **style**. *Bare* (2000), by Damon Intreabartolo (b. 1975), features a cast of teenage characters and was subtitled a "Pop Opera." Here, the substitution of the word *pop* in place of the word *rock* is appropriate not only as being descriptive of the style, but mirroring the youth of the cast as well.

pop wail. In **contemporary commercial music (CCM)**, a higher **belt style** needed to perform contemporary **popular music** and modern **musical theatre repertoire**. Also called **cry**, **belt-mix**, or **superbelt**.

popular music. A kind of music that is written for mass consumption and entertainment. Popular music is a wide umbrella that encompasses virtually all nonclassical musical **styles**. Not all music that is categorized as popular music is still popular in contemporary society, however. **Plantation songs**, **barbershop** music, and **jazz**, for instance, are all **forms** of popular music, but these styles have relatively little impact on contemporary culture and the current popular music industry. Popular music has always been distinct from **folk music** in that it is written down or recorded for posterity.

Porpora, Nicola (1686–1768). Italian singing teacher and composer. Porpora was born in Naples and graduated from its local conservatory, the Poveri di Gesù Cristo. Popora is primarily remembered as a singing teacher. His students included some of the greatest singers of the eighteenth century, including **Farinelli**, Caffarelli (1710–1783), and many others. Porpora was also trained as a composer, and he wrote many *opera seria* in the **style** of Alessandro Scarlatti (1660–1725), but few of these works are still performed.

port de voix. A French vocal **ornament** that was a stylistic hallmark of the **baroque** *air de cour*, the *port de voix* is essentially the French version of an *appoggiatura*. The *port de voix* was quickly appropriated by other **genres**, both vocal and instrumental.

portamento. The phenomenon of a singer "sliding" between two **pitches**, quickly passing through and encompassing each pitch in between. *Portamento* is usually a deliberate stylistic choice, and it is especially appropriate when performing the **genre** of **Italian opera** from the era of *bel canto* composers—Gioacchino Rossini (1792–1868), Gaetano Donizetti (1797–1848), and Vincenzo Bellini (1801–1835)—through the *verismo* operas of Giacomo Puccini (1858–1924).

portative organ. A small, portable pipe organ that is often used in **early music ensembles**. Portative organs are usually employed when performing **baroque sacred music** that was written before the invention of the piano in the late eighteenth century. The harpsichord is generally the instrument of choice for **secular music** written during this era. See also **positive organ**.

Portuguese art song. An often-neglected body of **art song repertoire** that exists in the shadow of **Spanish art song** and **Latin American art song**. Portuguese art song is distinct from these two **genres** not only in its language, but also through a repertoire created by a distinct roster of composers who drew inspiration from the poetry and **folk music** of Portugal and Brazil. Representative composers of Portuguese art song include Francisco Ernani Braga (1868–1945) and Heitor Villa-Lobos (1887–1959).

positive organ. Similar to a **portative organ**, but smaller and often placed on a table or the floor. Portative and positive organs are used extensively in **baroque sacred music** (whereas harpsichords are more often used in baroque **secular music**).

posterior cricoarytenoids (PCA). One of the two types of paired **cricoarytenoid muscles**. The **posterior cricoarytenoids** function as **vocal fold abductors**.

postlude. An instrumental section of music played after something else. See also **interlude**, **prelude**.

posttonal. Any music that is not tonal and doesn't follow traditional rules of **voice leading** and **harmonic progressions**. Music theorists credit the **Tristan chord** from Wagner's *Tristan und Isolde* (1865) as the beginning of the posttonal era, which reached its full flowering in the early twentieth century with the **expressionistic** works of Richard Strauss (1864–1949) and Arnold Schoenberg (1874–1951). The music of Claude Debussy (1862–1918) is also considered to be posttonal, as is much of the **art music** that continued to be written throughout the twentieth century.

posture. A general term describing the alignment of the human body. While the concept of singing posture can be controversial on minute levels, most singers and singing teachers agree that good posture is a basic prerequisite for healthy, efficient singing regardless of the **genre** or **style**. A good singing posture allows the singer to manage their breath efficiently by setting up a physical framework that is conducive to good *appoggio*. Thus, many singing teachers view posture as the first and most fundamental building block in vocal **technique**.

postvocalic. Refers to a **consonant** that follows a **vowel** sound.

power spectrum. An **acoustic** analysis method that allows one to visualize **spectral envelopes** (unique patterns of overtones). In a power spectrum, **amplitude** is displayed on the vertical axis and **frequency** on the horizontal axis, allowing the **fundamental frequency** and its **harmonics**

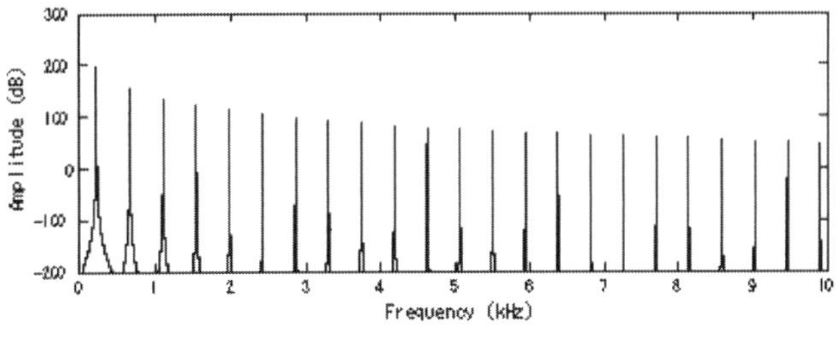

Figure 39. A power spectrum graph. *Courtesy Creative Commons.*

to be seen clearly. Power spectrums can be used to visualize any musical sound and are useful to singers, who have unique spectral envelopes that determine individual **timbres**. Singers can produce power spectrums using **voice analysis software** like **VoceVista**.

Practical Method of Italian Singing, A. One of the most commonly used **technique books**, written by Italian composer and singing teacher **Nicola Vaccai** in 1832. Although the original Italian title is *Metodo pratico di canto italiano per camera*, the work is almost universally recognized today by the English translation of the title. Vaccai's brief work consists of a graduated series of singing exercises that work progressively through the common **intervals**—smaller to larger—and through many other chromatic passages, **ornaments**, and articulations. The exercises are set to simple Italian texts that encourage **legato** and provide the opportunity for the balancing of **resonance** in the young singer. *A Practical Method of Italian Singing* is probably the most frequently used technique book in the **classical** voice studio, with *24 Progressive Vocalises*, by **Heinrich Panofka**, and *Vocal Method*, Op. 31, by **Mathilde Marchesi**, as close runners-up.

practice. To **rehearse** on one's own, usually to polish **technique** or prepare for a **rehearsal**. Individuals practice, two or more musicians rehearse.

praise music. Popular music style (usually **rock-** or **pop-**influenced) with Christian **lyrics** used during worship services in many circles of evangelical Christianity. While praise music is certainly a form of **contemporary Christian music**, the latter **genre** usually refers to the industry as a whole (which thrives upon airplay, **concerts**, and recordings), whereas praise music more narrowly refers to music performed during actual worship services. While praise music is often disrespected in **academic** and higher **liturgical** circles due to its lack of musical sophistication and (often) nonsubstantive lyrical content, it is a style that unapologetically panders to the masses, essentially guaranteeing its ubiquity and potential posterity within the field of church music.

precentor. The leader of a group of singers who **chant** the more elaborate portions of music in a **liturgical** worship service.

prelude. An instrumental section of music played before something else. See also **interlude**, **postlude**.

premiere. The first performance of a new musical work. Sometimes made more specific with a preceding adjective: world premiere, American premiere, and so forth. In **musical theatre** and **opera**, the premiere of a new show is usually called opening night.

prepalatal. In the study of **diction**, refers to a specific **point of articulation** of a **consonant** that involves the middle of the tongue and the area between the **alveolar ridge** and the **hard palate**. Common examples include [ʃ], [ʒ], [dʒ], [tʃ], [j], [ɲ], and [ʎ]. See also **alveolar, bilabial, dental, labiodental, palatal, velar.**

presentational. An acting term/concept that describes the relationship between the actor and the audience. In a theatrical performance, many actions and habits of the actor—for instance, gesture and not upstaging oneself—are "presentational" (as opposed to "real"). The actor is deliberately communicating to an audience, therefore acknowledging that the audience exists. Presentational acting is often contrasted with representational acting, which is a specific **style** that deliberately ignores the audience, allowing the spectator to be something of a voyeur. The latter style is not as common in **opera** and **musical theatre** performance.

Presley, Elvis (1935–1977). American singer, actor, and cultural icon. Presley was born in Tupelo, Mississippi, and moved to Memphis, Tennessee, in 1948, when he was thirteen years old. In Memphis, he met Sam Phillips (1923–2003), the owner of Sun Records, with whom Presley made his first recordings. Presley's earliest recordings were in the **rockabilly style**, which was something of a **fusion** of **country** music and **rhythm and blues**. An almost instant success, Presley soon signed with RCA records and began an illustrious career that lasted two decades. During this time, he also made many Hollywood movies. He died of prescription drug abuse in 1977, at the age of forty-two. One of the most influential and famous of all American musicians, Presley is widely known as the "King of Rock 'n' Roll" or simply the "King." His versatile vocalism encapsulated many styles, including **rock 'n' roll**, country, **gospel**, and **blues**.

prestissimo (It). Fastest. Faster than *presto*.

presto (It). Fast. Faster than *allegro*, but slower than *prestissimo*.

prevocalic. Refers to a **consonant** that precedes a **vowel** sound.

Price, Leontyne (b. 1927). African American **soprano**. Price was born and raised Laurel, Mississippi, as the only child of poor working-class parents. She studied music at an early age and, when she was fourteen, heard Marian Anderson sing in Jackson, Mississippi, an event that inspired her, in part, to pursue singing **professionally**. Price enrolled at the Juilliard School in 1949, where she performed the **role** of Alice Ford in Verdi's *Falstaff*. She was hired by Virgil Thomson (1896–1989) to appear in

a revival of his **opera** *Four Saints in Three Acts* in 1952. This was immediately followed by a world tour as the title role in Gershwin's *Porgy and Bess*. As Price's career progressed, she eventually settled into the Verdi–Puccini **repertory**; some of her signature roles included the title roles in Puccini's *Tosca* and *Madama Butterfly*, Leonora in Verdi's *Il trovatore*, and the title role in Verdi's *Aida*. She made her **Metropolitan Opera** debut as Leonora and created the role of Cleopatra in Barber's *Antony and Cleopatra*, which was **commissioned** for the opening of the Metropolitan Opera House at Lincoln Center in 1966. Price sang at **The Met** for many seasons, and she was one of the first African Americans to become a longtime member of the **company's** roster. She gave her farewell performance at the Metropolitan Opera as Aida on January 3, 1985. After her retirement from opera, Price made **recital** appearances for the next twelve years, retiring from singing altogether in 1997.

prima donna. Literally an Italian word meaning "first lady," the *prima donna* is the principal female character in an **opera**. Can carry a negative connotation similar to *diva*.

prima prattica (It). First practice. The term *prima prattica* was coined by Claudio Monteverdi (1567–1643) to refer to the **polyphonic** compositional practices of the **Renaissance** era. *Seconda prattica* (or "second practice") refers to the **bass**-driven **baroque style**.

primary muscles of expiration. See **expiration (primary muscles).**

primary muscles of inspiration. See **inspiration (primary muscles).**

primo passaggio. The Italian term for the lower of the two primary points of transition in singing. See also *passaggio*.

primo uomo. Literally an Italian word meaning "first man," the *primo uomo* is the principal male character in an **opera**.

Prince, Hal (b. 1928). **Broadway producer** and **director**. Prince is one of the most important and successful figures in the history of Broadway **theatre**, having won a record twenty-one **Tony Awards**. Prince was born in New York City and began his long career as a producer while still in his twenties, working as a producer of several important Broadway shows, including *The Pajama Game* (1954) and *West Side Story* (1957). He made his debut as a director with the original 1966 **production** of *Cabaret*. Prince also cultivated a longtime collaboration with Stephen Sondheim (b. 1930), serving as both director and producer of *Company* (1970), *Follies* (1971), *A Little*

Night Music (1972), and *Pacific Overtures* (1976). He also served as the director of Sondheim's *Sweeney Todd: The Demon Barber of Fleet Street* (1979) and *Merrily We Roll Along* (1981). In 2006, Prince received a special Tony Award for Lifetime Achievement in the Theatre.

process. See **vocal processes**.

processed singing. Refers to a specific kind of **amplified singing** that alters the voice through the use of **reverberation**, **Auto-Tune**, and other special effects. Processed singing has (somewhat controversially) become the standard in many **forms of contemporary commercial music (CCM)**. While amplified and processed singing have traditionally been considered to be heresy in **classical genres**, one could argue that the recording industry—with its practice of splicing and mixing—has been routinely processing singing of all genres for some time.

producer. In **musical theatre** and **opera**, the person in charge of financing the **production**. While in most cases producers are not directly involved in the artistic process—which is technically the job of the **stage director** and **musical director**—their ultimate authority over funding and public relations still grants them considerable power in such central issues as casting and production values. See also **impresario**.

production. A generic term that is used to refer to an **opera** or **musical** as a whole. Productions are administered and maintained by **producers**, along with an artistic staff that includes **stage directors**, **musical directors**, and technical assistants (who take charge of such areas as set design, costumes, and **props**).

professional. One who gets paid for a service (e.g., performing). The opposite of an **amateur**, who is unpaid.

program music. A piece of music with a narrative that tells a story, as opposed to absolute music. Since most vocal music sets texts, virtually all vocal music is program music.

progressive rock (also called prog rock). See **art rock**.

progressive voice injury. A type of **vocal injury** that is the result of illness and has a predictable outcome. **Acute laryngitis** is an example of a progressive voice injury. One of the three basic types of voice injuries, along with **constant voice injuries** and **episodic voice injuries**.

pronunciation. How a word is articulated within a particular language, **dialect**, region, **genre**, or **style**. This obvious and apparently elementary concept becomes surprisingly technical and complex and remains a central issue of study for singers of all genres and styles.

prop. An accessory used by a singer in an **opera** or **musical**. Short for "property," each prop is determined by the theatrical situation. **Songs** or **arias** performed outside of a theatrical context (for example, in a **recital**) also occasionally require props, as is the case with Leporello's "Catalog Aria" in Mozart's *Don Giovanni* (1787)—which requires the singer to page through a notebook—or Amalia's "Vanilla Ice Cream" from Bock and Harnick's *She Loves Me* (1963)—which is sung as she is writing a letter.

Proper. The movements of a **Mass** that change according to the **liturgical** calendar, as distinct from the **Ordinary** (the *Kyrie*, *Gloria*, *Credo*, *Sanctus-Benedictus*, and *Agnus Dei*), which remains the same. Like the Ordinary, the Proper also has five parts: the **introit**, **gradual**, **alleluia-verse** (or **tract**), **offertory**, and **communion**. However, while the texts in the Ordinary are standardized, the Proper texts rotate according to the liturgical season and the Sunday or feast within the season.

proprioception. The unconscious perception of movement and spatial orientation arising from stimuli within the body.

proscenium. The border that surrounds the front of a stage in a traditional **theatre**. To a singer or actor, the proscenium constitutes the **fourth wall**. Performers occasionally (in some shows) "break proscenium," which means that they venture past the fourth wall and interact with the audience.

proximity effect. In electronically **amplified singing**, the effect on the amplified sound created by changing the distance of the **microphone** from the mouth. This effect is found in cardioid microphones. When the sound source is near the center of the **diaphragm** of the microphone, the lower **frequencies** are accentuated. As the sound source is distanced from the center of the diaphragm, the lower frequencies are attenuated, and the resulting signal will be dominated by the upper frequencies. For more information, see the essay entitled "What Every Singer Needs to Know about Audio Technology."

psalter. A book containing musical settings of the 150 Psalms of David from the Old Testament of the Bible. Psalters have been used consistently in **liturgical** worship since the **medieval** era and can be set in many ways. Plainchant and **Anglican chant** are two of the most common types of psalm performance. See also **Bay Psalm Book**, **Gregorian chant**,.

psyche. The "mind" half of the philosophical dichotomy of "psyche and soma" ("mind and body"), usually attributed to the French philosopher René Descartes (1596–1650).

The **voice pedagogue Cornelius Reid** famously dovetailed this philosophical concept with a discourse on **voice pedagogy** through the publication of his 1975 **treatise** *Voice: Psyche and Soma*, the third and final part of a pedagogical trilogy that also includes *Bel Canto: Principles and Practices* (1950) and *The Free Voice: A Guide to Natural Singing* (1965).

puberphonia. See **mutational chink**.

public domain. Term used to describe any work of art that has existed long enough for the copyright to have expired, allowing it to be disseminated and performed freely in public use. Virtually all works from vocal **repertory** written before the early twentieth century are in public domain and can be performed without special permissions and royalties paid to the composer. Public domain **scores** are also ubiquitous on the Internet and can be legally downloaded, but these editions often pale in comparison to the accuracy of *Urtext* scores issued by reputable publishers. It should be noted that even if a composition is public domain, recent editions of a score—for instance, some of the very best *Urtext* editions—may still be subject to copyright law. Duration of copyright protection varies from one nation to another, so that a work in public domain in one nation may still be protected in another.

Pulitzer Prize. An annual award given by Columbia University to honor significant works of journalism, letters, drama, and music. The Pulitzer Prize in Music has been awarded annually since 1943. Vocal works that have won the Pulitzer Prize in Music include eight choral works, eight **operas**, and three **song cycles**. In addition, eight **musicals** have been awarded the Pulitzer Prize for Drama. A comprehensive list of these works appears in appendix F.

pulse. 1. Considered by some to be a **register** in singing. See **glottal fry**.
2. Another name for the **beat** in a piece of music.

punk. A **subgenre** of **rock** music that emerged in England during the 1970s. Punk was a **form** of social protest, and the **lyrics** of punk were usually intensely political in nature. Punk music was usually loud in volume, with an intense and harsh vocal **quality**. The music and lyrics—as well as the dress and behavior of the performers—was deliberately provocative. The Sex Pistols are credited as the originators of punk.

Q

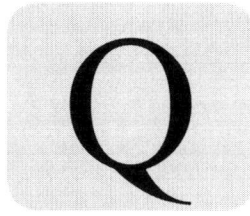

Qasimov, Alim (b. 1957). Azerbaijani vocalist known for his exceptional **improvisational** skills. Qasimov performs almost exclusively in the *mugam* **style**, a folk variation of the Iranian–Arabic–Turkish *maqam* modal system. To date, Qasimov has recorded nine albums and is universally acclaimed as one of the greatest living **world music** singers.

qawwali. The devotional music of Pakastani Sufis. Sufis represent the mystical branch of Islam. **Nusrat Fateh Ali Khan** is a famous exponent of *qawwali.*

quadratus lumborum muscles. In the Italian *appoggio* breathing **technique**, one of the six primary muscles of **expiration**. The other five include the **internal intercostal muscles, transverse abdominis muscles, internal oblique abdominis muscles, rectus abdominis muscles,** and **external oblique abdominis muscles.**

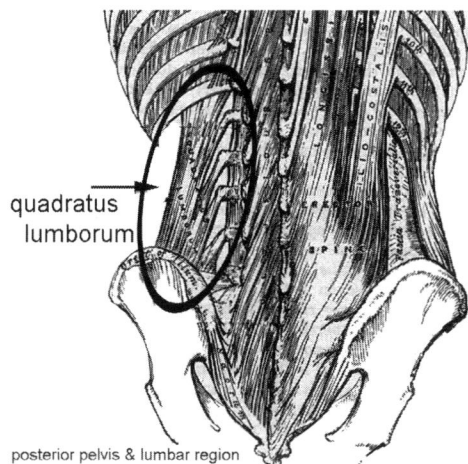

quadratus lumborum

posterior pelvis & lumbar region

Figure 40. Quadratus lumborum muscles. *Courtesy Gray's Anatomy,* with labeling by Scott McCoy; reprinted with permission from *Your Voice: An Inside View* (2004).

quadruple meter. A **meter** with four **beats**. There are two basic types of quadruple meter: **simple quadruple** and **compound quadruple.**

quality. 1. In **diction**, classifies whether a **vowel** is an **open vowel** or **closed vowel**. **Quality** is one of the two properties of vowels, along with **peak of the tongue arch (front vowels, central vowels,** or **back vowels).** Vowels can be classified as "open and front," "closed and back," and so forth. See also **vowel chart.**

2. To the singing teacher or **speech-language pathologist (SLP)**, the subjective assessment of the voice: whether it sounds "raspy," "forced," "breathy," and so on.

quartal. Harmonies that consist of pitches that are stacked in **intervals** of fourths. Similar to **quintal** (stacked in fifths) and **extended tertian** (stacked in thirds) sonorities. Quartal sonorities are a hallmark of certain kinds of contemporary **choral music.**

quartet. A type of **ensemble** for four singers or instrumentalists. Quartets can be all-male or all-female (as in the **barbershop harmony style**) or mixed (**SATB**). Many **liturgical** churches and community **choirs** also employ SATB quartets to serve as section leaders in choirs. In **opera**, a quartet can be any ensemble of four solo voices. Famous examples include quartets from Mozart's *Don Giovanni* (1787) and Verdi's *Rigoletto* (1851).

quasi (Lat). "As if." Somewhat opaque term tossed around by many singers and **pedagogues** as a prefix for a well-known term, for example, "quasi-legit" or "quasi-falsetto." Usually used when a well-established term is not available or appropriate, but the related one almost suffices (but not quite).

Quasthoff, Thomas (b. 1959). German **bass-baritone** and **concert** singer who is particularly renowned for singing German *Lieder*, as well as for his **interpretations** of Bach. During the final years of his career (during the first decade of the twenty-first century), Quasthoff also experimented with **jazz improvisations** and American popular **song**. In addition to his acclaimed **technique** and consummate artistry, Quasthoff is admired for overcoming severe physical handicaps that were the result of birth defects caused by the morning sickness drug thalidomide. His retirement in 2012 was due to persistent health concerns and artistic differences with his recording label, **Deutsche Grammophon Gesellschaft (DGG).**

Queen's Songbook, The. A book of traditional Hawaiian **songs**, most of which were originally compiled by Queen Lili'uokalani (1838–1917), who was the last monarch of Hawaii. Published in 1973, it remains the most widely disseminated collection of traditional Hawaiian songs. Many of these songs can be used pedagogically with beginners in the voice studio, as they are easily singable, possessing a limited **range** and a finite number of open and pure Hawaiian **vowels.**

Querelle des bouffons. A series of "pamphlet wars" that took place in Paris from 1752–1754 regarding the relative merits of **French opera** and **Italian opera**. The term *bouffons* derives from the Italian **genre** under fire—the *opera buffa*—which had appeared in France in 1752, with a **production** of Pergolesi's *La serva padrona* (1733).

quintal. **Harmonies** that consist of **pitches** that are stacked in **intervals** of fifths. Similar to **quartal** (stacked in fourths) and **extended tertian** (stacked in thirds)

sonorities. Quintal sonorities are a hallmark of certain kinds of contemporary **choral music.**

quintet. A type of **ensemble** for five singers or instrumentalists. Quintets can be all-male or all-female, but they are most frequently mixed ensembles. Famous examples of **operatic** quintets include those from Mozart's *Die Zauberflöte* (1791) and the quintet from Bizet's *Carmen* (1875).

***quodlibet* (Lat).** "What you please." A vocal composition in which two or more well-known melodies and texts are presented simultaneously, often in a deliberately incongruous manner. The *quodlibet* practice dates back to the **medieval** era, when it was used in **polyphonic secular music** to display compositional cleverness and **virtuosity**. In recent history, its most notable presence has been in light **opera**—for instance, **Gilbert and Sullivan ensembles**—and **musical theatre**, with examples including the "Pick-a-Little, Talk-a-Little"/"Goodnight Ladies" **number** in Willson's *The Music Man* (1957).

quotation. In music, the insertion of a preexisting melody—sometimes from a completely different piece by a completely different composer—into a musical work. Quotations are usually intended to be easily recognizable by the audience.

quotient. See **closed quotient (CQ).**

Qur'anic chant. The sung reading of the Qur'an (Koran), the sacred scripture of Muslims. Qur'anic chant is not notated; it is **improvisational** and highly **ornamental**. Daily chanting of the Qur'an is almost universally practiced throughout the Muslim world. Sometimes spelled Koranic chant.

R

R&B. Commonly used abbreviation for **rhythm and blues**.

rage aria. An **operatic aria** in which a character expresses his or her anger, usually as a **soliloquy**. Count Almaviva's "Hai già vinta la causa. . . . Vedrò mentr'io sospiro," from Mozart's *Le nozze di Figaro* (1786), is an example of a rage aria.

raï. A modern North African vocal **genre** that is the product of Algerian diaspora. *Raï*—which means "opinion" in Arabic—derives from the Bedouin **folk music** of the Cheikhas, but it is usually infused with a modern **pop style**. The **lyrics** of *raï*, which are usually in Arabic or French, are often provocative or political in nature. **Reinette l'Oranaise** (the "First Lady of North African Music") and **Khaled** (the "King of *Raï*") are famous exponents of the genre.

rallentando **(It).** Slowing down. Equivalent to *ritardando*.

ranchera. A **blues**-influenced **folk music** of Mexico, usually **scored** for voice and guitar. Like the blues, the **lyrics** of *ranchera* music are often about hard times and fond reminiscence. **Chavela Vargas** has gained international recognition as a performer of *rancheras*.

range. The span of notes—from bottom to top—possessed by an individual singer. Range, along with **tessitura** and **color**, is one of several factors in determining the **voice type** or *Fach* of the singer.

range of motion (ROM). The distance a movable object can travel while properly attached to another. In singing, almost always refers to a part of the body.

rap. An essential element of **hip-hop** and **reggae** music in which words are rhythmically spoken over a **pulse** or beat. Although rap is often associated with vocal **styles**, it is essentially rhythmic speaking as opposed to legitimate singing. "Emceeing" (or "MCing") is a synonym for rapping.

rarefaction. In **acoustics**, a decrease in density or a depressurization of air molecules. Rarefaction is the opposite of **compression**. Both rarefaction and compression travel in waves.

rarefaction wave. See **rarefaction**.

rasch, rascher **(Ger).** Quick, lively; quicker, livelier.

rave. An exceptionally positive **review**.

RCL. Abbreviation for **Revised Common Lectionary**, which is used in **liturgical** churches.

realism. A nineteenth-century theatrical movement that focused on the stories of common, everyday people, their **dialects**, and their mannerisms. Realism also focuses on the individual's power of choice in determining his or her destiny. Closely related to naturalism in **theatre** and *verismo* in **opera**.

realistic. A kind of acting advocated by **Uta Hagen** that deals with the "transference" or "substitution" of one's own psyche into that of the character being portrayed. Although Hagen did not identify herself as a **method actor**, there are some similarities between her school and the **Method**.

Received Pronunciation (RP). The standard English **pronunciation** in southern England. RP is also known as "standard English," "Oxford English," "BBC English," or the "Queen's English." **Classical singers** of English **repertoire** often utilize RP.

recital. A label given to a **concert** with a small number of performers, usually accompanied by a pianist. Can also describe **chamber music concerts**.

recitatif mesuré **(Fr).** Measured **recitative**. In French **baroque opera**, describes accompanied recitative in a consistent and steady **meter**.

recitatif simple **(Fr).** Simple **recitative**. In French **baroque opera**, describes a flexible recitative that constantly shifts between **duple meter** and **triple meter** to allow for a more natural **declamation** of the text.

recitation formula. In **medieval chant**, a simple melody that is adapted for a variety of different texts.

recitative. A type of singing that resembles speech and closely follows the natural **declamation** of the text. During the **baroque** and **classical** eras, recitative was used between **numbers** in **operas**, **oratorios**, and secular **cantatas**. Generally speaking, much more text is delivered during recitatives than **arias**. Thus, recitatives do much to further the narrative. The two major types of recitatives are *recitativo secco* and *recitativo accompagnato*.

recitativo **(It).** See **recitative**.

recitativo accompagnato **(It).** Literally meaning accompanied **recitative**, refers to a recitative that is **scored** for orchestral **accompaniment**. The opposite of *recitativo secco*, which is for **continuo** only.

recitativo secco **(It).** Literally meaning "dry **recitative**," refers to a recitative that is **scored** for **continuo** only. The opposite of *recitativo accompagnato*, which is scored for orchestral **accompaniment**.

reciting tone. The second most important note of a **church mode** (next to the **final**). The reciting tone is used for reciting text before the **chant cadences** at the final.

rectus abdominis muscles. In the Italian *appoggio* breathing **technique**, one of the six primary muscles of **expiration**. The other five include the **internal intercostal muscles, external oblique abdominis muscles, internal oblique abdominis muscles, transverse abdominis muscles,** and **quadratus lumborum muscles**.

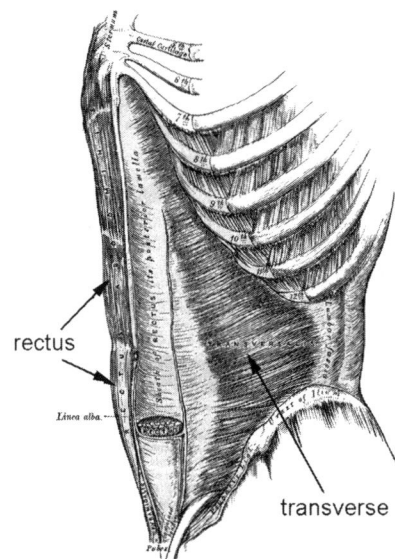

Figure 41. Rectus abdominis muscles. *Courtesy Gray's Anatomy,* with labeling by Scott McCoy; reprinted with permission from *Your Voice: An Inside View* (2004).

Redžepova, Esma (b. 1943). Macedonian Romani singer and songwriter. Redžepova was born in Yugoslavia as the youngest of six children. From an early age, she was steeped in Romani (Gypsy) music, and she began singing and playing in this **style** at the age of nine. After winning a prominent talent contest, Redžepova began touring and performing **professionally** at the age of fourteen. During the course of her long career, she has performed more than 9,000 concerts in more than thirty countries. Her fame as a singer has earned her the title "Queen of the Gypsies." Redžepova is also highly regarded for her tireless work as a humanitarian, particularly for her work with helping poor children with special needs.

reed (reedy). An imprecise, subjective adjective used to describe a bright or **nasal tone quality** in certain singers. In **contemporary commercial music (CCM) pedagogy**, reed can have a positive connotation, referring to an edgy tone quality desirable in **rock styles**.

reflux. See **acid reflux**.

reform opera. An **opera** that deliberately seeks to reinvent the **operatic** conventions of the time. *Orfeo ed Euridice* (1762), by Christoph Willibald Gluck (1714–1787), is the quintessential example of a reform opera.

refrain. Music—and often text—that is repeated at regular **intervals** throughout the course of a larger **song form**. **Burden** is a synonym for refrain that was employed during the **medieval** and **Renaissance** eras.

reggae. Popular music style associated with Jamaica and the Caribbean. The origins of reggae date back to the nineteenth century; however, the **style** began to take its current shape in the second half of the twentieth century with the emergence of **ska** and **rocksteady**. These important precursors to reggae absorbed the influence of **rock 'n' roll**, **rhythm and blues**, and swing band music. Contemporary reggae music refers to many **forms** of Caribbean **pop** music. Bob Marley (1945–1981) is the most famous exponent of reggae known outside of Jamaica.

Regina, Elis (1945–1982). Brazilian vocalist and one of the most beloved and revered figures of her country during the 1960s and 1970s. Born in Porto Alegre, in Rio Grande do Sul, Regina made her first **professional** appearance at the age of eleven on a children's radio show. She won her first singing contest in 1965, an event that launched her prolific recording career. She died of a drug overdose at the young age of twenty-six. Regina was held in particularly high regard for her exceptional **technique** and keen **intonation**, especially while singing chromatic passages. A pioneering figure in the **popular music style** that emerged in Brazil during the twentieth century that was known as the MPB (*Musica Popular Brasileira*), Regina helped to launch the careers of many Brazilian popular singers and musicians.

regional house. A smaller **opera company**, usually in a nonmetropolitan or smaller metropolitan area. Regional houses generally do only two or three **productions** per year, have apprentice programs for young artists, and are committed to community outreach.

regional theatre. A **professional** or **semiprofessional theatre company** in the United States that is not located in the New York City metropolitan area.

register. On a scientific and **objective** level, register refers to **laryngeal** function while singing. In this sense, there are two registers: **chest** voice (**TA/mode 1**) and **head** voice (**CT/mode 2**). While every **voice pedagogy** book tends to define vocal registers in a slightly different way, most would agree with the concise statement that a register is a series of contiguous **pitches** produced in the same way and containing the same essential **timbre**.

registration. The **register** choices made by the singer: whether he or she is in **chest** voice (**TA/mode 1**), **head** voice (**CT/mode 2**), or some sort of **mixed register**.

rehabilitation. The process of regaining skills that have been lost. The opposite of **habilitation**, which means to physically learn and keep new skills.

rehearsal. An event that occurs when two or more musicians assemble to polish a specific piece of music for an intended performance. Not to be confused with a

practice session, which occurs when a musician spends time alone refining his or her **technique** or preparing for a rehearsal or performance.

rehearsal pianist (rehearsal accompanist). The pianist who plays from a **vocal score** (or **piano-vocal score**) before **rehearsals** with the orchestra.

rehearse. A verb that describes the act of two or more musicians assembling to polish a specific piece of music for an intended performance. See also **practice**.

Reid, Cornelius (1911–2008). New York-based **voice pedagogue** of the twentieth century. Reid was also a prolific writer, best known for his pedagogical trilogy *Bel Canto: Principles and Practices* (1950), *The Free Voice: A Guide to Natural Singing* (1965), and *Voice: Psyche and Soma* (1975). He was known for his strong opinions and steely resolve; Reid was not bashful about standing his ground on controversial pedagogical issues, even if his perspective went against some of the groupthink of the profession. He maintains a loyal following far outside the New York area, with Reid disciples teaching throughout the country.

reinforced falsetto. Term used interchangeably with **male rock falsetto**.

Reinke's edema. A **voice disorder** that occurs when excess fluid builds up in the vocal fold **cover** of **Reinke's space**. Reinke's edema usually occurs bilaterally and is typically the result of repeated vocal abuse. It is often seen in the **vocal folds** of smokers. Named after the German anatomist Friedrich Reinke (1862–1919). Also called mucosal edema.

Reinke's space. Another name for the **superficial lamina propria** of the **vocal folds**. Combined with the epithelium, Reinke's space is part of the vocal fold **cover**. Named after the German anatomist Friedrich Reinke (1862–1919).

relative pitch. Imprecise term that refers to one's ability to hear **intervals** and **chords** in relation to a starting (or given) **pitch**. Musicians who do not have perfect pitch or **absolute pitch** sometimes claim to have relative pitch, meaning that they have similar abilities as long as they are given an initial reference point; however, as there is virtually no distinction between relative pitch and good **musicianship**, the label is somewhat meaningless. It is assumed that all trained musicians with the requisite talent to have a career will possess relative pitch.

release. The end of a sung **pitch** or **phrase** when **phonation** ceases. The release is a cultivated vocal **technique**, as the singer strives for a "clean" release in which the voice is well-supported through the end of a phrase. Release is the opposite of **onset**, which is the beginning of a sung pitch or phrase. Sometimes called **offset**, which also signifies the opposite of onset.

Renaissance. An era of music history lasting from approximately 1400–1600. Renaissance literally means "rebirth" and derives its name from the visual art movement of the same name. More broadly, the Renaissance was a general cultural movement that encompassed literature, visual art, music, science, diplomacy, and much more. The cradle of the Renaissance was Florence, and some scholars suggest that the era was precipitated by the flight of Greek scholars to Italy from Constantinople after its capture by the Turks. The Renaissance era occurred before the rise of instrumental music as a dominant force in Western **art music**, which was one of the catalysts for the beginning of the **baroque** era. This makes the Renaissance an especially rich era for vocalists, as virtually all Renaissance music was vocal music. Important Renaissance **genres** included the **Mass**, **motet**, **madrigal**, *chanson*, *frottola*, *lauda*, *villancico*, and *canzona*.

repertoire (repertory). Refers to an entire body of musical works. Thus, the **operatic** repertoire refers to all **operas**, whereas a particular singer's repertoire refers to everything that a singer performs. Used interchangeably with repertory.

repertory. See **repertoire**.

repertory actor. An actor who comes out of the English **repertory theatre** tradition. These actors are trained as **classical** actors and perform many **roles** from the traditional **canon** of theatre literature, including William Shakespeare (1564–1616), Molière (1622–1673), Henrik Ibsen (1828–1906), George Bernard Shaw (1856–1950), Anton Chekhov (1860–1904), and many others. The repertory tradition of acting emphasizes the technical facets of acting that deal with intense training, refinement of nuance, and physical discipline.

repertory theatre. A **theatre** or **opera company** that runs several different **productions** on various nights. See **in repertory**.

répétiteur. French term for vocal coach or **rehearsal pianist**.

Requiem. The **Latin Mass** for the dead. Also called the *Missa pro defunctis*. Many composers have written choral-orchestral settings of the Requiem Mass, including Wolfgang Amadeus Mozart (1756–1791), Hector Berlioz (1803–1869), Gabriel Fauré (1845–1924), and Maurice Duruflé (1902–1986). Johannes Brahms (1833–1897) famously composed an all-German Requiem with *Ein deutsches Requiem*, Op. 45 (1868) to biblical texts, and Paul Hindemith (1895–1963) wrote a unique Requiem entitled *When Lilacs Last in the Dooryard Bloom'd: A Requiem for Those We Love* (1946), a setting of the long poem by Walt Whitman (1819–1892).

resolution. In music, occurs when one moves from **dissonance** to **consonance**, usually through smooth **voice leading**.

resonance. Scientifically, resonance is the intensification and enriching of a musical **tone** through supplementary vibration. In all instruments (including the human voice), resonance is achieved through the cooperation of three elements: a power source, a vibrator, and a resonator. In the human voice, the power source is the breath, the vibrator is the **vocal folds**, and the resonator is the **vocal tract**, which includes the **pharynx**, **oral cavity**, **nasal cavity**, and **articulators**. There are two basic types of resonance: **forced resonance** and **free resonance**. The latter is more relevant to singers. The **acoustic** space of the room in which a singer performes also plays a **role** in the phenomenon of resonance.

respiration. The **inhalation** and **exhalation** of air. See **breath cycle**.

responsorial. In **sacred music**, describes the alternation between a soloist (**cantor**) and **chorus**.

retroflex r [ɹ]. See **American r**.

reverberation (reverb). The persistence of sound after the sound's source has ceased. Reverberation can occur **acoustically**—if one is in a "live" room with good acoustics—or it can be the result of electronic enhancement. Reverb is an essential element of the recording industry; many sound engineers add it to enhance the sound of singers.

review. A critic's evaluation of a musical performance, usually published in a newspaper, journal, or online blog. An exceptionally positive review is known as a **rave** review. An exceptionally negative review is known as a **pan**.

Revised Common Lectionary (RCL). In **liturgical** churches, a standardized prescribed set of scripture readings for a three-year cycle of church services. When **choirmasters** select **anthems** and other service music, they are restricted to choosing texts that are the same as—or related to—the lectionary readings for that particular service. They must also select **formulas** for the psalms prescribed by the RCL.

revue. An evening of **musical theatre** entertainment that lacks a single narrative point of view. Instead of embodying specific characters, actors in a revue usually present a series of tableaus and **songs**. If a revue features already-released material by a single composer, it is called a **catalog show**. The term *jukebox musical* is used if the songs were originally released by a popular artist in the **form** of commercial recordings.

rhetoric. A musical concept that has its origins in public speaking and literature, codified through the writings of Aristotle (384–322 BCE), Cicero (106–43 BCE), and Quintilian (35–100 CE). Cicero divides the discipline of rhetoric into five parts: invention, arrangement, **style**, memory, and delivery. During the **baroque** era, many composers and performers intimately knew and actively practiced the doctrine of rhetoric in music, making a basic understanding of rhetorical concepts essential for the **early music** performer.

rhythm and blues. Style of African American **popular music** that began in the 1940s and persisted through the 1960s. Although rhythm and blues was primarily a vocal **genre**, **dance** was also an essential element of the style. Rhythm and blues has its origins in the **twelve-bar blues songs** of its predecessor (**blues**), but it also incorporated elements of **jazz**, particularly through its instrumentation, which included the electric guitar, electric bass, drums, and wind instruments (especially saxophones). Rhythm and blues is considered to be an important precursor of **rock 'n' roll**, which emerged in the 1950s. Clyde McPhatter (1932–1972) and Sam Cooke (1931–1964) are two of the most well-known early rhythm and blues singers. Rhythm and blues is often abbreviated **RnB** or **R&B**.

ribbon microphone. A **microphone** designed with a thin metal ribbon suspended within a magnetic field. **Acoustic** vibrations set the ribbon into motion, thereby altering the magnetic field and sending an electrical signal to the amplifier. For more information, see the essay entitled "What Every Singer Needs to Know about Audio Technology."

riff. In **jazz** and **popular music**, a brief **motive** that is repeated, often in an **improvisational** way. Riffs can be either melodic, **ornamental**, or **accompanimental**.

riffing. A verb indicating that the singer is executing **riffs**.

Rilling, Helmuth (b. 1933). German choral **conductor**. Rilling was born in Stuttgart and studied organ, composition, and choral conducting at the Stuttgart College of Music. While still a student, he founded Gächinger Kantorei, a **professional ensemble** that he would go on to

conduct for the next sixty years. In 1967, he studied with Leonard Bernstein (1918–1990) in New York and was appointed professor of choral conducting at the Frankfurt Musikhochschule. With the American choral **director** Royce Salzman (b. 1928), he founded the Oregon Bach Festival in 1970, which eventually grew to become one of North America's major summer music festivals, with an all-professional chorus and orchestra; the festival also hosts an annual conducting **master class** that draws musicians throughout the world to study choral-orchestral works with Rilling. In 1972, Rilling embarked on a mission to become the first conductor to record the complete choral works of Johann Sebastian Bach (1685–1750), a goal that was realized in 1985. He founded the Internationale Bachakademie Stuttgart in 1981.

Like the late **Robert Shaw**, Rilling never became interested in the **historically informed performance practice (HIPP)** movement, and he continues to conduct and perform period works at **A=440** and on modern instruments. Unlike Shaw, however, Rilling tends to use much smaller forces and prefers to work with ensembles comprised of professional singers. Rilling's recordings are noteworthy for their rhythmic precision and flawless ensemble. In addition to Bach, Rilling's **repertoire** includes the major choral-orchestral works from the **baroque** through the **romantic** eras, and he has been equally committed to **new music**, commissioning new works from Arvo Pärt (b. 1935), Krzysztof Penderecki (b. 1933), Sven-David Sandström (b. 1942), Tan Dun (b. 1957), and Osvaldo Golijov (b. 1960). Rilling's recording of Penderecki's *Credo* (1998) at the Oregon Bach Festival won a **Grammy Award** for Best Choral Performance.

ring. A subjective term that refers to either the **resonance** or **timbre** of a singer's voice. Ring is roughly equivalent to **singer's resonance**. When a singer tunes his or her **formants** to achieve maximum resonance, he or she will also achieve considerable "ring" in the sound.

ring register. A slang term for **chest** or **TA register**.

rising diphthong. Two **vowel** sounds in the same syllable with a lengthening of the second vowel. Thus, a **glide** is created on the first vowel. Rising diphthongs are especially important in Italian **diction**. Examples include such words as più [pju], quando [kwando], and chiusa [kjuza].

ritardando **(It).** Slowing down. Equivalent to *rallentando*.

ritenuto **(It).** Held back.

RnB. Commonly used abbreviation for **rhythm and blues**.

Robeson, Paul (1898–1976). African American **bass-baritone**. Robeson was born in Princeton, New Jersey, and excelled at both music and sports during his high school years. He attended Rutgers University on an **academic** scholarship, where he played college football and graduated as the valedictorian of his class. After Rutgers, he attended Columbia Law School, where he graduated in 1923. Although Robeson was a multitalented polymath, he achieved national fame primarily through his singing and acting, which had always been a hobby for him. His most famous **role** was Joe—who sings "Ol' Man River"—in the musical *Show Boat* (1927), which he performed in the 1928 London **production**, the 1932 **Broadway** revival, and the 1936 film version. He also appeared in many plays and performed widely as a **concert** singer. In his later years, Robeson became widely known for his political activism, which at times overshadowed his formidable capabilities as a singer.

Figure 42. Scene from *Othello* with Paul Robeson and Margaret Webster (i.e., Uta Hagen as Desdemona). Theatre Guild production 1943–44.

rock. A **genre** of American **popular music** that emerged in the 1960s, a descendent of its predecessor, **rock 'n' roll**. Rock assumes a variety of musical **forms**, largely freeing itself from the rigid **twelve-bar blues** structure that persisted in both **rhythm and blues** and rock 'n' roll. Rock also largely abandons wind instruments, preferring electric, amplified instruments and drum sets. Rock remained popular as a genre for more than three decades, and it spawned many **subgenres**, including **jazz rock**, **art rock**, **folk rock**, **country rock**, **hard rock**, acid rock, **heavy metal**, **punk**, **new wave**, and **grunge**. As a result of these subgenres, vocal **styles** varied widely, with some styles—for example, the hard rock and heavy metal subgenres—adopting a harsh, edgy, and less melodic quality. Rock **lyrics** are often either intensely personal or political in nature.

rock 'n' roll (rock and roll). A type of American **popular music** originating in the 1950s. Rock 'n' roll was essentially a **form** of orchestrated **blues**, with the primary instruments including electric guitars, saxophones, and a rhythm section (drums, piano, and bass). Most rock 'n' roll **songs** were in simple **quadruple meter** (common time), with a strong emphasis on the first **beat** of each bar. **Rhythm and blues** was an important precursor of rock 'n' roll, and the vocal **styles** were quite similar. Unlike rhythm and blues, however, which was primarily an African American **genre**, many white musicians appropriated rock 'n' roll as well, including the songwriting and record producing team of Jerry Lieber (1933–2011) and Mike Stoller (b. 1933).

rock-mix. A description of a **contemporary commercial music (CCM)** singing **style** sometimes found in **musical theatre audition** listings (for instance, those found in magazines like *Backstage*). The subjective term may imply a **TA-dominant**, "heavier" **mix** associated with **rock** music, as opposed to **classic Broadway** or lighter, more **pop**-influenced styles.

rock opera. A term that originated in the recording industry to signify a **concept album** that told a narrative story. The rock band The Who is credited with the most famous examples of early rock opera with *Tommy* (1969) and *Quadrophenia* (1973). The **musical theatre** composer Andrew Lloyd Webber (b. 1948) and his **lyricist**, Tim Rice (b. 1944), then dovetailed the concept with the musical theatre industry, releasing a concept album for their "rock opera" *Jesus Christ Superstar* (1970) one year before the fully staged version was produced on **Broadway** in 1971. Webber and Rice then utilized the same concept with *Evita*, a 1976 concept album that preceded the 1978 **West End production**. Both *Jesus Christ Superstar* and *Evita* were highly successful endeavors. In contemporary usage, a rock opera can describe any musical theatre production with a **rock score**; however, while this was unusual in the 1970s, it is commonplace today. Hence, the term has lost most of its usefulness.

rockabilly. A **form** of American **popular music** that was a **fusion** of **country** music and early **rock 'n' roll**. Rockabilly was popular during the late 1950s, and its principal exponents were **Elvis Presley**, Carl Perkins (1932–1998), Johnny Cash (1932–2003), and Gene Vincent (1935–1971).

rocksteady. Jamaican **genre** that is rich in vocal **harmony**. A successor to **ska** and a precursor to **reggae**. In 2001, the American **rock** band No Doubt entitled their fifth studio album *Rock Steady*, attempting to recreate the sounds of a 1960s Jamaican **dance** hall.

Rodrigues, Amália (1920–1999). An internationally celebrated singer and actress whose name is inextricably linked with the Portuguese fado **genre**. Known as the "Queen of Fado" in her native Portugal, Rodrigues was almost single-handedly responsible for popularizing fado worldwide during the latter half of the twentieth century. In addition to her beauty and charisma, her singing is memorable for its unique **timbre**, careful attention to the nuances of text, and great depth of emotion. Rodrigues was born into poverty in the Alfama district of Lisbon. After a difficult childhood, she began performing as an **amateur** singer during her teenage years, landing her first **professional** engagement at the age of nineteen. She quickly rose to the top of her profession, becoming Portugal's most renowned singer and starring in the movie *Fado* in 1946. During this time, she began making frequent trips to South America, introducing and popularizing fado in Brazil and neighboring countries. She also began a prolific recording career that would continue for the rest of her life. At the time of her death in 1999, she had performed in more than twenty countries, receiving honors in France, Israel, Lebanon, the Netherlands, Portugal, Romania, and Japan. Rodrigues's stature in Portugal as an iconic celebrity whose name is synonymous with her art **form** is analogous to that of **Umm Kulthum** in Egypt, Édith Piaf (1915–1963) in France, **Sezen Aksu** in Turkey, and **Carlos Gardel** in Argentina.

role. The character sung in an **opera**, **oratorio**, or **musical**.

rolled *r*. Consists of multiple flips of the *r* **consonant**. Rolled *r* is used in **classical singing** in all four of the major languages—Italian, French, German, and English—in certain circumstances, but is not as common as the **flipped *r*** [ɾ]. Utilizes the [r] symbol in the **International Phonetic Alphabet (IPA)**. See also **American *r***.

ROM. Abbreviation for **range of motion**.

Roman Latin. See **church Latin**.

romance. 1. A French **song** that was an important precursor to the French *mélodie*. *Romances* generally consisted of straightforward melodies cast in a **strophic form** with simple piano **accompaniments**. French *romances* are somewhat analogous to the **Tin Pan Alley** songs of the American **sheet music** industry in the early twentieth century.
    2. A sentimental Russian song developed during the eighteenth and nineteenth centuries during the Imperial era of Russia.

Romani music (Gypsy music). The music of the Romani people, who were originally from Northern India but now live mostly in Europe. Romani music features folk-like tunes delivered in a **declamatory** vocal **style**. *Glissandi* are a prominent feature of the vocal style. **Accompaniment** often features percussive sounds (sometimes made from hand-clapping and tongue-clacking), accordions, and bass instruments (either **acoustic** or electric). A derogatory synonym for Romani music is Gypsy music. The word *Roma* is sometimes used to describe the Gypsy subgroup of the Romani people.

romantic. The period of Western **art music** immediately following the **classical** era (1750–1825). The romantic era is the only period of music named after a literary movement and, specifically, the German Romantic poetry that exemplified the spirit of the age (see **German Romanticism**). Musically, the romantic period begins with the late works of Ludwig van Beethoven (1770–1827), which broke free from the shackles of Viennese **classical** conventions. The romantic spirit also believed that **expression** should be prioritized above all else, dictating formal and technical choices in compositions. New **genres** also characterized the era, for example, the *Lied*, a quintessentially romantic art **form** due to its deep connection to poetry and use of the relatively recently invented piano. Idiomatic schools of **opera** also flourished in Italy, France, and Germany. The romantic era ended at the turn of the twentieth century with the **posttonal** compositions of Claude Debussy (1862–1918), Richard Strauss (1864–1949), and Arnold Schoenberg (1874–1951), ushering in the modern era of Western music.

Romanticism. See **German Romanticism**.

romanza. A nineteenth-century Spanish **song type**, the name *romanza* actually dates from the fourteenth century, describing a folk **song** that was passed down through oral tradition. In this sense, the *romanza* is a rough equivalent to the *Minnelieder* of **medieval** Germany or the *troubadour* and *trouvère* songs of **medieval** France. During the **Renaissance** era, instrumental **accompaniments**—for example, the guitar, lute, or *vilhuela*—were added to *romanzas*. In the nineteenth century, the keyboard emerged as the accompaniment of choice. *Romanzas* are usually **strophic** in **style** and have texts that deal with love and everyday life. Spanning more than 500 years, the *romanza* has few rivals for longevity among musical **genres**.

rondeau (pl. *rondeaux*). One of the three *formes fixes*, along with the *ballade* and *virelai*. The *rondeau* has the musical **form** of ABaAabAB, with capital letters indicating the music and text of the **refrain** and lowercase letters indicating the same music with different texts.

root position. Describes a **chord** whose root is the lowest voice, that is, a chord that is not in an **inversion**.

roots music. Term used to describe authentically American **genres** of music, including **blues**, **jazz**, **country**, and other types of ethnic and border music.

Rosenblatt, Yossele (1882–1933). Ukrainian-born Jewish **cantor** (*chazzan*) and composer. Rosenblatt is widely considered to be the greatest cantor of all time, and he is certainly the most famous. Although his strict religious upbringing prevented him from attending any formal institutions of musical study, his talent was recognized early in his life, when he sang in the **choir** of his local synagogue in Ukraine. At the age of seven, he moved with his family to Austria, and later accepted a full-time job as a cantor in Hungary at the age of eighteen. After a brief stint in Slovakia, he moved to Hamburg before settling in the United States, where he would spend most of the rest of his life.

Although he traveled widely, Rosenblatt's most important positions were in New York City, where he served as a cantor in Harlem and Brooklyn. Vocally, he was highly regarded for his extraordinary **technique**, perfect **intonation**, flawless **coloratura**, and great **expression**. His fame as a cantor spread beyond the Jewish community, and he was courted by Hollywood for an appearance in the 1927 film *The Jazz Singer*. Dubbed the "Jewish Caruso," Rosenblatt was offered a leading **role** at the **Metropolitan Opera**—in Halévy's *La Juive*—by Arturo Toscanini (1867–1957), but he turned down the offer, stating that his gifts as a singer were only to be used to serve God. In 2010, many of Rosenblatt's recordings were remastered and rereleased by Mendel Werdyger (b. 1958), owner of the Brooklyn store Mostly Music.

roster. The listing of names of individuals who are in an **ensemble**, for instance, a choral **ensemble** or **opera chorus**.

rote. A way of learning a piece of music that does not involve reading from a printed **score**. In rote learning, a **song** leader sings a **phrase**, and the singers then imitate what they hear. After several (or many) repetitions, the music is learned. Thus, rote learning relies on human memory as opposed to **sight-reading** skills. While learning by rote is part of the oral tradition inherent in many types of **folk music**, as well as many **forms** of **popular music** (including **blues** and **gospel**), it is generally discouraged among **classical** musicians. Even **amateur choir rehearsals** become quite inefficient unless the **choristers** possess basic sight-reading skills.

roulade. A specific kind of **ornament** found in vocal music of the eighteenth century. Essentially short **melismas**, *roulades* are always sung on an open **vowel** or on one syllable of text.

round note. In **early music** performance, the idea that a note is "tapered" or "shaped," rather than begun or released abruptly. Nuanced round notes often occur in more lyrical or softer sections of the music.

Royal Opera House. See **Covent Garden**.

royalty. A fee paid to the composer or licensing organization for the privilege of publicly performing a musical work.

RP. Abbreviation for **Received Pronunciation**.

rubato **(It).** "Robbed." Relates to **tempo**: the implication is that time is "stolen" from part of a **phrase** by delaying it, but it is "paid back" elsewhere via rushing. It is common, for example, for **jazz** or **pop** singers to lag behind the **beat** but ultimately come out with it. Precisely how *rubato* was applied in different eras and places is a controversial topic among performers and musccicologists.

ruhig **(Ger).** Quiet.

rumba. An Afro-Cuban **dance** and musical **style**. It is usually performed by a vocal soloist with a **chorus** and two or three conga drums. *Rumbas* are almost always fast and in **duple meter**.

run. In **theatre**, the number of times a **musical production** is performed.

Russian art song. Russian-language art song reached its full flowering in the mid-nineteenth century as a result of the nationalistic movement that swept many of the non-European countries. The **romances** of Mikhail Glinka (1804–1857)—the "Father of **Russian Opera**"—and Alexander Dargomyzhsky (1813–1869) were pioneering works that inspired future generations of Russian art song composers. The **Mighty Handful**—Aleksandr Borodin (1833–1887), César Cui (1835–1918), Mily Balakirev (1837–1910), Modest Musorgsky (1839–1881), and Nikolay Rimsky-Korsakov (1844–1908)—or **Russian Five**, all composed **songs**, with Musorgsky emerging as the group's most important composer of vocal music. A second, more European type of Russian art song flourished in the late nineteenth century with the songs of Pytor Il'yich Tchaikovsky (1840–1893) and Sergey Rakhmaninov (1873–1943). These songs were more melodic in nature and owed less to the folk idioms and rustic **harmonies** favored by the Mighty Handful.

While not as vast a **genre** as the German *Lied* repertoire, the Russian art song genre contains hundreds of works from some of Russia's greatest composers, not to mention settings of some of the greatest Russian poets. The recent proliferation of publications related to

Russian art song **IPA transcriptions** and Russian **diction** books has finally made this genre more accessible to Western singers and audiences.

Russian Five. A group of five nineteenth-century Russian composers who dedicated themselves to nationalistic principles. The members of the Russian Five were Aleksandr Borodin (1833–1887), César Cui (1835–1918), Mily Balakirev (1837–1910), Modest Musorgsky (1839–1881), and Nikolay Rimsky-Korsakov (1844–1908). They were also known as the **Mighty Handful**.

Russian opera. Like **Russian art song**, Russian opera is essentially a nineteenth-century development that is intensely nationalistic in flavor. The compositional **style** is indebted to the **harmonic** and melodic influences of Russian **folk music**, and **libretto** subjects often deal with Russian legends and historical subjects. Mikhail Glinka (1804–1857), considered to be the "Father of Russian Opera," wrote two important early **operas** that **form** the foundation of the **genre**: *A Life for the Tsar* (1832) and *Ruslan and Lyudmila* (1842). Of the **Russian Five**, all composed operas except Mily Balakirev (1837–1910). Modest Musorgsky (1839–1881) wrote some of the most well-known and idiomatic Russian operas, the most important of which is *Boris Godunov* (1869). Outside of the **Mighty Handful**, as the Russian Five were also known, the most important composers of Russian opera include Pyotr Il'yich Tchaikovsky (1840–1893), Sergey Prokofiev (1891–1953), and Dmitri Shostakovich (1906–1975). Although rarely heard in the West fifty years ago, Russian operas are increasing their visibility and are now regularly programmed in major **opera houses** throughout the world.

16-bar cut. A short excerpt of music offered by a **musical theatre** performer at an **audition**. A 16-bar cut is not necessarily sixteen bars; rather, it is an excerpt that is short in duration, usually only thirty to forty-five seconds in length. The singing actor usually offers several contrasting 16-bar cuts to the audition panel.

SAB. A common three-part voicing for pedagogically simplified **choral music**. Named for the three voice parts: **soprano**, **alto**, and **baritone**. SAB arrangements are commonly found in junior high school choral libraries.

sacred concerto. In the early **baroque** era, a composition on a sacred text for one or more singers and instrumental **accompaniment**. Used interchangeably with **vocal concerto**.

Sacred Harp, The. One of the best-known of the American shape-note tune books, published in 1844, and compiled by Benjamin Franklin White (1800–1879) and Elisha James King (1821–1844). Its name came to be applied to the **style** of American congregational **hymn** singing that was invented in 1801 and flourished during the nineteenth century. The style—which is also known as **shape note singing**—derives its name from its notation, a unique twist on the ***solfège*** system that features note heads of various shapes that correspond with respective **scale degrees**.

Figure 43. An example of *The Sacred Harp* notation. *Courtesy Creative Commons.*

Sacred Harp songs are performed *a cappella*. Most of the texts are sacred in nature, and Sacred Harp singing can occurs either at Sunday morning worship services or community social gatherings. Hugh McGraw (b. 1931), perhaps the best-known practitioner of sacred harp singing, received a National Endowment for the Arts Heritage Fellowship in 1982.

sacred music. An extremely vast **genre** of music that denotes any music that sets a religious text or is used in **liturgical** worship. The first recorded Western music was **Gregorian chant**, and sacred music comprised the majority of the **repertoire** written during the **medieval** and **Renaissance** eras. The invention of **opera** and the increase in instrumental music during the **baroque** era led to the rise in prominence of **secular music**, but sacred music continued to play a significant **role** in subsequent eras, particularly in the choral repertory. Sacred music is distinguished from secular music, which denotes any music that does not set a religious text or is not used in a religious context.

sainete. A short Spanish theatrical work intended as a sort of final "dessert" after the main work of the evening is performed.

Saint Cecilia (St. Cecilia). The patron saint of music. St. Cecilia was a Roman martyr who lived in the second century. Many composers—particularly British composers—have composed works in honor of St. Cecilia. Some of the most well-known include *Ode to St. Cecilia* (1692), by Henry Purcell (1659–1695); *Ode for St. Cecilia's Day* (1739), by George Frideric Handel (1685–1759); *Hymn to St. Cecilia*, Op. 27 (1942), by Benjamin Britten (1913–1976); *A Hymn to St. Cecilia* (1960), by Herbert Howells (1892–1983); and *For St. Cecilia*, Op. 30 (1947), by Gerald Finzi (1901–1956).

samba. An Afro-Brazilian **dance** established in Brazil at the beginning of the twentieth century. *Sambas* featured a vocal soloist and choral **refrains** over a distinctive syncopated rhythmic pattern. The **genre** was an important forerunner of *bossa nova*.

sample. In **hip-hop** music, a short melodic segment—usually sung but **processed**—that serves as a vocal **refrain** to **verses**, which are usually **rapped**.

Sanctus (Sanctus-Benedictus). One of the five standard parts of the **Ordinary** in a Catholic **Mass**.

sanft **(Ger).** Gentle.

Sangaré, Oumou (b. 1968). Malian singer commonly referred to as the "Songbird of Wassoulou." Sangaré was born in the Wassoulou region south of the Niger river in Mali, where she absorbed the traditional hunting **songs** from the region. Her talent was recognized at an early age, and she sang as a child to support her family after her father abandoned her mother. Sangaré rose to regional stardom after winning a talent contest in her teens. She soon began touring internationally, securing her fame on the **world music** scene. Sangaré is the most well-known ambassador of the **Wassoulou style**, and she is a fierce advocate for women's rights in Mali, opposing both child marriage and polygamy. She has released six albums, including the highly acclaimed *Oumou* (2004).

sans **(Fr).** Without.

Sarum chant. The **monophonic chant** performed in England—specifically at Salisbury Cathedral—between the thirteenth and sixteenth centuries.

SAS. Abbreviation for **Standard American Spanish**.

SATB. The standard four-part voicing for most types of **choral music**. Named for the four voice parts: **soprano**, **alto**, **tenor**, and **bass**.

Savoy Operas. The label given to the thirteen surviving **Gilbert and Sullivan comic operas**, named after the Savoy Theatre, at which most of them were **premiered**. Although their first four comic operas—*Trial by Jury* (1875), *The Sorcerer* (1877), *HMS Pinafore* (1878), and *The Pirates of Penzance* (1879)—were premiered before the opening of the Savoy, the label still generically applies to all **G&S** works.

Savoyard. The label given to a **Gilbert and Sullivan** performer or enthusiast. The name derives from London's Savoy Theatre, where most of Gilbert and Sullivan's **comic operas** were first performed.

scale. A collection of **pitches** arranged in a stepwise sequence from lowest to highest.

scale degree. In the **major** and **minor modes**, the labeling of the first through seventh **pitches** of the eight-note **scale** by using either a numeral—1, 2, 3, 4, 5, 6, 7—or *solfège* syllable—*do, re, mi, fa, sol, la, ti.* The eighth (final) note is always a repetition of the first **scale degree**. Scale degrees are an important aspect of **sight reading** (or **sightsinging**).

Scandinavian art song. A **genre** label sometimes used interchangeably with **Nordic art song**. Since Scandinavia proper only includes the countries of Denmark, Norway, and Sweden, Nordic art song is the more inclusive term, since it also includes the countries of Finland, Iceland, and the Faroe Islands.

scat. In **jazz**, the practice of vocally **improvising** on a series of meaningless syllables as opposed to a poetic text. When scatting, jazz singers seek to imitate the sounds made by jazz instrumentalists who also do not have a specific text to deliver during performance. Not every jazz vocalist improvises. Thus, not every jazz vocalist scats. In addition to revolutionizing the singing world with his unique vocal **style**, Louis Armstrong is credited as being one of the first singers who practiced scatting. Other jazz vocalists specifically remembered for their scatting/improvisational abilities include **Ella Fitzgerald**, Mel Tormé (1925–1999), Betty Carter (1929–1998), Sarah Vaughan (1924–1990), and Cab Calloway (1907–1994).

scena **(It).** Italian for "scene." In **opera**, a *scena* is a type of **aria** or **duet** that is more **recitative**-like than melodic in style. The *scena* can also refer to an introductory portion of an aria or duet written in this style before proceeding to the aria or duet proper.

scene. An organized portion of an **act** in an **opera** or **musical**.

scenic. One of the four basic **song forms** of *Lieder*. Scenic song forms are written in a clear, "sectional" **style** with earlier sections of music reprised later in the **song**. (If there is no repetition, then the song is **through-composed**.) "Frühlingstraum," from Schubert's *Winterreise*, D911 (1828), is an example of a scenic song; its **form** is ABCABC.

schleppen **(Ger).** "To drag." Gustav Mahler (1860–1911) frequently uses the marking *nicht schleppen* ("do not drag").

Schlummerlied **(Ger). Lullaby.** Also called *berceuse*, **slumber song**, *Wiegenlied*.

Schnarrbass. See *Strohbass*.

schnell, schneller (Ger). Quick, quicker.

Schubertiad. A **song recital** in a small, intimate space, for instance, the parlor of a private home. The term derives its name from the Austrian *Lied* composer Franz Schubert (1797–1828), who hosted many such soirées at his Viennese home in the early eighteenth century. See also *Liederabend*.

schwa [ə]. A neutral, mid-**central vowel** found in the middle of the **vowel chart**. Schwas are prevalent in unaccented syllables in English, French, and German, and they represent the "neutral" **vowel** sound in each language. While the [ə] **International Phonetic Alphabet (IPA)** symbol is used to represent the schwa sound, the **color** and roundness of the schwa subtly differs in each language.

Schwarzkopf, Elisabeth (1915–2006). German **soprano**. Schwarzkopf was born in the Posen province of Prussia as the daughter of a classics master. She attended the Berlin Hochschule für Musik for one year and soon joined the Berlin Städtische Oper, where she sang a variety of supporting **roles**. In 1942, she made her **professional** debut as a recitalist in Berlin. After the war ended in 1945, she joined the Vienna Staatsoper as a leading soprano, which eventually led to an illustrious international career at most of the world's leading **opera houses**. Her signature role was the Marschallin in Strauss's *Der Rosenkavalier*, in which she made her **Metropolitan Opera** debut in 1963. In addition to this role, Schwarzkopf is held in particularly high regard for her *Lieder* singing, which has been extensively preserved on record. Her most famous recordings include Wolf's *Spanisches Liederbuch* and *Italienisches Liederbuch*, with **Dietrich Fischer-Dieskau** and **Gerald Moore**, as well as Strauss's *Vier letzte Lieder*, with George Szell (1897–1970). An outstanding musician, Schwarzkopf was also committed to **new music**, creating the role of Ann Trulove in Stravinsky's *The Rake's Progress* in 1951. Her husband, Walter Legge (1906–1979)—the head of EMI records—also helped to advance her career with many recordings. Schwarzkopf is remembered for her personal beauty, the dark warmth of her **tone quality**, and her supreme musical intelligence and nuance, which is heard to particular advantage in the songs of Hugo Wolf (1860–1903) and Richard Strauss (1864–1949).

schwerer Spielbaß (*schwerer Baßbuffo*). A **voice type** in the **Kloiber Fach System** that is heavier than the *Spielbaß* (*Baßbuffo*) but positioned one spot higher on the chart than the *Charakterbaß* (*Baßbariton*). Examples include Daland in Wagner's *Der fliegende Holländer* (1843), Ochs in Strauss's *Der Rosenkavalier* (1911), and the title **role** in Puccini's *Gianni Schicchi* (1918). Although *schwerer Spielbaß* translates as "severe playful

bass," the literal translation is not descriptive of the actual *Fach*, which is simply a lower and heavier version of the *Spielbaß*. The *schwerer Spielbaß* is often—but not always—a comical role. See the *Fach* chart in appendix C.

score. The notated music from which a singer or instrumentalist performs, or from which a **conductor** conducts. Scores are usually published in several varieties, for example, **full scores**, **vocal scores** (or **piano-vocal scores**), and **choral scores**.

scratch vocal. The initial vocal and rhythm section track laid down in a recording studio that allows the engineer and artists to keep their place within the **song** on the "real" (subsequent) takes.

scream artist. In **genres** that call for it—for instance, **heavy metal** and **screamo**—one who screams.

screamo. A **genre** of music that alternates between sung and screamed passages.

screlt, screlting. A **contemporary commercial music (CCM)** term that has emerged recently in New York, meaning a "screamy **belt**." While some consumers might find this sound to be exciting, it more often carries a negative connotation. Some **pedagogues** argue that a true "screlt" sound is difficult to achieve in a healthy way.

SD. Abbreviation for **spasmodic dysphonia**.

sea shanty (sea chantey). A type of **work song** that was sung on large merchant sailing vessels during the nineteenth century.

sean-nós. A highly **ornamented style** of traditional Irish singing. *Sean-nós* is Irish for "old style," and most texts are in Gaelic.

season. In the musical world, the performance year, which generally coincides with the **academic** year: September through May. Summer seasons given by various musical organizations are usually called festivals.

second-act bass. A phenomenon in the **comic operas** of **Gilbert and Sullivan**, where an important character (who is always a **bass**) only appears in Act II of the two-**act** structure. Examples include the Sergeant of Police in *The Pirates of Penzance* (1879), Private Willis in *Iolanthe* (1882), and the title **role** in *The Mikado* (1885)

second inversion. See **inversion**.

second *passaggio*. See *secondo passaggio*.

second practice. See *seconda prattica*.

seconda prattica **(It).** Second practice. The term *seconda prattica* was coined by Claudio Monteverdi (1567–1643) to refer to the **bass**-driven **baroque style**, which allowed the rules of **Renaissance** counterpoint to be broken by the composer in favor of expressive setting of the text. *Prima prattica* (or "first practice") refers to the previous **polyphonic** compositional style of the Renaissance era.

secondo passaggio. The Italian term for the higher of the two primary points of transition in singing. See also *passaggio*.

secular music. Any music that is not religious in nature. Most **art songs**—and virtually all **operas**—are secular works, whereas most **oratorios** and many choral works can be classified as **sacred music**, or music that sets religious texts or is used in **liturgical** worship. It should be noted that strict classification of a work as sacred or secular is sometimes a gray area. Oratorios, for example, usually set biblical stories, but they are intended for public entertainment as opposed to worship services.

seguidilla. A quick, lively Spanish **dance** in **triple meter** that derives its name from the poetic **form** of the same name. The *seguidilla* achieved wide popularity in Europe, especially in Spain. Georges Bizet (1838–1875) famously wrote one of Carmen's **arias**—"Près des remparts de Séville"—in the **style** of a *seguidilla*. Its influence is also felt in many **Spanish art songs** from the late nineteenth and early twentieth centuries.

sehr (Ger). Very.

Sellars, Peter (b. 1957). American **opera** and **theatre director** particularly well-known for his provocative and creative stagings of both traditional and contemporary works. Sellars was born in Pittsburgh and attended Harvard University, where he pursued a number of outlandish experiments as a director of operas, plays, and musical **concerts**. His prodigious career as a **stage director** began almost immediately after his graduation from Harvard, with appearances at several important music festivals that generated significant attention from the press. His radical stagings of Mozart's three Lorenzo da Ponte (1749–1838) operas in the 1980s made him one of the most talked about figures in the opera world: Sellars set *Le nozze di Figaro* (1786) in New York City's Trump Tower, *Don Giovanni* (1787) in Spanish Harlem, and *Così fan tutte* (1790) in a diner on Cape Cod. He is also well-known for his stagings of contemporary works, including Hindemith's *Mathis de Maler* (1938), Ligeti's *Le grand macabre* (1978), Messiaen's *Saint Françoise* *d'Assise* (1983), and Saariaho's *L'amour de loin* (2000). In 2011, Sellars staged Adams's *Nixon in China* (1987) at the **Metropolitan Opera**.

semioccluded vocal tract. Roughly meaning "partially closed **vocal tract**," a semioccluded vocal tract occurs when one **phonates** through **lip trills** or a **bilabial fricative**, or sings an [u] **vowel**. **Straw phonation** is another example of a semioccluded vocal tract.

semiprofessional. A musical **ensemble** or organization that utilizes both **professional** (paid) musicians and **auditioned amateurs**. Many **symphony choruses** and regional **opera companies** are semiprofessional groups.

semitone. Synonym for **half step**. The term is used with more frequency in **popular music** and **jazz**.

sempre **(It).** "Always." Paired with an expressive adjective or **tempo** marking (i.e., *sempre legato*, etc.).

Senesino (1686–1758). Italian **castrato** and one of the most famous **opera** singers of his day. Senesino—whose real name was Francesco Bernardi—was born in Siena. Early in his career, he sang in many Italian **opera houses** before moving to Dresden in 1717, where he was fired for insubordination in 1720. In the same year, he accepted a contract with London's Royal Academy, where he began a long association with George Frideric Handel (1685–1759), who wrote many of his opera **roles** specifically for Senesino. Of these twenty roles, seventeen were **premiered** by Senesino, including the title roles in *Giulio Cesare* (1724), *Alessandro* (1726), *Admeto* (1727), *Riccardo Primo* (1727), *Siroe* (1728), *Tolomeo* (1728), *Poro* (1731), *Ezio* (1732), *Sosarme* (1732), and *Orlando* (1733). After the dissolution of the Royal Academy in 1728, he sang sporadically during the next ten years throughout Europe before retiring in 1740. Senesino was widely regarded for his warmth of **tone quality**, flawless **coloratura**, and clean **ornamentation**. Along with **Farinelli**, he is one of the two most famous castratos in history.

sensation. A subjective but essential element of vocal **technique** that involves how something feels to the individual singer.

sepulcra **(pl. *sepulcri*).** A type of **Passion** that is performed on Maundy Thursday.

sequence. A type of **trope**—an additional **Latin** text—used in **liturgical** worship. The **five great sequences** are the *Stabat Mater*, *Dies Irae*, *Lauda Sion*, *Veni Sancte Spiritus*, and *Victimae Paschali Laudes*.

serenade. A melody intended for evening performance and usually sung to either a lover or person of higher rank. The term also applies to melodic instrumental works written for special occasions.

serenata **(It). Serenade.**

seriöser Baß. Literally translating as "serious **bass**," the *seriöser Baß* is the twenty-ninth and lowest category in the **Kloiber Fach System. Roles** include Arkel in Debussy's *Pelléas et Mélisande* (1898), as well as many roles by Richard Wagner (1813–1883), including Fasolt and Fafner in *Das Rheingold* (1862), Hagen in *Götterdämmerung* (1876), and Gurnemanz in *Parsifal* (1878). A *seriöser Baß* is one **Fach** lower than a *Charakterbaß* **(Baßbariton)**. See the *Fach* chart in appendix C.

SES. Abbreviation for Standard European Spanish.

sextet. A type of **ensemble** for six singers or instrumentalists. Sextets can be all-male or all-female, but they are most frequently mixed ensembles. Famous examples of **operatic** sextets include those from Mozart's *Don Giovanni* (1787) and *Così fan tutte* (1790).

shadow vowel. The presence of a very short **schwa** after a final **consonant**. Shadow vowels are an important feature of exploded consonants in **acoustic singing** and an essential **technique** through which the **classical singer** can project with clear **diction**.

Shajarian, Mohammad-Reza (b. 1940). World's most famous singer of Iranian **classical** music. Shajarian was born in Khorasan, the northeastern region of Iran, and studied with Abdollah Davami (1891–1980), with whom he learned many Iranian classical **songs**, as well as the *radif*, a set of Persian **modes**. He became a national star after appearing on Iranian television in the 1970s. Shajarian has an intimate knowledge of Persian poetry, which forms the backbone for most of the texts he sings. He was a major figure in the Iranian cultural revolution.

Shakespeare, William (1849–1931). English **tenor** and **voice pedagogue.** Shakespeare studied in London at the Royal Academy of Music with William Sterndale Bennett (1816–1875), and in Milan with Francesco Lamperti (1813–1892), the father of **Giovanni Battista Lamperti**. In 1878, he was appointed professor of singing at the Royal Academy of Music, where he taught for most of his life. He is the author of several **treatises**, the most important of which are *The Art of Singing* (1899) and *Plain Words on Singing* (1924). Shakespeare the voice pedagogue should not be confused with the English **Renaissance** poet and dramatist also named William Shakespeare (1564–1616).

shape note singing. A **style** of group singing that flourished in the United States in the eighteenth century. Shape note singers perform congregational **hymns** that utilize notes in various shapes as a pedagogical tool to increase **sight-reading** facility. The style is named after the shape of the written note heads, which correspond to various **solmization** syllables. See also *The Sacred Harp*.

Shaw, Robert (1916–1999). American choral **conductor** and **pedagogue**, and one of the most influential figures on choral **pedagogy** in the twentieth century. Shaw was born in Red Bluff, California, and graduated from Pomona College in 1938. He spent the early part of his career as a symphonic **chorus master**, during which time he prepared works for Arturo Toscanini (1867–1957). He went on to found the Robert Shaw Chorale in 1946, with whom he toured and recorded until his appointment as **director** of the Atlanta Symphony Orchestra in 1967. In 1970, he founded the Atlanta Symphony Chorus, which quickly grew in stature under his direction. With the Atlanta Symphony Orchestra and Chorus, Shaw recorded numerous major works from the essential **canon** of the choral **repertory**. By the time of his death in 1999, Shaw had received fourteen **Grammy Awards**, a Guggenheim Fellowship, and the National Medal of the Arts.

While often criticized for his temper, rigidity, disdain for **professional** singers (his writings indicate his preference for **amateurs**), and unapologetic disregard for **historically informed performance practice (HIPP)**—his recording of Bach's *B Minor Mass*, for instance, features hundreds of amateur singers performing in **church Latin** with modern instruments—Shaw has undoubtedly had more influence on contemporary choral culture in the United States than any other single person. He almost single-handedly popularized the **count singing** pedagogical method, and his numerous recordings—which offer near-perfect **ensemble** singing and impeccable **blend** and **intonation**—offer **objective** proof of the practical success of his choral philosophy. Shaw's disciples comprise an entire generation of American choral conductors, many of whom studied with him through his **workshops**, eight of which were held at Carnegie Hall during the last decade of the twentieth century.

sheet music. Printed music that is bought and used in performance. In this sense, sheet music is synonymous with **score**. The sheet music industry narrowly refers to the **Tin Pan Alley** era of American **popular music**, when scores for individual **32-bar** popular songs were purchased for home use.

shelf equalizer. In audio technology, a type of **equalizer** that allows the user to **boost** or **cut** the uppermost or lowermost **frequencies**. Shelf equalizers are displayed on a graph with an upward or downward curve that then flattens out into a straight line. "Shelves" are found at the low and high ends of the frequency spectrum (named so because they literally look like steps or shelves). For more information, see the essay entitled "What Every Singer Needs to Know about Audio Technology."

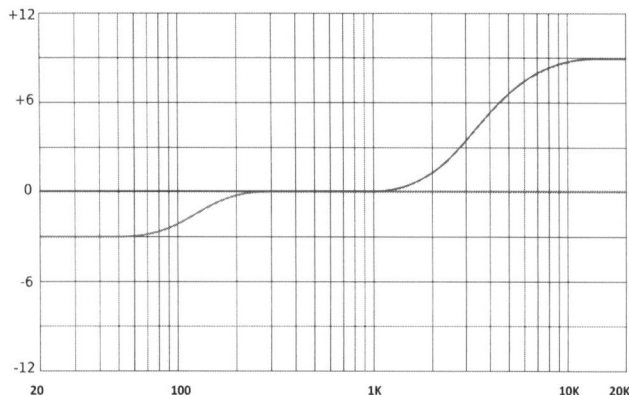

Figure 44. A shelf equalizer graph. *Courtesy Creative Commons.*

shimmer. Voice science term for a short-term fluctuation in **amplitude** (volume).

shotgun pattern. In audio technology, a descriptive phrase used to describe how a **microphone** will respond to **acoustic** energy directed at it. A shotgun pattern is a **pickup pattern** with a long, narrow oval emanating from the center of the posterior of the **diaphragm** and a shorter, narrow oval pattern emanating 180 degrees from the center of the diaphragm. Two smaller narrow ovals may also be found extending from the left and right of the center of the diaphragm. Figure 45 offers a visualization of a shotgun pickup pattern. This pattern is ideal in situations where it is difficult to place a microphone close

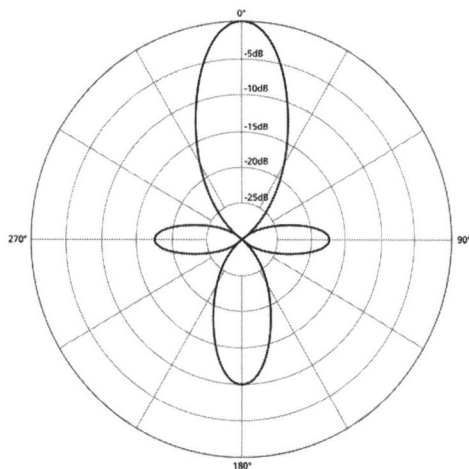

Figure 45. A shotgun microphone pattern. *Courtesy Creative Commons.*

to the sound source. For instance, shotgun microphones are popular amongst television news broadcasters and in the film industry, where microphones are often mounted to a boom that is positioned off-camera for the actor. For more information, see the essay entitled "What Every Singer Needs to Know about Audio Technology."

show choir. An American **genre** that combines **dance** with choral arrangements of popular tunes. Show choirs began in the 1960s and have found popularity mostly in high schools in the Southern and Midwestern United States. In 2009, the television series *Glee* sparked a show choir renaissance across the country, but the show's popularity was short-lived. Many music educators consider show choir to be a sport as opposed to a legitimate musical **ensemble**.

showstopper. In **musical theatre**, a significant or "showy" theatrical **number** that is strategically placed to generate audience enthusiasm. The showstopper derives its name from the audience reaction that the number receives, which tends to literally "stop the show." The performers must wait for the applause to die down, or even perform an **encore**, before resuming their performance.

sibilant. In **diction**, describes **fricative** and **affricate consonants** in which a stream of air is directed while the tongue rests against the teeth. When singers and choral **directors** refer to sibilants, they are primarily addressing the two **alveolar** hissing sibilants—[s] and [z]—which tend to be intrusive in singing and must be kept as short as possible. **Amplified singers** and recording artists often rely on electronic **de-essing** to keep the sibilants under control.

sight reading. The ability to read music at first sight. Sight reading is not an innate ability; rather, one becomes a strong sight reader through experience, training, and the development of strong **musicianship**. Sight-reading skills are especially important for choral artists, who are often partly hired on the basis of their ability to sight read. See also **sightsinging**.

sightsinging. Synonymous with **sight reading**. College and conservatory courses that develop sight-reading skills are often called sightsinging or "aural skills" courses.

signal chain. A term used to describe the path an electrical signal travels from the **microphone** to the speaker within an audio system. Elements of the signal chain often include—but are not limited to—the **microphone**, cables, mixer board, compressor, reverb unit, **equalizer**, amplifier, and speaker. Each element of the signal chain has the potential to alter the original **acoustic** signal.

signature. Indicators at the beginnings of staves musical **scores**, signatures can be of two types: **key signatures** or time signatures. Key signatures indicate the **major mode** or **minor** mode (or **key**) of the piece, whereas time signatures indicate the **meters** and note values.

Sills, Beverly (1929–2007). American **soprano**. Sills made her **operatic** début in 1947, as Frasquita in Bizet's *Carmen* with the Philadelphia Grand Opera Company. In 1955, she joined the New York City Opera, where she established a legendary career. Her greatest **roles** with New York City Opera included Cleopatra in Handel's *Giulio Cesare* and all three of Donizetti's Tudor queens: Elizabeth in *Roberto Devereux* and the title roles in *Anna Bolena* and *Maria Stuarda*. With the **company**, she also recorded the title role in Moore's *The Ballad of Baby Doe* for **Deutsche Grammophon Gesellschaft (DGG)** in 1959. Later in her career, Sills moved into administration, becoming the general **director** of the New York City Opera in 1980, chairman of the board of the Lincoln Center in 1994, and chairman of the **Metropolitan Opera** in 2002. The Beverly Sills Artist Award was established by the Metropolitan Opera in 2005.

silver age. Sometimes used to refer to a second **golden age** after a period of decline.

simple duple. A two-**beat meter** in which each beat is divided into a two-part **subdivision**. See **simple meter**.

simple meter. When each **beat** of a measure is divided into two **subdivisions**. There are three kinds of simple meter: **simple duple**, which has two beats per measure; **simple triple**, which has three beats per measure; and **simple quadruple**, which has four beats per measure.

simple quadruple. A four-**beat meter** in which each beat is divided into a two-part **subdivision**. See **simple meter**.

simple triple. A three-**beat meter** in which each beat is divided into a two-part **subdivision**. See **simple meter**.

Sinatra, Frank (1915 1998). American popular singer. Sinatra was born in Hoboken, New Jersey, to Italian immigrant parents. Although he was almost completely untrained as a singer, he achieved early success as a performer on the radio and with **big bands**. The bandleader Tommy Dorsey (1905–1956) hired him in 1940, and Sinatra soon became one of America's most famous singers, a stature he would hold until **Elvis Presley** arrived on the musical scene in the 1950s. Although Sinatra's **repertoire**—especially in his early career—was comprised of jazz standards, he never **improvised**. His **baritone** voice was warm and lyrical, and Sinatra's artistic achievement rests largely in his expressive power and nuanced delivery of **song** texts. Throughout the course of his lifetime, Sinatra won eleven **Grammy Awards**, and his prolific recording catalog has sold more than 150 million albums. His 1955 album *In the Wee Small Hours* is considered to be one of the first **concept albums** in the **popular music** industry.

sine nomine **(Lat).** Without name. The label given to a **Renaissance Mass** when the **cantus firmus** cannot be identified.

singer's formant. A region of strong **acoustic** energy, as shown by a **spectrogram**. In scientific terms, the singer's formant is a grouping of **harmonics** 3, 4, and 5 to create **ring** or **singer's resonance**. This phenomenon usually occurs between approximately 2,500–3,200 **Hz** and is accompanied by a spectrum peak near this location. It is this increase in energy at this **pitch** level that allows singers to project over an orchestra, which peaks at much lower **frequencies** (c. 500 Hz). The singer's formant is absent in speech and the spectra of many untrained singers.

singer's instinct. An unquantifiable talent for singing. The kinesthetic sense that some singers possess that enables them to organically produce good vocal sounds and express texts. While many aspects of singing can be taught, singer's instinct cannot. A performer who does not possess singer's instinct is likely to always have a certain amount of rigidity and lack **expression**.

singer's resonance. Refers to the presence of the **singer's formant** in **classical singing**. The term *singer's resonance* is often used interchangeably with **ring**.

singing exercise. See **vocalise**.

Singing: The Mechanism and the Technic. A 1967 **treatise** by **William Vennard**, and one of the most important and most influential books on **fact-based voice pedagogy** published in the twentieth century. *Singing: The Mechanism and the Technic* is perhaps the most significant precursor to **Richard Miller's** 1986 treatise *The Structure of Singing*.

singing voice specialist (SVS). A teacher of singing who works with injured singers as part of a **voice team**, along with an **otolaryngologist (ENT)** and **speech-language pathologist (SLP)**. Although the term has come into frequent use in recent decades, the label has become somewhat controversial in the medical community due to the wide variety of training among SVSs and the lack of a national oversight organization to ensure that SVSs are indeed qualified to work with injured singers. Most SVSs agree that it is imperative to rely on the expertise of the other two members of the voice team.

Singspiel. A German-language **form** of light **opera**. In *Singspiels*, spoken dialogue alternates with **songs** and **ensemble numbers**. Settings are usually in rural or exotic places. Some of the most famous examples of the **genre** include three *Singspiels* by Wolfgang Amadeus Mozart (1756–1791): *Bastien und Bastienne* (1768), *Die Entführung aus dem Serail* (1782), and *Die Zauberflöte* (1791).

sinus. Any cavity, recess, passage, or hollow bone in the body. In singing, usually refers to one of the hollow cavities in the skull connecting with the **nasal cavity**.

Six, Les. A group of six French composers in the first half of the twentieth century who modeled their art after the aesthetic and artistic principles of Erik Satie (1866–1925) and Jean Cocteau (1889–1963). Members of *Les Six* included Louis Durey (1888–1979), Arthur Honegger (1892–1955), Darius Milhaud (1892–1974), Germaine Taillefaire (1892–1983), Francis Poulenc (1899–1963), and Georges Auric (1899–1973). The name *Les Six* was given to them in 1920 by the French music critic Henri Collet (1885–1951).

ska. A **style** of Jamaican **popular music**. At its peak of popularity in the early 1960s, ska combined elements of Afro-Cuban **dance** music and New Orleans **jazz**. Along with **rocksteady**, ska is an important precursor of **reggae**.

slating. The information a **musical theatre** performer gives to an **audition** panel before singing their **song**.

SLP. Abbreviation for **speech-language pathologist**.

SLS. Abbreviation for **Speech Level Singing**.

slumber song. See **lullaby**. See also *berceuse*, *Schlummerlied*, *Wiegenlied*.

slur. In vocal music, a curved line inserted over several notes, indicating that those notes should be sung on a single syllable of text. Notes without slurs will each have their own syllables.

soft palate. The soft, fleshy portion of the back of the **palate** (the roof of the mouth).

soggetto cavato (It). "Carved from the words"; the complete **phrase** is *soggetto cavato dalle parole*. Almost always applies to a **cantus firmus** that is constructed using **pitches** of the Guidonian **solmization** system that correspond to the **vowels** of someone's name.

soleá. A **song** type of the **flamenco genre**, usually in either **simple triple** or **compound duple meter** with four-line **stanzas** similar to *coplas*.

solfège. The practice of assigning **solmization** syllables to various **scale degrees** when **sightsinging**. There are two basic types of *solfège*. Most North American universities, colleges, and conservatories utilize **movable do** *solfège*, which assigns the syllable *do* to the **tonic** of the **major key** or relative **minor** key. Some conservatories—particularly in Europe—utilize **fixed do** *solfège*, in which the note C is always *do*, D is always *re*, and so forth. **Chromatic fixed do** (another variation) also assigns unique syllables to chromatically altered notes: C♯ is always *di*, D♭ is always *ra*, and so on.

solfeggio (It). See *solfège*.

soliloquy. A **song** or **aria** delivered by one character who is alone on the stage. Soliloquies usually allow the audience to glimpse into the inner machinations of a character before they make a pivotal decision that will impact the **plot**. Billy Bigelow's "Soliloquy" from Rodgers and Hammerstein's *Carousel* (1945) is a famous example.

solmization. The assigning of syllables to the steps of a **scale**. The most common solmization system—of a **major** scale—utilizes the syllables *do, re, mi, fa, sol, la,* and *ti*. The names of the first six notes were originally assigned by the **medieval** music theorist Guido d'Arezzo (c. 991–1033), who took them from the first **verse** of the **Latin** hymn "Ut queant laxis." Chromatic solmization adds ten syllables to the five chromatic note possibilities: *di* (*ra*), *ri* (*me*), fi (*se*), si (*le*), and *li* (*te*). Solmization is used extensively in *solfège* and **sightsinging**.

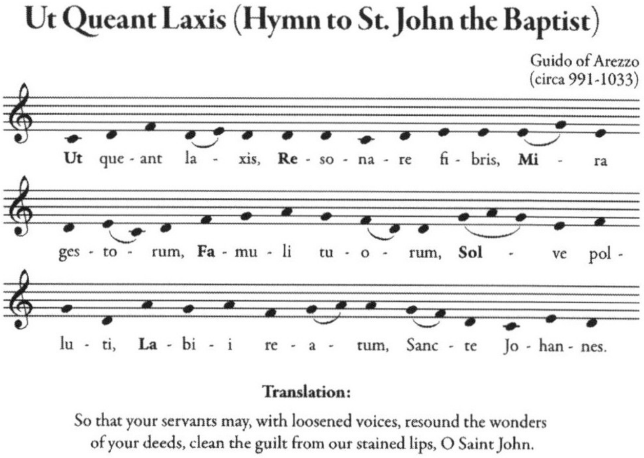

Ut Queant Laxis (Hymn to St. John the Baptist)

Guido of Arezzo
(circa 991-1033)

Ut que-ant la - xis, Re - so - na - re fi - bris, Mi - ra

ges - to - rum, Fa - mu - li tu - o - rum, Sol - ve pol -

lu - ti, La - bi - i re - a - tum, Sanc - te Jo - han - nes.

Translation:
So that your servants may, with loosened voices, resound the wonders of your deeds, clean the guilt from our stained lips, O Saint John.

Figure 46. Hymn: *Ut Queant Laxis*, early eleventh century. *Courtesy Creative Commons.*

soma. The "body" half of the philosophical dichotomy of "psyche and soma" ("mind and body"), usually attributed to the French philosopher René Descartes (1596–1650). The **voice pedagogue Cornelius Reid** famously dovetailed this philosophical concept into the discourse of **voice pedagogy** through the publication of his 1975 **treatise** *Voice: Psyche and Soma*, the third and final part of a pedagogical trilogy that also includes *Bel Canto: Principles and Practices* (1950) and *The Free Voice: A Guide to Natural Singing* (1965).

somatic. An adjective that describes an activity or approach that is holistic and body-centered. Advocates of somatic exercises believe in the transformative power of movement and self-awareness to promote psychological and physical well-being.

Somatic Voicework (SVW). A school of **voice pedagogy** founded by New York **pedagogue** Jeannette LoVetri (b. 1949). Also known as "The LoVetri Method," SVW is a body-based method of training based on voice science, classical voice training, speech training, acting, movement, and various **bodywork** methods. SVW is frequently associated with **contemporary commercial music (CCM) pedagogy**, and LoVetri is highly regarded as one of the world's most famous CCM **pedagogues**. Training in SVW is offered each summer at Shenandoah University's annual Contemporary Commercial Music Voice Pedagogy Institute, an extremely well-enrolled event that draws voice teachers from throughout the world to Winchester, Virginia, each July.

song. Any vocal composition consisting of melody and text. See also **art song**, **folk music**, **popular music**, **song collection**, **song cycle**, **song set**.

song collection. A large group of **songs** that are published in a single volume. Song collections are usually (but not always) by a single composer. Unlike **song cycles**, songs from song collections are not usually intended to be performed as a cohesive whole and can be excerpted in performance without the obligation of performing others from the **opus**. Famous examples of song collections include Schumann's *Myrthen*, Op. 25 (1840) and Wolf's *Spanisches Liederbuch* (1891) and *Italienisches Liederbuch* (1892–1896).

song cycle. A collection of **songs** by a single composer that are meant to be performed in order as a cohesive set. The texts of song cycles either feature a narrative—telling a unified story—or may simply be settings of poems that share a similar theme. Most (but not all) song cycles also feature texts by a single poet. The term *song cycle* (*Liederkreis* in German) was first used in the early nineteenth century, with Ludwig van Beethoven (1770–1827) being credited with the first important song cycle, *An die ferne Geliebte*, Op. 98 (1816). In addition to the many examples from the German *Lieder* **repertory**, there are also many examples of the song cycle in the French

mélodie repertoire, as well as examples in the English, American, Spanish, Russian, and Scandinavian **art song genres**. In recent years, contemporary **musical theatre** and **cabaret song** writers have also begun using the term to describe some of their songs that revolve around a particular theme. Examples of these contemporary song cycles include *Songs for a New World* (1995), by Jason Robert Brown (b. 1970), and *Elegies* (2003), by William Finn (b. 1952).

song form. Often used as a synonym for **32-bar song form** (AABA), song form most narrowly refers to the basic structure of popular **songs** in the **Great American Songbook**, the **golden era** of American songwriting from the 1920s to the 1950s. More broadly, songs can take on a variety of **forms**. In **classical** music—for example, German *Lieder* and French *mélodies*—four forms are the most common: **strophic**, modified strophic, **scenic**, and **through-composed**.

Song of Mary. See *Magnificat*.

Song of Simeon. See *Nunc dimittis*.

song set. A short grouping of **songs** that is usually published under a single **opus** number and not necessarily intended to be performed as a cohesive group. For example, Fauré's song set *Cinq mélodies de Venise*, Op. 58 (1891) can be performed sequentially as a set of five songs, or its songs can be excerpted and performed individually. Song sets usually contain far fewer songs than **song cycles** and **song collections**.

sonogram. See **spectrogram**.

sopranist (*sopranista*). See **male soprano**.

soprano. 1. The highest of the seven principal **classical** voice categories. The **Kloiber Fach System** identifies seven subcategories of sopranos: the *Soubrette*, *lyrischer Koloratursopran* (*Koloratursoubrette*), *dramatischer Koloratoursopran*, *lyrischer Sopran*, *judgendlich-dramatischer Sopran*, *dramatischer Sopran*, and *Charaktersopran*. The *spinto* soprano is another frequently referenced variety.

2. The highest voice part in four-part (**SATB**) **choral music**.

sostenuto (**It**). Sustained.

sotto voce (**It**). Softly, in a low voice.

Soubrette. In the **Kloiber Fach System**, the *Soubrette* is the highest *Fach* on the chart, positioned one notch above the *lyrischer Koloratursopran* (*Koloratursoubrette*).

Examples of *Soubrette* **roles** include Gianetta in Donizetti's *L'elisir d'amore* (1832), Barbarina in Mozart's *Le nozze di Figaro* (1786), and Papagena in Mozart's *Die Zauberflöte* (1791). The term *Soubrette* implies a character **type**, in addition to a **voice type**. They are usually young, teenage characters who are secondary in importance to the principal female **soprano** of an **opera**. The literal French translation is "maid." See the *Fach* chart in appendix C.

soul. **Genre** of American **popular music** that originated during the 1950s and 1960s. Soul music combines elements of **gospel** and **rhythm and blues**, two of its most important forerunners. A distinctly African American genre of music, most soul music features **call-and-response forms**, in addition to hand clapping and physical movements. **Ray Charles** and **Aretha Franklin** are two of the genre's most famous and recognizable performers.

source. The "vibrators"—as opposed to the resonators—in **acoustics**. In singing, the source is the **vocal folds**. See also **source/filter theory**.

source/filter theory. The way that current voice science describes voice production. The word *source* refers to the **vocal folds**, which generate periodic sound through **frequency**. The word *filter* refers to the resonators and **articulators** of the **vocal tract**.

source music. Another name for **diegetic** music.

Souzay, Gérard (1918–2004). French **baritone** best known as an interpreter of French *mélodies* and German *Lieder*. Souzay studied at the Paris Conservatoire, where his principal teachers included **Pierre Bernac** and Claire Croiza (1882–1946). He began his career as a recitalist in 1945, and soon moved into selected **operatic roles**, including Aeneas in Purcell's *Dido and Aeneas* and the title roles in Monteverdi's *Orfeo* and Mozart's *Don Giovanni*. His most frequently performed operatic role was Golaud in Debussy's *Pelléas et Mélisande*. Souzay is most famous for his prolific recording career, which includes the **song cycles** of Franz Schubert (1797–1828) and Schumann's *Dichterliebe*, Op. 48, as well as the *mélodies* of Gabriel Fauré (1845–1924), Henri Duparc (1848–1933), Ernest Chausson (1855–1899), Claude Debussy (1862–1918), Maurice Ravel (1875–1937), and Francis Poulenc (1899–1963). For more than three decades, Souzay's **recital** partner was **Dalton Baldwin**, who is the pianist featured on most of his recordings.

Spanish art song. 1. The **art song** of Spain. While Spain's singing tradition is rich, most Spanish vocal music written before the twentieth century was either popular in nature or written for the **theatre**. Spanish art song did not reach its zenith until the early twentieth century, making it a much younger cousin of the German *Lied* and French *mélodie*. The most important composers of Spanish song include Enrique Granados (1867–1916), Manuel de Falla (1876–1946), Joaquín Nin (1879–1949), Jesús Guridi (1886–1949), Federico Mompou (1893–1987), Fernando Obradors (1897–1945), Joaquín Rodrigo (1901–1999), and Xavier Montsalvatge (1912–2002). Songs written by these composers should always be performed using Standard European Spanish (**SES**), or **Castilian**.

2. Sometimes used in a broader sense to include any Spanish-language art song, thus including the **Latin American art song repertoire**, in addition to continental Spanish art song. Latin American song, however, should be performed in **Standard American Spanish (SAS)**.

spasmodic dysphonia (SD). A type of neurological **voice disorder** in which the muscles of the **larynx** go into spasm. Individuals who suffer from SD tend to struggle during **phonation** and sustained singing. Due to its neurological origin, singers who suffer from this condition may not respond well to traditional **voice therapy**. Different kinds of SD can directly affect **abduction** or **adduction**, and the disorder can thus be placed in two categories: abductor spasmodic dysphonia (abductor SD) and adductor spasmodic dysphonia (adductor SD).

spec sheets. In audio technology, a term that is short for "specification sheets." Spec sheets are technical documents included in the packaging of audio equipment. They include such information as **frequency response**, polar pattern, **microphone sensitivity**, **polarity**, connector type, weight, and dimensions. Spec sheets also often include technical drawings of the equipment for additional clarity.

spectacle. A nineteenth-century **genre** of **musical theatre** with an emphasis on lavish sets and costumes. See also **extravaganza**.

spectral envelope. The scientific term that explains why each singer has his or her own unique **timbre**. The spectral envelope describes the unique pattern of overtones produced by each individual singer. Spectral envelopes can be visualized using a **power spectrum**.

spectral slope. In voice science and **acoustics**, the rate at which **harmonics**—produced by the vibrating **vocal folds**—decrease in **amplitude** (become softer) as they rise in **frequency** (**pitch**). This decrease in amplitude is always relative to the **fundamental frequency**.

spectral waterfall. See **spectrogram**.

spectrogram. A visual representation of the spectrum of **frequencies**, intensities, and **durations**. In voice science and **vocology**, **voice analysis software** (for instance, **VoceVista**) makes frequent use of spectrograms. A spectrogram can also be called a **sonogram, spectral waterfall, voiceprint,** or **voicegram.** Spectrograms are useful in the study of **resonance.**

spectrograph. The electronic instrument that generates a **spectrogram.**

spectrum analyzer. A device that displays relative **amplitudes** of the overtones of the voice during **phonation.** A kind of **spectrogram.**

speech-language pathologist (SLP). A vocal health **professional** who works with injured voices and specializes in communication disorders. Also known informally as a speech therapist. SLPs who complete their clinical fellowship year (CFY) earn the **Certificate of Clinical Compliance (CCC),** thus granting them the professional letters **CCC-SLP.** Injured singers often work with a SLP as part of a three-member **voice team,** along with their singing teacher and an **otolaryngologist (ENT).**

Speech Level Singing (SLS). A school of **contemporary commercial music (CCM) pedagogy** developed by Seth Riggs (b. 1930). Clients of SLS include many important figures in the **popular music** and film industries.

speech melody. An **extended technique** first developed by Steve Reich (b. 1936) in his piece *Different Trains* (1988). Speech melody involves using recorded literal speech as its own **form** of "melody." The speech is then imitated by the instruments, who derive their **pitches** and rhythms directly from the speaking. Reich also used speech melody in two of his later works: *The Cave* (1993) and *City Life* (1995).

speechy. Used to negatively describe a singing sound that too closely resembles that of normal speech. Could be desirable or complimentary in **jazz** or **musical theatre** styles. In the Italian school, somewhat similar to *voce aperta* (as opposed to *voce chiusa*)

Spielalt. German *Fach* that literally translates as "playful alto." In the **Kloiber Fach System,** the *Spielalt* is positioned one spot lower on the chart than the *dramatischer Mezzosopran,* but one spot higher than the *lyrischer Alt.* Examples of *Spielalt* roles include Nancy in Flotow's *Martha* (1847), Meg Page in Verdi's *Falstaff* (1893), Lola in Mascagni's *Cavalleria Rusticana* (1890), and Florence Pike in Britten's *Albert Herring* (1947). See the *Fach* chart in appendix C.

Spielbaß (Baßbuffo). German *Fach* that literally translates as "playful **bass.**" In the **Kloiber Fach System,** the *Spielbaß (Baßbuffo)* is positioned one spot lower on the chart than the *Charakterbariton,* but one spot higher than the *schwerer Spielbaß (schwerer Baßbuffo).* Examples of *Spielbaß (Baßbuffo)* **roles** include Leporello in Mozart's *Don Giovanni* (1787), Don Alfonso in Mozart's *Così fan tutte* (1790), Dr. Bartolo in Rossini's *Il barbiere di Siviglia* (1816), the title role in Donizetti's *Don Pasquale* (1842), and the Doktor in Berg's *Wozzeck* (1925). See the *Fach* chart in appendix C.

Spieltenor (Tenorbuffo). German *Fach* that literally translates as "playful **tenor.**" In the **Kloiber Fach System,** the *Spieltenor (Tenorbuffo)* is positioned one spot lower on the chart than the *haute-contre,* but one spot higher than the *lyrischer Tenor.* Examples of *Spieltenor (Tenorbuffo)* **roles** include Basilio and Don Curzio in Mozart's *Le nozze di Figaro* (1786), Remendado in Bizet's *Carmen* (1875), Beppo in Leoncavallo's *Pagliacci* (1892), and Goro in Puccini's *Madama Butterfly* (1904). See the *Fach* chart in appendix C.

spinto. Literally translating as "pushed," an Italian adjective used to describe certain types of **sopranos** and **tenors** in **opera** who have a particular "edge" or "bite" in their sound. *Spintos* are generally considered to be heavier **voice types** than lyric sopranos or lyric tenors, sometimes sacrificing beauty or warmth in exchange for power. Although the term is used widely, the *spinto* is not an official category in the **Kloiber Fach System.** Sometimes called *lirico spinto.*

spiritual. African American religious folk **song** cultivated during the nineteenth and early twentieth centuries. Stylistically, spirituals usually employ a **call-and-response** format and **refrains.** Themes depict the struggles of a hard life combined with deep faith and a sense of determined optimism. Famous composers and arrangers of spirituals include Harry T. Burliegh (1866–1949), R. Nathaniel Dett (1882–1943), Hall Johnson (1888–1970), William Dawson (1899–1990), Jester Hairston (1901–2000), and Moses Hogan (1957–2003). Early versions of spirituals were also archived by nineteenth-century collectors in **shape note** publications.

Spolin, Viola (1906–1994). An important innovator of American **theatre** whose **acting technique** is widely advocated and practiced by teachers and students of acting. The Spolin **technique** focuses on **improvisation** as a means to making acting more **realistic**; the actor makes reactive choices as he or she would in real life. She called her acting exercises "theatre games," most of which are collected in *Improvisation for the Theatre* (1963). This book is an essential **treatise** for the **musical**

theatre performer, and its third edition was published in 1999. In theatrical training, Spolin's method is one of the most frequently referenced acting techniques, along with those of **Constantin Stanislavski**, **Stella Adler**, **Sanford Meisner**, **Michael Chekhov**, **Uta Hagen**, and the **Method**.

Sprechstimme. A vocal **quality** or **style** that lies somewhere in between speech and singing. Although exact **pitches** are notated—with an *x* over each note stem—and are expected to be performed with accuracy, it is also incumbent on the performer to give the vocal line a speech-like quality. *Sprechstimme* was invented by Engelbert Humperdinck (1854–1921) in his work *Königslieder* (1897), but the **technique** is most famously associated with Arnold Schoenberg (1874–1951) and his works *Pierrot lunaire*, Op. 21 (1912) and *Moses und Aron* (1932). Alban Berg (1885–1935) also made use of *Sprechstimme* in his **operas** *Wozzeck* (1925) and *Lulu* (1935).

Figure 47. *Sprechstimme* notation from Schoenberg's *Pierrot lunaire*, 1912. *Courtesy Creative Commons.*

squall. A pitched yell characterized by high phonatory intensities, distorted **timbre**, and strong **adduction** of the **thyroarytenoid** muscles and/or **supraglottic** structures. Squall is a frequent component of American **gospel** singing, and its use is generally restricted to moments of high emotional intensity.

square note. In **early music**, the idea that a note is sung at a consistent volume and then abruptly ended. Compare with **round note**. Not to be confused with **shape note singing** (which contains some printed notes with square symbols).

Stabat Mater. A **Latin sequence** for the Feast of the Seven Doulours. The text describes the Virgin Mary standing at the foot of the cross during the Crucifixion. Historically, the *Stabat Mater* is one of the sacred texts set most frequently by composers, resulting in major choral-orchestral works by Antonio Vivaldi (1678–1741), Giovanni Battista Pergolesi (1710–1736), Gioacchino Rossini (1792–1868), Antonín Dvořák (1841–1904),

Francis Poulenc (1899–1963), and others. The *Stabat Mater* is one of the **five great sequences**, along with the *Dies Irae*, *Lauda Sion*, *Veni Sancte Spiritus*, and *Victimae Paschali Laudes*.

staccato **(It).** Detached, with a space between each note. The opposite of **legato**.

stage director. In **opera** and **musical theatre**, the person who conceives and **blocks** the onstage action. In opera, the stage director usually serves under the **musical director**, who is also the **conductor**. In musical theatre, however, the opposite is true, and the stage director—who is simply called the **director**—serves as the artistic leader of the **production**. **Franco Zeffirelli** and **Peter Sellars** are two of the most famous opera stage directors in recent history, and **Hal Prince** and **Tommy Tune** are two examples of influential musical theatre stage directors. While some stage directors also choreograph **dance numbers**, that job is more often the province of the **choreographer**.

standard (jazz standard). A **song** that has become **canonized** in **jazz** and **popular music**. Standards are usually—but not always—in **32-bar song form**, and they generally originated in **Broadway musicals** and through the **Tin Pan Alley sheet music** industry. Standards, however, are widely known and usually not performed or remembered in their original contexts. They comprise a substantial portion of the jazz musician's **repertoire**. Most standards are also considered to be part of the **Great American Songbook**. Sometimes called jazz standards. Although most standards have **lyrics**, they are part of the repertory of both singers and instrumentalists. Well-known examples of jazz standards include "Star Dust" (1927), "My Funny Valentine" (1937), "All the Things You Are" (1939), and "Round Midnight" (1944).

Standard American Spanish (SAS). The **dialect** of Spanish common in the western hemisphere, as distinct from Standard European Spanish (SES) or **Castilian** Spanish. While the Spanish spoken by people of the Americas has many unifying features, there are still numerous subtle differences in Spanish **pronunciation** between various countries, with Argentina, Mexico, and Puerto Rico (for example) each maintaining their own distinct dialects. Singers of **Latin American art song** must carefully consider the poet and country of origin when making pronunciation decisions in their **repertoire**.

Standard European Spanish (SES). See **Castilian**.

standard Roman pronunciation (of Latin). See **church Latin**.

standing ovation. The practice of an audience standing while applauding at the end of a **concert**, **recital**, or theatrical **production** to pay tribute to an especially outstanding performance. While traditionally reserved for rare or special performances, the standing ovation phenomenon has become routine in contemporary culture, rendering it somewhat meaningless.

Stanislavski, Constantin (1863–1938). Russian actor and **theatre director** whose philosophies on acting have made him one of the most influential figures in theatrical history. Stanislavski's "system" advocates rigorous discipline, integrity, self-analysis, personal experience, reflection, and **emotional recall**, a quintessential Stanislavski concept. By shifting the focus away from raw **technique** and more toward the personal and emotional, Stanislavski is credited as the founder of modern theatre itself. He codified his system of acting in a series of writings, all of which were translated into English (some after his death). These books—collectively comprising a trilogy—include *An Actor Prepares* (1936), *Becoming a Character* (1948), and *Creating a Role* (1961). In the United States, **Lee Strasberg** became the major advocate of Stanislavski's teachings, which he codified into a system he called the **Method**. **Stella Adler** and **Sanford Meisner** also based their **acting techniques** in part on Stanislavski's ideas. A prevalent figure today among students of acting, no individual has had more influence on modern acting than Stanislavski.

stanza. A complete section of poetry, consisting of several lines.

steigern **(Ger).** Intensify, increase.

sternocleidomastoids. Muscles of the neck that connect the **sternum** and clavicle to the mastoid process, which is part of the jaw. Strained singing often visibly reveals the

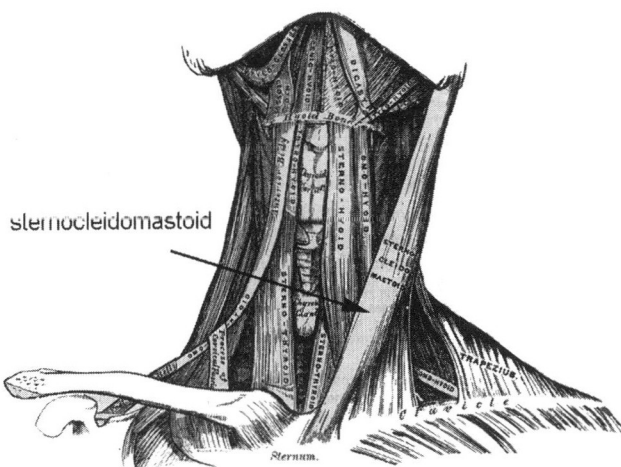

Figure 48. Sternocleidomastoid muscles. *Courtesy Gray's Anatomy*, with labeling by Scott McCoy; reprinted with permission from *Your Voice: An Inside View* (2004).

sternocleidomastoid muscles (although they are sometimes still visible in slender singers who exhibit good **technique**).

sternum. Flat bone located in the center of the **chest** that is connected to the ribs. A "raised sternum" is a characteristic of good singing **posture**.

steroid myasthenia. A **voice disorder** caused by long-term exposure to steroid inhalers. A symptom of steroid myasthenia is **chronic laryngitis**.

stile antico **(It).** "Ancient **style**." Refers to the *prima prattica* style of the **Renaissance** era.

stile concertato **(It).** "Concerted **style**." Refers to music from the **baroque** era that features contrasts between smaller and larger forces.

stile concitato **(It).** "Excited **style**." Term coined by Claudio Monteverdi (1567–1643) to describe music composed to portray anger. Rapid reiterations of a single note characterizes the *stile concitato* style.

stile moderno **(It).** "Modern **style**." Refers to the *seconda prattica* style of the **baroque** era.

stile rappresentativo **(It).** "Representative **style**." *Stile rappresentativo* describes the **recitative**-like **monodic** style composed by the first practitioners of **Italian opera** in the early seventeenth century. *Stile rappresentativo* is intended to "represent" human speech.

stock character. In **opera**, **operetta**, or **musical theatre**, a character that conforms to certain stereotypes, appearing in many different works of the **genre** with few changes except for the character's name. Examples include the **ingénue soprano**, the **romantic tenor**, or the villainous **bass**, or—in the case of **Gilbert and Sullivan**—the **patter baritone**. Stock characters vary in different eras of opera history. Wolfgang Amadeus Mozart (1756–1791), for instance, relegated his tenors to comical, supporting **roles**, but by the romantic era the tenor had emerged from the sidebar into the usual position of being the heroic leading male character.

Stockhausen, Julius (1826–1906). German **baritone** of the nineteenth century renowned for his **interpretation** of *Lieder*. Stockhausen gave the first public performances of many of Schubert's works, including *Die schöne Müllerin*, D795 (1823) in 1856. Johannes Brahms (1833–1897) also dedicated *Lieder* to Stockhausen. He studied in London with **Manuel García** (1805–1906) and wrote a two-volume singing method, which he published in

1886. Not to be confused with the ***avant-garde*** composer Karlheinz Stockhausen (1928–2007).

Figure 49. Photograph of Johannes Brahms and Julius Stockhausen, 1870.

Stollen. The A section of an AAB **bar form**.

straight tone. A **style** of singing that is absent of **vibrato**, therefore containing no variation of **pitch** in sustained notes. While often undesirable in much of Western **classical** solo singing, straight-tone singing is quite prevalent in some Western vocal styles, including most forms of **choral music**, **jazz**, and **barbershop** singing. Many **world music** styles also make effective use of straight-tone singing. One advantage to straight-tone singing is the greater potential to create overtones when harmonizing with other straight-tone singers. When **ensembles** sing with excessive vibrato, it is more difficult to produce overtones, as there is pitch variation in the lower **harmonics**.

Strasberg, Lee (1901–1982). American actor, **director**, and acting teacher. Strasberg is credited as the inventor of the **Method**, a codification of the teachings of **Constantin Stanislavski**. In 1931, Strasberg founded a theatrical collective in New York City known as the Group Theatre. Two of his students were **Stella Adler** and **Sanford Meisner**, who would later go on to develop their own **acting techniques**. In 1951, he founded the Actors Studio, which would become one of the most famous acting schools in the world, influencing an entire generation of Hollywood performers. Strasberg's acting philosophy rigidly adhered to the tenets of Stanislavski—including personal experience and **emotional recall**—and many actors and historians consider him to be the "Father of

Method Acting in America." In theatrical training, the Method is one of the most frequently referenced acting techniques, along with those of Stanislavski, Adler, Meisner, **Michael Chekhov**, **Anne Bogart**, and **Viola Spolin**.

stratified squamous epithelium. The outermost layer or **cover** of the **vocal folds**.

straw phonation. Vocal **warm-up** and therapeutic **technique** devised by Ingo Titze (b. 1945) that makes use of the **semioccluded vocal tract**. In this **exercise**, the singer **vocalizes** through a drinking straw, maximizing the efficiency of the **vocal folds** and **laryngeal**/pharyngeal space, as well as the **oral cavity**. The **soft palate** must remain in an engaged (back) position to ensure that no **nasal resonance** is occurring.

Streisand, Barbra (b. 1942). American popular singer and enduring figure of the **musical theatre** and film industries. Born in Brooklyn, Streisand sang in New York City nightclubs in the early 1960s before landing a featured **role** in the 1962 **Broadway musical** *I Can Get It for You Wholesale*, by Harold Rome (1908–1993). Her reputation soared after appearances on national television shows (including *The Ed Sullivan Show*), and, in 1964, Streisand was selected for the role of Fanny Brice in the Broadway **production** of *Funny Girl*, by Jule Styne (1905–1994). This role solidified her stardom, and Streisand won an Academy Award for Best Actress when she reprised the role three years later in the film version. She has also been prolific as a recording artist, recording more than fifty albums and winning ten **Grammy Awards**. Later in her career, she also moved into directing with the film *Yentl* (1983). Streisand is one of the only artists who has won all four major entertainment awards: the **Emmy**, Grammy, Oscar, and **Tony**. Her vocal **style** is unique and idiosyncratic, yielding very personalized **interpretations** that cannot be imitated without resorting to caricature. No one can hear the song "People," for example, without immediately associating it with Streisand's iconic rendition.

stretta* (It).** Drawn together or tightening. In **Italian opera**, the fast climax at the end of an **aria** or **ensemble**. More often used for ensembles than arias, where such a passage is then often called a ***cabaletta.

***stringendo* (It).** Pressing or becoming faster.

stroboscope (stroboscopy). An instrument used to visualize **vocal fold** vibration via a synchronized, flashing light that is passed through a flexible or rigid **endoscope**. An examination by stroboscope is called a stroboscopy.

Strohbass. A low **register** of the male voice produced by an intentionally pressed or lowered **larynx** to sing in a **range** below the natural speaking voice. More of an imposed **quality** than a true vocal register, some **pedagogues** question the health and freedom of *Strohbass* singing. Synonymous with *Schnarrbass*.

strophic. A **song form** in which the same music is repeated with different words for each **verse**. One of the four standard forms of German *Lieder*, strophic **forms** also appear ubiquitously in **folk music**, patriotic **songs**, and **hymns**.

Structure of Singing, The. Important 1986 pedagogical **treatise** by **Richard Miller** advocating a systematic approach to **voice pedagogy**. *The Structure of Singing* has arguably had more influence on modern **fact-based** voice pedagogy than any other single book, making it one of the most important treatises ever written in the discipline.

studio class. A weekly performance hour at a college, university, or conservatory when members of a particular voice studio sing for one another in preparation for more significant or high-profile performances.

style. The choices a performer makes when interpreting a musical work based on such factors as tradition, **genre**, history, and context. The concept of style comes from a rhetorical tradition that dates back to Aristotle (384–322 BCE). In this sense, style is distinct from content: *what* one says as opposed to *how* one says it. In music, each genre will have its own stylistic tendencies, and styles also vary widely within a single genre. One would not perform Giuseppe Verdi (1813–1901) the same way he or she would perform Claudio Monteverdi (1567–1643). A thorough understanding of style is essential for the modern singer.

subdivision. Microdivisions felt and measured within a particular **meter**. Singers of all **styles** "feel" subdivisions, which greatly influence accuracy and **expression**. For example, in a **simple quadruple meter** (common time), the experienced singer will likely feel a sixteenth-note subdivision at all times.

subdominant. In **tonal music**, the note a fifth below the **tonic** and the **chord** built on that note (IV).

subgenre. A **genre** within a genre.

subglottal (subglottic). Adjective meaning "below the **glottis**."

subjective pedagogy. Voice teaching that involves **imagery** and **sensation**. Not **fact-based**.

submediant. In **tonal music**, the note a third below the **tonic** and the **chord** built on that note (VI).

subtext. The layer of meaning behind a particular text. Singers often consider (or create) subtexts to convey a meaning or emotion that complements the actual words being sung. In certain situations, subtexts can also be ironic in nature.

subtonic. In **tonal music**, the note a **major** second below the **tonic** and the **chord** built on that note (♭VII).

succentor. The assistant to the **precentor** in a **liturgical** worship service.

succès d'estime. A show that is admired by critics and aficionados but fails to become a box-office success. Many of Stephen Sondheim's musicals fall into this category.

sulcus glottideus. See **sulcus vocalis**.

sulcus vocalis. A **voice disorder** in which a groove or infolding of mucus along the surface of the **vocal fold** appears due to a thinning of the **superficial lamina propria** tissue. Also known as sulcus glottideus.

superbelt. **Contemporary commercial music (CCM)** term originating in New York City at the turn of the twenty-first century to define a high **belt** that incorporates a level of **mix** into the sound. The superbelt **repertoire** includes many contemporary **musical theatre roles**—for example, Elphaba in Stephen Schwartz's *Wicked* (2003)—that require the female singer to belt above a C5. Essentially synonymous with high-belt or **belt-mix**.

supercardioid pattern. In audio technology, a descriptive **phrase** used to describe how a **microphone** will respond to **acoustic** energy directed at it. A supercardioid pattern

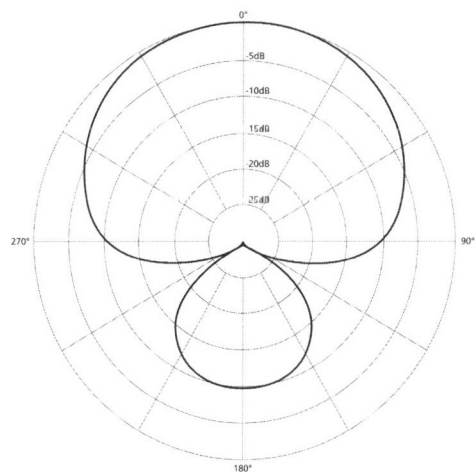

Figure 50. A supercardioid microphone pattern. *Courtesy Creative Commons.*

is a **pickup pattern** with a **cardioid pattern** shape at the anterior of the **diaphragm** and a circular pattern shape emanating from the posterior of the diaphragm. Figure 50 offers a visualization of a supercardioid pickup pattern. This pattern is similar to the cardioid pattern, with a slightly narrower **acceptance angle**. Unlike the standard cardioid pattern, the supercardioid pattern responds to noise from the posterior of the diaphragm, as well as the anterior. This allows the microphone to pick up some of the room's natural **reverb**, but it can also amplify room noise and contribute to **feedback**. For more information, see the essay entitled "What Every Singer Needs to Know about Audio Technology."

superficial lamina propria. The outermost layer of the **lamina propria**.

supertonic. In **tonal music**, the second **scale degree** and the **chord** built on that note (II).

support. The control of one's exhalation while singing, closely related to **breath management**.

supported. Singing that is **engaged**, or utilizes good *appoggio* **technique**.

supraglottal (supraglottic). Adjective meaning "above the **glottis**."

suspension. An **ornament** that consists of a **dissonant** note that occurs in a strong metrical position and resolves itself through downward, stepwise motion.

Sutherland, Joan (1928–2010). Australian **soprano** known for her flawless **coloratura** and penchant for the *bel canto* **repertoire**. Sutherland was born in Sydney, where she received her early training from her mother and John and Aida Dickens. In 1951, she moved to London to study with Clive Carey at the Royal Conservatory of Music. She made her debut at **Covent Garden** one year later as the First Lady in Mozart's *Die Zauberflöte* (1791). During the next decade, Sutherland secured her fame at Covent Garden, encouraged by the **conductor** Richard Bonynge (b. 1930), whom she married in 1952. Her most famous **roles** include Cleopatra in Handel's *Giulio Cesare* (1724), Gilda in Verdi's *Rigoletto* (1851), Desdemona in Verdi's *Otello* (1887), and the title role in Donizetti's *Lucia di Lammermoor* (1839). From the 1960s onward, Sutherland enjoyed wide acclaim in the world's greatest **opera houses** and recorded dozens of **opera** roles. She retired from singing in 1990 and was awarded the Order of Merit in 1991.

SVS. Abbreviation for **singing voice specialist**.

SVW. Abbreviation for **Somatic Voicework**.

Sweet Adelines International. One of two female **barbershop** societies, founded in 1945. The other is **Harmony, Incorporated**.

swing. 1. A **musical theatre** performer who **understudies** more than one **role**. Swings must be prepared to step into a role—often with little or no **rehearsal**—if the actor or singer in the leading role should become ill or injured.
2. A **genre** of **jazz** music commonly associated with the **big band era** of the 1930s.
3. An aspect of rhythm in jazz, and specifically **big-band** music. In this rhythmic practice, successive eighth notes are performed unevenly, with the first note slightly longer than the second. Understanding the swing style is relevant to the **scat** singer and the singer of jazz **standards**.

swing band. See **big band**.

swing band era. See **big band era**.

syllabic. A kind of text setting where one note directly corresponds to one syllable of text.

syllabification. 1. In **diction**, the act of dividing a word into its various syllables, separating the root from prefixes, suffixes, and verb endings. Rules for syllabification vary from language to language, but a thorough understanding of syllabification is necessary for correct **pronunciation**.
2. In vocal music, the composer's designation for which syllables of text are sung to which notes. In a good edition of a **vocal score**, syllabification is always clear, with words directly aligned beneath **pitches** and **slurs**, marking multiple notes that set a single syllable. Also known as **text underlay**.

symbolism. A French literary movement from the second half of the nineteenth century closely associated with the poets Charles Baudelaire (1821–1867), Stéphane Mallarmé (1842–1898), and Paul Verlaine (1844–1896). Although symbolism did not manifest itself as a musical movement per se, a basic understanding of symbolism is essential to the performer of French *mélodies*, many of which set symbolist poems. Likewise, symbolism is a close cousin of **impressionism**, and Debussy's **opera** *Pelléas et Mélisande* (1902)—itself a setting of a symbolist play by Maurice Maeterlinck (1862–1949)—is an excellent example of the merging of symbolism and impressionism in **opera**.

sympathetic resonance. In **acoustics**, the phenomenon that occurs when a passive vibratory body responds to systematic pedagogy • 173

external vibrations. In singing, sympathetic resonances are sometimes subjectively felt in the singer's body in areas beyond the **vocal tract** resonators.

symphonic choral music. An important **genre** of choral and **oratorio repertoire** that includes the major works written for **chorus**, orchestra, and soloists. Much of the symphonic choral music repertory was written by some of history's greatest composers.

symphony chorus. The resident **chorus** of a symphony orchestra, specializing in performing choral–orchestral **masterworks**.

systematic desensitization. A **technique** borrowed from cognitive behavior therapy and used for the management of **musical performance anxiety (MPA)**. During a period of weeks, months, or even years, the singer is slowly subjected to increasingly stress-inducing performance events, with anxiety management techniques being applied to each performance situation.

systematic pedagogy. A term associated with American **voice pedagogue Richard Miller**, who introduced a logical, "systematic" way to train singers technically. Miller advocated that all voice teachers should systematically address specific technical topics in every voice **lesson**, particularly with younger singers. These topics include **onset** and **release**, **breath management**, **agility** and **flexibility**, **resonance**, **vowel** differentiation and balance, resonance balancing, sustained singing, **register** unification, **range** extension and stabilization, *messa di voce*, **vibrato**, and **timbre**. Although primarily a technician, Miller also understood the necessity that voice pedagogues educate their students about vocal health and artistry. Hence, these nontechnical aspects of singing also play a **role** in his systemic **pedagogy**. In truth, great voice teachers from all generations addressed the multifarious layers of vocal **technique** that Miller addresses, but Miller, writing and benefiting from a newer era of scientific and **fact-based** pedagogy, is usually given credit as the most significant **pedagogue** who demystified vocal technique for the **voice pedagogy** community at large.

T

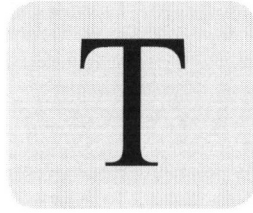

32-bar song form. The standard American popular **song form** used during the golden era of song (from approximately 1926–1950). The basic structure of 32-bar song form is simple: "AABA," with eight bars of music devoted to each section. While the **lyric** of a 32-bar song usually has four distinct lines, the third line (sung to the "B" music) often reveals a different mood, impregnating the returning "A" section of the final eight bars with greater wisdom or meaning. **Songs** cast in 32-bar song form (and variants of it) comprised the majority of **standards** in the **musical theatre** and **jazz repertories** during the 1920s, 1930s, and 1940s. Most of the songs from **Tin Pan Alley** and the **Great American Songbook** are in 32-bar song form, including most of the songs of Richard Rodgers (1902–1979) and Lorenz Hart (1895–1943), Cole Porter (1891–1964), Irving Berlin (1888–1989), Jerome Kern (1885–1945), and George Gershwin (1898–1937) and Ira Gershwin (1896–1983). Jazz, **cabaret**, and musical theatre specialists still perform this repertoire with regularity, and many contemporary composers in these **genres** continue to be influenced by this song form.

TA. Abbreviation for **thyroarytenoid**. Used as an adjective, describes one of the two basic **laryngeal** functions (along with **cricothyroid**).

TA-dominant. An adjective that describes a type of singing that is in **mode 1** or **chest** voice. Male singers (except for **countertenors** and falsettists) sing in a TA-dominant **style**. Likewise, many nonclassical female singers sing in a TA-dominant style, as most **contemporary commercial music (CCM)** styles do not favor a **CT-dominant** (or **mode 2**/**head** voice) production.

tactic. An acting term or concept. An actor's tactic helps to achieve his or her **objective**. **Opera**, **operetta**, and **musical theatre** singers must be familiar with this term,

as it is frequently used by **stage directors** and coaches in **rehearsal** for a **production**.

tag. A short snippet of **barbershop** music, usually deliberately composed as a short, several-measure composition in its own right and not an excerpt from a larger **song**.

tahrir. A vocal **ornamentation** in Persian **classical** music, similar to **yodeling**.

taille **(Fr). Tenor**. Occasionally found in French **scores**.

Taizé. Originally a religious community in Cluny, France, the term *Taizé* now commonly refers to a **repertory** of religious **choral music**. *Taizés* are simple repeated melodies that are **harmonized homophonically** and used in **liturgical** worship. The founding composers of the *Taizé* repertoire included Jacques Berthier (1923–1994) and Joseph Gelineau (1920–2008), who are also credited with conceiving and shaping the repertoire's **style** and liturgical use.

Tanglewood. One of the world's most important summer music festivals, located in Lenox and Stockbridge, Massachusetts, and formally known as the Tanglewood Music Center. Tanglewood has been the Boston Symphony Orchestra's place of summer residency each summer since 1937. The summer festival is an annual pilgrimage for many of the great artists of the **classical** music world, and the Tanglewood Music Center provides fellowships for young musicians who are in the **emerging artist** phase of their careers. Since 1966, Boston University has been responsible for the **academic** side of the operation, which includes college-level instruction, as well as shorter **workshops** for precollege students; this educational arm is known as the Boston University Tanglewood Institute. Tanglewood also hosts a **jazz** festival.

tango. A slow, **duple dance form** closely associated with Argentina. Primarily an instrumental **genre**, the tango is one of the most idiosyncratic dance **styles**, with six slow steps forward and six slow steps back, in repetition. **Carlos Gardel** is almost single-handedly credited with introducing the vocal version of the music, which is also known as the *tango canción*.

tarana. An **improvised** Indian vocal composition that is similar in nature to **scat** singing. *Taranas* usually function as the conclusion to a *khyal* performance. Also called *tillana*.

Tauber, Richard (1891–1948). American **tenor** widely regarded as one of the greatest singers of the twentieth century. Tauber was born and raised in Austria and spent his early career as a house singer in Dresden, Germany. There he sang most of the *lyrischer Tenor* **roles**, including Mozart's Belmonte in *Die Entführung aus dem Serail* and Ottavio in *Don Giovanni*, as well as Tamino in *Die Zauberflöte*. Later in his career, Tauber moved into the **operetta repertoire**, and he was particularly renowned as Prince Sou-Chong in Lehár's *Das Land des Lächelns*, a role that Tauber **premiered** in 1929. Also a composer, he wrote three operettas, music for films, and many **songs**.

Figure 51. Photograph of Richard Tauber, c. 1929.

TDP. Abbreviation for thyroarytenoid dominant production. **TA-dominant** is another frequently used adjective.

Te Deum. A **Latin hymn** of praise used **liturgically** at the end of matins and on feast days. Composers of major choral–orchestral settings include Joseph Haydn

(1732–1809), Giuseppe Verdi (1813–1901), Antonín Dvořák (1841–1904), and Zoltán Kodály (1882–1967). In the Anglican tradition, the English translation of the *Te Deum* is sung as a canticle during morning prayer.

Teatro alla Scala. See **La Scala**.

Teatro Colón. The principal **opera house** of Buenos Aires, Argentina, and the most well-known opera house in South America. The **theatre** opened its doors in 1908 and has 2,487 seats, with an additional 1,000 places for standing room. The Teatro Colón is particularly renowned for its excellent **acoustics** and is a favorite venue for **opera** singers to perform.

Teatro San Cassiano. The world's first public **opera house**, built in Venice, in 1637. In the years immediately following the opening of the Teatro San Cassiano, many other opera houses were built throughout Italy, with virtually every major city—Rome, Naples, and Milan—becoming a major center for **baroque opera**.

technique. The skill with which one performs. Most **voice pedagogues** would agree that a strong vocal technique is one that encourages healthy singing, ease of production, vocal facility, and endurance. Although vocal technique was considered to be a somewhat elusive ideal for centuries, recent innovations in voice science and **vocology** have helped to cultivate a more **fact-based** understanding of the discipline. Although individual **pedagogues** will always disagree on some of the finer points, vocal technique now stands alongside instrumental technique as a more well-defined endeavor. While different vocal **styles** occasionally call for slightly different vocal techniques, the ideals—healthy singing, facility, and endurance—remain virtually unchanged, regardless of the style.

technique book. A book of vocal exercises that progresses sequentially and systematically, addressing various aspects of vocal **technique**. **Nicola Vaccai**, **Mathilde Marchesi**, and **Heinrich Panofka** have written three of the most enduring technique books in the history of **voice pedagogy**. Also called a method book.

tempo (pl. tempi or tempos). The speed of a piece of music. The composer often indicates tempos with **metronome markings**, making the measurement precise. Many **expressive markings** also indicate or imply tempi.

tempo di mezzo. In nineteenth-century **Italian opera**, the second part of the formulaic structure of an **aria** or **duet**. Roughly (and idiomatically) translating as "the middle part," the *tempo di mezzo* is a transition that falls between a slow *cantabile* section and a fast and final *cabaletta*.

temporomandibular joint (TMJ) disorders. A group of conditions that cause pain and dysfunction in the jaw joint and the muscles that control jaw movement. Many singers who suffer from TMJ disorders experience discomfort or a lack of jaw mobility that negatively affects their singing. TMJ disorders can range from mild to severe. A singer who suffers from prolonged discomfort should consult his or her physician.

tenor. 1. One of the seven principal **classical** voice categories, and the highest male category with the exception of the **countertenor**. The **Kloiber Fach System** identifies six subcategories of tenors: the *haute-contre*, *Spieltenor* (*Tenorbuffo*), *lyrischer Tenor*, *jugendlicher Heldentenor*, *Heldentenor*, and *Charaktertenor*. The *leggiero* tenor and *spinto* tenor are other frequently referenced varieties. The countertenor—being a **CT-dominant voice type**—is best thought of as its own category separate from other kinds of tenors.
2. In **medieval polyphonic choral music**, the lowest voice part that sings the **cantus firmus**.

Terfel, Bryn (b. 1965). Welsh **bass-baritone**. Terfel was born in Pant Glas, in Caernafonshire, in North Wales. He began singing during childhood and, when he was eighteen, enrolled in the Guildhall School in London to study singing. Upon graduation from Guildhall, he won numerous prizes, including the Lieder Prize at the BBC Cardiff Singer of the World Competition. The early part of his career was devoted to the **roles** of Wolfgang Amadeus Mozart (1756–1791), particularly Leporello in *Don Giovanni* and the title role in *Le nozze di Figaro*. Terfel made both his **Covent Garden** and **Metropolitan Opera** debuts in the role of Mozart's Figaro. Terfel soon moved into the heavier roles, including several by Richard Wagner (1813–1883): Wolfram von Eschenbach in *Tannhäuser*, Hans Sachs in *Die Meistersinger von Nürnberg*, and Wotan in *Der Ring des Nibelungen*. Terfel is also known for his charming stage presence and versatility; he has made several recordings of **art songs** and **musical theatre** selections. In 2002, he appeared in the title role in *Sweeney Todd: The Demon Barber of Fleet Street*, by Stephen Sondheim (b. 1930), with the Lyric Opera of Chicago.

ternary form. Any three-part **song form** (**ABA**, ABC, etc.).

tertian. Stacked in thirds. See **extended tertian**.

tessitura. The limited **range** of notes in which a singer feels most comfortable singing for extended periods of time. While many **classically** trained singers possess at least a two-**octave** range, most trained singers would fatigue if they sang in the wrong tessitura—either too high or too low—for an extended period of time. Tessitura is also the property of a musical **score**, referring to the range of notes in which a piece of music primarily "lies" (or "sits"). Voice teachers often examine scores to determine whether the tessitura is right for the singer to whom he or she is assigning the **song** or **aria**.

text painting. See **word painting**.

text underlay. How syllables of text line up with the written notes of a vocal line. Text underlay is usually conveyed by both spacing (in a good edition of the **score**) and the use of **slur** markings. One slur marking over several notes indicates that one syllable is to be sung for the duration of the slur. See **syllabification**.

the Method. See **Method, the**.

theater. An American spelling variant of **theatre**.

theatre. 1. The art of acting and stagecraft.
2. A term used to distinguish **musicals** from **opera**. The performing art world considers these **genres** to be members of two distinct disciplines primarily based on the answer to the question, "What comes first: the music or the acting?" Straight plays and musicals are both considered to be part of the theatre industry, whereas opera is considered to be part of the musical world. Whether a work is considered to be a musical or an opera is ultimately determined by the composer (how he or she categorizes it) and the venue (whether it is written for a **Broadway** theatre or **opera house**, etc.).
3. A building designed to house dramatic **productions** (usually musicals or plays). Buildings designed for opera are called opera houses.
4. The British, old-fashioned American spelling of theatre. The spelling "theatre" still exists among many prominent regional companies, colleges, universities, and publications. Some people make a distinction in spelling when referring to the genre ("theatre") versus a physical building (a "theater"), but this distinction is unofficial and not standardized. For all practical purposes, the two spellings are both accepted and used interchangeably.

therapy. See **voice therapy**.

third inversion. See **inversion**.

thoracic breathing. A breathing **technique** that only involves the muscles of the **thorax** and not the abdominal engagement or **balanced breathing** associated with *appoggio*. See also *National Schools of Singing*.

thorax. The portion of the body that is located between the neck and abdomen, including the ribs and many vital organs (for instance, the heart and lungs).

three-mass model (of voice production). A theory of **vocal fold oscillation** that builds upon the concepts established by the **myoelastic-aerodynamic theory** and **one-mass model**. Like the one-mass model, the three-mass model includes the **vocal tract**, but it describes the **vocal folds** as three interconnected masses: the vocal fold itself (the **thyroarytenoid** muscle), the **lamina propria**, and the epithelium. This added complexity allows for asymmetry in the vertical phase difference of the **glottis**, which more accurately mimics what actually occurs during vocal fold oscillation. The three-mass model is not definitive, however, and vocologists are currently conducting research using computer simulations of sixteen-mass models.

throat singing. See **Tuvan throat singing**.

through-composed. Describes a piece of music that does not follow a formulaic pattern or structure. Rather, the composer continues to compose new music as the piece progresses. One of the four principal **art song** forms, along with **strophic**, modified strophic, and **scenic**.

thumri. Urban secular vocal **genre** from North India. Sung in Hindi, *thumris* are devotional and **romantic** in nature. They can be accompanied by a variety of instruments, including the tabla, tanpura, sarangi, violin, and harmonium.

thyroarytenoid dominant production. See **TA-dominant**.

thyroarytenoids. Paired muscles in the **larynx**, the thyroarytenoids form the main body of the **vocal folds**. They derive their name from their points of insertion: Each thyroarytenoid muscle stretches from the **thyroid**

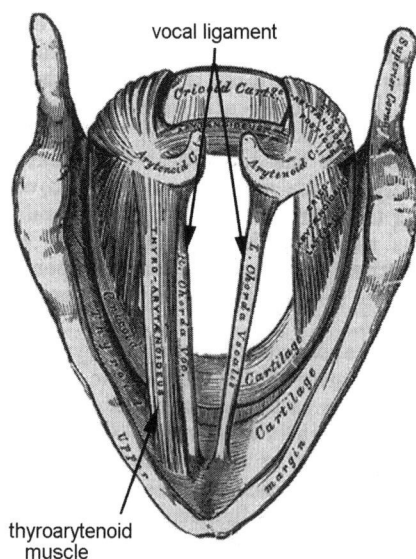

Figure 52. Thyroarytenoid muscles. *Courtesy Gray's Anatomy,* with labeling by Scott McCoy; reprinted with permission from *Your Voice: An Inside View* (2004).

cartilage to one of the two **vocal processes** of the **arytenoid cartilage**. The two thyroarytenoids are the principal muscles used in **mode 1** or **chest register**.

thyrohyoid membrane. The membranous curtain that connects the **thyroid cartilage** of the **larynx** to the **hyoid bone**.

thyroid cartilage. One of the three principal cartilages of the **larynx**. Shaped like a shield, the thyroid cartilage is the largest of the three and is located in the front of the larynx. See the anatomical drawings in appendix B.

thyrovocalis muscle. An internal division of the **thyroarytenoid** muscle. Also called the vocalis muscle. See the anatomical drawings in appendix B.

tiefer Alt. This designation—the lowest female category in the **Kloiber Fach System**—includes only four **roles**: Magdalena in Kienzl's *Der Evangelimann* (1895), Genoveva in Debussy's *Pelléas et Mélisande* (1902), Gaea in Strauss's *Daphne* (1938), and the Orchestra Soloist in Rihm's *Die Eroberung von Mexico* (1991). The literal translation is "low **contralto**." *Tiefer alts* are essentially **contraltos**, although this is technically not the correct term according to the *Fach* system. See the *Fach* chart in appendix C.

tillana. See *tarana*.

timbre. Roughly equivalent to **color**. In singing, refers to the **quality** of one's voice. For a list of adjectives often used to describe various vocal **timbres**, see appendix J.

Tin Pan Alley. The nickname commonly given to the American **sheet music** industry of the early twentieth century. The Tin Pan Alley era spanned from the 1880s through the 1950s, when the phonograph and LP records finally replaced live music at the piano as the principal **form** of home entertainment. "Tin Pan Alley" can also be used to describe the **style** of **songs** that came out of the industry. A "Tin Pan Alley song" is formulaic, usually in **32-bar song form** with an introductory **verse**. The later years of Tin Pan Alley are closely related to the **Great American Songbook**.

TMJ disorders. See **temporomandibular joint disorders**.

Tomatis, Alfred A. (1920–2001). Called the "Father of Psychoacoustics," Tomatis invented the electronic ear to rehabilitate the listening function of **opera** singers after research led him to conclude that the voice only contains the sounds that the ear hears. Tomatis's theory that the ear controls vocal emission was verified by Raul Husson and Pierre Grassé before the Academy of Science in Paris, in 1957. His text *L'oreille et la voix* (*The Ear and the Voice*, 2001) presents his theories relating to the singer's audio–vocal control and the role of the ear in language and learning, as well as higher brain function.

tonadilla. A Spanish theatrical **song form** popular in the eighteenth century. It was also the name of a form of **musical comedy** that took place in Spain at this same time. *Tonadillas* were also popular in Cuba and other Spanish-speaking Latin American countries.

tonal music. Music that is organized around a tonal center, or **tonic**. Tonal music is generally written in either a **major mode** or **minor** mode (**key**) and follows rules of **harmonic progression** and **voice leading**. Most Western music written since the late seventeenth century is tonal. Before tonal music, the **church mode** system prevailed, and music was usually considered to be **modal** in nature. In addition, **posttonal** music emerged in **art music** at the turn of the twentieth century. Most **forms** of **popular music** remain tonal.

tone. Refers to the beauty (or **quality**) of the singing voice. While it is a profoundly subjective term, there is somewhat of a consensus that a good vocal **tone quality** in the realm of Western music is one that can be labeled with such adjectives as "warm," "rich," "focused," and "well-supported." Different **genres**, as well as different cultures, also cultivate a different aesthetic consensus with regard to what constitutes beauty (and, by extension, good tone quality). Tone is distinct from **intonation**, which refers to how accurately **pitches** are centered.

tone cluster. Three or more **pitches** sounded simultaneously that do not comprise a **functional chord**. Tone clusters are usually **dissonant** in nature. See also **cluster**.

tone quality. The subjective quality of a voice. How beautiful (or not) one's voice is. Virtually a synonym for **tone**.

tonic. In **tonal music**, the first **scale degree** and the **chord** built on that note (I).

Tony Awards. More formally known as the Antoinette Perry Awards for Excellence in Theatre, these annual awards for **Broadway theatre** are more commonly known as the Tony Awards. The awards are sponsored by the American Theatre Wing and the Broadway League, and they have been given each season since 1947. Of special interest to singers are the annual awards given for Best Musical, Best Revival of a Musical, Best Performance by a Leading Actor in a Musical, Best Performance by a Leading Actress in a Musical, Best Performance by a Featured Actor in a Musical, and Best Performance by a Featured Actress in a Musical. See appendix G for a complete listing of Tony Award winners for Best Musical from 1949 to 2015.

Tosi, Pier Francesco (c. 1653–1732). Italian **castrato**, composer, and writer of music. Tosi is best known for his early **treatise** on singing, *Opinioni de' cantori antichi, e moderni* (1723), which is one of the first **voice pedagogy** treatises to have been preserved in its entirety. Published in England, in 1743, in translation as *Observations on the Florid Song*, the work is especially valuable for its catalog of various **baroque ornaments** utilized by singers at the time.

trachea. The tube that connects the **pharynx** and **larynx** to the lungs. Colloquially called the windpipe. See the anatomical drawings in appendix B.

tracking. 1. A term used in recording studios to describe the process of recording multiple tracks of instrumental or vocal parts that are later combined into one final track. Tracking is an important aspect of the "studio sound" that cannot be replicated in live performance.
  2. See **formant tuning**.

tract. 1. A section of the **Proper** in the **Mass** that replaces the **alleluia-verse** during Lent.
  2. See **vocal tract**.

traditional belt. A label used to describe a traditional **belt** voice heard in the classic **Broadway style**. The traditional belt is in contrast to a **contemporary belt**, which is likely to have a higher **range** extension with the incorporation of **mix**. Also called a **call**.

tragédie en musique. A type of **French opera** in the late seventeenth and early eighteenth centuries that combined conventions from **classical** French **theatre** with **ballet** traditions. Jean-Baptiste Lully (1632–1687) is credited as the inventor of the *tragédie en musique*. Later in his career, Lully began using a new label for this **genre**—the *tragédie lyrique*—which is virtually identical in **style** to its predecessor.

tragédie lyrique. The successor to the *tragédie en musique*. Both terms were coined by the **French opera** composer Jean-Baptiste Lully (1632–1687).

transducer. An element within an electronic system that converts one form of energy to another. In the case of a **microphone**, the transducer transforms **acoustic** vibrations into electric impulses. In the case of a speaker, the transducer transforms electric impulses into acoustic vibrations.

transliteration. The conversion of a text from one script to another. This recasting of a language for singers occurs most frequently with Russian **repertoire**, which uses the Cyrillic alphabet. Russian transliterations utilize phonetic syllables spelled out with **Latin** letters familiar to the English speaker. With the explosion of **IPA transcriptions** throughout the past several decades, the use of transliterations has declined, with most **classical singers** preferring to transcribe **International Phonetic Alphabet (IPA)** symbols from the original Cyrillic characters.

transposition. A piece of music that is removed from its original **key** and sung or played at either a higher or lower **pitch**. In **musical theatre** and **popular music**, transposition happens frequently, and **songs** are commonly transposed to a key that is best suited to the singer's voice. Likewise, many **art songs** are available in several transpositions and published in high, medium, and low editions. In **opera**, however, transposition is more unusual; opera singers are generally not permitted to request key changes for **arias** in an effort to make them more comfortable.

transverse abdominis muscles. In the Italian *appoggio* breathing **technique**, one of the six primary muscles of **expiration**. The other five include the **internal intercostal muscles**, **external oblique abdominis muscles**, **internal oblique abdominis muscles**, **rectus abdominis muscles**, and **quadratus lumborum muscles**.

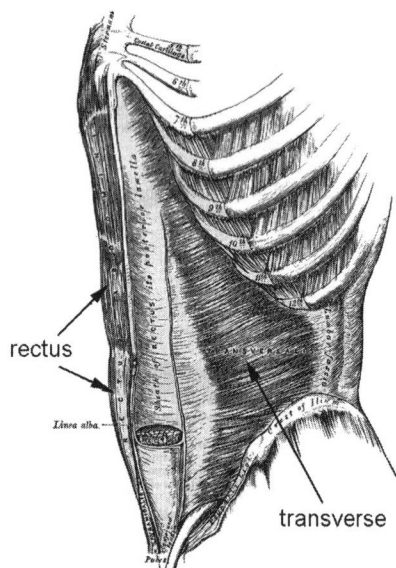

Figure 53. Transverse abdominis muscles. *Courtesy Gray's Anatomy,* with labeling by Scott McCoy; reprinted with permission from *Your Voice: An Inside View* (2004).

traumatic laryngitis. A type of **laryngitis** brought on by vocal abuse, including overuse, screaming, singing, or speaking with inadequate **technique**, or **vocal fatigue** brought on by spending long periods of time speaking in

a noisy environment. Traumatic laryngitis can usually be resolved through **vocal rest** and removing oneself from the abusive situation.

travesti. See **pants role**.

treatise. A written discourse on a scientific or pedagogical subject. Treatises are usually longer in length than an essay. There are many treatises that have been important in the history of **voice pedagogy**. Two examples include *Singing: The Mechanism and the Technic* (1967), by **William Vennard**, and *The Structure of Singing* (1986), by **Richard Miller**.

treble. 1. The highest voice part, usually written in the **soprano range**.
2. In the Anglican tradition, the name for a **boy soprano**.

tremolo. A pejorative term for a fast **vibrato** that exceeds 7.5 **pulses** per second. The opposite of a **wobble**.

très (Fr). Very.

trill. A kind of **ornament** that features a rapid alternation between the notated **pitch** and the diatonic pitch directly above that note. In singing, trilling is a cultivated **technique** that only singers of great **agility** can truly master. Generally speaking, higher voices trill more frequently than lower voices, and **CT-dominant** voices (women and **countertenors**) trill more easily than **TA-dominant** voices (**tenors**, **baritones**, and **basses**).

trillo. A type of vocal **ornament** used in **early music** that consists of the rapid repetition of the same note through repeated **onset** and **offset**.

trio. A type of **ensemble** for three singers or instrumentalists. "Soave sia il vento," from Mozart's *Così fan tutte* (1790), and "Three Little Maids from School," from **Gilbert and Sullivan's** *The Mikado* (1885), are two famous examples of trios from **opera** and **comic opera**, respectively.

triphthong. Three **vowels** in succession within a single syllable. Triphthongs are considerably less common than **diphthongs**, but they still occur on a somewhat regular basis in Italian. Common examples include "miei" [mjɛ:i], "tuoi" [twɔ:i], and "vuoi" [vwɔ:i].

triple bill. Three **one-act operas** or other relatively short **productions** presented on the same evening.

triple meter. A **meter** with three **beats**. There are two basic types of triple meter: **simple triple** and **compound triple**.

triple motet. A thirteenth-century **motet** for four voices. In a triple motet, each voice above the **tenor** is set to a different text.

triplum. In **medieval polyphony**, the third voice from the bottom. The *triplum* is immediately above the *duplum*.

Tristan chord. A **nonfunctional chord** composed by Richard Wagner (1813–1883) and associated with his 1865 **opera** *Tristan und Isolde*. The four notes in the Tristan chord—from bottom to top—are F, B, D♯, and G♯. Through smooth chromaticism, the Tristan chord ultimately "resolves," but to a new **dominant** chord that seems completely unrelated to the Tristan chord.

Figure 54. Tristan chord (from the opening bars of Wagner's *Tristan und Isolde*, 1865. *Courtesy Creative Commons.*

This startling break from the rules and expectations in **voice leading** and **harmonic progressions** in **tonal music** signaled a new era in music. Many music theorists believe that the Tristan chord marks the beginning of musical modernism. It is perhaps the mostly widely discussed and prolifically written about chord in the history of Western music. The opening bars of *Tristan und Isolde* are also perhaps Wagner's most frequently recognized *leitmotif*.

triste **(Fr).** Sad.

trobairitz. A female *troubadour*.

trope. A new **Latin** text sung to **liturgical chant** during the **medieval** era. Many tropes involved adding texts to an existing **melisma**. Tropes were occasionally sung to newly composed melodies

troubadour. A poet-composer from Southern France during the **medieval** era. *Troubadours* composed and performed **monophonic secular songs**. The poems were written in Occitan, otherwise known as *langue d'oc*. *Troubadours* flourished during the twelfth and thirteenth centuries and were analogous to the *trouvères* of Northern France.

troupe. A group of theatrical performers. Sometimes called a **company**.

trouser role. See **pants role**.

trouvère. A poet-composer from Northern France during the **medieval** era. *Trouvères* composed and performed **monophonic secular songs**. The poems were written in Old French, otherwise known as *langue d'oïl*. *Trouvères* flourished during the twelfth and thirteenth centuries and were analogous to the *trouvères* of Southern France.

trunk song. A **song** composed by a **musical theatre** composer that has not yet found its way into an actual **musical**. Some composers find venues for trunk songs in retrospective **revues** of their work.

Tune, Tommy (b. 1939). A prolific **Broadway director**, actor, dancer, and **choreographer**. Tune has received nine **Tony Awards** in four different categories, including one for Best Featured Actor in a Musical (for *Seesaw*, 1973), one for Best Actor in a Musical (for *My One and Only*, 1983), four for Best Choreographer (for *A Day in Hollywood/A Night in Ukraine*, 1980; *My One and Only*, 1983; *Grand Hotel*, 1989; and *The Will Rogers Follies*, 1991), and three for Best Director of a Musical (for *Nine*, 1982; *Grand Hotel*, 1989; and *The Will Rogers Follies*, 1991). Tune is one of the most decorated and ubiquitous figures in the Broadway industry.

tuning fork. A two-pronged steel device that, when struck, gives off a reliably accurate **pitch**, often A=440. **Professional** choral **ensembles** who specialize in **classical** *a cappella* **repertoire** usually get their pitches from a tuning fork as opposed to a **pitch pipe**, which is the preferred device for **amateur** situations or **popular music**, for example, **barbershop** ensembles. With a tuning fork, the **conductor** or designated **chorister** can silently procure the pitch, which he or she then softly hums just loudly enough for the ensemble to hear. Professional singers also usually carry a tuning fork, which they reference while studying **scores** in public places or while traveling.

turba **(pl.** *turbae***).** **Latin** word meaning "turmoil" or "uproar." In **Passion** settings, the *turba* refers to a crowd of people. *Turba* passages are sung by the **chorus**.

turning. The phenomenon that happens at the *secondo passaggio* of the male **classical** voice—**vowel** modification or **cover** to cultivate a certain warmth or depth—is sometimes referred to as the voice "turning." At the second *passaggio*, one needs to "turn" his voice to avoid a "shouty" or "spread" sound. More scientifically, turning occurs when the second **harmonic** passes above the first **formant**.

tutti **(It).** All. Usually used to instruct all of the forces—both singers and instrumentalists—to perform.

Tuvan throat singing. An eccentric singing **technique** that involves specific manipulation of the singer's jaw, lips, mouth, and sinuses to produce several **overtones** simultaneously. The **fundamental** note that produces these overtones is always a specific **pitch** in the **TA/mode 1 register**.

twang. A certain **timbre**—often distinguished by brightness or **nasality**—often found in **country** music. As **pop** music and **musical theatre** have appropriated some aspects of the country **style**, twang can occasionally be heard in these **genres** as well. Twang is the opposite of **loft**.

twelve-bar blues (12-bar blues). A standard **song form**, the twelve-bar blues is the underpinning of the **blues genre**. It is the basis for not only the blues genre, but it is also ubiquitous in **jazz** and **rock 'n' roll**. **Musical theatre**, a genre inextricably intertwined with trends in **popular music**, also occasionally contains **songs** that are written in a twelve-bar blues style. The texts of blues often have a gritty, sardonic character. The basic **harmonic progression** is as follows: I-I-I-I/IV-IV-I-I/V-IV-I-I (I = **tonic**; IV = **subdominant**; V = **dominant**).

twelve-tone music (dodecaphonic music). A **style** of **post-tonal** music written during the first half of the twentieth century in which a sequential row of all twelve chromatic **pitches** forms the basis of a composition. Arnold Schoenberg (1874–1951) is credited as the inventor of the **technique**, which was also practiced by Anton Webern (1883–1945), Alban Berg (1885–1935), and Igor Stravinsky (1882–1971).

type. A **musical theatre** (and acting) designation that designates the kind of character the actor or actress is likely to play. Standard types include **ingénue, character actor/actress**, and **leading man/woman**. Types often carry with them specific vocal demands. For example, a character actress will almost always be required to **belt**. Vocal expectations can, however, vary greatly depending upon which period of theatrical history one examines. The Rodgers and Hammerstein ingénue is almost always a **legit soprano**, whereas contemporary ingénues frequently sing in a **pop/rock, TA-dominant style**. In **classical** music, the term *voice type* can refer to a singer's *Fach*.

U

ululation. A long, wavering high-pitched vocal sound produced by the deliberate and rapid manipulation of the tongue. An ululation is a distinct and idiomatic sound heard in certain types of **world music**.

umlaut (¨). A **diacritical marking** in German that often occurs over the **vowels** *ä*, *ö*, *ü*, and vowel combination *äu*. *Umlauts* are an essential element of German **diction**, as they change the **pronunciation** of the vowel or vowel combination, essentially creating new and additional vowels and **diphthongs**. Although the same diacritical marking is used, *umlauts* should not be confused with the French *diérèse*, which is used to delineate two separate (but adjacent) vowel sounds. In German, *umlaut* literally means "round sound."

un peu (**Fr**). A little.

unaccompanied. Singing without instrumental **accompaniment**, either as a soloist or in a small or large **ensemble**. **Genres** that are almost exclusively unaccompanied include **Gregorian chant**, **barbershop**, contemporary *a cappella* groups, and many types of **folk music**. Many choral compositions are also unaccompanied, including most of the **repertoire** from the **medieval** and **Renaissance** eras. Unaccompanied is often used as a synonym with *a cappella*, although some *a cappella* music of the Renaissance and **baroque** eras occasionally doubled the vocal parts with instruments.

underengaged. Singing that is not **engaged** or **supported**, or does not utilize good *appoggio* technique.

underscoring. Instrumental music that accompanies spoken dialogue, usually in a **musical** or **operetta**. Also occurs in **melodrama**.

understudy. A **musical theatre** performer, usually in a supporting **role**, who also studies a leading role so that he or she can step in in case of illness or emergency. An understudy is similar to a **cover** in **opera**.

undersupported. Singing that is not **supported** or **engaged**, or does not utilize good *appoggio* technique. Used interchangeably with **underengaged**.

unidirectional microphone. A **microphone** that can pick up sound from only one direction, the opposite of an **omnidirectional** microphone (which can pick up sound from any direction).

unilateral. Describes **voice disorders** that occur on only one **vocal fold**. The opposite of **bilateral** (which means to occur on both vocal folds).

unison. Occurs when two or more singers or instrumentalists play the same **pitches** at the same time. Unison singing or playing can literally occur at the same pitch level or in **octaves**.

unvoiced. A **phoneme** created without the use of the **vocal folds**. **Consonants** are unvoiced when **phonation** is not necessary to produce them. The opposite of **voiced** (which involves phonation). For example, the only difference between [b] and [p] is that the former is voiced and the latter is not.

uptune. A commonly used term referring to a faster, uptempo **jazz song**. In this context, it is the opposite of a **ballad**, which is slower and more lyrical. Historically, **musical theatre** singers were asked to offer both a ballad and an uptune in singing **auditions**, but this practice has largely been replaced by the offering of two contrasting **16-bar cuts**.

urban blues. One of the three basic **subgenres** of **blues**, along with **country blues** and **classic blues**. Urban blues added electric **amplification** to the blues sound and featured more **virtuosic** instrumental playing than country and classic blues. The urban blues **style** was performed in larger cities, especially Chicago, during the late 1940s. Howlin' Wolf (1910–1976) and B. B. King (b. 1925) are examples of urban blues musicians. Urban blues eventually developed into **rhythm and blues**.

Urtext. A German word meaning "original." To musicians, an *Urtext* is a scholarly edition of a published **score** that reflects the original intentions of the composer. Critical commentary often accompanies *Urtext* editions, indicating information about the original sources, historical background, and textual variants. *Urtext* editions are often more expensive than cheaper **public domain** alternatives, but they are generally free from error and represent an authoritative edition of a work. **Classical singers** often check their less-expensive trade editions against an *Urtext* edition to ensure musical accuracy.

uvula. Fleshy, protruding pendant lobe that hangs from the middle of the posterior part of the **soft palate**.

uvular trill. A **consonant**-like sound sometimes utilized when producing **vocal distortion** in **contemporary commercial music (CCM) styles**. The uvular trill is produced by directing the air stream toward the uvula, thus sending it into vibration against and between the tonsils. A version of the uvular trill can be found in the French language and is represented in the **International Phonetic Alphabet (IPA)** by the symbol [R].

V

Vaccai, Nicola (1790–1848). Italian **opera** composer and singing teacher best remembered for his technical **treatise** entitled *Metoda pratico de canto* (1832). Most contemporary voice teachers know this work by its English title: *A Practical Method of Italian Singing* (1832). It is perhaps the **technique book** most widely used today, standing alongside those written by **Heinrich Panofka**, **Mathilde Marchesi**, and others.

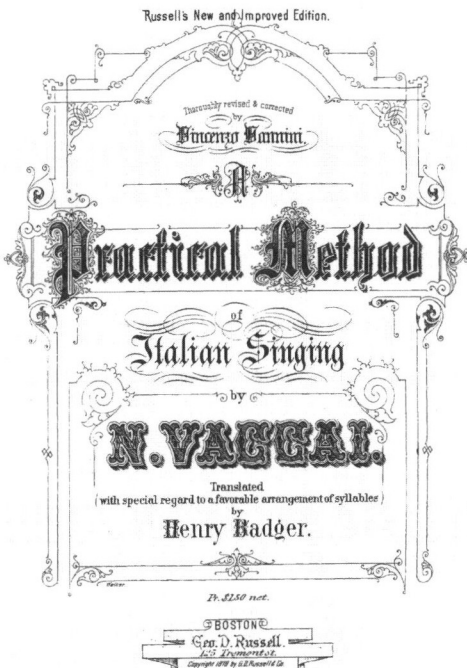

Figure 55. Cover of Vaccai's *A Practical Method of Italian Singing*, 1832.

Vargas, Chavela (1919–2012). Costa Rican-born Mexican singer and the name most frequently associated with the *ranchera* **genre** of **world music**. Born Isabel Vargas Lizano, she began using the name Chavela (a childhood pet name for Isabel) when she started performing as a teenager in Mexico. Her first album, *Noche de Bohemia* (*Bohemian Night*), was released in 1961. During the course of the rest of her life, she would record more than eighty albums and appear in numerous films. The Spanish film director Pedro Almodóvar (b. 1949) was particularly infatuated with Vargas and featured her in many of his films, most notably *La flor de mi secreto* (*The Flower of My Secret*, 1995). Her influence upon other performers of Spanish-language **popular music** has been enormous. In addition to *ranchera*, Vargas also sang a variety of other Latin American popular **styles**.

variety show. An evening of many diverse acts and talent displays, some of which may involve singing. **Vaudeville** was a specific kind of variety show.

varix (pl. varices). A vascular disorder in the **vocal fold** caused by dilation of the small capillaries. Varices can burst under certain conditions, leading to **vocal fold hemorrhages**. Varices are similar to **vascular ectasias**.

vascular ectasias. A **voice disorder** that consists of dilated vessels in the **cover** of the **vocal folds**, resulting in bumps. Vascular ectasias are usually the result of overuse, poor singing or speaking **technique**, or some other **form** of vocal abuse.

vaudeville. An important precursor to the **Broadway musical**, vaudeville was a type of stage entertainment consisting of many short, unrelated, and unconnected presentations by performers displaying a wide array of skills, most of which were unrelated to music. While variety shows were taking place in many parts of the United States, vaudeville proper is usually thought of as a New York City **genre** that peaked during the period between 1880–1920. Especially the province of various immigrant communities, specific types of vaudeville are often clarified with the addition of a preceding "ethnic" adjective: Jewish vaudeville, Italian vaudeville, Irish vaudeville, and so forth. In addition to **songs**, featured entertainments also included instrumental **numbers**, comic routines, magic tricks, lectures, monologues, dancing, acrobatic feats, and circus-like animal tricks. Almost any creative stage presentation was fair game and included under the genre. Vaudeville should not be confused with the **minstrel show**. Although the two genres share some similarities in their "variety" nature, the minstrel show was more formulaic and specific in structure.

velar. In the study of **diction**, refers to **consonants** that have a specific **point of articulation** involving the back of the tongue and the **soft palate**. Specific examples include [g], [k], [ŋ], and [x]. See also **alveolar**, **bilabial**, **dental**, **labiodental**, **palatal**, **prepalatal**.

velum. Another name for the **soft palate**.

Vennard, William (1909–1971). Important American **voice pedagogue** of the twentieth century. Vennard is best known for his **treatise** *Singing: The Mechanism and the Technic* (1967), a pioneering work and landmark in the evolution of **fact-based voice pedagogy**. This important publication became the standard voice pedagogy text in colleges and universities for decades. The majority of Vennard's teaching career was spent as chair of the voice department at the University of Southern California, where he taught from 1950 until his death in 1971. He served as national president of the **National Association of Teachers of Singing (NATS)** from 1964–1966.

ventricle. Any chamber within the body.

ventricular folds. See **false vocal folds**.

ventricular dysphonia. A **voice disorder** that occurs when the **false vocal folds** close abnormally above the real **vocal folds**. This phenomenon interferes with normal **phonation**. The cause of ventricular dysphonia is often unknown, but the disorder can typically be resolved through proper **voice therapy**.

Venturi effect. Named after the Italian physicist Giovanni Battista Venturi (1746–1822), the Venturi effect is specifically the increase in air (fluid) pressure that results when air flows through a constricted section of a tube or pipe. In **vocal production**, the Venturi effect occurs at the **laryngeal** level. When air passes through the narrow passage between the **vocal folds**, speed and pressure increase, creating suction and aiding in full **adduction** (closure) of the **vocal folds**. See also **Bernoulli's principle**.

Verdi baritone. A specific kind of **baritone** voice roughly equivalent to the *Heldenbariton* in the **Kloiber Fach System**. Verdi baritones have a certain **dramatic** "bite" in their sound, with a lot of depth in the higher **range**. Named after the **operatic repertoire** of Giuseppe Verdi (1813–1901), which has many baritone **roles** that require this **voice type**. A Verdi baritone is roughly the baritone equivalent to a *spinto* voice in the **soprano** or **tenor** ranges; the term *spinto baritone* is never used, however.

verismo. A specific **style** of **Italian opera** in vogue toward the end of the nineteenth century. *Verismo* (meaning "real" or "truthful") **opera** sets **librettos** that feature ordinary people—as opposed to historical subjects or great literary figures—who find themselves in dangerous, violent, or life-threatening situations. *Verismo* operas almost always end with the death—usually murder or suicide—of one or more of the principal characters. Intense, **dramatic** orchestral music perfectly complements the tragic events unfolding on the stage. *Cavalleria rusticana* (1890), by Pietro Mascagni (1863–1945), and *Pagliacci* (1892), by Ruggero Leoncavallo (1857–1919), are usually credited as being the first famous examples of the **genre**. Giacomo Puccini (1858–1924) built on this tradition, contributing three *verismo* operas that still occupy the very core of the **operatic repertory**: *La bohème* (1896), *Tosca* (1900), and *Madama Butterfly* (1904). Although it was a **French opera** written fifteen years before *Cavalleria rusticana*, many musicologists view *Carmen* (1875), by Georges Bizet (1838–1875), as an important forerunner of the *verismo* **formula** and style.

vers mesurée **(Fr).** Measured verse. See also *musique mesurée*.

verse. 1. Any of the A sections of a simple, **strophic song form**.
2. A specific **stanza** of poetry in a **song** text.
3. An introductory, nonrecurring portion of many AABA popular songs in the **style** of the **Great American Songbook**.
4. In **verse-chorus song form**, the portions of music that precede the **chorus**. In this sense, each **verse** will share the same music, but the words are different with each repetition (as opposed to the chorus, which usually features the same words and music each time it appears).
5. Similar to verse-chorus song form, verses can also be found alternating with **refrains** in secular songs of the **medieval** and **Renaissance** eras, as well as in nineteenth- and twentieth-century sacred **hymns**.

verse anthem. An Anglican **anthem** for **chorus** and soloists during the **Renaissance** and **baroque** eras. The soloist sections alternate between full choral sections. A verse anthem differs from a **full anthem**, which has no soloists.

verse-chorus song form. A popular contemporary **song form** that alternates between two sections of music, creating a repetitive ABABAB **form**. The exact number of repetitions varies from **song** to song. In verse-chorus song form, the A sections of music (the **verses**) usually repeat the same music with different texts, whereas the B sections (the **choruses**) are virtually identical to one another, repeating the same music and text. A bridge (a C section) often substitutes for a later verse, providing some musical variety before a final repetition of the chorus. In contemporary **pop** and **rock styles** (styles that greatly influence contemporary **musical theatre** songs), a **half-step modulation** upward often occurs upon the last repetition of the chorus.

verse-refrain song form. See **verse-chorus song form**.

vestibular folds. See **false vocal folds**.

Viardot, Pauline (1821–1910). French **mezzo-soprano** of Spanish origin. Viardot was the daughter of the elder **Manuel García** (1775–1832); she was the younger sibling of **Manuel García** (1805–1906) and **Maria Malibran**. One of the most important **operatic** figures of the nineteenth century, Viardot was known and respected by the most famous composers of the nineteenth century, including Hector Berlioz (1803–1869), Frédéric Chopin (1810–1849), Franz Liszt (1811–1886), Giacomo Meyerbeer (1791–1864), Camille Saint-Saëns (1835–1921), Robert Schumann (1810–1856), and Richard Wagner (1813–1883). Many of these composers wrote works specifically for her voice. In addition to singing, she also composed more than 100 **songs**, setting texts in multiple languages. She also published a **technique book**, *Une heure d'étude: exercises pour voix de femmes* (1861), which closely follows the method of vocal **technique** advocated by the younger Manuel García.

vibrato. A **pitch** fluctuation in singing that occurs in most trained voices and is used for expressive and stylistic purposes. Vibrato is the result of neurological impulses that occur when singers balance the power source (**breath management**) with the proper coordination of their vibrators (**vocal folds**) and resonators (**laryngopharynx, oropharynx**, and **nasopharynx**). Most **classical pedagogues** also view the presence of an even vibrato as a hallmark of good vocal **technique** and a sign of relaxed, "open" singing that is free of unnecessary tension. Vibrato rate and extent can vary widely among singers, even among singers of the same **genre** and **style**. Most Western **classical singers** strive for an even vibrato rate of approximately six to seven cycles per second (cps), but amplitude can vary greatly within that **range**. For some singers, a vibrato is a carefully controlled **tone** with good **intonation**, whereas for others, it is a more extreme

fluctuation, sometimes up to a **semitone** on either side of the intended pitch. **Jazz** and **pop** singers often deliberately employ **straight tone** as their default, using vibrato sparingly and only for expressive purposes. Minimal vibrato is often the ideal in **professional** choral singing and **early music** communities, as well as **treble** and boy choirs, which are almost always straight-tone **ensembles**. Vibrato frequencies and amplitudes vary greatly among various **world music** singing genres. Vibrato is *not* the same as *oscillazione*, **tremolo**, or *trillo*.

Victorian art song. Named after Queen Victoria (1819–1901), the **art song** that was published in England during the nineteenth century and before the songs of Ralph Vaughan Williams (1872–1958), Roger Quilter (1877–1953), George Butterworth (1885–1916), and Ivor Gurney (1890–1937). An underperformed and underappreciated **repertoire**, the Victorian art song is often neglected due to a long-held bias that it is of inferior quality to the great flowering of **English art songs** that occurred toward the turn of the century. Composers of Victorian art song included John Liptrot Hatton (1809–1896), Henry Hugo Pearson (1815–1873), William Sterndale Bennett (1816–1875), and Arthur Sullivan (1842–1900).

Victorian comic opera. See **English comic opera**, **Gilbert and Sullivan**.

video laryngoscope (video laryngoscopy). A type of modern **laryngoscope** that allows the **otolaryngologist (ENT)** or **speech-language pathologist (SLP)** to digitally view the **vocal folds** of the client. An examination by video laryngoscope is called a video laryngoscopy.

Viennese operetta. A **form** of light **opera** that emerged in Vienna during the 1870s. Viennese operetta is a **waltz-based**, "cleaner" version of its predecessor, the bawdy French cousin *opéra bouffe* that features dialogue, dancing, and memorable tunes. The **genre's libretti** usually feature members of the aristocracy, who embark on comical romps of mayhem and infidelity, only to have it all work out in the end. *Die Fledermaus* (1874), by Johann Strauss (1825–1899), represents the apotheosis of the genre and the **golden age** of Viennese operetta. In the 1780s and 1790s, the genre was at its peak. Somewhat waning in popularity by the beginning of the twentieth century, **operetta** was almost single-handedly revived by *Die lustige Witwe* (1905), by Franz Lehár (1870–1948). This work ushered in a new **silver age** of Viennese operetta. When *Die lustige Witwe* was revived two years later in New York City, it was immensely popular, and the 1907 American **production** of *The Merry Widow* (the English translation of *Die lustige Witwe*) is credited with the birth of **merchandizing** through souvenirs—"Merry Widow" cigars, chocolates, scarves, and so forth—a practice that has been a staple commercial practice of the **Broadway** industry ever since.

In addition to Johann Strauss and Franz Lehár, other significant composers of Viennese operettas include Oscar Straus (1870–1954), Robert Stolz (1880–1975), Franz von Suppé (1819–1895), Karl Millöcker (1842–1899), Emmerich Kálmán (1882–1953), Leo Fall (1873–1925), Eduard Künneke (1885–1953), and Walter Goetze (1883–1961). Although the **repertoire** is vast, few Viennese operettas are still performed today beyond German and Austrian borders, with the significant exceptions of *Die Fledermaus* and *Die lustige Witwe*, which receive hundreds of international performances each year. Germany, Austria, and Hungary still mount productions of *Die Fledermaus* as an annual New Year's Day tradition.

Viewpoints. Late twentieth-century acting school developed by **Anne Bogart**. Many **musical theatre** performers pursue this training, which involves **improvisational ensemble**-building based on "The Six Viewpoints," a dance concept developed by Mary Overlie (b. 1946). Viewpoints training is often coupled with Suzuki, an intense physical acting training developed by Tadashi Suzuki (b. 1939).

Vignoles, Roger (b. 1945). English **collaborative pianist**. Vignoles was born in Cheltenham and educated at Magdalene College and the Royal College of Music. He has performed with many of the world's finest singers, including **Thomas Hampson**, **Kathleen Battle**, Anne Sofie von Otter (b. 1955), Kiri Te Kanawa (b. 1944), Wolfgang Holzmair (b. 1952), and Thomas Allen (b. 1944). Recent projects include the complete **songs** of Richard Strauss (1864–1949) for **Hyperion Records**.

villancico. A Spanish poetic and musical **genre** of the late fifteenth and early sixteenth centuries. *Villancicos* are comprised of multiple **verses** (called *coplas*) that alternate with a **refrain** (called an *estribillo*). The subject of many *villancico* texts is Christmas, making the *villancico* something of a Spanish version of a **carol**. Closely related to the **madrigal** genre, they are part of the **Renaissance** choral **repertory**. Joaquín Rodrigo (1901–1999) adapted the *villancico* **form** to the **art song** genre in his three *Villancicos* (1952) for voice and guitar.

villanelle. A **genre** of vocal music popular in Italy during the sixteenth and seventeenth centuries. *Villanelles* are usually written in three voices and performed *a cappella*. Similar to the *canzonetta*, they are closely linked with the **madrigal** genre and are part of the **Renaissance** choral **repertory**.

virelai. One of the three *formes fixes* of the fourteenth and fifteenth centuries, along with the *ballade* and *rondeau*.

The *virelai* has the pattern of AbbaA; the A section acts as a **refrain**, and the bba **stanzas** feature alternate music in the b sections and the same music (but different words) in the a sections.

virtuosic. Adjective that means "like a **virtuoso**."

virtuoso. A highly skilled performer possessing formidable **technique**. A female virtuoso is properly called a "virtuosa."

vital capacity. The maximum amount of air that can be expired after maximum **inhalation**.

vite **(Fr).** Fast.

vivace **(It).** Lively.

vivacissimo **(It).** Very fast and lively.

vivo **(It).** Lively.

vocal coach (coach). See **collaborative pianist**.

vocal concerto. An early **baroque genre** for several voices and **continuo** that emerged at the end of the sixteenth century. Throughout the seventeenth century, it was a term used to broadly categorize any piece for multiple voices and orchestra. Most vocal concertos were written for **liturgical** use and fall under the genre of sacred **choral music**, although some secular **madrigals**—for instance, the *Seventh Book of Madrigals* (1619), by Claudio Monteverdi (1567–1643)—can rightly be called vocal concertos. The vocal concerto was primarily a seventeenth-century genre, and the term should not be used generically to describe music of subsequent centuries. Unlike the instrumental concerto, the term *vocal concerto* does not simply refer to a piece for solo voice and orchestra. The term was obsolete by the late baroque era.

While many singers routinely compete in university and regional concerto competitions, they usually do so with **orchestral songs** and **opera arias**, not vocal concertos. As an exception to the normal definition of the vocal concerto, Reinhold Glière (1875–1956) wrote a "vocal concerto" for **soprano** and orchestra in 1946.

vocal cords. Dated (but still frequently encountered) term that has been replaced by the more accurately descriptive **vocal folds**.

vocal distortion. A certain kind of processed singing in amplified **contemporary commercial music (CCM) styles** that deliberately distorts the natural qualities of the singing voice.

vocal division. Refers to the voice, **diction**, **pedagogy**, and **opera** faculty in a college, conservatory, or university school of music. The vocal division is usually distinct from the **choral division**. Does not refer to one's vocal **registers** or *passaggio*.

vocal fatigue. A tiring of the voice due to either overuse, illness, inadequate **technique**, or some combination of these factors.

vocal fold cover. See **cover** (4).

vocal fold cysts. A **voice disorder** that consists of egg-shaped masses just under the **cover** of the **vocal fold**. Vocal fold cysts resemble vocal fold polyps, but they usually extend more deeply into the **lamina propria** or—in some extreme cases—the **thyroarytenoid** muscle. Cysts are usually unilateral, only affecting one of the two vocal folds. They are often the result of trauma, but they can be **idiopathic** in origin. **Voice therapy** alone cannot treat cysts; they must be treated by a **laryngologist** who specializes in **phonosurgery**.

vocal fold hemorrhage. A type of **voice disorder** that occurs when a blood vessel ruptures within the **vocal folds**. Vocal fold hemorrhages are generally caused by trauma or abuse. After a hemorrhage, the voice will quickly become impaired due to blood accumulation in the vocal fold, which prevents normal **mucosal wave** formation.

vocal fold oscillation. Describes normal **vocal fold** vibration. Several theories have been put forth to explain vocal fold oscillation, including the **myoelastic-areodynamic theory**, **neurochronaxic theory**, **one-mass model**, and **three-mass model**.

vocal fold paralysis. A neurological disorder resulting in the paralysis of one or both **vocal folds**. Vocal fold paralysis stems from problems with either the superior or recurrent **laryngeal** nerves.

vocal fold paresis. A **vocal fold** weakness in one or both vocal folds. The disorder is similar to **vocal fold paralysis**, although not as severe. Vocal fold paresis usually does not result in full vocal fold paralysis, but it is a similar type of disorder, stemming from problems with either the superior or recurrent **laryngeal** nerves.

vocal fold polyps. A type of **voice disorder** that consists of **lesions** that develop on the **vocal folds** as a result of trauma. Vocal fold polyps are usually **unilateral**, occurring on only one vocal fold. A vocal fold polyp is often preceded by a **vocal fold hemorrhage**.

vocal fold varices. See **varix**.

vocal folds. A paired system of tissue layers in the **larynx** that can vibrate to produce sound, resulting in **phonation**. The structure of each vocal fold is in five layers, consisting of the **stratified squamous epithelium**, **superficial lamina propria**, **intermediate lamina propria**, **deep lamina propria**, and **thyroarytenoid** muscle. Historically called the "**vocal cords**," the term *vocal folds* is now preferred as being more descriptive and accurate.

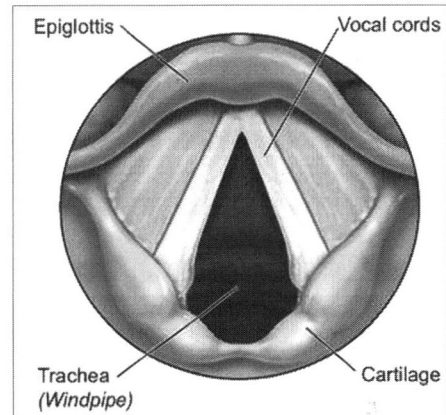

Figure 56. An anatomical drawing of the vocal folds (or cords). *Courtesy Creative Commons.*

vocal fry. See **glottal fry**.

vocal injury. A **voice disorder** that is acquired either through abuse, illness, or chemical imbalance in the body (e.g., medication side effects). There are three basic types of voice injuries: a **progressive voice injury**, an **episodic voice injury**, and a **constant voice injury**.

vocal ligaments. A pair of ligaments that pass through the **intermediate lamina propria** layer of each **vocal fold**.

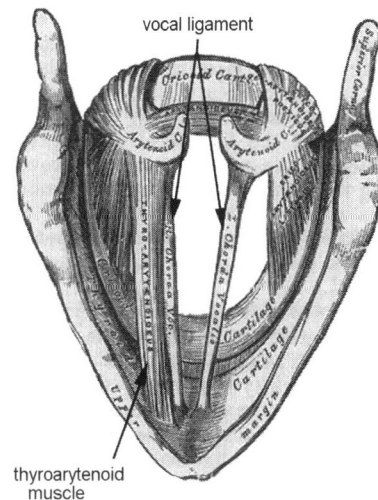

Figure 57. Vocal ligament and thyroarytenoid muscle. *Courtesy Gray's Anatomy*, with labeling by Scott McCoy; reprinted with permission from *Your Voice: An Inside View* (2004).

Vocal ligaments connect the **thyroid cartilage** to the two **arytenoids** at the **vocal processes**.

vocal percussion. See **beat boxing**.

vocal process granulomas. See **granulomas**.

vocal processes. The two points of connection at the **arytenoids** for the two **vocal ligaments**, which connect the arytenoids to the **thyroid cartilage**. This term can be confusing to students of singing, as "process," in this case, refers to a point of connection as opposed to an action. A process can describe any prominence of bone or cartilage within the body.

vocal processing. See **processed singing**.

vocal production. A specific focus of **voice pedagogy** and voice science that addresses **phonation**, **resonance**, and vocal health. Maximum efficiency in vocal production is a primary concern among **voice pedagogues** and **vocologists**.

vocal range. See **range**.

vocal rest. An indeterminate length of time when a singer does not sing, usually due to **vocal fatigue**. Vocal rest can be a simple reduction in singing or speaking activities, or complete cessation of **phonation**. Vocal rest can be either self-imposed or requested by a voice teacher, **speech-language pathologist (SLP)**, or **otolaryngologist (ENT)**.

vocal score. For musical works with orchestral **accompaniment**, a **score** that publishes vocal or choral parts, in addition to a **piano reduction** of the original orchestral part. While conductors use **full scores**—which include all of the instrumental parts—singers almost always learn their **roles** and perform from vocal scores. Sometimes called a **piano-vocal score**.

vocal technique. See **technique**.

vocal tract. Refers to the area of the human body where sound begins (at the **source**) and the tube through which it is filtered. The vocal tract includes the **larynx** (which houses the **vocal folds**) and its resonators: the **pharynx**, **oral cavity**, **nasal cavity**, and **articulators** (including the lips and tongue).

vocal trill. An **extended technique** that involves wild and rapid **oscillation** between two **pitches** not necessarily adjacent to one another. Not the same as a traditional **trill**.

Vocal Wisdom. Famous 1957 **treatise** attributed to **Giovanni Battista Lamperti**. Subtitled *Maxims of Giovanni*

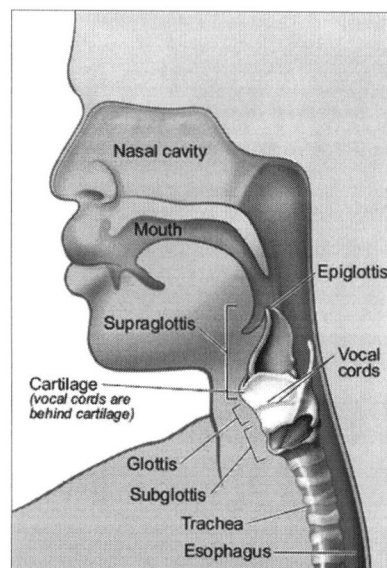

Figure 58. An anatomical drawing of the vocal tract. *Courtesy Creative Commons.*

Battista Lamperti, Vocal Wisdom is actually a collection of Lamperti quotations that were transcribed by his student, William Earl Brown (1863–1945), during his studies with Lamperti in Dresden, Germany, from 1891–1893. Lamperti's teaching is firmly rooted in the **bel canto** tradition of the **International Italian School**. Although the book predates modern voice science and the advent of **fact-based voice pedagogy**, there is little in *Vocal Wisdom* that is questionable by today's standards, revealing Lamperti as a gifted, intuitive voice teacher and one of the great **voice pedagogues** of the late nineteenth century. Along with *On Studying Singing* (1950), by Sergius Kagen (1909–1964), *Vocal Wisdom* is a perennial basic reading assignment in many freshmen voice seminars at conservatories, colleges, and universities.

vocalic. In **diction**, refers to how a **consonant** relates to a **vowel**. Consonants can be **prevocalic**, **intervocalic**, or **postvocalic** (occurring before a vowel, between two vowels, or after a vowel). See also **vocalic harmonization**, which roughly means "to harmonize the vowels."

vocalic harmonization. Vocalic harmonization is the matching of **vowel** sounds in adjacent syllables. The term has its origins in the study of French **diction**: When an **open vowel** directly precedes a **closed** version of the same vowel, both are then closed. This usually only occurs with two specific vowel pairs—[ɛ] and [e]—as in the word *baiser* [beze], and [œ] and [ø], as in the word *heureux* [hørø]. While vocalic harmonization originated as part of the French spoken language (and was systemized in French dictionaries), **Nico Castel**—in his extensive **IPA transcription** series published by Leyerle Publications—adapts vocalic harmonization as a helpful singing **technique** in both Italian and French, changing the **quality** of vowels in either direction (either open to closed or closed to open) so that adjacent vowels match. This often helps the singer technically—that is, a **soprano** may benefit from an open vowel in her higher **range**, just as a **tenor** may benefit from a closed vowel in his *passaggio*—even if those vowel choices are not technically correct in terms of the **International Phonetic Alphabet (IPA)** symbol one would find in the dictionary. In this situation, when vocalic harmonization is applied to directly improve vocal technique, it essentially becomes a form of vowel modification, a technique that skilled **classical singers** routinely use when striving for even, consistent **resonance** throughout their entire vocal range.

vocalis muscle. See **thyrovocalis muscle**.

vocalise. 1. A technical exercise that does not employ any text. Vocalises are often only performed on **vowel** sounds, and a single vowel is sometimes exclusively used throughout the entire vocalise. Vocalises are similar to—and often used as a synonym for—**warm-ups**, but they go further in the sense that they address a specific aspect of vocal **technique**. Published vocalises are found in **treatises** and **technique books**, but they are also often adapted and even created spontaneously by **voice pedagogues** to meet the needs of individual students. A widely accepted fundamental building block of vocal technique, a series of vocalises usually begins most voice **lessons** and individual practice sessions.

2. A **concert** piece for solo voice with no words, usually with orchestral or piano **accompaniment**. Vocalises are sung on either one or several vowels. In this sense, the voice is used instrumentally, as opposed to being a vehicle to deliver the text. The most famous example of this seldom-performed **genre** is the *Vocalise*, Op. 34, No. 14 (1912), by Sergei Rachmaninoff. Other well-known examples include the *Vocalise-étude* (1907), by Gabriel Fauré (1845–1924); the *Vocalise-étude en forme de habanera* (1907), by Maurice Ravel (1875–1937); the *Three Vocalises* for **soprano** and clarinet (1958), by Ralph Vaughan Williams (1872 1958); and the *Vocalise* (1961), by Wilbur Chenoweth (1899–1980).

vocalization. The singing of a **vocalise**, usually either as a **warm-up** or in a singing **lesson**.

vocalize. Verb that is closely related to **vocalization**. When one vocalizes, he or she is singing a vocalization.

voce aperta. Italian term meaning "open voice." In **voice pedagogy**, this is a pejorative term, describing a sound that is, by *bel canto* standards, "ugly" (i.e., not "tall," "round," or "beautiful"). In the Italian tradition, skilled singers must strive to sing with "*voce chiusa*": a more

skillful, aesthetically pleasing sound with even, well-balanced **resonance**.

voce chiara. Italian term meaning "clear voice." Often refers to voices that are bright in **quality**. *Voce chiara* is descriptive and neither complimentary nor pejorative.

voce chiusa. Italian term meaning "closed voice." In the Italian *bel canto* tradition, *voce chiusa* is an ideal toward which a singer should strive at all times. **Classical singers** desiring *voce chiusa* strive for a "tall," "round," and "beautiful" sound through proper **vowel** modification and well-balanced **resonance**. *Voce chiusa* is often addressed by **voice pedagogues** when addressing the higher **range** of the male voice (i.e., in the upper portion of the *zona di passaggio* and above *secondo passaggio*). In this sense, *voce chiusa* is closely linked with the concept of **cover**. See also *voce coperta*.

voce coperta. Italian term for "blanketed voice." Synonymous with **cover**, an important concept in **classical singing** referring to **vowel** modification in the upper **range** of voices (particularly male voices).

voce di petto. Italian term meaning "**chest** voice." See also **mode 1**, **registration**, **TA**.

voce di testa. Italian term meaning "**head** voice." See also **CT**, **mode 2**, **registration**.

voce finta. Italian term meaning "feigned voice." Describes a vocal **quality** that is "off the voice"; in other words, a singer chooses to deliberately not use his or her full voice. *Voce finta* is used to great effect in more intimate **genres**, for instance, **art song**, when a singer is prioritizing **expression** as opposed to **resonance**, either when employing text painting or evoking a specific character within the narrative. *Voce finta* is always deliberate; "thin" vocal sounds that are the result of fatigue or poor vocal **technique** should not be described as *voce finta*.

voce intermedia. See *zona di passaggio*.

voce mista. Italian term meaning "mixed voice." See also **mix**, **registration**.

voix mixte. French term for *voce mista*.

voce piena. Italian term meaning "full voice." Singing with full **resonance** and requisite **support** for **classical singing** in the Italian **operatic** tradition.

VoceVista. A software package developed by Donald Grey Miller (b. 1930) that is designed to give **voice pedagogues** and students visual feedback via a computer monitor while singing. This contrasts with traditional, "aural-only" approach that still characterizes the vast majority of voice **lessons** taught in the twenty-first century. VoceVista appropriately translates as "seen voice." The program incorporates two electronic signals: a real-time spectrum analysis (or **spectrograph**) and an **electroglottograph** (**EGG**). After some basic training, singers and teachers can "see" various aspects of vocal **technique** and **resonance** as opposed to merely relying on aural perception. While voice scientists and other research specialists have used **voice analysis software** for several decades, VoceVista is by far the most widely used, inexpensive voice analysis software used by voice pedagogues and their students. In 2008, Miller published *Resonance in Singing: Voice Building Through Acoustic Feedback*, which includes a copy of the VoceVista software. This **treatise** further clarifies the use of VoceVista and advocates for its routine use in voice studios of all types.

vocology. Term coined by Ingo Titze (b. 1945), director of the **National Center for Voice and Speech (NCVS)**, as a single word essentially meaning voice science. Vocology is the science and practice of voice **habilitation**, including evaluation, diagnosis, and intervention. NCVS is based in Salt Lake City and offers summer courses in vocology for **voice pedagogues** who desire a more thorough grounding in voice science and voice habilitation. While the discipline of vocology also includes the study of the speaking voice, NCVS is particularly devoted to the scientific study of the singing voice, hence vocology's special relevance to singers and voice pedagogues.

Vogl, Johann Michael (1768–1840). Austrian **baritone**. Vogl is of great historical importance due to his close acquaintance with Franz Schubert (1797–1828), who wrote many **songs** for him. Vogl **premiered** "Erlkönig," D328 (1815), "Aufenthalt," D957/8 (1828), and "Die Taubenpost," D957/14 (1828), as well as many other German *Lieder*. He was one of the most celebrated singers of his day, and his devotion to Schubert and dedication to the *Lied* did much to solidify Schubert's reputation as master of the **genre**.

voice (verb). 1. A verb used in singer's **diction**. One can either "voice" a **consonant**—meaning that the **vocal folds** are **phonating** while pronouncing it—or leave the consonant **unvoiced**.

2. To experiment with seating within a specific section of a **choir**. A choral **director** "voices" individual sections of his or her choir until a homogenous **blend** is achieved.

voice analysis software. A computer program that **objectively** measures properties of the singing voice, including (but not limited to) **frequency (pitch)**, amplitude

(loudness), and **harmonics**. Voice analysis software usually features some sort of visual component (for example, spectrograph), allowing users to "see" results as well. **VoceVista** is a commonly used voice analysis software program.

voice box. Informal colloquial term for the **larynx**.

voice care team. See **voice team**.

voice crossing. In **choral music**, voice crossing occurs when two adjacent vocal parts cross one another (e.g., the **alto** line dips below the **tenor**). When two vocal parts share the same staff of music—for example, a tenor and **bass** written in bass clef on a single stave—voice crossing can be a source of confusion. In these instances, the singer must follow the direction of note stems: upward stems indicate the upper part, lower stems indicate the lower part.

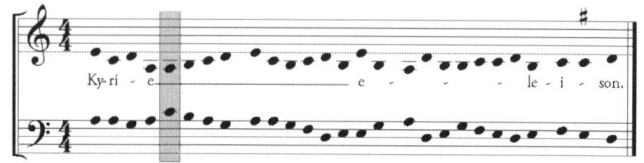

Figure 59. An example of voice crossing in first species counterpoint. *Courtesy Creative Commons.*

voice disorder. A malfunction at the **laryngeal** level, usually as the result of either disease or injury. When singers develop voice disorders, they usually have trouble with proper function of the **larynx** and **vocal folds**, which can result in abnormal **pitch**, loudness, or **quality**. Voice disorders can be grouped into five broad categories: structural changes in the vocal fold, **neurogenic** voice disorders, systemic disease contributors to laryngeal pathology, disorders of voice use, and **idiopathic** voice disorders. Specific voice disorders discussed in this volume include **epithelial dysplasia: carcinoma, epithelial hyperplasia: leukoplakia, epithelial hyperplasia: hyperkeratosis, Reinke's edema, laryngeal webs, contact ulcers, granulomas, papillomas, laryngitis, nodules, cysts, lesions and masses, vascular ectasias, polyps, sulcus vocalis, vocal fold paralysis, vocal fold paresis, spasmodic dysphonia (SD), acid reflux, muscle tension dysphonia (MTD), ventricular dysphonia, aphonia, diplophonia, hyperfunction,** and **hypofunction**. Specific symptoms and treatments of voice disorders vary widely.

voice exchange. In **polyphonic** vocal music (either solo or choral), when identical music is repeated but assigned to different voice parts.

Voice Foundation. A Philadelphia-based **professional** organization for voice professionals ranging from medical specialists to **voice pedagogues**. The mission of the Voice Foundation is to enhance knowledge, care, and training of the voice through educational programs and publications for voice care professionals and public and professional voice users, and through supporting and funding research. Founded in 1969, the Voice Foundation brings together physicians, scientists, **speech-language pathologists (SLPs)**, performers, and teachers to share their knowledge and expertise in the care of the professional voice user. Since 1989, the Voice Foundation has been led by Robert Thayer Sataloff (b. 1949), an internationally renowned **otolaryngologist (ENT)** who is also a professional singer and **conductor**, as well as author of more than 600 publications, including more than thirty-six textbooks. The Voice Foundation hosts a symposium in Philadelphia each year during the first weekend in June.

voice leading. The motion of several simultaneous voices—either **homophonic** or **polyphonic**—as they move through a **harmonic progression**. The **pedagogy** of music theory often involves the imposition of strict rules of voice leading—rules that are the *bêtes noires* of many a music student.

voice pathology. See **voice disorder**.

voice pedagogue. A teacher of singing. While any practicing voice teacher is a voice pedagogue, the most influential voice pedagogues are known to the international **pedagogy** community through presentations of their research and ideas via publications, conferences, and **workshops**. Many of their **treatises** have profoundly influenced the discipline of **voice pedagogy**. In this sense, the most famous voice pedagogues are **academics** and scholars.

voice pedagogy. The study and practice of voice teaching. Almost as long as there have been singers, there have been singing teachers; therefore, voice pedagogy has existed for centuries. As a formal discipline, voice pedagogy seems specifically rooted in Italy, where the characteristics of the Italian language and the music written by its **opera** composers seemed particularly conducive to codifying the ideals of healthy **vocal production**. The concept of *bel canto*—which means different things in different historical contexts, but always refers to "beautiful singing"—persists today, and most **classical** voice teachers ally themselves with some aspect of the **International Italian School** of singing.

In the latter part of the twentieth century, discoveries in voice science gave way to a modern school of voice pedagogy often referred to as **fact-based** voice pedagogy. As science and technology revealed more about how the singing voice functions, voice teachers were able to apply new research to their teaching, making the art of singing less elusive than in previous decades. **Vocology** emerged as a sister discipline to voice pedagogy; however, these new innovations did not render the International Italian School obsolete. Rather, voice science merely affirmed much of what had been rightly in practice for centuries. The wide dissemination of fact-based pedagogical research among singing teachers has nonetheless informed the language of teachers and their manner of explaining concepts to their students. Younger generations of singing teachers often explain the same concepts as their teachers but in a more fact-based way.

While voice pedagogy has historically been associated with classical vocal **styles**, recent decades have seen a proliferation of pedagogical research as it applies to **contemporary commercial music (CCM)** styles, including **musical theatre**, **rock**, **pop**, **jazz**, and **world music**. The most widely practiced schools of CCM voice pedagogy are fact-based in nature, convincingly arguing that nonclassical sounds can be produced in a technically sound and healthy way. This suggestion—increasingly accepted among contemporary **voice pedagogues** contradicts (and in some circles, mythologizes) a widely held concept that the International Italian School is the only road to healthy singing.

The history and discipline of voice pedagogy is primarily studied through the reading of **treatises** of voice pedagogues. For a comprehensive list of these treatises, see the timeline in appendix E, as well as the comprehensive bibliography. Many additional terms in this book also relate to voice pedagogy. See also *appoggio*, **balanced breathing**, **chest**, *coup de glotte*, **CT-dominant**, **false vocal fold contraction**, **head**, **historical pedagogy**, **hyperfunction**, **hypofunction**, **methodologist**, **mode 1**, **mode 2**, **psyche**, **soma**, **systematic pedagogy**, **TA-dominant**.

voice science. See **vocology**.

voice teacher. See **voice pedagogue**.

voice team. When teaching vocally injured singers, a **voice pedagogue** depends on the expertise of vocal health **professionals**, specifically **otolaryngologists (ENTs)** and **speech-language pathologists (SLPs)**. These three professionals—the singing teacher, the ENT, and the SLP—are sometimes referred to as a "voice team." The singer must depend on all three for a full recovery. Voice teachers who have pursued advanced training in areas of vocal health sometimes market their specialization with injured voices by referring to themselves as **singing voice specialists (SVSs)**, but this does not negate the importance of a three-member voice team. Injured singers should still seek out multiple specialists to resolve their injury, pathology, or disorder.

voice therapy. The act of routinely going to a **speech-language pathologist (SLP)** for treatment after being diagnosed with a **voice disorder** or voice injury.

voice type. A descriptive term that attempts to group many individual singers into basic categories. Singers of the same voice type will tend to possess similar **ranges**, **colors**, and **tessituras**. In **classical singing**, the seven basic voice types are **soprano, mezzo-soprano, contralto, counter-tenor, tenor, baritone,** and **bass**. These seven voice types are further divided into subcategories (and *Fächer*), with specific **operatic roles** matching specific voice types. Adjectives are often added to general voice types to arrive at specificity (e.g., **dramatic** soprano, **lyric** baritone, etc.). The **castrato** can be thought of as an eighth (and now extinct) voice type. Some **voice pedagogues** think of the **bass-baritone** as its own specific voice type as well.

Voice types should not be confused with the four basic choral parts: soprano, **alto**, tenor, and bass. While many singers may find that they are most comfortable on the choral part that has the same name as their voice type, their part assignment is often a general label and not reflective of their true, specific vocal identity. *Spinto* and dramatic sopranos, for example, will often sing alto, countertenors may sing either soprano or alto, and baritones will usually sing bass in **choirs**. Thus, a voice "type" is a somewhat casual designation compared to the twenty-nine *Fächer* of the **Kloiber Fach System**, the categories and roles of which are much more specifically defined.

voiced. Any **phoneme** that involves **phonation**. Voiced is an adjective used in singer's **diction** indicating that a **consonant** is **pitched**, that is, the **vocal folds** are phonating during **production** of the consonant. These consonants are described as **voiced consonants**, whereas all other consonants (ones that do not involve phonation) are described as **unvoiced**. Voicing is an essential element of diction, as many consonants are only distinguishable from one another through voicing. For example, the only difference between [b] and [p] is that the former is voiced and the latter is not. These consonants are referred to as **consonant pairs**. In some languages, the same letter is pronounced differently in different situations. For example, in German, voiced consonants become unvoiced when they occur at the ends of words.

voiced consonants. Consonants that are produced, in part, with **phonation** of the **vocal folds**. Common voiced consonants include [b], [d], [g], [v], [z], [dʒ], [ʒ], and [ð]. Most voiced consonants also have an **unvoiced** "partner," and together those two consonants constitute a **consonant pair**.

voicegram. See **spectrogram**.

voiceprint. See **spectrogram**.

VoiceWorks. A Los Angeles-based system of vocal **technique** developed by Lisa Popeil (b. 1956). VoiceWorks is one of several methods that directly deal with **contemporary commercial music (CCM) styles**, along with **Somatic Voicework (SVW)**, **Complete Vocal Technique (CVT)**, and **Speech Level Singing (SLS)**. Popeil disseminates her method through a series of "Total Singer" **workshops** and numerous books, including *The Total Singer* (1996) and *Sing Anything* (2012).

voicing. A practice used by choral **directors** to seat choral artists within their respective sections. When a director "voices" a section, he or she experiments with singers in different positions until an ideal **blend** is achieved. Advocates of voicing argue that correct and careful seating within a section is essential for good blend and **intonation**.

vorig **(Ger).** Former or previous.

Vortrag **(Ger). Interpretation** or performance. Often used in combination with adjectives. (e.g., *mit freiem Vortrag* means "in a free **style**").

vowel. One of two principal categories of **phonetic sounds** (along with **consonants**). Vowels are pronounced with an uninterrupted **vocal tract**, resulting in the ability for all vowels to be sustained for indeterminate periods of time; therefore, vowels are an essential element of **legato** and **resonance** in singing **technique**. Different vowels are formed as the shape of the vocal tract changes, mostly through the movement of the lips and tongue. They can be categorized by **quality** (**front vowels** and **back vowels**) and by the **peak of the tongue arch** (**front vowels**, **central vowels**, or **back vowels**). Two other families of vowels include **mixed vowels**, which blend together qualities of two separate and distinct vowel sounds, and **nasal vowels**, which alter the sounds of pure vowels through a lowered (unengaged) **soft palate**. While mixed vowels occur with frequency in German, French, and Nordic languages, the four nasal vowels are an idiomatic characteristic of French and Portuguese. When two adjacent vowel sounds are strung together, **diphthongs** result, and three adjacent vowels create **triphthongs**. Vowel precision and mastery is an essential element of **classical singing** technique. Vowels are often modified at the extremes of one's vocal **range** to track the **singer's formant** and ensure consistent resonance from top to bottom. When striving for one's foreign language **diction** to sound indigenous, the singer must thoroughly understand the unique nature of vowel formations within each particular language.

vowel chart. A drawing or diagram that organizes different vowels—almost always conveyed through the **International Phonetic Alphabet (IPA)**—according to **quality** (**front vowels** and **back vowels**) and **peak of the tongue arch** (**front vowels**, **central vowels**, or **back vowels**). **Mixed vowels** and **nasal vowels** are also frequently diagrammed. Vowel charts assume different shapes in different publications.

VOWELS

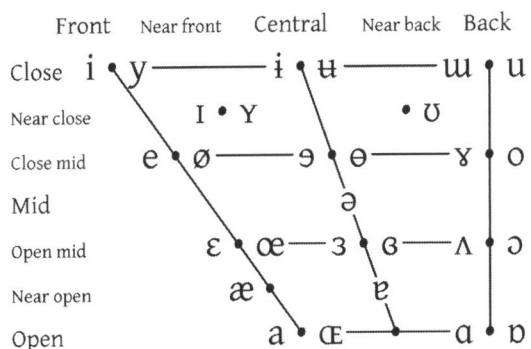

Vowels at right & left of bullets are rounded & unrounded.

Figure 60. The phonetic vowel chart. *Courtesy Creative Commons.*

vowel migration. The shifting of a **vowel**, either intentionally or unintentionally, consciously or unconsciously. Unintentional vowel migration is scientific and an aspect of the physics of sound. For instance, as female voices ascend toward and past G5, all vowels tend to migrate toward [a] regardless of the vowel attempted by the singer. Likewise, experienced singers who strive for a unified **tone quality** throughout their entire vocal **range** will deliberately modify their vowels toward more desirable ones in various parts of their range. In this sense, vowel migration is closely related to **formant tuning**. Among **amateur** singers, unintentional vowel migration can also occur for nonscientific and nontechnical reasons. On longer **melismas**, for instance, inexperienced singers might "forget" which syllable of a word they are supposed to be singing, resulting in the incorrect vowel being sung by the end of the passage.

vowel tuning. See **formant tuning (formant tracking)**.

W

waltz. Type of couple **dance** in **triple meter** popular in the late eighteenth and early nineteenth centuries, particularly in Vienna. **Viennese operetta** is heavily influenced by the waltz, with waltzes appearing in virtually every **score** in the **genre**.

War of the Buffoons. See *Querelle des bouffons*.

warm-up. Technical exercises undertaken by a singer before progressing to more difficult **vocalizations** and **repertoire**. Most practice sessions and voice **lessons** begin with warm-up exercises. Common warm-ups include stretching, humming, **lip trills**, and **straw phonation**.

Warren, Leonard (1911–1960). American **baritone**. Warren was born in New York to Russian immigrant parents. In 1938, he won a contract with the **Metropolitan Opera**, where he became one of the **company's** principal singers for the next twenty-two years. Warren's rich baritone voice and effortless high range made him ideally suited for the **Verdi baritone repertory**. Out of his 610 performances at **The Met**, 359 were in Verdi **operas**, and eighty-nine of those were as the title role in *Rigoletto*. He was also highly regarded as Tonio in Leoncavallo's *Pagliacci* and Scarpia in Puccini's *Tosca*. Warren died of a cerebral hemorrhage onstage at the Metropolitan Opera on March 1, 1960, during a **production** of Verdi's *Simon Boccanegra* (1857, rev. 1881).

Wassoulou. A **genre** of West African **popular music** that is generally performed by women. The **lyrics** of Wassoulou **songs** focus on such feminine issues as childbearing, fertility, and polygamy. **Oumou Sangaré** is the most well-known ambassador of the genre, and she is called the "Songbird of Wassoulou."

waulking song. A type of Scottish folk **song** that was historically sung by women as they "waulked" (cleansed material during clothmaking). Most waulking songs are in the Gaelic language.

wavelength. In a sinusoidal sound wave, the wavelength is the distance measured between two **frequency** peaks. Wavelength is represented by the Greek symbol lambda (λ).

web. See **laryngeal web**.

Wells, Kitty (1919–2012). Country music singer and one of the first significant female performers of country music. Wells was born Ellen Muriel Deason in Nashville, Tennessee. She was the first female country performer to attain true stardom. "It Wasn't God Who Made Honky Tonk Angels" (1952) made her an overnight celebrity and launched a solo career that earned her the nickname the "Queen of Country Music." Wells was one of the leading country performers of the 1950s, and many of her hit **songs** reflected a feminine point of view. She was the wife of country musician Johnnie Wright (b. 1914), and she toured and performed with him throughout her long career. "It Wasn't God Who Made Honky Tonk Angels" was the first number-one hit by a female artist. The record it set—six weeks at number one—has only been surpassed once, by Connie Smith (b. 1941), with "Once a Day" (1964). In 2000, Faith Hill (b. 1967) tied Wells's six-week run with "Breathe" (1999).

Weltliche (Ger) "Worldly." *Weltliche* is a German adjective meaning secular. The term was famously used by Hugo Wolf (1860–1903) to describe the final thirty-four songs—the *Weltliche Lieder*—of his *Spanisches Liederbuch* (1889) **song collection**. The opening ten songs (the sacred ones) were designated as *Geistliche Lieder* (sacred songs; *Geistliche* means "of the spirit").

wenig (Ger). Little, not much.

West End. Short for **West End Theatre**.

West End Theatre. The English equivalent to American **Broadway** named after West End Avenue in London. Next to Broadway, the West End Theatre District is the second most important **musical theatre** industry in the world. In recent decades, there has been a strong symbiotic relationship with Broadway, with the two often sharing similar **repertoires**. Historically, however, distinctly British **musicals** had their origins in the West End. West End Theatre has its roots in **English comic opera**, beginning with the fourteen Victorian works of **Gilbert and Sullivan**. Although Queen Victoria reigned until 1901, the Edwardian era of English comic opera is generally labeled as the period beginning after the breakup of Gilbert and Sullivan in the mid-1890s through the beginning of World War I. This era was dominated by the **comic operas** and **musical comedies** of Sidney Jones (1861–1946), Ivan Caryll (1861–1921), and Lionel Monckton (1861–1924). Frederic Norton (1869–1946) scored perhaps the biggest hit of the late Edwardian era with *Chu Chin Chow* (1916), a musical comedy based on the story *Ali Baba and the 40 Thieves*.

The period between World War I and World War II gave rise to a new generation of English musical theatre composers, the most prolific of these being Noël Coward (1899–1973), Vivian Ellis (1903–1996), and Ivor Novello (1893–1951). Novello was arguably the most successful of the three, and all eight of his lavish **musicals** composed between 1935–1951 feature a unique brand of lyrical nostalgia that captured the hearts of British audiences. The most significant musical comedies to emerge in the postwar years were *Salad Days* (1954), by Julian Slade (1930–2006) and Dorothy Reynolds (1913–1977), and *The Boy Friend* (1954), by Sandy Wilson (b. 1924).

The most important British composer of the last four decades has been Andrew Lloyd Webber (b. 1948), whose long list of musicals and **megamusicals** have dominated the West End and given rise to a "British invasion" of Broadway that began in the 1980s. Since the 1970s and Lloyd Webber, there has been considerably more parity between the repertoires of the West End and Broadway, with many successful shows finding their way across the Atlantic to run in both **theatre** districts. These blockbuster musicals (by Lloyd Webber and many others) have also been translated into many other languages and have played throughout the world. With occasional exceptions, the West End now refers to the British musical theatre industry, and the distinctly British musical as a repertory piece has now given way to a more cosmopolitan international **style**.

whistle register. A commonly used term that refers to **flageolet register**.

whole step. An **interval** of two **half steps**. See **whole-tone scale**.

whole-tone scale. A six-note **scale**—as opposed to the seven-note scale that characterizes all **major**, **minor**, and **modal** scales—that is comprised entirely of **whole steps**. Since there are no **half-step**/whole-step patterns (and thus no landmarks), there is no sense of the first **scale degree** ("do"), and whole-tone scales are not designated according to **pitch** names; a "C whole-tone scale," for example, would be meaningless. As a result, there are only two whole-tone scales possible, each comprised of six completely distinct sets of pitches.

Figure 61. Two incarnations of the whole-tone scale. *Courtesy Creative Commons.*

Figure 62. Two incarnations of the whole-tone scale. *Courtesy Creative Commons.*

Whole-tone scales were used most frequently by Claude Debussy (1862–1918) and his immediate contemporaries. Singers of these French *mélodies* and **French operas** must feel comfortable singing whole-tone scales. See also **octatonic scale**, *solfège*.

Wiegenlied (Ger). **Lullaby**. Also called *berceuse*, **slumber song**, *Schlummerlied*.

Williams, Hank (1923–1953). Classic **country** music singer. Williams's penchant for lyrical depth earned him the nickname the "Hillbilly Shakespeare." He spent his childhood in Alabama and began writing **songs** at the age of fourteen. During World War II, Williams worked at a shipyard in Mobile and performed on local radio. His original compositions attracted the attention of Fred Rose (1898–1954), which led to a Nashville contract with Acuff-Rose Music. In 1947, Williams signed his first record deal. His major hit was "Lovesick Blues" (1948), which spent sixteen weeks at the number-one spot. In 1949, Williams joined the cast of the **Grand Ole Opry**.

Although he produced many more hits throughout the next three years, Williams began his descent into the alcoholism and drug addiction that resulted in his eventual firing from the Grand Ole Opry in 1952. While Williams possessed many gifts, he is probably best remembered for his talent as a songwriter.

windscreen. See **pop filter**.

wobble. A distasteful, wide, or erratic **vibrato** that is either a result of flawed vocal **technique** (often inadequate *appoggio*) or a compromise of the vocal apparatus due to pathologies or excessive age of the singer. Some **vocologists** measure a wobble as a vibrato of less than 5.5 **pulses** per second. In this context, a wobble is the opposite of a **tremolo**, which is a vibrato that is too fast (exceeding 7.5 pulses per second). Wobble is also a pejorative term used by singers and **conductors** (usually fellow choral artists) to describe the sound of choral groups that do not achieve good **blend**. A **choir** that "wobbles" is also usually **out-of-tune** and is the antithesis of a choir that "blends" and strives for good **intonation**. Erratic vibrato or an **operatic singer's resonance** that are inappropriate for the **style** are common causes of choral wobble.

woodshedding. The process a **barbershop quartet** goes through as they **improvise harmonies** around a tune. While some barbershop quartets **rehearse** from published and precomposed arrangements, other groups prefer woodshedding four-part harmony from a melody alone.

word painting. The practice of musically illustrating the meaning of words in vocal music. In vocal music of all eras, composers practiced word painting. Clichéd examples include requiring a singer to sing a high note on the words *sky* or *heaven*, or a low note on the words *valley* or *grave*. More subtle examples include falling **motives** for **laments** (to indicate sobbing), or **coloratura** passages to indicate anger (for example, in Handelian **rage arias**). **Harmony** also plays a significant **role** in word painting, with **dissonance** and resolution being inextricably linked with the dramatic situation occurring in the text or the emotional state of the character. See also **declamation**.

work song. A **song** that synchronizes the rhythm of a group task, usually hard physical labor. Work songs are most closely associated with African American slaves who brought the **style** and custom from West Africa. Many are in **call-and-response form**. Work songs are an important forerunner of **blues**, **jazz**, **gospel**, and **spiritual** styles. See also **field holler**.

workshop. An early **production** of a new **musical theatre** work, usually in the presence of the composer and **lyricist**. Workshops give the creators the chance to "try out" a new work before taking it to a more high-profile venue. Revisions usually ensue after an initial workshop.

world music. Term used to denote virtually any **form** of non-Western music, either in the **art music** or **popular music** vein. World music is an extraordinarily vast collection of **genres** that is rapidly gaining more ubiquity and influence in Western culture. Many forms of world music, in both indigenous and popular **styles**, feature singing as a prominent element. The growing field of ethnomusicology has increased the prevalence of world music **ensembles** in the West, and the **fusion** between world music and various Western popular styles has made world music styles increasingly relevant to the modern singer and student of singing. World music vocal styles are as varied as the cultures from which they originate, and each must be studied on its own terms within its own social context. World music styles specifically addressed in this dictionary include Beijing/**Peking opera** (China), *bossa nova* (Brasil), *fado* (Portugal), *Noh* or *Nogaku* (Japan), *qawwali* (Pakistan), *raï* (Algeria), *ranchera* (Mexico), *tahrir* (Iran), **tango** (Argentina), *xoomei* or **Tuvan throat singing** (Tuva/Mongolia), and **yodeling** (Switzerland). Some of the world music singers featured in this volume include **Sezen Aksu, Asha Bhosle, Björk, Fairuz, Youssou N'Dour, João Gilberto, Víctor Jara, Salif Keita, Nusrat Fateh Ali Khan, Umm Kulthum, Kongar-ool Ondar, Alim Qasimov, Elis Regina, Amália Rodrigues,** and **Mohammad-Reza Shajarian**. See also **ethnic and border music**.

X

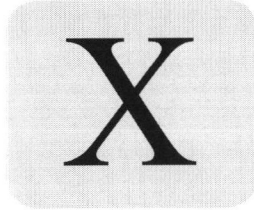

XLR. In audio technology, a type of cable used to transmit audio signals from a **microphone** to a sound system or recording interface. XLR cables used for audio applications have three pins: ground (pin 1), positive (pin 2), and negative (pin 3). For more information, see the essay entitled "What Every Singer Needs to Know about Audio Technology."

xoomei. An alternate spelling for *khoomei.* See **Tuvan throat singing**.

Y

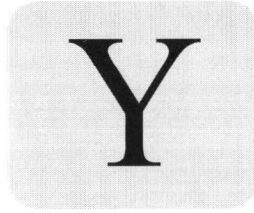

YAP. Abbreviation for **young artist program**.

YAP Tracker. An online resource for **young artists** interested in **auditioning** for **young artist programs (YAPs)**, **apprenticeships**, and competitions. YAP Tracker lists more than 2,500 opportunities for singers each year and allows singers to upload their materials to a central source for online application. In addition to U.S. programs, YAP Tracker also lists opportunities in Canada and Europe.

yodeling. A **style** of singing often associated with **folk music** of the Swiss Alps. Yodeling features the singing of leaps and a rapid alternation between the two principal vocal **registers** (**TA** and **CT**). A "yodel" can also be a short section of yodeling, sung on a single breath. Derived from the (middle-high) German verb *jôlen*, meaning "to call," yodeling is thought to have originated as a call between mountain peoples. Whether there was a practical use for yodeling is unclear, but its popularity as a folk music endures. Due to the use of both registers, yodelers often have an extensive **range** of three **octaves** or more. A yodeler is a singer who yodels or practices yodeling.

yoga. A type of **bodywork** meant to unite mind and body. Meaning "union" in Sanskrit, yoga incorporates breath control **techniques** (*pranayama*) that can help singers with **breath management**, as well as **music performance anxiety (MPA)**. Yoga's physical **postures** or poses (*asanas*) encourage healthy body alignment and develop **kinesthetic** awareness. Yoga also involves meditation practice to calm and center the mind through positive affirmations (*mantras*) and **chanting** (*kirtan*). Yoga has become a common part of the training in a **young artist program (YAP)** or collegiate **opera workshop**.

young artist. One who participates in a **young artist program (YAP)**. Also called an apprentice.

young artist program (YAP). An **opera** or **art song** program intended for young or emerging **professional classical singers**. While many YAPs are summer programs affiliated with festivals, most regional **opera houses** now offer YAPs during their normal September through May seasons. **Young artists**—often labeled apprentices—usually sing *comprimario* **roles**, participate in opera **chorus** work, **cover** leading **roles**, and engage in promotional work and educational outreach. Often used interchangeably with **apprenticeship**.

Z

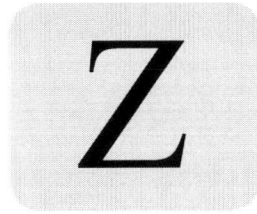

zart (**Ger**). Tender, delicate, or soft.

zarzuela. Zarzuela is a **form** of light **opera** developed in Spain. Although the earliest examples of this **genre** were written for the court of King Philip IV in the seventeenth century, *zarzuela* finally achieved popularity in the nineteenth century and international recognition in the twentieth century. *Zarzuela* literally translates as "bramble bush," but its name derives from the name of the palace of King Philip IV (1621–1665)—"La Zarzuela." The genre eventually found its way into the cosmopolitan **theatres** of Madrid and Barcelona, gradually assuming some of the characteristics of other forms of light opera—Italian *opera buffa*, German *Singspiel*, and **Viennese operetta** in particular. Important composers of *zarzuela* have included Juan Hidalgo (1614–1685), Francisco Asenjo Barbieri (1823–1894), Emilio Arieta (1823–1894), Tomás Bretón (1850–1923), Amadeo Vives (1871–1932), Francisco Alonso (1887–1948), and Federico Moreno Tórroba (1891–1982). One **subgenre** of *zarzuela* is the *tonadilla*, a one-**act** satirical *zarzuela* that reached the height of its popularity in the mid-eighteenth century. The *tonadilla* often featured traditional Spanish **dances**, for instance, the *seguidilla*. Another eighteenth-century form is the *género chico,* another one-act form of *zarzuela* that featured more dialogue, traditional Spanish folk songs, and a working-class perspective.

Zauberoper (**pl.** *Zauberopern*). Literally meaning "magic **opera**," this term is another label given to a *Singspiel* or **German Romantic opera** that has fairy tale or other magical elements in the **plot**. Mozart's *Die Zauberflöte* (1791) and Weber's *Der Freischütz* (1821) are examples of *Zauberopern*.

Zeffirelli, Franco (b. 1923). Italian opera and film **director**. Zeffirelli was born and raised in Florence, where he later studied art and architecture at the University of Florence. Increasingly attracted to the **theatre**, he actually began his career in the film industry, assisting several prominent **directors**, including Vittorio de Sica (1901–1974), Luchino Visconti (1906–1976), and Roberto Rossellini (1906–1977). Although the public at large primarily knows Zeffirelli as a film director—his most famous film is the 1968 version of *Romeo and Juliet*—he has also been active since the 1950s as an **opera** director on several continents. He was a frequent collaborator with **Joan Sutherland**, and his work with the **Metropolitan Opera** has included several high-profile **productions** of Puccini's operas, including *La bohème* (1896), *Tosca* (1900), and *Turandot* (1926). In addition, Zeffirelli has directed movie versions of many operas—starring such luminaries as **Placido Domingo**—and made several documentaries about **Maria Callas**, including the fictionalized 2002 biopic *Callas Forever*. Zeffirelli is also active in Italian politics and has served as a member of the Italian senate.

Zeitmaß (**Ger**). **Tempo**.

ziemlich (**Ger**). Somewhat or rather.

zipper effect. The zipper effect is a concept developed by Seth Riggs (b. 1930), the creator of **Speech Level Singing (SLS)**. The term *zipper effect* is used to describe the zipper-like process in which the **vocal folds** dampen along the posterior two-thirds of the folds, thus only using the front third of the folds for vibration at the *primo passaggio*. The zipper effect theory was challenged in 2011, when a study published in the *Journal of Singing* by Randy Buescher (b. 1961) reported that no such action exists in the vocal folds.

zögernd (**Ger**). Hesitating.

zona di passaggio. Literally translating to "zone of passage," the area of the classically trained voice that lies between the *primo passaggio* and *secondo passaggio*. It is in this *zona di passaggio* that *aggiustamento* or **vowel** modification occurs as singers strive for consistent **resonance** and an even **tone quality** from top to bottom. This "balancing" of the two primary vocal **registers**—commonly called **head (CT/mode 2)** and **chest (TA/mode 1)** voice—in the *zona di passaggio* is often called a **mixed register** or coordinated register.

Zwischenfach. Someone who "swings" between two *Fachs* (German plural, *Fächer*), usually adjacent ones (i.e., **mezzo-soprano** and **soprano**, **tenor** and **baritone**, etc.). True *Zwischenfach* singing is rare at the highest echelon of the **professional** world and is usually only found at the regional and **amateur** levels. A young dramatic **soprano**, for instance, might primarily sing mezzo-soprano **repertory** while occasionally "trying out" heavier soprano arias and before attempting an entire dramatic soprano **role**. While professionals occasionally shift *Fächer* (and thus repertories) as they age, most professional singers tend to focus on one *Fach* at a time (and for an extended period of time). The demands of certain types of **contemporary commercial music (CCM) styles** have given birth to some hybrid terminology—for example, "**baritenor**"—but these terms usually represent a new, descriptive *Fach*, not two simultaneous ones.

zydeco. Louisiana two-step **dance** music related to Cajun music. *Zydeco* primarily differs from Cajun music in the sense that *zydeco* is usually played by black Creole bands. While often thought of as an instrumental **genre**, much of the *zydeco* **repertory** features singing. While the instrumental and **harmonic** content is distinct and idiomatic, the vocal **style** of both Cajun and *zydeco* is similar to that of American **blues**. **Clifton Chenier** is known as the "King of Zydeco."

Classical and Contemporary Commercial Music: A Comparison

Jeannette LoVetri

The diversity of popular styles of music continues to expand, particularly in the United States, but internationally as well. From simple roots, these styles have emerged to be the dominant force in the musical world and the ones that most music enthusiasts appreciate. Classical music is no longer the only genre of music deserving of serious scholarly and academic study. Our popular styles, now called contemporary commercial music, grouped together as a genre, are taking their place as being different from, but equal to, classical styles, and deserving of the same study, respect, and investigation by everyone who has an interest in them.

For approximately sixty years, classical music was the only style of music taught in undergraduate and graduate degree programs in colleges and universities. In the 1980s, the first music theatre bachelor's degrees began to emerge, and the number of programs continues to expand throughout the United States. There is a high demand for institutions of higher learning to offer programs that train students to become accomplished in music theatre and other styles.

Training for instrumental musicians is offered in both classical and jazz degree programs, and the stylistic and philosophical differences of each genre are taught differently for both. For vocalists, however, the differences are more pronounced, and they can be significant enough to cause confusion that might interfere with overall success.

The need for a new term became increasingly apparent during the last half of the twentieth century, due to the use of the word *nonclassical* to describe any style that was, in fact, not classically based. The implication of this term was that classical music was somehow the baseline by which all music should be evaluated. It placed any style that was not classical against a preconceived assumption that what was not classical was somehow of lesser value or lacking in worth. The prefix "non" is defined by the World English Dictionary[1] as follows:

non—prefix, from Latin non—not
  1. indicating negation
  2. indicating refusal or failure: noncooperation
  3. indicating exclusion from a specified class of persons or things: nonfiction
  4. indicating lack or absence, especially of a quality associated with what is specified: nonobjective; nonevent

It presupposes that classical music, which also has many styles, sets the standard, but this flies in the face of the statistics about the music marketplace, which has long established that other styles are far more popular than classical styles, that they generate a great deal more money, and that they are highly complex and diverse in both skill and execution in their own right. The disparity served no useful purpose and demanded that a new term be found.

In 2000, the term *contemporary commercial music*, abbreviated CCM, was announced at the Science and the Singing Teacher in the New Millennium conference, sponsored by the New York Singing Teachers' Association (NYSTA) and Mount Sinai Medical Center, in New York City. This term, meant to collect all the styles previously called "nonclassical" under one umbrella, was also designed to stop the practice of defining these styles by what they were not. The term has subsequently been used in articles, research papers, and presentations, and at conferences and congresses throughout the United States and in several foreign countries. It has awakened the academic community, in particular, to the validity of these styles and allowed them to be seen as being united by their common roots. While the term does not yet extend to the category of music called "world music," it may someday include these styles as well.

The New York City Performing Arts Library at Lincoln Center, considered by many to be among the premier musical libraries in the world, has its CD collection divided along similar lines. The groupings it uses for its CD collection are as follows:

Pop
Music theater
Gospel
Jazz
R&B/soul
U.S. folk
Blues
Country
Hip-hop
Metal
Rock
Electronic

World
Latin/pop
Raggae/raggaeton
Salsa

Opera
Nonoperatic vocal music
Vocal music

CCM encompasses all the styles on the top part of this list. The National Association of Teachers of Singing (NATS) now has two divisions for its competition, classical, and music theatre. These organizations' separations of musical categories further advance the notion that the styles are distinct from classical music styles, but equal to them. Such a position demands, then, that a good, neutral term be used to cover them all, and CCM is the answer to that need. This is a correlate with classical, a term that encompasses the styles of opera, operetta, art song/recital, orchestral music with vocal solos, chamber music, early music, oratorio, and contemporary or experimental styles. The many styles of CCM born in the United States have flourished and subsequently traveled the world during the last one hundred years. We have reached a junction where these styles deserve formal recognition by the academic, musical, and performing communities.

WHY CALL THEM CONTEMPORARY COMMERCIAL MUSIC?

In the United States, the term *contemporary*, when used alone, is often associated with works written by living classical composers, but it can sometimes also mean any work from the twentieth century to the present. The word *commercial* can mean music written for a TV or radio commercial, or it can refer to the part of the music business that deals with various aspects of music making, including electronic music and music marketing. Used together, however, these two words, *contemporary commercial*, did not have any previous meanings.

In the new term, the word *contemporary* was taken to be anything originating from approximately the turn of the twentieth century onward, but that could also have roots going back even further, which folk and gospel music definitely do. The word *commercial* was taken to mean "for profit," as opposed to "not-for-profit," which is a legal definition. Commercial theatre is any theatre that is produced through money raised from investors who seek to have a return on their investments. Not-for-profit theatre funds are raised primarily through grants and donations. Commercial music is any kind of music that is in the music marketplace driven by consumers; however, from an artistic point of view, the level of quality of the product of both commercial and not-for-profit arts organizations can be exactly the same.

CLASSICAL STYLES: DIFFERENT ORIGINS, DIFFERENT HERITAGE

Western classical music has its original roots in Europe, in the church and in the commissions of aristocracy and royalty, going back to the late Middle Ages, being more firmly established at the end of the sixteenth century. Classical music did not become accessible to the general populace until the mid-1800s, although exposure to various composers' works through religious services was ongoing.

Composers of classical music can now be found worldwide, and classical music has also broadened in its scope and form. Classical music of twentieth- and twenty-first-century composers continues to be created successfully, and all forms, including opera, have expanded the breadth of sounds that enthusiasts can enjoy, although it also maintains many of its older conventions. Some of the music written has changed quite a bit in terms of style, but the singers, trained in the traditional manner, continue to be heard in ways that remain close to the vocal production originally captured in the earliest recordings.

Classical music is taught in most of the programs for vocalists through undergraduate and graduate training, regardless of whether the music sung is classical or some other style.[2] The first formal training for singing at a university conservatory was a bachelor's in voice at Oberlin Conservatory in Ohio, in 1934, and that was followed in 1938 by a similar degree at the Juilliard School in New York City. These first degrees codified training into a cohesive whole for a college curriculum. Prior to that, singing training was strictly a situation of one teacher working with one student at a time, but not in a school setting. This singing training was aimed at classical repertoire, primarily art song literature and perhaps also opera.

THE ROOTS OF CONTEMPORARY COMMERCIAL MUSIC: MUSIC OF THE COMMON PERSON

To further appreciate the criteria and parameters of the main styles of CCM, those that have had a significant impact on the social and cultural fabric of society, we need to briefly investigate their beginnings. The other styles are certainly important, but these examples will suffice to illustrate how the individual styles have come to their current points of development. While being a cursory overview, the following information will indicate the validity of these styles and the reasons why they deserve to be taken seriously on their own terms.

Jazz Is Born

At the beginning of the 20th century, jazz was emerging in the Deep South. The great artists of that era, most of whom were from New Orleans, and who can still be heard today through recordings, launched a unique style of music that would grow and develop throughout the rest of the century, spawning several, then dozens, of offshoot styles. The "Roaring Twenties," sometimes called the "Jazz Age," was associated with a severe break in many social and cultural standards. It was a time when young people took up jazz in large numbers, sometimes to the consternation of their parents. In the 1920s,

> What many young people wanted to do was dance: the Charleston, the cakewalk, the black bottom, and the flea hop. Jazz bands played at dance halls like the Savoy in New York City and the Aragon in Chicago; radio stations and phonograph records (100 million of which were sold in 1927 alone) carried their tunes to listeners across the nation. Some older people objected to jazz music's "vulgarity" and "depravity" (and the "moral disasters" it supposedly inspired), but many in the younger generation loved the freedom they felt on the dance floor.[3]

By the end of the 1920s, jazz vocalists were beginning to sing with big bands broadcasting through the airwaves into people's living rooms, where the large speakers on the family's radio made it seem like the songsters were right there, singing to them. At the same time, recordings became widely available, and you could purchase any kind of music to play at home on your phonograph, as many times as you wished. For the first time, the average person had a chance to determine who was successful by purchasing records or movie tickets. "Popular music" became a big business and has remained so ever since.

Early training for jazz musicians was primarily through imitation and personal experience, but the demand for training by young enthusiasts eventually produced organized courses and led to the first college degree, offered by the University of North Texas. The bachelor's degree was in jazz studies, with a major in "dance band" or dance music.[4]

The Two Worlds Are Separate but Not Equal

In the early decades of the twentieth century, the two forms of music—classical and jazz—were separate in every way. This was perhaps because the music was originally born in New Orleans of African Americans, or because it was taken up by young people who were perceived by their elders as being "rowdy" and "vulgar," or maybe for other reasons only to be speculated about, jazz carried a slightly tainted reputation in sophisticated society until it was integrated into the big bands and taken up by Caucasian vocalists who became celebrities. And because jazz was learned through informal apprenticeships by younger musicians and singers who were mentored by older, more experienced players for quite some time, jazz did not develop an organized written form until the big bands began to require arrangements. Some of these arrangements were written after they had been inspired by "jam sessions," or improvisational rounds of music making, which was and still is a hallmark of jazz expression. Other composers, particularly George Gershwin and Cole Porter, were strongly influenced by jazz's syncopated rhythms, and many vocalists copied the great Bessie Smith, Ma Rainey, and Ethel Waters, alongside such vaudeville singers as Sophie Tucker and Al Jolson. Jazz had "arrived," and its influences had spread throughout the country and across the oceans by the 1930s.

Simultaneously, in various locations throughout the United States, local people were playing music for their own enjoyment and in religious services. These styles were locked within geographic areas of the country, only to be heard live by local people until electronic amplification intervened and brought them to a national audience. With the invention of the microphone at the end of the 1920s, and the emergence of radio as a national form, music that had previously only been heard in a specific locale, one performance at a time, was suddenly available to anyone who had a radio or phonograph, or anyone who could attend a Hollywood movie at their local theatre. Music emerging in other parts of the country was also being seen in films and heard on the radio. Country music out of the southeast and "cowboy" music from Texas showed up on radio and in films in the early and mid-1930s. There was also growing influence from Chicago, New York, and Hollywood, as artists were intrigued and inspired by the variances of style that continued to spin into new forms, decade by decade.

With the growth of media and the more complex electronic forms that emerged as equipment got more sophisticated, popular styles continued to diversify and expand. Recording equipment improved in quality, allowing the sounds to be captured more vividly and authentically. Record quality and playback was also better, giving the listener a richer aural experience. Films had gone from silent to "talkies" and then from black-and-white to color, ultimately bringing musical spectacles from Hollywood to millions of fans. They became acquainted with the performers who had been seen in vaudeville or heard on the radio by watching them on the silver screen. It was only a short journey then, for many of these same entertainers would move to television when it became widely available in the early 1950s.

Music Theatre: Changing Every Decade

Music theatre in the United States slowly grew out of various traveling shows, early theatrical productions with music, and early vaudeville or variety shows. It was also influenced by English music hall productions. In 1927, Jerome Kern and Oscar Hammerstein II created the first "book" musical, *Show Boat*, which is a play that contains songs that are part of the plot. The subsequent decades saw the rise of this form as the predominant one on Broadway, and it became the pattern for hundreds of shows that followed. Music written for Broadway became a familiar part of life for millions by exposure through recordings and movies. The style of music found on Broadway changed with every decade to reflect the tastes of the public at large. In the late 1960s, rock and roll arrived on Broadway, and its influence has grown strongly ever since.

Music theatre has several unique characteristics that are found on Broadway and in the West End in London—and in no other part of the music industry. Singers are expected to sing in specific vocal qualities and with designated vocal characteristics, frequently in precise pitch ranges. These quantifiers are not found elsewhere, although classical music, particularly opera and oratorio, do have designations called "*fachs*," which are categories that suit certain types of singers and voices. It is a vast and complex field that now flourishes throughout the world, but the strongholds are still in New York and London, where most shows are created.

A Sound Explosion in the 1950s Still Being Heard around the World

There is controversy about the origins of rock and roll. Many believe it emerged in Memphis or another city in the southeast, while others favor Chicago. Its arrival heralded a shift in musical tastes that has lingered for more than sixty years and is likely to continue for decades to come. Rock, as it became, is a derivative of jazz, but it was likely influenced by other styles, including Southern blues, bluegrass, or even ragtime. The early rock singers combined a new rhythmic beat, energetic sound, and simple lyrics to capture the hearts of the youth of the mid-twentieth century and, with some significant help from such network television shows as Ed Sullivan's, took the country by storm. Popular music became the official domain of the young, much to the chagrin of their parents, who had perhaps been chastised for doing something quite similar decades earlier. Rock is also a

large field, with many famous star singers and influences. It is always changing, but many of the groups from the 1950s and 1960s, rock's early days, are still touring or performing in "revival shows" to audiences full of fans.

More Styles Born in the United States: Country, Gospel, and Homegrown Folk

During this time, Nashville continued to flourish in its own right, and it, too, became a recognizable national force in the music marketplace. Stars from the Grand Ole Opry sang on the radio and later appeared in films and on television. A few, like "Tennessee" Ernie Ford and Gene Autry, emerged to become stars of their own TV shows in the 1950s. Gospel singing, which many believe has its roots in the songs of the slaves of the South or perhaps also with the camp meetings, open to all races, was concurrently being heard on the radio and in recordings. In the 1950s, gospel singing made it to mainstream TV through Mahalia Jackson's program. Hearing her rich, powerful voice singing the words with deep devotion was a moving experience for many who were unfamiliar with this style.

With the coming of each decade, new popular styles were born, and during the last fifty years of the twentieth century, a plethora of styles was easily available through the newly minted outlet of the Internet, as well as the tried and true media forms of TV and radio, film and live performance.

In the 1960s and 1970s, folk music became popular, and although each country has its own version of folk music, in the United States, that tradition has variations in all geographic locations and probably goes back farther in history than any other style. It became a form universally embraced by young people during the turbulent Vietnam War era and emerged as another producer of names that continue to be recognized in the twenty-first century.

VOICE SCIENCE INTERVENES

With the invention of new tools in voice-science research in the early and middle twentieth century, it was possible for the first time to take a real-time look at the larynx of a vocalist during singing without causing injury. Acoustic measurements of singers' voices also became more accurate. In 1977, *Scientific American* published a definitive article by Johan Sundberg, PhD, on vocal acoustics.[5] It has been discovered that classical singers' voices exhibit a certain amount of consistency in terms of both physiologic response and acoustic parameters. These hallmark characteristics are some of the ingredients classical singers need to acquire, either through training or by natural tendency, or both, if they are to succeed at the highest levels.

Later in the century, voice scientists began to examine other kinds of singers, particularly those who sang using the vocal quality called "belting," a type of sound quite different than that made by a classical vocalist, less refined but perhaps more closely related to speech. Belting is a kind of intense vocal production that allows the voice to carry easily but does not have the characteristics of a classical sound. It can be found in many styles of world music and has its early roots in American music in many of the aforementioned styles. It was later found on vaudeville stages in the singing of many performers and made its way to the Broadway stage as well. The research produced a body of work that indicates that the responses of belters' throats are quite different than those of classical singers, and that these differences have an impact on both the mode of vocal production and the output of the vocal acoustics.

WHY SINGING IN EACH GENRE IS DIFFERENT

A brief synopsis of what is currently known in voice science about both qualities (classical and belting) is that they require different amounts of breath pressure and produce a different type of closure in the vocal folds themselves. In addition, the configuration of the throat and mouth (coupled together as a tube) differs in shape with each. While this is a large generalization, the point is that the two genres are not only different musically, they are different because of the way the vocalists in each mode produce sound.

There is also a third kind of sound, one that is neither belting nor classical. This genre is frequently referred to as "mix." This sound has attributes of both classical and belting and is the quality used in most vocal music that is not obviously classical or belting.

In academia, primarily in the United States, training for vocalists continued to be exclusively classical, but a few universities added music theatre degrees in the 1980s. In these programs, young vocalists were allowed to participate in music theatre productions done at their schools. Shortly thereafter, outside of academia, the first training programs for vocalists who were seeking information about how to approach other styles emerged. These programs, which are still being offered, bring new information to singers and teachers of singing about performing each style optimally.

CONCLUSION

CCM and classical music are two broad categories defining genres of music, with many divisions within each category. They are two terms with positive connotations that allow each genre to be considered equally, but separately. They also help to clarify the continuous blurring of the lines between styles. The term *contemporary commercial music*, perhaps one day to transform into something else, does the job it was intended to do, which is give each style in the formerly labeled "non-classical" category a way to be respected through its own

criteria and parameters without apology or explanation, and it links them all through their common heritage of arising from average people for their own expression. It allows us to move forward into the twenty-first century, with both genres, classical and CCM, being seen as having value and worth.

NOTES

1. "Non-," *World English Dictionary*, http://dictionary.reference.com/browse/non- (accessed 25 November 2013).

2. E. M. Weekly and J. LoVetri, "Follow-Up Contemporary Commercial Music (CCM) Survey: Who's Teaching What in Non-classical Music," *Journal of Voice* 23, no. 3 (2009): 367–75.

3. "The Roaring Twenties," *History.com*, www.history.com/topics/roaring-twenties (accessed 25 November 2013).

4. "Timeline of Jazz Education," *Wikipedia.org*, http://en.wikipedia.org/wiki/Timeline_of_jazz_education (accessed 25 November 2013).

5. J. Sundberg, "The Acoustics of the Singing Voice," *Scientific American* 236, no. 3 (2007): 82–91.

REFERENCES

"Non-." *World English Dictionary*, http://dictionary.reference.com/browse/non- (accessed 25 November 2013).

"The Roaring Twenties." *History.com*, www.history.com/topics/roaring-twenties (accessed 25 November 2013).

Sundberg, J. "The Acoustics of the Singing Voice." *Scientific American* 236, no. 3 (2007): 82–91.

"Timeline of Jazz Education." *Wikipedia.org*, http://en.wikipedia.org/wiki/Timeline_of_jazz_education (accessed 25 November 2013).

Weekly, E. M., and J. LoVetri. "Follow-Up Contemporary Commercial Music (CCM) Survey: Who's Teaching What in Non-classical Music." *Journal of Voice* 23, no. 3 (2009): 367–75.

Jeannette LoVetri is artist-in-residence at Shenandoah Conservatory in Winchester, Virginia. She is also guest faculty at the University of Michigan, Ann Arbor, Medical Center; University of Central Oklahoma; and University of Massachusetts Dartmouth. In addition, LoVetri is singing specialist with the Brooklyn Youth Chorus and lecturer in the Drexel University College of Medicine. Her students have appeared on Broadway, at Carnegie and Avery Fisher halls, at the Rose Room at the Lincoln Center, at Albert Hall in London, and at Madison Square Garden. LoVetri is author of numerous pedagogical and scientific articles, as well as two reference book chapters, and editor of a third chapter in a book published for the Australia Association of Teachers of Singing. She lectures, presents, and teaches on various topics worldwide and is a recipient of the Van Lawrence Fellowship from NATS and the Voice Foundation, where she is on the Advisory Board. LoVetri is a past president of NYSTA and a member of NATS and the American Academy of Teachers of Singing.www.thevoiceworkshop.com.

Criteria for Selecting Repertoire

John Nix

Imagine the following scenario: It is the beginning of the new school term. In the midst of looking for repertoire for your students, you find yourself thinking, "I sang 'Deh vieni, non tardar' when I was in undergraduate school, so a young light soprano like Debbie should be able to get through it, too." Yet, at midterm, Debbie still cannot "get through" Susanna's aria, and both you and Debbie are very frustrated. You feel confused and wonder if you are to blame for not helping her progress, while she feels defeated by the piece and is discouraged about practicing it. Compounding this unfortunate situation are deadlines: NATS competitions, semester juries, scholarship auditions—all of which are fast approaching. Debbie and her classmates need the right repertoire selected at the beginning of the term rather than having it selected through trial and error as classes go along. What can be done to prevent this mid-semester crisis from happening? How can repertoire be systematically selected to best fit the needs of each student?

To begin this discussion, it must be stated unequivocally that few singers can overcome the difficulties caused by repertoire that is not suited for their voice. Even singers who sing at a world-class level (performers at the Metropolitan Opera, for instance) find miscalculations in repertoire selection to be vocally hazardous or even career-threatening. By the same logic, it follows that no matter how talented and knowledgeable the teacher is in assisting the singer in establishing a technical foundation through vocalises, the same teacher can hamper the student's rate of development or even tear down the technique he or she helped the student acquire by assigning inappropriate literature. Secure technique, good health habits, *and* singing the proper repertoire are the keys to a long, successful career as a singer. It is the teacher's task to carefully choose repertoire that ensures success and progress, at the same time that it challenges, but does not defeat, the student.

Many criteria must be considered when choosing repertoire for singers. These criteria fall into four broad categories: the physical limitations of the singer, the voice classification of the singer, expressive/emotional factors, and musicianship skills. Depending on the type of student—beginning, intermediate, advanced, or professional—these criteria take on differing levels of importance. For the beginning singer, physical limitations and voice classification issues are paramount; for intermediate, advanced, or professional singers, emotional factors and musicianship skills also become important.

The first category, physical limitations, includes three considerations: the age of the student, the length of time the student has been studying, and the individual technical problems the student is experiencing. Age is important in understanding what state the singer's instrument is in developmentally. For example, the larynx of a forty-year-old male singer is capable of performing tasks that few eighteen-year-old larynxes can manage. A young male singer does not have the laryngeal or extrinsic muscular stability to withstand a long piece with a high tessitura like an older singer can. The laryngeal cartilages of a forty-year-old are also less flexible than those of a teenager, which increases the stability of the laryngeal framework.

So, consider the physical maturation of the singer: Is he or she physically mature enough for the demands of the piece? The length of study is also important. How long has this singer been training his or her muscles and mind for the act of singing? How established are certain technical habits? How long has he or she been studying with the same teacher? Again, consider the case of the eighteen-year-old student and the forty-year-old student. What if the teenager has been studying voice for several years, while the forty-year-old singer is a beginner? The younger singer would be developmentally less stable than his or her older counterpart, but he or she would probably be more technically advanced with regards to some aspects of singing, having had more instruction in breath management, for instance. Finally, what technical issues is this singer dealing with?

For example, does he or she have difficulties with a register bridge? If so, assigning a piece that repeatedly traverses the troublesome bridge might be of limited use in the studio as a technical exercise, but it would not be a good piece for the student to perform publicly. Are certain vowels or consonants especially easy or troublesome? A female student who is reticent to sufficiently open her mouth for higher pitches needs pieces with such open vowels as [a] on the high notes before she ever tackles pieces that feature the closed front vowel [i] on high notes. Is the student capable of managing his or her breath skillfully throughout a long phrase? If not, finding repertoire that has phrases of various lengths and frequent rests may be necessary until the proper *appoggio* is acquired. Is the student in transition from a lower voice classification to higher one? Finding repertoire that features descending phrases might help such a student access the newer, less familiar light mechanism in a musical context. At the risk of stating the obvious, helping the student succeed in making a free sound is the first priority.

The second category to be considered in repertoire selection, voice classification, includes the following considerations: the pitch location of register bridges in the singer's voice, the tessitura of the voice, the timbre of the voice, and range. The first two considerations, the location of register bridges and tessitura, are widely considered to be the most accurate ones to use in determining voice classification, although all factors deserve consideration. Relating these factors to repertoire selection, it is essential that a teacher have accurate information about the location of each student's register bridges when selecting repertoire. Assigning a student a piece that has a great deal of full-voiced singing immediately below a major bridge can invite a singer, particularly a less-experienced one, to carry a heavy production higher than is optimal. This is one reason why young tenors and sopranos should not be given arias by verismo composers, which frequently feature such full singing in the upper middle voice. Young singers typically do not cope well with a sustained high tessitura, as has been previously mentioned. Pieces with a wide range and that contain passages requiring agility but have few high sustained phrases are often more effective repertoire choices until muscular stability and endurance increase.

Vocal timbre must also be considered. A singer's unique timbre is the result of several factors, including vocal tract length, the amount of vocal fold adduction used during singing, the thickness of the vocal fold mucosa, prior training, and personal preference. Timbre is often important in determining subclassifications within a voice category, and, as such, it plays a crucial role in revealing a stage character's personality. For example, a singer with the register bridges, tessitura, and range of a lyric coloratura but who has a warm timbre might find the soubrette roles (like Susanna, Zerlina, Despina) to be a better fit for her voice than a singer who possesses a brighter timbre. In a similar fashion, a tenor with a brilliant timbre would find "Sound an Alarm" from

Judas Maccabeus by Handel much more congenial for his voice than a darker-voiced colleague would trying to sing the same piece. The singer's timbre must match the style of the music and the text; however, because of the many factors that influence timbre, teachers should be careful when assigning repertoire to not assume that a darker timbre means that the student is a lower voice type, nor should they assume a bigger voice is a heavier voice.

Finally, pieces selected for a singer must match that student's range. This means not only the obvious "you need a high A and a low C to sing all the notes in this piece," but also the context of the notes: How are the extremes of the piece approached? By leap or by step? Are they part of a scale pattern or rolled over in an arpeggio? How long are the crucial notes? Are they staccato, or are they whole notes? Is the high or low note isolated, or are there several high notes in quick succession? What vowels are set on the crucial notes? Pieces that have high notes on the low first formant vowels [i], [I], [u], [ʊ], and [e] tend to work better for male singers than female singers, as such vowels require significant modification in the upper octave of the female voice. What consonants are paired with those vowels on the high and low notes? Voiced consonants can be quite problematic on high pitches. Are most of the phrases ascending or descending, or is there a good balance between the two? Ascending phrases invite a singer to bring weight up, while descending phrases help a singer blend the lighter mechanism downward. And last, is the text set in a syllabic or melismatic fashion in the *passaggio* and at the extremes?

For more information on registers and classification schemes, readers may find the following sources helpful: pages 72–81 of the fourth edition of Meribeth Bunch's *Dynamics of the Singing Voice* (1997); pages 99–136 of Richard Miller's *English, French, German, and Italian Techniques of Singing* (1977); pages 195–198 of the second edition of Barbara Doscher's *The Functional Unity of the Singing Voice* (1994); pages 78–79 (paragraphs 277–284) of William Vennard's *Singing: The Mechanism and the Technic* (1967); and pages 169–178 of Ingo Titze's *Principles of Voice Production* (1994).

Expressive and emotional factors, the third category, include such considerations as the emotional maturity of the singer, the singer's temperament or personality, and the singer's personal preferences with regard to styles of music and poetry. At eighteen, few singers, no matter how vocally gifted they may be, can draw upon life experiences to understand and fully appreciate the *Kindertotenlieder* of Mahler. A middle-aged mother of two might find studying these same songs an overwhelming emotional experience. Along these same lines, however, a sensitive singer in his twenties and a singer of fifty might find John Duke's setting of "Loveliest of Trees" equally enjoyable, although each might offer very different perspectives on the poetry.

Temperament is also an important factor in repertoire selection. Some types of music and poetry demand a forthright, visceral, assertive presentation, while others require a subtle, intellectual approach. Few shy, retiring personalities would emotionally connect with performing Bill's "Soliloquy" from *Carousel*, for example, while the same singers might find lute songs from the late Renaissance quite rewarding.

Finally, all singers have particular types of music and poetry that they enjoy performing. Singers tend to sing most expressively those musical styles that they like the most. These personal preferences are based upon a host of musical and extramusical factors—a mathematically inclined student may be attracted to the ornate structure of Bach's vocal music, for instance, while another singer who grew up in a deeply religious family might find gospel music and spirituals satisfying. In any case, it cannot be stated strongly enough that accurate discernment of these criteria depends upon the singer and the teacher building a long-term relationship of trust and mutual understanding. Through such a relationship and careful observation, a teacher can fine-tune his or her selections to match the student's maturity, personality, and likes and dislikes.

The final category, musicianship skills, concerns the ability of the singer to negotiate the composer's instructions accurately and clearly deliver the text. Beginning singers typically need literature that is predictable in terms of melody, harmony, rhythm, dynamics, and articulation. At this stage of development, making their voices accurately respond to their brains' commands is difficult enough; combining good body use, breathing, and phonation with a musical idea is quite a challenge. Beginners need not be overwhelmed with awkward intervals, dissonant harmonies, and odd rhythms, nor should they be asked to sing too softly or too loudly. Scalar or triadic-based melodies, clear harmonies, and simple dance rhythms sung at a healthy mezzo-forte dynamic are the road to success. By the same logic, beginners are best served by texts that are in their native language. As technical proficiency is acquired, more demanding literature in other languages can be approached. Still, each student must be treated individually. There are those singers who are gifted with fine instruments and excellent techniques who are not strong musicians or have difficulty with delivering a foreign language. There are also a number of singers who have the opposite problem, that is, they possess great sight-reading skills, perfect pitch, outstanding tonal memory, an excellent sense of rhythm, and have a knack for languages, yet they struggle with a lesser natural endowment or severe technical issues. In either case, the overriding commandment to know the student's strengths and weaknesses and select repertoire that will give them the best chance for success must be obeyed.

At the beginning of this article, the well-known aria "Deh vieni, non tardar" was mentioned. Looking through Susanna's solo with the aforementioned considerations in mind, we can now systematically examine the challenges this aria holds for singers. We can also begin to answer the question of whether it is appropriate for an undergraduate soprano like our hypothetical singer, Debbie.

On a physical limitations level, the age of the singer is important in this piece. It is a long aria for a young singer. There are many extended phrases throughout the middle range at a slow tempo. The accompanying texture is thin, so any problems in the singer's voice will be exposed; however, the singer must be of an age where she can be believable as a young maid. Thus, a balance must be struck between a singer who is vocally stable enough to handle the long phrases and exposed texture and a singer young enough to be accepted as the character. The length of study is also a factor. A beginning singer rarely possesses an even enough scale or has the breath management skill to sing the phrases of this aria. In terms of technical problems the piece poses, the tessitura and exposed phrases require the singer to have a fine middle voice; the register bridges between chest/middle voice and middle/head voice must be seamless. There are a number of nasal consonants preceding vowels on higher pitches, especially in measure 14 ("non venite il mio diletto"), measure 31 ("Deh vieni"), measure 37 ("Finchè non splende"), and measures 64, 68, and 70 ("incoronar"). Most singers must deemphasize the amount of nasal coupling and duration of nasals on higher pitches. There are numerous instances of low first-formant vowels in the text being set on higher pitches, particularly in measure 12 ("Timide cure"), measures 14 and 31 again, measure 41 ("bruna e il mondo"), and measure 46 ("ruscel qui scherza"). In each case, these vowels have first formants that are up to one octave below the written pitch. The singer must modify the vowel to match the first formant with the fundamental pitch to reinforce the fundamental and maintain an even dynamic level.

The next category to consider in our systematic approach is voice classification issues: How might these issues clarify what kinds of singers should perform "Deh vieni"? There are a number of crucial notes in the melodic line that are on or near register bridges. These important notes, in particular F#4, B4 (the leading tone of the dominant key), and F5 (the tonic), must have precise intonation for melodic and harmonic reasons. Yet, it is these same notes that can often be problematic to sing with good intonation because of their proximity to register bridges, especially for singers with larger voices. Teachers must be sensitive to this when assigning this aria to singers with intonation difficulties just above the chest voice/middle voice bridge, and just below and in the upper *passaggio*. The tessitura of the recitative is slightly lower than the aria; the recitative centers around Bb4, while the aria sits around C5. The singer must be comfortable with singing for several minutes in this middle region of her voice. In terms of timbre, the aria needs a voice that is warm in color, yet light in weight. Susanna's humanity and youthfulness are revealed as much through this vocal aspect as they are through Da Ponte's text or Mozart's melodic line. As for range issues, the aria encompasses two octaves, from A3 to A5. This is a wide range for any singer, especially a beginning-level student. The lowest note is approached by step and is at the end of a phrase, while the highest note is approached by a leap of a major third and is in the middle of an arching phrase. While there are many sustained F5s, the high A5 is only an eighth note in duration. Although the vowel on the highest note is /ɑ/, there are a number of closed vowels on high pitches, as was previously mentioned. Finally, the text is generally set in a syllabic fashion, except for the passages approaching and leaving the climatic A5.

We now come to the third category, expressive and emotional factors. "Deh vieni" needs a singer who is emotionally mature enough to understand love and marriage, yet youthful enough to portray innocence in a credible fashion. The role calls for a quick-witted, lively personality; this is made apparent in this otherwise andante aria through the energetic opening lines of the recitative, especially in the accompaniment. After the recitative, the aria requires the singer to spin out a lovely Mozartean line. To do this, one must truly enjoy the classical period style of melodic writing and enjoy sharing that love for an elegant line with an audience.

The final category, musicianship skills, includes musical and textual aspects. The aria opens with a *recitativo accompagnato*. As many Mozart scholars have pointed out, a character's personality is more clearly revealed in the orchestrally accompanied recitatives than in the secco recitatives. In this recitative, the singer must find a way to show Susanna's pert nature, while gradually slowing down the tempo to more closely match the tempo of the aria. This subtlety of pacing and inflection only comes with experience. On a positive note for younger singers, the melodic line is triadic. There are only a few crucial chromatic notes outside of the basic harmony. There are several wide leaps, however, including 6ths, 7ths, and even one minor 9th. In general, the wider intervals are descending intervals rather than ascending. Less experienced singers need to be careful to not overshoot the lower note of each wide leap. The aria is solidly diatonic and begins in F major; after briefly modulating to the dominant, it returns to F. The accompaniment is generally supportive and subordinate to the vocal line.

Rhythmically, the singer first has to find the proper balance between free running speech inflection and a notated melody to render the recitative correctly. This is a skill that takes time and experience with the Italian language to perfect. In the aria itself, there are no major rhythmic challenges; the line rocks along in a gentle 6/8 meter. Care must be taken in measures 63 and 67 on the word *fronte* to not overstress the last syllable of the word, due to the stepwise rise in the melodic line on this syllable and the dotted eighth-sixteenth-eighth rhythm.

Dynamically, finesse is required in shaping the long phrases, especially at the end of the aria, where there are several crucial sustained notes. The singer must strike a balance between singing at a high enough dynamic level to "make" the long phrases in terms of breath and not losing subtlety in the process.

Textually, the singer needs a good command of Italian diction. Care must be taken with double consonants; Da Ponte is notorious for stringing several words with double consonants in a row, as in "senza affanno in braccio all'idol mio." There are also other Italian challenges—singing several vowels that share the same note, for instance, as we find in measures 40 and 41: "finchè l'aria è ancor bruna, e il mondo."

Finally, there is the issue of being expressive in another language. "Deh vieni" is in Italian, not English. Hence, young American singers have a foreign language to deal with when singing this aria in its original language. Some young singers and teachers might be tempted to listen to a number of recordings and copy what Italian native singers do. While this can be valuable in terms of understanding performance traditions, mimicking what a native does on a recording is not being expressive, it is being a parrot. A young singer must understand why the words may be shaded in a particular way and how such shading changes the meaning of the words before he or she can be truly expressive. As was stated earlier, beginning singers first need to learn how to be expressive while singing their own language. With experience and language study, they can begin to transfer this skill into other literature outside of their native tongue.

This process may seem tedious and overly methodical to some readers. It is methodical and systematic, but such caution saves time and heartache in the long run. There is an old saying in the carpentry trade that a good craftsman measures the piece of wood twice before cutting; then he only has to cut it once. The same is true with vocal repertoire selection: It is better to be methodical and assign literature for students only after much patient deliberation; getting it right the first time is much easier and effective than trial and error.

In conclusion, we return to Debbie and her struggles. Given what has been revealed about the potential pitfalls of a casual approach to repertoire selection, even in an aria as familiar as "Deh vieni," it becomes clear that if she is assigned pieces based upon what her teacher remembers singing at that age, Debbie will succeed in proportion to the amount her voice resembles her teacher's voice at that age. Every student is unique. It is poor judgment for a teacher to assume that experiences they had as young singers were typical or similar to those their students are currently dealing with. If, however, Debbie is assigned pieces based upon a careful examination of the aforementioned criteria, she stands a much better chance of succeeding—and with success comes the motivation to continue to study voice and learn new and challenging pieces.

REFERENCES

Bunch, Meribeth. *Dynamics of the Singing Voice*. New York: Springer, 1997.

Doscher, Barbara. *The Functional Unity of the Singing Voice*, 2nd ed. Metuchen, NJ: Scarecrow Press, 1994.

Miller, Richard. *English, French, German, and Italian Techniques of Singing*. Metuchen, NJ: Scarecrow Press, 1977.

Titze, Ingo. *Principles of Voice Production*. Englewood Cliffs, NJ: Prentice Hall, 1994.

Vennard, William. *Singing: The Mechanism and the Technic*. New York: Carl Fischer, 1967.

Tenor **John Nix** is associate professor of voice pedagogy at the University of Texas at San Antonio (UTSA), coordinator of the Vocal Area for the 2011–2014 academic years, and founding director of the UTSA Vocal Arts Laboratory. He was previously on the staff of the National Center for Voice and Speech in Denver, where he worked with Ingo Titze. Nix has also served on the music faculties of the University of Colorado at Denver and Eastern New Mexico University. He holds degrees in arts administration from Florida State University and vocal performance from the University of Georgia and the University of Colorado at Boulder, and as well as a certification in vocology from the University of Iowa. At the University of Colorado, he studied voice and pedagogy with the late Barbara Doscher and the Alexander Technique with James Brody.

Nix's current and former students include a member of the Mormon Tabernacle Choir; two Santa Fe Opera apprentices; members of the Army Soldiers' Chorus; a second-place winner in the National Federation of Music Clubs competition; a two-time finalist in the American Traditions competition; and faculty members at universities in Montana, Texas, Wyoming, and New York. UTSA students of his have gone on to win graduate fellowships to such institutions as Indiana University. Nix's work has been funded by the San Antonio Area Foundation, the Grammy Foundation, and UT-San Antonio, and he has received two R-13 grants from the National Institutes of Health. Nix was the 2006 winner of the National Association of Teachers of Singing (NATS)/Voice Foundation Van Lawrence Award.

Nix's published articles have appeared in the *NATS Journal*, the *New York Opera Newsletter*, *Otolaryngology–Head and Neck Surgery*, the *Journal of Voice*, the *Journal of Singing*, the *International Journal of Research in Choral Singing*, *Vocalease*, *Australian Voice*, and the *Opera Journal*. He is editor and annotator of *From Studio to Stage: Repertoire for the Voice*, compiled by Barbara Doscher (Scarecrow Press, 2002); vocal music section editor for *The Oxford Handbook of Music Education* (2011); and a general editor and author for *The Oxford Handbook of Singing* (2012).

Reprinted with permission of Dr. Richard Sjoerdsma, editor-in-chief. *The Journal of Singing*, Jan./Feb. 2002, Vol. 58, No. 3.

Practicing 101: Ten Tips for Making the Most of Your Time between Lessons

Dean Southern

The old anecdote has been told a thousand times and in at least as many versions—a New York cabbie (or Heifitz or Rubinstein) is stopped by a tourist on the street and asked, "How do you get to Carnegie Hall?" The reply: "Practice, practice, practice!" While the wisdom of this little joke is obvious, the reality for singers is that they often don't know how to practice efficiently or effectively. By the time they enter college, most violinists, pianists, and other instrumentalists have been working on their instruments in solitude for ten or more years; however, many singers first learned to use their instruments in their school choirs, and the prospect of practicing on their own can be mystifying.

Success in singing, like almost any worthwhile endeavor, is dependent on individual discipline, self-sacrifice, and hard work. In *Vocal Wisdom*, the legendary pedagogue Giovanni Battista Lamperti is quoted as saying,

> "Know thyself" applies to singer more than to other professions, because to sing well, body, soul, and mind are tuned together to do it. The only things you can learn from others are to breathe slowly, and deeply, to pronounce correctly and distinctly, and to listen intensely and carefully. The coordination of these three must come from yourself. Know thyself.[1]

Where does one gain this knowledge? In the practice room.

The following tips are intended as a guide to getting the maximum benefit from your practice time. By gradually implementing these suggestions, your practicing will become more efficient, more effective, and more enjoyable.

1. Schedule your practice time. The cornerstone of steady, measurable progress is consistent, regular practice, and, conversely, the consequence of practicing in fits and spurts is uncertainty; therefore, the first thing you should think at the start of each day is, "When am I going to practice?" Plan your practice time as you would your work or class schedule, and stick to it. In addition, try to practice at optimal times, rather than leaving it until the end of the day, when you are physically and mentally exhausted.

2. Make the practice room your sacred space. Learning to concentrate is the key to good singing, and you cannot learn to concentrate if you are distracted. E-mails, phone calls, and texts can wait, so put away your laptop, and turn off your cell phone, iPhone, or Blackberry while you are practicing. Be sure that your practice space allows you the privacy to sing and experiment with your voice freely. Singing while driving your car is unsafe and does not count as practicing.

3. Set goals for your practice session. When you enter the practice room, have specific goals in mind, both large and small. Larger goals are those that stay with you each time you practice, for example, learning to sing as effortlessly and expressively as possible. Smaller goals might include giving specific attention to various physical aspects of your singing (alignment, breath, neck, jaw, tongue, etc.). Or maybe you learn the pitches and rhythms of a new piece on a single vowel, while trying to master the diction, phrasing, or dramatic understanding of another.

4. Use your lesson as a blueprint for your practicing. In addition to making suggestions and correcting errors, your teacher is showing you how to practice. Assume that what you do in your lesson is what you should do in the practice room. Recreate what you and your teacher accomplish in your lesson by repeating the process on your own; make it part of your regular behavior, and apply it to other aspects of your singing. If you are studying with a new teacher, ask him or her about continuing to use old vocal exercises and practice habits; what worked before may not be as useful now.

5. Start over every day. One of the most important things about being a singer is the ability to find your voice every day. It is tempting to start your practice session with the tonal and physical memory of where you ended on the previous day, but this can lead to vocal fatigue and frustration.

6. Warm up gradually. Singers are breath athletes. As with any athletic activity, it is important to slowly stretch the muscles of your body and, thus, your instrument. Sing for a couple of minutes in a comfortable range and then stop, resuming a few minutes later. This gradual procedure is essential to your vocal health, and exercising your voice in this way will help you avoid bad habits and physical tension. Your endurance and stamina will eventually increase as the muscles of your instrument become stronger, more limber, more responsive, and more finely coordinated.

7. Set limits for time spent singing and divide it up throughout the day. While the singing voice is a miraculous and resilient mechanism, its physical limitations are real and should be taken seriously. For that reason, practice as much as you can every day without becoming vocally fatigued. Opinions vary, but it is generally accepted that the maximum one should spend singing in one day is two hours. Otherwise, the muscles of the vocal apparatus fail to function as efficiently, and you run the risk that your singing will not be as healthful. Divide your practice time into increments of twenty or thirty minutes throughout the day, and have the discipline to stop, even when "it feels good." This ensures that your brain remains alert and that any resulting vocal fold swelling has the opportunity to subside.

8. Break your music up into manageable sections. One of the main purposes of practicing is to build muscle coordination, which varies depending upon what you are singing. Especially with new repertoire, your brain will be able to send the proper commands to the body more effectively if it is sending a limited number of commands at a time. You can only remember so much, so try practicing each phrase of a song or aria separately until it is accurate and easy. Then progressively put phrases together until you can sing the whole piece with ease, confidence, and the ability to think ahead. In the long run, this will be much more successful than singing the piece in its entirety every time you practice it. Another useful method is to practice the final phrase first and then work back to the beginning phrase by phrase.

9. Find effective ways of practicing without singing. While singers cannot beneficially sing for the same number of hours as their instrumental counterparts practice, there are limitless nonsinging activities that will contribute to your success. For example, with the various languages in which singers are expected to communicate effectively, language study is a never-ending subject to which one's time can be devoted. Likewise, song and aria texts can be examined and deconstructed repeatedly to find ever deeper layers of meaning and nuance. Studying a variety of audio and video recordings of your pieces from different eras can provide you with a wealth of musical information; they connect you to the legacy of performance traditions and help you develop your own musical values and interpretations. By miming your repertoire, you can routine almost all of the physical and mental activities involved in singing without actually phonating. This can be done endlessly without costing you any vocal capital. It will train your brain to send the proper signals and create positive muscle memory. A good rule of thumb is think ten times, sing once. These types of activities are especially useful if you have lengthy choir, opera, or other rehearsals during a particular day.

10. Memorize your music deliberately and early, and review it often. Effective memorization is not something that happens accidentally; it takes conscious effort. Rather than memorizing your piece by mindlessly singing it over and over again, try writing the text repeatedly on a piece of paper. Memorize the meaning of foreign-language texts while you memorize the pronunciation. Don't put off memorizing your music; the longer you sing it from memory, the more secure you will be. In addition, review your score constantly to keep details of the music freshly in mind.

Learning to practice is an integral part of learning to sing. An improved ability to practice will result in greater personal satisfaction in the practice room, as well as greater confidence and success on the stage.

NOTE

1. Giovanni Battista Lamperti, *Vocal Wisdom: Maxims of Giovanni Battista Lamperti*, enlarged ed. Transcribed by William Earl Brown. Edited by Lillian Strongin (New York: Taplinger Publishing, 1957), p. 32.

REFERENCES

Lamperti, Giovanni Battista. *Vocal Wisdom: Maxims of Giovanni Battista Lamperti*, enlarged ed. Transcribed by William Earl Brown. Edited by Lillian Strongin. New York: Taplinger Publishing, 1957.

Baritone **Dean Southern** has performed in opera, oratorio, and recital throughout the United States and Europe, including Carnegie Hall's Weill Recital Hall in New York, Kennedy Center in Washington, D.C., and the Festival dei Due Mondi in Spoleto, Italy. His students have been accepted to prestigious young artist programs and graduate schools and awarded the Fulbright grant, and they have gone on to successful careers as performers and voice teachers. Southern regularly gives master classes at universities and conservatories in the United States and abroad, including the Kungliga Musikhögskolan (Royal College of Music) in Stockholm, Sweden, the Conservatorio Profesional de Música in Valencia, Spain, and the Interlochen Arts Academy in Michigan. Since 2004, he has spent his summers on the faculty of the American Institute of Musical Studies in Graz, Austria, where he teaches voice and gives the Henry Pleasants lecture series on historic singers.

Southern is author of the "Distant Voices" column in *Classical Singer* magazine. The magazine has also published several of his articles, including "Practicing 101: Ten Tips for Making the Most of Your Time between Lessons" and the three-part series "Distant Voices: Listening to Singers of the Past." He frequently presents "Distant Voices: Listening to Singers of the Past"—a multimedia, guided tour through the first half-century of recorded vocal history—at colleges, universities, and arts organizations throughout the United States.

Southern is a graduate of Luther College, in Decorah, Iowa, and he holds master's degrees in piano performance from the University of Missouri as a student of Jane Allen, and in voice performance from the University of Akron as a student of Clifford Billions. He earned the doctor of musical arts degree in voice performance at the Cleveland Institute of Music, where he studied with the noted pedagogue Mary Schiller.

From 2008–2012, Southern was assistant professor at the University of Miami Frost School of Music in Coral Gables, Florida, where he taught voice pedagogy and served as stage director for the Frost Opera Theater. He was appointed to the faculty of the Cleveland Institute of Music in 2012.

Originally appeared in the September 2009 issue of *Classical Singer* magazine, Sara Thomas, editor.

Coping with Musical Performance Anxiety

Heather Winter Hunnicutt

There are many terms used for that phenomenon that makes singers freeze in their concert heels or run from the stage with tux tails in tow: stage fright, nervousness, panic attack, butterflies in the stomach, and a vast assortment of other colloquial labels. No matter what the teacher or student may call it, music performance anxiety (MPA), a state of apprehension, uncertainty, and fear resulting from the anticipation of a realistic or fantasized threat in the context of musical performance, is widespread, normal, and manageable with the right strategies for the effected singer.

While a singer experiencing the debilitating symptoms of MPA may feel that he or she is the center of some cosmic conspiracy to prevent their success, the truth that every performer and teacher must understand is how common the problem really is. While numerous publications spout different statistics, the lowest published prevalence rates are in the 80 percent range,[1] and some studies report that as many as 90.6 percent of performers face this issue.[2] It occurs at all levels of musicianship, as well as all ages, ethnicities, and genders.[3] Actually, musicians are more prone to mood disorders than the general population, making MPA particularly likely among singers.[4] You are far from alone. In fact, those who experience no anxiety about performing are the atypical singers.

"Why is this happening to me?" is a common and fair question, and the answer is simple: because anxiety is useful, even helpful. But before you throw this book across the room in response to that notion, consider this: MPA is a result of our bodies' natural "fight or flight" response.[5] Our bodies are brilliantly efficient in their daily functions as the various systems communicate with one another to protect and preserve. The "fight or flight" response refers to how the body jumps into overdrive for maximum energy and strength in response to a threat. It's how a mother suddenly becomes capable of lifting a car off of her infant, how a hiker is able to outrun a mountain lion, and how a child can

pull their unconscious parent from a burning building. Mental health professionals call the car, mountain lion, or fire that is able to provoke a nearly superhuman body response the "fear stimulus." In the case of MPA, the fear stimulus is the performance itself or various individual aspects connected to it, for instance, the audience, particular individuals in the audience, fear of failure, fear of success, fear of lack of adequate preparation, fear of uncontrollable variables in the performance, etc.

The human body's nervous system is made up of the central nervous system (the brain and spinal cord) and the peripheral nervous system (all other nerves and connections). The peripheral nervous system uses conscious control over the somatic nervous system and unconscious control over the autonomic nervous system. In the unconscious autonomic nervous system, the parasympathetic division is responsible for sedate activities like digestion or breathing. The other division of the autonomic nervous system is called the sympathetic division, and it is responsible for the invocation of fight or flight. Through one or more of the five senses, the brain perceives the existence of the fear stimulus and quickly communicates that presence to the brain. The brain instantly responds by giving the body fuel to go full throttle in the form of epinephrine (adrenaline). The brain sends the order to the endocrine system for the adrenal gland to send out its fuel into the nervous system, which it does, where alpha and beta receptors throughout the body receive it and respond accordingly. The result is usually an elevated heart rate, rapid respiration, internal temperature change, extra gastrointestinal activity, and, most important, the brain sending strong messages that say "fight" (stay and deal with the situation) and/or "fly" (run away).

So, while the body's reaction that prompts MPA may be inconvenient and frustrating when it interferes with your ability to perform to the best of your ability, you will be thankful for it the next time you have a car headed toward you at 60 miles per hour and have to quickly get out of its path. This is why it is perfectly normal to experience MPA. It's your body backing you up and protecting you. Now it simply becomes a matter of harnessing that fuel in a constructive manner rather than a counterproductive one.

Each person experiences the symptoms of MPA in a different way because our bodies and brains are so varied. While one person may sweat like crazy, another may have a body that looks as cool as a cucumber, but his or her mind is racing a mile a minute. On a broad level, symptoms of MPA are divided into three types: physical, cognitive, and behavioral.[6] Physical symptoms are what your body involuntarily does as a response to increased adrenaline: sweaty palms, upset stomach, numbness in the extremities, shaking hands or knees, dilated pupils, shallowness of breath, etc. Cognitive symptoms are involuntary thoughts that the brain concocts as a response to adrenaline: feelings of inadequacy, contemplating worst-case scenarios, discounting the positives, etc. Behavioral symptoms are usually the most difficult to understand. These manifestations are actions that one voluntarily takes, but the choice to adopt those actions is strongly influenced by the anxiety one is feeling: avoiding practicing, stopping mid-song, postponing a performance, binge eating when unsatisfied with the product, self-medicating with alcohol and illicit drugs, etc.

The level to which performers experience MPA also varies and is divided into three tiers: mild, moderate, and severe. Mild is adaptive and increases arousal for better performance. Moderate is normal but maladaptive, and the individual could benefit from self or professional help. Severe, as we will discuss in more detail later, is a psychological condition requiring professional intervention. Severe symptoms are defined as those so debilitating that a performance cannot be accomplished without intervention, and roughly 14 to 16 percent of individuals who experience MPA fall into the severe category.[7] These levels can be applied to the different types of symptoms and overall symptomatology of the individual. For example, John Doe might have mild behavioral symptoms (maybe once a month after a bad voice lesson he puts off practicing) and cognitive symptoms (he occasionally engages in overly negative self-talk), but also severe physical symptoms (when performing, his body goes into a mode where he is sweating through his shirt, his breathing is so fast that he can't sustain phrases, his heart rate is so elevated that his vibrato nearly doubles its normal speed, and his neck is so tense that he can't achieve any of the freedom in his sound that he regularly achieves in the practice room). Most individuals have some combination of two or all three types of symptoms.[8] For mild and moderate symptoms, self-help and educational interventions (help from the teacher or other nonmedical professionals) is usually sufficient to tame symptoms to a manageable level. For an individual experiencing severe symptoms, the help of a medical professional (usually a psychologist and/or psychiatrist) should be sought.

For the severe cases, there are a number of tactics that mental health professionals may choose to employ in treatment. Pharmaceutical approaches can be extremely effective for those with moderate to severe physical symptoms, and certain medicines can also help lessen cognitive symptoms. Various beta blockers (Inderal, Propranolol, etc.) work by preventing much of the body's reuptake of adrenaline. By regulating how much adrenaline the body is working with, beta blockers mitigate the symptoms caused by the overproduction of adrenaline in the fight or flight response. Different forms of tranquilizers/sedatives (Xanax, Valium, Ativan, etc.) work by slowing down the central nervous system; however, because of the nondiscriminatory way in which they dull overall energy levels, they can be a highly counterproductive choice for individuals who are not off the charts in terms of anxiety levels. Antihistamines (Vistril, Atarax, etc.) may occasionally be considered for their sedative effects, but these are generally not a good choice for singers, as they are very dehydrating. Longer-term pharmaceutical possibilities include selective serotonin reuptake inhibitors (Prozac, Paxil, Celexa, Zoloft, etc.) and serotonin and norepinephrine reuptake inhibitors (Effexor, Cymbalta, Pristiq, etc.). These treatments are most often used for individuals with depression, generalized anxiety, and other mood disorders because they work to restore normal levels of chemicals at work in the brain during a period of weeks, months, or years. Because individuals with severe MPA often have high generalized anxiety levels as well, this can be a useful treatment. These are off-label but common uses for these prescriptions.

Medications are often paired with psychotherapy of some sort, or psychotherapy may be employed without additional medication. Psychotherapy generally involves multiple sessions of retraining the brain to be more reasonable in performance or daily life situations. Cognitive behavior therapy (CBT) is an approach that has perhaps the most science and statistics behind it for this purpose.[9] CBT has three main components within its process: skills training, cognitive restructuring, and exposure and response prevention. The skills training segment incorporates such principles as relaxation training, breathing retraining, thought stopping, taming distractions, positive imagery, and the use of coping cards. Cognitive restructuring is a process of retraining the brain by identifying maladaptive cognitions when they occur and replacing them with adaptive ones. Exposure and response prevention is a system during which the individual is slowly desensitized to the fear stimulus in a safe environment.

For the majority of singers experiencing MPA, however, approaches that do not involve a mental health professional are highly effective. In determining the right way to personally manage MPA, the singer must first determine what characterizes his or her own case. First, determine what your specific fear stimuli are. What is it that provokes the MPA response in you? Is it wondering what your peers will think?

Is it that you want to be a successful singer so badly that you think every performance is "do or die"? Is it that you are afraid of forgetting the words? Is it that you are worried about whether your teacher will think you did a good job? Once you can identify exactly what about the performance sends you into fight or flight, you can hone in on making adjustments to those areas.

Next, determine how MPA manifests itself in you. Make a list of everything that happens to you. Do your hands freeze up so that you can't even feel them? Do you keep telling yourself that you are going to forget your French text? Do you contemplate over and over again how to get out of singing in that master class? Do you have an image of yourself in your head tripping over your dress and falling on your face? Are you unable to hold phrases as long as you can in the practice room? Write your symptoms down on paper. Now rewrite the list, dividing it into types of symptoms: hands freezing = physical symptom, convincing yourself that you are going to forget the French = cognitive symptom, trying to edge out of performing in a master class = behavioral symptom.

Once you have divided up your symptoms, take a good look at where they fall. Give yourself a rating in each category of mild, moderate, or severe, and give yourself an overall score in one of those three tiers. Then have someone who knows you and your singing well (a teacher or friend) score you from an outsider's perspective. Do you have a reasonable view of your own symptoms, or do you see things differently than someone outside your own head does?

Now you know where to focus most of your efforts. Perhaps you have discovered that you have lots of physical symptoms and a few cognitive because your fear stimuli are connected to worrying that you are ill-prepared for performances. Then you know that you will always have to overprepare for each performance to mitigate those symptoms, and that beta blockers might be the next step because they can selectively reduce the siege of adrenaline in your body. Knowing more about your MPA, you can now choose the best management methods for you. There are many methods out there—some concentrating more on the physical, others more on the cognitive—and each can be quite effective depending upon the individual. Some of these include meditation, the Alexander Technique, coping cards, flooding, graded task assignments, systematic desensitization, and cognitive restructuring at an educational level.

As previously mentioned, MPA is widespread, with as many as 90.6 percent of musicians experiencing it. It is a normal response, because it is a natural reaction of the body that is both useful and protective. And it is manageable. With an understanding of what is happening and why, that excess energy can be refocused on a more useful purpose of creating a powerfully energized and creative performance.

NOTES

1. E. A. Plaut, "Psychotherapy of Performance Anxiety," *Medical Problems of Performing Artists* 5, no. 3 (1990): 28–36.

2. Wendy J. Cox and Justin Kenardy, "Performance Anxiety, Social Phobia, and Setting Effects in Instrumental Music Students," *Journal of Anxiety Disorders* 7, no. 1 (1993): 55.

3. Alice G. Brandfonbrener, "An Overview of the Medical Problems of Musicians," *Journal of American College Health* 34, no. 2 (1986): 165–69.

4. Diane K. Miller and Judith R. F. Kupersmith, "Louisville-PACH: Psychiatric Problems of Performing Artists," *Medical Problems of Performing Artists* 5, no. 1 (1990): 19–22.

5. R. May, *The Meaning of Anxiety* (New York: Norton & Company).

6. Paul Salmon, "A Psychological Perspective on Musical Performance Anxiety: A Review of the Literature," *Medical Problems of Performing Artists* 5, no. 1 (1990): 2–11.

7. J. L. Abel and K. T. Larkin, "Anticipation of Performance among Musicians: Physiological Arousal, Confidence, and State-Anxiety," *Psychology of Music* 18, no. 2 (1990): 171–82.

8. Heather Nicole Winter, "Predicting the Unpredictable: A Guide for the Voice Teacher to Diagnose Various Types of Musical Performance Anxiety in Voice Students and a Plan for Effective Treatment" (DM document, Indiana University, 2006), 10–18.

9. Duncan B. Clark and W. Stewart Agras, "The Assessment and Treatment of Performance Anxiety in Musicians," *American Journal of Psychiatry* 148, no. 5 (1991): 598–605; Margaret J. Kendrick, Kenneth D. Craig, David M. Lawson, and Park O. Davidson, "Cognitive and Behavior Therapy for Musical Performance Anxiety," *Journal of Consulting and Clinical Psychology* 50, no. 3 (1982): 353–62; Julie Jaffee Nagel, David P. Himle, and James D. Papsdorf, "Cognitive-Behavioral Treatment of Musical Performance Anxiety," *Psychology of Music* 17, no. 1 (1989): 12–21.

REFERENCES

Abel, J. L., and K. T. Larkin. "Anticipation of Performance among Musicians: Physiological Arousal, Confidence, and State-Anxiety." *Psychology of Music* 18, no. 2 (1990): 171–82.

Brandfonbrener, Alice G. "An Overview of the Medical Problems of Musicians." *Journal of American College Health* 34, no. 2 (1986): 165–69.

Clark, Duncan B., and W. Stewart Agras. "The Assessment and Treatment of Performance Anxiety in Musicians." *American Journal of Psychiatry* 148, no. 5 (1991): 598–605.

Cox, Wendy J., and Justin Kenardy. "Performance Anxiety, Social Phobia, and Setting Effects in Instrumental Music Students." *Journal of Anxiety Disorders* 7, no. 1 (1993): 55.

Kendrick, Margaret J., Kenneth D. Craig, David M. Lawson, and Park O. Davidson. "Cognitive and Behavior Therapy for Musical Performance Anxiety." *Journal of Consulting and Clinical Psychology* 50, no. 3 (1982): 353–62.

May, R. *The Meaning of Anxiety*. New York: Norton & Company.

Miller, Diane K., and Judith R. F. Kupersmith. "Louisville-PACH: Psychiatric Problems of Performing Artists." *Medical Problems of Performing Artists* 5, no. 1 (1990): 19–22.

Nagel, Julie Jaffee, David P. Himle, and James D. Papsdorf. "Cognitive-Behavioral Treatment of Musical Performance Anxiety." *Psychology of Music* 17, no. 1 (1989): 12–21.

Plaut, E. A. "Psychotherapy of Performance Anxiety." *Medical Problems of Performing Artists* 5, no. 3 (1990): 28–36.

Salmon, Paul. "A Psychological Perspective on Musical Performance Anxiety: A Review of The Literature." *Medical Problems of Performing Artists* 5, no. 1 (1990): 2–11.

Winter, Heather Nicole. "Predicting the Unpredictable: A Guide for the Voice Teacher to Diagnose Various Types of Musical Performance Anxiety in Voice Students and a Plan for Effective Treatment." DM document, Indiana University, 2006.

DEMOGRAPHIC INFORMATION

Name (your name will never be printed in published materials and will only be used for the primary researcher's reference): _____

Gender: _____

Age on date of performance event: _____

Number of years studying voice: _____

Age when starting musical instruction of any kind: _____

Current degree program: _____

Anticipated completion of degree (date): _____

Voice type/part: _____

Number of professional performances given (approximate): _____

Number of total performances given (approximate): _____

Medical conditions affecting respiratory or vocal function (asthma, etc.): _____

_____

_____

Number of alcoholic drinks per day/week/month: _____

Use of recreational drugs: _____

Blood pressure or anxiety medication(s): _____

Professional plans/career goals: _____

_____

_____

MPA QUESTIONNAIRE: FIVE-POINT SCALE QUESTIONS

For the following questions, please answer with a number between 1 and 5, 1 meaning "strongly disagree," 2 meaning "disagree," 3 meaning "undecided" or "neutral," 4 meaning "agree," and 5 meaning strongly agree." Circle the appropriate number.

I have perfect pitch/absolute pitch.	1	2	3	4	5
I have strong relative pitch.	1	2	3	4	5
I consider myself to be a good musician.	1	2	3	4	5
I learn music easily.	1	2	3	4	5
I memorize easily.	1	2	3	4	5
My voice teacher and I have a good relationship.	1	2	3	4	5
I am critical of myself in my lessons.	1	2	3	4	5
I am critical of myself in my practicing.	1	2	3	4	5
I enjoy performing more than most activities.	1	2	3	4	5
I tend to get sick when a performance is nearing.	1	2	3	4	5
I am a healthy person.	1	2	3	4	5
My diet is healthy.	1	2	3	4	5
I get enough sleep on a regular basis.	1	2	3	4	5
I exercise regularly.	1	2	3	4	5
I regularly drink enough water to support my body and voice.	1	2	3	4	5
I deal with stress well.	1	2	3	4	5
I am stressed more often than I should be.	1	2	3	4	5
I am a generally anxious person.	1	2	3	4	5
People who know me would say I am an anxious or stressed person.	1	2	3	4	5
I feel like I belong at this school.	1	2	3	4	5
I feel like I belong in my teacher's studio of students.	1	2	3	4	5
I feel comfortable in my teacher's voice studio.	1	2	3	4	5
I feel comfortable singing in front of my colleagues.	1	2	3	4	5
My teacher believes in me and my voice.	1	2	3	4	5
My family believes in me and my voice.	1	2	3	4	5
I believe in me and my voice.	1	2	3	4	5
My teacher understands my musical goals.	1	2	3	4	5
My teacher understands who I am as a person.	1	2	3	4	5
I am a confident singer.	1	2	3	4	5
I am a confident performer.	1	2	3	4	5
I am easily distractible.	1	2	3	4	5
I easily maintain my focus when singing.	1	2	3	4	5
I easily maintain my focus when practicing.	1	2	3	4	5
I easily maintain my focus when performing.	1	2	3	4	5
Staying focused during a performance can be a struggle.	1	2	3	4	5

I believe I will have a good audience turnout for my performance.	1	2	3	4	5
As a child, I was a natural performer.	1	2	3	4	5
I consider myself to be a natural performer.	1	2	3	4	5
Those who know me would consider me to be a natural performer.	1	2	3	4	5
I am sometimes down or depressed.	1	2	3	4	5
I am often down or depressed.	1	2	3	4	5
I like who I am as a person.	1	2	3	4	5
I like who I am as a singer.	1	2	3	4	5
I am a good singer.	1	2	3	4	5
I am a physically attractive person.	1	2	3	4	5
Others consider me to be a physically attractive person.	1	2	3	4	5
I have a good relationship with my family.	1	2	3	4	5
I have good relationships with my friends.	1	2	3	4	5
I am involved in a long-term romantic relationship.	1	2	3	4	5
I am involved in a short-term romantic relationship.	1	2	3	4	5
I am happy with my romantic relationship.	1	2	3	4	5
I date regularly.	1	2	3	4	5
I sometimes have low self-esteem.	1	2	3	4	5
I often have low self-esteem.	1	2	3	4	5
I have other activities I take part in and enjoy aside from singing.	1	2	3	4	5
A career as a professional singer is important to me.	1	2	3	4	5
A career in music is very important to me.	1	2	3	4	5
I prefer performances to auditions.	1	2	3	4	5
Auditions make me nervous.	1	2	3	4	5
I consider myself to be a perfectionist.	1	2	3	4	5
Those who know me well would consider me to be a perfectionist.	1	2	3	4	5
I am a competitive person by nature.	1	2	3	4	5
I am now competitive because of my career plans.	1	2	3	4	5
I enjoy a challenge.	1	2	3	4	5
I enjoy a competition.	1	2	3	4	5
I tend to have anxiety about performances.	1	2	3	4	5
I tend to have anxiety about auditions.	1	2	3	4	5
My teacher fully understands my performance anxiety.	1	2	3	4	5
Only a small percentage of singers will actually sing for a living.	1	2	3	4	5
I am disheartened by the odds for success as a singer.	1	2	3	4	5
I believe that, even if I don't sing for a living, I will be happy.	1	2	3	4	5
Singing is my top priority.	1	2	3	4	5
I consider myself to be a religious or spiritual person.	1	2	3	4	5
I regularly attend religious services.	1	2	3	4	5
I believe that a higher power is looking out for me.	1	2	3	4	5

I believe that things happen for a reason.	1	2	3	4	5
I believe that I choose what happens in my own life.	1	2	3	4	5
I believe that much of my life has already been decided for me.	1	2	3	4	5
I have complete control over the course my career takes.	1	2	3	4	5
I have too little control over the course my career takes.	1	2	3	4	5
I like to be in control.	1	2	3	4	5
I feel uncomfortable if I don't have enough control.	1	2	3	4	5
I feel uncomfortable if I have too much control.	1	2	3	4	5
I deal well with conflicts.	1	2	3	4	5
I am a nonconfrontational person.	1	2	3	4	5
My family and friends come to support me during my performances.	1	2	3	4	5
I have a good support system in my family and/or friends.	1	2	3	4	5
There are people who care about me succeeding as much as I do.	1	2	3	4	5
I have a plan for combating any performance anxiety I might experience.	1	2	3	4	5
I have a method for coping with stress that works.	1	2	3	4	5
I plan too much for myself.	1	2	3	4	5
I am good about setting boundaries and not taking on too much.	1	2	3	4	5
I have personally experienced performance anxiety in my life.	1	2	3	4	5
I have personally experienced performance anxiety in the recent past.	1	2	3	4	5
I used to get nervous but don't tend to do that anymore.	1	2	3	4	5
I am an introverted individual.	1	2	3	4	5
I am an extroverted individual.	1	2	3	4	5
I fear the future.	1	2	3	4	5
I am a positive thinker.	1	2	3	4	5
I'm often negative.	1	2	3	4	5
Important people will be at my performances.	1	2	3	4	5
I am embarrassed by my nervousness.	1	2	3	4	5
I get physical symptoms when I'm nervous.	1	2	3	4	5
I get emotional symptoms when I'm nervous.	1	2	3	4	5
Nervousness is negatively affecting my vocal progress.	1	2	3	4	5
I am driven to do my best.	1	2	3	4	5
My quality of performing/singing is consistent.	1	2	3	4	5
I start new projects with lots of energy.	1	2	3	4	5
I fear success.	1	2	3	4	5
I function well at a high energy level.	1	2	3	4	5
I am able to quiet mental chatter.	1	2	3	4	5
I frequently imagine the worst.	1	2	3	4	5
I need to learn how to relax.	1	2	3	4	5
No matter how much I prepare, something always goes wrong.	1	2	3	4	5

Soprano **Heather Winter Hunnicutt, DM**, serves on the faculty of Georgetown College as chair of the Music Department, associate professor of voice, coordinator of vocal studies, and director of the Lyric Theatre Program. She teaches applied voice, voice pedagogy, lyric diction, and music education courses, and directs the opera workshop and full-scale operas. She received undergraduate, graduate, and doctoral degrees in voice from the Indiana University Jacobs School of Music. Her various research, speaking, and singing endeavors have taken her to such cities as Bangkok, Paris, Salzburg, Munich, Honolulu, Philadelphia, and Minneapolis. Professional memberships include the National Association of Teachers of Singing (NATS), College Music Society, National Association of Music Education, National Opera Association, and Mu Phi Epsilon. Winter Hunnicutt completed the NATS Intern Program in the summer of 2009, at Shorter College in Rome, Georgia.

What Every Singer Needs to Know about Audio Technology

Matthew Edwards

Each generation encounters unique challenges in the pursuit of a singing career. In 1892, Louis Lombard commented on the lack of skilled European instructors to provide proper training in the United States.[1] In 1937, voice teacher Marcia Davenport wrote in the *Saturday Evening Post* about the lack of nonacademic training programs and limited opportunities outside of the Metropolitan Opera.[2] The modern singer no longer struggles with those challenges. Our conservatories are now recognized as some of the world's finest, and there are numerous opportunities outside of the Metropolitan Opera, as well as a plethora of professional training programs. Academia has also evolved and now includes programs that specialize in musical theatre, jazz, and commercial music. While training opportunities are less of a concern than before, the technological revolution has produced a new hurdle to overcome. The modern singer must now face the reality of an increasing reliance on live sound enhancement and a growing tendency to modify recorded performances.

Audio technology is hardly new; singers were facing the challenges of the microphone as early as 1925.[3] At first, the microphone was isolated to recording studios and radio stations. It was quickly incorporated into live performance, beginning with big-band music, and then eventually found its way into rock and roll and musical theatre.[4] Now, technology is found in nearly all performance venues. Rock artists tour with systems capable of remembering unique sound designs for each individual song.[5] Broadway shows utilize sound systems that rival those in use by major pop/rock touring acts.[6] Even the Metropolitan Opera has begun to incorporate audio technology in its HD broadcasts, utilizing equalization, compression, and reverb to enhance the sound captured by the microphones.[7] The twenty-first-century singer, whether classical or contemporary commercial music (CCM), will work with audio equipment at some point during their career.

Performers can make sounds on a microphone that may sound unpleasant without one and vice versa; therefore, it is becoming increasingly important for the singing teacher to integrate audio equipment into the teaching studio. For the reader who is focused on performing and not teaching, it is still beneficial to become familiar with basic sound equipment to retain control over the final product. The following information is intended to give you a basic knowledge of the elements you are most likely to encounter as a singer and/or teacher.

SIGNAL CHAIN

The path an audio signal travels from input to output of a sound system is called the signal chain. The singer's voice enters the signal chain through a microphone, which transforms the acoustic energy of the singing voice into electrical impulses. The electrical impulses generated by the microphone are sent through a series of components that modify the signal before the speakers transform it back into acoustic energy. Audio engineers possess a thorough understanding of the intricacies of these systems. With their knowledge, they are capable of making a nearly infinite variety of alterations to the original signal. While some engineers strive to replicate the original sound source as accurately as possible,[8] others use the capabilities of the system to alter the sound for artistic effect.[9] There are additional components and variations available to engineers that cannot be discussed in just a few pages. The components described here are found in most of the systems you will encounter and serve as a great starting point for understanding the basics of audio technology.

MICROPHONES

As previously mentioned, the microphone is the first element in the signal chain. The three most common types of microphones a singer will encounter are dynamic, condenser, and ribbon. Each of these offers various advantages and disadvantages that make them ideal for different settings and uses. Before we discuss the various types of microphones, let us first look at the basic specifications you should understand.

Frequency Response

Frequency response is a term used to define how accurately the microphone captures the original audio spectrum. Alterations to the audio spectrum of a singer's voice can potentially alter the singer's timbre.[10] Therefore, understanding this aspect of audio technology is not only important for amplifying live performances and capturing recordings, but also for obtaining and interpreting acoustic measurements in scientific research.

A "flat response" microphone captures the original signal with little to no signal alteration. These microphones are also sometimes called measurement mikes because they are ideal for situations where accurate measurements of the audio signal are required. Most microphones that are not designated as "flat" have some type of cut or boost within the audio spectrum. For instance, the Shure SM58 cuts the signal drastically below 300 Hz and boosts the signal in the 3-kHz range by 6 dB, the 5-kHz range by nearly 8 dB, and the 10-kHz range by approximately 6 dB (see figure 1). The Oktava 319 cuts the frequencies below 200 Hz, while boosting everything above 300 Hz with nearly 5 dB between 7 kHz and 10 kHz (see figure 1). In practical terms, recording a bass with the Shure SM58 would drastically cut the amplitude of the fundamental frequency, while the Oktava 319 would produce a slightly more consistent boost in the range of the singer's formant. Both of these options could be acceptable depending upon the needs of the singer being recorded, but they must be considered before making the recording.

Amplitude Response

The amplitude response of a microphone can vary depending upon the angle at which the singer is positioned in relation to the axis of the microphone. To visualize the amplitude response of a microphone at various angles, microphone manufacturers publish polar pattern diagrams (sometimes called a directional pattern or pickup pattern). Polar pattern diagrams usually consist of six concentric circles divided into twelve equal sections. The center point of the microphone's diaphragm is labeled "0°" and is referred to as "on-axis," while the opposite side of the diagram is labeled "180°" and is described as "off-axis."

Although polar pattern diagrams are drawn in two-dimensions, they actually represent a three-dimensional response to acoustic energy.[11] The outermost circle of the diagram indicates that the sound pressure level of the signal is transferred without any amplitude reduction, indicated in decibels (dB). Each of the inner circles represents a –5 dB reduction in the amplitude of the signal up to –25 dB. For example, look at figure 2. If the microphone's response circle crossed point A on this diagram, we would know that the strength of the signal at that point would be reduced by 10 dB. The examples in figure 3 show the most common polar patterns.

When you are using a microphone with a polar pattern other than omnidirectional (a pattern that responds to sound equally from all directions), you may encounter frequency response fluctuations, in addition to amplitude fluctuations. Cardioid microphones, in particular, are known for their tendency to boost lower frequencies at close proximity to the sound source, while attenuating those same frequencies as the distance between the sound source and the microphone increases. This is known as the "proximity effect." Some manufacturers will notate these frequency response changes on their polar pattern diagrams by using a combination of various lines and dashes alongside the amplitude response curve.

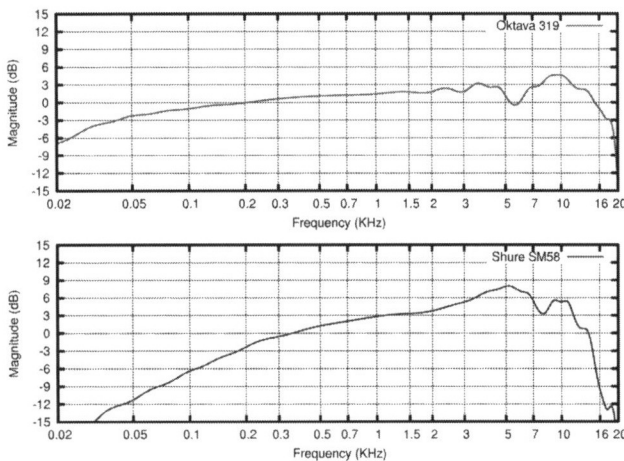

Figure 1. Frequency Response Graphs for the Oktava 319 and Shure SM58. *Courtesy Creative Commons.*

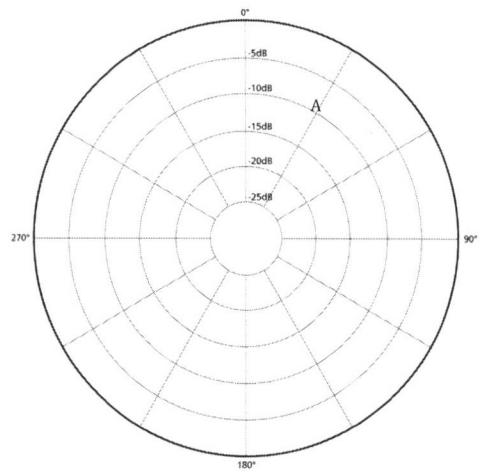

Figure 2. An example of a microphone polar pattern diagram. *Courtesy Creative Commons.*

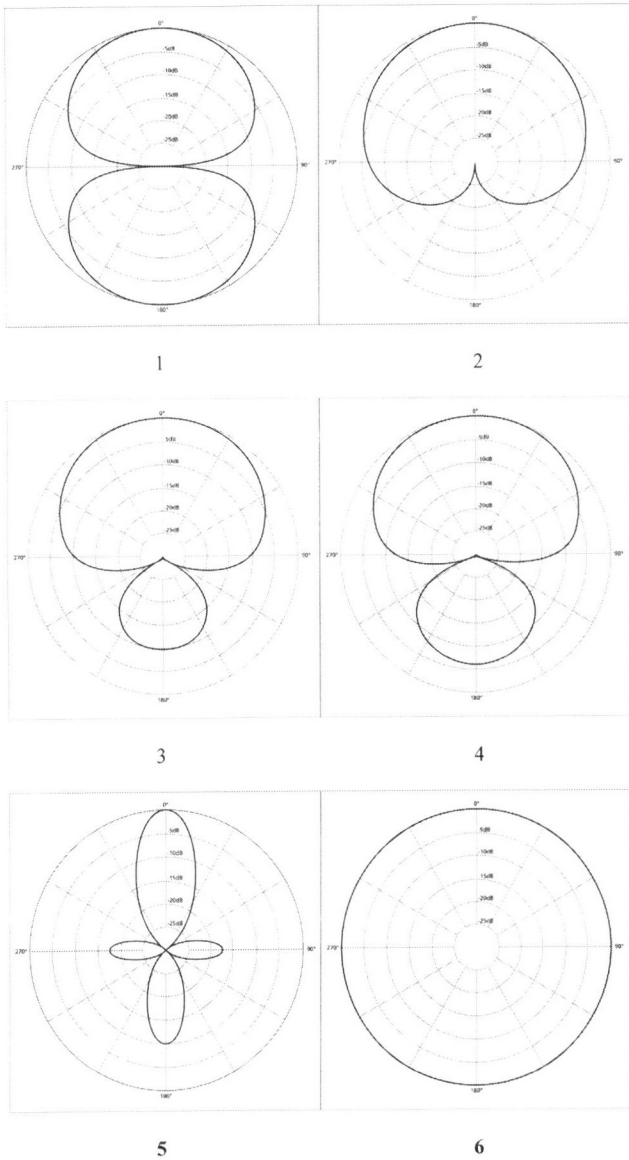

Figure 3. Diagram 1 represents a bidirectional pattern; diagram 2 represents a cardioid pattern; diagram 3 represents a supercardioid pattern; diagram 4 represents a hypercardioid pattern; diagram 5 represents a shotgun pattern; and diagram 6 represents an omnidirectional pattern sensitivity. *Courtesy Creative Commons.*

Sensitivity is difficult to explain without going into an in-depth discussion of electricity and electrical terminology. Microphones are tested with a 1-kHz tone at 94 dB to determine how sensitive the microphone's diaphragm will be to acoustic energy. Microphones with greater sensitivity can be placed farther from the sound source without excessive noise in the signal. Microphones with lower sensitivity will need to be placed closer to the sound source to keep excess noise at a minimum. When shopping for a microphone, you should audition several microphones next to one another with the same volume settings. As you sing on each microphone, the sensitivity variations will become clear.

Microphone Types

When choosing a microphone, you will not only need to make a choice about which polar pattern you want (omni-directional, cardioid, etc.), but you will also need to specify what type of diaphragm you will need. Singers will most often encounter three basic diaphragm types: dynamic, condenser, and ribbon.

Dynamic

Dynamic microphones use a Mylar diaphragm, moving within a magnetic field, to turn acoustic vibrations into an electrical signal that can be amplified. The industry standard for live performance is the Shure SM58. These microphones are affordable, nearly indestructible, and easy to use. Dynamic microphones have a lower sensitivity than condenser microphones and are proficient at avoiding feedback. This feature makes them an excellent choice for rock singers who must deal with a high level of stage noise when performing; however, this feature is largely because their ability to amplify sound quickly dissipates with distance. Therefore, softer voiced singers (i.e., crooners) often sing with their lips touching or barely touching the metal screen to achieve their optimal tone. At louder dynamic levels, you want to create some distance between yourself and the microphone, but usually no more than three to four inches.

Condenser

Condenser microphones use two electrically charged, thin metal plates separated by a layer of insulation to transform acoustic sound into an electrical signal. As acoustic vibrations send the anterior metal plate into motion, the distance between the two plates varies, which creates an electric signal that is then sent to the amplifier. The magnets in a standard condenser microphone are powered by a system called "phantom power." Phantom power is a component of the soundboard that sends a forty-eight-volt power supply through the microphone cable to the microphone's diaphragm to power the magnetic field. If you are planning to use a condenser microphone, be sure that your sound system or recording console supplies phantom power.[12] Without a power source, standard condenser microphones will not work. There are also microphones on the market called electret condenser microphones that do not require phantom power. Electret microphones are usually found in smaller systems. These microphones contain a permanently charged magnetic element within the diaphragm, thus eliminating the need for an external power source. Head mounted microphones, laptop computers, and smart phones all utilize electret condenser microphones.

Condenser microphones are the microphones of choice for recording applications due to their high level of sensitivity. They are also sometimes used by jazz and folk singers, as well as in head-mounted microphones on Broadway.

With a condenser microphone, performers can sing at nearly inaudible levels acoustically to create a final tone that is intimate and earthy. The same vocal effects can be produced with a dynamic microphone, but not with the same clarity of a condenser.

Ribbon

Ribbon microphones utilize a thin metal ribbon placed between two magnets to capture acoustic vibrations. When the ribbon is set into motion by the sound source, the magnetic field is altered, creating an electric signal. Ribbon microphones of the past were easily broken and failed to gain the same popularity as condenser and dynamic microphones; however, recent advances in technology have enabled manufacturers to develop products that are more durable, causing ribbon microphones to experience a boost in popularity. It is important to never use phantom power with a ribbon microphone. The phantom power signal will ruin the microphone and often void the warranty.

EQUALIZATION

Equalizers are components that enable the engineer to alter the audio spectrum of the sound source. While many classical singers spend considerable time learning about spectral analysis, formant tuning, and acoustics to alter their timbre, audio engineers are able to make tone adjustments with a few simple tweaks on an equalizer. Equalizers come in three main types: shelf, parametric, and graphic.

Shelf

Shelf equalizers allow you to cut or boost the uppermost and lowermost frequencies of an audio signal in a straight line (see figure 4). While this style of equalization (EQ) is not very useful for fine-tuning a singer's tone quality, it can be effective in removing room noise. For instance, if there is an air conditioner creating a 60 Hz hum in the recording studio, the shelf can be set at 65 Hz, with a steep slope. This setting would only allow frequencies above 65 Hz to be heard, which would eliminate the hum from the recording.

Parametric

Parametric units allow the engineer to control the center frequency of the area to be adjusted, the amount of cut or boost applied to the area, and the width of frequencies to be covered within the bell curve surrounding the center frequency, called the "Q" (see figure 5). These controls are usually found on the individual channels of live performance soundboards since they take up a minimal amount of space and offer sufficient control for most situations. They can also be found on control boards in recording studios.

With the advent of digital workstations, engineers can now use computer software to fine-tune the audio quality of each individual channel in both live and recording studio settings. Still, many engineers prefer to use the parametric controls, as they are easier to adjust throughout the course of a performance, and they are usually sufficient for experienced artists with a high level of vocal ability.

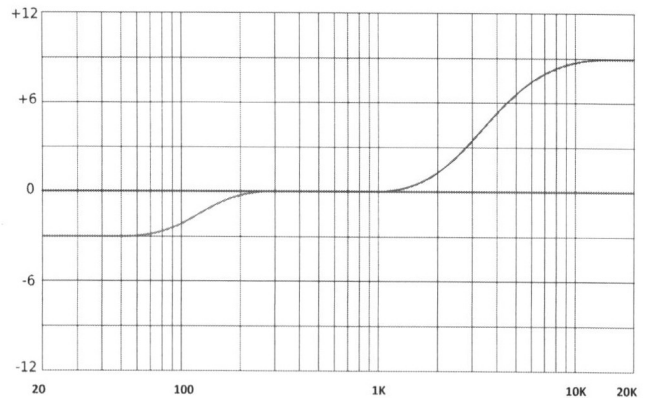

Figure 4. The frequency amplitude curves above show the effect of applying a shelf EQ to an audio signal. *Courtesy Creative Commons.*

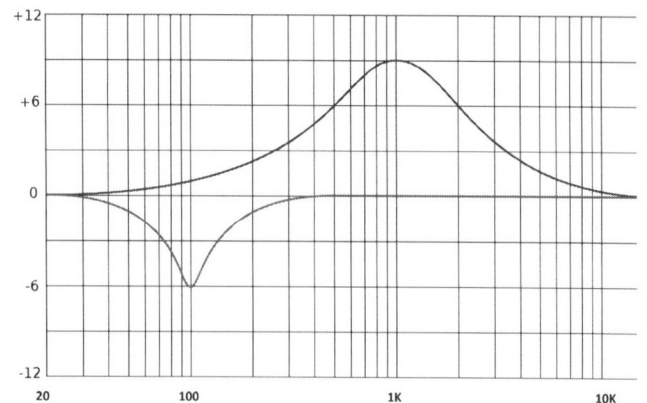

Figure 5. The frequency amplitude curves display two parametric EQ settings. The top curve represents a boost of +8 dB set at 1 kHz with a relatively large bell curve—a low Q. The lower curve represents a high Q set at 100 Hz with a cut of 6dB. *Courtesy Creative Commons.*

Graphic

Graphic equalizers allow engineers to specify a specific frequency for boost or cut with a fixed frequency bandwidth. On a ten-band equalizer, the typical frequencies include (in Hz) 31, 63, 125, 250, 500, 1 k, 2 k, 4 k, 8 k, and 16 k. Graphic equalizers are often the third-to-last element in the signal chain of a live system, preceding the amplifier and speakers. In this position, they can be used to adjust the overall sound quality of the entire mix.

Utilizing Equalization

Opinions on the usage of EQ vary amongst engineers. Some engineers believe that EQ should only be used to remove or reduce frequencies that were not part of the original signal, while others only use EQ when adjustments in microphone placement have failed to yield acceptable results. Engineers seeking a processed sound may use EQ quite liberally to intentionally change the vocal quality of the singer. For instance, if the singer's voice sounds dull, the engineer could add "ring" or "presence" to the voice by boosting the equalizer in the 2- to 10-kHz range. Using EQ to its full effect, a singer can easily brighten or darken their voice as needed in the studio or live performance without resorting to vocal constriction.

COMPRESSION

CCM singers often use a wide variety of vocal colors and volume levels in their performance. When using amplification, this can prove problematic for the sound team since dramatic volume shifts require adjustments at the soundboard. To help solve this problem, engineers often use a component called compression.

Compressors limit the output of a sound source by a specified ratio. The user sets a maximum acceptable amplitude level for the output called the "threshold." The user then sets a ratio to reduce the output once it surpasses the threshold. The typical ratio for a singer is usually between 3:1 and 5:1. A 4:1 ratio indicates that for every 4 dB beyond the threshold level, the output will only increase by 1 dB. For example, if the singer went 24 dB beyond the threshold with a 4:1 ratio, the output would only be 6 dB beyond the threshold level (see figure 6).

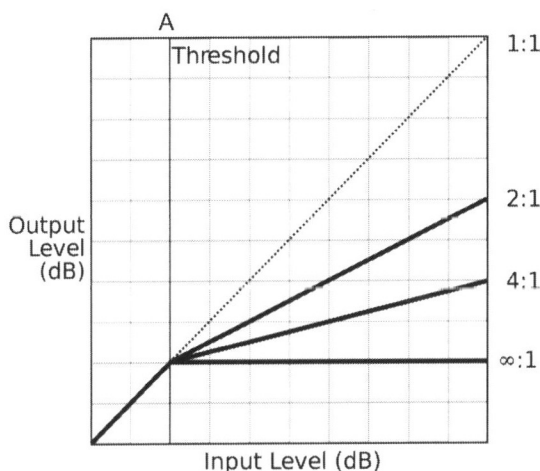

Figure 6. A representation of the effects of various compression ratios applied to a signal. The 1:1 angle represents no compression. The other ratios represent the effect of compression on an input signal with the threshold set at line A. *Courtesy Creative Commons.*

Microphone technique can provide some of the same results and is preferable for the experienced artist; however, compression tends to be more consistent and gives the singer freedom to focus on performing and telling a story. This additional freedom is ideal for musical theatre performers, singers using head-mounted microphones in performance, and those new to performing with a microphone. Compression can also be helpful for classical singers whose dynamic abilities can be impressive live, but often difficult to record in a manner that allows for consistent listening levels through a stereo system.

MULTIBAND COMPRESSION

If a standard compressor causes unacceptable alterations to the tone quality, engineers can turn to a multiband compressor. Multiband compressors allow the engineer to isolate a specific frequency range within the signal and set an individual compression setting for that range. For instance, if a tenor's placement creates a dramatic boost in the 4-kHz area every time he sings above an A4, a multiband compressor can be used to limit the signal only in that part of the voice. By setting a 3:1 ratio in the 4-kHz area at a threshold that corresponds to the amplitude peaks that appear when the performer sings above A4, the engineer can eliminate the forward placement from the sound on only those notes that are offensive, while leaving the rest of the signal untouched. These units are available for live and studio use and can be a great alternative to compressing the entire signal.

REVERB

Reverb is one of the easier effects for singers to identify. Natural reverb occurs when the audience hears the direct signal from the singer, and then milliseconds later, they hear the voice again as it is reflected off the sidewalls of the performance hall. In many CCM venues and recording studios, the spaces are designed to inhibit natural reverb. Without at least a little reverb, even the best singer can sound harsh and even amateurish. Early reverb units sent the audio signal through a metal spring, which added supplementary vibrations to the sound. While some engineers still use spring reverb to obtain a specific effect, most now use digital units. Common settings on digital reverb units include wet/dry, bright/dark, and options for delay time. The wet/dry control adjusts the amount of direct signal (dry) and the amount of reverberated signal (wet). The bright/dark control helps simulate the effects of various surfaces within a natural space. For instance, harder surfaces, such as stone, create a brighter tone quality, while softer surfaces, such as wood, create a darker tone quality. The delay time, which is usually adjustable from milliseconds to seconds, adjusts the amount of time between when the dry signal and wet signal reach the ear. Engineers can transform almost any room into a chamber music hall or concert stadium by adjusting the various settings.

AUTO-TUNE

Auto-Tune has gained a bad reputation in the last few years. It was first used in studios as a useful way to clean up minor imperfections in otherwise perfect performances; however, it has now turned into an industry standard that many artists use, even if they are not willing to admit it.[13] Whether or not a singer or teacher agrees with the use of Auto-Tune, it is a reality in today's market, and it must be understood.

The two primary developers of Auto-Tune technology are Antares and Melodyne. Auto-Tune comes in two types: "auto" and "graphical." "Auto" Auto-Tune allows the engineer to set specific parameters for pitch correction that are then computer controlled. "Graphical" Auto-Tune tracks the pitch in the selected area of a recording and plots the fundamental frequency on a linear graph. The engineer can then select specific notes for pitch correction. They can also drag selected pitches to a different frequency, add or reduce vibrato, and change formant frequencies above the fundamental.

While this may sound like cheating to some classical vocal artists, it must be mentioned that even the Metropolitan Opera uses its own version of Auto-Tune. Engineers at The Met record the rehearsals leading up to the final HD broadcast. If a singer misses a high note or makes any other mistake during the broadcast performance, the engineers will take the recording from the rehearsal and splice it into the final mix before releasing it commercially.[14]

DIGITAL VOICE PROCESSORS

Digital voice processors are still relatively new to the market and have yet to gain widespread usage among singers. Although several brands of vocal effects processors are available, the industry leader as of this printing is a company called TC-Helicon. TC-Helicon manufactures several different units that span from consumer to professional grade. TC-Helicon's premiere performer controlled unit is called the VoiceLive 3. The VoiceLive 3 incorporates more than twelve vocal effects, eleven guitar effects, and a multi-track looper with 250 factory presets and 250 memory slots for user presets. The VoiceLive 3 puts the effects at the singer's feet in a programmable stomp box that also includes phantom power, MIDI in/out, a USB connection, guitar input, and monitor out. Onboard vocal effects include equalization, compression, reverb, and "auto" Auto-Tune. The unit also offers μMod (an adjustable voice modulator), a doubler (for thickening the lead vocal), echo, delay, reverb, and several other specialized effects.

One of the most impressive features of these units is the ability to add computer-generated harmonies to the lead vocal. The processor identifies the fundamental frequency and then adds digitized voices at designated intervals above and below the lead singer. The unit also offers the option to program each individual song with specific settings for every verse, chorus, and bridge.

THE BASICS OF LIVE SOUND SYSTEMS

Live sound systems come in a variety of sizes, from small practice units to state-of-the-art stadium rigs. Most singers only need a basic knowledge of the components commonly found in systems with one to eight inputs. Units beyond that size usually require an independent sound engineer and are beyond the scope of this chapter.

Following the microphone, the first element in the signal chain is usually the mixer. Basic portable mixers provide controls for equalization, volume level, auxiliary (usually used for such effects as reverb and compression), and, on some units, controls for built-in digital effects processors. Mixers are available in powered and unpowered units. Powered mixers combine an amplifier with a basic mixer, providing a compact solution for those who do not need a complex system. Unpowered mixers do not provide amplification; when using these systems, it is necessary to add a separate amplifier to power the speakers.

The powered mixer or amplifier then connects to speaker cabinets, which usually contain, at a minimum, a "woofer" and a "tweeter." The "woofer" is a large round speaker that handles the bass frequencies, while the "tweeter" is a horn-shaped speaker[15] that handles the treble frequencies. The frequencies are separated and sent to the appropriate speaker (woofer or tweeter) by a device called a crossover. Speaker cabinets come in two forms: active and passive. Passive cabinets require a powered mixer or an amplifier to operate. Active cabinets have a built-in amplifier and do not require an external amplifier.

Perhaps the most important element of the live sound system for a singer is the monitor. A monitor is a speaker that faces the singer and allows them to hear their voice through the system as they perform. Onstage volume levels can vary considerably, with drummers often producing sound levels as high as 120 dB. For the singer, these volume levels make it nearly impossible to receive acoustic feedback while performing. Just as a classical singer is prone to pushing in a poor acoustic environment, so are CCM singers. Monitors can improve aural feedback and reduce the urge to oversing. Powered monitors offer the same advantages as powered speaker cabinets and can be a great option for amplification in the private studio, for practice, and as a backup plan for singers performing in venues that do not supply monitors. In-ear monitors are another option for performers; however, research has shown that there is little to no reduction in the preferred listening level of performers. Thus, they offer little benefit in regards to hearing safety.[16]

CONCLUSION

As an undergraduate conservatory student, most of my colleagues and professors viewed audio enhancement with great disdain. Various professors talked about the great singers of the past and the lack of such singers in our generation, as well as the preceding one. Perhaps singers and teachers of older generations have always lamented the loss of the great singers of the past, while criticizing the youngest generation of rising stars. In the nineteenth century, Giovanni Lamperti defined what he believed to be the "Golden Age of Song," the period when Bellini, Donizetti, and Rossini were still composing.[17] In 1937, voice teacher Marcia Davenport recalled such great singers as Emma Eames and Geraldine Farrar of the early twentieth century, who were "polished, mature, and seasoned," unlike young singers of the 1930s, who she believed were "coddled" and were "wasting their time."[18] Voice teachers of the 1930s also criticized popular crooners of their era. Teachers considered crooners to be a "perversion of the natural production of the singing voice," and they accused crooners of singing in a style that was "injurious to the voice," with "words and sounds of the gutter."[19] By 1958, Frank Sinatra, one of the original crooners, was testifying in front of Congress about the "most brutal, ugly, desperate, vicious form of expression it has been my misfortune to hear"—rock and roll.[20] Clearly, these types of debates have existed for many decades, possibly even centuries, and they are not going away.

Whether we approve of it or not, audio enhancement is here to stay. Just as prior generations have adapted and evolved with the marketplace, so must our generation. While we may long for the talents and performance practices of the past, the reality is that our culture is evolving faster than ever. Due to the Internet and the abundant opportunities for consumers and producers to gain mass-media attention,[21] the public now plays a greater role in determining which artists succeed and which do not. As we, the teachers, increase our knowledge of audio technology, we can adjust our teaching and improve our dialogue with those on the other side of the operating board. If we combine our efforts with these highly skilled professionals, we can capture recordings and enhance live performances in a manner that truthfully represents the talents of the singer. For those who desire a manufactured sound, we, as teachers, can assist them in achieving such sounds without causing vocal damage. While the task may seem daunting, it is our duty to our students and, for singers, their duty to themselves, to learn about this technology and embrace it.

NOTES

1. Irving Lowens and Louis Lombard, "Louis Lombard's 'Our Conservatories,'" *American Music* 3, no. 3 (1985): 347–51.

2. Marcia Davenport, "What Makes a Singer?" *Saturday Evening Post*, 11 December 1937, 20–21, 83–88.

3. Paula Lockheart, "A History of Early Microphone Singing, 1925–1939: American Mainstream Popular Singing at the Advent of Electronic Microphone Amplification," *Popular Music and Society* 26, no. 3 (2003): 367–85.

4. Elizabeth L. Wollman, *The Theatre Will Rock: A History of the Rock Musical* (Ann Arbor: University of Michigan Press, 2006).

5. S. Benzuly, "Sir Paul McCartney Tour Profile," *MixOnline.com*, 1 September 2011, http://mixonline.com/live/tourprofiles/sir_paul_mccartney_tour/ (accessed 21 June 2012).

6. Gaby Alter, "Broadway Sound: Four Shows, Four Dramatically Different Designs," *Mix*, October 2009, 46–49.

7. Gary Eskow, "Opera Hits a High Note with High-Tech Broadcasts," *MixOnline.com*, 1 April 2008, http://mixonline.com/post/features/audio_new_yorks_met/ (accessed 21 June 2012).

8. For instance, refer to recordings by such artists as Joss Stone and Bonnie Raitt.

9. For example, listen to "Pumped Up Kicks," as performed by Foster the People, or " Believe," by Cher.

10. K. Omori, A. Kacker , L. M. Carroll, W. D. Riley, and S. M. Blaugrund. "Singing Power Ratio: Quantitative Evaluation of Singing Voice Quality." *Journal of Voice* 10, no. 3 (1996): 228–35. Available online at www.ncbi.nlm.nih.gov/pubmed/8865093 (accessed 21 June 2012).

11. The concept of the three-dimensional response of a diaphragm can be difficult to visualize. Think of a round balloon as a three-dimensional polar pattern diagram. Position the tied end away from your mouth and the opposite end directly in front of your lips. In this position, you are singing on-axis, and the tied end of the balloon is 180^0, also known as off-axis. If you were able to split the balloon in half vertically and horizontally (in relationship to your lips), you would find the center point of the balloon. That imaginary center represents the diaphragm of the microphone. If you were to extend a 45^0 angle in any direction from the imaginary center and then drew a circle around the inside of the balloon following that angle, you would have a visualization of the three-dimensional application of the two-dimensional polar pattern drawing.

12. The button used to activate phantom power on a soundboard is usually indicated by the lettering "+48v."

13. WENN.com, "Bieber Admits Studio Vocal Help," *Toronto Sun*, 4 July 2012, www.torontosun.com/2012/07/04/bieber-admits-studio-vocal-help (accessed 21 June 2012).

14. Eskow, "Opera Hits a High Note with High-Tech Broadcasts."

15. Some units do contain circular tweeters; however, the horn shape is the most common.

16. Jeremy Federman and Todd Ricketts, "Preferred and Minimum Acceptable Listening Levels for Musicians While Using Floor and In-Ear Monitors," *Journal of Speech, Language, and Hearing Research* 51, no. 1 (2008): 147–59.

17. Giovanni Battista Lamperti, *Vocal Wisdom: Maxims of Giovanni Battista Lamperti*. Transcribed by William Earl Brown. Edited by Lillian Strongin (New York: Taplinger Publishing, 1957), p. ii.

18. Davenport, "What Makes a Singer?," 20–21, 83–88.

19. Allison McCracken, "'God's Gift to Us Girls': Crooning, Gender, and the Re-Creation of American Popular Song, 1928–1933," *American Music* 17, no. 4 (1999): 381.

20. David Szatmary, *A Time to Rock: A Social History of Rock 'n' Roll* (New York: Schirmer Books, 1996), p. 27.

21. For instance, Justin Bieber, who was discovered on YouTube in 2008.

REFERENCES

Alter, Gaby. "Broadway Sound: Four Shows, Four Dramatically Different Designs." *Mix*, October 2009, 46–49.

Benzuly, S. "Sir Paul McCartney Tour Profile." *MixOnline.com*, 1 September 2011, http://mixonline.com/live/tourprofiles/sir_paul_mccartney_tour/ (accessed 21 June 2012).

Davenport, Marcia. "What Makes a Singer?" *Saturday Evening Post*, 11 December 1937, 20–21, 83–88.

Eskow, Gary. "Opera Hits a High Note with High-Tech Broadcasts." *MixOnline.com*, 1 April 2008, http://mixonline.com/post/features/audio_new_yorks_met/ (accessed 21 June 2012).

Federman, Jeremy, and Todd Ricketts. "Preferred and Minimum Acceptable Listening Levels for Musicians While Using Floor and In-Ear Monitors." *Journal of Speech, Language, and Hearing Research* 51, no. 1 (2008): 147–59.

Lamperti, Giovanni Battista. *Vocal Wisdom: Maxims of Giovanni Battista Lamperti*. Transcribed by William Earl Brown. Edited by Lillian Strongin. New York: Taplinger Publishing, 1957.

Lockheart, Paula. "A History of Early Microphone Singing, 1925–1939: American Mainstream Popular Singing at the Advent of Electronic Microphone Amplification." *Popular Music and Society* 26, no. 3 (2003): 367–85.

Lowens, Irving, and Louis Lombard. "Louis Lombard's 'Our Conservatories.'" *American Music* 3, no. 3 (1985): 347–51.

McCracken, Allison. "'God's Gift to Us Girls': Crooning, Gender, and the Re-Creation of American Popular Song, 1928–1933." *American Music* 17, no. 4 (1999): 365–95.

Omori, K., A. Kacker, L. M. Carroll, W. D. Riley, and S. M. Blaugrund. "Singing Power Ratio: Quantitative Evaluation of Singing Voice Quality." *Journal of Voice* 10, no. 3 (1996): 228–35.

Szatmary, David. *A Time to Rock: A Social History of Rock 'n' Roll*. New York: Schirmer Books, 1996.

WENN.com. "Bieber Admits Studio Vocal Help." *Toronto Sun*, 4 July 2012, www.torontosun.com/2012/07/04/bieber-admits-studio-vocal-help (accessed 21 June 2012).

Wollman, Elizabeth L. *The Theatre Will Rock: A History of the Rock Musical*. Ann Arbor: University of Michigan Press, 2006.

Equally at home in classical and CCM styles, **Matthew Edwards** has performed operatic and musical theatre roles with such companies as Tri-Cities Opera, Ash Lawn Opera Festival, New Jersey Opera, Atlantic Coast Opera Festival, Bay View Music Festival, the Acadiana Symphony Orchestra, Dayton Philharmonic Pops, Hudson Valley Symphony, Miami Valley Symphony, Cincinnati Opera Outreach, and Lyric Opera Cleveland Outreach. As a guitarist, keyboardist, and singer, he has also performed pop/rock as a soloist and in bands. He has directed and acted with the Theater Lab (Dayton), Canal Days Festival, and KNOW Theater (Binghamton). Edwards has also served on the production staff of the Dayton International Air Show's 100th Anniversary of Flight Celebration and the Radio City Christmas Spectacular in Cleveland, Ohio.

A specialist in working with contemporary singers, Edwards's current and former students have performed on *American Idol*, on and Off-Broadway, on national tours, on TV, on cruise ships, and in bands throughout the United States. He has worked with independent recording studios and record labels as a vocal and performance coach and frequently works with classical singers who are learning how to "crossover."

Matthew Edwards is assistant professor of voice at Shenandoah University. He was a member of the National Association of Teachers of Singing (NATS) Intern Program, where he was mentored by Jeanette Lovetri and Dr. Scott McCoy. He completed Level I–III certification in Somatic Voicework™ and is now on the faculty of the CCM Voice Pedagogy Institute at Shenandoah University, where he teaches Somatic Voicework™ each summer. His research and workshops have been presented at the NATS National Conference, the Voice Foundation Annual Symposium: Care of the Professional Voice, the International Congress of Voice Teachers (ICVT), the National Center for Voice and Speech (NCVS), the Southeastern Theatre Conference (SETC), the Musical Theatre Educators Alliance (MTEA), and at numerous universities throughout the United States. He has authored articles for *VOICEPrints: The Official Journal of NYSTA*, *The Journal of Voice*, *The Journal of Singing*, *Southern Theatre Magazine*, and *American Music Teacher*. His book, *So You Want to Sing Rock?*, a joint project with the National Association of Teachers of Singing (NATS), is available through Rowman & Littlefield. Please read more online at EdwardsVoice.com and AuditioningForCollege.com.

APPENDIX A

IPA Vowel Chart, Consonant Chart, and Symbol Chart

*VOWEL CHART

The IPA symbols with English examples provide an approximation of the vowel sound. Actual vowel formation and resonance must be defined for each language.

TONGUE VOWELS are also called front vowels. They require a front arch of the tongue. There are two fundamental closed front vowels: [i] and [e]. Each closed vowel has a corresponding open vowel form.

      closed [i] _see_ < open [ɪ] _bit_   closed [e] _chaos_ < open [ɛ] _said_

LIP VOWELS are also called back vowels. They require lip rounding and a back tongue arch. There are two fundamental closed back vowels: [u] and [o]. Each closed vowel has a corresponding open vowel form.

      closed [u] _blue_ < open [ʊ] _look_   closed [o] _provide_ < open [ɔ] _ought_

MIXED VOWELS require lip rounding and a front tongue arch. There are two fundamental closed mixed vowels with a corresponding open vowel form: closed [y] < open [ʏ]   closed [ø] < open [œ]

      [i] tongue + [u] lip = [y] _früh, une_   <   [ɪ] tongue + [ʊ] lip = [ʏ] _Glück_
      [e] tongue + [o] lip = [ø] _schön, yeux_   <   [ɛ] tongue + [ɔ] lip = [œ] _möcht, cœur_

CENTRAL VOWELS do not require lip rounding.

      There are four central vowels: dark [ɑ] _father_, bright [a] _voilà_, [æ] _sat_, [ʌ] _up_ (optional: [ɒ] _hot_)
      There are two r colored vowels: English [ɜ] _bird_, German [ʁ] _der_

NASAL VOWELS resonate in the height of the yawn space with a small amount of shared resonant space in the nasal cavity. There are four nasal vowels: [ɑ̃], [ɛ̃], [õ] (Grubb) or [ɔ̃] (dictionary), and [œ̃].

CHART DESCRIPTION: The front vowels are on the left side of the chart, the back vowels are on the right side of the chart, and the mixed vowels are at the top and bottom (the arrows indicate vowel mixing). The schwa is not included since its pronunciation varies from language to language. The points indicate closed vowels, the broader spaces indicate open vowels, and the center space is reserved for central vowels.

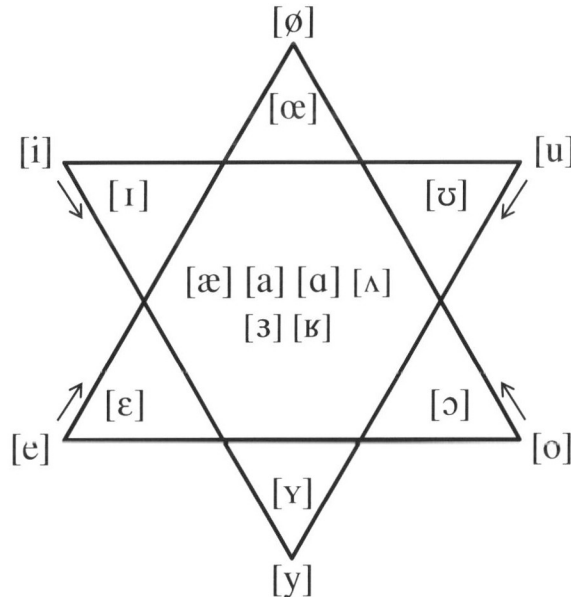

*From the _Lyric Diction Workbook Series_ by Cheri Montgomery, published by S.T.M. Publishers

Chart AA.1. IPA Vowel Chart

*CONSONANT CHARTS

VOICING groups consonants in one of two categories. Voiced consonants engage the vocal cords. Voiceless consonants employ air flow without vocalized tone.

	Bilabial	Labiodental	Dental and Alveolar	Prepalatal and Palatal	Velar	Glottal
Voiceless	[p], [ʍ] _when_	[f]	[θ] _thin_, [t], [s]	[ʃ] _sheep_, [tʃ] _chair_, [ç] _hue_	[k], [χ] GR a_ch_	[h], [ʔ] _each_
Voiced	[b], [w], [m]	[v]	[ð] _them_, [d], [z] [n], [l], rolled [r], flipped [ɾ], retroflex [ɹ]	[ʒ] _vision_, [dʒ] _judge_, [j] _yes_ [ɲ] IT si_gn_ore, [ʎ] IT g_li_	[g] [ŋ] _sing_	

POINT OF ARTICULATION identifies the formation of each consonant by indicating the point of contact or near point of contact made by the articulators.

Points of Articulation	English	Italian	German	French
Bilabial [baɪˈlɛɪbiəl] Refers to the lips	[p] [b] [m] [ʍ][w]	[p] [b] [m] [w]	[p] [b] [m]	[p] [b] [m] [w]
Labiodental [lɛɪbioˈdɛntəl] Involves the lower lip and the upper row of teeth	[f] [v]	[f] [v]	[f] [v] [pf]	[f] [v]
Dental [ˈdɛntəl] Involves the tongue tip and the back of the upper row of teeth	[θ] [ð]	[t] [d] [s] [z] [l] [n] [ɾ] [r] [ts] [dz]	[s] [z] [l]	[t] [d] [s] [z] [l] [n] [ɾ]
Alveolar [ʔælˈviələɪ] Involves the tongue tip and the ridge behind the upper teeth	[t] [d] [s] [z] [l] [n] [ɾ] [ɹ]		[t] [d] [n] [ɾ] [ts]	
Prepalatal [pɹiˈpælətəl] Involves the tongue and area between the alveolar ridge and hard palate	[ʃ] [ʒ] [tʃ] [dʒ]	[ʃ] [tʃ] [dʒ] [j] [ɲ] [ʎ]	[ʃ] [tʃ]	[ʃ] [ʒ] [j] [ɲ] [ɥ]
Palatal [ˈpælətəl] Involves a middle arch of the tongue and the hard palate	[j]		[j] [ç]	
Velar [ˈviləɪ] Involves a back arch of the tongue and the soft palate	[k] [g] [ŋ]	[k] [g] [ŋ]	[k] [g] [ŋ] [χ]	[k] [g]
Glottal [ˈglɑtəl] Involves the air flow and the opening between the vocal cords	[ʔ] [h]		[ʔ] [h]	

MANNER OF ARTICULATION describes how air moves past the articulators during the enunciation of a consonant.

Manner of Articulation	English	Italian	German	French
Stop [stɑp] A momentary closure of the air flow passage **Plosive** [ˈploʊsɪv] A stop released without aspiration (for Italian & French)	[p] [b] [t] [d] [k] [g] [ʔ]	[p] [b] [t] [d] [k] [g]	[p] [b] [t] [d] [k] [g] [ʔ]	[p] [b] [t] [d] [k] [g]
Fricative [ˈfɹɪkətɪv] Produced by directing the air flow past a set of articulators	[f] [v] [s] [z] [ʍ] [ʃ] [ʒ] [h] [θ] [ð]	[f] [v] [s] [z] [ʃ]	[f] [v] [s] [z] [ʃ] [h] [ç] [χ]	[f] [v] [s] [z] [ʃ] [ʒ]
Affricate [ˈʔæfɹɪkət] A stop or plosive that is followed by a fricative	[tʃ] [dʒ]	[ts] [dz] [tʃ] [dʒ]	[tʃ] [pf] [ts]	
Nasal [ˈneɪzəl] Produced by directing vocalized tone through the nasal passages	[m] [n] [ŋ]	[m] [n] [ŋ] [ɲ]	[m] [n] [ŋ]	[m] [n] [ɲ]
Lateral [ˈlætəɹəl] Produced by directing vocalized tone over the sides of the tongue	[l]	[l] [ʎ]	[l]	[l]
Glide [glɑɪd] Produced by directing vocalized tone past the articulators without friction	[j] [w]	[j] [w]	[j]	[j] [w] [ɥ]
Trill [tɹɪl] Formed by taps of the tongue tip against the alveolar ridge and/or teeth	[ɾ]	[ɾ] [r]	[ɾ]	[ɾ]
Retroflex [ˈɹɛtɹoʊflɛks] Produced with rounded lips and the tongue tip curled up	[ɹ]			

*From the _Lyric Diction Workbook Series_ by Cheri Montgomery, published by S.T.M. Publishers

Chart AA.2. Consonant Chart

*IPA SYMBOLS WITH SAMPLE WORDS

VOWELS	ENGLISH	ITALIAN	GERMAN	FRENCH
[i]	see [si]	ivi ['ivi]	Lied [li:t]	ici [i'si]
[ɪ]	wit [wɪt]		Bitte ['bɪttə]	
[e]		perché [per'ke]	Erde ['ʔeːrdə]	été [e'te]
[ɛ]	bell [bɛl]	bene ['bɛne]	Feld [fɛlt]	rêve ['rɛvə]
[u]	blue [blu]	luna ['luna]	Ruh [ru:]	jour [ʒur]
[ʊ]	look [lʊk]		jung [jʊŋ]	
[o]	obey [ʔo'beɪ]	solo ['solo]	Mond [mo:nt]	pauvre ['povrə]
[ɔ]	ought [ʔɔt]	core ['kɔre]	Sonne ['zɔnnə]	aurore [ɔ'rɔrə]
[æ]	glad [glæd]			
[a]		cara ['kara]	allein [ʔal'laen]	voilà [vwa'la]
[ɑ]	father ['fɑðə]		Abend ['ʔaːbɔnt]	âme ['amə]
[ʌ]	up [ʔʌp]			
[y]			Blüte ['bly:tə]	sûr [syr]
[ʏ]			Küsse ['kʏssə]	
[ø]			schön [ʃø:n]	feu [fø]
[œ]			könnt [kœnnt]	seul [sœl]
[ɜ]	bird [bɜd]			
[ʁ]			Vater ['faːtɐ]	
[ã]				enfant [ã'fã]
[ɛ̃]				bien [bjɛ̃]
[õ]				ombre ['õbrə]
[œ̃]				humble ['œblə]

CONSONANTS	ENGLISH	ITALIAN	GERMAN	FRENCH
[p]	pure [pjʊə]	pace ['patʃe]	Perle ['pɛrlə]	porte ['pɔrtə]
[b]	beauty ['bjutɪ]	bella ['bɛlla]	Bild [bɪlt]	beauté [bo'te]
[ʍ]	wheat [ʍit]			
[w]	wish [wɪʃ]	uomo ['wɔmo]		oui [wi]
[m]	mist [mɪst]	mondo ['mondo]	Meer [me:r]	même ['mɛmə]
[f]	faith [fɛɪθ]	fiore ['fjore]	Fest [fɛst]	fois [fwa]
[v]	voice [vɔɪs]	vita ['vita]	Welt [vɛlt]	voix [vwa]
[pf]			Pfade ['pfaːdə]	
[θ]	thin [θɪn]			
[ð]	them [ðɛm]			
[t]	tone [toʊn]	tempo ['tempo]	Tag [ta:k]	tête ['tɛtə]
[d]	dance [dans]	donna ['dɔnna]	Dank [daŋk]	désir [de'zir]
[s]	sing [sɪŋ]	spesso ['spesso]	Wasser ['vassɐ]	soir [swar]
[z]	zeal [zil]	sdegno ['zdeɲɲo]	Seele ['ze:lə]	zéphyr [ze'fir]
[ts]		senza ['sɛntsa]	Zeit [tsaet]	
[dz]		mezzo ['mɛddzo]		
[n]	night [naɪt]	nome ['nome]	Nebel ['ne:bəl]	noir [nwar]
[l]	little ['lɪtəl]	luce ['lutʃe]	Liebe ['li:bə]	lune ['lynə]
[ɾ]	thread [θrɛd]	parola [pa'rola]	rot [ro:t]	riche ['riʃə]
[ɹ]	rose [roʊz]			
[r]		rosa ['roza]	Herr [hɛrr]	

CONSONANTS	ENGLISH	ITALIAN	GERMAN	FRENCH
[ʃ]	shine [ʃaɪn]	lascia ['laʃʃa]	Sterne ['ʃtɛrnə]	chant [ʃã]
[ʒ]	vision ['vɪʒən]			jamais [ʒa'mɛ]
[tʃ]	child [tʃaɪld]	cielo ['tʃelo]	Deutsch [dɔøtʃ]	
[dʒ]	judge [dʒʌdʒ]	gioia ['dʒɔja]		
[ɲ]		sogno ['soɲɲo]		vigne ['viɲə]
[ʎ]		figlio ['fiʎʎo]		
[ç]	huge [çjudʒ]		Licht [lɪçt]	
[j]	young [jʌŋ]	miei [mjɛːi]	Jahr [ja:r]	yeux [jø]
[ɥ]				nuit [nɥi]
[k]	kiss [kɪs]	casa ['kaza]	Kind [kɪnt]	cœur [kœr]
[g]	good [gʊd]	guida ['gwida]	gern [gɛrn]	guerre ['gɛrə]
[ŋ]	wing [wɪŋ]	lungo ['luŋgo]	Engel ['ʔɛŋəl]	
[χ]			Nacht [naχt]	
[ʔ]	eyes [ʔaɪz]		Augen ['ʔaogən]	
[h]	health [hɛlθ]		Herz [hɛrts]	

STRESS MARKS, LONG MARK AND SCHWA

	ENGLISH	ITALIAN	GERMAN	FRENCH
[']	above [ʔʌ'bʌv]	così [ko'zi]	wohin [vo:'hɪn]	
[,]	melancholy ['mɛlən,kalɪ]		rosenbaum ['ro:zən,baom]	
[:]		mio ['mi:o]	Boot [bo:t]	
[ə]	listen ['lɪsən]		Geliebte [gə'li:ptə]	petite [pə'titə]

*From the *Lyric Diction Workbook Series* by Cheri Montgomery, published by S.T.M. Publishers

Chart AA.3. Symbol Chart

APPENDIX B

Anatomy Diagrams

MUSCLES OF INSPIRATION

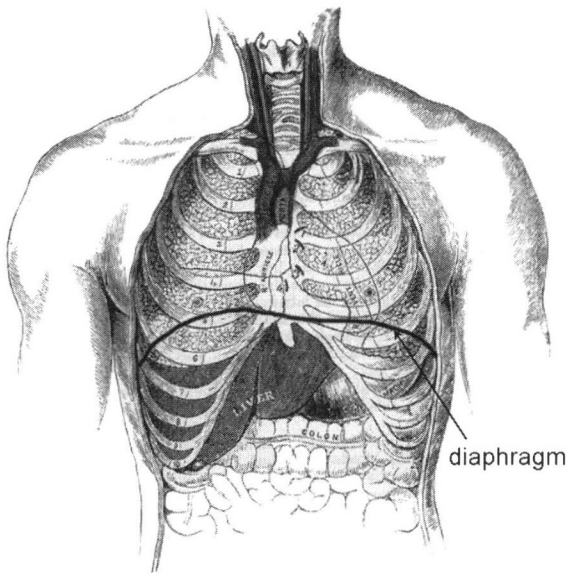

Figure AB.1. Location of diaphragm in thorax/torso. *Courtesy Gray's Anatomy*, with labeling by Scott McCoy; reprinted with permission from *Your Voice: An Inside View* (2004).

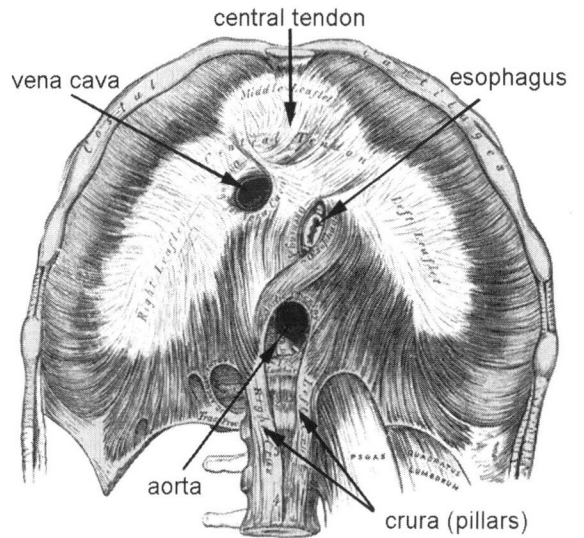

Figure AB.2. Inferior view of diaphragm. *Courtesy Gray's Anatomy*, with labeling by Scott McCoy; reprinted with permission from *Your Voice: An Inside View* (2004).

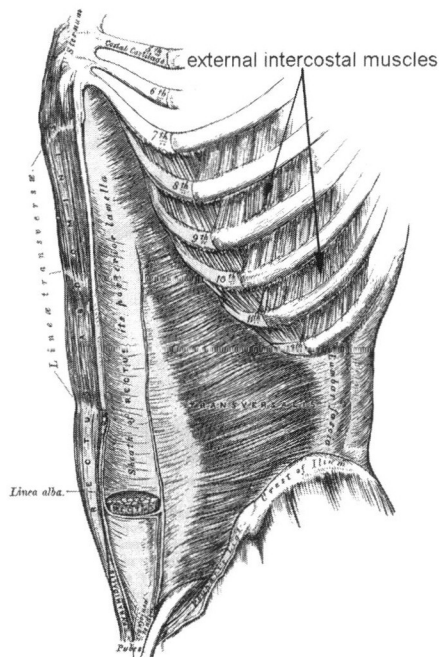

Figure AB.3. External intercostal muscles. *Courtesy Gray's Anatomy*, with labeling by Scott McCoy; reprinted with permission from *Your Voice: An Inside View* (2004).

MUSCLES OF EXPIRATION

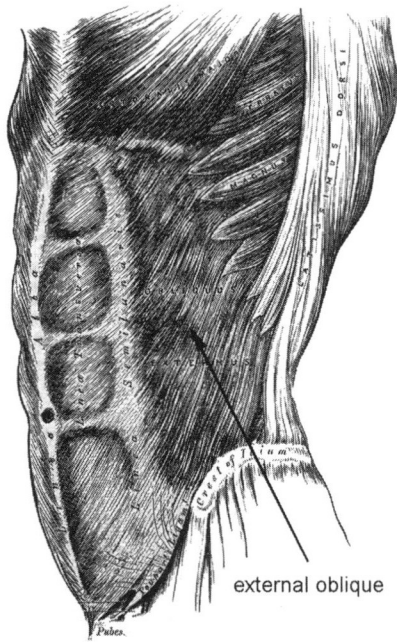

Figure AB.4. External oblique abdominis muscles. *Courtesy Gray's Anatomy*, with labeling by Scott McCoy; reprinted with permission from *Your Voice: An Inside View* (2004).

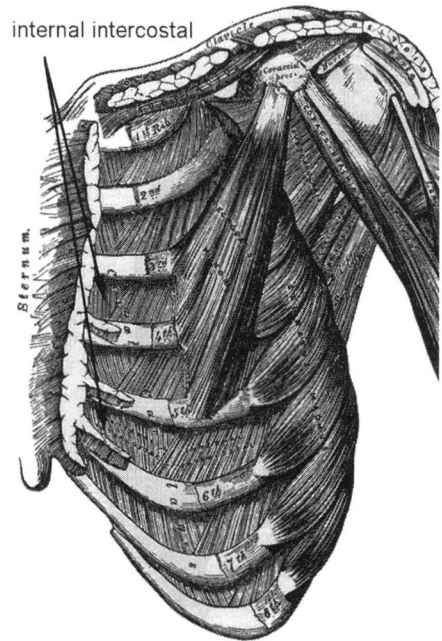

Figure AB.5. Internal intercostal muscles. *Courtesy Gray's Anatomy*, with labeling by Scott McCoy; reprinted with permission from *Your Voice: An Inside View* (2004).

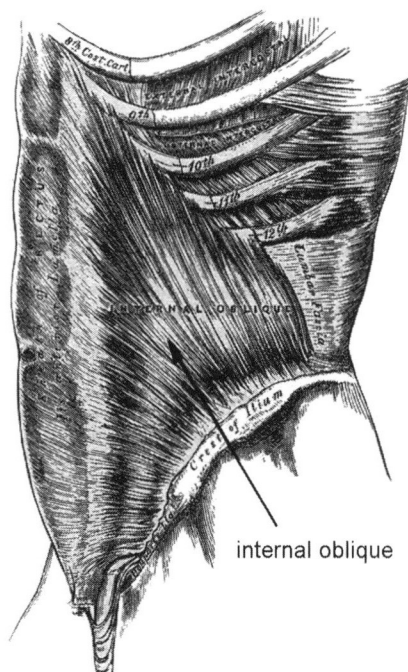

Figure AB.6. Internal oblique abdominis muscles. *Courtesy Gray's Anatomy*, with labeling by Scott McCoy; reprinted with permission from *Your Voice: An Inside View* (2004).

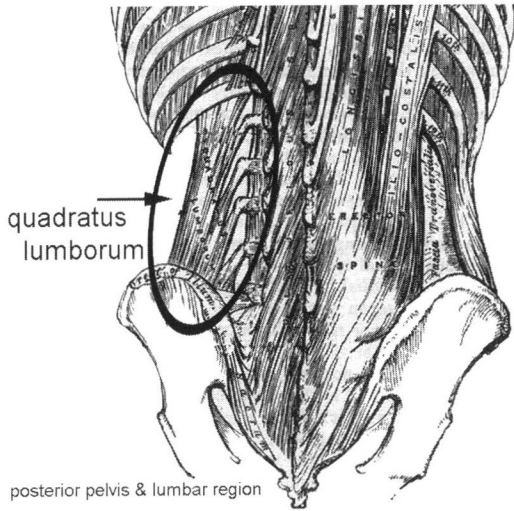

quadratus lumborum

posterior pelvis & lumbar region

Figure AB.7. Quadratus lumborum muscles. *Courtesy Gray's Anatomy*, with labeling by Scott McCoy; reprinted with permission from *Your Voice: An Inside View* (2004).

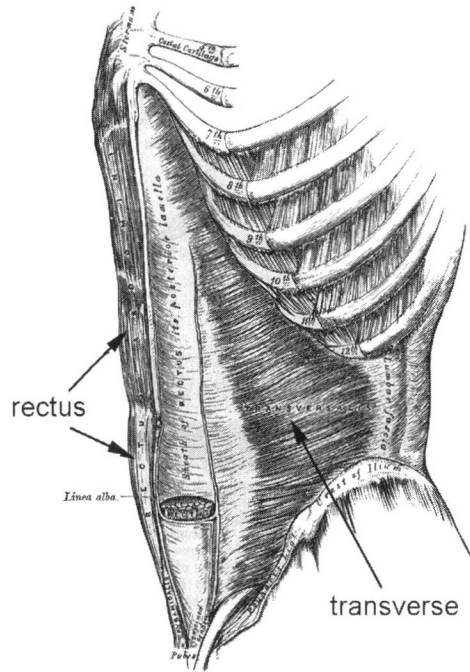

rectus

transverse

Figure AB.8. Rectus abdominis muscles. *Courtesy Gray's Anatomy*, with labeling by Scott McCoy; reprinted with permission from *Your Voice: An Inside View* (2004).

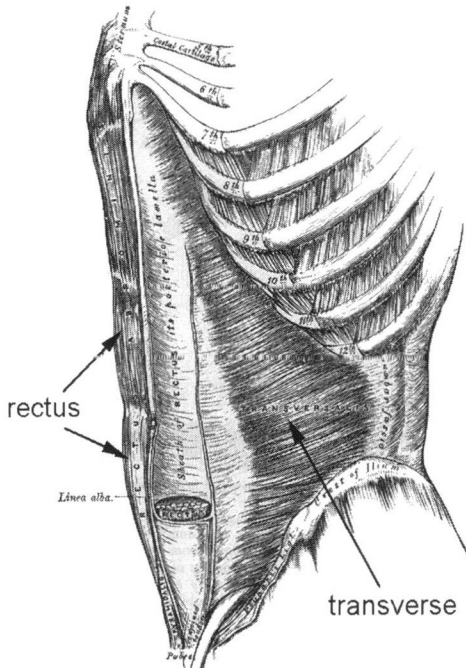

rectus

transverse

Figure AB.9. Transverse abdominis muscles. *Courtesy Gray's Anatomy*, with labeling by Scott McCoy; reprinted with permission from *Your Voice: An Inside View* (2004).

VOCAL TRACT, LARYNX, VOCAL FOLDS

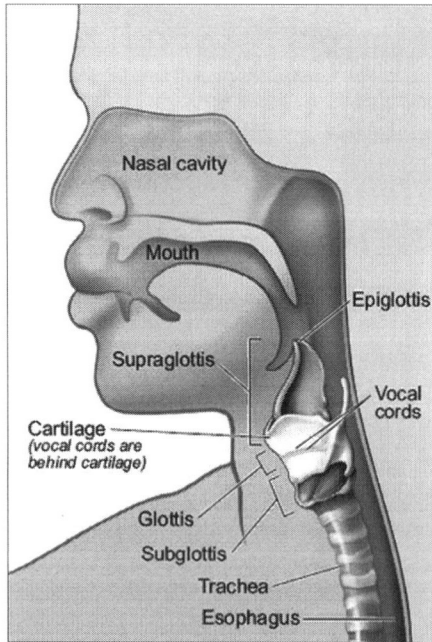

Figure AB.10. An anatomical drawing of the vocal tract.
Courtesy Creative Commons.

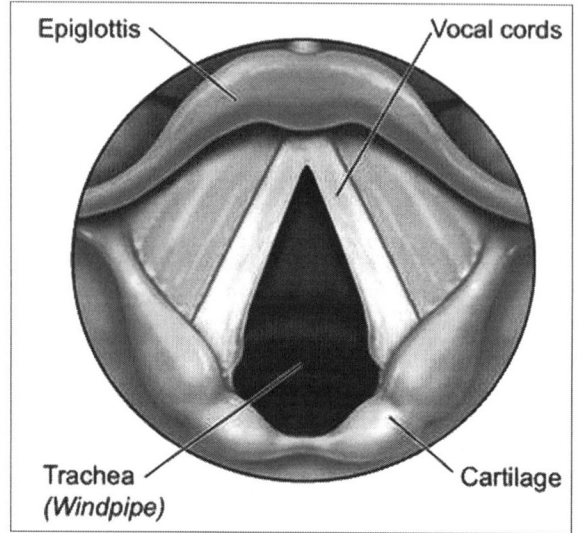

Figure AB.11. An anatomical drawing of the vocal folds (or cords).
Courtesy Creative Commons.

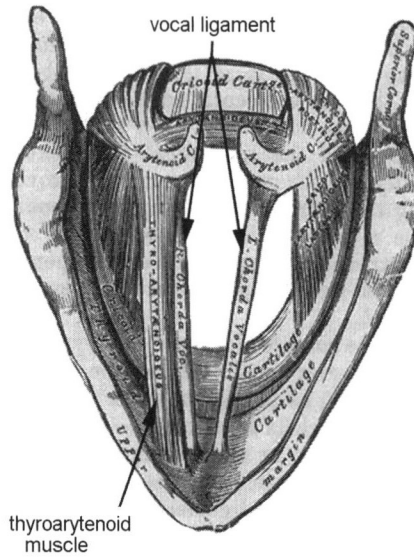

Figure AB.12. Vocal ligament and thyroarytenoid muscle.
Courtesy Gray's Anatomy, with labeling by Scott McCoy;
reprinted with permission from *Your Voice: An Inside View* (2004).

APPENDIX C

Fach Chart

The following chart is intended to clarify the various *Fächer* as outlined by Rudolf Kloiber (1899–1973) in his *Handbuch der Oper* (13th edition, 2011). Each of Kloiber's twenty-nine categories are outlined in this section, with rough English translations of the German *Fach* name and three sample roles for each category. For a more comprehensive listing of roles, one should consult the *Handbuch der Oper*. The reader should also consult the individual *Fach* entries in this dictionary for more information, as well as the entries for *Fach*, German Fach System, and Kloiber Fach System. The dictionary also contains many additional entries for other voice categories and classifications that are not found among Kloiber's twenty-nine official *Fächer*, but they are nevertheless used with regularity by singers, voice teachers, and industry professionals.

Table AC.1. *Fach* Chart

Fach	Translation	Role	Opera	Composer
Soubrette	NA (Fr: "maid") NB: usually a young, teenage character	Barbarina Papagena Gianetta	*Le nozze di Figaro* (1786) *Die Zauberflöte* (1791) *L'elisir d'amore* (1832)	Mozart Mozart Donizetti
lyrischer Koloratursopran (*Koloratursoubrette*)	"lyric coloratura soprano"	Blonde Musetta Sophie	*Die Entführung aus dem Serail* (1782) *La bohème* (1896) *Der Rosenkavalier* (1911)	Mozart Puccini Strauss
dramatischer Koloratursopran	"dramatic coloratura soprano"	Cleopatra Königin der Nacht Manon	*Giulio Cesare* (1724) *Die Zauberflöte* (1791) *Manon Lescaut* (1893)	Handel Mozart Puccini
lyrischer Sopran	"lyric soprano"	Pamina Michaëla Sophie	*Die Zauberflöte* (1791) *Carmen* (1875) *Werther* (1892)	Mozart Bizet Massenet
jugendlich-dramatischer Sopran	"young dramatic soprano"	Elsa Mimì Marie	*Lohengrin* (1850) *La bohème* (1896) *Wozzeck* (1925)	Wagner Puccini Berg
dramatischer Sopran	"dramatic soprano"	Leonore Brünnhilde Tosca	*Fidelio* (1805, rev. 1814) *Der Ring des Nibelungen* (1876) *Tosca* (1900)	Beethoven Wagner Puccini
Charaktersopran	"character soprano" NB: "character" ≠ "comic"	La Folie Volpino Mélisande	*Platée* (1745) *Lo speziale* (1768) *Pelléas et Mélisande* (1902)	Rameau Haydn Debussy
koloratur-Mezzosopran	"coloratura mezzo-soprano"	Rinaldo Isabella Rosina	*Rinaldo* (1711) *L'italiana in Algeri* (1813) *Il barbiere di Siviglia* (1816)	Handel Rossini Rossini
lyrischer Mezzosopran	"lyric mezzo-soprano"	Dorabella Charlotte Suzuki	*Così fan tutte* (1790) *Werther* (1892) *Madama Butterfly* (1904)	Mozart Massenet Puccini
dramatischer Mezzosopran	"dramatic mezzo-soprano"	Fricka Dalila Octavian	*Der Ring des Nibelungen* (1876) *Samson et Dalila* (1877) *Der Rosenkavalier* (1911)	Wagner Saint-Saëns Strauss
Spielalt	"playful contralto"	Meg Page Lola Florence Pike	*Falstaff* (1893) *Cavalleria rusticana* (1890) *Albert Herring* (1947)	Verdi Mascagni Britten
lyrischer Alt	"lyric contralto"	Floßhilde Mrs. Quickly Ciesca	*Der Ring des Nibelungen* (1876) *Falstaff* (1893) *Gianni Schicchi* (1918)	Wagner Verdi Puccini

(continued)

Table AC.1. *Fach* Chart (*continued*)

Fach	Translation	Role	Opera	Composer
dramatischer Alt	"dramatic contralto"	Lucia	*Cavalleria rusticana* (1890)	Mascagni
		Hexe	*Hänsel und Gretel* (1893)	Humperdinck
		Mother	*The Consul* (1950)	Menotti
tiefer Alt	"low contralto"	Magdalena	*Der Evangelimann* (1895)	Kienzl
		Genoveva	*Pelléas et Mélisande* (1902)	Debussy
		Gaea	*Daphne* (1938)	Strauss
contratenor (*countertenor*)	NA (Lat: "against the tenor") NB: a male falsettist	Nerone	*L'incoronazione di Poppea* (1642)	Monteverdi
		Cesare	*Giulio Cesare* (1724)	Handel
		Oberon	*A Midsummer Night's Dream* (1960)	Britten
haute-contre	NA (Fr: "against the tenor") NB: a high tenor	Atys	*Atys* (1676)	Lully
		Castor	*Castor et Pollux* (1737)	Rameau
		Orfeo	*Orfeo ed Euridice* (1762)	Gluck
Spieltenor (*Tenorbuffo*)	"playful tenor"	Basilio	*Le nozze di Figaro* (1786)	Mozart
		Beppo	*Pagliacci* (1892)	Leoncavallo
		Goro	*Madama Butterfly* (1904)	Puccini
lyrischer Tenor	"lyric tenor"	Tamino	*Die Zauberflöte* (1791)	Mozart
		Alfredo	*La traviata* (1853)	Verdi
		Pinkerton	*Madama Butterfly* (1904)	Puccini
jugendlicher Heldentenor	"young heroic tenor"	Samson	*Samson et Dalila* (1877)	Saint-Saëns
		Rudolfo	*La bohème* (1896)	Puccini
		Palestrina	*Palestrina* (1917)	Pfitzner
Heldentenor	"heroic tenor"	Tristan	*Tristan und Isolde* (1865)	Wagner
		Otello	*Otello* (1887)	Verdi
		Peter Grimes	*Peter Grimes* (1945)	Britten
Charaktertenor	"character tenor" NB: "character" ≠ "comic"	Mime	*Der Ring des Nibelungen* (1876)	Wagner
		Dr. Cajus	*Falstaff* (1893)	Verdi
		Herodes	*Salome* (1905)	Strauss
lyrischer Bariton	"lyric baritone"	Papageno	*Die Zauberflöte* (1791)	Mozart
		Malatesta	*Don Pasquale* (1842)	Donizetti
		Harlekin	*Ariadne auf Naxos* (1916)	Strauss
Kavalierbariton	"cavalier baritone" NB: a *lyrischer Bariton* with more edge	Don Giovanni	*Don Giovanni* (1787)	Mozart
		Escamillo	*Carmen* (1875)	Bizet
		Ford	*Falstaff* (1893)	Verdi
Heldenbariton	"heroic baritone"	Hans Sachs	*Die Meistersinger von Nürnberg* (1868)	Wagner
		Wotan	*Der Ring des Nibelungen* (1876)	Wagner
		Dr. Schön	*Lulu* (1935)	Berg
Charakterbariton	"character baritone" NB: "character" ≠ "comic"	Beckmesser	*Die Meistersinger von Nürnberg* (1868)	Wagner
		Alberich	*Der Ring des Nibelungen* (1876)	Wagner
		Scarpia	*Tosca* (1900)	Puccini
Spielbaß (*Baßbuffo*)	"playful bass"	Leporello	*Don Giovanni* (1787)	Mozart
		Dr. Bartolo	*Il barbiere di Siviglia* (1816)	Rossini
		Don Pasquale	*Don Pasquale* (1842)	Donizetti
schwerer Spielbaß (*Schwerer Baßbuffo*)	"severe playful bass" NB: a lower, heavier *Spielbaß*	Daland	*Der fliegende Holländer* (1843)	Wagner
		Ochs	*Der Rosenkavalier* (1911)	Strauss
		Gianni Schicchi	*Gianni Schicchi* (1918)	Puccini
Charakterbaß (*Baßbariton*)	"character bass" NB: "character" ≠ "comic"	Monterone	*Rigoletto* (1851)	Verdi
		Alberich	*Der Ring des Nibelungen* (1876)	Wagner
		Timur	*Turandot* (1926)	Puccini
seriöser Baß	"serious bass" NB: the lowest and heaviest bass *Fach*	Hagen	*Der Ring des Nibelungen* (1876)	Wagner
		Gurnemanz	*Parsifal* (1878)	Wagner
		Arkel	*Pelléas et Mélisande* (1902)	Debussy

APPENDIX D

Bel Canto: A Definition

In his 1999 book *Bel Canto: A History of Vocal Pedagogy*, James Stark offers an in-depth exploration of the historical schools of voice pedagogy during the course of 300 pages. Toward the conclusion of his book, he includes an essay entitled "*Bel Canto*: Context and Controversy," which discusses how the term *bel canto* has meant different things to different singers, pedagogues, and eras. Stark synthesizes this multitude of meanings into his own definition of *bel canto* as follows:

> *Bel canto* is a concept that takes into account two separate but related matters. First, it is a highly refined method of using the singing voice in which the glottal source, the vocal tract, and the respiratory system interact in such a way as to create the qualities of *chiaroscuro*, *appoggio*, register equalization, malleability of pitch and intensity, and a pleasing vibrato. The idiomatic use of this voice includes various forms of vocal onset, *legato*, *portamento*, glottal articulation, crescendo, decrescendo, *messa di voce*, *mezza voce*, floridity and trills, and *tempo rubato*. Second, *bel canto* refers to any style of music that employs this kind of singing in a tasteful and expressive way. Historically, composers and singers have created categories of recitative, song, and aria that took advantage of these techniques, and that lent themselves to various types of vocal expression. *Bel canto* has demonstrated its power to astonish, to charm, to amuse, and especially to move the listener. As musical epochs and styles have changed, the elements of *bel canto* adapted to meet new musical demands, thereby ensuring the continuation of *bel canto* in our own time.[1]

The reader is encouraged to consult Stark's entire study for an in-depth exploration of the *bel canto* concept within the context of historical voice pedagogy.

NOTE

1. James Stark, *Bel Canto: A History of Vocal Pedagogy* (Toronto: University of Toronto Press, 1999), p. 189.

APPENDIX E

A History of Singing: A Timeline

c. 425 BCE	Psalms of David are collected.
c. 750	Gregorian chant is developed.
c. 950	Gregorian chant is first put into notation.
c. 1151	Hildegard von Bingen's *Ordo Virtutum*.
c. 1200	Perotin's four-voice *organa*.
c. 1322	Philippe de Vitry's *Ars nova notandi*.
c. 1364	Machaut's *Messe de Notre Dame*.
1436	Du Fay's *Nuper rosarum flores*.
c. 1515	Josquin's *Missa Pange lingua*.
1562	Palestrina's *Missa pape marcelli*.
1583	The Florentine Camerata holds its first meeting
1598	Peri's *Dafne* becomes the first opera in history.
1605	Monteverdi's *Fifth Book of Madrigals*.
1607	Monteverdi's *Orfeo*.
1637	The Teatro San Cassiano, the world's first opera house, opens.
1643	Monteverdi's *L'incoronazione di Poppea*.
c. 1700	The piano is invented by Bartolomeo Cristofori.
1719	Handel forms the Royal Academy of Music.
1722	Rameau's *Traité de l'harmonie*.
	J. S. Bach's *Das wohltemperierte Klavier*.
1723	J. S. Bach is appointed at the Thomaskirche in Leipzig.
	Pier Francesco Tosi's *Observations on the Florid Song*.
1725	Fux's *Gradus ad Parnassum*.
1762	Gluck's *Orfeo ed Eurydice*.
1774	Mancini's *Practical Reflections on the Figurative Art of Singing*.
1786	Mozart's *Le nozze di Figaro*.
1798	Haydn's *Die Schöpfung*.
1815	Schubert writes 140 *Lieder*.
1816	Rossini's *Il barbiere di Siviglia*.
1822	*Exercises pour la voix* by Manuel García I.
1824	Beethoven's *Missa solemnis*, Op. 123, and *Symphony No. 9*, Op. 125.
1828	Schubert's *Winterreise*, D911, and *Schwanengesang*, D957.
1831	Bellini's *Norma*.
1832	Donizett's *L'elisir d'amore*.
1837	Gilbert Duprez sings a high C in full operatic head voice.
1840	Schumann writes 168 *Lieder*.
	Traité complet de l'art du chant by Manuel García II.
1853	Verdi's *La traviata* and *Il trovatore*.
1855	Manuel García II invents the laryngoscope.
1858	Offenbach's *Orphée aux enfers*.
1863	Hermann von Helmholtz's *On the Sensations of Tone*.
1865	Wagner's *Tristan und Isolde*.
1867	The New England Conservatory opens in Boston.
1868	Brahms's *Ein deutsches Requiem*, Op. 45.
1874	Johann Strauss's *Die Fledermaus*.
1876	Wagner's *Der Ring des Nibelungen*.
	Emile Berliner invents the microphone.
1877	Francesco Lamperti's *A Treatise on the Art of Singing*.
1878	Thomas Edison invents the phonograph.
1881	The Savoy Theatre opens in London.
1884	Julius Stockhausen's *Method of Singing*.
1886	Mathilde Marchesi's *Méthode de chant théorique et pratique*.
1887	Emile Berliner patents the gramophone.
1894	Manual García's *Hints on Singing*.
1895	Guglielmo Marconi sends and receives the first radio signal.
1896	Brahms's *Vier ernste Gesänge*, Op. 121.
	Wolf completes the *Italienisches Liederbuch*.
	Liber Usualis is published by the monks of Solesmes.
1897	The International Phonetic Alphabet is invented.
1899	William Shakespeare's *The Art of Singing*.

1900	Puccini's *Tosca*.	1964	Ella Fitzgerald records her last *Songbook*.
1901	Mathilde Marchesi's *Ten Singing Lessons*.	1966	The Metropolitan Opera House opens in Lincoln Center.
1902	Lilli Lehmann's *How to Sing*.		
	Debussy's *Pelléas et Mélisande*.	1967	Vennard's *Singing: The Mechanism and the Technic*.
1903	Pope Pius X establishes standard Roman pronunciation of church Latin.		D. Ralph Appelman's *The Science of Vocal Pedagogy*.
1905	Strauss's *Salome*.		David Munrow and Christopher Hogwood form the Early Music Consort.
	Giovanni Battisa Lamperti's *The Technics of Bel Canto*.	1968	*Hair* opens on Broadway.
1906	The New York Singing Teachers Association is founded.	1970	Robert Shaw forms the Atlanta Symphony Chorus.
1907	Franz Lehár's *The Merry Widow* opens in New York.	1972	Luciano Pavarotti garners seventeen curtain calls at the Metropolitan Opera.
1911	Mahler's *Das Lied von der Erde*.	1973	Christopher Hogwood forms the Academy of Ancient Music.
1912	Schoenberg's *Pierrot lunaire*, Op. 21.	1975	Cornelius Reid's trilogy on singing is issued by Joseph Patelson.
1921	Fauré's *L'horizon chimérique*, Op. 118.		
1922	Allesandro Moreschi, the last castrato, dies.	1976	Glass's *Einstein on the Beach*.
1924	William Shakespeare's *Plain Words on Singing*.	1977	Richard Miller's *National Schools of Singing*.
1925	Berg's *Wozzeck*.		Johann Sundberg's "Acoustics of the Singing Voice."
1926	Louis Armstrong records "Heebie Jeebies."	1979	"Rappers Delight" by the Sugarhill Gang.
	Pierre Bernac meets Francis Poulenc.	1980	Coffin's *Overtones of Bel Canto*.
1927	*Show Boat* opens on Broadway.	1981	MTV is launched.
1930	Ethel Merman stars in *Girl Crazy*.	1982	The compact disc (CD) is invented.
1931	*Vocal Wisdom: Maxims of Giovanni Battista Lamperti* is published.		James McKinney's *The Diagnosis and Correction of Vocal Faults*.
1936	The American Standards Association recommends A=440 Hz.	1983	Michael Jackson's *Thriller*.
1943	*Oklahoma!* opens on Broadway.	1985	Helmuth Rilling releases the complete choral works of J. S. Bach.
1944	The National Association of Teachers of Singing is founded.	1986	Richard Miller's *The Structure of Singing*.
1948	The long-playing (LP) vinyl record is invented.	1988	Barbara Doscher's *The Functional Unity of the Singing Voice*.
	Alfred Deller forms the Deller Consort.	1990	Robert Shaw's first Carnegie Hall Choral Workshop is held.
	Robert Shaw forms the Robert Shaw Chorale.	1993	MP3 audio format is invented.
1949	The first Tony Award for Best Musical is awarded to *Kiss Me, Kate*.	1994	Ingo Titze's *Principles of Voice Production*.
1950	Sergius Kagen's *On Studying Singing*.	1996	Oran Lathrop Brown's *Discover Your Voice*.
1954	Alfred A. Tomatis invents the Electronic Ear.		Donald Miller introduces VoceVista.
1955	Marian Anderson becomes the Metropolitan Opera's first black performer.	2001	Alfred A. Tomatis's *L'oreille et la voix* (*The Ear and the Voice*).
1956	Elvis Presley records "Hound Dog."	2002	*American Idol* premieres.
1958	Cage's *Aria*.	2004	Scott McCoy's *Your Voice: An Inside View*.
1961	Russell Oberlin sings in Britten's *A Midsummer Night's Dream*.		
1962	Britten's *War Requiem*.		

APPENDIX F

The Pulitzer Prize and Grawemeyer Award: Vocal Works

PULITZER PRIZE

The Pulitzer Prize is an annual award given by Columbia University to honor significant works in journalism, letters, drama, and music. The Pulitzer Prize in Music has been awarded annually since 1943. Vocal works that have won the Pulitzer Prize in Music include the following:

Choral

Secular Cantata No. 2: A Free Song (1943)	William Schumann (1910–1992)
The Canticle of the Sun (1946)	Leo Sowerby (1895–1968)
Meditations on Ecclesiastes (1957)	Norman Dello Joio (1913–2008)
The Flight into Egypt (1987)	John Harbison (b. 1938)
Blood on the Fields (1997)	Wynton Marsalis (b. 1961)
On the Transmigration of Souls (2003)	John Adams (b. 1947)
The Little Match Girl Passion (2008)	David Lang (b. 1957)
Partita for Eight Voices (2013)	Caroline Shaw (b. 1982)

Opera

The Consul (1950)	Gian Carlo Menotti (1911–2007)
Giants in the Earth (1951)	Douglas Moore (1893–1969)
The Saint of Bleecker Street (1955)	Gian Carlo Menotti (1911–2007)
Vanessa (1958)	Samuel Barber (1910–1981)
The Crucible (1962)	Robert Ward (1917–2013)
Life Is a Dream (2000)	Lewis Spratlan (b. 1940)
Madame White Snake (2011)	Zhou Long (b. 1953)
Silent Night (2012)	Kevin Puts (b. 1972)

Art Song

From the Diary of Virginia Woolf (1975)	Dominick Argento (b. 1927)
Canti del sole (1984)	Bernard Rands (b. 1934)
Lilacs (1996)	George Walker (b. 1922)

Each year since 1918, a Pulitzer Prize in Drama has also been awarded. In this category, the following Broadway musicals have been awarded a Pulitzer Prize:

Of Thee I Sing (1932)	Lyrics by Ira Gershwin (1896–1983)
	Music by George Gershwin (1898–1937)
South Pacific (1950)	Lyrics by Oscar Hammerstein II (1895–1960)
	Music by Richard Rodgers (1902–1979)
Fiorello! (1960)	Music by Jerry Bock (1928–2010)
	Lyrics by Sheldon Harnick (b. 1924)
How to Succeed in Business without Really Trying (1962)	Music and Lyrics by Frank Loesser (1910–1969)
A Chorus Line (1976)	Lyrics by Edward Kleban (1939–1987)
	Music by Marvin Hamlisch (1944–2012)
Sunday in the Park with George (1984)	Music and Lyrics by Stephen Sondheim (b. 1930)
Rent (1996)	Music and Lyrics by Jonathan Larson (1960–1996)
Next to Normal (2010)	Music by Tom Kitt (b. 1974)
	Lyrics by Brian Yorkey (b. 1970)

GRAWEMEYER AWARD

The Grawemeyer Award is an annual award given by the University of Louisville. The awards honor specific achievements in five categories: education, the improvement of world order, religion, psychology, and music composition. The composition award is the oldest of the Grawemeyer Awards and was first presented in 1985. Vocal works that have won the Grawemeyer Award for Music Composition have included four operas and two art song cycles:

Opera

The Mask of Orpheus (1987)	Harrison Birtwistle (b. 1934)
Marco Polo (1998)	Tan Dun (b. 1957)
L'amour de loin (2003)	Kaija Saarijaho (b. 1952)
La commedia (2011)	Louis Andriessen (b. 1939)

Art Song

Ad ora incerta (1997)	Simon Bainbridge (b. 1952)
Neruda Songs (2008)	Peter Lieberson (1946–2011)

APPENDIX G

The Tony Award for Best Musical

1949	*Kiss Me, Kate*
1950	*South Pacific*
1951	*Guys and Dolls*
1952	*The King and I*
1953	*Wonderful Town*
1954	*Kismet*
1955	*The Pajama Game*
1956	*Damn Yankees*
1957	*My Fair Lady*
1958	*The Music Man*
1959	*Redhead*
1960	*The Sound of Music* and *Fiorello!* (tie)
1961	*Bye Bye Birdie*
1962	*How to Succeed in Business without Really Trying*
1963	*A Funny Thing Happened on the Way to the Forum*
1964	*Hello, Dolly!*
1965	*Fiddler on the Roof*
1966	*Man of La Mancha*
1967	*Cabaret*
1968	*Hallelujah, Baby!*
1969	*1776*
1970	*Applause*
1971	*Company*
1972	*Two Gentlemen of Verona*
1973	*A Little Night Music*
1974	*Raisin*
1975	*The Wiz*
1976	*A Chorus Line*
1977	*Annie*
1978	*Ain't Misbehavin'*
1979	*Sweeney Todd: The Demon Barber of Fleet Street*
1980	*Evita*
1981	*42nd Street*
1982	*Nine*
1983	*Cats*
1984	*La Cage aux Folles*
1985	*Big River*
1986	*The Mystery of Edwin Drood*
1987	*Les Misérables*
1988	*The Phantom of the Opera*
1989	*Jerome Robbins' Broadway*
1990	*City of Angels*
1991	*The Will Rogers Follies*
1992	*Crazy for You*
1993	*Kiss of the Spider Woman*
1994	*Passion*
1995	*Sunset Boulevard*
1996	*Rent*
1997	*Titanic*
1998	*The Lion King*
1999	*Fosse*
2000	*Contact*
2001	*The Producers*
2002	*Thoroughly Modern Millie*
2003	*Hairspray*
2004	*Avenue Q*
2005	*Monty Python's Spamalot*
2006	*Jersey Boys*
2007	*Spring Awakening*
2008	*In the Heights*
2009	*Billy Elliot the Musical*
2010	*Memphis*
2011	*Book of Mormon*
2012	*Once*
2013	*Kinky Boots*
2014	*A Gentleman's Guide to Love and Murder*
2015	*Fun Home*

APPENDIX H
Essential Operas

The following is a basic list of opera's greatest masterworks or, at the very least, excellent and representative teaching pieces for each major composer of opera. While not all-inclusive, it does represent the basic canon of opera in the Western classical tradition. The student of classical singing should familiarize himself or herself with the basic plots and stylistic features of each work. The name given in brackets following each opera is the librettist for the work.

Claudio Monteverdi (1567–1643)
Orfeo (1607) [Striggio]
L'incoronazione di Poppea (1643) [Busenello]

Jean-Baptiste Lully (1632–1687)
Alceste (1674) [Quinault]
Atys (1676) [Quinault]
Armide (1686) [Quinault]

Henry Purcell (1659–1695)
Dido and Aeneas (1689) [Tate]

Jean-Philippe Rameau (1683–1764)
Hippolyte et Aricie (1733) [Pellegrin]
Les Indes galantes (1735) [Fuzelier]
Castor et Pollux (1737) [Bernard]

George Frideric Handel (1685–1759)
Acis and Galatea, HWV 49 (1718) [Gay, with others]
   (technically not an opera)
Radamisto, HWV 12 (1720) [anonymous]
Giulio Cesare in Egitto, HWV 17 (1724) [Haym]
Ariodante, HWV 33 (1735) [anonymous, after Ariosto]
Serse, HWV 40 (1738) [anonymous, after Minato]

Christoph Willibald Gluck (1714–1787)
Orfeo ed Euridice (1762) [Calzabigi]
Iphigénie en Aulide (1774) [Leblanc]
Iphigénie en Tauride (1779) [Guillard]

Wolfgang Amadeus Mozart (1756–1791)
Le nozze di Figaro, K492 (1786) [da Ponte]
Don Giovanni, K527 (1787) [da Ponte]
Così fan tutte, K588 (1790) [da Ponte]
Die Zauberflöte, K620 (1791) [Schikaneder]

Ludwig van Beethoven (1770–1827)
Fidelio, Op. 72 (1805) [Sonnleithner/Treitschke]

Carl Maria von Weber (1786–1826)
Der Freischütz (1821) [Kind]

Giacomo Meyerbeer (1791–1864)
Les Huguenots (1836) [Scribe/Deschamps]

Gioachino Rossini (1792–1868)
L'italiana in Algeri (1813) [Anelli]
Il barbiere di Siviglia (1816) [Sterbini,
   after Beaumarchais]
La Cenerentola (1817) [Ferretti, after Perrault]

Gaetano Donizetti (1797–1848)
L'elisir d'amore (1832) [Romani]
Lucia di Lammermoor (1835) [Cammarano,
   after Scott]
Don Pasquale (1843) [Ruffini]

Vincenzo Bellini (1801–1835)
La sonnambula (1831) [Romani]
Norma (1831) [Romani]

Hector Berlioz (1803–1869)
Les Troyens (1863) [Berlioz, after Virgil]

Richard Wagner (1813–1883)
Der fliegende Holländer (1843) [Wagner]
Tannhäuser (1845) [Wagner]
Lohengrin (1850) [Wagner]
Tristan und Isolde (1859) [Wagner]
Der Ring des Nibelungen (cycle of four operas,
   1862–1876) [Wagner]
   I.   *Das Rheingold* (1862) [Wagner]
   II. *Die Walküre* (1862) [Wagner]
   III. *Siegfried* (1876) [Wagner]
   IV. *Götterdämmerung* (1876) [Wagner]
Die Meistersinger von Nürnberg (1862) [Wagner]
Parsifal (1878) [Wagner]

Giuseppe Verdi (1813–1901)
Nabucco (1842) [Solera]
Rigoletto (1851) [Piave, after Hugo]
Il trovatore (1853) [Cammarano/Bardare]
La traviata (1853) [Piave, after Dumas]
Un ballo in maschera (1859) [Somma]
Don Carlos (1867) [Méry/du Locle]
Aida (1871) [Ghislanzoni]
Otello (1887) [Boito, after Shakespeare]
Falstaff (1893) [Boito, after Shakespeare]

Charles Gounod (1818–1893)
Faust (1859) [Barbier/Carré, after Goethe]

Jacques Offenbach (1819–1880)
Orphée aux enfers (1858) [Crémieux/Halévy]
Les contes d'Hoffman (1881) [Barbier]

Johann Strauss (1825–1899)
Die Fledermaus (1874) [Haffner/Genée,
    after Meilhac/Halévy]

Georges Bizet (1838–1875)
Carmen (1875) [Meilhac/Halévy]

Modest Musorgsky (1839–1881)
Boris Godunov (1874) [Musorgsky, after Pushkin]

Pyotr Il'yich Tchaikovsky (1840–1893)
Yevgeny Onegin, Op. 24 (1879) [Tchaikovsky,
    after Pushkin]

Arthur Sullivan (1842–1900)
HMS Pinafore, or The Lass That Loved a Sailor (1878)
    [Gilbert]
The Pirates of Penzance, or The Slave of Duty (1879)
    [Gilbert]
The Mikado, or The Town of Titipu (1885) [Gilbert]

Jules Massenet (1842–1912)
Manon (1884) [Meilhac/Gille, after Prévost]
Werther (1892) [Blay/Milliet/Hartmann, after Goethe]
Cendrillon (1899) [after Perrault]

Leoš Janáček (1854–1928)
Jenůfa (1904) [Janáček]
Kát'a Kabanová (1921) [Janáček]

Ruggero Leoncavallo (1857–1919)
Pagliacci (1892) [Leoncavallo]

Giacomo Puccini (1858–1924)
La bohème (1896) [Giacosa/Illica]
Tosca (1900) [Giacosa/Illica]
Madama Butterfly (1904) [Giacosa/Illica]

Il trittico (1918) [Adami/Forzano]
Turandot (1926) [Adami/Simoni]

Claude Debussy (1862–1918)
Pelléas et Mélisande (1902) [Debussy, after Maeterlinck]

Pietro Mascagni (1863–1945)
Cavalleria rusticana (1890) [Targioni-Tozzetti/Menasci]

Richard Strauss (1864–1949)
Salome, Op. 54 (1905) [Strauss, after Wilde]
Elektra, Op. 58 (1909) [Hofmannsthal, after Sophocles]
Der Rosenkavalier, Op. 59 (1911) [Hofmannsthal]
Capriccio, Op. 85 (1942) [Krauss/Strauss]

Hans Pfitzner (1869–1949)
Palestrina (1917) [Pfitzner]

Arnold Schoenberg (1874–1951)
Moses und Aron (1954) [Schoenberg]

Alban Berg (1885–1935)
Wozzeck (1925) [Berg, after Büchner]
Lulu (1937) [Berg, after Wiedekind]

Douglas Moore (1893–1969)
The Ballad of Baby Doe (1956) [Latouche]

George Gershwin (1898–1937)
Porgy and Bess (1935) [Heyward]

Aaron Copland (1900–1990)
The Tender Land (1954) [Everett]

Samuel Barber (1910–1981)
Vanessa, Op. 32 (1958) [Menotti]

Gian Carlo Menotti (1911–2007)
The Consul (1950) [Menotti]
The Saint of Bleecker Street (1954) [Menotti]

Benjamin Britten (1913–1976)
Peter Grimes (1945) [Slater, after Crabbe]
Albert Herring (1947) [Crozier, after Maupassant]
Billy Budd (1951) [Forster/Crozier, after Melville]
A Midsummer Night's Dream (1960) [Britten/Pears,
    after Shakespeare]

Carlisle Floyd (1926–)
Susannah (1955) [Floyd]

Karlheinz Stockhausen (1928–2007)
Licht (cycle of seven operas, 1977–2003) [Stockhausen]

Philip Glass (1937–)
Einstein on the Beach (1976) [Wilson]

APPENDIX I

Major Song Cycles, Collections, and Sets

In addition to the songs in the anthology, the student singer who studies classically should become familiar with the following song cycles, collections, and/or important larger works for solo voice. While not all-inclusive, the major works included in this appendix represent the basic canon of Western art song.

GERMAN

Ludwig van Beethoven (1770–1827)
An die ferne Geliebte, Op. 98 (1816) [Jeitteles]

Franz Schubert (1797–1828)
Die schöne Müllerin, D795 (1823) [Müller]
Winterreise, D911 (1827) [Müller]
Schwanengesang, D957 (1828) [Rellstab, Heine, Seidl]

Robert Schumann (1810–1856)
Liederkreis, Op. 24 (1840) [Heine]
Liederkreis, Op. 39 (1840) [Eichendorff]
Frauenliebe und Leben, Op. 42 (1840) [Brentano]
Zwölf Gedichte von Justinus Kerner, Op. 45 (1840) [Kerner]
Dichterliebe, Op. 48 (1840) [Heine]

Johannes Brahms (1833–1897)
Die schöne Magelone, Op. 33 (1869) [Tieck]
Vier ernste Gesänge, Op. 121 (1896) [biblical]

Hugo Wolf (1860–1903)
Mörike-Lieder (1888) [Mörike]
Spanisches Liederbuch (1891) [trans. Heyse/Geibel]
Italienisches Liederbuch (1892/1896) [trans. Heyse]

Gustav Mahler (1860–1911)
Lieder eines fahrenden Gesellen (1885) [Mahler]
Des Knaben Wunderhorn (1885/1899) [Brentano]
Kindertotenlieder (1904) [Rückert]
Rückert-Lieder (1905) [Rückert]

Richard Strauss (1864–1929)
Krämerspiegel, Op. 66 (1918) [Kerr]
Brentano-Lieder, Op. 68 (1918) [Brentano]
Vier letzte Lieder (1948) [Hesse, Eichendorff]

Arnold Schoenberg (1874–1951)
Das Buch der hängenden Gärten (1909) [George]

FRENCH

Gabriel Fauré (1845–1924)
La bonne chanson, Op. 61 (1894) [Verlaine]
La chanson d'Ève, Op. 95 (1910) [Lerberghe]
Le jardin clos, Op. 106 (1914) [Lerberghe]
Mirages, Op. 113 (1919) [Brimont]
L'horizon chimérique, Op. 118 (1921) [Mirmont]

Claude Debussy (1862–1918)
Ariettes oubliées (1887) [Verlaine]
Cinq poèmes de Charles Baudelaire (1890) [Baudelaire]
Proses lyriques (1895) [Debussy]
Chansons de Bilitis (1898) [Louÿs]
Ballades de François Villon (1910) [Villon]

Maurice Ravel (1875–1937)
Shéhérazade (1903) [Klingsor]
Histoires naturelles (1906) [Renard]
Cinq mélodies populaires grecques (1907) [Calvocoressi]
Don Quichotte à Dulcinée (1932) [Morand]

Francis Poulenc (1899–1963)
Le bestiaire (1919) [Apollinaire]
Chansons gaillardes (1926) [anonymous]
Tel jour, telle nuit (1937) [Éluard]
Fiançailles pour rire (1939) [Vilmorin]
Banalités (1940) [Apollinaire]
Calligrammes (1948) [Apollinaire]
La fraîcheur et le feu (1950) [Éluard]
Le travail du peintre (1956) [Éluard]
La courte paille (1960) [Carême]

Jacques Leguerney (1906–1997)
Poèmes de la Pléiade, Vols. I–VIII (1947) [Ronsard]
Sept poèmes de François Maynard (1949) [Maynard]
La solitude (1951) [de Viau]
La nuit (1951) [Saint-Amant]
Le carnaval (1952) [Saint-Amant]

ENGLISH

Ralph Vaughan Williams (1872–1958)
Songs of Travel (1904) [Stevenson]
House of Life (1904) [Rossetti]

Roger Quilter (1877–1953)
To Julia, Op. 8 (1906) [Herrick]
Seven Elizabethan Lyrics, Op. 12 (1908) [various]

George Butterworth (1885–1916)
Six Songs from A Shropshire Lad (1912) [Housman]
Bredon Hill and Other Songs (1912) [Housman]

Gerald Finzi (1901–1956)
A Young Man's Exhortation, Op. 14 (1929) [Hardy]
Earth and Air and Rain, Op. 15 (1932) [Hardy]
Let Us Garlands Bring, Op. 18 (1942) [Shakespeare]
Before and After Summer, Op. 16 (1949) [Hardy]
Till Earth Outwears, Op. 19a (1955) [Hardy]
I Said to Love, Op. 19b (1956) [Hardy]

Benjamin Britten (1913–1976)
Seven Sonnets of Michelangelo, Op. 22 (1940) [Michelangelo]
The Holy Sonnets of John Donne, Op. 35 (1945) [Donne]
A Charm of Lullabies, Op. 41 (1947) [various]

AMERICAN

Charles Ives (1874–1954)
114 Songs (1922) [various]

Aaron Copland (1900–1990)
Twelve Poems of Emily Dickinson (1950) [Dickinson]
Old American Songs (1950/1952) [traditional]

Samuel Barber (1910–1981)
Dover Beach, Op. 3 (1931) [Arnold]
Knoxville Summer of 1915, Op. 24 (1947) [Agee]
Hermit Songs, Op. 29 (1953) [anonymous]

Ned Rorem (b. 1923)
Flight for Heaven (1950) [Herrick]
Poems of Love and the Rain (1963) [various]
Evidence of Things Not Seen (1997) [various]

Dominick Argento (b. 1927)
From the Diary of Virginia Woolf (1974) [Woolf]
The Andrée Expedition (1983) [Andrée]

SPANISH

Isaac Albéniz (1860–1909)
Seis baladas italianas (1887) [de Balaños]

Enrique Granados (1867–1916)
Colección de tonadillas (1914) [Periquet]
Canciones amatorias (1915) [various]

Manuel de Falla (1876–1946)
Siete canciones populares españolas (1914) [traditional]

Joaquín Nin (1879–1949)
Vente cantos populares españoles (1923) [traditional]

Joaquín Turina (1882–1949)
Poema en forma de canciones, Op. 19 (1918) [Campoamor]
Canto a Sevilla, Op. 37 (1927) [San Román]

Jesús Guridi (1886–1961)
Seis canciones castellanas (1939) [Guridi]

Oscar Esplá (1886–1976)
Cinco canciones playeras españolas (1930) [Alberti]

Fernando Obradors (1897–1945)
Canciones clásicas españolas, Vols. I–IV (1921–1940) [various]

Federico García Lorca (1898–1936)
Trece canciones españolas antiguas (1965) [various]

Joaquín Rodrigo (1901–1999)
Cuatro madrigales amatorios (1947) [various]

Xavier Montsalvatge (1912–2002)
Cinco canciones negras (1945) [various]

RUSSIAN

Modest Musorgsky (1839–1881)
The Nursery (1872) [Musorgsky]
Sunless (1874) [Golenishev-Kutuzov]
Songs and Dances of Death (1877) [Golenishev-Kutuzov]

Dmitri Shostakovich (1906–1975)
Suite on Verses of Michelangelo, Op. 145 (1974) [trans. Efros]

SCANDINAVIAN

Edvard Greig (1843–1907)
Haugtussa, Op. 67 (1895) [Garborg]

APPENDIX J

Listening to Singers

When one listens to singers, a wide lexicon of vocabulary is used to descibe what one hears. While some terms are objective in nature (pitch, loudness, duration, etc.), many are subjective and difficult to measure scientifically. Dr. Scott McCoy's book *Your Voice: An Inside View* (second edition, 2012) outlines fifteen different categories for subjective listening on a scale.

Each of these categories is a separate entity in and of itself. A singer can fall anywhere within the spectrum of each, measuring differently (to different listeners) on multiple categories simultaneously. It should be restated that these fifteen categories are subjective in nature; they cannot be objectively and quantifiably mesured by scientific means. Please refer to Dr. McCoy's book for more information.

1.	Bright	Dark
2.	Twang	Loft
3.	Forward	Back
4.	Lyric	Dramatic
5.	Clear	Breathy
6.	Clean	Raspy
7.	Healthy	Damaged
8.	Conversational	Ringing
9.	Nasal	Nonnasal
10.	Free	Forced
11.	Vibrant	Straight-Tone
12.	Wobble	Flutter
13.	In-Tune	Out-of-Tune
14.	Good Diction	Poor Diction
15.	Stylistically Correct	Stylistically Incorrect

APPENDIX K

The Singer's Ten Steps to Wellness

Karen Wicklund

The following article is a modified excerpt from Karen Wicklund's 2010 *Singing Voice Rehabilitation: A Guide for the Voice Teacher and Speech-Language Pathologist*. It is used with permission of DelMar Cengage Learning.

The vocal hygiene guidelines in chapter 6 of Karen Wicklund's *Singing Voice Rehabilitation: A Guide for the Voice Teacher and Speech-Language Pathologist* include twenty-three points. Because some singers find it difficult to remember such a lengthy list of precautions, the following provides a step-by-step daily list that will remind the singer of vocal hygiene habits at different points throughout the day. While some of these steps, for example, exercise, might occur later in the day, all of the steps should be done on a daily basis.

1. RISE two to three hours before having to vocalize, after adequate rest.
   RATIONALE: Rest gives the body time to recover from the stress of the previous day. "A fair amount of sleep is essential for good general health and for proper functioning and resilience of the vocal organs" (Brodnitz, 1988).

2. HYDRATE. Try to drink at least two cups or more of water on rising, to start you on your daily goal of half your body weight in ounces of water.
   RATIONALE: Your body loses water overnight in respiration and perspiration and needs replenishment immediately on rising (Batmanghelidj, 1997).

3. EXERCISE: Move your body! Walking, running, elliptical—whatever form of aerobic movement you like, you need at least twenty minutes at least four times per week. If you are a weight trainer, take care not to strain your neck muscles while weight training.
   RATIONALE: Studies have shown that without exercise, the cardiovascular system declines 30 percent between ages thirty and seventy in its ability to deliver blood to the tissues (Smith and Zook, 1986). And, other studies have shown that exercise maintains the elasticity of the lungs, allowing them to retain their capacity for residual volume (Milic-Emili, Petit, and Deroanne, 1962).

4. EAT something before warming up the voice.
   RATIONALE: The act of chewing and swallowing warms up the vocal mechanism. Though it is probably not a good idea to eat a large meal right before a performance, some singers feel better after eating a moderately sized meal a couple of hours before (Ware, 1998). Adequate nutrition throughout the day maintains blood sugar levels and provides energy for singing (Harvey and Miller, 1998).

5. WARM-UP the voice/vocalize daily.
   RATIONALE: "A pitcher knows better than to throw a fastball before a number of warm-up throws . . . yet most singers will start belting high notes with hardly any exercise. . . . Avoid singing any high notes until your voice is thoroughly warmed up. . . . Start with exercises of limited range and then move to wider ones as the voice becomes more responsive" (McKinney 1994, p. 179).

6. STUDY singing. Engage in consistent study of the voice by seeing your teacher on a regular basis.
   RATIONALE: "An alert singing teacher may detect deficits in support, breath control, pitch, or other speaking habits that may produce voice fatigue and aggravate laryngeal injury" (Sataloff, 1991, pp. 249–50).

7. SUPPORT the speaking voice in the same way as the singing voice.
   RATIONALE: The singer should learn to use a supported, properly placed tone in the proper range for that individual singer (Westerman-Gregg, 1995). Those speakers who manage vocal demands by increasing both breath support and laryngeal resistance experience less vocal fatigue than those who deal with the problem solely at the laryngeal level (Kostyk and Rochet, 1998). Also, a recent research study found that a group of teachers with voice disorders who used an amplification system reported that the result was more "clarity of their speaking and singing voice" (Roy et al., 2002). In addition, a recent study showed that in singers using

microphone systems, risk of noise exposure was alleviated more by use of in-ear monitors than with floor monitors (Federman and Ricketts, 2008).

8. MONITOR stress levels hourly by taking deep breaths, stretching, and relaxing the body and vocal mechanism.

   RATIONALE: Studies regarding prolonged periods of stress have shown a link between voice dysfunction and stress and/or anxiety symptoms (Tolkmitt and Scherer, 1986; Long, 1988; Sapir, 1993; Goldman et al., 1996).

9. AVOID SMOKING/SECOND-HAND SMOKE or toxic/irritating chemicals in the atmosphere.

   RATIONALE: Smoking causes edema of the vocal folds and generalized inflammation in the vocal tract (Sataloff, 1991). Cigarette smoking is also a primary causative factor in emphysema, bronchitis, and lung cancer, as well as other diseases (Estes, 2006). Singers should also avoid exposure to stage smoke and the chemicals in the air of print shops or hair salons.

10. AVOID EATING within two to three hours of going to bed.

    RATIONALE: Laryngopharygeal reflux disease (LPRD) can be exacerbated by a singer's prone position during sleep and also by lifestyle factors, because singers often eat late at night (Sataloff, 1991). Management can include acid-blocker medications, elevation of the head of the bed, and, in extreme cases, surgery to tighten the lower and/or upper esophageal sphincters (LES and UES).

REFERENCES

Anticaglia, J., M. Hawkshaw, and R. Sataloff. "The Effects of Smoking on Voice Performance." *Journal of Singing* 61, no. 2 (2004): 167–72.

Batmanghelidj, F. *Your Body's Many Cries for Water*. Falls Church, VA: Global Health Solutions, 1997.

Brodnitz, F. *Keep Your Voice Healthy*, 2nd ed. Austin, TX: ProEd, 1988.

Estes, M. *Health Assessment and Physical Examination*, 3rd ed. Clifton Park, NY: Thomson Delmar Learning, 2006.

Federman, J., and T. Ricketts. "Preferred and Minimum Acceptable Listening Levels for Musicians While Using Floor and In-Ear Monitors." *Journal of Speech, Language, and Hearing Research* 51 (2008): 147–59.

Goldman, S., J. Hargrave, R. Hillman, E. Holmberg, and C. Gress. "Stress, Anxiety, Somatic Complaints, and Voice Use in Women with Vocal Nodules." *American Journal of Speech-Language Pathology* 5 (1996): 44–54.

Harvey, P., and S. Miller. "Nutrition and the Professional Voice User." In *Vocal Health and Pedagogy*, edited by Robert T. Sataloff, 210–211. San Diego, CA: Singular Publishing, 1998.

Kostyk, B. E., and A. P. Rochet. "Laryngeal Airway Resistance in Teachers with Vocal Fatigue: A Preliminary Study." *Journal of Voice* 12, no. 3 (1998): 287–99.

Long, G. "The Relationship of Voice Stress, Anxiety, and Depression to Life Events and Personal Style Variables. *Social Behavior and Personality* 16, no. 2 (1988): 133–45.

McKinney, J. *Diagnosis and Correction of Vocal Faults*. Nashville, TN: Genovox Music Group, 1994.

Milic-Emili, G., J. M. Petit, and R. Deroanne. "Mechanical Work of Breathing during Exercise in Trained and Untrained Subjects." *Journal of Applied Physiology* 17 (1962): 43–46.

Roy, N., B. Weinrich, S. D. Gray, K. Tanner, S. W. Toledo, H. Dove, et al. "Voice Amplification versus Vocal Hygiene Instruction for Teachers with Voice Disorders: A Treatment Outcomes Study." *Journal of Speech, Language, and Hearing Research* 45 (2002): 625–38.

Sapir, S. "Vocal Attrition in Voice Students: Survey Findings." *Journal of Voice* 7, no. 1 (1993): 69–74.

Sataloff, R. *Professional Voice: The Science and Art of Clinical Care*. New York: Raven Press, 1991.

Smith, E., and S. Zook. "The Aging Process: Benefits of Physical Activity." *Journal of Physical Education, Recreation, and Dance* 57, no. 1 (1986): 32–34.

Tolkmitt, F., and K. Scherer. "The Effect of Experimentally Induced Stress on Vocal Parameters." *Journal of Experimental Psychology: Human Perception and Performance* 12, no. 3 (1986): 302–13.

Ware, C. *Basics of Vocal Pedagogy*. New York: McGraw-Hill, 1998.

Westerman-Gregg, J. "Speaking and Singing with One Voice." Proceedings of the NATS Winter Workshop, Las Vegas, Nevada, 1995.

Wicklund, K. "Singer's Health Issues: The Efficacy of a Wellness Model for Singers." Doctoral diss., Northwestern University, 1996.

Karen Wicklund, DM, MHS CCC-SLP has collaborated as a singing voice specialist (SVS) and/or SLP with the voice teams of Dr. Bastian, Dr. Sims, Dr. Akst, and Dr. Heman-Ackah as director of the Chicago Center for Professional Voice, and at Western Michigan University, where she is a voice professor and SLP. She is currently teaching her SVS certification training workshops in Chicago, Kalamazoo, and Arizona. A reknowned singer's wellness specialist, her website (www.singershealth.com) provides health information and referrals for singers worldwide. Dr. Wicklund has also published articles in *Medical Problems of Performing Artists*, the *Journal of Singing*, *ASHA Leader*, and *American Organist*, and presented at the international conferences of NATS, PAS, and ASHA, as well as the Occupational Voice Symposium in London and the Voice Foundation in Philadelphia. She has sung leading roles with the San Francisco, Santa Fe, Omaha, Lake George, and other American opera companies.

"The Singer's Ten Steps to Wellness" originally appeared in *Singing Voice Rehabilitation: A Guide for the Voice Teacher and Speech-Language Pathologist* (Clifton Park, NY: Delmar/Cengage Learning, 2010). It is reprinted with permission.

APPENDIX L

Medications and Their Effects on the Voice

The following list was compiled by Dr. Ingo Titze and the National Center for Voice and Speech (NCVS). It is reprinted with their permission. It was created with the aid of an experienced pharmacist and voice scientists of NCVS. The chart is provided as information only and is not meant to supersede a physician's counsel. All pharmacological choices should be done with consultation of one's doctor. See nvcs.org for more information.

Table AL.1. Medications and Their Effects on the Voice

Brand Name	Generic Name	Drug Class	Effects on Voice or Speech
Abilify	aripiprazole	atypical antipsychotic	No effects on voice or speech mechanisms have been reported.
Accolate	zafirlukast	antihistamine-leukotriene receptor antagonist	No effects on voice or speech mechanisms have been reported.
Accupril	quinapril	cardiovascular-ACE inhibitor	Excessive coughing has been associated with the use of ACE inhibitors, which, in turn, may lead to hoarseness and possibly vocal tissue damage.
Accutane	isotretinoin	antiacne-oral retinoid	Adverse mucocutaneous effects are frequently reported. Cheilitis (inflammation of the lips) occurs in more than 90 percent of patients and appears to be dose-related. Other mucocutaneous effects frequently encountered include xerosis, xerostomia, epistaxis, peeling, and pruritus. The mucocutaneous drying effects of isotretinoin are dose-related and are usually reversible following discontinuation.
Aciphex	rabeprazole	proton pump inhibitor	These agents have a favorable effect on the voice in that they reduce damage caused by gastroesophageal reflux disease (GERD). Uncontrolled acidic spillage of stomach acids into the larynx is harmful to delicate vocal fold tissues.
Actonel	risedronate	osteoporosis-bisphosphonate	Adverse effects with oral risedronate during the clinical trials were reported as generally mild and primarily affected the gastrointestinal system. The specific events reported were acid regurgitation (4.1 percent), including pyrosis (heartburn); flatulence (4.1 percent); gastroesophageal reflux disease (GERD) (0.7 percent); dyspepsia (3.4 percent); diarrhea (1.4 percent); abdominal pain (2.1 percent); and nausea (2.1 percent).
Actos	pioglitazone	antidiabetic-insulin sensitizer	No effects on voice or speech mechanisms have been reported.
Adalat CC	nifedipine	cardiovascular-CCB	No effects on voice or speech mechanisms have been reported.

(continued)

Table AL.1. Medications and Their Effects on the Voice (*continued*)

Brand Name	Generic Name	Drug Class	Effects on Voice or Speech
Adderall	amphetamine/ dextroamphetamine	stimulant	Adderall may have a drying effect on vocal fold tissues, which can lead to hoarseness, soreness, voice changes, and laryngitis. In addition, dry vocal tissues may be more prone to such injuries as nodules.
Advair-diskus	fluticasone and salmeterol	antiasthmatic-steroid/ bronchodilator	Patients using inhaled steroids sometimes experience voice changes (including complete loss of voice). The onset and severity of symptoms is highly variable among patients. Studies show that discontinuation of inhaled steroids restores the voice in dysphonic patients, but symptoms may not resolve immediately.
Aldactone	spironolactone	cardiovascular-diuretic	Diuretics have a drying effect on mucous membranes, including those used to speak and sing. Hoarseness, sore throat, voice changes, or laryngitis are possible symptoms. In addition to irritation effects, dry vocal folds may be more prone to such injuries as nodules.
Allegra	fexophenadine	antihistamine	Antihistamines have a drying effect on mucous membranes that may cause hoarseness, sore throat, voice changes, or laryngitis. In addition to irritation, dry vocal folds may be more prone to such injuries as nodules.
Altace	ramipril	cardiovascular-ACE inhibitor	Excessive coughing has been associated with the use of ACE inhibitors, which, in turn, may lead to hoarseness and possibly vocal tissue damage.
Amaryl	glimepiride	antidiabetic-sulfonylurea	No effects on voice or speech mechanisms have been reported.
Ambien	zolpidem	sedative/hypnotic	The use of sedatives may produce an uninhibited or diminished drive to speak. Symptoms of dysarthria (slow, slurred, and uncoordinated speech movements) may also be linked to sedative use.
Amoxil	amoxicillin	antibiotic-penicillin	In general, no effects on voice or speech mechanisms are associated with antibiotic use. It should be noted, however, that antibiotic abuse/misuse can lead to an overgrowth of Candida in the body, possibly leading to laryngeal thrush.
Antivert	meclizine	antihistamine	Antihistamines have a drying effect on mucous membranes that may cause hoarseness, sore throat, voice changes, or laryngitis. In addition to irritation, dry vocal folds may be more prone to such injuries as nodules.
Aricept	donepezil	cholinergic function enhancer for Alzheimer's patients	Infrequent voice and speech effects may include tongue edema, (swelling), pharyngitis (sore throat), and bronchitis.
Astelin	azelastine	antihistamine	Antihistamines have a drying effect on mucous membranes that may cause hoarseness, sore throat, voice changes, or laryngitis. In addition to irritation, dry vocal folds may be more prone to such injuries as nodules.
Ativan	lorazepam	antianxiety-benzodiazepine	Less than 1 percent of patients who take benzodiazepines experience slurred speech and symptoms of dysarthria (slow, uncoordinated speech).
Atrovent	ipratropium	antiasthmatic-bronchodilator	Inhaled bronchodilators sometimes dry or irritate tissues in the mouth and throat and may lead to hoarseness, soreness, voice changes, or laryngitis. Dry vocal tissues may be more prone to such injuries as nodules.

(continued)

Table AL.1. Medications and Their Effects on the Voice (*continued*)

Brand Name	Generic Name	Drug Class	Effects on Voice or Speech
Augmentin	amoxicillin clavulenate	antibiotic-penicillin	In general, no effects on voice or speech mechanisms are associated with antibiotic use. It should be noted, however, that antibiotic abuse/misuse can lead to an overgrowth of Candida in the body, possibly leading to laryngeal thrush.
Avapro	irbesartan	cardiovascular-AGII antagonist	Although excessive coughing has been associated with the use of ACE inhibitors and, to a lesser extent, AGII inhibitors, which may lead to hoarseness and possible vocal tissue damage, this effect has *not* been reported with the use of Avapro.
Avelox	moxifloxacin	antibiotic-fluoroquinolone	In general, no effects on voice or speech mechanisms are associated with antibiotic use. It should be noted, however, that antibiotic abuse/misuse can lead to an overgrowth of Candida in the body, possibly leading to laryngeal thrush.
Avodart	dutasteride	BPH-5 alpha reductase inhibitor	No effects on voice or speech mechanisms have been reported.
Axid	nizatidine	gastrointestinal-H2 blocker	Two effects exist: 1) The antihistamine component has a drying effect on mucous membranes that may cause hoarseness, sore throat, voice changes, or laryngitis. In addition to irritation, dry vocal folds may be more prone to such injuries as nodules. 2) However, this medication may benefit the voice if it is taken to reduce acidity of gastroesophageal reflux. Uncontrolled spillage of stomach acids into the larynx is harmful to delicate vocal fold tissues.
Azmacort	triamcinolone	antiasthmatic-steroid inhaled	Patients using inhaled steroids sometimes experience voice changes (including complete loss of voice). The onset and severity of symptoms is highly variable among patients. Studies show that discontinuation of inhaled steroids restores the voice in dysphonic patients, but symptoms may not resolve immediately
Bactrim	sulfamethox/trimethoprin	antibiotic-sulfa	In general, no effects on voice or speech mechanisms are associated with antibiotic use. It should be noted, however, that antibiotic abuse/misuse can lead to an overgrowth of Candida in the body, possibly leading to laryngeal thrush.
Bactroban	mupirocin	antibiotic	No effects on voice or speech mechanisms have been reported.
Benadryl	diphenhydramine	antihistamine	Antihistamines have a drying effect on mucous membranes that may cause hoarseness, sore throat, voice changes, or laryngitis. In addition to irritation, dry vocal folds may be more prone to such injuries as nodules.
Benicar	olmesartan	cardiovascular-AGII antagonist	An infrequently reported adverse reaction is coughing, which, in turn, may cause hoarseness and possible vocal tissue damage.
Bentyl	dicyclomine	antispasmotic	The following adverse effects are frequently associated with the use of anticholinergic agents like dicyclomine, at both therapeutic and subtherapeutic levels: blurred vision, cycloplegia, mydriasis, photophobia, anhidrosis, xerostomia (dry mouth), urinary retention, sinus tachycardia, palpitations, and constipation. Saliva substitutes may be administered to relieve dry mouth.

(continued)

Table AL.1. Medications and Their Effects on the Voice (*continued*)

Brand Name	Generic Name	Drug Class	Effects on Voice or Speech
Biaxin	clarithromycin	antibiotic-macrolide	In general, no effects on voice or speech mechanisms are associated with antibiotic use. It should be noted, however, that antibiotic abuse/misuse can lead to an overgrowth of Candida in the body, possibly leading to laryngeal thrush.
Boniva	ibandronate	osteoporosis-bisphosphonate	Adverse events of the digestive system were reportedly the most common reason for withdrawal from clinical trials of orally administered ibandronate. In addition to dyspepsia, other reported adverse events included constipation (2.5–4 percent), diarrhea (6.8 percent ibandronate vs. 5 percent placebo), esophagitis, gastritis (2.2 percent vs. 1.9 percent), pharyngitis (2.5 percent vs. 1.5 percent), and nausea/vomiting (2.7 percent vs. 2.1 percent).
Botox	botulinum toxin type A	onabotulinumtoxinA	Indicated for treatment of blepharospasms. Side effects can include increased incidence of upper respiratory tract infections, cough, bronchitis, and possible dry mouth.
Buspar	buspirone	antianxiety	No effects on voice or speech mechanisms have been reported.
Byetta	exenatide	antidiabetic-incretin mimetics	Other notable gastrointestinal events included diarrhea (13 percent vs. 6 percent placebo) and dyspepsia (6 percent vs. 3 percent placebo). Anorexia (reported as decreased appetite) and gastroesophageal reflux were also reported in 1–5 percent of patients and at a higher rate than placebo.
Caduet	amlodipine/atorvastatin	cardiovascular-CCB/statin	Calcium channel blockers like amlodipine should be used cautiously in patients with gastroesophageal reflux disease (GERD) or hiatal hernia associated with reflux esophagitis. The drugs relax the lower esophageal sphincter. Note that voice production can be adversely affected by GERD.
Calan	verapamil	cardiovascular-CCB	Calcium channel blockers like verapamil should be used cautiously in patients with gastroesophageal reflux disease (GERD) or hiatal hernia associated with reflux esophagitis. The drugs relax the lower esophageal sphincter. Note that voice production can be adversely affected by GERD.
Cardizem CD	diltiazem	cardiovascular-CCB	Calcium channel blockers like diltiazem should be used cautiously in patients with gastroesophageal reflux disease (GERD) or hiatal hernia associated with reflux esophagitis. The drugs relax the lower esophageal sphincter. Note that voice production can be adversely affected by GERD.
Cardura	doxazosin	cardiovascular-alpha blocker	No effects on voice or speech mechanisms have been reported.
Catapres	clonidine	cardiovascular-alpha agonist	No effects on voice or speech mechanisms have been reported.
Ceftin	cefuroxine	antibiotic-cephalosporin	In general, no effects on voice or speech mechanisms are associated with antibiotic use. It should be noted, however, that antibiotic abuse/misuse can lead to an overgrowth of Candida in the body, possibly leading to laryngeal thrush.
Cefzil	cefprozil	antibiotic-cephalosporin	In general, no effects on voice or speech mechanisms are associated with antibiotic use. It should be noted, however, that antibiotic abuse/misuse can lead to an overgrowth of Candida in the body, possibly leading to laryngeal thrush.

(continued)

Table AL.1. Medications and Their Effects on the Voice (*continued*)

Brand Name	Generic Name	Drug Class	Effects on Voice or Speech
Celebrex	celecoxib	analgesic-NSAID-COX 2 inhibitor	Less common gastrointestinal effects (0.1–1.9 percent incidence) that occurred with celecoxib regardless of causality included anorexia, constipation, diverticulitis, gastritis, gastroenteritis, gastroesophageal reflux disease (GERD), hemorrhoids, hiatal hernia, melena, stomatitis, and xerostomia.
Celexa	citalopram	antidepressant-SSRI	Increased cough and gastroesophageal reflux have been reported, both of which can adversely affect the voice. Asthma, laryngitis, bronchospasm, or sputum increase may rarely occur.
Chantix	varenicline	nicotine receptor agonist	Among the most common (> 5 percent, and twice the rate seen in placebo) adverse reactions to varenicline were constipation and flatulence. Other common adverse reactions (>= 1 percent and at least 0.5 percent more than placebo) included abdominal pain (including discomfort, tenderness, distension), anorexia, appetite stimulation, asthenia, dysgeusia, dyspepsia, dyspnea, gastroesophageal reflux, malaise, rhinorrhea, and xerostomia.
Cialis	tadalafil	ED-phosphodiesterase (PDE) type 5 inhibitor	No effects on voice or speech mechanisms have been reported.
Cipro	ciprofloxacin	antibiotic-fluoroquinolone	In general, no effects on voice or speech mechanisms are associated with antibiotic use. It should be noted, however, that antibiotic abuse/misuse can lead to an overgrowth of Candida in the body, possibly leading to laryngeal thrush.
Claritin	loratadine	antihistamine	Antihistamines have a drying effect on mucous membranes that may cause hoarseness, sore throat, voice changes, or laryngitis. In addition to irritation, dry vocal folds may be more prone to such injuries as nodules.
Cleocin	clindamycin	antibiotic	In general, no effects on voice or speech mechanisms are associated with antibiotic use. It should be noted, however, that antibiotic abuse/misuse can lead to an overgrowth of Candida in the body, possibly leading to laryngeal thrush.
Climara	estradiol	hormone-estrogen topical	No effects on voice or speech mechanisms have been reported.
Clomid	clomiphene	nonsteroidal fertility agent	No effects on voice or speech mechanisms have been reported.
codeine sulfate	codeine sulfate	analgesic-narcotic	Narcotics may produce an uninhibited or diminished drive to speak. Symptoms of dysarthria (slow, slurred, and uncoordinated speech movements) may also be linked to narcotic use.
Combivent	ipratropium/albuterol	antiasthmatic-bronchodilator	Inhaled bronchodilators sometimes dry or irritate tissues in the mouth and throat and may lead to hoarseness, soreness, voice changes, or laryngitis. Dry vocal tissues may be more prone to such injuries as nodules.
Concerta	methylphenidate	stimulant	Complaints of xerostomia or dysgeusia may be limited by sucking sugarless hard candy, crushed ice, and drinking plenty of water or other fluids.

(continued)

Table AL.1. Medications and Their Effects on the Voice (*continued*)

Brand Name	Generic Name	Drug Class	Effects on Voice or Speech
Coreg	carvedilol	cardiovascular-alpha and beta blocker	Beta blockers can cause bronchospasm, dyspnea, or wheezing in patients with asthma or pulmonary disease. Nonselective beta blockers like carvedilol are more likely than selective agents to precipitate bronchospasm. Patients with preexisting bronchospastic disease are at greater risk. Two cases of death from status asthmaticus have been reported in patients receiving single doses of carvedilol. Rare postmarketing reports describing interstitial pneumonitis associated with carvedilol therapy do exist.
Coumadin	warfarin	anticoagulant	Vocal performers, particularly, should be cautious about using medications that decrease platelet function during periods of strenuous voicing demands, due to an increased possibility of vocal fold hemorrhage.
Covera-hs	verapamil	cardiovascular-CCB	Calcium channel blockers like verapamil should be used cautiously in patients with gastroesophageal reflux disease (GERD) or hiatal hernia associated with reflux esophagitis. The drugs relax the lower esophageal sphincter. Note that voice production can be adversely affected by GERD.
Cozaar	losartan	cardiovascular-AGII antagonist	An infrequently reported adverse reaction is coughing, which, in turn, may cause hoarseness and possible vocal tissue damage.
Crestor	rosuvastatin	cardiovascular-statin	The manufacturer provides the following adverse events, which occurred in >= 2 percent of patients receiving rosuvastatin vs. placebo during premarketing trials (regardless of causality): pharyngitis (9 percent vs. 7.6 percent placebo), headache (5.5 percent vs. 5 percent), diarrhea (3.4 percent vs. 2.9 percent), dyspepsia (3.4 percent vs. 3.1 percent), nausea/vomiting (3.4 percent vs. 3.1 percent), muscle pain (2.8 percent vs. 1.3 percent), asthenia (2.7 percent vs. 2.6 percent), back pain (2.6 percent vs. 2.4 percent), flu-like syndrome (2.3 percent vs. 1.8 percent), urinary tract infection (2.3 percent vs. 1.6 percent), rhinitis (2.2 percent vs. 2.1 percent), and sinusitis (2 percent vs. 1.8 percent).
Cycrin	medroxyprogesterone	hormone-progestin	No effects on voice or speech mechanisms have been reported.
Cymbalta	duloxetine	antidepressant-serotonin–norepinephrine reuptake inhibitor	Pharyngitis has been frequently reported during duloxetine administration (9 percent vs. 5 percent placebo). In clinical trials, cough was reported in 3–6 percent of those on duloxetine versus 3 percent of those receiving placebo.
Darvocet-n	propoxyphene/acetaminophen	analgesic-narcotic	Narcotics may produce an uninhibited or diminished drive to speak. Symptoms of dysarthria (slow, slurred, and uncoordinated speech movements) may also be linked to narcotic use.
Daypro	oxaprozin	analgesic-NSAID	Those who use their voices rigorously should be cautious about using medications that decrease platelet function during periods of strenuous voicing demands, due to an increased possibility of vocal fold hemorrhage.
Decadron	dexamethasone	steroid-glucocorticoid	Dexamethasone's effect is advantageous when used to shrink swollen vocal tissues, although patients taking dexamethasone should be carefully monitored by a physician. It is not advised for patients with vocal fold ulcers, hemorrhages, or acute laryngitis.

(continued)

Table AL.1. Medications and Their Effects on the Voice (*continued*)

Brand Name	Generic Name	Drug Class	Effects on Voice or Speech
Deltasone	prednisone	steroid-glucocorticoid	Prednisone's effect is advantageous when used to shrink swollen vocal tissues, although patients taking prednisone should be carefully monitored by a physician. It is not advised for patients with vocal fold ulcers, hemorrhages, or acute laryngitis.
Depakote	valproic acid	antiseizure	Anticonvulsants may produce an uninhibited or diminished drive to speak. Symptoms of dysarthria (slow, slurred, and uncoordinated speech movements) may also be linked to their use.
Desyrel	trazodone	antidepressant	No effects on voice or speech mechanisms have been reported.
Detrol	tolterodine	anticholinergic-overactive bladder	Adverse effects consistent with the actions of antimuscarinic agents and reported in < 1percent of patients treated with tolterodine in controlled clinical studies were confusion, gastroesophageal reflux, and flushing of the skin.
Diabeta	glyburide	antidiabetic-sulfonylurea	No effects on voice or speech mechanisms have been reported.
Diflucan	fluconazole	antifungal	No effects on voice or speech mechanisms have been reported.
Dilantin	phenytoin	antiseizure	Anticonvulsants may produce an uninhibited or diminished drive to speak. Symptoms of dysarthria (slow, slurred. and uncoordinated speech movements) may also be linked to their use.
Dilaudid	hydromorphone	analgesic-narcotic	Narcotics may produce an uninhibited or diminished drive to speak. Symptoms of dysarthria (slow, slurred, and uncoordinated speech movements) may also be linked to narcotic use.
Diovan	valsartan	cardiovascular-AGII antagonist	Excessive coughing has been associated with the use of ACE inhibitors or, to a lesser extent, AGII inhibitors, which, in turn, may lead to hoarseness and possibly vocal tissue damage.
Dolophine	methadone	analgesic-narcotic	Narcotics may produce an uninhibited or diminished drive to speak. Symptoms of dysarthria (slow, slurred, and uncoordinated speech movements) may also be linked to narcotic use.
Doryx	doxycycline	antibiotic-tetracycline	In general, no effects on voice or speech mechanisms are associated with antibiotic use. It should be noted, however, that antibiotic abuse/misuse can lead to an overgrowth of Candida in the body, possibly leading to laryngeal thrush.
Duragesic	fentanyl	analgesic-narcotic	Narcotics may produce an uninhibited or diminished drive to speak. Symptoms of dysarthria (slow, slurred, and uncoordinated speech movements) may also be linked to narcotic use.
Dyazide	hydrochlorothiazide/ triamterene	cardiovascular-diuretic	Diuretics have a drying effect on mucous membranes, including those used to speak and sing. Hoarseness, sore throat, voice changes, or laryngitis are possible symptoms. In addition to irritation effects, dry vocal folds may be more prone to such injuries as nodules.
Effexor	venlafaxine	antidepressant-serotonin–norepinephrine reuptake inhibitor	Effexor may have a drying effect on the body, including vocal fold tissues, which can lead to hoarseness, soreness, voice changes, or laryngitis. In addition, dry vocal tissues may be more prone to such injuries as nodules.

(continued)

Table AL.1. Medications and Their Effects on the Voice (*continued*)

Brand Name	Generic Name	Drug Class	Effects on Voice or Speech
Elavil	amitriptyline	antidepressant-TCA	Tricyclic antidepressants may affect coordination, including the speech production system. Slow or slurred speech may be observed. They also have a drying effect on vocal fold tissues, which can lead to hoarseness, soreness, voice changes, or laryngitis. In addition, dry vocal tissues may be more prone to such injuries as nodules.
Erytab	erythromycin	antibiotic-macrolide	In general, no effects on voice or speech mechanisms are associated with antibiotic use. It should be noted, however, that antibiotic abuse/misuse can lead to an overgrowth of Candida in the body, possibly leading to laryngeal thrush.
Eskalith	lithium	bipolar disorder-monovalent cation	Dry mouth may occur with lithium treatment. Slurred speech may indicate the need for dose adjustment.
Estrace	estradiol	hormone-estrogen	No effects on voice or speech mechanisms have been reported.
Estraderm	estradiol	hormone-estrogen topical	No effects on voice or speech mechanisms have been reported.
Estring	estradiol vaginal ring	hormone-estrogen	No effects on voice or speech mechanisms have been reported.
Fastin	phentermine	stimulant	Dry mouth may occur.
Fioricet	butalbital/APAP/caffeine	analgesic-barbiturate-pain combo	Narcotics may produce an uninhibited or diminished drive to speak. Symptoms of dysarthria (slow, slurred, and uncoordinated speech movements) may also be linked to narcotic use.
Flagyl	metronidazole	antibiotic	In general, no effects on voice or speech mechanisms are associated with antibiotic use. It should be noted, however, that antibiotic abuse/misuse can lead to an overgrowth of Candida in the body, possibly leading to laryngeal thrush.
Flexeril	cyclobenzaprine	antispasmotic	The use of muscle relaxers may produce an uninhibited or diminished drive to speak. Symptoms of dysarthria (slow, slurred, and uncoordinated speech movements) may also be linked to sedative use. Muscle relaxers may affect coordination, including the speech production system. Slow or slurred speech may be observed. They also have a drying effect on vocal fold tissues, which can lead to hoarseness, soreness, voice changes, or laryngitis. In addition, dry vocal tissues may be more prone to such injuries as nodules.
Flomax	tamsulosin	BPH-alpha blocker	The use of Flomax rarely causes pharyngitis (sore throat) or increased cough. Excessive coughing may lead to hoarseness and possible vocal tissue damage.
Flonase	fluticasone	antiallergy-steroid topical	Throat irritation and dryness, cough, hoarseness, and voice changes are all possible adverse reactions.
Flovent	fluticasone	antiallergy-steroid topical	Patients using inhaled steroids sometimes experience voice changes (including complete loss of voice). The onset and severity of symptoms is highly variable among patients. Studies show that discontinuation of inhaled steroids restores the voice in dysphonic patients, but symptoms may not resolve immediately.

(continued)

Table AL.1. Medications and Their Effects on the Voice (*continued*)

Brand Name	Generic Name	Drug Class	Effects on Voice or Speech
Fosamax	alendronate	osteoporosis-bisphosphonate	Adverse effects with alendronate during the clinical trials were reported as generally mild and primarily affected the gastrointestinal system. The specific events reported were acid regurgitation (4.1 percent), including pyrosis (heartburn); flatulence (4.1 percent); gastroesophageal reflux disease (GERD) (0.7 percent); dyspepsia (3.4 percent); diarrhea (1.4 percent); abdominal pain (2.1 percent); and nausea (2.1 percent).
Gardasil	HPV vaccine	vaccine	No effects on voice or speech mechanisms have been reported.
Geodon	ziprasidone	atypical antipsychotic	Dry mouth may occur.
Glucophage	metformin	antidiabetic-oral biguanide agent	No effects on voice or speech mechanisms have been reported.
Glucotrol	glipizide	antidiabetic-sulfonylurea	No effects on voice or speech mechanisms have been reported.
Humalog	insulin lispro	antidiabetic-insulin	No effects on voice or speech mechanisms have been reported.
Humulin-N	insulin isophane (human)	antidiabetic-insulin	No effects on voice or speech mechanisms have been reported.
Humulin-R	insulin regular	antidiabetic-insulin	No effects on voice or speech mechanisms have been reported.
Hydrodiurel	hydrochlorothiazide	cardiovascular-diuretic	Diuretics have a drying effect on mucous membranes, including those used to speak and sing. Hoarseness, sore throat, voice changes, or laryngitis are possible symptoms. In addition to irritation effects, dry vocal folds may be more prone to such injuries as nodules.
Hytrin	terazosin	cardiovascular-alpha blocker	No effects on voice or speech mechanisms have been reported.
Hyzaar	losartan/HCTZ	cardiovascular-AGII antagonist/diuretic	An infrequently reported adverse reaction is coughing, which, in turn, may cause hoarseness and possible vocal tissue damage. Diuretics have a drying effect on mucous membranes, including those used to speak and sing. Hoarseness, sore throat, voice changes, or laryngitis are possible symptoms. In addition to irritation effects, dry vocal folds may be more prone to such injuries as nodules.
Imdur	isosorbide mononitrate	cardiovascular-vasodilator	Voice-related effects may occur, including vocal tissue dryness (which, in addition to irritation effects, may be more prone to such injuries as nodules). Bronchitis, bronchospasm, and pharyngitis (sore throat) are other possible effects.
Imitrex	sumatriptan	antimigrane	No effects on voice or speech mechanisms have been reported.
Inderal	propranolol	cardiovascular-beta blocker	No effects on voice or speech mechanisms have been reported.
Indocin	indomethacin	analgesic-NSAID	Those who use their voices rigorously should be cautious about using medications that decrease platelet function during periods of strenuous voicing demands, due to an increased possibility of vocal fold hemorrhage.
Januvia	sitagliptin	antidiabetic-dipeptidyl-peptidase-IV (DPP-IV) inhibitors	No effects on voice or speech mechanisms have been reported.
Kariva	desogestrel/ethinyl estradiol	hormone-birth control	The use of oral contraceptives has not been shown to significantly affect female voices.

(continued)

Table AL.1. Medications and Their Effects on the Voice (*continued*)

Brand Name	Generic Name	Drug Class	Effects on Voice or Speech
Keflex	cephalexin	antibiotic-cephalosporin	In general, no effects on voice or speech mechanisms are associated with antibiotic use. It should be noted, however, that antibiotic abuse/misuse can lead to an overgrowth of Candida in the body, possibly leading to laryngeal thrush.
Keppra	levetiracetam	antiseizure	Anticonvulsants may produce an uninhibited or diminished drive to speak. Symptoms of dysarthria (slow, slurred, and uncoordinated speech movements) may also be linked to their use.
Klonopin	clonazepam	antianxiety-benzodiazepine	Less than 1 percent of patients who take benzodiazepines experience slurred speech and symptoms of dysarthria (slow, uncoordinated speech).
Klor Con	potassium chloride	supplement	No effects on voice or speech mechanisms have been reported.
Lamictal	lamotrigine	antiseizure	Anticonvulsants may produce an uninhibited or diminished drive to speak. Symptoms of dysarthria (slow, slurred, and uncoordinated speech movements) may also be linked to their use.
Lamisil	terbinafine	antifungal	No effects on voice or speech mechanisms have been reported.
Lanoxin	digoxin	cardiovascular-digitalis inotropic agent	No effects on voice or speech mechanisms have been reported.
Lantus	insulin glargine	antidiabetic-insulin	No effects on voice or speech mechanisms have been reported.
Lasix	furosemide	cardiovascular-diuretic	Diuretics have a drying effect on mucous membranes, including those used to speak and sing. Hoarseness, sore throat, voice changes, or laryngitis are possible symptoms. In addition to irritation effects, dry vocal folds may be more prone to such injuries as nodules.
Lescol	fluvastatin	cardiovascular-statin	No effects on voice or speech mechanisms have been reported.
Levaquin	levofloxacin	antibiotic-fluoroquinolone	In general, no effects on voice or speech mechanisms are associated with antibiotic use. It should be noted, however, that antibiotic abuse/misuse can lead to an overgrowth of Candida in the body, possibly leading to laryngeal thrush.
Levemir	insulin detemir	antidiabetic-insulin	No effects on voice or speech mechanisms have been reported.
Levitra	vardenafil	ED-phosphodiesterase (PDE) type 5 inhibitor	Gastrointestinal adverse reactions occurring in at least 2 percent of patients taking vardenafil film-coated tablets and more frequently than placebo included dyspepsia (4 percent vs. 1 percent) and nausea/vomiting (2 percent vs. 1 percent). Dyspepsia also occurred in 2.8 percent of patients receiving the orally disintegrating tablets. Gastrointestinal effects that occurred in less than 2 percent of patients included abdominal pain, diarrhea, dysphagia, esophagitis, gastritis, gastroesophageal reflux, vomiting, and xerostomia.
Levothroid	levothyroxine	hormone-thyroid replacement	No effects on voice or speech mechanisms have been reported.
Levoxyl	levothyroxine	hormone-thyroid replacement	No effects on voice or speech mechanisms have been reported.
Lexapro	escitalopram	antidepressant-SSRI	Xerostomia occurred in 4 percent of patients receiving 10 mg., versus 3 percent on placebo. Xerostomia (9 percent) at least doubled in incidence when the 20 mg. dose was utilized.

(continued)

Table AL.1. Medications and Their Effects on the Voice (*continued*)

Brand Name	Generic Name	Drug Class	Effects on Voice or Speech
Lipitor	atorvastatin	cardiovascular-statin	No effects on voice or speech mechanisms have been reported.
Lodine	etodolac	analgesic-NSAID	Those who use their voices rigorously should be cautious about using medications that decrease platelet function during periods of strenuous voicing demands, due to an increased possibility of vocal fold hemorrhage.
Lopid	gemfibrizil	cardiovascular-lipid reduction	No effects on voice or speech mechanisms have been reported.
Lopressor	metoprolol tartrate	cardiovascular-beta blocker	No effects on voice or speech mechanisms have been reported.
Lortab	hydrocodone/ acetaminophen	analgesic-narcotic	Narcotics may produce an uninhibited or diminished drive to speak. Symptoms of dysarthria (slow, slurred, and uncoordinated speech movements) may also be linked to narcotic use.
Lotensin	benazepril	cardiovascular-ACE inhibitor	Excessive coughing has been associated with the use of ACE inhibitors, which, in turn, may lead to hoarseness and possibly vocal tissue damage.
Lotrel	amolodipine/benazepril	cardiovascular-CCB/ACEi combo	Calcium channel blockers like amolodipine should be used cautiously in patients with gastroesophageal reflux disease (GERD) or hiatal hernia associated with reflux esophagitis. The drugs relax the lower esophageal sphincter. Note that voice production can be adversely affected by GERD. Excessive coughing has been associated with the use of ACE inhibitors, which, in turn, may lead to hoarseness and possibly vocal tissue damage.
Lotrisone	clotrimoxazole/ betamethasone	antifungal/steroid topical	No effects on voice or speech mechanisms have been reported.
Lovaza	omega-3-acid ethyl esters	omega-3 fatty acid	No effects on voice or speech mechanisms have been reported.
Lumigan	bimatoprost	antiglaucoma-synthetic prostamide	No effects on voice or speech mechanisms have been reported.
Lunesta	eszopiclone	sedative/hypnotic	The use of sedatives may produce an uninhibited or diminished drive to speak. Symptoms of dysarthria (slow, slurred, and uncoordinated speech movements) may also be linked to sedative use.
Lupron	leuprolide	hormonal antagonist	No effects on voice or speech mechanisms have been reported.
Lyrica	pregabalin	antiseizure	Anticonvulsants may produce an uninhibited or diminished drive to speak. Symptoms of dysarthria (slow, slurred, and uncoordinated speech movements) may also be linked to their use.
Macrobid	nitrofurantoin	antibiotic-nitrofuran	In general, no effects on voice or speech mechanisms are associated with antibiotic use. It should be noted, however, that antibiotic abuse/misuse can lead to an overgrowth of Candida in the body, possibly leading to laryngeal thrush.
Medrol	methylprednisolone	steroid-glucocorticoid	Methylprednisolone's effect is advantageous when used to shrink swollen vocal tissues, although patients taking methylprednisolone should be carefully monitored by a physician. It is not advised for patients with vocal fold ulcers, hemorrhages, or acute laryngitis.
Mevacor	lovastatin	cardiovascular-statin	No effects on voice or speech mechanisms have been reported.

(continued)

Table AL.1. Medications and Their Effects on the Voice (*continued*)

Brand Name	Generic Name	Drug Class	Effects on Voice or Speech
Miacalcin	calcitonin salmon	osteoporosis-calcitonin	Adverse reactions reported by 3 percent or more patients using intranasal calcitonin were rhinitis (12 percent), nasal symptoms (12 percent), epistaxis (3.5 percent), headache (3.2 percent), and sinusitis (2.3 percent). Nasal symptoms were the most commonly reported and cover a wide variety of symptoms, including crusting, nasal dryness, redness or erythema, infection, itching, nasal congestion, stenosis, and uncomfortable feeling and soreness across the bridge of the nose. Nasal irritation is mild to moderate in 95 percent of cases. Nasal symptoms were often only reported once and usually improved with continued use or discontinuation.
Micronase	glyburide	antidiabetic-sulfonylurea	No effects on voice or speech mechanisms have been reported.
Miralax	polyethylene glycol 3350	laxative-osmotic	No effects on voice or speech mechanisms have been reported.
Mirapex	pramipexole	antiparkinson-dopamine agonist	Dry mouth may occur.
Mirena	levonorgestrel-releasing intrauterine system	hormone-birth control	The use of oral contraceptives has not been shown to significantly affect female voices.
Mobic	meloxicam	analgesic-NSAID	Those who use their voices rigorously should be cautious about using medications that decrease platelet function during periods of strenuous voicing demands, due to an increased possibility of vocal fold hemorrhage. Less common gastrointestinal effects (< 1 percent incidence) that occurred with meloxicam regardless of causality included colitis; xerostomia (dry mouth); peptic ulcer disease (duodenal or gastric ulcer); eructation; gastritis; gastroesophageal reflux; gastrointestinal bleeding (hemorrhagic duodenal or gastric ulcer); hematemesis; melena; pancreatitis; gastrointestinal perforation (perforated duodenal or gastric ulcer, intestinal perforation); and stomatitis, including oral ulceration.
Monopril	fosinopril	cardiovascular-ACE inhibitor	Excessive coughing has been associated with the use of ACE inhibitors, which, in turn, may lead to hoarseness and possibly vocal tissue damage.
Motrin	ibuprofen	analgesic-NSAID	Those who use their voices rigorously should be cautious about using medications that decrease platelet function during periods of strenuous voicing demands, due to an increased possibility of vocal fold hemorrhage.
MS-Contin	morphine sulfate	analgesic-narcotic	Narcotics may produce an uninhibited or diminished drive to speak. Symptoms of dysarthria (slow, slurred, and uncoordinated speech movements) may also be linked to narcotic use.
Naprosyn	naproxen	analgesic-NSAID	Those who use their voices rigorously should be cautious about using medications that decrease platelet function during periods of strenuous voicing demands, due to an increased possibility of vocal fold hemorrhage.
Nasonex	mometasone	antiallergy-steroid topical	Throat irritation and dryness, cough, hoarseness, and voice changes are all possible adverse reactions. Oral or nasal candidiasis rarely occur.
Neurontin	gabapentin	antiseizure	Anticonvulsants may produce an uninhibited or diminished drive to speak. Symptoms of dysarthria (slow, slurred, and uncoordinated speech movements) may also be linked to their use.

(continued)

Table AL.1. Medications and Their Effects on the Voice (*continued*)

Brand Name	Generic Name	Drug Class	Effects on Voice or Speech
Nexium	esomeprazole	proton pump inhibitor	These agents have a favorable effect on the voice in that they reduce damage caused by gastroesophageal reflux disease (GERD). Uncontrolled acidic spillage of stomach acids into the larynx is harmful to delicate vocal fold tissues.
Nitrostat	nitroglycerin	cardiovascular-nitrate-vasodilation	No effects on voice or speech mechanisms have been reported.
Nolvadex	tamoxifen	hormone-antiestrogen	No effects on voice or speech mechanisms have been reported.
Norco	hydrocodone/acetaminophen	analgesic-narcotic	Narcotics may produce an uninhibited or diminished drive to speak. Symptoms of dysarthria (slow, slurred, and uncoordinated speech movements) may also be linked to narcotic use.
Norvasc	amlodipine	cardiovascular-CCB	Calcium channel blockers like amlodipine should be used cautiously in patients with gastroesophageal reflux disease (GERD) or hiatal hernia associated with reflux esophagitis. The drugs relax the lower esophageal sphincter. Note that voice production can be adversely affected by GERD.
Nuvaring	etonogestrel/ethinyl estradiol vaginal ring	hormone-birth control	The use of oral contraceptives has not been shown to significantly affect female voices.
Nystatin	nystatin	antifungal	No effects on voice or speech mechanisms have been reported.
Oxycontin	oxycodone	analgesic-narcotic	Narcotics may produce an uninhibited or diminished drive to speak. Symptoms of dysarthria (slow, slurred, and uncoordinated speech movements) may also be linked to narcotic use.
Paxil	paroxetine	antidepressant-SSRI	Paxil may have a drying effect on mucous membranes that can cause hoarseness, sore throat, voice changes, or laryngitis. In addition to irritation, dry vocal folds may be more prone to such injuries as nodules.
Penicillin-vk	penicillin	antibiotic-penicillin	In general, no effects on voice or speech mechanisms are associated with antibiotic use. It should be noted, however, that antibiotic abuse/misuse can lead to an overgrowth of Candida in the body, possibly leading to laryngeal thrush.
Pepcid	famotidine	gastrointestinal-H2 blocker	Two effects exist: 1) The antihistamine component has a drying effect on mucous membranes that may cause hoarseness, sore throat, voice changes, or laryngitis. In addition to irritation, dry vocal folds may be more prone to such injuries as nodules. 2) However, this medication may benefit the voice if it is taken to reduce acidity of gastroesophageal reflux. Uncontrolled spillage of stomach acids into the larynx is harmful to delicate vocal fold tissues.
Percocet	oxycodone/acetaminophen	analgesic-narcotic	Narcotics may produce an uninhibited or diminished drive to speak. Symptoms of dysarthria (slow, slurred, and uncoordinated speech movements) may also be linked to narcotic use.
Phenergan	promethazine	antinausea-phenothiazine	Antihistamines have a drying effect on mucous membranes that may cause hoarseness, sore throat, voice changes, or laryngitis. In addition to irritation, dry vocal folds may be more prone to such injuries as nodules.

(*continued*)

Table AL.1. Medications and Their Effects on the Voice (*continued*)

Brand Name	Generic Name	Drug Class	Effects on Voice or Speech
Plan-b	levonorgestrel	hormone-birth control	The use of oral contraceptives has not been shown to significantly affect female voices.
Plavix	clopidogrel	cardiovascular-platelet aggregation inhibitor	Those who use their voices rigorously should be cautious about using medications that decrease platelet function during periods of strenuous voicing demands, due to an increased possibility of vocal fold hemorrhage.
Plendil	felodipine	cardiovascular-calcium channel blocker	No effects on voice or speech mechanisms have been reported.
Pravachol	pravostatin	cardiovascular-statin	No effects on voice or speech mechanisms have been reported.
Prednisone	prednisone	steroid-glucocorticoid	Prednisone's effect is advantageous when used to shrink swollen vocal tissues, although patients taking prednisone should be carefully monitored by a physician. It is not advised for patients with vocal fold ulcers, hemorrhages, or acute laryngitis.
Premarin	congugated estrogens	hormone-estrogen	No effects on voice or speech mechanisms have been reported.
Prempro	congugated estrogens/ medroxyprogesterone	hormone-estrogen/ progestin combo	No effects on voice or speech mechanisms have been reported.
Prevacid	lansoprazole	proton pump inhibitor	These agents have a favorable effect on the voice in that they reduce damage caused by gastroesophageal reflux disease (GERD). Uncontrolled acidic spillage of stomach acids into the larynx is harmful to delicate vocal fold tissues.
Prilosec	omeprazole	proton pump inhibitor	These agents have a favorable effect on the voice in that they reduce damage caused by gastroesophageal reflux disease (GERD). Uncontrolled acidic spillage of stomach acids into the larynx is harmful to delicate vocal fold tissues.
Prinivil	lisinopril	cardiovascular-ACE inhibitor	Excessive coughing has been associated with the use of ACE inhibitors, which, in turn, may lead to hoarseness and possibly vocal tissue damage.
Procardia	nifedipine	cardiovascular-calcium channel blocker	No effects on voice or speech mechanisms have been reported.
Prometrium	progesterone	hormone-progestin	No effects on voice or speech mechanisms have been reported.
Protonix	pantoprazole	proton pump inhibitor	These agents have a favorable effect on the voice in that they reduce damage caused by gastroesophageal reflux disease (GERD). Uncontrolled acidic spillage of stomach acids into the larynx is harmful to delicate vocal fold tissues.
Proventil	albuterol	antiasthmatic-bronchodilator	Inhaled bronchodilators sometimes dry or irritate tissues in the mouth and throat and may lead to hoarseness, soreness, voice changes, or laryngitis. Dry vocal tissues may be more prone to such injuries as nodules.
Provera	medroxyprogesterone	hormone-progestin	No effects on voice or speech mechanisms have been reported.
Provigil	modafinil	stimulant	Bronchospasm (i.e., asthma), dyspnea, epistaxis, pharyngitis, and rhinitis may occur.
Prozac	fluoxetine	antidepressant-SSRI	Prozac may have a drying effect on mucous membranes that can cause hoarseness, sore throat, voice changes, or laryngitis. In addition to irritation, dry vocal folds may be more prone to such injuries as nodules.

(continued)

Table AL.1. Medications and Their Effects on the Voice (*continued*)

Brand Name	Generic Name	Drug Class	Effects on Voice or Speech
Pulmicort-respules	budesonide	antiasthmatic-steroid inhaled	Patients using inhaled steroids sometimes experience voice changes (including complete loss of voice). The onset and severity of symptoms is highly variable among patients. Studies show that discontinuation of inhaled steroids restores the voice in dysphonic patients, but symptoms may not resolve immediately
Reglan	metoclopramide	antinausea-phenothiazine	Pseudoparkinsonism may develop, including bradykinesia, tremor, cogwheel rigidity, and mask-like facies. The parkinsonian-like symptoms generally subside within 2–3 months following the discontinuation of metoclopramide. Tardive dyskinesia has been reported with long-term and high-dose use and especially among patients being treated for longer than 3 months. Tardive dyskinesia includes such symptoms as repetitive and involuntary movements of the extremities, lip smacking, grimacing, tongue protrusion, rapid eye movements, blinking, puckering and pursing of the lips, or impaired movement of the fingers. The symptoms are often irreversible, and there is no known treatment. Tardive dyskinesia occurs more frequently in elderly patients, especially females. Although tardive dyskinesia is more likely to occur after prolonged therapy or high dosage, relatively brief therapy has been associated with this effect as well.
Relafen	nabumetone	analgesic-NSAID	Those who use their voices rigorously should be cautious about using medications that decrease platelet function during periods of strenuous voicing demands, due to an increased possibility of vocal fold hemorrhage.
Remeron	mirtazepine	antidepressant-piperazinoazepines	Dry mouth may occur.
Restoril	temazepam	sedative/hypnotic	The use of sedatives may produce an uninhibited or diminished drive to speak. Symptoms of dysarthria (slow, slurred, and uncoordinated speech movements) may also be linked to sedative use.
Rhinocort-Aqua	budesonide	antiallergy-steroid topical	Throat irritation and dryness, cough, hoarseness, and voice changes are all possible adverse reactions. Oral or nasal candidiasis rarely occur.
Risperdal	risperadone	atypical antipsychotic	Risperdal may have adverse effects on speech, including difficulty in articulating words.
Ritalin	methylphenidate	stimulant	Complaints of xerostomia or dysgeusia may be limited by sucking sugarless hard candy or crushed ice and drinking plenty of water or other fluids.
Robaxin	methocarbamol	antispasmotic	Muscle relaxants have a drying effect on mucous membranes that may cause hoarseness, sore throat, voice changes, or laryngitis. In addition to irritation, dry vocal folds may be more prone to such injuries as nodules. The use of sedatives may produce an uninhibited or diminished drive to speak. Symptoms of dysarthria (slow, slurred, and uncoordinated speech movements) may also be linked to sedative use.
Roxicodone	oxycodone	analgesic-narcotic	Narcotics may produce an uninhibited or diminished drive to speak. Symptoms of dysarthria (slow, slurred, and uncoordinated speech movements) may also be linked to narcotic use.
Septra	sulfamethox/trimethoprin	antibiotic-sulfa	In general, no effects on voice or speech mechanisms are associated with antibiotic use. It should be noted, however, that antibiotic abuse/misuse can lead to an overgrowth of Candida in the body, possibly leading to laryngeal thrush.

(continued)

Table AL.1. Medications and Their Effects on the Voice (*continued*)

Brand Name	Generic Name	Drug Class	Effects on Voice or Speech
Serevent	salmeterol	antiasthmatic-bronchodilator	Inhaled bronchodilators sometimes dry or irritate tissues in the mouth and throat and may lead to hoarseness, soreness, voice changes, or laryngitis. Dry vocal tissues may be more prone to such injuries as nodules.
Seroquel	quetiapine	atypical antipsychotic	Among the most frequent adverse events associated with the use of quetiapine is xerostomia. In clinical trials for schizophrenia, xerostomia was reported in 7 percent of patients receiving immediate-release quetiapine. In clinical trials of immediate-release quetiapine, rhinitis was reported in 3 percent of patients treated with quetiapine, and it was among the adverse effects that occurred in more than 2 percent of patients treated with the active drug and was reported more frequently than in placebo-treated patients. Treatment-emergent adverse effects as reported in clinical trials of patients with bipolar depression, which occurred in at least 5 percent of patients and with an incidence greater than placebo, included nasal congestion (5 percent vs. 3 percent).
Serzone	nafazodone	antidepressant	No effects on voice or speech mechanisms have been reported.
Sinemet	carbidopa/levodopa	anti-Parkinson-dopamine agonist	Dyskinesia and sporadic movements are the most common of the serious effects of carbidopa; levodopa therapy can include choreiform reaction and dystonic reaction. These effects occur in up to 80 percent of patients receiving levodopa therapy for >= 3 years. Involuntary movements, including chewing, bruxism, gnawing, twisting, protrusion of the tongue, opening and closing the mouth, bobbing of the head, rhythmic movements of the feet or hands, quick movements of the shoulder, and ballismus, have been reported and may necessitate dosage reduction. Blepharospasm (which may indicate toxicity), muscle twitching, ataxia, myoclonia during sleep, and hand tremor also have been reported.
Singulair	montelukast	antiasthmatic-leukotriene receptor antagonist	No effects on voice or speech mechanisms have been reported.
Skelaxin	metaxalone	antispasmotic	No effects on voice or speech mechanisms have been reported. The use of sedatives may produce an uninhibited or diminished drive to speak. Symptoms of dysarthria (slow, slurred, and uncoordinated speech movements) may also be linked to sedative use.
Soma	carisoprodol	antispasmotic	No effects on voice or speech mechanisms have been reported. The use of sedatives may produce an uninhibited or diminished drive to speak. Symptoms of dysarthria (slow, slurred and uncoordinated speech movements) may also be linked to sedative use.
Spiriva	tiotropium	anticholinergic-COPD	The incidence of xerostomia with tiotropium use is roughly 10 percent. As with most anticholinergic agents, constipation may occur if significant amounts of tiotropium are absorbed. Postmarketing reports indicate that other gastrointestinal-related effects have occurred, including dysphagia, epistaxis, hoarseness, gastrointestinal obstruction (e.g., paralytic ileus), oral candidiasis, and throat irritation, although the exact incidences of these adverse reactions have not been established.
Strattera	atomoxetine	stimulant	Dry mouth may occur.

(continued)

Table AL.1. Medications and Their Effects on the Voice (*continued*)

Brand Name	Generic Name	Drug Class	Effects on Voice or Speech
Suboxone	buprenorphine/naloxone	analgesic-narcotic	Narcotics may produce an uninhibited or diminished drive to speak. Symptoms of dysarthria (slow, slurred, and uncoordinated speech movements) may also be linked to narcotic use.
Sumycin	tetracycline	antibiotic-tetracycline	In general, no effects on voice or speech mechanisms are associated with antibiotic use. It should be noted, however, that antibiotic abuse/misuse can lead to an overgrowth of Candida in the body, possibly leading to laryngeal thrush.
Synthroid	levothyroxine	hormone-thyroid replacement	No effects on voice or speech mechanisms have been reported.
Tagamet	cimetidine	gastrointestinal-H2 blocker	Two effects exist: 1) The antihistamine component has a drying effect on mucous membranes that may cause hoarseness, sore throat, voice changes, or laryngitis. In addition to irritation, dry vocal folds may be more prone to such injuries as nodules. 2) However, this medication may benefit the voice if it is taken to reduce acidity of gastroesophageal reflux. Uncontrolled spillage of stomach acids into the larynx is harmful to delicate vocal fold tissues.
Tamiflu	oseltamivir	antiviral	No effects on voice or speech mechanisms have been reported.
Tegretol	carbemazepine	antiseizure	Anticonvulsants may produce an uninhibited or diminished drive to speak. Symptoms of dysarthria (slow, slurred, and uncoordinated speech movements) may also be linked to their use.
Tenormin	atenolol	cardiovascular-beta blocker	No effects on voice or speech mechanisms have been reported.
Tiazac	diltiazem	cardiovascular-calcium channel blocker	No effects on voice or speech mechanisms have been reported.
Timoptic	timolol ophthalmic	antiglaucoma-beta blocker	No effects on voice or speech mechanisms have been reported.
Topamax	topiramate	antiseizure	Anticonvulsants may produce an uninhibited or diminished drive to speak. Symptoms of dysarthria (slow, slurred, and uncoordinated speech movements) may also be linked to their use.
Toprol-XL	metoprolol succinate	cardiovascular-beta blocker	No effects on voice or speech mechanisms have been reported.
Toradol	ketorolac	analgesic-NSAID	Those who use their voices rigorously should be cautious about using medications that decrease platelet function during periods of strenuous voicing demands, due to an increased possibility of vocal fold hemorrhage.
Treximet	sumatriptan/naproxen	migraine treatment	Those who use their voices rigorously should be cautious about using medications that decrease platelet function during periods of strenuous voicing demands, due to an increased possibility of vocal fold hemorrhage.
Tricor	fenofibrate	cardiovascular-fibrate	No effects on voice or speech mechanisms have been reported.
Trileptal	oxcarbazepine	antiseizure	Anticonvulsants may produce an uninhibited or diminished drive to speak. Symptoms of dysarthria (slow, slurred, and uncoordinated speech movements) may also be linked to their use.

(continued)

Table AL.1. Medications and Their Effects on the Voice (*continued*)

Brand Name	Generic Name	Drug Class	Effects on Voice or Speech
Trusopt	dorzolamide ophth sol	antiglaucoma	The possibility of systemic adverse reactions to dorzolamide is small, but there have been occasional reports of headache, nausea, asthenia, fatigue, skin rash, and urolithiasis. Contact dermatitis, xerostomia (dry mouth), epistaxis, and throat irritation have been reported during post-market surveillance.
Tussionex	hydrocodone/guaifenesin	analgesic-narcotic	Narcotics may produce an uninhibited or diminished drive to speak. Symptoms of dysarthria (slow, slurred, and uncoordinated speech movements) may also be linked to narcotic use.
Tylenol	acetaminophen	analgesic	No effects on voice or speech mechanisms have been reported.
Tylenol-codeine	acetaminophen/codeine	analgesic-narcotic	Narcotics may produce an uninhibited or diminished drive to speak. Symptoms of dysarthria (slow, slurred, and uncoordinated speech movements) may also be linked to narcotic use.
Ultracet	tramadol/acetaminophen	analgesic	No effects on voice or speech mechanisms have been reported.
Ultram	tramadol	analgesic	No effects on voice or speech mechanisms have been reported.
Valium	diazepam	antianxiety-benzodiazepine	Less than 1 percent of patients who take benzodiazepines experience slurred speech and symptoms of dysarthria (slow, uncoordinated speech).
Valtrex	valacyclovir	antiviral	No effects on voice or speech mechanisms have been reported.
Vancomycin	vancomycin	antibiotic-glycopeptide	In general, no effects on voice or speech mechanisms are associated with antibiotic use. It should be noted, however, that antibiotic abuse/misuse can lead to an overgrowth of Candida in the body, possibly leading to laryngeal thrush.
Vasotec	enalapril	cardiovascular-ACE inhibitor	Excessive coughing has been associated with the use of ACE inhibitors, which, in turn, may lead to hoarseness and possibly vocal tissue damage.
Viagra	sildenafil	ED-phosphodiesterase (PDE) type 5 inhibitor	Adverse reactions affecting hearing or otic special senses and occurring in < 2percent of patients in controlled clinical trials of sildenafil included hearing loss, otalgia, and tinnitus. In addition, 29 reports of sudden changes in hearing, including hearing loss or a decrease in hearing, usually in 1 ear only, have been reported to the FDA during postmarketing surveillance in patients taking sildenafil, tadalafil, or vardenafil; the reports are associated with a strong temporal relationship to the dosing of these agents. The hearing changes are often accompanied by vestibular effects, including dizziness, tinnitus, and vertigo. Follow-up has been limited in many of the reports; however, in approximately one-third of the patients, the hearing loss was temporary. Concomitant medical conditions or patient factors may play a role, although risk factors for the onset of sudden hearing loss have not been identified. Patients should be instructed to contact their physician if they experience changes in hearing.
Vicodin	hydrocodone/ acetaminophen	analgesic-narcotic	Narcotics may produce an uninhibited or diminished drive to speak. Symptoms of dysarthria (slow, slurred, and uncoordinated speech movements) may also be linked to narcotic use.

(continued)

Table AL.1. Medications and Their Effects on the Voice (*continued*)

Brand Name	Generic Name	Drug Class	Effects on Voice or Speech
Vistaril	hydroxyzine	antihistamine	Antihistamines have a drying effect on mucous membranes that may cause hoarseness, sore throat, voice changes, or laryngitis. In addition to irritation, dry vocal folds may be more prone to such injuries as nodules.
Voltaren	diclofenac	analgesic-NSAID	Those who use their voices rigorously should be cautious about using medications that decrease platelet function during periods of strenuous voicing demands, due to an increased possibility of vocal fold hemorrhage.
Vytorin	simvastatin/ezetimibe	cardiovascular-statin/lipid reduction	No effects on voice or speech mechanisms have been reported.
Vyvanse	lisdexamfetamine	stimulant	Dry mouth may occur.
Wellbutrin	buproprion	antidepressant-aminoketone	No effects on voice or speech mechanisms have been reported.
Xalatan	latanoprost	antiglaucoma-synthetic prostamide	No effects on voice or speech mechanisms have been reported.
Xanax	alprazolam	antianxiety-benzodiazepine	Less than 1percent of patients who take benzodiazepines experience slurred speech and symptoms of dysarthria (slow, uncoordinated speech).
Xenical	orlistat	gastrointestinal lipase inhibitor	No effects on voice or speech mechanisms have been reported.
Xyzal	levocetirizine	antihistamine	Antihistamines have a drying effect on mucous membranes that may cause hoarseness, sore throat, voice changes, or laryngitis. In addition to irritation, dry vocal folds may be more prone to such injuries as nodules.
Zanaflex	tizanidine	antispasmotic	Dry mouth may occur. The use of sedatives may produce an uninhibited or diminished drive to speak. Symptoms of dysarthria (slow, slurred, and uncoordinated speech movements) may also be linked to sedative use.
Zantac	ranitidine	gastrointestinal-H2 blocker	Two effects exist: 1) The antihistamine component has a drying effect on mucous membranes that may cause hoarseness, sore throat, voice changes, or laryngitis. In addition to irritation, dry vocal folds may be more prone to such injuries as nodules. 2) However, this medication may benefit the voice if it is taken to reduce acidity of gastroesophageal reflux. Uncontrolled spillage of stomach acids into the larynx is harmful to delicate vocal fold tissues.
Zestoretic	lisinopril/HCTZ	cardiovascular-ACE inhibitor/diuretic	Two adverse reactions are possible: 1) Excessive coughing has been associated with the use of ACE inhibitors, which, in turn, may lead to hoarseness and possible vocal tissue damage. 2) The diuretic component may have a drying effect on mucous membranes, including those used to speak and sing. Hoarseness, sore throat, voice changes, and laryngitis are possible symptoms. In addition to irritation effects, dry vocal folds may be more prone to such injuries as nodules.
Zestril	lisinopril	cardiovascular-ACE inhibitor	Excessive coughing has been associated with the use of ACE inhibitors, which, in turn, may lead to hoarseness and possibly vocal tissue damage.
Zetia	ezetimibe	cardiovascular-lipid reduction	No effects on voice or speech mechanisms have been reported.

(continued)

Table AL.1. Medications and Their Effects on the Voice (*continued*)

Brand Name	Generic Name	Drug Class	Effects on Voice or Speech
Ziac	bisoprolol/HCTZ	cardiovascular-beta blocker/diuretic	Diuretics have a drying effect on mucous membranes, including those used to speak and sing. Hoarseness, sore throat, voice changes, or laryngitis are possible symptoms. In addition to irritation effects, dry vocal folds may be more prone to such injuries as nodules.
Zithromax	azithromycin	antibiotic-macrolide	In general, no effects on voice or speech mechanisms are associated with antibiotic use. It should be noted, however, that antibiotic abuse/misuse can lead to an overgrowth of Candida in the body, possibly leading to laryngeal thrush.
Zocor	simvastatin	cardiovascular-statin	No effects on voice or speech mechanisms have been reported.
Zoloft	sertraline	antidepressant-SSRI	Zoloft may have a drying effect on mucous membranes that can cause hoarseness, sore throat, voice changes, or laryngitis. In addition to irritation, dry vocal folds may be more prone to such injuries as nodules.
Zovirax	acyclovir	antiviral	No effects on voice or speech mechanisms have been reported.
Zyban	buproprion	antidepressant-aminoketone	No effects on voice or speech mechanisms have been reported.
Zyloprim	allopurinol	antigout	No effects on voice or speech mechanisms have been reported.
Zyprexa	olanzepine	atypical antipsychotic	Infrequent effects may include coughing, pharyngitis (sore throat), or (nondefined) voice alterations.
Zyrtec	cetirizine	antihistamine	Antihistamines have a drying effect on mucous membranes that may cause hoarseness, sore throat, voice changes, or laryngitis. In addition to irritation, dry vocal folds may be more prone to such injuries as nodules.

Bibliography

Note: In some instances, a book falls into more than one category and is listed in two different locations. This is deliberate and intended for the convenience of the reader, whom, it is assumed, is consulting the bibliography to research a particular topic.

CONTENTS

SINGING (GENERAL)

Jander, Owen, Ellen T. Harris, David Fallows, and John Potter. "Singing." *Grove Music Online*, edited by Deane Root, oxfordmusiconline.com (accessed 1 May 2013).

Potter, John, ed. *The Cambridge Companion to Singing*. New York: Cambridge University Press, 2000.

Potter, John, and Neil Sorrell. *A History of Singing*. New York: Cambridge University Press, 2012.

VOICE PEDAGOGY

Alderson, Richard. *The Complete Handbook of Voice Training*. Mira Loma, CA: Parker Publishing, 1979.

Appelman, D. Ralph. *The Science of Vocal Pedagogy: Theory and Application*. Bloomington: Indiana University Press, 1986.

Blades-Zeller, Elizabeth. *A Spectrum of Voices: Prominent American Voice Teachers Discuss the Teaching of Singing*. Lanham, MD: Scarecrow Press, 2002.

Boytim, Joan Frey. *The Private Studio Handbook: A Practical Guide to All Aspects of Teaching*. New York: Hal Leonard, 2003.

Brown, Oren L. *Discover Your Voice: How to Develop Healthy Voice Habits*. San Diego, CA: Singular Publishing, 1996.

Bybee, Ariel, and James E. Ford. *The Modern Singing Master: Essays in Honor of Cornelius L. Reid*. Lanham, MD: Scarecrow Press, 2004.

Caldwell, Robert, and Joan Wall. *Excellence in Singing: Multilevel Teaching and Multilevel Learning*. 5 vols. Redmond, WA: Caldwell Publishing, 2001.

Chapman, Janice. *Singing and Teaching Singing: A Holistic Approach to Classical Voice*, 2nd ed. San Diego, CA: Plural Publishing, 2011.

Coffin, Berton. *Overtones of Bel Canto: Phonetic Basis of Artistic Singing with 100 Chromatic Vowel-Chart Exercises*. Lanham, MD: Scarecrow Press, 1980.

———. *Sounds of Singing: Principles and Applications of Vocal Technique with Chromatic Vowel Chart*, 2nd ed. Lanham, MD: Scarecrow Press, 1987.

Dayme, Maribeth. *Dynamics of the Singing Voice*, 5th ed. New York: Springer, 2009.

Doscher, Barbara. *The Functional Unity of the Singing Voice*, 2nd ed. Lanham, MD: Scarecrow Press, 1994.

Hines, Jerome. *The Four Voices of Man*. Milwaukee, WI: Limelight Editions, 2004.

Kagen, Sergius. *On Studying Singing*. New York: Dover Publications, 1950.

McCoy, Scott. *Your Voice: An Inside View*, 2nd ed. Delaware, OH: Inside View Press, 2012.

McKinney, James C. *The Diagnosis and Correction of Vocal Faults: A Manual for Teachers of Singing and Choir Directors*. Long Grove, IL: Waveland Press, 2005.

Miller, Richard. *English, French, German, and Italian Techniques of Singing: A Study in National Tonal Preferences and How They Relate to Functional Efficiency*. Lanham, MD: Scarecrow Press, 1977.

———. *National Schools of Singing: English, French, German, and Italian Techniques of Singing Revisited*. Lanham, MD: Scarecrow Press, 1997.

———. *On the Art of Singing*. New York: Oxford University Press, 1996.

———. *Securing Baritone, Bass-Baritone, and Bass Voices*. New York: Oxford University Press, 2008.

———. *Solutions for Singers: Tools for Every Performer and Teacher*. New York: Oxford University Press, 2004.

———. *The Structure of Singing*. New York: Schirmer Books, 1986.

———. *Training Soprano Voices*. New York: Oxford University Press, 2000.

———. *Training Tenor Voices*. New York: Schirmer Books, 1993.

Sell, Karen. *The Disciplines of Vocal Pedagogy: Toward a Holistic Approach*. Farnham, Surrey, UK: Ashgate, 2005.

Smith, W. Stephen, with Michael Chipman. *The Naked Voice: A Wholistic Approach to Singing*. New York: Oxford University Press, 2007.

Reid, Cornelius. *Bel Canto: Principles and Practices*, reprint ed. New York: Joseph Patelson Music House, 1975.

———. *A Dictionary of Vocal Terminology*. Huntsville, TX: Recital Publications, 1983.

———. *Essays on the Nature of Singing*. Huntsville, TX: Recital Publications, 1992.

———. *The Free Voice*, reprint ed. New York: Joseph Patelson Music House, 1975.

———. *Voice: Psyche and Soma*, reprint ed. New York: Joseph Patelson Music House, 1975.

Vennard, William. *Singing: The Mechanism and the Technic*, rev. ed. New York: Carl Fisher, 1967.

Ware, Clifton. *Basics of Vocal Pedagogy*. New York: McGraw-Hill, 1997.

HISTORICAL PEDAGOGY

Coffin, Berton. *Historical Vocal Pedagogy Classics*. Lanham, MD: Scarecrow Press, 1989.

Duey, Philip A. *Bel Canto in Its Golden Age: A Study of Its Teaching Concepts*. New York: Columbia University Press, 1951.

García, Manuel. *Hints on Singing*. London: Lowe & Brydone, 1894.

Lamperti, Giovanni Battista. *Vocal Wisdom: Enlarged Edition*. Transcribed by William Earl Brown. New York: Taplinger Publishing, 1931.

Manén, Lucie. *Bel Canto: The Teaching of the Classical Italian Song-Schools, Its Decline and Restoration*. New York: Oxford University Press, 1987.

Miller, Richard. "Historical Overview of Vocal Pedagogy." In *Vocal Health and Pedagogy: Volume II—Advanced Assessment and Treatment*, 2nd ed, edited by Robert T. Sataloff, 301–7. San Diego, CA: Plural Publishing, 2006.

Stark, James. *Bel Canto: A History of Vocal Pedagogy*. Toronto: University of Toronto Press, 1999.

Toft, Robert. *Bel Canto: A Performer's Guide*. New York: Oxford University Press, 2013.

VOCOLOGY (VOICE SCIENCE)

Bozeman, Kenneth W. *Practical Vocal Acoustics: Pedagogic Applications for Teachers and Singers*. Hillsdale, NY: Pendragon Press, 2013.

McCoy, Scott. *Your Voice: An Inside View*, 2nd ed. Delaware, OH: Inside View Press, 2012.

Sataloff, Robert T. *Voice Science*. San Diego, CA: Plural Publishing, 2005.

Sundberg, Johann. *The Science of the Singing Voice*. DeKalb: Northern Illinois University Press, 1989.

Sundberg, Johann, Edward C. Carterette, and Morton P. Friedman. *The Science of Musical Sounds*. Waltham, MA: Academic Press, 1991.

Titze, Ingo. *Fascinations with the Human Voice*. Salt Lake City, UT: National Center for Voice and Speech, 2010.

———. *The Myoelastic Aerodynamic Theory of Phonation*. Salt Lake City, UT: National Center for Voice and Speech, 2006.

———. *Principles of Voice Production*. Salt Lake City, UT: National Center for Voice and Speech, 2000.

Titze, Ingo, and Katherine Verdolini Abbott. *Vocology: The Science and Practice of Voice Habilitation*. Salt Lake City, UT: National Center for Voice and Speech, 2012.

Tomatis, Alfred A. *The Ear and the Voice*. Lanham, MD: Scarecrow Press, 2005.

VOCAL HEALTH

Baken, Ronald J., and Robert F. Orlikoff. *Clinical Measurement of Speech and Voice*. San Diego, CA: Singular Publishing, 1999.

Colton, Raymond H., Janina K. Casper, and Rebecca Leonard. *Understanding Voice Problems: A Physiological Perspective for Diagnosis and Treatment*, 4th ed. Baltimore, MD: Lippincott, Williams, & Wilkins, 2011.

DeVore, Kate, and Starr Cookman. *The Voice Book: Caring for, Protecting, and Improving Your Voice*. Chicago: Chicago Review Press, 2009.

Hixon, Thomas J. *Respiratory Function in Singing: A Primer for Singers and Singing Teachers*. San Diego, CA: Plural Publishing, 2007.

Lessac, Arthur. *The Use and Training of the Human Voice: A Bio-Dynamic Approach to Vocal Life*, 3rd ed. New York: McGraw-Hill, 1997.

Linklater, Kristin. *Freeing the Natural Voice*. Hollywood, CA: Drama Publishers, 1976.

McClosky, David Blair, and Members of the McClosky Institute of Voice. *Your Voice at Its Best: Enhancement of the Healthy Voice, Help for the Troubled Voice*. Long Grove, IL: Waveland Press, 2011.

Rubin, John S., Robert T. Sataloff, and Gwen S. Korovin. *Diagnosis and Treatment of Voice Disorders*, 3rd ed. San Diego, CA: Plural Publishing, 2005.

Sataloff, Robert T. *Vocal Health and Pedagogy: Volume I—Science and Assessment*, 2nd ed. San Diego, CA: Plural Publishing, 2006.

———. *Vocal Health and Pedagogy: Volume II—Advanced Assessment and Treatment*, 2nd ed. San Diego, CA: Plural Publishing, 2006.

Wicklund, Karen. *Singing Voice Rehabilitation: A Guide for the Voice Teacher and Speech-Language Pathologist*. Clifton Park, NY: Cengage Learning, 2010.

DICTION

General

Adams, David. *A Handbook of Diction for Singers: Italian, German, French*, 2nd ed. New York: Oxford University Press, 2008.

International Phonetic Association. *Handbook of the International Phonetic Association*. New York: Cambridge University Press, 1999.

Karna, Duane Richard, ed. *The Use of the International Phonetic Alphabet in the Choral Rehearsal*. Lanham, MD: Scarecrow Press, 2012.

Moriarty, John. *Diction: Italian, Latin, French, German . . . the Sounds and 81 Exercises for Singing Them*. New York: Schirmer Books, 1975.

Pullum, Geoffery K., and William A. Laduslaw. *Phonetic Symbol Guide*, 2nd ed. Chicago: University of Chicago Press, 1996.

Stapp, Marcie. *The Singer's Guide to Languages*. San Francisco, CA: Teddy's Music Press, 1987.

Wall, Joan. *International Phonetic Alphabet for Singers: A Manual for English and Foreign Language Diction*. Redmond, WA: Pst, 1989.

———. *Diction for Singers*, 2nd ed. Redmond, WA: Caldwell Publishing, 2009.

Pronunciation Dictionaries

de Boor, Helmuth, Hugo Moser, and Christian Winkler. *Siebs Deutsche Aussprache: Reine und Gemässigte Hochlautung mit Aussprachewörterbuch*. Berlin, Germany: Walter de Gruyter, 1969.

Garzanti Linguistica Staff, eds. *Grande Dizionario Garzanti in Italiano*. New York: French and European Publications, 2012.

Jones, Daniel. *Cambridge English Pronouncing Dictionary*, 18th ed. Edited by Peter Roach, Jane Setter, and John Esling. New York: Cambridge University Press, 2011.

Kenyon, John Samuel, and Thomas Albert Knott. *A Pronouncing Dictionary of American English*, 2nd ed. Springfield, MA: Merriam-Webster, 1953.

Mangold, Max. *Duden's Das Aussprache Wörterbuch*, 6th ed. Evanston, IL: Adler's Foreign Books, 2006.

Upton, Clive, William Kretzmar Jr., and Rafal Konopka. *Oxford Dictionary of Pronunciation for Current English*. New York: Oxford University Press, 2003.

Warnant, Leon. *Dictionnaire de la prononciation française dans sa norme actuelle*. Paris: Duculot, 1987.

German

Johnston, Amanda. *English and German Diction for Singers: A Comparative Approach*. Lanham, MD: Scarecrow Press, 2011.

Montgomery, Cheri. *German Lyric Diction Workbook*, 3rd ed. Nashville, TN: STM Publishers, 2006.

Odom, William. *German for Singers: A Textbook of Diction and Phonetics*, 2nd ed. New York: Schirmer Books, 1997.

French

Bernac, Pierre. *The Interpretation of French Song*. New York: W. W. Norton & Company, 1970.

Davis, Eileen. *Sing French: Diction for Singers*. Columbus, OH: Éclairé Press, 2010.

Grubb, Thomas. *Singing in French: A Manual of French Diction and French Vocal Repertoire*. Belmont, CA: Simon & Schuster, Macmillan, 1979.

Hunter, David. *Understanding French Verse: A Guide for Singers*. New York: Oxford University Press, 2005.

Montgomery, Cheri. *French Lyric Diction Workbook*, 3rd ed. Nashville, TN: STM Publishers, 2006.

Italian

Colorni, Evelina. *Singer's Italian: A Manual of Diction and Phonetics*. New York: Schirmer Books, 1995.

Montgomery, Cheri. *Italian Lyric Diction Workbook*, 3rd ed. Nashville, TN: STM Publishers, 2009.

English

Blizzard, John. *Singing American English: Textbook for Diction for Singers*. Raleigh, NC: Lulu Press, 2002.

Forward, Geoffery G. *American Diction for Singers*. Van Nuys, CA: Alfred, 2001.

Johnston, Amanda. *English and German Diction for Singers: A Comparative Approach*. Lanham, MD: Scarecrow Press, 2011.

LaBouff, Kathryn. *Singing and Communicating in English: A Singer's Guide to English Diction*. New York: Oxford University Press, 2007.

Marshall, Madeleine. *The Singer's Manual of English Diction*. New York: Schirmer Books, 1953.

Montgomery, Cheri. *English Lyric Diction Workbook*, 3rd ed. Nashville, TN: STM Publishers, 2006.

Spanish

Castel, Nico. *A Singer's Manual of Spanish Lyric Diction*. New York: Excalibur Publishing, 1994.

Draayer, Suzanne. *Pronunciation Guides Found in Canciones de España: Songs of Nineteenth-Century Spain*. 6 vols. Lanham, MD: Scarecrow Press, 2005.

Russian

Belov, Anton. "The Sounds of Russian." In *Twenty Arias for Baritone*, edited by Anton Belov, 151–63. Geneseo, NY: Leyerle Publications, 2005.

Olin, Emily. *Singing in Russian: A Guide to Language and Performance*. Lanham, MD: Scarecrow Press, 2011.

Piatak, Jean. *Russian Songs and Arias: Phonetic Readings, Word by Word Translations*. Redmond, WA: Pst, 1991.

Scandinavian/Nordic Languages

Ellingboe, Bradley. *Forty-Five Songs of Edvard Grieg*, corrected ed. Geneseo, NY: Leyerle Publications, 1988.

Holman, Eugene, with Gustav Djuosjöbacka and Donald Adamson. *Singing in Finnish: A Manual for Singers and Vocal Coaches*. Helsinki, Finland: Academy of Finnish Art Song, 2005.

Johansson, Annette. *Thirty Songs of Wilhelm Stenhammar*. Geneseo, NY: Leyerle Publications, 1999.

Rosenberg-Wolff, Carita, with Gustav Djuosjöbacka. *Singing in Swedish: A Manual for Singers and Vocal Coaches*. Helsinki, Finland: Academy of Finnish Art Song, 2011.

Other

Boire, Paula. *Romanian Art Songs*. 2 vols. Geneseo, NY: Leyerle Publications, 2004.

Cheek, Timothy. *Singing in Czech*. Lanham, MD: Scarecrow Press, 2001.

Dechario, Joseph. *Timeless Jewish Songs: Hebrew, Yiddish, and Ladino Texts with IPA Transcriptions*. 2 vols. Geneseo, NY: Leyerle Publications, 1994.

Zhong, Mei. *Newly Arranged Chinese Folk Songs*. Geneseo, NY: Leyerle Publications, 2005.

———. *Traditional and Modern Chinese Art Songs*. Geneseo, NY: Leyerle Publications, 2009.

Leslie de'Ath's regular column in the *Journal of Singing* is frequently devoted to languages that are off the beaten path.

IPA TRANSCRIPTIONS AND TRANSLATIONS

General

Retzlaff, Jonathan, and Cheri Montgomery. *Exploring Art Song Lyrics: Translation and Pronunciation of the Italian, German, and French Repertoire*. New York: Oxford University Press, 2012.

Opera Libretti

Belov, Anton. *Libretti of Russian Operas:* Ruslan and Lyudmila *(Glinka);* Boris Godunov *(Mussorgsky);* Eugene Onegin *and* The Queen of Spades *(Tchaikovsky);* Aleko *(Rachmaninoff); and* The Golden Cockerel *(Rimsky-Korsakov)*. Geneseo, NY: Leyerle Publications, 2004.

Castel, Nico. *The Complete Puccini Libretti: Volume I—La bohème, Edgar, La fanciulla del West, Madama Butterfly, and Manon Lescaut*. Edited by Marcie Stapp. Geneseo, NY: Leyerle Publications, 1994.

———. *The Complete Puccini Libretti: Volume II—La rondine, Tosca, Il trittico (Il tabarro, Suor Angelica, and Gianni Schicchi), and Le villi*. Edited by Marcie Stapp. Geneseo, NY: Leyerle Publications, 1994.

———. *The Complete Verdi Libretti: Volume I—Aida, Alzira, Aroldo, Attila, Un ballo in maschera, La battaglia di Legnano, and Il corsaro*. Geneseo, NY: Leyerle Publications, 1996.

———. *The Complete Verdi Libretti: Volume II—Don Carlo, I due Foscari, Ernani, Falstaff, La forza del destino, Giovanna d'Arco, and Un giorno di regno*. Geneseo, NY: Leyerle Publications, 1996.

———. *The Complete Verdi Libretti: Volume III—I Lombardi; Luisa Miller; Macbeth; I masnadieri; Nabucco; Oberto, conte di San Bonifacio; and Otello*. Geneseo, NY: Leyerle Publications, 1996.

————. *The Complete Verdi Libretti: Volume IV—Rigoletto, Simon Boccanegra, Stiffelio, La traviata, Il trovatore, and I vespri siciliani.* Geneseo, NY: Leyerle Publications, 1996.

————. *Four Strauss Opera Libretti: Der Rosenkavalier, Elektra, Salome, and Ariadne auf Naxos.* Edited by Marcie Stapp. Geneseo, NY: Leyerle Publications, 2002.

————. *French Opera Libretti: Volume I—Werther and Chérubin (Massenet); Carmen (Bizet); Samson et Dalila (Saint-Saëns); Lakmé (Delibes); Pelléas et Mélisande (Debussy); Don Carlos (Verdi); and Les contes d'Hoffman (Offenbach).* Edited by Marcie Stapp. Geneseo, NY: Leyerle Publications, 1999.

————. *French Opera Libretti: Volume II—Faust and Roméo et Juliette (Gounod); La Juive (Halévy); Mignon and Hamlet (Thomas); Thaïs and Manon (Massenet); and Les pêcheurs de Perles (Bizet).* Edited by Marcie Stapp. Geneseo, NY: Leyerle Publications, 1999.

————. *French Opera Libretti: Volume III—Le prophète and Les Huguenots (Meyerbeer); Cendrillon and Don Quichotte (Massenet); Louise (Charpentier); and Les Troyens (Berlioz).* Edited by Marcie Stapp. Geneseo, NY: Leyerle Publications, 1999.

————. *German Miscellaneous Opera Libretti: Tannhäuser, Lohengrin, and Der fliegende Holländer (Wagner); Die lustigen Weiber von Windsor (Nicolai); Hänsel und Gretel (Humperdinck); Fidelio (Beethoven); and Der Freischütz (Weber).* Edited by Marcie Stapp. Geneseo, NY: Leyerle Publications, 2005.

————. *Gluck and Monteverdi Opera Libretti: Orfeo ed Euridice, Alceste, Iphigénie en Aulide, and Iphigénie en Tauride (Gluck); L'Orfeo, Il ritorno d'Ulisse in Patria, and L'incoronazione di Poppea (Monteverdi).* Edited by Marcie Stapp. Geneseo, NY: Leyerle Publications, 2008.

————. *Handel Opera Libretti: Volume I—Rodelinda, Alcina, Agrippina, Giulio Cesare, Rinaldo, and Ottone.* Edited by Hemdi Kfir. Geneseo, NY: Leyerle Publications, 2005.

————. *Handel Opera Libretti: Volume II—Ariodante, Serse, Orlando, Partenope, Tamerlano, Radamisto, and Lotario.* Edited by Marcie Stapp. Geneseo, NY: Leyerle Publications, 2005.

————. *Italian Belcanto Opera Libretti: Volume I—Il barbiere di Siviglia and Il turco in Italia (Rossini); Lucia di Lammermoor, L'elisir d'amore, and Lucrezia Borgia (Donizetti); and Norma and I Capuleti e I Montecchi (Bellini).* Edited by Scott Jackson Wiley. Geneseo, NY: Leyerle Publications, 2000.

————. *Italian Belcanto Opera Libretti: Volume II—La Centerentola and L'italiana in Algeri (Rossini); La sonnambula and I puritani (Bellini); Anna Bolena, Maria Stuarda, Roberto Devereux, and Don Pasquale (Donizetti).* Edited by Marcie Stapp. Geneseo, NY: Leyerle Publications, 2000.

————. *Italian/French Belcanto Opera Libretti: Volume III—Il viaggio a Reims, Semiramide, and Otello (Rossini); Beatrice di Tenda (Bellini); La fille du régiment and La favorite (Donizetti); Le comte Ory and Guillaume Tell (Rossini).* Edited by Marcie Stapp. Geneseo, NY: Leyerle Publications, 2000.

————. *The Libretti of Mozart's Completed Operas: Volume I—Basien und Bastienne, La clemenza di Tito, Così fan tutte, Don Giovanni, Die Entführung aus dem Serail, La finta giardiniera, and La finta semplice.* Geneseo, NY: Leyerle Publications, 1998.

————. *The Libretti of Mozart's Completed Operas: Volume II—Idomeneo; Lucio Silla; Mitridate, re die Ponto; Le nozze di Figaro; Il re pastore; Der Schauspieldirektor; and Die Zauberflöte.* Geneseo, NY: Leyerle Publications, 1998.

————. *Der Ring des Nibelungen: Das Rheingold, Die Walküre, Siegfried, and Götterdämmerung.* Edited by Marcie Stapp. Geneseo, NY: Leyerle Publications, 2003.

————. *Three Wagner Opera Libretti: Die Meistersinger von Nürnberg, Tristan und Isolde, and Parsifal.* Edited by Marcie Stapp. Geneseo, NY: Leyerle Publications, 2006.

————. *Verismo Opera Libretti: Andrea Chénier and Fedora (Giordano); Adriana Lecouvreur (Cilea); La bohème and Pagliacci (Leoncavallo); Mefistofele (Boito); Cavalleria rusticana and L'amico Fritz (Mascagni); and La gioconda (Ponchielli).* Edited by Scott Jackson Wiley. Geneseo, NY: Leyerle Publications, 2000.

————. *Viennese Operetta Libretti: Franz Lehár's Die lustige Witwe (The Merry Widow).* Edited by Marcie Stapp. Geneseo, NY: Leyerle Publications, 2006.

————. *Viennese Operetta Libretti: Johann Strauss's Die Fledermaus (The Bat).* Edited by Marcie Stapp. Geneseo, NY: Leyerle Publications, 2006.

German Lieder

Glass, Beaumont. *Brahms' Complete Song Texts.* Geneseo, NY: Leyerle Publications, 1999.

————. *Hugo Wolf's Complete Song Texts.* Geneseo, NY: Leyerle Publications, 2000.

————. *Schubert's Complete Song Texts: Volume 1.* Geneseo, NY: Leyerle Publications, 1996.

————. *Schubert's Complete Song Texts: Volume 2.* Geneseo, NY: Leyerle Publications, 1996.

————. *Schumann's Complete Song Texts.* Geneseo, NY: Leyerle Publications, 2002.

————. *Selected Song Texts of Great German Lieder.* Geneseo, NY: Leyerle Publications, 2004.

————. *Richard Strauss' Complete Song Texts.* Geneseo, NY: Leyerle Publications, 2004.

Magner, Candace A. *Phonetic Readings of Brahms Lieder.* Lanham, MD: Scarecrow Press, 1995.

————. *Phonetic Readings of Schubert Lieder.* Lanham, MD: Scarecrow Press, 1994.

Reinhard, Thilo. *The Singer's Schumann.* New York: Rosen Publishing, 1989.

French Mélodies

Bathori, Jane. *On the Interpretation of the Melodies of Claude Debussy.* Hillsdale, NY: Pendragon Press, 1998

Dibbern, Mary, Carol Kimball, and Patrick Choukroun. *The Songs of Jacques Leguerney: A Guide for Study and Performance.* Hillsdale, NY: Pendragon Press, 2002.

Gartside, Robert. *Interpreting the Songs of Gabriel Fauré.* Geneseo, NY: Leyerle Publications, 1996.

————. *Interpreting the Songs of Maurice Ravel.* Geneseo, NY: Leyerle Publications, 1992.

Néron, Martin. *Francis Poulenc: Selected Song Texts.* Geneseo, NY: Leyerle Publications, 2010.

Rohinsky, Marie-Claire. *The Singer's Debussy.* New York: Rosen Publishing, 1987.

Italian Art Song

Gerhart, Martha. *Italian Song Texts from the Seventeenth through the Twentieth Centuries: Volume I.* Geneseo, NY: Leyerle Publications, 2002.

———. *Italian Song Texts from the Seventeenth through the Twentieth Centuries: Volume II.* Geneseo, NY: Leyerle Publications, 2002.

———. *Italian Song Texts from the Seventeenth through the Twentieth Centuries: Volume III.* Geneseo, NY: Leyerle Publications, 2014.

Russian Art Song

Challis, Natalia. *The Singer's Rachmaninoff.* New York: Rosen Publishing, 1989.

Piatak, Jean. *Russian Songs and Arias: Phonetic Readings, Word by Word Translations.* Redmond, WA: Pst, 1991.

Richter, Laurence R. *Mussorgsky's Complete Song Texts.* Geneseo, NY: Leyerle Publications, 2002.

———. *Prokofiev's Complete Song Texts.* Geneseo, NY: Leyerle Publications, 2008.

———. *Rachmaninov's Complete Song Texts.* Geneseo, NY: Leyerle Publications, 2000.

———. *Selected Nineteenth Century Russian Song Texts.* Geneseo, NY: Leyerle Publications, 2005.

———. *Shostakovich's Complete Song Texts.* Geneseo, NY: Leyerle Publications, 2007.

———. *Tchaikovsky's Complete Song Texts.* Geneseo, NY: Leyerle Publications, 1999.

Scandinavian/Nordic Art Song

Ellingboe, Bradley. *Forty-Five Songs of Edvard Grieg,* corrected ed. Geneseo, NY: Leyerle Publications, 1988.

Holman, Eugene, with Gustav Djuosjöbacka and Donald Adamson. *Singing in Finnish: A Manual for Singers and Vocal Coaches.* Helsinki, Finland: Academy of Finnish Art Song, 2005.

Johansson, Annette. *Thirty Songs of Wilhelm Stenhammar.* Geneseo, NY: Leyerle Publications, 1999.

Rosenberg-Wolff, Carita, with Gustav Djuosjöbacka. *Singing in Swedish: A Manual for Singers and Vocal Coaches.* Helsinki, Finland: Academy of Finnish Art Song, 2011.

Other Art Song Languages

Adams, David. *The Song and Duet Texts of Antonín Dvořák.* Geneseo, NY: Leyerle Publications, 2003.

Boire, Paula. *Romanian Art Songs.* 2 vols. Geneseo, NY: Leyerle Publications, 2004.

Cheek, Timothy. *Singing in Czech.* Lanham, MD: Scarecrow Press, 2001.

Dechario, Joseph. *Timeless Jewish Songs: Hebrew, Yiddish, and Ladino Texts with IPA Transcriptions.* 2 vols. Geneseo, NY: Leyerle Publications, 1994.

Sobrer, Josep Miquel. *The Singer's Anthology of Twentieth-Century Spanish Song.* Edited by Edmon Colomer. Buffalo, NY: Rosen Publishing, 1987.

Wilson, Kathleen. *The Art Song in Latin America: Selected Works by Twentieth-Century Composers.* Hillsdale, NY: Pendragon Press, 1998.

Zhong, Mei. *Newly Arranged Chinese Folk Songs.* Geneseo, NY: Leyerle Publications, 2005.

———. *Traditional and Modern Chinese Art Songs.* Geneseo, NY: Leyerle Publications, 2009.

Leslie de'Ath's regular column in the *Journal of Singing* is frequently devoted to languages that are off the beaten path.

TRANSLATIONS (WITHOUT IPA TRANSCRIPTIONS)

General

Miller, Philip L. *The Ring of Words: An Anthology of Song Texts.* New York: W. W. Norton & Company, 1973.

German Lieder

Fischer-Dieskau, Dietrich. *The Fischer-Dieskau Book of Lieder.* Translated by George Bird and Richard Stokes. Milwaukee, WI: Limelight Publications, 1977.

Mercier, Richard. *The Songs of Hans Pfitzner: A Guide and Study.* Westport, CT: Greenwood Press, 1998.

———. *The Songs of Max Reger: A Guide and Study.* Lanham, MD: Scarecrow Press, 2008.

Sams, Eric. *The Songs of Hugo Wolf.* London: Faber Finds, 2008.

———. *The Songs of Johannes Brahms.* New Haven, CT: Yale University Press, 2000.

———. *The Songs of Robert Schumann.* London: Faber Finds, 2008.

Stokes, Richard. *The Book of Lieder: The Original Texts of over 1,000 Songs.* London: Faber & Faber, 2005.

Wigmore, Richard. *Schubert: The Complete Song Texts.* New York: Schirmer Books, 1988.

French Mélodies

Bernac, Pierre. *Francis Poulenc: The Man and His Songs.* London: Kahn & Averill, 2002.

———. *The Interpretation of French Song.* London: Kahn & Averill, 2002.

Johnson, Graham. *Gabriel Fauré: The Songs and Their Poets.* Translated by Richard Stokes. Farnham, Surrey, UK: Ashgate, 2011.

Johnson, Graham, and Richard Stokes. *A French Song Companion.* New York: Oxford University Press, 2002.

Italian Art Song

Lakeway, Ruth C., and Robert C. White Jr. *Italian Art Song.* Bloomington: Indiana University Press, 1989.

Spanish Art Song

Cockburn, Jacqueline, and Richard Stokes. *The Spanish Song Companion.* Lanham, MD: Scarecrow Press, 2006.

Draayer, Suzanne. *A Singer's Guide to the Songs of Joaquín Rodrigo*. Lanham, MD: Scarecrow Press, 2003.

Russian Art Song

Sylvester, Richard D. *Tchaikovsky's Complete Songs: A Companion with Texts and Translations*. Bloomington: Indiana University Press, 2004.

ART SONG

General

Banfield, Stephen. *Sensibility and English Song: Critical Studies of the Early Twentieth Century*. New York: Cambridge University Press, 1989.

Dunsby, Jonathan. *Making Words Sing: Nineteenth- and Twentieth-Century Song*. New York: Cambridge University Press, 2004.

Emmons, Shirlee, and Stanley Sonntag. *The Art of the Song Recital*. Long Grove, IL: Waveland Press, 2001.

Emmons, Shirlee, and Wilbur Watkins Lewis. *Researching the Song: A Lexicon*. New York: Oxford University Press, 2006.

Goleeke, Thomas. *Literature for Voice: An Index of Songs in Collections and Source Book for Teachers of Singing*. Lanham, MD: Scarecrow Press, 1994.

Hall, James Husst. *The Art Song*. Norman: University of Oklahoma Press, 1953.

Kimball, Carol. *Art Song: Linking Poetry and Music*. Milwaukee, WI: Hal Leonard, 2013.

———. *Song: A Guide to Art Song Style and Literature*, rev. ed. Milwaukee, WI: Hal Leonard, 2006.

Stevens, Denis, ed. *A History of Song*. New York: W. W. Norton & Company, 1961.

Turnbridge, Laura. *The Song Cycle*. New York: Cambridge University Press, 2010.

German Lieder

Gorrell, Lorraine. *The Nineteenth-Century German Lied*. Portland, OR: Amadeus Press, 1993.

Hallmark, Rufus. *German Lieder in the Nineteenth Century*, 2nd ed. New York: Routledge, 2009.

Kramer, Lawrence. *Franz Schubert: Sexuality, Subjectivity, Song*. New York: Cambridge University Press, 2003.

Kravitt, Edward F. *The Lied: Mirror of Late Romanticism*. New Haven, CT: Yale University Press, 1996.

Malin, Yonatin. *Songs in Motion: Rhythm and Meter in the German Lied*. New York: Oxford University Press, 2010.

Parsons, James, ed. *The Cambridge Companion to the Lied*. New York: Cambridge University Press, 2004.

Stein, Deborah, and Robert Spillman. *Poetry into Song: Performance and Analysis of Lieder*. New York: Oxford University Press, 1996.

Youens, Susan. *Heinrich Heine and the Lied*. New York: Cambridge University Press, 2011.

French Mélodies

Barzun, Jacques. *An Essay on French Verse for Readers of English Poetry*. New York: New Directions Publishing, 1990.

Daykin, Frank. *Encyclopedia of French Art Song: Fauré, Debussy, Ravel, Poulenc*. Hillsdale, NY: Pendragon Press, 2013.

Hunter, David. *Understanding French Verse: A Guide for Singers*. New York: Oxford University Press, 2005.

Meister, Barbara. *Nineteenth-Century French Song: Fauré, Chausson, Duparc, and Debussy*. Bloomington: Indiana University Press, 1998.

Noske, Fritz. *French Song from Berlioz to Duparc*, 2nd ed. Mineola, NY: Dover Publications, 2012.

English Art Song

Pilkington, Michael. *English Solo Song: A Guide for Singers, Teachers, Librarians, and the Music Trade of Songs Currently Available*. London: Thames Publishing, 1997.

American Art Song

Carman, Judith E., William K. Gaeddert, and Rita M. Resch. *Art Song in the United States, 1759–2011: An Annotated Bibliography*, 4th ed. Lanham, MD: Scarecrow Press, 2013.

Clifton, Keith E. *Recent American Art Song*. Lanham, MD: Scarecrow Press, 2008.

Friedberg, Ruth, and Robin Fisher. *American Art Song and American Poetry*, 2nd ed. Lanham, MD: Scarecrow Press, 2012.

Villamil, Victoria Etnier. *A Singer's Guide to the American Art Song: 1870–1980*. Lanham, MD: Scarecrow Press, 2004.

Spanish and Latin American Art Song

Draayer, Suzanne. *Art Song Composers of Spain: An Encyclopedia*. Lanham, MD: Scarecrow Press, 2009.

Hoover, Maya, ed. *A Guide to the Latin American Art Song Repertoire*. Bloomington: Indiana University Press, 2010.

Individual Composers

Fischer-Dieskau, Dietrich. *Robert Schumann: Words and Music*. Translated by Reinhard G. Pauly. Portland, OR: Amadeus Press, 2003.

———. *Schubert's Songs: A Biographical Study*. Translated by Kenneth S. Whitton. Milwaukee, WI: Limelight Editions, 1984.

Foster, Beryl. *The Songs of Edvard Grieg*, rev. ed. Rochester, NY: Boydell Press, 2007.

Miller, Richard. *Singing Schumann: An Interpretive Guide for Performers*. New York: Oxford University Press, 2005.

Moore, Gerald. *Poet's Love: The Songs and Cycles of Schumann*. London: Hamish Hamilton, 1981.

———. *The Schubert Song Cycles: With Thoughts on Performance*. London: Hamish Hamilton, 1975.

Pilkington, Michael. *Campion, Dowland, and the Lutenist Songwriters*. Bloomington: Indiana University Press, 1989.

———. *Delius, Bridge, and Somervell*. London: Thames Publishing, 1993.

———. *Gurney, Ireland, Quilter, and Warlock*. Bloomington: Indiana University Press, 1989.

———. *Purcell*. London: Thames Publishing, 1994.

Poulenc, Francis. *Diary of My Songs*. Translated by Winifred Radford. London: Kahn & Averill, 2007.

Reed, John. *The Schubert Song Companion*. London: Mandolin, 1997.

Stark, Lucien. *A Guide to the Solo Songs of Johannes Brahms*. Bloomington: Indiana University Press, 1995.

Suurpää, Lauri. *Death in Winterreise: Musico-Poetic Associations in Schubert's Song Cycle*. Bloomington: Indiana University Press, 2013.

Wood, Vivian Lee Poates. *Poulenc's Songs: An Analysis of Style*. Jackson: University Press of Mississippi, 1979.

Youens, Susan. *Hugo Wolf: The Vocal Music*. Princeton, NJ: Princeton University Press, 1992.

———. *Hugo Wolf and His Mörike Songs*. New York: Cambridge University Press, 2006.

———. *Retracing a Winter's Journey: Schubert's Winterreise*. Ithaca, NY: Cornell University Press, 1991.

———. *Schubert, Müller, and Die schöne Müllerin*. New York: Cambridge University Press, 1997.

———. *Schubert's Late Lieder: Beyond the Song Cycles*. New York: Cambridge University Press, 2002.

———. *Schubert's Poets and the Making of Lieder*. New York: Cambridge University Press, 1999.

REPERTOIRE

Boldrey, Richard. *Guide to Operatic Duets*. Redmond, WA: Caldwell Publishing, 1994.

———. *Guide to Operatic Roles and Arias*. Redmond, WA: Caldwell Publishing, 1994.

Clark, Mark Ross. *Guide to the Aria Repertoire*. Bloomington: Indiana University Press, 2007.

Coffin, Berton. *The Singer's Repertoire: Complete Edition*. Whitefish, MT: Literary Licensing, 2012.

DeVenney, David P. *The New Broadway Song Companion: An Annotated Guide to Musical Theatre Literature by Voice Type and Song Style*, 2nd ed. Lanham, MD: Scarecrow Press, 2009.

Doscher, Barbara M. *From Studio to Stage: Repertoire for the Voice*. Edited by John Nix. Lanham, MD: Scarecrow Press, 2002.

Hopkin, J. Arden. *Songs for Young Singers: An Annotated List for Developing Voices*. Lanham, MD: Scarecrow Press, 2002.

Kimball, Carol. *Art Song: Linking Poetry and Music*. Milwaukee, WI: Hal Leonard, 2013.

———. *Song: A Guide to Art Song Style and Literature*, rev. ed. Milwaukee, WI: Hal Leonard, 2006.

Ord, Alan J. *Songs for Bass Voice: An Annotated Guide to Works for Bass Voice*. Lanham, MD: Scarecrow Press, 1994.

Singher, Martial. *An Interpretive Guide to Operatic Arias: A Handbook for Singers, Coaches, Teachers, and Students*. State College, PA: Penn State University Press, 2003.

OPERA

Abbate, Carolyn. *In Search of Opera*. Princeton, NJ: Princeton University Press, 2003.

Abbate, Carolyn, and Roger Parker. *A History of Opera*. New York: W. W. Norton & Company, 2012.

Batta, Andras. *Opera: Composers, Works, Performers*. Potsdam, Germany: H. F. Ullman, 2012.

Charlton, David, ed. *The Cambridge Companion to Grand Opera*. New York: Cambridge University Press, 2003.

Clark, Mark Ross. *Singing, Acting, and Moving in Opera: A Guide to Singer-getics*. Bloomington: Indiana University Press, 2009.

Cooke, Mervyn, ed. *The Cambridge Companion to Twentieth-Century Opera*. New York: Cambridge University Press, 2006.

DelDonna, Anthony R., and Pierpaolo Polzonetti, eds. *The Cambridge Companion to Eighteenth-Century Opera*. New York: Cambridge University Press, 2009.

Grout, Donald J., and Hermine Weigel Williams. *A Short History of Opera*, 4th ed. New York: Columbia University Press, 2003.

Helgot, Daniel. *The Third Line: The Opera Performer as Interpreter*. New York: Schirmer Books, 1993.

Kloiber, Rudolf, Wulf Konold, and Robert Maschka. *Handbuch der Oper*. Munich, Germany: Bärenreiter-Verlag Kassel, 1985.

Macy, Laura. *The Grove Book of Opera Singers*. New York: Oxford University Press, 2008.

Sadie, Stanley, and Laura Macy. *The Grove Book of Operas*. New York: Oxford University Press, 2009.

Simon, Henry W. *100 Great Operas and Their Stories: Act-by-Act Synopses*. New York: Anchor Books, 1989.

Till, Nicholas, ed. *The Cambridge Companion to Opera Studies*. New York: Cambridge University Press, 2012.

OPERA DIRECTING

Cathcart, Kathryn, and Willene Gunn. *Teaching Opera: The Role of the Opera Workshop with Scene Catalog*. Geneseo, NY: Leyerle Publications, 2008.

Eaton, Quaintance. *Opera Production: A Handbook*. Minneapolis: University of Minnesota Press, 1961.

Eaton, Quaintance, and Randolph Mickelson. *Opera Production II: A Handbook*. Minneapolis: University of Minnesota Press, 1974.

Gerbrandt, Carl. *Sacred Music Drama: The Producer's Guide*, 2nd ed. Bloomington: AuthorHouse, 2006.

Goldovsky, Boris. *Bringing Opera to Life: Operatic Acting and Stage Direction*. Upper Saddle River, NJ: Pearson-Prentice Hall, 1968.

Goldovsky, Boris, and Arthur Schoep. *Bringing Soprano Arias to Life*. Lanham, MD: Scarecrow Press, 1990.

Summers, Franklin W. *Operas in One Act: A Production Guide*. Lanham, MD: Scarecrow Press, 1996.

OPERETTA

Bordman, Gerald. *American Operetta: From HMS Pinafore to Sweeney Todd*. New York: Oxford University Press, 1981.

Bradley, Ian. *The Complete Annotated Gilbert and Sullivan*. New York: Oxford University Press, 1996.

———. *O Joy! O Rapture! The Enduring Phenomenon of Gilbert and Sullivan*. New York: Oxford University Press, 2005.

Eden, David, and Meinhard Saremba, eds. *The Cambridge Companion to Gilbert and Sullivan*. New York: Cambridge University Press, 2009.

Traubner, Richard. *Operetta: A Theatrical Study.* New York: Routledge, 2003.

Williams, Carolyn. *Gilbert and Sullivan: Gender, Genre, Parody.* New York: Columbia University Press, 2011.

Wren, Gayden. *A Most Ingenious Paradox: The Art of Gilbert and Sullivan.* New York: Oxford University Press, 2001.

CHORAL MUSIC AND ENSEMBLE SINGING

Blocker, Robert, ed. *The Robert Shaw Reader.* New Haven, CT: Yale University Press, 2004.

de Quadros, André, ed. *The Cambridge Companion to Choral Music.* New York: Cambridge University Press, 2012.

Dürr, Alfred. *The Cantatas of J. S. Bach: With Their Librettos in German-English Parallel Text.* Translated by Richard D. P. Jones. New York: Oxford University Press, 2006.

Emmons, Shirlee, and Constance Chase. *Prescriptions for Choral Excellence.* New York: Oxford University Press, 1996.

Garretson, Robert L. *Choral Music: History, Style, and Performance Practice.* Upper Saddle River, NJ: Pearson-Prentice Hall, 1993.

Green, Jonathan D. *A Guide to the Choral-Orchestral Works of Johann Sebastian Bach.* Lanham, MD: Scarecrow Press, 2000.

Jeffers, Ron. *Translations and Annotations of Choral Repertoire: Volume I—Sacred Latin Texts.* Corvalis, OR: Earthsongs, 1988.

Jeffers, Ron, and Gordon Paine. *Translations and Annotations of Choral Repertoire: Volume II—German Texts.* Corvalis, OR: Earthsongs, 2000.

Jordan, James, and Matthew Mehaffey. *Choral Ensemble Intonation.* Chicago: GIA Publications, 2001.

Mussulman, Joseph A. *Dear People . . . Robert Shaw,* 2nd ed. Chapel Hill, NC: Hinshaw Music, 1996.

Nash, Ethan, and Joshua Jacobson. *Translations and Annotations of Choral Repertoire: Volume IV—Hebrew Texts.* Corvalis, OR: Earthsongs, 2009.

Paine, Gordon. *Translations and Annotations of Choral Repertoire: Volume III—French and Italian Texts.* Corvalis, OR: Earthsongs, 2007.

Robinson, Ray, ed. *Choral Music: A Norton Historical Anthology.* New York: W. W. Norton & Company, 1978.

Shrock, Dennis. *Choral Repertoire.* New York: Oxford University Press, 2009.

Steinberg, Michael. *Choral Masterworks: A Listener's Guide.* New York: Oxford University Press, 2005.

Strimple, Nick. *Choral Music in the Nineteenth Century.* Portland, OR: Amadeus Press, 2008.

———. *Choral Music in the Twentieth Century.* Portland, OR: Amadeus Press, 2002.

CLASS VOICE

Christy, Van Ambrose, and John Glenn Paton. *Foundations in Singing: A Basic Textbook in Vocal Technique and Song Interpretation,* 5th ed. New York: William C. Brown, 1990.

Dayme, Maribeth, and Cynthia Vaughn. *The Singing Book,* 2nd ed. New York: W. W. Norton & Company, 2007.

Schmidt, Jan, and Heidi Counsell Schmidt. *Basics of Singing,* 6th ed. Clifton Park, NY: Cengage Learning, 2007.

Ware, Clifton. *Adventures in Singing: A Process for Exploring, Discovering, and Developing Vocal Potential,* 4th ed. New York: McGraw-Hill, 2007.

PERFORMANCE PRACTICE

Donington, Robert. *Baroque Music: Style and Performance: A Handbook.* New York: W. W. Norton & Company, 1982.

———. *The Interpretation of Early Music,* rev. ed. New York: W. W. Norton & Company, 2008.

Duffin, Ross W. *How Equal Temperament Ruined Harmony (and Why You Should Care).* New York: W. W. Norton & Company, 2008.

Elliott, Martha. *Singing in Style: A Guide to Vocal Performance Practices.* New Haven, CT: Yale University Press, 2006.

McGee, Timothy J., A. G. Rigg, and David N. Klausner. *Singing Early Music: The Pronunciation of European Languages in the Late Middle Ages and the Renaissance.* Bloomington: Indiana University Press, 1996.

Neumann, Frederick. *Ornamentation in Baroque and Post-Baroque Music.* Princeton, NJ: Princeton University Press, 1983.

NEW MUSIC

Mabry, Sharon. *Exploring Twentieth-Century Vocal Music: A Practical Guide to Innovations in Performance and Repertoire.* New York: Oxford University Press, 2002.

Manning, Jane. *New Vocal Repertory: Volume 1.* New York: Oxford University Press, 1994.

———. *New Vocal Repertory: Volume 2.* New York: Oxford University Press, 1999.

CHAMBER MUSIC

Klaus, Kenneth S. *Chamber Music for Solo Voice and Instruments, 1960–1989: An Annotated Guide.* Berkeley, CA: Fallen Leaf Press, 1994.

Winchester, Barbara, and Kay Dunlap. *Vocal Chamber Music: A Performer's Guide,* 2nd ed. New York: Routledge, 2008.

CHURCH MUSIC

Daw, Carl P., Jr. and Thomas Pavlechko. *Liturgical Music for the Revised Common Lectionary: Year A.* New York: Church Publishing, 2009.

———. *Liturgical Music for the Revised Common Lectionary: Year B.* New York: Church Publishing, 2009.

———. *Liturgical Music for the Revised Common Lectionary: Year C.* New York: Church Publishing, 2009.

Laster, James. *Catalogue of Choral Music Arranged in Biblical Order,* 2nd ed. Lanham, MD: Scarecrow Press, 1996.

———. *Catalogue of Choral Music Arranged in Biblical Order: Supplement.* Lanham, MD: Scarecrow Press, 2002.

MUSIC PSYCHOLOGY

Green, Barry, with W. Timothy Gallwey. *The Inner Game of Music*. New York: Doubleday, 1986.

Hallam, Susan, Ian Cross, and Michael Thaut, eds. *The Oxford Handbook of Music Psychology*. New York: Oxford University Press, 2009.

Hemsley, Thomas. *Singing and Imagination: A Human Approach to a Great Musical Tradition*. New York: Oxford University Press, 1998.

Honing, Henkjan. *Musical Cognition: A Science of Listening*. Newark, NJ: Transaction Publishers, 2011.

Huron, David. *Sweet Anticipation: The Music and the Psychology of Expectation*. Cambridge, MA: MIT Press, 2008.

Jourdain, Robert. *Music, the Brain, and Ecstasy: How Music Captures Our Imagination*. New York: William Morrow and Company, 2008.

Levitan, Daniel J. *This Is Your Brain on Music: The Science of a Human Obsession*. New York: Plume/Penguin, 2007.

———. *The World in Six Songs: How the Musical Brain Created Human Nature*. Plume/Penguin, 2009.

Meyer, Leonard B. *Emotion and Meaning in Music*. Chicago: University of Chicago Press, 1961.

Parncutt, Richard, and Gary E. McPherson. *The Science and Psychology of Music Performance*. New York: Oxford University Press, 2002.

Patel, Aniruddh D. *Music, Language, and the Brain*. New York: Oxford University Press, 2010.

Sachs, Oliver. *Musicophilia: Tales of Music and the Brain*, rev. ed. New York: Vintage Books, 2008.

Storr, Anthony. *Music and the Mind*. New York: Ballantine Books, 1993.

Thompson, William Forde. *Music, Thought, and Feeling: Understanding the Psychology of Music*. New York: Oxford University Press, 2008.

Williamson, Aaron. *Musical Excellence: Strategies and Techniques to Enhance Performance*. New York: Oxford University Press, 2004.

Zbikowski, Lawrence M. *Conceptualizing Music: Cognitive Structure, Theory, and Analysis*. New York: Oxford University Press, 2005.

INSPIRATION

Cameron, Julia. *The Artist's Way*. New York: G. P. Putman's Sons, 1992.

Dayme, Meribeth Bunch. *The Performer's Voice: Realizing Your Vocal Potential*. New York: W. W. Norton & Company, 2005.

Edwards, Betty. *Drawing on the Right Side of the Brain*, 4th ed. New York: Tarcher, 2012.

Emmons, Shirlee, and Alma Thomas. *Power Performance for Singers: Transcending the Barriers*. New York: Oxford University Press, 1998.

Eustis, Lynn. *The Singer's Ego: Finding a Balance between Life and Music*. Chicago: GIA Publications, 2005.

———. *The Teacher's Ego: When Singers Become Voice Teachers*. Chicago: GIA Publications, 2012.

Herrigel, Eugen. *Zen in the Art of Archery*. New York: Random House, 1953/1981.

Jordan, James. *The Musician's Soul*. Chicago: GIA Publications, 1999.

———. *The Musician's Spirit: Connecting to Others through Story*. Chicago: GIA Publications, 2002.

———. *The Musician's Walk: An Ethical Labyrinth*. Chicago: GIA Publications, 2005.

Jordan, James, Mark Moliterno, and Nova Thomas. *The Musician's Breath: The Role of Breathing in Human Expression*. Chicago: GIA Publications, 2011.

Jordan, James, Nova Thomas, and James Conlon. *The Art of Being for Musicians, Actors, Dancers, and Teachers*. Chicago: GIA Publications, 2010.

Langer, Ellen J. *On Becoming an Artist: Reinventing Yourself through Mindful Creativity*. New York: Ballantine Books, 2005.

Mabry, Sharon. *The Performing Life: A Singer's Guide to Survival*. Lanham, MD: Scarecrow Press, 2012.

Ristad, Eloise. *A Soprano on Her Head: Right-Side-Up Reflections on Life and Other Performances*. Moab, UT: Real People Press, 1982.

Ware, Clifton. *The Singer's Life: Goals and Roles*. St. Paul, MN: Birth Grove Publishing, 2005.

THE BUSINESS

Beeching, Angela Myles. *Beyond Talent: Creating a Successful Career in Music*, 2nd ed. New York: Oxford University Press, 2010.

Dornemann, Joan, and Maria Ciaccia. *Complete Preparation: A Guide to Auditioning for Opera*. Tucson, AZ: Excalibur Publishing, 1992.

Lenson, Benny, Dorothy Maddison, and Gail Sullivan. *Kein' Angst Baby! A Singer's Guide to German Auditions in the 1990s*. London: Rhinegold Publishing, 1994.

Mabry, Sharon. *The Performing Life: A Singer's Guide to Survival*. Lanham, MD: Scarecrow Press, 2012.

Shepard, Philip, and Sarah Kristine Schäfer. *What the Fach?! The Definitive Guide for Opera Singers Auditioning and Working in Germany, Austria, and Switzerland*, 2nd ed. Seattle, WA: CreateSpace Independent Publishing Platform, 2010.

Tindall, Blair. *Mozart in the Jungle: Sex, Drugs, and Classical Music*. New York: Grove Press, 2006.

GREAT SINGERS

Blyth, Alan. *Song on Record: Volume I*. New York: Cambridge University Press, 1986.

———. *Song on Record: Volume II*. New York: Cambridge University Press, 1988.

Hines, Jerome. *Great Singers on Great Singing*, 7th ed. Milwaukee, WI: Limelight Editions, 2004.

Pleasants, Henry. *The Great American Popular Singers: Their Lives, Careers, and Art*, rev. ed. New York: Simon & Schuster, 1985.

———. *The Great Singers: From Jenny Lind and Caruso to Callas and Pavarotti*, rev. ed. Minnetonka, MN: Olympic Marketing Corporation, 1985.

Steane, J. B. *The Grand Tradition: Seventy Years of Singing on Record*, 2nd ed. Portland, OR: Amadeus Press, 1993.

————. *Singers of the Century: Volume 1*. Portland, OR: Amadeus Press, 1996.

————. *Singers of the Century: Volume 2*. Portland, OR: Amadeus Press, 2003.

————. *Singers of the Century: Volume 3*. Portland, OR: Amadeus Press, 2003.

————. *Voices, Singers, and Critics*. Portland, OR: Amadeus Press, 2002.

Villamil, Victoria Etnier. *From Johnson's Kids to Lemonade Opera: The American Classical Singer Comes of Age*. Boston: Northeastern University Press, 2004.

MUSIC HISTORY

General

Burkholder, J. Peter, and Claude V. Palisca. *Norton Anthology of Western Music: Volume 1—Ancient to Baroque*, 6th ed. New York: W. W. Norton & Company, 2009.

————. *Norton Anthology of Western Music: Volume 2—Classic to Romantic*, 6th ed. New York: W. W. Norton & Company, 2009.

————. *Norton Anthology of Western Music: Volume 3—Twentieth Century*, 6th ed. New York: W. W. Norton & Company, 2009.

Burkholder, J. Peter, Donald J. Grout, and Claude V. Palisca. *A History of Western Music*, 8th ed. New York: W. W. Norton & Company, 2009.

Taruskin, Richard. *Oxford History of Western Music: Volume 1—Music from the Earliest Notations to the Sixteenth Century*. New York: W. W. Norton & Company, 2005.

————. *Oxford History of Western Music: Volume 2—Music in the Seventeenth and Eighteenth Centuries*. New York: W. W. Norton & Company, 2005.

————. *Oxford History of Western Music: Volume 3—Music in the Nineteenth Century*. New York: W. W. Norton & Company, 2005.

————. *Oxford History of Western Music: Volume 4—Music in the Early Twentieth Century*. New York: W. W. Norton & Company, 2005.

————. *Oxford History of Western Music: Volume 5—Music in the Late Twentieth Century*. New York: W. W. Norton & Company, 2005.

Medieval

Everist, Mark. *The Cambridge Companion to Medieval Music*. New York: Cambridge University Press, 2011.

Fassler, Margot. *Anthology for Music in the Medieval West*. New York: W. W. Norton & Company, 2013.

————. *Music in the Medieval West*. New York: W. W. Norton & Company, 2013.

Haines, John. *Medieval Song in Romance Languages*. New York: Cambridge University Press, 2010.

Hoppin, Richard H. *Anthology of Medieval Music*. New York: W. W. Norton & Company, 1978.

————. *Medieval Music*. New York: W. W. Norton & Company, 1978.

Yudkin, Jeremy. *Music in Medieval Europe*. Upper Saddle River, NJ: Pearson-Prentice Hall, 1989.

Renaissance

Atlas, Allan W. *Anthology of Renaissance Music*. New York: W. W. Norton & Company, 1998.

————. *Renaissance Music*. New York: W. W. Norton & Company, 1998.

Brown, Howard M. *Music in the Renaissance*. Upper Saddle River, NJ: Pearson-Prentice Hall, 1976.

Freedman, Richard. *Anthology for Music in the Renaissance*. New York: W. W. Norton & Company, 2013.

————. *Music in the Renaissance*. New York: W. W. Norton & Company, 2013.

Baroque

Heller, Wendy. *Anthology for Music in the Baroque*. New York: W. W. Norton & Company, 2013.

————. *Music in the Baroque*. New York: W. W. Norton & Company, 2013.

Hill, John Walter. *Anthology of Baroque Music*. New York: W. W. Norton & Company, 2005.

————. *Baroque Music: Music in Western Europe, 1580–1750*. New York: W. W. Norton & Company, 2005.

Classical

Downs, Philip G. *Anthology of Classical Music*. New York: W. W. Norton & Company, 1992.

————. *Classical Music: The Era of Haydn, Mozart, and Beethoven*. New York: W. W. Norton & Company, 1992.

Pauly, Reinhard G. *Music in the Classic Period*. Upper Saddle River, NJ: Pearson-Prentice Hall, 1973.

Ratner, Leonard G. *Classic Music: Expression, Form, and Style*. New York: Schirmer Books, 1985.

Rice, John A. *Anthology for Music in the Eighteenth Century*. New York: W. W. Norton & Company, 2012.

————. *Music in the Eighteenth Century*. New York: W. W. Norton & Company, 2012.

Till, Nicholas. *Mozart and the Enlightenment: Truth, Virtue, and Beauty in Mozart's Operas*. New York: W. W. Norton & Company, 1996.

Romantic

Frisch, Walter. *Anthology for Music in the Nineteenth Century*. New York: W. W. Norton & Company, 2012.

————. *Music in the Nineteenth Century*. New York: W. W. Norton & Company, 2012.

Longyear, Rey M. *Nineteenth-Century Romanticism in Music*. Upper Saddle River, NJ: Pearson-Prentice Hall, 1988.

Plantinga, Leon. *Anthology of Romantic Music*. New York: W. W. Norton & Company, 1985.

————. *Romantic Music*. New York: W. W. Norton & Company, 1985.

Modern

Auner, Joseph. *Anthology for Music in the Twentieth and Twenty-First Centuries*. New York: W. W. Norton & Company, 2013.

————. *Music in the Twentieth and Twenty-First Centuries*. New York: W. W. Norton & Company, 2013.

Morgan, Robert P. *Anthology of Twentieth-Century Music*. New York: W. W. Norton & Company, 1991.

————. *Twentieth-Century Music*. New York: W. W. Norton & Company, 1991.

Ross, Alex. *Listen to This*. New York: Farrar, Straus and Giroux, 2010.

————. *The Rest Is Noise: Listening to the Twentieth Century*. New York: Picador Books, 2008.

Salzman, Eric. *Twentieth-Century Music: An Introduction*. Upper Saddle River, NJ: Pearson-Prentice Hall, 2001.

MUSIC THEORY AND SIGHTSINGING

Aldwell, Edward, Carl Schachter, and Allen Cadwallader. *Harmony and Voice Leading*, 4th ed. Clifton Park, NY: Cengage Learning, 2010.

Bell, John, and Steven R. Chicurel. *Music Theory for Musical Theatre*. Lanham, MD: Scarecrow Press, 2008.

Cadwallader, Allen, and David Gagné. *Analysis of Tonal Music: A Schenkerian Approach*, 3rd ed. New York: Oxford University Press, 2010.

Chafe, Eric. *Analyzing Bach Cantatas*. New York: Oxford University Press, 2003.

Christensen, Thomas, ed. *The Cambridge History of Western Music Theory*. New York: Cambridge University Press, 2002.

Clendinning, Jane Piper, and Elizabeth West Marvin. *The Musician's Guide to Theory and Analysis*, 2nd ed. New York: W. W. Norton & Company, 2010.

Edlund, Lars. *Modus Novus: Studies in Reading Atonal Melodies*. Wappingers Falls, NY: Beekman Books, 1964.

————. *Modus Vetus: Sight Singing and Ear Training in Major/ Minor Tonality*. Wappingers Falls, NY: Beekman Books, 1963.

Gauldin, Robert. *A Practical Approach to Eighteenth-Century Counterpoint*. Long Grove, IL: Waveland Press, 1995.

————. *A Practical Approach to Sixteenth-Century Counterpoint*. Long Grove, IL: Waveland Press, 1995.

Hindemith, Paul. *Elementary Training for Musicians*, 2nd ed. Mainz, Germany: Scott Music, 1984.

Kennan, Kent. *Counterpoint*, 4th ed. Upper Saddle River, NJ: Pearson-Prentice Hall, 1998.

Laitz, Steven G. *The Complete Musician: An Integrated Approach to Tonal Theory, Analysis, and Listening*, 3rd ed. New York: Oxford University Press, 2011.

Manoff, Tom. *The Music Kit*, 4th ed. New York: W. W. Norton & Company, 2001.

Ottman, Robert W., and Nancy Rogers. *Music for Sight Singing*, 8th ed. Upper Saddle River, NJ: Pearson-Prentice Hall, 2010.

Salzer, Felix, and Carl Schachter. *Counterpoint in Composition: The Study of Voice Leading*. New York: Columbia University Press, 1989.

Stein, Deborah, ed. *Engaging Music: Essays in Music Analysis*. New York: Oxford University Press, 2004.

Stein, Deborah, and Robert Spillman. *Poetry into Song: Performance and Analysis of Lieder*. New York: Oxford University Press, 1996.

Straus, Joseph N. *Introduction to Post-Tonal Theory*, 3rd ed. Upper Saddle River, NJ: Pearson-Prentice Hall, 2004.

Temperley, David. *The Cognition of Basic Musical Structures*. Cambridge, MA: MIT Press, 2004.

————. *Music and Probability*. Cambridge, MA: MIT Press, 2010.

CCM PEDAGOGY

Bell, Jeffrey E. "American Musical Theatre Songs in the Undergraduate Vocal Studio: A Survey of Current Practice, Guidelines for Repertoire Selection, and Pedagogical Analysis of Selected Songs." DMA diss., Ball State University, 1996.

Burdick, Barbara. "Vocal Techniques for Music Theater: The High School and Undergraduate Singer." *Journal of Singing* 61, no. 3 (January 2005): 261.

Edwin, Robert. "Apples and Oranges: Belting Revisited." *Journal of Singing* 57, no. 2 (November 2000): 43.

————. "Belt Yourself." *Journal of Singing* 60, no. 3 (January 2004): 285

————. "Belting 101." *Journal of Singing* 55, no. 1 (September 1998): 53.

————. "A Broader Broadway." *Journal of Singing* 59, no. 5 (May 2003): 431.

————. "Contemporary Music Theater: Louder Than Words." *Journal of Singing* 61, no. 3 (January 2005): 291.

LeBorgne, Wendy Lynn DeLeo. "Defining the Belt Voice: Perceptual Judgments and Objective Measures." Ph.D. diss., University of Cincinnati, 2001.

LoVetri, Jeannette. "Contemporary Commercial Music: More Than One Way to Use the Vocal Tract." *Journal of Singing* 58, no. 3 (January 2002): 249.

————. "Female Chest Voice." *Journal of Singing* 60, no. 2 (November 2003): 161.

————. "Who's Minding the Store?" *Journal of Singing* 59, no. 4 (March 2003): 345.

McCoy, Scott. "A Classical Pedagogue Explores Belting." *Journal of Singing* 63, no. 5 (May 2007): 545.

Melton, Joan. *Singing in Musical Theatre: The Training of Singers and Actors*. New York: Allworth Press, 2007.

Nix, John. "Criteria for Selecting Repertoire." *Journal of Singing* 58, no. 3 (January 2002): 217.

Popeil, Lisa. "Comparing Belt and Classical Techniques Using MRU and Video Fluoroscopy." *Journal of Singing* 56, no. 2 (November 1999): 27

————. "The Multiplicity of Belting." *Journal of Singing* 64, no. 1 (September 2007): 77.

Spivey, Norman. "Music Theatre Singing . . . Let's Talk. Part 1: On the Relationship of Speech and Singing." *Journal of Singing* 64, no. 4 (March 2008): 483.

————. "Music Theater Singing . . . Let's Talk. Part 2: Examining the Debate on Belting." *Journal of Singing* 64, no. 5 (May 2008): 607.

Titze, Ingo. "Belting and a High Larynx Position." *Journal of Singing* 63, no. 5 (May 2007): 557.

MUSICAL THEATRE

Alper, Steven M. *Next! Auditioning for Musical Theatre*. Portsmouth, NH: Heinemann, 1995.

Bloom, Ken. *The Routledge Guide to Broadway*. New York: Routledge, 2006.

Blumenfield, Robert. *Blumenfield's Dictionary of Musical Theater*. Milwaukee, WI: Limelight Editions, 2010.

Bordman, Gerald. *American Musical Comedy: From Adonis to Dreamgirls*. New York: Oxford University Press, 1982.

———. *American Musical Revue: From the Passing Show to Sugar Babies*. New York: Oxford University Press, 1985.

DeVenney, David P. *The New Broadway Song Companion: An Annotated Guide to Musical Theatre Literature by Voice Type and Song Style*, 2nd ed. Lanham, MD: Scarecrow Press, 2009.

Everett, William A., and Paul R. Laird. *Historical Dictionary of the Broadway Musical*. Lanham, MD: Scarecrow Press, 2008.

Forte, Allen. *The American Popular Ballad of the Golden Era: 1925–1950*. Princeton, NJ: Princeton University Press, 1995.

———. *Listening to Classic American Popular Songs*. New Haven, CT: Yale University Press, 2001.

Green, Stanley. *Broadway Musicals Show by Show*, 7th ed. Revised and updated by Cary Ginell. New York: Applause Books, 2011.

Hischak, Thomas S. *Off-Broadway Musicals since 1919: From Greenwich Village Follies to the Toxic Avenger*. Lanham, MD: Scarecrow Press, 2011.

———. *The Oxford Companion to the American Musical: Theatre, Film, and Television*. New York: Oxford University Press, 2008.

Miller, D. A. *Place for Us: Essay on the Broadway Musical*. Cambridge, MA: Harvard University Press, 1998.

Mordden, Ethan. *Beautiful Mornin': The Broadway Musical of the 1940s*. New York: Oxford University Press, 1999.

———. *Coming Up Roses: The Broadway Musical of the 1950s*. New York: Oxford University Press, 2000.

———. *The Happiest Corpse I've Ever Seen: The Last Twenty-Five Years of the Broadway Musical*. New York: Palgrave Macmillan, 2004.

———. *Make Believe: The Broadway Musical of the 1920s*. New York: Oxford University Press, 1997.

———. *One More Kiss: The Broadway Musical of the 1970s*. New York: Palgrave Macmillan, 2004.

———. *Open a New Window: The Broadway Musical of the 1960s*. New York: Palgrave Macmillan, 2002.

———. *Sing for Your Supper: The Broadway Musical of the 1930s*. New York: Palgrave Macmillan, 2005.

Sondheim, Stephen. *Finishing the Hat: Collected Lyrics (1954–1981) with Attendant Comments, Principles, Heresies, Grudges, Whines, and Anecdotes*. New York: Alfred A. Knopf, 2010.

———. *Look, I Made a Hat: Collected Lyrics (1981–2011) with Attendant Comments, Amplifications, Dogmas, Harangues, Digressions, Anecdotes, and Miscellany*. New York: Alfred A. Knopf, 2011.

Stempel, Larry. *Showtime: A History of the Broadway Musical Theater*. New York: W. W. Norton & Company, 2010.

Wolf, Stacy. *A Problem Like Maria: Gender and Sexuality in the American Musical*. Ann Arbor: University of Michigan Press, 2002.

OTHER STYLES

American and Roots Genres

Averill, Gage. *Four Parts, No Waiting: A Social History of American Barbershop Harmony*. New York: Oxford University Press, 2003.

Cohen, Norm. *Ethnic and Border Music: A Regional Exploration*. Westport, CT: Greenwood Press, 2007.

———. *Folk Music: A Regional Exploration*. Westport, CT: Greenwood Press, 2005.

Cohen, Ronald. *Folk Music: The Basics*. New York: Routledge, 2006.

Crawford, Richard, and Larry Hamberlin. *An Introduction to America's Music*, 2nd ed. New York: W. W. Norton & Company, 2012.

LeBlanc, Eric. *Blues: A Regional Exploration*. Westport, CT: Greenwood Press, 2013.

Malone, Bill C., and Jocelyn R. Neal. *Country Music, USA*, 3rd ed. Austin: University of Texas Press, 2010.

Tribe, Evan. *Country: A Regional Exploration*. Westport, CT: Greenwood Press, 2006.

Wiessman, Dick. *Blues: The Basics*. New York: Routledge, 2004.

Rock Genres

Campbell, Michael. *Popular Music in America: The Beat Goes On*, 3rd ed. Clifton Park, NY: Cengage Learning, 2008.

Campbell, Michael, and James Brody. *Rock and Roll: An Introduction*, 2nd ed. Clifton Park, NY: Cengage Learning, 2007.

Charlton, Katherine. *Rock Music Styles*, 6th ed. New York: McGraw-Hill, 2010.

Covach, John, and Andrew Flory. *What's That Sound? An Introduction to Rock and Its History*, 3rd ed. New York: W. W. Norton & Company, 2012.

Robins, Wayne. *A Brief History of Rock, Off the Record*. New York: Routledge, 2007.

Stuessy, Joe, and Scott D. Lipsomb. *Rock and Roll: Its History and Development*, 6th ed. Upper Saddle River, NJ: Pearson-Prentice Hall, 2008.

Walser, Robert. *Running with the Devil: Power, Gender, and Madness in Heavy Metal Music*. Middletown, CT: Wesleyan University Press, 1993.

Jazz

Gioia, Ted. *The History of Jazz*, 2nd ed. New York: Oxford University Press, 2011.

———. *The Jazz Standards: A Guide to the Repertoire*. New York: Oxford University Press, 2012.

Gridley, Mark C. *Jazz Styles. History and Analysis*, 10th ed. Upper Saddle River, NJ: Pearson-Prentice Hall, 2008.

Meeder, Christopher. *Jazz: The Basics*. New York: Routledge, 2007.

Megill, Donald D., and Richard S. Demory. *Introduction to Jazz History*, 6th ed. Upper Saddle River, NJ: Pearson-Prentice Hall, 2003.

Walser, Robert. *Keeping Time: Readings in Jazz History*. New York: Oxford University Press, 1998.

Whitehead, Kevin. *Why Jazz? A Concise Guide*. New York: Oxford University Press, 2011.

Yanow, Scott. *Jazz: A Regional Exploration*. Westport, CT: Greenwood Press, 2005.

World Music

Alves, Williams. *Music of the Peoples of the World*, 2nd ed. Clifton Park, NY: Cengage Learning, 2008.

Bakan, Michael. *World Music: Traditions and Transformations*. New York: McGraw-Hill, 2011.

Miller, Terry E., and Andrew Shahriari. *World Music: A Global Journey*, 3rd ed. New York: Routledge, 2012.

Nettl, Bruno, Thomas Turino, Isabel K. F. Won, and Charles Capwell. *Excursions in World Music*, 5th ed. Upper Saddle River, NJ: Pearson-Prentice Hall, 2007.

Nidel, Richard O. *World Music: The Basics*. New York: Routledge, 2005.

Titon, Jeff Todd, Timothy J. Cooley, David Locke, David P. McAllester, and Anne K. Rasmussen. *Worlds of Music: An Introduction to the Music of the World's Peoples*. Clifton Park, NY: Cengage Learning, 2008.

Wald, Elijah. *Global Minstrels: Voices of World Music*, new ed. New York: Routledge, 2006.

BODYWORK

General

Conable, Barbara. *The Structures and Movement of Breathing: A Primer for Choirs and Choruses*. Chicago: GIA Publications, 2000.

Dimon, Theodore. *Your Body, Your Voice: The Key to Natural Singing and Speaking*. Berkeley, CA: North Atlantic Books, 2011.

Malde, Melissa, Mary Jean Allen, and Kurt-Alexander Zeller. *What Every Singer Needs to Know about the Body*, 2nd ed. San Diego, CA: Plural Publishing, 2012.

Alexander Technique

Alexander, F. Matthias, and Edward Maisel. *The Alexander Technique: The Essential Writings of F. Matthias Alexander*. London: Thames and Hudson, 1990.

Conable, Barbara, and William Conable. *How to Learn the Alexander Technique: A Manual for Students*. Columbus, OH: Andover, 1995.

de Alcantara, Pedro. *The Alexander Technique: A Skill for Life*. Marlborough: Crowood, 1999.

———. *Indirect Procedures: A Musician's Guide to the Alexander Technique*. Oxford: Clarendon, 1997.

Gelb, Michael. *Body Learning: An Introduction to the Alexander Technique*. New York: Holt, 1995.

Harer, John B., and Sharon Munden. *The Alexander Technique Resource Book*. Lanham, MD: Scarecrow Press, 2008.

Heirich, Jane Ruby. *Voice and the Alexander Technique*, 2nd ed. Berkeley, CA: Mornum Time Press, 2011.

Jones, Frank Pierce. *Freedom to Change: The Development and Science of the Alexander Technique*. London: Mouritz, 1997.

Jones, Frank Pierce, Theodore Dimon, and Richard A. Brown. *Frank Pierce Jones: Collected Writings on the Alexander Technique*. Cambridge, MA: Alexander Technique Archives, 1998.

McEvenue, Kelly, and Patsy Rodenburg. *The Actor and the Alexander Technique*. New York: Palgrave Macmillan, 2006.

Nettl-Fiol, Rebecca, and Luc Vanier. *Dance and the Alexander Technique: Exploring the Missing Link*. Urbana: University of Illinois Press, 2011.

Vineyard, Missy. *How You Stand, How You Move, How You Live: Learning the Alexander Technique to Explore Your Mind-Body Connection and Achieve Self-Mastery*. New York: Marlowe & Sons, 2007.

Feldenkrais

Feldenkrais, Moshé. *Awareness through Movement: Easy-to-Do Health Exercises to Improve Your Posture, Vision, Imagination, and Personal Awareness*. New York: HarperOne, 2009.

———. *Body Awareness as Healing Therapy: The Case of Nora*, 2nd ed. Berkeley, CA: Frog Books, 1993.

———. *The Elusive Obvious, or Basic Feldenkrais*. Soquel, CA: Meta Publications, 1981.

———. *Embodied Wisdom: The Collected Papers of Moshé Feldenkrais*. Edited by Elizabeth Beringer. Berkeley, CA: North Atlantic Books, 2010.

———. *The Potent Self: A Study of Spontaneity and Compulsion*. Berkeley, CA: Frog Books, 2002.

Nelson, Samuel H., and Elizabeth Blades-Zeller. *Singing with Your Whole Self: The Feldenkrais Method and Voice*. Lanham, MD: Scarecrow Press, 2002.

Yoga

Carman, Judith E. *Yoga for Singing: A Developmental Tool for Technique and Performance*. New York: Oxford University Press, 2012.

Lister, Linda. *Yoga for Singers: Freeing Your Voice and Spirit through Yoga*. Raleigh, NC: Lulu Press, 2011.

ACTING

Adler, Stella. *The Art of Acting*. New York: Applause Books, 2000.

Bogart, Anne. *And Then, You Act: Making Art in an Unpredictable World*, new ed. New York: Routledge, 2007.

———. *Conversations with Anne*. New York: Theatre Communications Group, 2012.

———. *A Director Prepares: Seven Essays on Art and Theatre*. New York: Routledge, 2001.

———. *The Viewpoints Book: A Practical Guide to Viewpoints and Composition*. New York: Theatre Communications Group, 2004.

Brunetti, David. *Acting the Song*. Seattle, WA: BookSurge Publishing, 2006.

Chekhov, Michael. *On the Technique of Acting*. New York: Harper Perennial, 1993.

Cohen, Robert. *Acting Power*. Palo Alto, CA: Mayfield Publishing, 1998.

Hagen, Uta. *A Challenge for the Actor*, 10th ed. New York: Scribner, 1991.

———. *Respect for Acting*, 2nd ed. New York: Wiley, 2008.

Mamet, David. *True and False: Heresy and Common Sense for the Actor*. New York: Vintage Books, 1999.

Meisner, Sanford, and Dennis Longwell. *Sanford Meisner on Acting*. New York: Vintage Books, 1987.

Moore, Tracey, and Allison Bergman. *Acting the Song: Performance Skills for Musical Theatre*. New York: Allworth Press, 2008.

Ostwald, David F. *Acting for Singers: Creating Believable Singing Characters*. New York: Oxford University Press, 2005.

Spolin, Viola. *Improvisation for the Theater: A Handbook of Teaching and Directing Techniques*, 3rd ed. Chicago: Northwestern University Press, 1999.

Stanislavski, Constantin. *An Actor Prepares*. Translated by Elizabeth Reynolds Hapgood. New York: Routledge, 1989.

———. *Becoming a Character*. Translated by Elizabeth Reynolds Hapgood. New York: Routledge, 1989.

———. *Creating a Role*. Translated by Elizabeth Reynolds Hapgood. New York: Routledge, 1989.

Strasberg, Lee. *A Dream of Passion: The Development of the Method*. New York: Plume, 1988.

RECOMMENDED ANTHOLOGIES FOR VOICE TEACHERS

The following bibliographic entries are annotated because of their particular importance to voice instructors.

First and Second Book Series

Edited by Joan Frey Boytim (b. 1934). Published by Schirmer in twenty volumes.

Affectionately known as "The Boytim Books," this colossal series gathers together a wealth of age-appropriate repertoire for the high school and first-year college student. Organized by voice type, the "First Book" series is published in three volumes for soprano, mezzo-soprano, tenor, and baritone, and the "Second Book" series in two volumes for the same four voice categories.

The Singer's Musical Theater Anthology

Published by Hal Leonard in twenty-two volumes.

The Singer's Musical Theater Anthology is the industry standard for musical theatre performers and teachers. Five volumes are published for each of four voice categories, including soprano, mezzo-soprano/belter, tenor, and baritone/bass, as well as two volumes on duets. The songs are published in their original keys, and the accompaniments are not simplified, appearing as they did in the original piano-vocal scores.

The Singer's Library of Musical Theatre

Published by Alfred in eight volumes.

This additional eight volumes of musical theatre repertoire was introduced many years after the Hal Leonard *Singer's Musical Theater Anthology* (SMTA) appeared, and while there are a few repeat selections, this series largely contains repertoire not found in SMTA. It is recommended that musical theatre singers and their teachers own both collections.

Canzone Scordate

Edited by Arne Dørumsgaard (1921–2006). Published by Recital Publications in twenty-two volumes.

Arne Dørumsgaard's *Canzone Scordate* is a classic collection of art-song arrangements of Renaissance, baroque, sacred, and folk songs in five languages: Italian, German, French, Spanish, and English.

Variazoni-Cadenze Tradizioni

Edited by Luigi Ricci (1893–1981). Published by Ricordi in two volumes and two appendixes.

Luigi Ricci's vast collection of operatic cadenzas is a classic anthology and a must-own series for students of opera. The series is published in two volumes (for female voice and male voice) and two appendixes (a supplemental volume for all voice types and an all-Rossini collection).

La Flora

Edited by Knud Jeppesen (1892–1974). Published by Wilhelm Hansen in three volumes.

Knud Jeppesen's *La Flora* is a pedagogical collection of Italian *arie antiche* by Renaissance and baroque composers. This series is excellent for building technique and flexibility in young singers.

Great Opera Composers for Young Singers

Edited by Gabriella Ravazzi (b. 1942). Published by Ricordi in seven volumes.

Gabriella Ravazzi's collection gathers together age-appropriate arias for beginning singers. The series serves as a pedagogical building block before singers advance to standard aria anthologies.

Pathways of Song

Edited by Frank LaForge (1879–1953) and Will Earhart (1871–1960). Published by Alfred in four volumes and two keys.

This work is a classic American collection of art songs, many of which are off the beaten path and seldom performed in the twenty-first century. *Pathways of Song* is a perfect series for younger, less-experienced singers.

Resonance

Edited by the Royal Conservatory Music Development Program. Published by Frederick Harris in twelve volumes.

Resonance is a graded vocal method with level-appropriate songs. There are nine volumes of repertoire (numbered as a "preparatory volume" and then numbered one through eight) and three volumes of vocalises and recitatives, the final one published in two keys. The Royal Conservatory recently paired with the National Association of Teachers of Singing to create the "Achievement Program," a tiered curriculum for high school and avocational students of singing.

The New Millennium Series

Published by Conservatory Canada in four volumes.

Conservatory Canada's *New Millennium Series* is a preconservatory, graded collection designed for private studio use. Each book is paired with a syllabus and a guided rubric for assessment.

METHODOLOGIES AND TECHNIQUE BOOKS

While there are many technique books available for purchase, most methodologies used in North American voice studios are in the public domain and can therefore be downloaded free of charge from such websites as imslp.org. Another collection entitled *Vocal Exercises: The Ultimate Collection* is available from CD Sheet Music, LLC. This volume includes all the major vocalise collections of Franz Abt (1819–1885), Pasquale Bona (1808–1878), Giovanni Marco Bordogni (1789–1856), Giuseppe Concone (1801–1861), Adolphe-Léopold Dannhauser (1835–1896), Louis Lablache (1794–1858), Franscesco Lamperti (1811–1892), Giovanni Battista Lamperti (1839–1910), B. Lütgen (1835–1870), Mathilde Marchesi (1821–1913), Salvatore Marchesi (1822–1908), Henrich Panofka (1807–1887), Auguste Mathieu Panseron (1796–1859), Gioacchino Rossini (1792–1868), Giovanni Battista Rubini (1794–1854), William Shakespeare (1849–1931), Ferdinand Sieber (1822–1895), Max Spicker (1858–1912), Nicola Vaccai (1790–1848), and Pauline Viardot (1821–1910).

Professional Organizations for Singers

NATIONAL ASSOCIATION OF TEACHERS OF SINGING (NATS)

Founded in 1944, National Association of Teachers of Singing, Inc. (NATS) is the largest professional association of teachers of singing in the world, with more than 7,000 members in the United States, Canada, and more than twenty-five other countries. NATS offers a variety of lifelong learning experiences to its members, including workshops, intern programs, master classes, and conferences. The association also annually provides chapter and regional auditions for students of singing, as well as artist-level competitions for classical and musical theatre performers. NATS CHATS is a monthly web-based program enjoyed by voice professionals worldwide, and the *Journal of Singing* is regarded as the premiere voice pedagogy journal in the world.

NEW YORK SINGING TEACHERS ASSOCIATION (NYSTA)

The New York Singing Teachers Association (NYSTA), founded in 1906, and centered in New York, is the oldest professional association of singing teachers and voice professionals, with local, national, and international members. NYSTA is dedicated to inspiring and educating those who work with the singing voice in all musical genres and around the globe. The association is a leader in online education, offering professional development courses online through the Oren Lathrop Brown Professional Development Program. Voice professionals who complete the program earn the NYSTA's Distinguished Voice Professional certificate. The organization also publishes a professional journal, *VOICEPrints*, five times annually.

THE VOICE FOUNDATION (TVF)

The mission of the Voice Foundation (VF) is to enhance knowledge, care, and training of the voice through educational programs and publications for voice care professionals, the public, and professional voice users, and through supporting and funding research. Founded in 1969, the VF brings together physicians, scientists, speech-language pathologists, performers, and teachers to share their knowledge and expertise in the care of the professional voice user. Since 1989, the foundation has been led by Robert Thayer Sataloff, MD, DMA, FACS, an internationally renowned otolaryngologist who is also a professional singer and conductor, and author of more than 600 publications, including more than thirty-six textbooks.

MUSIC TEACHERS NATIONAL ASSOCIATION (MTNA)

Founded in 1876, the Music Teachers National Association (MTNA) is a nonprofit organization of independent and collegiate music teachers committed to furthering the art of music through teaching, performance, composition, and scholarly research. MTNA also hosts an annual national convention that is linked to the prestigious national MTNA Young Artist Competition. The association publishes *American Music Teacher* bimonthly and offers a national certification program through which members can become a Nationally Certified Teacher of Music.

AMERICAN CHORAL DIRECTORS ASSOCIATION (ACDA)

Founded in 1959, the American Choral Directors Association (ACDA) is a nonprofit music-education organization whose central purpose is to promote excellence in choral music through performance, composition, publication, research, and teaching. In addition, ACDA strives through arts advocacy to elevate choral music's position in American society. The association is particularly known for its national and regional conferences, as well as for its monthly publication, the *Choral Journal*.

EARLY MUSIC AMERICA (EMA)

Early Music America (EMA) is a nonprofit service organization devoted to early music. Founded in 1985, EMA expands awareness of and interest in the music of the medieval, Renaissance, baroque, and classical periods performed on period instruments using historically informed performance practice. EMA's members receive a quarterly magazine, an annual directory, and a wide array of benefits. With its broad membership, including professional performers, ensembles, presenters, instrument makers, amateur musicians, and audience members, the organization serves as an advocate for the field throughout North America.

AMERICAN GUILD OF MUSICAL ARTISTS (AGMA)

The American Guild of Musical Artists (AGMA) is the official American labor union for opera singers. AGMA represents approximately 8,000 current and retired opera singers, as well as ballet and other dancers, opera directors, backstage production personnel at opera and dance companies, and figure skaters. The guild claims exclusive jurisdiction over all aspects of the work of its members and shares some Broadway jurisdiction with its sister union, Actors Equity Association. Any artist who performs at principal American opera or dance companies works under AGMA contracts. The organization was founded in 1936, in an effort to eliminate exploitation of opera singers who were being forced into oppressive contracts without benefits or protections. Throughout the years, the guild has expanded its jurisdiction to include dancers (including athletes who dance on ice) and production personnel.

OPERA AMERICA (OA)

Opera America (OA) is a service organization based in North America promoting the creation, presentation, and enjoyment of opera. Almost all professional opera companies and some semiprofessional companies in the United States are members of OA, including such opera companies as the Metropolitan Opera, San Francisco Opera, Lyric Opera of Chicago, and Dallas Opera. OA also includes internationally affiliated opera companies the likes of the Canadian Opera Company and Opera Australia, businesses, educational institutions, libraries, foundations, guilds, and such opera artists as singers and composers.

NATIONAL OPERA ASSOCIATION (NOA)

The National Opera Association (NOA) is a national organization founded in 1955 that seeks to promote a greater appreciation of opera and musical theatre and encourages opera education programs in the United States. The NOA hosts annual competitions in singing and for collegiate opera scenes and publishes an academic journal entitled the *Opera Journal*. The association's membership includes professionals from the United States, Canada, Europe, Asia, and Australia.

VOICE AND SPEECH TRAINERS ASSOCIATION (VASTA)

The Voice and Speech Trainers Association (VASTA) is a nonprofit organization founded, grown, and guided by volunteers in the profession that services the needs of voice and speech professionals worldwide. VASTA is the only organization in the United States dedicated to fostering excellence in the field of voice and speech training. The association's current membership includes approximately 500 members from around the globe. These include professors; performers; voice, speech, text, and dialect coaches; speech/language pathologists; otolaryngologists; coaches in private practice and acting; singing specialists who are seeking to integrate disciplines; and others interested in the art and science of the human voice.

MUSICAL THEATRE EDUCATORS ALLIANCE (MTEA)

The Musical Theatre Educators Alliance (MTEA) is a forum for discussing all matters relating to the recruitment, training, and placement of professionally bound college and conservatory-affiliated music theatre students. The MTEA was formed to serve the following purposes: to facilitate the conversations among the diverse teaching population who are involved in the practical training of music theatre students; promote high standards; share solutions; broaden visibility; strengthen credibility within the larger academic community and the profession; and exchange curricular, production, and professional ideas and information.

SOUTHEASTERN THEATRE CONFERENCE (SETC)

The Southeastern Theatre Conference (SETC) is a dynamic membership organization that serves a diverse constituency and reaches out to ten states in the Southeastern United States and beyond. SETC is the strongest and broadest network of theatre practitioners in the United States. The organization provides extensive resources and year-round opportunities for constituents. The SETC's services, publications, and products contribute significantly to the careers of emerging artists, seasoned professionals, and academicians. The group energizes the practical, intellectual, and creative profile of theatre in the United States.

NATIONAL FEDERATION OF
MUSIC CLUBS (NFMC)

Since its founding in 1898, the National Federation of Music Clubs (NFMC) has grown into one of the world's largest music organizations, with club and individual members of all ages. The NFMC is chartered by the Congress of the United States and is the only music organization member of the United Nations. The federation provides both local events and national competitions for its members.

About the Author

Matthew Hoch is assistant professor of voice at Auburn University, where he teaches applied voice, diction, and opera workshop. He earned his BM, *summa cum laude*, from Ithaca College, with a triple major in vocal performance, music education, and music theory; his MM from the Hartt School, with a double major in vocal performance and music history; and his DMA in vocal performance and literature from the New England Conservatory. A graduate of the Pennsylvania Governor's School for the Arts, he holds the diploma in art history from the University of Hartford and has pursued advanced training with Dr. Ingo Titze at the Summer Vocology Institute (SVI) at the National Center for Voice and Speech (NCVS).

From 2006–2012, Dr. Hoch served as assistant professor of voice at Shorter College, where his voice students won fifty-six awards at chapter and regional National Association of Teachers of Singing (NATS) auditions. During his time at Shorter, Dr. Hoch also served as coordinator of vocal studies, director of the Guest Artist Series, and founder of both the New Music Series and Musical Theatre Master Class Series. Dr. Hoch's students were accepted into top graduate programs and won numerous competitions, including the district Metropolitan Opera National Council auditions, chapter and regional Music Teachers National Association Young Artist Competition auditions, and chapter and regional NATS auditions. Equally at home as a musical theatre pedagogue, his students have been accepted into many professional training and summer stock programs, were top scorers at the Georgia Theatre Conference, and have included fourteen Kennedy Center American College Theater Festival Irene Ryan nominees, including the 2011 Best Musical Theatre Performer in the Southeast Region.

As a voice pedagogue, Dr. Hoch has been extremely active in the nation's two largest organizations for teachers of singing: the National Association of Teachers of Singing (NATS) and the New York Singing Teachers Association (NYSTA). With NATS, he coordinated the NATS CHATS program from 2006–2011, and has served on the nominating committee as well as two terms as chair of the professional development committee for the national board of directors. With SER-NATS, he has served as registrar and repertoire consultant, as well as on numerous task forces. With GA-NATS, he has served as registrar, repertoire consultant, and historian, repertoire consultant. In 2010, he adjudicated the final round of the TEXOMA-NATSAA auditions. Hoch is an alumnus of the 2006 NATS Intern Program, where he was apprenticed to national NATS president Dr. Donald Simonson. As a recipient of the 2007 NATS Voice Pedagogy Award, he studied CCM voice pedagogy with Jeannette Lo-Verti at Shenandoah University's Music Theatre Vocal Pedagogy Institute, where he earned three levels of certification in Somatic Voicework Training™—the LoVetri Method. He coordinated and hosted the 2009 NATS Intern Program at Shorter College.

With NYSTA, Dr. Hoch currently holds the office of vice president, and he has served as editor-in-chief of *VOICE-Prints: The Official Journal of NYSTA* since 2008. He is also a member of the Board of Directors, the Professional Development Program Committee, and the Internet Technology Committee. Dr. Hoch completed the five-course core curriculum of NYSTA's Oren Lathrop Brown Professional Development Program and has been awarded the NYSTA's Distinguished Voice Professional certificate. In 2013, he was selected as a master teacher for NYSTA's annual Comparative Pedagogy Weekend.

Dr. Hoch has performed as a Bach soloist with many professional organizations, including the Atlanta Baroque Orchestra (in Bach's cantatas BWV 56 and BWV 173a), and at the Oregon Bach Festival (in Bach's *St Matthew Passion*), the Hartford Symphony (in Bach's *Magnificat*), and the Vox Consort and New Haven Oratorio Choir (in Bach's *St John Passion*). His professional oratorio experience includes more than a dozen other works by J. S. Bach; Handel's *Messiah*; Haydn's *Paukenmesse*; Mozart's *Coronation Mass*;

Mendelssohn's *Elijah*; Brahms's *Ein deutsches Requiem*; Fauré's *Requiem*; Duruflé's *Requiem*; Puccini's *Messa di Gloria*; Vaughan Williams's *Five Mystical Songs*, *Fantasia on Christmas Carols*, and *Dona nobis pacem*; Dvořák's *Te Deum*; Bernstein's *Chichester Psalms*; Rutter's *Mass of the Children*; Stainer's *The Crucifixion*; Saint-Saëns's *Oratorio de Noël*; and Orff's *Carmina Burana*. As a chamber musician, Dr. Hoch has performed with the United States Coast Guard Chamber Players, the Balkan String Quartet, and the Blue Mountain Chamber Players.

Operatic credits have included Horace Tabor in *The Ballad of Baby Doe*, Melchior in *Amahl and the Night Visitors*, Ben in *The Telephone*, David in *A Hand of Bridge*, Falke in *Die Fledermaus*, Don Alhambra in *The Gondoliers*, Jupiter in *Orphée aux enfers*, Fiorello in *Il barbiere di Siviglia*, Silvio in *Un ballo in maschera*, Count Almaviva in *Le nozze di Figaro*, and the title roles in *Gianni Schicchi* and *Dido and Aeneas*. Dr. Hoch has held summer apprenticeships with Ash Lawn Opera and the College Light Opera Company on Cape Cod. From 2003–2005, he was the baritone soloist at historic Trinity Church on Copley Square in Boston. At Ithaca College and the Hartt School, he was a winner of both schools' prestigious concerto competitions.

A champion of art song and recital singing, Dr. Hoch recently performed Wolf's *Italienisches Liederbuch* at Spivey Hall. Other repertoire includes major cycles and sets by Schubert, Schumann, Brahms, Strauss, Beethoven, Fauré, Debussy, Ravel, Poulenc, Leguerney, Vaughan Williams, Finzi, Britten, Copland, Barber, and de Falla. Also interested in new music, Dr. Hoch can be heard as a soloist on the Navona recording of Kile Smith's *Vespers*, with the Piffaro Renaissance Band and the Crossing. Through the Weill Music Institute at Carnegie Hall, he studied twentieth-century vocal techniques in New York City with Meredith Monk, a workshop that resulted in his solo and conducting debuts in Carnegie's Zankel Hall. As a soloist, he has sung world premieres by Robert Kyr, Daniel Asia, Jocelyn Hagen, Norman Mathews, Denis von Paris, and Sorrel Hayes. His voice teachers have included Larry Weller, Mark St Laurent, Joanna Levy, Mitchell Piper, Susan Clickner, Carol McAmis, Randie Blooding, and Donald Nally.

As a professional chorister, Dr. Hoch has performed and recorded with some of the premiere choral ensembles in the United States, including the Santa Fe Desert Chorale, Conspirare, the Minnesota Chorale, the Handel and Haydn Society, the Woodland Scholars, the Vox Consort, CONCORA, the Cayuga Vocal Ensemble, the Alchemy Project, the Crossing, and the Festival dei due Mondi in Spoleto, Italy. In Spoleto, he recorded Gian Carlo Menotti's *The Saint of Bleecker Street* and *Cantatas* under the direction of Gian Carol Menotti, Richard Hickox, and Donald Nally;

both recordings are available on the Chandos label. He has been a regular participant in the Carnegie Hall Choral Workshops, where he has sung under the batons of Peter Schreier, Charles Dutoit, Robert Spano, and Helmuth Rilling. From 2005–2012, Dr. Hoch sang as a tenured member of the Oregon Bach Festival Chorus under the direction of Maestro Rilling. With this Grammy Award-winning group, he recorded the complete cycle of Haydn's late masses for Hänssler Classics and sang the world premieres of Felix Mendelssohn's *Der Onkel von Boston* (2005) and Sven-David Sandström's *Messiah* (2009). In 2012, he served as the bass section leader for the OBF Youth Choral Academy under the direction of Anton Armstrong.

As a scholar, Dr. Hoch has researched, written, presented, and published on a variety of topics, including Richard Strauss, French art song, classical and popular singers, choral literature, and the female "belt" voice. He has been selected as a presenter at many conferences and symposia, including ICVT (international), IHS (international), HICAH (international), NCVS (national), SETC (national), CMS (national), NOA (national), AMS (mega-regional), GMEA (state), GMTA (state), CMENC (state), the International Conference on the Arts in Society (Kassel, Germany), and the New Vocal Educators Symposium (Bloomington, Indiana). His articles have appeared in *The Journal of Singing*, *The Opera Journal*, *VOICEPrints: The Official Journal of NYSTA*, the *Journal of the Association of Anglican Musicians*, and the *Triangle of Mu Phi Epsilon*. He is a two-time recipient of the Mu Phi Epsilon Musicological Research Award and was awarded the 2010 Bettylou Scandling Hubin Grant for World Music/Multicultural Studies by the Mu Phi Epsilon Foundation. His critical editions of the late songs of Richard Strauss are published by Classical Vocal Reprints.

Dr. Hoch is a member of Mu Phi Epsilon, Phi Mu Alpha Sinfonia, Pi Kappa Lambda, Phi Kappa Phi, Phi Beta, Pi Lambda Theta, Kappa Delta Pi, and Phi Delta Kappa. He is a lifetime member of ACDA, MENC, SRME, AMS, and SEM, and an active member of NATS, NYSTA, MTNA, SMT, AAM, AAUP, AGO, SETC, the International Phonetic Association, and the Voice Foundation. He is recognized as a Nationally Certified Teacher of Music by MTNA.

In addition to his academic life, Dr. Hoch also maintains a secondary career as an Episcopal choirmaster. He is currently choirmaster and minister of music at Holy Trinity Episcopal Church in Auburn, Alabama, where he plans, rehearses, and conducts service music and anthems in the Anglican tradition. He previously served in a similar position as choirmaster and director of music at St Peter's Episcopal Church in Rome, Georgia. He lives in Auburn, Alabama, with his wife, Theresa, and their three children, Hannah, Sofie, and Zachary.